FIELD GUIDE TO
TREES
OF SOUTHERN AFRICA

FIELD GUIDE TO
TREES
OF SOUTHERN AFRICA

BRAAM VAN WYK & PIET VAN WYK

Struik Publishers (Pty) Ltd
(a member of Struik Publishing Group (Pty) Ltd)
80 McKenzie Street
Cape Town 8001

Reg. No 54/00965/07

First published 1997

ISBN 1 86825 922 6

Editor: Peter Joyce
Designer: Dean Pollard
Cartographers: John Hall and Dean Pollard
Cover design: Dean Pollard
Design assistant: Lellyn Creamer
Editorial assistant: Helena Reid
Proofreader: Tessa Kennedy

Reproduction by cmyk Prepress
Printed and bound by Kyodo Printing Co
(S'Pore) Pte Ltd

Front cover, main photograph : *Adansonia digitata* (Baobab); embellishing photographs (left to right): *Combretum mossambicense* (Knobbly creeper), *Greyia sutherlandii* (Natal bottlebrush), *Erythrina caffra* (Coast coral tree), *Combretum mkuzense* (Tonga bushwillow), *Pappea capensis* (Jacket-plum), *Trichilia emetica* (Natal mahogany), *Bolusanthus speciosus* (Tree wisteria). Spine photograph: *Cyphostemma currorii* (Cobas); Half-title page: Pods and seeds of *Erythrina lysistemon* (Common coral tree). Title page: *Aloe pillansii* (Giant quiver tree). Contents page, top: *Acacia tortilis* (Umbrella thorn), bottom: *Pachypodium namaquanum* (Halfmens tree or Elephant's trunk). Back cover: *Rhigozum brevispinosum* (Short-thorn pomegranate).

PHOTOGRAPHIC CREDITS

All the photographs in this book were taken by Piet van Wyk with the exception of those listed below

BO = Bernie Olbrich; BVW = Braam van Wyk; CNC = Cape Nature Conservation; DJ = David Johnson;
DR = Dave Richardson; EVJ = Ernst van Jaarsveld; GD = Gerhardt Dreyer; GN = Geoff Nichols;
IC = Isabella Claassen; JO = Jo Onderstall; LH = Lesley Henderson; LVH = Lanz von Hörsten;
MCP = Meg Coates Palgrave; NBI = National Botanical Institute; ND = Nigel Dennis; NH = Norbert Hahn;
PJ = Pitta Joffe; RW = Rosemary Williams; SIL = Struik Image Library; SN = Stefan Neser; WM = Wayne Matthews;

Title page LVH; Contents page, bottom photograph LVH; Page 35 bottom right RW; 45 top left GD/SIL, bottom right
NH; 47 centre left NBI; 49 centre right and bottom centre BVW; 51 bottom right BVW; 55 top left JO, top right EVJ;
59 top left, centre right and bottom MCP, centre left IC, top right NBI; 65 top left DR, top right, centre left, bottom left,
bottom centre BO; 67 top right CNC; 69 bottom left LH; 85 bottom left BVW; 93 centre, centre right DJ; 95 bottom left
WM, bottom right GN; 113 top left and centre left BVW; 123 centre left BVW; 129 top centre NBI; 133 bottom centre
BVW; 137 bottom right BVW; 143 bottom left BVW; 149 top left BVW; 157 3rd row from top, right BVW; 161 top
right BVW; 165 top left ND/SIL, bottom left JO, bottom right NH; 179 top left EVJ; 201 2nd row from top, right BVW;
203 centre left CNC; 205 top right, centre left BVW; 215 bottom left BVW; 231 bottom left CNC, bottom centre SN;
245 centre left BVW; 255 bottom left WM, bottom right BVW; 261 centre right BVW; 265 top left BVW; 269 top right
and bottom left NH, bottom centre BVW; 283 bottom right BVW; 289 2nd row from top, right BVW; 295 bottom right
BVW; 297 centre right BVW; 299 centre right BVW; 309 centre right BVW; 319 centre right and bottom right BVW;
339 centre middle; 343 centre left BVW; 349 top left PJ/NBI; 363 top left, centre and right BVW; 373 top right PJ/NBI;
377 centre left WM; 393 bottom left and right BVW; 411 centre left BVW; 417 3rd row from top, right BVW; 435 top
centre BVW; 437 bottom left BVW; 441 2nd row from top, right BVW; 447 top centre and top right BVW; 453 top left
BVW; 471 bottom left EVJ; 475 2nd row from top, left BVW; 487 2nd row from top, centre NBI; 495 bottom left
BVW; 505 bottom right BVW; 521 all BVW.

CONTENTS

PREFACE 6

INTRODUCTION 7

MAPS: VEGETATION AND CENTRES OF ENDEMISM 8

IDENTIFYING TREES 10

HOW TO USE THIS BOOK 12

GUIDE TO THE SPECIES ACCOUNTS 13

KEY TO THE GROUPS 16

FAMILY DESCRIPTIONS 19

SPECIES ACCOUNTS 34

GLOSSARY OF TERMS 516

SELECTED REFERENCES AND CONTACT ADDRESSES 523

ACKNOWLEDGMENTS 524

INDEX 525

QUICK GUIDE TO THE GROUPS INSIDE BACK COVER

PREFACE

This book is intended primarily as a field manual to enable the reader to identify trees in their natural environment. It describes and illustrates about 815 of the most common native and naturalized alien tree species in southern Africa, which is about half the total number of trees known from this botanically diverse part of the continent. In many cases the names and diagnostic characters of closely related species are also mentioned, bringing the total number of trees we cover, and which can be identified with the use of the book, to well over 1 000. We would have liked to include all tree species native to the region, but unfortunately such a volume would have been prohibitively costly to produce and much too unwieldy for practical use.

As an aid to quick and positive identification, the trees in this book have been classified into groups, the arrangement based on easy-to-observe vegetative features. Colour illustrations of flowers and/or fruits, as well as a distribution map, accompany each species. Entries also cover plant usage, and include references to closely related species. Emphasis is placed throughout on family recognition. No keys have been attempted, partly because not all species are included and partly because the botanical detail required makes it impossible to devise a key simple enough to be helpful to the non-botanist.

This book contains the most comprehensive collection of photographs ever published on southern African trees. Most of the slides used were taken specifically for use in the book by one of us (PvW) who, since 1992, has covered over 160 000 km in his bid to photograph every known species of tree native to the region, both in flower and in fruit. These efforts have already yielded a collection of more than 30 000 colour photographs, and the project is continuing.

Trees form a very important part of most natural and artificial landscapes. They are remarkable organisms, commanding respect and admiration for their beauty, size, hardiness and longevity. To study tree diversity and to learn about the very special place they occupy in nature and in human culture is an enriching experience. Tree identification, particularly in a species-rich area such as ours, is intellectually challenging and stimulating. Not only does it involve the physical handling of living organisms usually much older than ourselves, but it also deepens one's appreciation and enjoyment of nature. We hope this book will provide its readers with many hours of pleasure and contribute towards a greater love and a richer understanding of our extraordinarily diverse tree flora.

Braam van Wyk
Piet van Wyk
Pretoria, February 1997

The authors gratefully acknowledge the substantial support – assistance that enabled them to complete the field work for the book – extended by the three Principal Sponsors, namely Total SA (Pty) Ltd (fuel), Mazda Wildlife Fund (transport) and Agfa (film).

MAZDA WILDLIFE FUND   TOTAL SA   AGFA

Generous financial and institutional support were also received from APBCO Insurance Brokers • Letaba Tyres • Persetel (Pty) Ltd • Rand Afrikaans University • University of Pretoria • VDO Architects.

INTRODUCTION

For the purposes of this book, southern Africa is defined as the mainland region of the African continent south of the Cunene, Okavango and Zambezi rivers, a geopolitical region comprising Namibia, Botswana, Zimbabwe, South Africa, Swaziland, Lesotho and that part of Mozambique south of the Zambezi River.

The distinction between shrubs and trees is somewhat artificial and often breaks down in practice. Here, we define a tree, broadly, as any perennial woody plant growing to a height of at least 2 m. Although a typical tree has a single trunk, it may be multistemmed. Our definition also embraces robust, woody climbers.

An estimated 1 700 tree species are native to southern Africa, and well over 100 more, introduced from other parts of the world, are now naturalized in the region. Many of these aliens have become invader weeds, penetrating and replacing indigenous vegetation.

Trees occur in a wide range of vegetation types, with many species found only in specific floristic regions and centres of endemism (see further on).

Climatic conditions (rainfall, temperature, the incidence of fire) largely determine the nature of the various principal vegetation types – forest, grassland, savanna, desert, fynbos and so forth – which are so classified according to the general effect produced in a particular area by the growth form of some or all plant species in combination. Large areas which are relatively uniformly covered by any one of these broad vegetation types usually represent major biotic zones and are often referred to as biomes.

Biomes themselves can be divided into smaller, more homogeneous ecological units or vegetation types, based upon such criteria as the dominant plant species, plant density and height. Mopane woodland, thorn bushveld and miombo woodland are examples of such vegetation types found in parts of southern Africa. These types often reflect more localized conditions – mean annual rainfall, for example, and the nature of the soil. A simplified vegetation map of southern Africa appears on page 8. Note, however, that the vegetation depicted is that which would have been prevalent today had the destruction wrought by human encroachment never taken place. At present very little (no more than 10 per cent) remains of some vegetation types, particularly within the Grassland and Fynbos biomes. As may be expected, vegetation types dominated by woody species are usually rich in tree diversity. In southern Africa, the greatest diversity of trees is found mainly within the Forest and Savanna (bushveld) biomes.

The geographical distribution of individual plant species (which, taken together, comprise the flora of a region) rarely covers precisely the same range as the vegetation type(s). Climate, though the main determinant of vegetation type, is clearly not the only phenomenon to be considered when trying to interpret present-day tree species distributions. A complex combination of many other factors, such as the evolutionary history of the species, continental drift, past climatic change, geology, soil characters, topography and interaction with other plants and animals (including human beings), must also be taken into account.

When the distribution of native plants is mapped, certain recurring patterns emerge within the great diversity. Particularly interesting are those areas that tend to embrace high concentrations of species with very restricted distributions. Commonly referred to as centres of endemism, or 'hot spots', these are parts of the region in which rare and unusual trees are most likely to be encountered. Some of the principal floristic centres of endemism in southern Africa are shown in the map on page 9. By far the three richest floristic areas in Africa are embraced within the southern subcontinent. These are: Cape Floristic Region (about 8 600 plant species; this is also one of the world's six Floristic Kingdoms); Maputaland-Pondoland Region (about 7 000 species), and the Succulent Karoo Region (about 5 000 species).

Areas especially rich in endemic trees are the Pondoland, Maputaland, Albany and Kaokoveld centres. Many southern African tree species also appear to be confined to the Chimanimani-Nyanga Centre. In reality, however, most of these are not endemic to that region, but are merely tropical African species at the southernmost limit of their ranges. Because of their restricted distribution, most of these rare endemics and peripheral tropical species have not been included in this book.

Overleaf: The first map is a simplified representation of the biomes and vegetation types of southern Africa; adapted from White (1983) and Low & Rebelo (1996). The second map shows the region's principal centres of endemism; based on unpublished data of one of the authors (BvW) and on Davis *et al.* (1994).

BIOMES AND VEGETATION TYPES

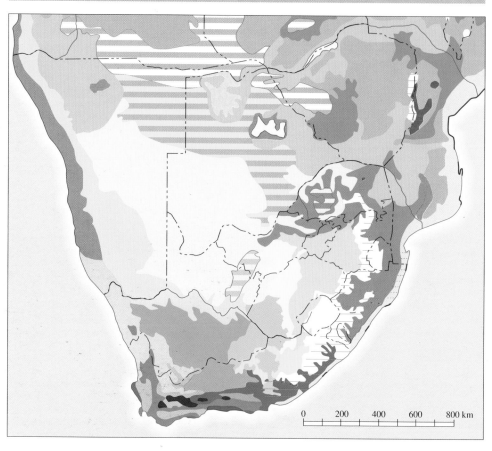

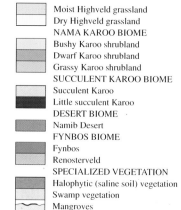

FOREST BIOME
Afromontane and inland forest (with grassland/fynbos)
Coastal dune & swamp forest (with grassland/bushveld)
Sand forest
SAVANNA (BUSHVELD) BIOME
Miombo (*Brachystegia-Julbernardia-Isoberlinia*) woodland
Mopane woodland and shrub woodland
Baikiaea plurijuga-Pterocarpus antunesii woodland
Thorn (*Acacia*) bushveld
Acacia-Colophospermum-Terminalia Kalahari bushveld
Undifferentiated bushveld and woodland
East Coast thorn bushveld, valley bushveld & thicket
Waterberg mountain bushveld
Tarchonanthus camphoratus-Grewia flava bushveld
GRASSLAND BIOME
Coastal grassland (associated with forest/bushveld)
Moist mountain grassland (with isolated forest patches)
Dry (Karroid) mountain grassland

Moist Highveld grassland
Dry Highveld grassland
NAMA KAROO BIOME
Bushy Karoo shrubland
Dwarf Karoo shrubland
Grassy Karoo shrubland
SUCCULENT KAROO BIOME
Succulent Karoo
Little succulent Karoo
DESERT BIOME
Namib Desert
FYNBOS BIOME
Fynbos
Renosterveld
SPECIALIZED VEGETATION
Halophytic (saline soil) vegetation
Swamp vegetation
Mangroves

CENTRES OF PLANT DIVERSITY AND ENDEMISM

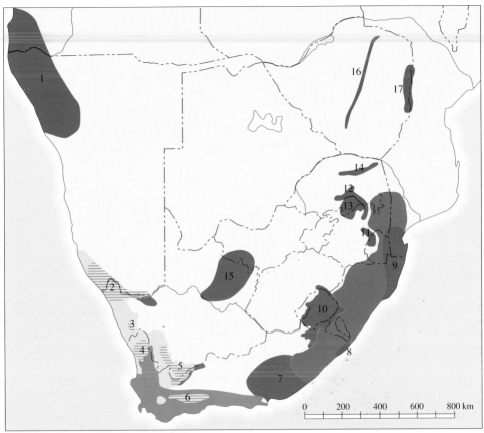

PRINCIPAL REGIONS OF PLANT DIVERSITY
AND ENDEMISM

	Succulent Karoo Region
	Cape Floristic Region
	Maputaland-Pondoland Region

PRINCIPAL LOCAL CENTRES OF PLANT ENDEMISM

1	Kaokoveld Centre
2	Gariep Centre
3	Kamiesberg Centre
4	Knersvlakte (Vanrhynsdorp) Centre
5	Western Mountain Karoo Centre

6	Little Karoo Centre
7	Albany Centre
8	Pondoland Centre
9	Maputaland Centre
10	Drakensberg Alpine Centre
11	Barberton Centre
12	Wolkberg Centre
13	Sekhukhuneland Centre
14	Soutpansberg Centre
15	Griqualand West Centre
16	Great Dyke Centre
17	Chimanimani-Nyanga Centre

IDENTIFYING TREES

By observing the many and various identifying tree features, or characters, listed below, you will be able to build a composite picture of and arrive at a name for the particular plant you are observing. Turn to the Glossary on pages 516–522 if you are unsure of some of the technical terms (the numbers that appear in square brackets refer to the appropriate Glossary illustrations).

Apart from the book itself, your most valuable items of equipment are a pair of sharp eyes, a retentive mind, and a small field notebook and pencil. A 10x handlens or a magnifying glass can also be a great help when studying a small object. Alternatively, reverse a pair of binoculars and look though the 'wrong' end. Binoculars are also useful in identifying leaf details, flowers and fruit in the upper parts of trees (and for bird-spotting!). A pair of small secateurs and a plastic bag can come in handy when collecting material for later study.

However, you should really accumulate as much information about the tree as you can while you are in the field. Certain characters can only be reliably observed in living specimens (for example, the presence or absence of latex). Positive identification of most trees requires physical handling of the plant material, so do not be afraid to touch and smell as well as look.

Tree size, form and foliage colour: Note the size and shape of the tree, as well as the colour of the crown, from a distance. Basic tree shape is genetically determined; each species has a specific tree architecture, though one that can be modified, within limits, by environmental and physiological conditions. Shape and colour are the two most useful features for identifying trees, especially in savanna areas, from a distance.

Bark: Note the bark of the tree. Every species has its own characteristic mature bark pattern. Mature trees with a flaky or rough and thick covering usually have thin smooth bark when young. Therefore you should examine only mature specimens when attempting to identify trees by their bark characters.

Branches and twigs: Note the surface texture and colour of branches and twigs. Young twigs are often marked with small, light-coloured pustules called lenticels [45]. Check whether twigs and older branches are round, flattened or more or less square in cross section. In deciduous species, thick twigs tend to indicate compound leaves. Record the presence of any spines or thorns, and note their arrangement.

Latex: Test for the presence of latex [53, 54]. Any abundant liquid exudate, whether watery (clear), cloudy, milky, or otherwise coloured, is here referred to as such. Pick a healthy green leaf, preferably one from an actively growing shoot; break it off at the point where the stalk (petiole) is attached to the stem, and check immediately whether any liquid oozes out at the broken end or from the scar on the stem. The exudate needs to be fairly copious, preferably forming a drop that completely covers the wound. If no latex is detected, check a few other leaves from different parts of the tree to confirm the fact.

Leaf samples: Always examine a variety of leaves, preferably from the canopy of the tree, to determine characters such as size, shape, colour, texture and degree of hairiness. A single leaf can be misleading. Leaves on coppice shoots may differ substantially from those in the canopy.

Simple and compound leaves: Determine at the outset whether the leaves are simple (undivided) [1, 2] or compound (that is, made up of separate leaflets) [3–8]. If in doubt, look for the axillary bud to determine whether the leaf is really compound or not. There is a small bud (which can develop into a leafy shoot, or a flower) in the axil between the stem and the petiole, but not between the rachis and stalk of a leaflet. Moreover, in a compound leaf there is no growing tip at the end of the rachis.

Leaf arrangement: Note how the leaves are arranged on the stem [9–12]. Are they alternate, opposite, or whorled? In compound leaves, these characteristics refer to the leaves themselves, not the individual leaflets. Clustered leaves are nearly always alternate, unless the clusters themselves are arranged in opposite pairs.

Leaf texture and hairiness: Touch the leaves on both sides. Are they smooth or rough, thin or leathery, woolly, hairless, or sticky?

External glands: Check for the presence of external glands on the leaf. These are often located at the point where the petiole is attached to the blade in simple leaves, or on the petiole or rachis in the case of compound leaves [55, 56].

Leaf margins: Are the leaf edges smooth, toothed, scalloped, wavy, lobed or rolled under? [35–38]

Venation: Note the venation pattern. Is there only a single midrib, or several veins from the base of the blade? Are the veins prominently raised or obscure on one or both surfaces? Are the lateral veins more or less parallel and terminating at the margin without forming an intramarginal vein? Check for the presence of domatia [57, 58] in the axils of the principal lateral veins.

Secretory cavities: Test for the presence of these cavities in the leaf blade [59]. Hold the leaf up to the sun (other light sources are invariably not bright enough) and look for translucent dots. These are extremely small (the size of pinpricks) and uniformly scattered all over the blade (here, the use of a handlens is recommended). Practise looking at a leaf known to contain them (for instance, any citrus or eucalypt species).

Bacterial nodules: These nodules [60] are also detected by holding the leaf up to the sun. These structures should be sought only in plants with opposite leaves and interpetiolar stipules [50]. They are much larger than secretory cavities, dark-coloured, not translucent and are easily visible although often confined to a specific area of the blade, particularly towards the midrib.

Odour: Crush the leaf and check its smell. Leaves with secretory cavities are usually strongly aromatic, but not all aromatic leaves have secretory cavities.

Stipules: Check for the presence of stipules at the base of the petiole [1, 46–49]. This is best done with young leaves near the tips of actively growing shoots. These structures can be very small and, again, a handlens is recommended. Stipules are often deciduous or shrivelled in mature leaves and, if the stipules have been shed, a distinct scar is usually left on the stem. In the case of opposite leaves, look out for the presence of interpetiolar stipules [50, 51].

Flowers: Look carefully for flowers [39] which, on many trees, are small and inconspicuous. Although we have tried to limit the use of floral technicalities in this book, four easy-to-observe characters are particularly useful (especially for family recognition), namely: flowers regular or irregular [43, 44]; petals free or united; stamens many (more than 10) or very few (4 or less); ovary superior or inferior [41, 42].

Fruit: Examine the tree carefully to establish whether the mature fruit is dry (pod, capsule, nut) or fleshy (berry, drupe). If you don't see any fruit, look on the ground directly beneath the tree: one can often find old pods, capsules, nuts and seeds (in this way, even the leaves of deciduous species can be studied). Make sure you understand the difference between a fruit and a seed; the two concepts are often confused.

Collecting material: It is always worthwhile collecting one or more twigs with a number of leaves attached (a single leaf does not show the leaf arrangement) together with any other fertile material that might be present, for more leisurely examination. These samples may be kept for several days in a moist plastic bag, provided that it is kept cool and not exposed to direct sunlight. If your attempts to identify the tree are unsuccessful, the material can be pressed and dried as a specimen, which you could then submit to an individual expert or herbarium (see next section).

HOW TO USE THIS BOOK

Once you have examined the tree carefully (see previous section), and have material in hand, you are ready to begin the identification process. The following steps will enable you to narrow down the possible species to which a sample may belong.

1. The trees in this book have been classified into 43 groups based on easy-to-observe vegetative features. Begin with the key on page 16. This key consists of pairs of choices (leads), and employs easily seen vegetative characters, some of which are illustrated in the Glossary (pages 516–522). Start at the first choice and establish which description matches your plant. At the end of each choice, there is either the name of a group, or a line leading to the next pair of choices. After arriving at the name of a group, turn to that particular section in the book.

Each group starts with a concise statement of its diagnostic characters. This statement is essentially a summary of the most important choices you have made in the key. You will appreciate, however, that it takes just one incorrect choice to arrive at the wrong group. So it is important that you verify the group's identification by checking that it agrees with the group characters. If there is any discrepancy you must, at some point in the key, have gone astray.

In addition, the icon accompanying each group is a pictorial representation which summarizes some of the group's diagnostic features. With a little practice you should be able to recognize the group simply by looking at the icons – which will save you having to work through all the choices. For convenience, all these icons are reproduced, in the form of a quick-reference key, on the inside back cover of the book.

2. Having established the group into which your plant falls, geographical distribution becomes the next clue to its identity (unless, of course, you know its family; see further on). Each species entry in the main section of this book has its range map. Concentrate only on those species likely to occur in the area from which your plant comes.

3. Compare your plant carefully with the photographs of those species with a relevant geographical distribution. Once you have found a picture that seems to match the material in hand, compare it carefully with the accompanying description. Pay particular attention to those diagnostic features which are highlighted in bold. Check the specimen against the family description (pages 19–33). If you cannot find a matching picture, check the cross references listed at the beginning of some of the groups.

If you cannot identify the species, don't be disheartened. With so many different trees in southern Africa, even seasoned botanists are quite often totally baffled. Remember also that this book does not feature every southern African tree. Ask a local expert, or try some of the books listed here as references (page 523). If the tree lacks fertile material, revisit it during a different season. You can also send your material to a herbarium that undertakes the naming of plants. Always write or phone to ask if the institution would be willing to help (contact addresses are listed at the back of this book). Establish whether there are any costs involved. Some herbaria charge a so-called handling fee, whereas others provide a free service. Make sure you send your plants in the form of good, properly dried, properly packed herbarium specimens, together with all the relevant data you have.

Knowing the family to which your plant belongs will obviously help a lot to speed up the identification process, but family recognition requires some experience and botanical knowledge and, in any event, it should be possible to identify most specimens without the use of family features. Nevertheless, novices are advised to familiarize themselves with the diagnostic characters of the principal tree families in southern Africa (see pages 19–33).

Mastering this skill, indeed, is an essential step towards becoming truly competent in the field of plant identification. Naturally it will involve practice, but you might be surprised how quickly you will be able to recognize families on sight. Most of our trees belong to a relatively small number of families, and it is of course much easier to recall the names of families than those of species.

GUIDE TO THE SPECIES ACCOUNTS

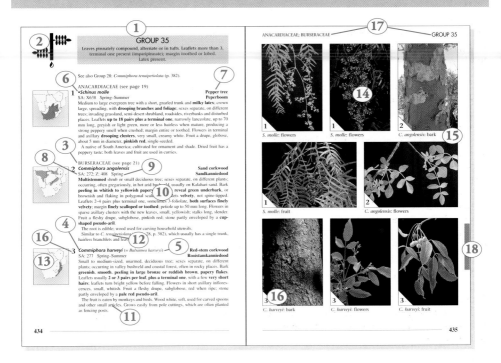

In this section the layout of the main text is briefly explained. The species entries, or accounts, contain a wealth of information, which is presented in concise and consistent fashion. To get the most out of the book, it is essential that you understand the meaning of all the various components numbered in the miniaturized sample spread shown above. Each is described, under a matching number, below.

1. GROUP The species described in this book are arranged in 43 groups based on easy-to-observe leaf and stem characters. For a key to the groups, see page 16. Diagnostic group characters are summarized at the start of each of the 43 sections and should be used to confirm the options offered in the key.

2. GROUP ICON Each of the 43 groups has its own icon, which appears as an identification and reference aid on every text page. An icon is a diagrammatic representation of a plant, or a stem with leaves, and it summarizes a group's diagnostic characters. As a quick reference to the groups, all the icons are repeated, arranged together, on the inside back cover of the book.

3. FAMILY NAME Just as species are brought together in inclusive units called genera, so genera are arranged in families. Within the 43 groups into which the main part of this book is organized, species appear alphabetically according to family. The families also appear in alphabetical sequence. It should be noted that four of the families represented in this book may also be referred to by an alternative name (which is the one used by us). These families and their alternative names are, respectively, the Compositae/Asteraceae; Guttiferae/Clusiaceae; Palmae/Arecaceae and Umbelliferae/Apiaceae. We have separated the legumes into three different families: the Mimosaceae, Caesalpiniaceae and the Fabaceae (narrowly defined; also referred to as Papilionaceae). Some authors combine these three families into a single inclusive family, the Leguminosae/Fabaceae (broadly defined).

4. SCIENTIFIC NAME A species name is made up of two parts. The first part is the genus name (e.g. *Ficus*; comparable to a person's surname). The second part is the specific epithet (e.g. *lutea*; comparable to a first name). The name of subspecies or varieties (which are variants within a species) consists of the name of the species in which it is classified, followed by a word indicating its rank (subsp. or var.), then the subspecific or varietal epithet. For the most part we have followed the scientific names accepted by the National Herbarium in Pretoria. For reference purposes and as a source of historical information, scientific names are often followed by one or more personal names, sometimes abbreviated. These so-called authority citations are of little use to laypeople and they have been omitted in this book.

5. SYNONYMS The names under which a plant was previously known, or are alternatively referred to, are its synonyms. Many people find name changes perplexing and even downright annoying, so it is worth outlining briefly why plant names change, or why at any one time a species may have more than one name.

Plants often have to be reclassified following the discovery of new information. As a result, a species may be transferred from one genus to another, or a single species may be split into two or more species. By the same token, two or more species may be combined into a single one, or what has previously been considered a subspecies or variety may be given specific rank. In certain circumstances a name may also change if an older published name is found.

Botanists also differ in their choice of classification systems, and this sometimes means that a single species bears two or more alternative and equally valid names, each one correct within its own particular system. One classification system may, for example, emphasize the similarities between certain species and so tend to lump them together. Another may emphasize the differences between the same species, splitting them up into different entities. The tree *Acacia albida*, for instance, also bears the name *Faidherbia albida*. The former reflects the similarities that this species shares with the genus *Acacia*; the latter the differences between this species and other *Acacia* members.

Synonyms are preceded by an equal sign (=) and placed in brackets. In this book we supply very few synonyms and then only from fairly recent name changes. Synonyms may facilitate cross-referencing between this book and other publications on trees, particularly older ones. When searching the literature to find out more about a particular tree species, you should not only use its currently accepted correct name, but also its synonyms.

6. ALIEN SPECIES A bullet (•) preceding a name signifies an alien plant invader. These are non-native plants that have been introduced into southern Africa from other parts of the world, and which have become naturalized – that is, capable of reproducing and spreading without human agency. Although by far the majority of tree species in southern African gardens and parks are aliens, most have not become naturalized and are therefore not treated in this book.

7. COMMON NAMES Common names are often confusing. The same name may apply to two or more different species, or the same species may have more than one common name. To provide a measure of stability, so-called standardized English and Afrikaans names were proposed for many native and alien trees (Von Breitenbach 1989, 1995).

With a few exceptions, these are the names used in this book, supplemented with a few newly proposed ones where suitable names did not previously exist. Names in other official and regional languages have been omitted, pending further efforts towards standardization, probably and preferably by mother tongue speakers, of tree names in each particular language.

8. NATIONAL TREE NUMBERS These have been proposed as a handy means of marking trees along highways and hiking trails, in nature reserves and recreation resorts, and also as a general quick-reference guide. The SA-numbers refer to those proposed for South Africa, Namibia, Botswana, Swaziland and Lesotho (based on Von Breitenbach 1989, 1995). Numbers of aliens are preceded by an X. The Z-numbers refer to the equivalent ones used in Zimbabwe (based on Drummond 1981).

9. FLOWERING TIME In a few tree species the peak flowering time occurs within fairly narrow limits. In many others, however, it may vary significantly from year to year over a species' distribution range, and even between two trees of the same species standing next to each other. We have therefore decided to give seasonal indicators rather than specific months. Our seasonal concepts are intended as a rough guide only: spring = August–November; summer = November–March; autumn = March–May; winter = May–August. Fruiting logically follows directly on flowering (except in the case of male trees of unisexual species).

10. DESCRIPTIVE TEXT The text for each species begins with an indication of duration, habit and habitat. Duration (whether deciduous or evergreen) is very variable in some species and not known with certainty in many others, and this aspect is not therefore described consistently. The location of vegetation types and centres of endemism mentioned in the text are shown in the maps on pages 8 and 9. Salient features of the bark, branchlets, leaves, inflorescence, flowers and fruit are then described. Particularly significant diagnostic characters are printed in bold. These characters, in combination, are normally essential for the positive identification of a species. Although we have tried to use language that can be readily understood by the layperson, some botanical terminology has been unavoidable (see Glossary, page 516).

11. PLANT USAGE Trees are not, of course, significant only for their place in the natural order and for the grace and beauty they bring to the land. They have immense practical value as food, medicine, tools, furniture, building materials, shelter and fuel. Selective mention is made of specific uses for some of the species. This feature has often had to be kept very short, or even omitted altogether, because of space constraints. Many of the healing properties ascribed to tree parts have not yet been scientifically proven, nor have any potentially negative side-effects been established. We have therefore refrained from mentioning specific medicinal usages, unless these have been validated by research.

12. RELATED SPECIES Where appropriate, the names of closely related species and their diagnostic characters are provided. The diagnostic characters of easily confused species are also given.

13. DISTRIBUTION MAPS Each species exhibits a certain pattern of distribution, which is one aspect of its definition. The distribution maps are compiled on a range style: the shaded areas are presented as a rough guide to the geographical limits of a particular species. The perimeter of a species distribution is approximate and, indeed, somewhat arbitrary. It does not indicate specific localities, nor does it give any indication whether a species is evenly spread over the area or occurs only in isolated localities. The colour of the shading will tell you whether a species is endemic – that is, restricted – to southern Africa (green), native to the region but also found further north in Africa (orange), or a naturalized alien (blue).

14. COLOUR PHOTOGRAPHS Each species description is accompanied, on the facing page, by one or more photographs. Thus all pertinent information relating to a tree appears on one spread. Illustrations showing features that are particularly helpful in identification (flowers, fruit, vegetative characteristics) have been selected. Growth forms and bark patterns have been included only if these are especially diagnostic.

15. CAPTIONS Label captions give the scientific name for the species, and the part(s) illustrated.

16. ENTRY NUMBERS The number adjacent to each species entry corresponds with the number of the species illustration(s) on the opposite page.

17. RUNNING HEADS These itemize the family or families that feature on the left hand (text) page, and the group into which they fall.

18. THUMB INDEXES The colour of these corresponds with the colour of the relevant group panel appearing in the Key to the Groups (pages 16–18) and in the Quick Guide on the inside back cover.

KEY TO THE GROUPS – Diagram A

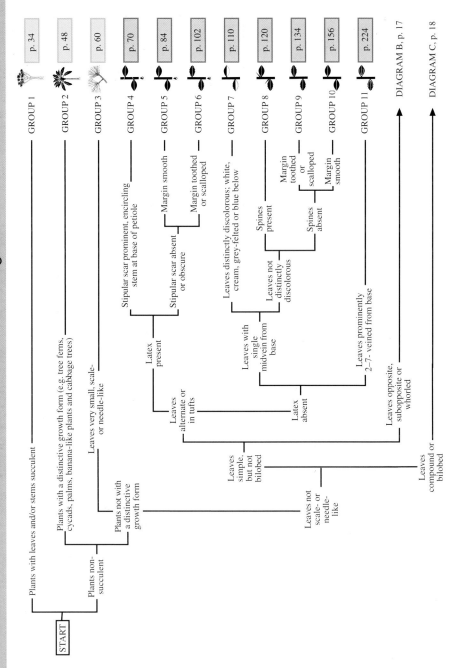

START

Plants with leaves and/or stems succulent — **GROUP 1** — p. 34

Plants non-succulent

Plants with a distinctive growth form (e.g. tree ferns, cycads, palms, banana-like plants and cabbage trees) — **GROUP 2** — p. 48

Plants not with a distinctive growth form

Leaves very small, scale- or needle-like — **GROUP 3** — p. 60

Leaves not scale- or needle-like

Latex present

Stipular scar prominent, encircling stem at base of petiole — **GROUP 4** — p. 70

Stipular scar absent or obscure

Margin smooth — **GROUP 5** — p. 84

Margin toothed or scalloped — **GROUP 6** — p. 102

Latex absent

Leaves simple, but not bilobed

Leaves alternate or in tufts

Leaves with single midvein from base

Leaves distinctly discolorous; white, cream, grey-felted or blue below — **GROUP 7** — p. 110

Leaves not distinctly discolorous

Spines present — **GROUP 8** — p. 120

Spines absent

Margin toothed or scalloped — **GROUP 9** — p. 134

Margin smooth — **GROUP 10** — p. 156

Leaves prominently 2–7- veined from base — **GROUP 11** — p. 224

Leaves opposite, subopposite or whorled — **DIAGRAM B, p. 17**

Leaves compound or bilobed — **DIAGRAM C, p. 18**

Diagram B

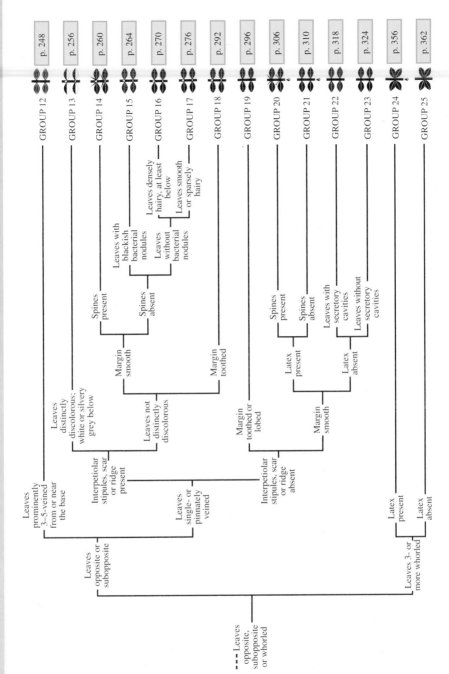

Leaves opposite, subopposite or whorled

- Leaves opposite or subopposite
  - Leaves prominently 3–5-veined from or near the base
    - Interpetiolar stipules, scar or ridge present
      - Leaves distinctly discolorous; white or silvery grey below
        - Spines present — **GROUP 12** — p. 248
        - Spines absent — **GROUP 13** — p. 256
      - Margin smooth — **GROUP 14** — p. 260
      - Leaves not distinctly discolorous — **GROUP 15** — p. 264
    - Leaves with blackish bacterial nodules — **GROUP 16** — p. 270
    - Leaves without bacterial nodules
      - Leaves densely hairy, at least below — **GROUP 17** — p. 276
      - Leaves smooth or sparsely hairy — **GROUP 18** — p. 292
  - Leaves single- or pinnately veined
    - Margin toothed — **GROUP 19** — p. 296
    - Interpetiolar stipules, scar or ridge absent
      - Margin toothed or lobed
        - Latex present
          - Spines present — **GROUP 20** — p. 306
          - Spines absent — **GROUP 21** — p. 310
      - Margin smooth
        - Leaves with secretory cavities — **GROUP 22** — p. 318
        - Latex absent
          - Leaves without secretory cavities — **GROUP 23** — p. 324
- Leaves 3- or more whorled
  - Latex present — **GROUP 24** — p. 356
  - Latex absent — **GROUP 25** — p. 362

17

Diagram C

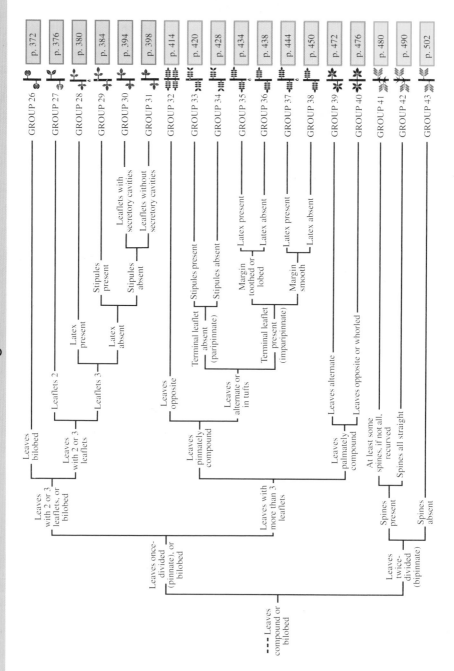

GROUP 26	p. 372
GROUP 27	p. 376
GROUP 28	p. 380
GROUP 29	p. 384
GROUP 30	p. 394
GROUP 31	p. 398
GROUP 32	p. 414
GROUP 33	p. 420
GROUP 34	p. 428
GROUP 35	p. 434
GROUP 36	p. 438
GROUP 37	p. 444
GROUP 38	p. 450
GROUP 39	p. 472
GROUP 40	p. 476
GROUP 41	p. 480
GROUP 42	p. 490
GROUP 43	p. 502

Leaves bilobed

Leaves with 2 or 3 leaflets

Leaflets 2

Leaflets 3

Latex present

Latex absent

Stipules present

Stipules absent

Leaflets with secretory cavities

Leaflets without secretory cavities

Leaves opposite

Leaves alternate or in tufts

Leaves pinnately compound

Terminal leaflet absent (paripinnate)

Terminal leaflet present (imparipinnate)

Stipules present

Stipules absent

Margin toothed or lobed

Margin smooth

Latex present

Latex absent

Latex present

Latex absent

Leaves palmately compound

Leaves alternate

Leaves opposite or whorled

Spines present

At least some spines, if not all, recurved

Spines all straight

Spines absent

Leaves with 2 or 3 leaflets, or bilobed

Leaves with more than 3 leaflets

Leaves once-divided (pinnate), or bilobed

Leaves twice-divided (bipinnate)

--- Leaves compound or bilobed

18

When identifying trees, a lot of time can be saved if one is familiar with the most important plant families in an area, especially as botanical keys — the formally accepted analytical devices for the determination of plant names – tend to be rather long and difficult to use. Thus anyone interested in southern African trees should be able to recognize, on sight, members of such prominent families as the Rubiaceae, Euphorbiaceae, Mimosaceae, Anacardiaceae, Fabaceae, Proteaceae, Celastraceae, Caesalpiniaceae, Combretaceae, Moraceae, Capparaceae, Asteraceae, Apocynaceae, Tiliaceae, Ebenaceae, Burseraceae, Flacourtiaceae and Sapindaceae. Together these 18 families, which we have ranked in descending order of importance, account for more than 1 000 native tree species, or nearly 65 per cent of the region's tree flora.

Each family entry appearing below begins with a brief summary of the features that distinguish its members in southern Africa. As the technical floral characters by which most plant families are defined are so obscure and esoteric (usually involving a determination of ovule number, placement and orientation), the emphasis here is on the more easily observed features which could assist in field identification. This section is followed by examples of the most important economic plants in each family, with the emphasis on those species and products which are known worldwide and with which readers might be familiar. Numerous examples of local usage are mentioned in the main section of this book.

Acanthaceae (Acanthus family) A family mainly of herbs and shrublets, well represented in southern Africa but with only about five species reaching tree size. Readily recognized by the opposite, estipulate leaves which arise from more or less swollen nodes. Stems are often slightly swollen immediately above each node. Flowers are conspicuously 2-lipped, and usually subtended by conspicuous bracts. The fruit is characteristically narrowly obovate, 2-valved, with elastic dehiscence. • Species from many genera are used as garden ornamentals, among them *Beloperone*, *Barleria*, *Acanthus*, *Hypoestes*, *Thunbergia* and *Justicia*. The deeply dissected, spiny leaves of *Acanthus* inspired the ornamental motifs on the Corinthian columns of classical Greek temples. (Groups 19, 23)

Anacardiaceae (Mango family) This is the fourth largest tree family in southern Africa, comprising at least 80 native tree species. Unfortunately, though, it is rather a difficult family to distinguish. Several members have alternate, imparipinnate leaves with a watery, rather than milky latex. Stipules are absent. Crushed leaves usually have a strong turpentine-like or resinous odour. Flowers are small, unisexual and inconspicuous. The genera are much easier to recognize. *Rhus*, for instance, has trifoliolate leaves with a resinous smell; and the leaves of *Ozoroa*, *Protorhus* and *Heeria* are simple with numerous more-or-less parallel side veins and watery or milky latex. The family can be confused with the latex-containing Burseraceae, but the latter often has bark that flakes in papery pieces. The pinnate leaves are also reminiscent of Sapindaceae and Meliaceae, both which lack any kind of milky latex. • Common edible fruit and seeds are the mango (*Mangifera indica*), pistachio nut (*Pistacia vera*) and cashew nut (*Anacardium occidentale*). The resinous exudate is poisonous in many species, causing severe irritation of the skin, as in poison ivy (*Toxicodendron* spp.) and the indigenous *Smodingium argutum*. The pepper tree (*Schinus molle*) from South America is widely planted for shade and ornament, particularly in arid regions. (Groups 5, 6, 24, 31, 35, 37)

Annonaceae (Custard apple family) A large family of mainly tropical trees and shrubs. About 20 native species are found in the southern African region. All its members have simple, entire, aromatic leaves arranged in two ranks and without stipules. The flowers, which tend to be greenish and inconspicuous, are usually bent to one side and downwards (nodding). They are very distinctive, with the perianth in two whorls of three, and with numerous, peculiar, short, thick stamens and usually several separate carpels instead of a single ovary (the latter is present in *Monodora*). The separate carpels, which have almost no style, are most prominent during fruiting, often developing into clusters of several fleshy fruits radiating from the tip of the original flower stalk. • Numerous species produce edible fruits, which for the most part are consumed locally rather than marketed for profit, and which are sometimes collectively known as 'custard apples' (from the custard-like flavour of many of them). Oil of ylang-ylang, one of the principal ingredients of French perfume, is distilled from the flowers of *Artabotrys odoratissimus*. (Group 10)

Apiaceae/Umbelliferae (Carrot family) A predominantly herbaceous family with only four or so tree species native to our area. Easily distinguished by the alternate, usually much-divided or pinnate leaves, with the petiole forming a sheath at the base. Crushed leaves have a strong, often carrot-like, smell. The flowers, borne in simple or compound umbels, are small, with an inferior ovary and two separate styles. • The family includes vegetables (carrot, parsnip), as well as numerous herbs, spices and flavouring plants (among them celery, parsley, fennel, dill, anise, angelica, coriander, cumin, and caraway). Many species, some of which are poisonous (for example hemlock, which brought about the death of the Athenian philosopher Socrates), are used in the preparation of medicines. (Groups 36, 38)

Apocynaceae (Oleander family) An easy to recognize, woody plant family with about 40 native tree species in the region. The combination of opposite or whorled leaves and milky or watery latex is definitive. All members have flowers with 5 petals, which are fused into a tube, and twisted in bud. Clusiaceae has a similar leaf arrangement, but the latex tends to be yellowish. • The family is rich in alkaloids, and several members are toxic or are used medicinally. Ornamentals include the oleander (*Nerium oleander*), Madagascar periwinkle (*Catharanthus roseus*), both which have become naturalized in the region, and the frangipani (*Plumeria*). (Groups 1, 20, 21, 24)

Aquifoliaceae (Holly family) A widespread family of trees and shrubs, but poorly represented in our region by just a single native species (*Ilex mitis*). Family characteristics are therefore unimportant in the context of this book. • Holly (*Ilex aquifolium*), with its attractive spiny foliage and bright red berries, has become a basic ingredient of Western-style Christmas decorations. (Group 10)

Araliaceae (Cabbage tree family) Closely related to the Apiaceae, but predominantly woody; with about 15 native species. Plants are usually conspicuous because of their large, palmately or pinnately lobed/compound leaves. The latter are alternate with stipules. The flowers have an inferior ovary, and are usually borne in umbels or spikes, which are often further compounded into large and complex umbels, racemes or panicles. • Cultivars of ivy (*Hedera helix*) are widely grown as ornamentals. Ginseng, a popular traditional medicine, is obtained from the roots of *Panax quinquefolia* and *P. pseudoginseng*. (Groups 2, 11, 38, 39)

Arecaceae/Palmae (Palm family) A distinctive family with an unmistakable habit, poorly represented in our region: there are only seven native species. The leaves are very large, palmately or pinnately divided (simple in Musaceae) and spirally arranged (2-ranked in Strelitziaceae). • Important economic products include coconuts (*Cocos nucifera*), dates (*Phoenix dactylifera*), sago (starch from the stem pith of *Metroxylon* spp.), fibres (coir from husks of coconut; raffia from leaflets of *Raphia*) and rattan cane (stems of *Calamus* spp.). *Elaeis guineensis* (African oil palm) is one of the world's most important sources of edible and soap-making oils. Many palms are cultivated as ornamentals. (Group 2)

Asteraceae/Compositae (Daisy family) Among the largest families of flowering plant in the world, and one that is predominantly herbaceous. Vegetative features are variable and the 40 or so species which reach tree size in our area are best recognized at generic or species level. However, many members tend to have cobwebby hairs on the stems and/or leaves. The small tubular flowers (called florets) are characteristically clustered in dense heads, subtended by bracts (an involucre) arranged in one or more whorls, the whole resembling a single flower. The ovary is inferior with a single ovule, and the fruit is small and often tipped by a tuft of hairs. • Important crop plants include lettuce (*Lactuca sativa*) and sunflower (*Helianthus annuus*). Among the many garden ornamentals are all the so-called daisies, everlastings (*Helichrysum*), marigolds (*Tagetes*), chrysanthemums and dahlias. Many common weeds belong to this family, among them cocklebur (*Xanthium*), cosmos (*Bidens formosa*), blackjack (*Bidens pilosa*), paraffin weed (*Chromolaena odorata*) and khaki weed (*Tagetes minuta*). (Groups 1, 3, 7, 9, 10, 19)

Balanitaceae (Green thorn family) A small family represented in our area by four species of *Balanites*. These are easily distinguished by their stalked, 2-foliolate leaves. • The family is of little economic importance. It is often included in the Zygophyllaceae. (Group 27)

Bignoniaceae (Jacaranda family) A very distinctive family of woody shrubs, trees and lianas, with about 11 native species. The leaves are pinnately compound, opposite or whorled and without stipules. Flowers are large, bell- or funnel-shaped and very showy. In several species the fruit is dehiscent and resembles a long, narrow pod, usually with winged seeds. • Ornamental trees and shrubs include Cape honeysuckle (*Tecomaria capensis*), yellow elder (*Tecoma stans*), jacaranda (*Jacaranda mimosifolia*) and the African flame tree (*Spathodea campanulata*). Many garden creepers with showy flowers – including golden shower (*Pyrostegia venusta*), trumpet vine (*Campsis grandiflora*), cat's claw (*Macfadyena unguis-cati*) and Mexican blood-trumpet (*Distictis buccinatoria*) – belong to the family. (Groups 8, 29, 32, 43)

Bombacaceae (Kapok family) A small family of tropical trees, with two species native to our area. Many species have thick, bottle-shaped or barrel-shaped trunks. The leaves are alternate, often palmately compound, with stipules. The flowers are large and showy, with 5 free petals and numerous stamens. • Kapok is derived from the fruit of silk cotton trees (*Bombax, Ceiba*). The durian (*Durio zibethinus*) is an extremely popular edible fruit in Southeast Asia. *Ochroma pyramidale* is the source of balsa wood. *Chorisia speciosa* (Brazil kapok) is an attractive flowering tree in tropical gardens. (Group 39)

Boraginaceae (Forget-me-not family) A predominantly herbaceous family with some ten tree species in our region. The leaves are alternate, simple, without stipules and are often harsh (sandpapery) to the touch. Twigs tend to be round. The flowers are regular, with 5 united petals and 5 stamens arising from the corolla tube. The sepals are often persistent in fruit. • Many members of the family are used as garden ornamentals, among them forget-me-not (*Myosotis*); and in traditional medicine, including comfrey (*Symphytum officinale*) and borage (*Borago officinalis*). (Groups 9, 10, 11)

Buddlejaceae (Wild sage family) A small family represented by seven or so native tree species, all belonging to the genus *Buddleja*. Easily recognized by the opposite or 3-whorled leaves, often with star-shaped hairs. Interpetiolar stipules, or a stipular ridge, are usually present between the petioles. Leaf margins are often toothed, which distinguishes them from the Rubiaceae. The flowers have 4 petals, united into a short tube, and 4 free stamens. • Certain species of *Buddleja* are used as garden ornamentals. (Groups 13, 23)

Burseraceae (Myrrh family) *Commiphora*, with about 35 tree species, is the only genus of the family in southern Africa. Species are conspicuous in arid bushveld and semi-desert areas; many are confined to Namibia's Kaokoveld region. Plants of the family are usually easy to recognize by the pinnately compound or trifoliolate (rarely simple) leaves, and strongly aromatic, often turpentine-like odour. All parts contain a milky or cloudy latex. Several species have bark which peels in thin, papery pieces, and this may help to distinguish them from the closely related Anacardiaceae. The flowers are small and insignificant. Seeds are usually covered by a bright red or yellowish aril-like structure. • Frankincense comes from the latex of certain species of *Boswellia*; myrrh from the latex of *Commiphora abyssinica, C. myrrha* and a number of other species cultivated in Ethiopia and Arabia. (Groups 5, 6, 28, 35, 37)

Buxaceae (Box-tree family) A small family of evergreen shrubs and trees, represented by only two native species in our area. These are vegetatively indistinct, with opposite, leathery leaves, without stipules. The flowers are inconspicuous, unisexual, with 3-chambered ovaries, the latter developing into very distinct capsules tipped by 3 slender horns. • A few species are grown as foliage plants, often as hedges or border edgings. (Group 23)

Cactaceae (Cactus family) A large, unmistakable family of mainly leafless stem succulents, almost exclusively confined to the semi-desert regions of North, Central and South America. Only one species, a small herbaceous shrublet or epiphyte, is indigenous to southern Africa. All tree forms in the area have been introduced. Most species have spines, often with tufts of tiny barbed hairs, which arise from cushions or areoles. Some resemble species of *Euphorbia*, but lack milky latex. The ovary is inferior, 1-chambered and many-seeded. • Prickly pears (*Opuntia*) are grown commercially for their fruit. Many species are valued as ornamentals. (Group 1)

FAMILY DESCRIPTIONS

Caesalpiniaceae (Bauhinia family) This is one of the ten largest woody plant families in our region (more than 50 species), and is particularly well represented in the miombo woodlands of south-central Africa. The leaves are alternate and characteristically paripinnate with opposite leaflets, 2-foliolate or deeply 2-lobed. A few species have imparipinnate or bipinnate leaves. Stipules are always present, at least in young growth, and are rarely spiny. An outstanding vegetative feature is the pulvinus, a conspicuous thickening at each petiole and petiolule base. The flowers are relatively large and showy, slightly irregular, with 10 or fewer stamens. This is one of three families characterized by a pod (legume) as fruit type, the other two being the Mimosaceae and Fabaceae. They are often combined into a single family, the Leguminosae. • Garden ornamentals include several species of *Bauhinia*, *Caesalpinia*, *Cassia*, and the flamboyant (*Delonix regia*). Various alkaloids, including the purgative senna, are obtained from species of *Cassia* and *Senna*. (Groups 26, 27, 33, 37, 38, 41, 43)

Capparaceae (Caper family) An important family in southern Africa (about 40 tree species), but difficult to identify in the absence of flowers or fruit. Leaves are alternate, simple, trifoliolate or palmately compound. Flowers are usually conspicuous, with 4 free petals, numerous long stamens and an ovary which is carried on a distinctive stalk (gynophore). In fruiting material the gynophore is clearly visible as a well-developed neck between the swollen (globose, oval or strongly elongated and pod-like) fruit and the fruit stalk proper, from which it is clearly demarcated by a scar (thickening) left by the receptacle and perianth. • Commercial capers are derived from the flower buds of *Capparis* species. The spider flower (*Cleome spinosa*) is a herbaceous annual grown for its attractive white or pink flowers. (Groups 8, 10, 29, 39)

Casuarinaceae (Beefwood family) A small family of leafless, woody, flowering plants from Australasia and Southeast Asia. Characterized by peculiar jointed branchlets (which function as leaves), superficially resembling pine needles. Represented by introduced species of *Casuarina* in our area. • The wood of several species is extremely hard and valued for furniture. (Group 3)

Celastraceae (Spike thorn family) With about 60 tree species in southern Africa, the Celastraceae counts as one of the ten largest tree families in the region. This is a rather indistinct family, although familiarity with the group leads to the recognition of a distinct, though difficult to describe, celastraceous 'look'. Young twigs tend to be greenish, somewhat angular, and in *Gymnosporia*, the largest genus in southern Africa, the plants are usually armed with spinescent shoots. The leaves are usually alternate or in clusters, leathery, with the venation on the lower surface somewhat translucent. In a few species elastic (rubbery) threads are visible on breaking the lamina. In our region these threads are only encountered in one other family, the closely related Hippocrateaceae. Stipules are present and usually minute, brown and shrivelled. Although small, the white or greenish flowers are more distinctive, being rather flat with a conspicuous nectar-secreting disc around the ovary, and a very short style. In species with capsular fruit the seeds are partly or completely covered by a fleshy orange or whitish aril. • The family is of more local than general economic importance. A few species are grown as ornamentals, mainly for their attractive, often variegated foliage (for example, *Celastrus*, *Euonymus*). The leaves of *Catha edulis*, known as khat, are a popular social drug in the Horn of Africa and parts of the Middle East. (Groups 8, 9, 10, 18, 19, 23)

Chenopodiaceae (Beetroot family) A large, mainly herbaceous family, with many species capable of growing in saline soils, often in arid regions. The genus *Salsola* has several species in the semi-desert parts of southern Africa, at least two of which may become small trees. They are all rather similar looking, with small, reduced leaves and inconspicuous flowers. • Different cultivars of *Beta vulgaris* (beetroot, sugar beet, spinach) are of major agricultural importance. A number of species, notably the saltbushes (*Atriplex*), are cultivated as fodder in arid areas. (Groups 3, 10)

Chrysobalanaceae (Coco plum family) A large tropical family of trees and shrubs. Poorly represented in our area by three native species, two of which reach tree size. A rather indistinct family with alternate, simple and entire leaves, with stipules; closely related to the Rosaceae. Two small glands are often present at the extreme base of the leaf blade (in our area, only in *Maranthus goetzeniana*). The fruit is always single-seeded. • The coco plum

(*Chrysobalanus icaco*) is cultivated for its fruit. Timber is provided by a number of species. Oil may be extracted from the seeds of many species. (Group 7)

Clusiaceae/Guttiferae (Mangosteen family) A family of about ten native tree species. They have opposite (rarely whorled), entire leaves (almost sessile in *Hypericum*), with very distinctive yellow or orange latex in some genera. Some species of *Garcinia* have leaves with many conspicuously parallel secondary and intersecondary veins. Flowers of *Hypericum* are unmistakable, with 5 free, yellow petals and many stamens, basally united into 5 bundles. • The mangosteen (*Garcinia mangostana*), a delicious fruit from Southeast Asia, is probably the best known family member. Gamboge, a yellow pigment used in watercolour paints, is prepared from the latex of *Garcinia hanburyi*. It has been used for centuries in the Far East as a dye to colour the orange-brown silk robes of Buddhist monks and priests. Timber and medicines are derived from various lesser known species. (Groups 21, 23, 24)

Combretaceae (Combretum family) This family is well represented in southern Africa, particularly in bushveld. More than 50 species reach tree size. The leaves are entire, alternate or opposite, and without stipules. *Combretum*, our largest genus, has opposite leaves which reminds one of Rubiaceae, but it lacks the characteristic stipules of the latter. Members of the second largest genus, *Terminalia*, often have a very distinctive pagoda-like tree architecture, known as Aubréville's Model. The main stem produces whorls of horizontal lateral branches. Each lateral branch is made up of a succession of branchlet units, each with the tip turned up and a cluster of leaves at its apex. The flowers are usually inconspicuous, small, greenish or yellowish white, and clustered in axillary heads or spikes. The ovary is inferior, elongated, and easily mistaken for the flower stalk. Fruits of *Combretum* are (with one exception) characteristically 4-winged. In most other members the fruit is surrounded by a single wing. • A few species, notably *Terminalia catappa* (Indian almond), are occasionally planted for ornament in the coastal regions of KwaZulu-Natal. The Rangoon creeper, *Quisqualis indica*, is widely grown for its attractive flowers. (Groups 8, 10, 23)

Cornaceae (Dogwood family) A small family of mainly northern hemisphere trees and shrubs, together with a few herbs. Poorly represented in our area, with only two native species. Vegetatively rather indistinct. The flowers are inconspicuous, with an inferior ovary which develops into drupes or berries, characteristically tipped by the calyx, or by a circular scar. • Species of *Cornus* (dogwood) have flowers that are surrounded by large, showy, white bracts, and are widely grown as ornamentals. (Group 18)

Crassulaceae (Crassula family) A large family of mainly succulent-leaved herbs. The native tree-like members (about three species) are recognized by their opposite, simple, succulent leaves and flowers with 5 separate ovaries. Vegetatively very similar to Portulacaceae, which has flowers with a single, 1-chambered ovary. • Popular collector plants among succulent enthusiasts. Some species are valued as rock-garden ornamentals. (Group 1)

Cunoniaceae (Wild alder family) A family of trees and shrubs, mainly from the southern hemisphere. Poorly represented in our area by two native species. Leaves are opposite, trifoliolate or pinnately compound, the leaflets having toothed margins. Stipules are present, and often large and united in pairs over the growing tips. • The family is of little economic importance. (Groups 29, 32)

Cupressaceae (Cypress family) A family of conifers (gymnosperms), usually with scale-like mature leaves arranged in opposite pairs or in whorls. Juvenile leaves tend to be needle-like. Three species are native to our area. The female cones are more or less globose, with the scales arranged in opposite pairs. • Timber is obtained from many species. The family also yields resins and flavourings, and some members are cultivated as ornamentals (including many cultivars of hardy, dwarf conifers with bluish, golden or variegated foliage). (Group 3)

Cyatheaceae (Tree fern family) There are about four species of tree fern native to our region, all from forest or wet areas in associated grassland. Tree ferns are unmistakable, having large, much-divided leaves which unfurl from coiled tips and usually have scales and/or prickles at the base of the petiole. Plants reproduce by means of spores, which are borne in fertile parts (sori) on the lower surface of the leaves. • A few species are grown as ornamentals; the family is otherwise of little economic importance. (Group 2)

Dipterocarpaceae (Meranti family) A woody family centred in the tropical rain forests of Southeast Asia. Poorly represented in our area, with three woodland tree species; easily identified by the large gland at the base of the midrib. The fruit is a nut enclosed in the persistent, winged and membranous calyx. • The family is the world's main source of hardwood timber; among useful genera are *Dipterocarpus, Hopea, Shorea* (meranti) and *Vatica*. Forest species grow very tall, with straight and unbranched boles and relatively small crowns. (Groups 7, 10)

Dracaenaceae (Dragon tree family) A distinct monocot family of large, perennial herbs or small trees, with four native tree species. The leaves are long and tapering, parallel-veined and often clustered in dense terminal rosettes. The flowers are very similar to those of the Liliaceae. • Ornamentals include species of *Sansevieria* (mother-in-law's tongue), *Cordyline* and *Dracaena* (dragon trees). (Group 2)

Ebenaceae (Ebony family) A woody family with about 35 tree species native to southern Africa. Vegetatively rather indistinct with simple, entire leaves without stipules. The two native genera are much easier to recognize: *Euclea* has hard, leathery leaves which tend to be opposite and with undulate margins; *Diospyros* has alternate leaves and fruit that is subtended or enclosed by the persistent and enlarged calyx. • Commercial ebony is the hard, black heartwood of certain species of *Diospyros*. The best known fruits are the persimmons (among others *Diospyros kaki* and *D. virginiana*). (Groups 10, 23)

Ericaceae (Heath family) A family with about 700 species in southern Africa (mainly in the Western Cape), but with probably fewer than 20 reaching tree size. Readily recognized (in our region) by the needle-like, leathery and alternate leaves which lack stipules. The flowers are small, with 5 united petals and 10 stamens. A distinctive feature are the anthers, which open with pores to release the pollen. The family can be confused with narrow-leaved members of the Rosaceae (with stipules) and Thymelaeaceae (with tough, fibrous bark). • The azaleas (*Rhododendron*) are popular garden ornamentals. Blueberries, cranberries and bilberries are obtained from species of *Vaccinium*. *Arbutus unedo* (strawberry tree) is often cultivated in gardens. (Group 3)

Erythroxylaceae (Cocaine family) A woody, mainly tropical family, poorly represented by about six species in our region. Readily recognized by the alternate, entire leaves with intrapetiolar stipules. *Erythroxylon* has the young stems conspicuously flattened towards the ends, whereas *Nectaropetalum* has its growing buds covered by united stipules, which are conspicuously spike- or horn-like. • The drug cocaine is extracted from the leaves of the South American *Erythroxylon coca*. (Group 10)

Escalloniaceae (Escallonia family) A mainly temperate southern hemisphere family of shrubs and trees. The leaves are alternate, simple, with toothed margins. A rather indistinct family, with just one native species. • Species of *Escallonia* are grown as ornamentals; otherwise the family is of little economic importance. (Group 9)

Euphorbiaceae (Euphorbia family) With just over 100 native tree species, this is the second largest woody family in southern Africa. Very heterogeneous, the vegetative and floral structures showing great variation. The vast majority of its species can readily be recognized by combinations of milky or watery latex, simple alternate leaves, a pair of glands at the petiole apex or base of leaf blade, and the presence of stipules or stipule scars. However, there are exceptions to each one of these. In the great majority of cases the fruit is characteristically 3-lobed and often crowned by the 3 persistent stigmas. The combination of stem succulence and milky latex, and of toothed leaf margins and milky latext, are definitive for the family. Succulent members are also characterized by specialized inflorescences (cyathia) that mimic flowers. • Most of the world's natural rubber is obtained from *Hevea brasiliensis*. Cassava or tapioca (starchy tubers of *Manihot esculenta*) is a staple food in many tropical countries. Numerous members are poisonous and/or have medicinal uses, including castor oil (*Ricinus communis*). The poinsettia (*Euphorbia pulcherrima*) is widely grown in gardens. (Groups 1, 5, 6, 9, 10, 11, 13, 25, 39)

Fabaceae (Pea family) A well represented family (sometimes referred to under the name Papilionaceae) in southern Africa, with about 80 tree species. The alternate leaves are usually imparipinnate or 3-foliolate, but sometimes simple. Stipules are always present, although deciduous with age in some species. An outstanding vegetative feature is the pulvinus, a conspicuous thickening at each petiole and petiolule base. Easily recognized as a family by the very characteristic butterfly-like flower type. The petals are unequal, with the uppermost (standard or banner) the largest, the two side ones small and stalked (wings), and the two basal ones united into a boat-shaped structure (keel). This is one of three families characterized by a pod (legume) as fruit type, the other two being the Mimosaceae and Caesalpiniaceae. They are often combined into a single family, the Leguminosae. • Seeds and pods of many of the herbaceous species are sources of human food, including garden pea (*Pisum sativum*), various types of beans (*Glycine, Phaseolus, Vicia*) and the peanut (*Arachis hypogea*). The cowpea (*Vigna sinensis*), clover (*Trifolium*) and lucerne (*Medicago sativa*) are widely used as forage plants. Liquorice is obtained from the dried roots and rhizomes of several *Glycyrrhiza* species. Garden ornamentals include lupin (*Lupinus*), broom (*Cytisus*), sweet pea (*Lathyrus*), blue rain (*Wisteria*) and several coral trees (*Erythrina*). Most members have root nodules containing nitrogen fixing bacteria, and play an important role in the nitrogen enrichment of soils. (Groups 10, 29, 33, 38)

Flacourtiaceae (Wild peach family) A family of woody plants with more than 30 tree species, found mainly in the subtropical parts of our region. This is a difficult family to distinguish, particularly vegetatively. Leaves are always simple and usually alternate. The flowers (which are often unisexual) tend to have 5 free petals, numerous free stamens, and a superior, 1-chambered ovary (later a 1-chambered fruit). • The family contains few plants of economic importance. (Groups 7, 8, 9, 10, 11, 19)

Greyiaceae (Wild bottlebrush family) An exclusively southern African family of one genus (*Greyia*) and three species. Easily recognized by the alternate, simple leaves, with more or less palmate venation, irregularly toothed margins, and sheathing leafbases. The scarlet, bell-shaped flowers are arranged in showy heads or spikes. • Often cultivated as ornamentals. (Group 11)

Hamamelidaceae (Witch hazel family) A woody family, poorly represented in our area by four forest species and vegetatively rather indistinct. The flowers in some species (including all native ones) are clustered in dense heads and have very characteristic, ribbon-shaped petals. • Storax, a fragrant gum used in perfumery and medicine, is derived from certain species of *Liquidambar*. This genus also yields excellent timber (American sweet gum or red gum). *Liquidambar styraciflua* (sweet gum) is often cultivated for its ornamental autumn foliage. Witch hazel lotion, from *Hamamelis virginiana*, is widely used to treat cuts and bruises. (Groups 7, 23)

Hernandiaceae (Hernandia family) A small tropical family with just a single native species in our area. *Gyrocarpus americanus* is a very distinct species and there is no need to dwell on family characters. • The family has no significant economic value. (Group 11)

Heteropyxidaceae (Lavender tree family) A small family (closely related to Myrtaceae) with two species in southern Africa and one in Mauritius. The local genus (*Heteropyxis*) has alternate, entire, simple leaves with secretory cavities. These emit a pleasant smell when crushed. The flowers are small and inconspicuous. • The family has no significant economic value. (Group 10)

Icacinaceae (White pear family) Vegetatively a rather indistinct woody family, poorly represented in our region. The two native tree genera, *Apodytes* (three species) and *Cassinopsis* (two species), are much easier to recognize than the family. • The family has no significant economic value, although a few species yield excellent timber, and several others have local uses. (Groups 10, 17, 18)

Lauraceae (Avocado family) An almost exclusively woody family, best represented in tropical forests, with about ten native tree species. Vegetatively rather indistinct, with alternate (opposite in *Dahlgrenodendron*), non-

2-ranked, simple, entire leaves, and no stipules. A useful diagnostic leaf character is the very fine reticulum of tertiary veins (as in Rhamnaceae). Twigs are usually green and without prominent lenticels. Leaves contain oil cells (not visible against the light) and are usually aromatic when crushed. The flowers are small, inconspicuous, with 6 tepals and unmistakable anthers which dehisce by flap-like valves. • Economic products include cinnamon and camphor (*Cinnamomum*), bay leaves (*Laurus nobilis*), timber (*Ocotea*) and the avocado (*Persea americana*). (Groups 7, 10, 11)

Lecythidaceae (Brazil nut family) A family of tropical trees centred in South America, with a single native species in southern Africa. The leaves are alternate, large and simple, usually without stipules. Most species have large, showy but very short-lived flowers. These have a fluffy appearance due to the numerous stamens. Fruits are usually hard and woody, with a lid through which the seeds are released. • Brazil or Pará nuts are the seeds of *Bertholletia excelsa*. (Group 10)

Liliaceae (Lily family) This is a family that is not usually associated with trees: members are predominantly herbaceous, many are bulbous plants. The tree forms (at least 25 species) in our region all belong to the genus *Aloe*, a distinct and easy to recognize group. Floral characters are very diagnostic for the family. All have 6 perianth segments ('petals'), 6 stamens and a 3-chambered, superior ovary. • A horticulturally important family: many species have beautiful flowers, among them tulips (*Tulipa*), lilies (*Lilium*), day lilies (*Hemerocallis*), hyacinths (*Hyacinthus*) and red-hot pokers (*Kniphofia*). Numerous food crops are derived from members of the genus *Allium*, including the onion, garlic, leek, shallot and chive. Several species are used medicinally. (Group 1)

Loganiaceae (Wild elder family) A predominantly woody family with about 20 tree species native to southern Africa. The leaves are opposite or whorled, simple, and often with reduced stipules (sometimes with a stipular line between the petioles). All species have flowers with 4- or 5-lobed tubular corollas, and 4 or 5 stamens which are attached to the petals. *Strychnos* is unmistakable with its opposite, 3-veined leaves. • Many species are rich in alkaloids and extremely poisonous (*Strychnos* species yield strychnine and curare). (Groups 12, 17, 19, 25)

Lythraceae (Pride-of-India family) A mainly tropical family of herbs, trees and shrubs. The single native tree species, *Galpinia transvaalica*, is very distinct, and there is no need to dwell on family characters. • Henna, a reddish brown dye, is obtained from *Lawsonia inermis*. Cultivars of pride-of-India (*Lagerstroemia indica*) are hardy trees with attractive flowers. *Cuphea* species are small shrublets often grown in gardens. (Group 23)

Malvaceae (Hibiscus family) For the most part a family of herbs and shrublets, with about eight native tree species. Closely related to Tiliaceae, Sterculiaceae and Bombacaceae, with which it shares alternate, simple, often lobed leaves which are 3- or more-veined from the base, stipules and star-shaped hairs. The flowers are very distinctive, with 5 free petals and numerous stamens united into a tube around the style; often subtended by an epicalyx (lower calyx whorl). • Cotton (seed fibres of *Gossypium*) is the most important product. Okra is a common vegetable in tropical regions (young fruit of *Hibiscus esculentus*). The family produces many garden ornaments, notably species of *Hibiscus* and hollyhocks (*Althaea*). (Group 11)

Melastomataceae (Dissotis family) A large, mainly tropical family, especially common in South America. Twigs are more or less 4-angled, with simple, glossy and rather leathery, entire leaves. Four of the five native tree species have leaves with pinnate venation (rather anomalous for the family). They are vegetatively easily confused with Myrtaceae, but can be distinguished by the lack of secretory cavities. The one remaining species (*Memecylon sousae*) has leaves that are more typically 3-veined from the base, and resembles the genus *Strychnos*. The ovary is inferior, resulting in a fruit tipped by the persistent calyx. • Several of the herbaceous members (*Dissotis, Medinilla, Tibouchina*) are cultivated for their showy flowers. (Group 12, 23)

Meliaceae (Mahogany family) A large, tropical, woody family with about 20 native species. Vegetatively rather diverse, with both simple and pinnately compound leaves. These are always alternate and without stipules. Species with compound leaves can be distinguished from the rather similar Anacardiaceae by the lack of latex. They also resemble pinnate-leaved members of the Sapindaceae, but the latter tend to have an aborted rachis apex. The flowers, however, are very distinct, with 5 free petals, and 8–10 stamens which are united into a cylindrical tube around the style. • A very important tropical timber family. True mahogany is derived from species of *Swietenia* and sapele from *Entandrophragma cylindricum*. The family contains certain bitter-tasting chemical compounds, many of which have insecticidal properties. Langsat (*Lansium domesticum*) is a popular edible fruit in Southeast Asia. *Melia azedarach* is widely cultivated for shade and ornament, and has now become a troublesome invader weed in our region. (Groups 10, 34, 38, 43)

Melianthaceae (White ash family) A small family, endemic to Africa and perhaps best known from the herbaceous genus *Melianthus*. *Bersama*, with five native tree species, is an exclusively woody genus. This is the only family in our region with alternate, pinnately compound leaves, with intrapetiolar stipules. • Species of *Melianthus* are grown as garden ornamentals. *Bersama* bark is widely used in traditional medicine. (Groups 36, 38)

Mimosaceae (Thorn-tree family) This is the third largest woody plant family in southern Africa, embracing about 100 tree species. The genera *Acacia* and *Albizia* are an important ecological component of bushveld vegetation throughout the region. The family is easily recognized by the bipinnate leaves, usually with petiolar or rachis glands. Stipules (or a stipular scar) are always present, and are often modified into thorns or spines (*Acacia*). An outstanding vegetative feature is the pulvinus, a conspicuous thickening at each petiole and petiolule base. The flowers are small, regular, with numerous exserted stamens, and arranged into dense capitate or spicate inflorescences. Many species have leaflets that fold up at night (so-called sleeping movements). This is one of three families characterized by a pod (legume) as fruit type, the other two being the Caesalpiniaceae and Fabaceae. The three are often combined into a single family, the Leguminosae. • Various commercial products are obtained from *Acacia* (tan-bark, wood, gums) and the family also produces a few ornamentals, including *Calliandra* (powderpuff), *Acacia* and *Albizia*. Gum arabic (from *Acacia senegal*) is used to thicken many convenience foods, pharmaceuticals and cosmetics, and may be a component of water-colour paints and printing inks. Pods of mesquite trees (*Prosopis*) are an important stock feed in arid areas. Most members have root nodules containing nitrogen-fixing bacteria, playing a significant role in the nitrogen enrichment of soils. Several species of *Acacia* from Australia (so-called wattles) have become serious invader weeds in southern Africa. The latter are all spineless. (Groups 10, 11, 41, 42, 43)

Monimiaceae (Lemonwood family) A medium-sized family of shrubs and trees, mainly from tropical areas in the southern hemisphere. The leaves are opposite, without stipules, leathery, with toothed margins, and they usually contain aromatic oils. *Xymalos monospora*, a distinct forest species, is the only representative in our area. The latter was previously included in Trimeniaceae (not found in Africa), a family which it resembles in having a superior, single-carpelled ovary. • The family is valued locally for timber, aromatic oils and medicine. (Group 19)

Moraceae (Fig family) This family is well represented in warmer, frost-free parts of the region, particularly so by the genus *Ficus*, which has more than 35 tree species. The family is easily recognized by the combination of alternate leaves, milky latex and a distinctive conical stipule that covers the apical bud. The stipule is deciduous and leaves an obvious circular or semicircular scar on falling. Flowers of all Moraceae are tiny, inconspicuous, and clustered into often complicated inflorescences – for example a 'fig' – which is a hollow, vase-like receptacle containing numerous tiny flowers. • Edible fruits include breadfruit and jackfruit (*Artocarpus*), figs (*Ficus*) and mulberries (*Morus*). Timber is obtained from *Chlorophora* (iroko-wood or fustic). Several species of *Ficus* are grown for ornamental purposes. The rubber plant (*F. elastica*) and weeping fig (*F. benjamina*) are common indoor and outdoor container plants in southern Africa. (Groups 4, 39)

Moringaceae (Horse-radish tree family) A small family of about 12 pale-barked, deciduous trees, only one (*Moringa ovalifolia*) of which is native to our area. All have graceful leaves, which are 2 or 3 times pinnate. Fruit a long, pod-like capsule. • Ben oil, used in salads and soap, comes from *Moringa oleifera* seeds. (Group 43)

Musaceae (Banana family) Tropical monocots with an unmistakable habit. *Ensete ventricosa* is the only native representative in our area. All species have large, oblong or oblong-elliptic leaf blades, borne spirally at the end of a pseudostem formed by the tightly overlapping leaf sheaths. The leaves resemble those in tree forms of Strelitziaceae, but the latter has true stems, and leaves arranged in a single plane. • The banana (bred in Southeast Asia from *Musa acuminata* and *M. balbisiana*) is a major food crop. (Group 2)

Myricaceae (Waxberry family) A woody family with about five species that reach tree size in our region. The leaves are alternate, simple and leathery, with more or less toothed margins. They are very distinctly dotted with minute, golden yellow glandular hairs (particularly below) and are aromatic when crushed. The flowers are inconspicuous, naked (without perianth) and borne in dense axillary spikes. • In former times the fruits of some species were boiled to produce wax. (Group 9)

Myrsinaceae (Myrsine family) A rather indistinct woody family, poorly represented in our region. It is much easier to familiarize oneself with the diagnostic features of the seven or so native tree species than to try and recognize the family. • The family is of little economic importance. (Groups 9, 10)

Myrtaceae (Guava family) A predominantly woody family, mostly tropical and subtropical, which is represented by some 25 native tree species. Easily recognized in our area by the combination of opposite, simple, entire leaves with secretory cavities. The flowers tend to have many showy stamens and the ovary is invariably inferior, resulting in fruit tipped by the remains of the calyx. The introduced eucalypts (*Eucalyptus*) are unusual in having mature leaves that are apparently alternate. • The eucalypts (which are predominantly Australian) yield valuable timber, and several species are grown in commercial plantations. Important spices produced by the family include allspice or pimento (*Pimenta dioica*) and cloves (the dry flower buds of *Syzygium aromaticum*; what appears to be a stalk is the inferior ovary). The guava (*Psidium guajava*) is probably the most popular edible fruit. Garden ornamentals include the bottlebrushes (*Callistemon* and *Melaleuca*) and tea bushes (*Leptospermum*). (Groups 10, 22)

Ochnaceae (Wild plane family) A family with just over 20 tree species in our region, nearly all of them members of the genus *Ochna*. These are characterized by alternate, simple leaves, with more or less finely toothed margins, and many closely spaced, parallel lateral veins. All species have narrow stipules, often borne somewhat in the leaf axil. The axillary and apical buds tend to be elongated and covered by overlapping, brownish, scale-leaves. The flowers are usually yellow (rarely white to cream or pink), with free, somewhat stalked petals and many free stamens. • The family includes few plants of economic value. (Groups 9, 10)

Olacaceae (Sourplum family) A family of woody, often hemiparasitic plants with just five or so native species. A rather indistinct family in flower or in sterile condition, but the species are easy to recognize. *Ximenia* has branch spines. • The family is of no major economic value, though some species produce useful timber and edible fruit. (Groups 8, 10)

Oleaceae (Olive family) A mainly woody family with about 15 tree species in southern Africa. Rather indistinct vegetatively, with both simple or pinnately compound leaves. These are always opposite, entire-margined and lack stipules. Branchlets almost always have at least a few small, whitish, raised lenticels. The flowers are regular, with 4, 5 or more united petals and 2 stamens arising from the petals. • The family contains several genera of economic or horticultural importance, among them *Olea* (olive), *Fraxinus* (ash), *Jasminum* (jasmine), *Ligustrum* (privet, liguster) and *Syringa* (lilac). The best baseball bats are made from the wood of the ash. (Groups 23, 32)

Oliniaceae (Hard pear family) A small family of about ten species of trees and shrubs endemic to southern and eastern Africa. *Olinia* is the only genus. Rather indistinct with opposite, simple, entire leaves, without stipules. The twigs tend to be 4-angled. Crushed leaves often smell of almonds. The flowers have an inferior ovary (fruit tipped by a circular scar). • The family is of no significant economic value. (Group 23)

Pedaliaceae (Sesame family) A small family of mainly annual or perennial herbs. The three native tree species (*Sesamothamnus*) are spiny and easy to identify. The irregular, tubular flowers have 5 united petals and are reminiscent of Scrophulariaceae. The fruits are often winged, or armed with hooks or spines. • Sesame seed and oil are obtained from *Sesamum indicum*. Tubers of the devil's claw (*Harpagophytum procumbens*) are a widely used herbal remedy. (Group 8)

Pinaceae (Pine family) The largest family of conifers, and one that is essentially confined to the northern hemisphere. There are invasive aliens but no native species in our area. Readily distinguished by the needle-shaped leaves borne in small clusters. Female cones are woody and conspicuous. • This is the most economically important gymnosperm family, providing the bulk of the world's requirements in soft-wood timber and wood pulp. It also yields various oils and turpentine. Species of *Pinus* are extensively grown in commercial plantations in the high-rainfall areas of southern Africa. (Group 3)

Pittosporaceae (Cheesewood family) A medium-sized family of evergreen trees and shrubs, with its greatest diversity in Australia and Southeast Asia. Poorly represented in our area, by a single indigenous species (*Pittosporum viridiflorum*). Crushed leaves have a resinous smell, but otherwise a rather indistinct family. • *Hymenosporum flavum* (sweet cheesewood) and several species of *Pittosporum* (cheesewood) are cultivated as garden ornamentals. (Group 10)

Podocarpaceae (Yellowwood family) A widespread family of gymnosperms, with four species of *Podocarpus* in our area. The genus is readily distinguished by the alternate, narrow, stiff and leathery, simple leaves, with a strong midvein and indistinct lateral veins. • Several species yield valuable timber; yellowwood was much used in house construction, in the building of wagons and for furniture in the early years of white settlement at the Cape. (Group 10)

Polygalaceae (Milkwort family) Vegetatively an indistinct family, with about four tree species in our area. The flowers, however, are very characteristic, pea-like, and superficially resemble those of Fabaceae. They are irregular, with 5 sepals, of which the inner two are wing-like and look like petals. The petals are reduced (well developed in Fabaceae), often with a brush-like appendage. The ovary is 2-chambered, unlike that of the single-chambered Fabaceae. • The family is of little economic importance. (Group 10)

Portulacaceae (Purslane family) A family of mainly succulent-leaved herbs, often with hairy leaf axils. Only three tree species occur in our area. The opposite and simple succulent leaves of *Portulacaria* are very similar to those of Crassulaceae. Some species of *Ceraria* are very distinctive by virtue of their narrow, cylindrical leaves, which are arranged in clusters. • Members of *Portulaca* are valued as ornamentals for their showy flowers. Purslane (*P. oleracea*) is a common weed, widely used as a pot herb. (Groups 1, 3)

Proteaceae (Protea family) An ancient, woody, southern hemisphere (Gondwana) family, in our region best represented in the Western Cape. More than 60 species may be considered trees. The leaves are simple, alternate, entire, leathery and without stipules (*Brabejum stellatifolium*, with leaves whorled and toothed, is a notable exception). The flowers, which are usually congested in showy heads or spikes, are very characteristic. Each has 4 petal-like sepals with reflexed tips, and 4 stamens which are opposite and fused to the sepals, often with only the anthers free or with very short filaments. The ovary is superior, with a long style. • Plants are mainly cultivated for ornament and cut flowers (for example, *Banksia*, *Grevillea* and *Protea*). The wood is very characteristic: it has broad rays, and makes beautiful furniture (*Grevillea*, *Faurea*). The macadamia nut (*Macadamia integrifolia*) is the only significant commercially grown food crop. (Groups 3, 10, 25)

Ptaeroxylaceae (Sneezewood family) A small African family, apparently related to Rutaceae. The single native species (*Ptaeroxylon obliquum*) is easily recognized by its opposite, imparipinnate leaves. • The family is of no significant economic importance. (Group 32)

Rhamnaceae (Buffalo-thorn family) A woody family with about 20 native tree species. Members are often thorny with simple, glossy leaves. The venation tends to be diagnostic – particularly the tertiary one, which forms a very fine and regular reticulum of minute squares or rectangles. In this respect the family resembles the Lauraceae. The flowers are usually inconspicuous, with a prominent disc, and 5 reduced petals very characteristically borne opposite to, and often embracing, the 5 stamens. Flowers of Celastraceae also have a well-developed disc, but the petals alternate with the stamens. • The family includes few plants of economic value. *Ceanothus* contains many attractive flowering shrubs, which are widely cultivated. Many species are used locally in traditional medicine. (Groups 3, 9, 11, 23)

Rhizophoraceae (Onionwood family) A predominantly woody tropical family, most notable for the many species known as mangroves. About ten species are native to our area. The leaves are opposite and simple, usually hairless, with interpetiolar stipules, and thus resemble some Rubiaceae. The stipules fall early, leaving a line between the petioles. In *Cassipourea*, the only inland genus in our region, the leaves are usually more or less toothed and the ovary is superior, so differing from Rubiaceae (which has entire margins and inferior ovaries). • Apart from many local uses (for food, and in traditional medicine), the family is of little economic importance. (Groups 17, 18, 25)

Rosaceae (Rose family) A family that is at its most abundant in temperate regions of the northern hemisphere; poorly represented in our area, with fewer than eight native tree species and a number of naturalized aliens. The leaves are alternate, simple or compound, usually with toothed margins (needle-shaped in some species of *Cliffortia*). Stipules are present and often conspicuous. The flowers are showy (unisexual and very inconspicuous in *Cliffortia*), regular, with 5 free, short-stalked petals, numerous free stamens and an often inferior ovary (superior in *Prunus*). • Economically an extremely important family, yielding many fruit crops. Among these are *Prunus* (almond, apricot, cherry, nectarine, peach, plum, prune), *Pyrus* (pear), *Fragaria* (strawberry), *Eriobotrya* (loquat), *Malus* (apple), quince (*Cydonia*), *Rubus* (blackberry, raspberry). The family also produces many garden ornamentals, most notably the rose (*Rosa*) itself. Rose oil is one of the world's most valuable oils, used as the base for most perfumes; the principal centre of production is Bulgaria. (Groups 7, 9, 36)

Rubiaceae (Coffee family) This is the largest family of trees in southern Africa, comprising about 160 native species, and extremely easy to recognize by its opposite leaves and interpetiolar stipules. The leaves are always entire and often have domatia in the axils of the side veins. Interpetiolar stipules occur between the opposite petiole bases, and often fall off at an early stage, leaving a distinct line or scar connecting the opposite petioles. The ovary is inferior, which means the fruit is either crowned by the persistent remains of the calyx, or by a circular scar. Inconspicuous interpetiolar stipules or lines are also found in Acanthaceae, Rhizophoraceae and Buddlejaceae, but these families usually have toothed leaf margins. • The family is rich in alkaloids and is widely used medicinally. Coffee (mainly from *Coffea arabica* and *C. canephora*), quinine (*Cinchona*) and ipecacuanha (*Cephaelis*) are the best known products. Coffee is said to be second only to petroleum as a revenue earner among the world's natural products. Ornamental plants include species of *Gardenia, Hamelia, Ixora, Pentas* and *Serissa*. (Groups 14, 15, 16, 17, 25)

Rutaceae (Citrus family) About 26 tree species are native to our area. An easy family to recognize vegetatively: trees with palmate, trifoliolate or pinnate leaves with secretory cavities in the lamina are invariably members of Rutaceae. Crushed leaves, typically, have a pungent, often citrus-like odour. All local members have alternate leaves except *Calodendrum capense*, which is unusual in that it has both opposite and simple leaves, and thus resembles species in the family Myrtaceae. Flowers of Rutaceae usually have 10 or fewer stamens and a superior ovary, whereas those of Myrtaceae have numerous stamens and an inferior ovary. • The family is of great economic importance, yielding various commercial citrus fruits including lemons, oranges, tangerines, mandarins, limes and grapefruit (all species of *Citrus*). Rue (*Ruta graveolens*) is widely grown in herb gardens as a medicinal plant. Numerous species are cultivated for their essential oils (among them bergamot oil) used in perfumes. Some forest species yield attractive, often yellowish, wood that is used for furniture. (Groups 22, 30, 32, 36)

Salicaceae (Willow family) A mainly temperate northern hemisphere family of deciduous trees and shrubs. Poorly represented in our area, with five or so native taxa, all confined to the banks of streams or rivers. The leaves are alternate, narrow, toothed and stipulate. Flowers, which lack sepals and petals, are inconspicuous, clustered into erect or pendulous spikes. • Willows (*Salix*) and poplars (*Populus*) provide timber and are also grown for ornament, shade and shelter. Willow wood (*Salix alba* var. *caerulea*) is used in the making of cricket bats; poplar wood is used for matches. (Groups 7, 9)

Salvadoraceae (Mustard family) A small family of trees and shrubs with four unspectacular native species. An indistinct family with opposite, simple, entire leaves. Best recognized at species level. • The family is of no major economic importance. Leaves and fruit of *Salvadora persica* are claimed by some to be the source of the 'mustard' of biblical times. Present-day mustard is made from the powdered seeds of species of *Brassica* (family Brassicaceae/Cruciferae). (Group 23)

Santalaceae (Sandalwood family) A large family of herbs, shrubs and trees, most of which are hemiparasites on the roots of other plants. The two native tree species have bluish green, simple, entire leaves with obscure secondary and tertiary veins. The flowers are inconspicuous with inferior ovaries. The family is closely related to some of the mistletoes (Loranthaceae). • The sandalwood tree (*Santalum album*) is probably the best known member of the family. It yields sandal oil and a fragrant timber. (Groups 10, 23)

Sapindaceae (Litchi family) More than 30 members of this predominantly woody family occur in the region. The leaves are always alternate and lack stipules. They are usually trifoliolate, paripinnate or imparipinnate, rarely simple (*Dodonaea* and *Pappea*) or 2-foliolate (*Aphania*). *Allophylus*, with trifoliolate leaves, resembles species of *Rhus*, but lacks the resinous smell of the latter when crushed. Pinnate leaves often have the rachis ending in a very diagnostic aborted rachis apex (resembling an inactive terminal growth tip). Flowers in local species are small and inconspicuous, and the seeds are often surrounded by a fleshy aril. • The fleshy arils of many species are edible (the best known example being the litchi, *Litchi chinensis*). *Koelreuteria paniculata* (golden-rain tree) is a popular garden ornamental. (Groups 9, 10, 31, 34, 38)

Sapotaceae (Milkwood family) A predominantly woody plant family with about 22 native species, and easily recognized by the combination of milky latex, and simple, entire, alternate leaves, which lack large stipules or conspicuous stipular scars (as in Moraceae). Young growth often has a rusty or brownish colour. All local members have fleshy fruit, and the seeds are shiny, brown, with a broad scar at the point of attachment. • The latex of some species was once a source of various rubber-like substances – used, for example, in golf balls (gutta-percha) and as the elastic component of chewing gum. The coating of top quality golf balls is currently made from balata rubber, prepared from the latex of trees belonging to the genus *Manilkara*. (Group 5)

Scrophulariaceae (Snapdragon family) A predominantly herbaceous family, with seven or so native tree species. Easily recognized from a combination of vegetative and floral features. Leaves opposite or whorled, simple, without stipules. Stems 4-angled. Flowers irregular, 2-lipped, with 5 united petals, 4 stamens (2 longer than the others) attached to the petals. The fruits are many-seeded. • The family produces many garden ornamentals, among them snapdragons (*Antirrhinum*), beard tongues (*Penstemon*) and slipper flowers (*Calceolaria*). The drugs digitalin and digoxin are obtained from *Digitalis*. The family is rich in hemiparasitic plants, including a few troublesome weeds (*Striga, Alectra*). (Groups 19, 23, 25)

Simaroubaceae (Tree-of-heaven family) Poorly represented in southern Africa by four native tree species. A rather indistinct woody family with alternate, imparipinnate leaves, usually without stipules. The leaflets usually have toothed margins, which distinguishes it from Meliaceae. Distinguished from pinnate-leaved Anacardiaceae and Burseraceae by the lack of latex, from Rutaceae by the lack of secretory cavities in the leaves, and from Sapindaceae by the lack of the aborted terminal rachis-projection. • *Ailanthus altissima* (tree-of-heaven) is widely grown in gardens, but the family is otherwise of little economic importance. (Group 36)

Solanaceae (Tomato family) A vegetatively diverse family, poorly represented among native trees (about ten species). The leaves are simple, alternate, without stipules, often with an unpleasant scent when crushed. They are often spiny in members of *Solanum*. The flowers are regular, with 5 united petals and 5 stamens (often coherent, but not fused in *Solanum*). The fruit is either a many seeded berry or a capsule. • Food plants include potato (*Solanum tuberosum*), egg fruit (*S. melongena*), tomato (*Lycopersicon esculentum*) and peppers (*Capsicum*). The family is rich in poisonous alkaloids, producing, among others, the nicotine in tobacco (*Nicotiana tabacum*). Many species are used in traditional medicine. *Datura ferox* and *D. stramonium* (thorn-apples) are troublesome weeds. (Groups 7, 8, 10)

Sterculiaceae (Cacao family) A family with some 22 native tree species. Closely related to the Malvaceae, Tiliaceae and Bombacaceae, from which it is best distinguished by floral technicalities. Features shared by these families are alternate, simple leaves – which are often lobed and 3- or more-veined from the base – stipules and star-shaped hairs. Sterculiaceae flowers tend to have many (10 or more) stamens, with 2-thecate anthers, the filaments of which are often shortly fused around the ovary. The fruits are usually large and dehiscent, often divided into segments and containing hairs that may cause severe irritation on contact with the skin. • Best known economic products are cacao (used in the manufacture of chocolate and cocoa), extracted from the seeds of *Theobroma cacao*, and cola (used in popular beverages) from seeds of *Cola nitida* and *C. acuminata*. Species of *Brachychiton* (flame trees, kurrajong) are widely cultivated for ornament. (Groups 10, 11, 39)

Strelitziaceae (Crane-flower family) A small family of banana-like plants. The three native tree species are easily recognized by their crowns of alternate, large, simple and distinctly stalked leaves arranged in a fan (2-ranked). The flowers are borne in large, boat-shaped bracts. • Several species are grown as ornamentals, notably *Strelitzia reginae* (crane-flower or bird of paradise flower) and lobster's claw (*Heliconia*). (Group 2)

Tamaricaceae (Tamarisk family) A small family of trees and shrubs, characterized by slender branches with alternate, small, scale-like leaves. Many species can tolerate saline soils (halophytes). The flowers are minute, and either pink or white. Only one species occurs naturally in southern Africa. • Several species of *Tamarix* are grown for ornament. Manna is an edible, white, sweet, gummy substance secreted by *T. mannifera* as a result of insect activity. (Group 3)

Thymelaeaceae (Fibre-bark family) Well represented in the region by small, more or less woody shrublets. Only about ten species, however, reach tree size. Members usually have a tough fibrous bark, making it very difficult to break off twigs (if a leaf is picked, a long strip of bark comes off with it). The leaves are alternate, simple, entire and without stipules. The flowers are tubular (sepals appearing petaloid), except in the wind-pollinated genus *Passerina*, where they are much reduced. • Economically not an important family. It produces a few lesser known garden ornamentals. (Groups 3, 10, 23)

Tiliaceae (Linden family) Best represented among native trees by the genus *Grewia*, which has more than 30 tree species in the region. The leaves are alternate, in two ranks, usually asymmetrical with toothed margins, 3-veined from the base, with star-shaped hairs and stipules. The flowers are attractive, axillary or leaf-opposed, with many free stamens. Closely related to the Malvaceae, Sterculiaceae and Bombacaceae. • Jute is obtained from the bark fibres of *Corchorus* spp. Excellent timber is obtained from species of *Tilia* (European limes, lindens, American basswood). Several species of *Tilia* are also cultivated for ornament, particularly in temperate regions of the northern hemisphere. (Group 11)

Ulmaceae (Elm family) A woody family of trees and shrubs; poorly represented in our area (five native species). Leaves are alternate, simple, with toothed margins and often unequal sided bases, and stipules. The flowers are greenish and inconspicuous, yet very characteristic in having one stamen opposite each sepal (petals absent). • Species of *Ulmus* (elm) produce excellent timber. They are also valued as ornamental trees, as are species of *Celtis*. (Groups 8, 11)

Urticaceae (Nettle family) A family of herbs and woody plants, represented by four native tree species. Plants have watery latex and tough, fibrous bark. The leaves are alternate, simple, 3-veined, often armed with coarse stinging hairs, and stipulate. Flowers are small, greenish and inconspicuous. • Ramie fibre, which is used in the textile industry, is obtained from the bark of *Boehmeria nivea*. *Urtica dioica* (stinging nettle) is a widespread weed. (Groups 5, 11)

Verbenaceae (Verbena family) Vegetatively a rather indistinct family, with about 22 native tree species. The leaves are opposite or whorled, simple, or palmately compound as in *Vitex*. Crushed leaves are usually strongly aromatic (often unpleasantly so) and the twigs tend to be 4-angled. The flowers have 5 united petals and are usually more or less irregular (2-lipped), with 4 stamens arising from the corolla. • The most economically important species is *Tectona grandis* from Southeast Asia, the source of teak, a much valued timber. A number of species are cultivated for ornament, including the lemon verbena (*Lippia citriodora*), Chinese hat plant (*Holmskioldia sanguinea*), purple wreath (*Petrea volubilis*) and various species of *Verbena*. *Lantana camara* is a serious alien invader weed in southern Africa. (Groups 19, 23, 25, 40)

Violaceae (Violet family) Vegetatively an indistinct family; poorly represented in our area by about seven species of forest trees. The leaves are alternate, simple, stipulate and usually toothed. The ovary (fruit) is 1-chambered, with numerous ovules (seeds) attached to the walls. • Many species of *Viola* (pansies, violets) are grown as garden ornamentals, and for essential oils used in perfumes and toiletries. (Group 9)

Vitaceae (Grape family) A distinct family of climbing shrubs or woody vines, with tendrils opposite the leaves and more or less swollen nodes (about ten native tree species). The leaves are alternate, simple (usually palmately veined) or palmately compound. Inflorescences are borne opposite the leaves. Flowers are small, greenish, inconspicuous, with a ring-like or lobed disk. The stamens are equal in number to the petals and opposite to them (as in Rhamnaceae). • Grapes, wine, raisins, sultanas and currants (from *Vitis vinifera*) are the main economic products. Species of *Parthenocissus* (for example, Virginia creeper) are widely cultivated to cover fences, pergolas and the walls of buildings. (Groups 1, 11, 29)

Zamiaceae (Cycad family) Members of this family are living descendants of an ancient group of cone-bearing plants (gymnosperms) which dominated the earth's vegetation about 145 million years ago. Tree forms (at least 22 species in our area) are palm-like, with thickset stems densely covered with persistent leaf-bases, and a crown of thick, leathery, pinnately compound leaves. Most species have a very local distribution and are rarely encountered in the wild. The large cones (male and female on separate plants) are very distinctive. • Because of their rarity, many species have acquired considerable monetary value. Illegal removal of plants from the wild has brought certain species to the brink of extinction. (Group 2)

GROUP 1
Plants with leaves and/or stems succulent.

See also Group 3: *Ceraria namaquensis* (p. 66); Group 8: *Sesamothamnus guerichii* (p. 132) and *S. lugardii* (p. 132); Group 9: *Chrysanthemoides monilifera* (p. 134); Group 39: *Adansonia digitata* (p. 472); Group 43: *Moringa ovalifolia* (p. 514).

APOCYNACEAE (see page 20)

1 Adenium multiflorum (= *A. obesum* var. *multiflorum*)   **Impala lily**
SA: 647.3; Z: 925   Winter   **Impalalelie**
Thickset spineless succulent shrub or small tree, with **watery latex**; occurring in hot, low-altitude bushveld, often on brackish flats or in rocky places. Leaves crowded at ends of branches, obovate to oblong-obovate, rather fleshy, **glossy dark green** to bluish green above, hairless; margin entire, wavy. Flowers in clusters, **white or pale pink with a crimson border**, very showy, produced in winter when plants are leafless. Fruit paired cylindrical follicles, each up to 240 mm long, light brown when mature, dehiscent; seeds with a tuft of silky, golden-brown hairs at each end.
    The plant is browsed by stock and game. Has medicinal applications although toxic and once used as arrow poison.
    A. boehmianum (**1.1**), found in northern Namibia and southern Angola, has showy pink to mauve flowers with a darker throat.

2 Pachypodium lealii   **Bottle tree**
SA: 648   Winter   **Bottelboom**
Thickset **spiny** succulent shrub or small tree up to 6 m high, with **watery latex**; trunk often somewhat bottle-shaped with a few upright branches; occurring in semi-desert areas and arid bushveld, usually on rocky hillsides. Spines slender, up to 30 mm long. Leaves **crowded near ends of branchlets**, obovate-oblong, with short hairs on both surfaces; margin entire, **wavy**. Flowers in clusters when trees are leafless, **white, flushed with pink on the outside**, showy. Fruit paired cylindrical follicles, each up to 110 mm long, dehiscent; seeds with a tuft of silvery silky hairs at one end.
    The latex is toxic, and was once used for arrow poison.
    P. namaquanum (**2.1**), the well known halfmens tree from the Richtersveld and adjacent areas, has an erect, spiny, succulent stem up to 5 m high, unbranched or with a few short branches near the top. The leaves are crowded at the apex of the stem which is usually bent towards the north.

ASTERACEAE (see page 20)

3 Lopholaena platyphylla   **Broad-leaved fluff bush**
SA: –   Winter   **Breëblaarpluisbos**
Soft-wooded shrub or small tree with a sparse and rather untidy crown; occurring on grassy hillsides in bushveld. Branchlets rough with persistent leaf bases. Leaves **sessile**, clustered towards ends of shoots, soft and fleshy, broadly elliptic to obovate, **60–180 x 30–120 mm**, light green to grey-green, hairless; margin entire. Flowerheads in axillary clusters, whitish to pale orange. Fruit a small nutlet, tipped with a tuft of silky hairs.

A. *multiflorum*: flowers

A. *multiflorum*: flowers

A. *boehmianum*: flowers

P. *lealii*: tree

P. *lealii*: fruit

P. *lealii*: flowers

P. *namaquanum*: tree

L. *platyphylla*: flowerhead

CACTACEAE (see page 21)

1 **•*Cereus jamacaru***   **Queen of the night**
SA: – Summer   **Nagblom**
Small tree with **upright succulent stems** and a short, woody trunk; invading bushveld, particularly on rocky ridges. Branches blue-green to green, 4–9-angled, constricted at intervals; margin with **straight spines, arranged in tufts of 5–10.** Flowers **up to 250 mm long**, white, showy, opening at night. Fruit a berry, usually pink or red, oval, about 60 mm long, with white flesh and numerous black seeds.

A native of South America; cultivated for ornament and hedging. A declared weed in South Africa. Previously incorrectly referred to as *C. peruvianus.*

Resembles the indigenous *Euphorbia ingens* (p. 40), which is distinguished by milky latex exuding from cut stems, and by spines arranged in pairs.

2 **•*Opuntia ficus-indica***   **Sweet prickly pear**
SA: X759; Z: – Spring   **Boereturksvy**
Branched, succulent shrub or small tree, with some of the **branches flattened to form leaf-like structures (cladodes)**; invading arid bushveld, thicket and karroid vegetation. Cladodes greyish green, 300–600 x 60–150 mm, with tufts of sturdy spines or almost spineless. Flowers borne on cladode margins, yellow or orange. Fruit a berry, oval, about 80 mm long, ripening through yellow to reddish, with tufts of minute, irritating (to skin on contact) spines.

A native of Central America; cultivated for its edible fruit, as animal fodder and as security hedging. This is a declared weed in South Africa.

O. lindheimeri has flattened and rounded cladodes whose spines are up to 50 mm long, usually single, rarely up to 3 per tuft. An invader of thicket in the Eastern Cape.

CRASSULACEAE (see page 23)

3 **Crassula ovata** (= *C. portulacea*)   **Kerky-bush**
SA: 137.3 Winter   **Kerkeibos**
Shrub or small sturdy tree up to 5 m high; occurring on rocky outcrops in thicket, dry river valleys and sand forest. Leaves sessile, succulent, **elliptic to elliptic-oblanceolate**, about **20–40 x 10–22 mm**, glossy green, **usually without a white, powdery coating**; apex rounded with a distinct point; margin entire, with or without red horny edge. Flowers in dense roundish terminal clusters, white to pink. Fruit 3–5 separate follicles, oval, up to 6 mm long, dehiscent.

Widely grown in gardens. The young leaves are eaten by stock and game. Roots once eaten by the Khoikhoin; used medicinally.

C. arborescens has leaves which are round to broadly obovate, about 20–50 x 20–50 mm, grey-green with a distinct, white, powdery coating. It flowers in late spring and summer.

C. jamacaru: tree

C. jamacaru: flower

C. jamacaru: fruit

O. ficus-indica: flowers

C. ovata: flowers

O. ficus-indica: tree

C. ovata: tree

C. ovata: trunk

EUPHORBIACEAE (see page 24)
Members of the *Euphorbia* genus contain a milky latex which is poisonous and may cause damage to the eyes and intense irritation to the skin. These plants should therefore be handled with caution. Tree euphorbias are especially common in the valley bushveld of the Eastern Cape and are often difficult to identify as belonging to particular species without expert knowledge.

1 *Euphorbia confinalis*   **Lebombo euphorbia**
SA: 345; Z: 520   Winter   **Lebombo-naboom**
Spiny, succulent candelabra-like tree up to 10 m high, with a sturdy main stem and **small rounded crown**, often with secondary stems along main trunk; occurring in bushveld, usually on rocky hill slopes and associated with the Lebombo Range. Branchlets 3- or 4-angled (subsp. *confinalis*), **40–70 mm in diameter**, constricted at intervals, forming segments with parallel sides; spines paired, slender, up to 6 mm long, borne on an **interrupted horny strip** along each ridge. Flowers in clusters, greenish yellow. Fruit a 3-lobed capsule, up to 10 mm in diameter, wine-red. Subsp. *rhodesiaca* from Zimbabwe is more robust with a branched stem and 5- or 6-angled branches.
   E. zoutpansbergensis is a more graceful plant with branches 6-angled and much more slender (20–35 mm in diameter), and is endemic to the Soutpansberg region. *E. sekukuniensis*, from the Steelpoort River Valley and adjacent areas, has 4- or 5-angled, slightly constricted branches which are even more slender (15–20 mm in diameter), with a continuous horny strip along each margin.

2 *Euphorbia cooperi*   **Transvaal candelabra tree**
SA: 346; Z: 521   Spring   **Transvaalse kandelaarnaboom**
Spiny, succulent candelabra-like tree up to 7 m high, with a sturdy main stem and **large rounded crown**; occurring in bushveld, usually on rocky hill slopes. Branchlets 4–6-angled, **up to 120 mm in diameter**, deeply constricted at intervals, forming **heart-shaped** segments 50–150 mm long; spines paired, slender, up to 8 mm long, borne on a **continuous horny strip** along each ridge. Flowers in clusters, greenish yellow. Fruit a 3-lobed capsule, up to 10 mm in diameter, dull red. Branchlets 4–6-angled with wing margins 5–6 mm wide in var. *cooperi* (widespread), 3–4-angled and 3 mm wide in var. *calidicola* (confined to Zambezi Valley).
   The latex is highly toxic, and has an acrid smell; used as fish poison.

3 *Euphorbia evansii*   **Lowveld euphorbia**
SA: 348   Spring   **Laeveldnaboom**
Spiny, succulent tree **up to 10 m high**, with a sturdy main stem and **several trunk-like branches, each ending in a candelabra-like crown of slender, erect branches**; occurring in bushveld, usually on rocky hill slopes. Branchlets 3- or 4-angled, 15–20 mm in diameter, **not segmented**, twisted; spines paired, slender, up to 6 mm long, borne on an **interrupted** horny strip along each ridge. Flowers in clusters of 3, greenish yellow. Fruit a 3-lobed capsule, up to 6 mm in diameter, green, flushed with red.
   The young shoots are eaten by livestock in times of drought.
   Compare *E. grandidens* (p. 40).

E. confinalis: flowers

E. confinalis: fruit

E. cooperi: fruit

E. confinalis: trees

E. cooperi: trees

E. cooperi: flowers

E. evansii: flowers

E. evansii: tree

1 *Euphorbia grandidens* **Valley-bush euphorbia**
SA: 350   Spring **Valleibosnaboom**
Spiny, succulent tree **up to 16 m high**, with a **sturdy main stem and often with several stem-like branches, each topped with a small candelabra-like crown**; occurring in dry bushveld and forest in hot valleys, usually in rocky places. Branchlets 2- or 3-angled, 10–20 mm in diameter, **not segmented**; spines paired, slender, up to 6 mm long, borne on **interrupted** horny cushions along each ridge, frequently **with a pair of tiny prickles** above them, sinuate between the spine tubercles. Flowers in clusters of 3, greenish yellow. Fruit a 3-lobed capsule, up to 8 mm in diameter, maroon-red.
 The latex has been used as a glue, and to seal the hulls of boats.
 Compare *E. evansii* (p. 38).

2 *Euphorbia ingens* **Common tree euphorbia**
SA: 351; Z: 527   Autumn–Winter **Gewone naboom**
Spiny, succulent tree up to 10 m high, with a short stem and **massive**, dark green crown; **lower branches not shed with age** as in other species; occurring in bushveld, often on rocky outcrops or deep sand, also on termitaria. Branchlets 4- or 5-angled, up to 120 mm in diameter, irregularly constricted, forming **segments with parallel sides**; spines paired, reduced, up to 2 mm long, borne on separate cushions that do not form a continuous ridge. Flowers in clusters, greenish yellow. Fruit an almost globose capsule, up to 15 mm in diameter, reddish.
 The latex is very toxic and caustic; used medicinally and as a fish poison. The town of Naboomspruit in the Northern Province derives its name from this tree.

3 *Euphorbia tetragona* **Honey euphorbia**
SA: 354   Winter–Spring **Heuningnaboom**
Spiny, succulent tree up to 13 m high; main stem single or branched, each with a small, candelabra-like crown; occurring in valley bushveld, often in dense stands. Branchlets 4- or 5-angled with **flat sides** (appearing square-shape), 25–50 mm in diameter, **shallowly constricted** at intervals; spines paired, up to 12 mm long, borne on **separate horny cushions**, sometimes spineless. Flowers in clusters of 3, greenish yellow. Fruit an almost globose capsule, up to 10 mm in diameter, reddish.
 The latex is used medicinally. Honey (known as 'noors honey') is made from the flowers of this and several other members of *Euphorbia*, though it is unpleasantly flavoured and causes a hot, burning sensation in the mouth.

4 *Euphorbia tirucalli* **Rubber euphorbia**
SA: 355; Z: 532   Summer **Kraalnaboom**
Spineless shrub or small to medium-sized succulent tree, with a rounded crown; occurring in bushveld, usually on rocky hill slopes and at old kraal-sites; widely used as a hedge around homesteads. Branchlets **cylindrical**, 5–8 mm in diameter, smooth. Leaves small and slender, up to 12 x 2 mm, fall very early and are rarely seen. Flowers in clusters towards tips of branches, yellowish green. Fruit a weakly 3-lobed capsule, about 12 mm in diameter, green, often flushed with pink.
 The latex is toxic; used medicinally, to repel or kill insects and as a fish poison. Browsed by black rhino. Reportedly effective in keeping moles away.

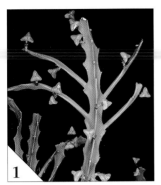

E. grandidens: fruit

E. ingens: flowers

E. ingens: fruit

E. grandidens: fleshy stems

E. tetragona: fruit

E. tirucalli: flowers

E. ingens: tree

E. tirucalli: flowers & fruit

GROUP 1

1 *Euphorbia triangularis*   **River euphorbia**
SA: 356   Winter   **Riviernaboom**
Spiny, succulent tree up to 18 m high; main stem single or branched, each with a small, **yellowish green**, candelabra-like crown with **branches tending to ascend from the base**; occurring in valley bushveld, often in dense stands, particularly common in the Eastern Cape. Branchlets are 3-angled (mainly Eastern Cape) or 5-angled (mainly KwaZulu-Natal), 40–90 mm in diameter, angles **wing-like**, **deeply constricted** at intervals, forming segments 50–300 mm long, with parallel sides and somewhat wavy margins; spines paired, slender, up to 8 mm long, borne on separate or continuous horny cushions. Flowers in clusters, greenish yellow. Fruit an almost globose capsule, up to 8 mm in diameter, **distinctly stalked**, reddish.
   The tree is traditionally planted, by the Xhosa of the Eastern Cape, outside their huts after the birth of and to protect twins.
   E. curvirama (from the Eastern Cape) has darker green stems, which arise horizontally from the main stem before curving upwards, and almost stalkless fruit.

LILIACEAE (see page 26)
There are approximately 150 species of *Aloe* in southern Africa, at least 30 of which may be considered trees or tree-like. Only a small sample number are featured here. Van Wyk & Smith (1996) and West (1992) provide illustrations and descriptions of all the South African and Zimbabwean species respectively.

2 *Aloe africana*   **Uitenhage aloe**
SA: 28.2   Winter   **Uitenhaagsaalwyn**
Single-stemmed, unbranched leaf succulent; stem densely covered with old dry leaves; occurring in valley bushveld. Leaves dull green, spineless on both surfaces, or with a few spines on the midline near the apex; margin with sharp, reddish brown teeth. Inflorescence branched; flower spikes erect, 40–60 mm long; flowers reddish in bud, opening yellow-orange, with an **up-turned** tube. Fruit a capsule.

3 *Aloe arborescens*   **Krantz aloe**
SA: 28.1; Z: 19   Autumn–Winter   **Kransaalwyn**
Much-branched shrub or small tree with somewhat obliquely disposed leaf rosettes; stem with old dry leaves below the leaf rosette only; occurring in high-rainfall montane grassland and forest areas, usually in rocky places. Leaves curved, **dull greyish or bluish green**, spineless on both surfaces, margin with pale teeth. Flowers usually in unbranched, erect spikes, 200–300 mm long, 2–4 per rosette; flowers scarlet, orange or yellow, occasionally bi-coloured. Fruit a capsule.
   A decorative garden plant. It is also grown as a live fence around cattle kraals. Pulp from the leaves is used medicinally.

4 *Aloe barberiae* (= *A. bainesii*)   **Tree aloe**
SA: 28   Winter   **Boomaalwyn**
Small to medium-sized tree with a **thickset trunk** and **rounded crown**; occurring in wooded ravines and coastal bush. Leaves **deeply channelled**, recurved, dark green, spineless on both surfaces; margin edged with a whitish line and small brown-tipped teeth. Inflorescence branched; flower spikes erect, 20–30 mm long; flowers rose-pink or orange (Maputaland coastal form). Fruit a capsule.

42

E. triangularis: stem & leaves *E. triangularis*: fruit

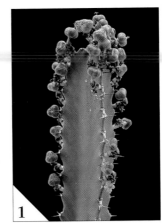

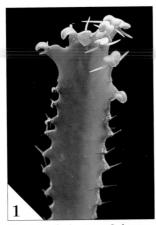

A. africana: flowers *A. barberiae*: flowers *A. barberiae*: tree

A. arborescens: flowers

1 Aloe dichotoma   Quiver tree
SA: 29   Winter   Kokerboom
Small tree with a **thickset trunk** and **dense, rounded** crown; occurring in desert and semi-desert areas, usually on rocky ridges. Leaves blue-green or yellowish green, spineless on both surfaces; margin with small yellowish brown teeth that may be obscure in old leaves. Inflorescence branched, **borne terminally** above the leaf rosette; flower spikes about 300 mm long; flowers bright yellow. Fruit a capsule.

The soft branches were once used by the San as quivers for their arrows. A favourite nesting site for social weaver birds.

Closely related to, and often associated with, *A. ramosissima*, a smaller plant which is usually multistemmed.

A. pillansii (**1.1**) has a taller trunk with fewer, more erect branches and a sparse crown. The inflorescences are somewhat drooping and borne below the leaf rosette. It is confined to the Richtersveld and adjacent areas.

2 Aloe ferox   Bitter aloe
SA: 29.2   Winter–Spring   Bitteraalwyn
Single-stemmed, unbranched leaf succulent; stem densely covered with old dry leaves; occurring in valley bushveld, karroid vegetation, coastal bush and grassland, usually on rocky hillsides. Leaves dull green, both surfaces with or without spines; margin with stout, brownish red teeth. Inflorescence branched; flower spikes **erect**; flowers golden orange to scarlet, occasionally white, with tips of inner perianth lobes usually **brown or black**. Fruit a capsule.

The sap from the leaves is harvested commercially: it yields a drug known as 'Cape aloes', which is widely used in pharmaceutical preparations. An excellent jam is prepared from the leaves. Often planted as a live fence around cattle kraals. Ash from dried leaves is mixed with tobacco snuff.

A. candelabrum, found in KwaZulu-Natal, is very similar, but the tips of its inner perianth lobes tend to be white.

3 Aloe marlothii subsp. *marlothii*   Mountain aloe
SA: 29.5;   Autumn–Winter   Bergaalwyn
Single-stemmed, unbranched leaf succulent; stem densely covered with old dry leaves; occurring in bushveld, usually on rocky hillsides. Leaves dull grey-green to green, both surfaces usually with **many sharp, hard spines**; margin with sharp, reddish brown teeth. Inflorescence branched; flower spikes carried **more or less horizontally**; flowers purplish in bud, opening orange, with purple stamens. Fruit a capsule.

Ash from the dried leaves is mixed with tobacco snuff. The leaves and sap are used medicinally.

A. dichotoma: tree

A. pillansii: tree

A. dichotoma: flowers

A. ferox: trees

A. ferox: flowers

A. marlothii: tree

1 *Aloe thraskii*   **Strand aloe**

SA: 30.7   Winter   **Strandaalwyn**

Single-stemmed, unbranched leaf succulent; stem densely covered with old dry leaves; occurring **on coastal dunes seldom more than a few hundred metres from the sea**, often directly exposed to the salt-laden spray. Leaves **deeply channelled, recurved**, bright green to yellowish grey-green, spineless above, with a few spines on the midline towards the apex below; margin with small reddish teeth. Inflorescence branched; flower spikes erect, about 250 mm long; flowers greenish yellow in bud, opening deep yellow, with bright orange stamens. Fruit a capsule.

A most decorative garden plant, best grown within sight of the sea.

PORTULACACEAE (see page 29)

2 *Portulacaria afra*   **Porkbush**

SA: 104   Summer   **Spekboom**

Sprawling shrub or small tree; occurring in karroid areas and bushveld, usually in rocky places; dominant in parts of the Eastern Cape (spekboomveld). Leaves **opposite, almost circular or obovate, up to 25 x 17 mm**, fresh green or pale grey, fleshy. Flowers in many-flowered panicles, small, pale pink to purplish. Fruit a small capsule, about 5 mm long, 3-winged.

The leaves are edible, with a pleasant acid taste earlier in the day, less acidic towards evening. Heavily browsed by game and stock and a valuable fodder plant in parts of the eastern Karoo. Leaves used medicinally. Dried stems flattened and used as thatch. Host to the mistletoe, *Viscum crassulae*, which has remarkably similar succulent leaves.

VITACEAE (see page 33)

3 *Cyphostemma currorii*   **Cobas**

SA: 456   Spring   **Kobas**

Thickset succulent tree up to 7 m high; occurring in semi-desert areas, usually on rocky hillsides. Bark **peeling in yellow papery pieces**, revealing a whitish to pinkish surface. Leaves **3-foliolate**; leaflets elliptic, large, **up to 300 x 200 mm**, thick, fleshy, **light green**; petiole **not winged**. Flowers in terminal, flat-topped, branched heads, small, yellowish green. Fruit a berry, oval, about 10 mm in diameter, red.

Sap from trunk is used medicinally and for veterinary purposes.

Three other tree-like cyphostemmas occur in Namibia. *C. bainesii* is rarely more than 1 m high, its leaflets up to 270 x 110 mm, bright green to bluish green, often with a red margin. *C. juttae* has blue-green leaves, simple and deeply lobed when juvenile, 3-foliolate when mature, with stalks winged. *C. uter* has 5-foliolate leaves.

A. thraskii: flowers

P. afra: fruit

A. thraskii: tree

P. afra: flowers

C. currorii: tree

C. currorii: leaf

C. currorii: flowers

GROUP 2

Plants with a distinctive growth form, usually unbranched or only sparingly branched. Leaves large, usually in terminal clusters.

See also Group 11: *Cussonia natalensis* (p. 224); Group 39: *Adansonia digitata* (p. 472); Group 41: *Acacia robynsiana* (p. 486); Group 43: *Moringa ovalifolia* (p. 514).

ARALIACEAE (see page 20)

1 *Cussonia arborea*   Octopus cabbage tree
Z: 813   Spring   Seekatkiepersol
Small to medium-sized deciduous tree; occurring in *Brachystegia* woodland, often in rocky places. Bark corky, rough and light brown. Leaves palmately compound with 5 or more leaflets, **simple** and variously lobed in young plants or sucker shoots, **250–500 mm in diameter**; leaflets with margin **scalloped or toothed**; petiole up to 300 mm long. Flowers in terminal groups of **slender spikes**, each **up to 600 mm long** (reminiscent of octopus arms, hence the common names), yellowish green. Fruit fleshy, almost globose, up to 7 mm in diameter, dark purple.
The wood is light, and strong; used for cupboards and traditional xylophone keys.

2 *Cussonia paniculata*   Highveld cabbage tree
SA: 563   Summer–Winter   Hoëveldse kiepersol
Small tree with a sturdy trunk, sparsely branched; occurring in bushveld and wooded grassland, usually in rocky places. Leaves clustered near ends of branches, **once compound**, with 7–11 radiating leaflets which are **not subdivided**; leaflets blue-green. Flowers in a branched **panicle of spikes**, greenish yellow. Fruit a fleshy drupe, globose, purple. Margin of leaflets deeply lobed or wavy in subsp. *sinuata* (found in central and northern parts of range), entire or sparsely toothed in subsp. *paniculata* (mainly southern Karoo and Eastern Cape).
The wood is soft, light, and was once used for the brake-blocks of wagons. A decorative and frost-tolerant garden feature plant.

3 *Cussonia sphaerocephala*   Natal forest cabbage tree
SA: 564.2   Summer   Natalse boskiepersol
Tall, slender, **sparsely branched**, evergreen tree; occurring in forest. Leaves clustered in **neat round heads** at ends of stems, **twice compound**, with 6–12 subdivided primary leaflets, leathery, glossy dark green above. Flowers in terminal **double umbels** of short, thick spikes, each 80–140 x 40–60 mm, greenish yellow. Fruit a fleshy drupe, obconical, about 6 mm in diameter, purplish.

4 *Cussonia spicata*   Common cabbage tree
SA: 564; Z: 815   Spring–Summer   Gewone kiepersol
Small to medium-sized evergreen tree, with spreading, **much-branched**, rounded crown; occurring in bushveld, on forest margins and on rocky outcrops in grassland. Leaves clustered at ends of branches, **twice compound**, with 5–9 subdivided primary leaflets, thickly leathery, **dark green**. Flowers in terminal **double umbels** of 8–12 spikes per unit, each 50–150 x 15–40 mm, greenish yellow. Fruit a fleshy drupe, round to angular, about 6 mm in diameter, purplish.
The root is poisonous, and used medicinally. Cultivated in gardens; frost-tender. Stems are split, hollowed-out and used as feeding trays for pigs and chickens.

C. arborea: leaves

C. paniculata: flowers

C. arborea: flowers

C. paniculata: tree

C. sphaerocephala: tree

C. sphaerocephala: leaf

C. spicata: tree

C. spicata: flowers & fruit

1 Cussonia transvaalensis   Transvaal cabbage tree
SA: 564.3   Spring – Summer   Transvaalkiepersol
Small to medium-sized evergreen tree, usually single-stemmed, with a small, **sparsely branched** crown; occurring in bushveld, usually on rocky ridges of quartzite or sandstone. Leaves clustered in rosettes at ends of branches, **twice compound**, with 7–9 subdivided primary leaflets, leathery, **blue- to grey-green**. Flowers in terminal **double umbels** of 7–11 spikes per unit, each 115–150 mm long, greenish yellow. Fruit a fleshy drupe, conical, about 10 mm long, purple.
    An attractive, frost-tolerant garden subject.

2 Cussonia zuluensis   Zulu cabbage tree
SA: 561   Spring   Zoeloekiepersol
Small, multi-stemmed, sparsely branched tree with a **rather spindly** shape; occurring in bushveld and coastal scrub and forest. Leaves clustered near ends of branches, **twice compound**, with 8–12 subdivided primary leaflets, leathery, **glossy dark green** above. Flowers in terminal **simple umbels** of 8–26 spikes, each 200–300 x 30–50 mm, greenish yellow, on stalks up to 20 mm long. Fruit a fleshy drupe, goblet-shaped, about 8 x 5 mm, mauve.
    Closely related to *C. nicholsonii* from southern KwaZulu-Natal, which has stalkless flowers and obconical fruit. *C. arenicola* is a small, slender, single-stemmed, usually understorey shrub endemic to Maputaland's sand and coastal forests.

ARECACEAE (see page 20)
3 Hyphaene coriacea (= *H. natalensis*)   Lala palm
SA: 23; Z: 16   Spring   Lalapalm
Palm **3–7 m high**; stem erect or reclining, often suckering and forming clumps; sexes separate, on different trees; occurring in low-altitude bushveld and coastal bush, often forming extensive stands in coastal grassland, particularly in Maputaland. Leaves **fan-shaped**, 1,5–2 m long (including petiole), **greyish green**; leaflets with base asymmetric; petiole with **black thorns**. Flowers in drooping clusters. Fruit small, oval to **somewhat pear shaped, 40–60 mm in diameter**, ripening from green through orange to glossy dark brown.
    The tree is heavily browsed by elephant. The sap is tapped to produce palm wine (an important local industry in coastal areas of Maputaland). Hard white kernel of the seed ('vegetable ivory') is carved into small ornaments and to adorn walking sticks. Palm swifts (*Cypsiurus parvus*) roost and nest in these trees. Leaves extensively used for such woven items as mats, baskets and hats.
    Borassus aethiopum (**3.1**) a similar looking tree from low-altitude bushveld, often along rivers and mainly north of the Limpopo River) has an erect stem up to 20 m in height, with a prominent swelling about half way up. The fruit is globose and considerably larger (120–180 mm in diameter).

C. transvaalensis: leaf

C. transvaalensis: flowers

C. transvaalensis: tree

C. zuluensis: flowers

H. coriacea: tree

H. coriacea: fruit

B. aethiopum: tree

1 Hyphaene petersiana (= *H. benguellensis* var. *ventricosa*)   **Real fan palm**
SA: 24; Z: 15   Spring   **Opregte waaierpalm**
Palm **up to 18 m** high; stem usually erect, often suckering and forming clumps, occasionally with a bulge near the middle or in the upper parts; sexes separate on different trees; occurring in low-altitude bushveld and along swamps, pans and rivers, often forming extensive stands. Leaves **fan-shaped**, 1,5–2 m long (including petiole), greyish green; leaflets with base asymmetric; petiole with **black thorns**. Flowers in drooping clusters. Fruit small, **more or less globose, 40–60 mm in diameter**, ripening from green through orange to glossy dark brown.

The kernel (pith) of the stem and the young leaves are edible. The leaves are also shredded into thin strips and used for weaving baskets. Sap tapped to make palm wine. Seeds eaten in times of famine; liquid inside the kernel resembles coconut milk in flavour and colour. For uses by animals see *H. coriacea*.

2 Phoenix reclinata   **Wild date palm**
SA: 22; Z: 14   Spring   **Wildedadelpalm**
Palm up to 10 m high; stem **slender** (up to 300 mm in diameter), erect or reclining, suckering and **forming dense clumps**; sexes separate on different trees; occurring in low-altitude bushveld, especially along rivers and on coastal dunes. Leaves **feather-shaped (pinnate)**, 3–4 m long, arching, **glossy light to dark green**, lower leaflets reduced to **yellowish spines**. Flowers in bunches. Fruit a drupe, **oval (date-like)**, up to **15 mm long**, orange-brown.

The tree is browsed by elephant. Fruit edible, sweet-tasting and reminiscent of dates. Stems made into brooms. Rachis of leaves used as uprights to construct fish kraals at Kosi Bay. Kernels of stems and stem apex are sometimes eaten. Sap tapped to make palm wine. Leaves used to make baskets. Spines on petiole used medicinally. Larval food plant for the butterfly *Zophopetes dysmephila*.

Lower leaflets of *Jubaeopsis caffra* are not reduced to spines and the fruit is round and fibrous, about 20 mm in diameter. This is a rare species, restricted to sandstone cliffs close to the mouth of the Msikaba and Mtentu Rivers in Pondoland.

3 Raphia australis   **Kosi palm**
SA: 26   Irregular   **Kosipalm**
Massive palm up to 24 m high; stem erect, not suckering, usually with breathing roots growing up from the soil below the tree; plants flower once, after about 30 years, and then die after setting fruit; occurring in **swamp forest**, often in dense groves. Leaves **feather-shaped (pinnate)**, very large, **up to 10 m long**, spreading, dark green to bluish green, with midrib (rachis) often **reddish**; leaflets with margin and midrib **spiny**. Flowers in a massive (up to 3 m high), conical, **apical inflorescence exserted above the crown of leaves**. Fruit oval, about 90 mm long, shiny brown, with conspicuous, thick, **overlapping scales**.

The leaves are used as a thatch material, and the petioles for hut construction, fences and rafts. Palmnut vultures (*Gypohierax angolensis*) nest in the trees and feed on the fruit.

R. vinifera (found in eastern and northern Zimbabwe) has less impressive, drooping inflorescences produced from the axils of the leaves.

H. petersiana: trees

P. reclinata: flowers

P. reclinata: tree

H. petersiana: fruit

H. petersiana: leaf bases

R. australis: inflorescence

P. reclinata: fruit

R. australis: fruit

CYATHEACEAE (see page 23)

1 Cyathea dregei (= *Alsophila dregei*)　　　　**Common tree fern**
SA: 1; Z: 2　　　　　　　　　　　　　　　**Gewone boomvaring**
Tree fern up to 5 m high, stem erect, usually unbranched, **200–450 mm in diameter**; occurring on forest margins and along streams in ravines and montane grassland. Leaves arching, up to 3 m long, **leathery**; leaflets hairless or with loose, minute, brownish, hair-like scales below, basal leaflets **do not form root-like structures**, the ultimate segments in mature foliage are entire or weakly toothed.

　　C. thomsonii (found in the Eastern Highlands of Zimbabwe) is very similar, but with slender stems (about 100 mm in diameter) and leaflets with minute, pale, stiff, twisted hairs along the veins on the lower surface. *C. capensis* (**1.1**) has slender (100–150 mm in diameter) stems and thinly textured, arching leaves with the basal leaflets modified into a tangled mass of green or brown root-like structures. It occurs in shaded, moist, forested ravines. *C. manniana* (from the Eastern Highlands of Zimbabwe) has slender (about 100 mm in diameter), often reclining stems with sharp prickles. The latter are also present on the petiole and rachis.

DRACAENACEAE (see page 24)

2 Dracaena aletriformis (= *D. hookeriana*)　　　**Large-leaved dragon tree**
SA: 30.9　Summer　　　　　　　　　　　**Grootblaardrakeboom**
Shrub or small tree up to about 5 m high; stem unbranched or branched, stout; occurring in coastal bush, montane forest and bushveld, usually in shady places. Leaves clustered towards ends of stems, narrow to broadly strap-shaped, **500–1000 x 25–110 mm**, leathery, **bright green**, with conspicuous **white edges**. Flowers in large, loose, terminal panicles (with **greenish branches**) up to 1,5 m long, greenish white, opening at night, sweetly scented. Fruit a berry, globose or 2- or 3-lobed, up to 20 mm in diameter, **smooth** orange or red.

　　An excellent indoor and outdoor subject for shady places. Larval food plant for the butterfly *Artitropa erinnys*.

　　Often confused with *D. transvaalensis*, a species associated with exposed xerophytic conditions, and restricted to a small area between the Dublin Mine in the Northern Province and the Penge area of Mpumalanga. It is a much-branched small tree with greyish green, stiff, long and narrow leaves in dense rosettes, and distinctly papillate fruit.

　　D. steudneri (**2.1**) is a sparsely branched tree up to 12 m high (from the Eastern Highlands of Zimbabwe), with leaves in terminal rosettes, up to 800 x 100 mm, and large terminal inflorescences with orange-yellow branches. An attractive garden subject widely cultivated in Zimbabwe.

3 Dracaena mannii (= *D. usambarensis*)　　　**Small-leaved dragon tree**
SA: 30.8; Z: 29　Spring　　　　　　　　　**Kleinblaardrakeboom**
Shrub or small tree up to about 5 m high; stem often **much-branched, slender**; occurring in swamp and dune forest, usually in moist places. Leaves clustered towards ends of stems, narrowly oblong-elliptic with a stem-clasping base, **up to 400 x 20 mm**, stiff and thinly leathery, glossy dark green to grey-green, **without white edges**. Flowers in terminal panicles (with yellow to orange branches) up to 0,5 m long, greenish white to cream, opening at night, sweetly scented. Fruit a berry, globose or 2- or 3-lobed, 10–30 mm in diameter, ripening through brown to orange-red.

　　A decorative plant for frost-free gardens.

1

C. dregei: trees

1.1

C. capensis: tree

2

D. aletriformis: flowers

2

D. aletriformis: fruit

2.1

D. steudneri: tree

3

D. mannii: fruit

3

D. mannii: flowers

MUSACEAE (see page 28)

1 *Ensete ventricosum* **Wild banana**
SA: 31; Z: 33   Spring **Wildepiesang**
Banana-like tree with a thickset stem of tightly overlapping leaf bases and **spirally** arranged leaves; flowers once after about 8 years and then dies after fruiting; occurring in forest, usually along streams. Leaves large and banana-like, about 2,5 x 1 m, fresh green with a **pinkish red** midrib; petiole almost absent. Flowers in **large drooping racemes**, cream, concealed by large, maroon bracts. Fruit leathery, resembling small bananas, with hard globose seeds.
Widely cultivated as an accent plant in gardens, fast growing but frost-sensitive. Easily grown from seed.

STRELITZIACEAE (see page 32)

2 *Strelitzia caudata* **Transvaal wild banana**
SA: 33; Z: 34   Spring **Transvaalse wildepiesang**
Banana-like tree up to 6 m high, with a conspicuous **fan-shaped** crown, usually growing in dense clumps; occurring **in areas of montane forest**, usually found between rocks on steep grassy slopes. Leaves arranged in two vertical ranks, up to 2 x 0,6 m, grey-green, blade becoming split by the wind, with a distinct, channelled petiole. Inflorescence simple, consisting of a **single**, purplish blue, **boat-shaped spathe**; flowers several per spathe, opening in succession, white, with spreading sepals and a narrow, blue, arrow-shaped structure formed by the petals, lowest sepal **with slender tail-like projection** from middle of keel below. Fruit a woody capsule, 3-lobed, dehiscent; seeds black with a tuft of bright orange hairs.
Closely related to *S. alba* (found in the Knysna-Humansdorp districts of the southern coastal region), all of whose sepals and petals are white. The plants that grow in the Eastern Highlands of Zimbabwe are *S. caudata* and not, as has been claimed in literature, *S. nicolai*.

3 *Strelitzia nicolai* **Natal wild banana**
SA: 34   Spring–Summer **Natalse wildepiesang**
Banana-like tree up to 12 m high, with a conspicuous **fan-shaped** crown, usually growing in dense clumps; occurring in **coastal dune vegetation** and **adjacent inland areas**. Leaves arranged in two vertical ranks, up to 2 x 0,6 m, glossy green, blade becoming split by the wind, with a distinct, channelled petiole. Inflorescence compound, consisting of **up to five** purplish-blue, **boat-shaped spathes**, each one arising at right angles from the preceding one; flowers several per spathe, opening in succession, white, with spreading sepals and a narrow, blue, arrow-shaped structure formed by the petals. Fruit a woody capsule, 3-lobed, dehiscent; seeds black with a tuft of bright orange hairs.
The plant is widely cultivated in gardens. Dried petioles are used as a binding material. Immature seeds edible, with a pleasant taste. Larval food plant for the butterfly *Moltena fiara*.

E. ventricosum: tree

E. ventricosum: inflorescence

S. caudata: flowers

S. nicolai: flowers

S. nicolai: trees

S. nicolai: fan-shaped crown

ZAMIACEAE (see page 33)
Although only two species of *Encephalartos* are illustrated in this book, about 18 more may attain tree-size in southern Africa. Most species have a restricted range and are rarely encountered in the wild. Reliable identification often requires expert knowledge. Goode (1989) provides illustrations and descriptions of all the members of the group known at the time. A few more have subsequently been described.

1 *Encephalartos altensteinii*   **Eastern Cape cycad**
SA: 3   Irregular   **Oos-Kaapse broodboom**
Palm-like tree up to 7 m high; stem usually unbranched, covered with persistent leaf bases; sexes separate, on different plants; occurring in coastal grassland and scrub forest, usually on rocky hillsides. Leaves crowded at the stem apex, up to 3,5 m long; leaflets up to 150 x 25 mm, dark green, lowermost ones **not reduced to a series of spines**, with 2–5 teeth along both margins. Cones yellowish green when mature, hairless. Seeds oval, about 25 mm long, scarlet.
    The fleshy cover of the seeds is edible, but the seed itself should be considered poisonous.
    E. natalensis (widespread in KwaZulu-Natal) and *E. senticosus* (Lebombo Mountains) are very similar, both with their lowermost leaflets reduced to a series of spines. Leaflets in the former are broader (up to 45 mm wide) than those in the latter (not more than 25 mm wide).

2 *Encephalartos transvenosus*   **Modjadji cycad**
SA: 13   Irregular   **Modjadjibroodboom**
Palm-like tree up to 13 m high; stem occasionally branched, erect, with golden-brown woolly crown; sexes separate, on different plants; occurring on forest margins and in bushveld on rocky hillsides. Leaves clustered towards the stem apex, up to 2,5 m long, glossy dark green; leaflets 100–200 x 20–35 mm, with 2–5 small teeth along upper and 1–3 along the lower margin, lowermost leaflets **reduced to spines**. Cones golden-yellow, hairless when mature. Seeds oval, up to 50 mm long, orange-red, rarely yellow.
    The fleshy layer around the seeds is eaten by children. Substantial numbers of this cycad occur in the Modjadji Nature Reserve near Duiwelskloof in the Northern Province. Here, plants of the species have been protected by the Rain Queens of the Lovedu Tribe.

E. *altensteinii*: trees

E. *altensteinii*: female cones

E. *altensteinii*: male cones

E. *transvenosus*: trees

E. *transvenosus*: female cones

E. *transvenosus*: trees with cones

GROUP 3
Leaves very small, scale- or needle-like.

See also Group 10: *Podocarpus falcatus* (p. 206).

ASTERACEAE (see page 20)

1 *Metalasia muricata*   White bristle bush
SA: 736.4 All year   Witsteekbos
Much-branched rounded shrub or small tree, with **erect branches**, occurring on
coastal dunes and in mountainous areas, often along streams or between rocks.
Branchlets **white-felted**. Leaves in tufts or scattered, sessile, somewhat twisted, up
to 18 x 2 mm, **sharp-tipped**, often with white woolly hairs; margin rolled under.
Flowers in **branched, terminal heads**, white, often tinged with pink or purple,
sweetly scented. Fruit a small nutlet with a crown of bristles.
    The tree is browsed by stock. Leaves used as a kind of tea. Plays a useful role in
the stabilization of coastal dunes.

CASUARINACEAE (see page 22)

2 •*Casuarina cunninghamiana*   Beefwood
SA: X245 Winter   Kasuarisboom
Evergreen, **pine-like** tree, with large, rather untidy, greyish green crown; invading
coastal dunes and riverbeds. What appear to be needle-shaped leaves are in fact
short branches, clearly distinguished from pine needles by being **jointed**, with several nodes and internodes; internodes longitudinally grooved, with the ridges
rounded; true leaves reduced to a whorl of minute scales at each node, blackish
with a **transverse brown band**. Flowers in small yellowish spikes (male) or globose heads (female), small, inconspicuous. The fruit resembles a small cone, oval,
about 20 mm long, brown.
    A native of Australia; cultivated for dune stabilization, ornament and shelter.
Considered one of the best fuel woods in the world.
    C. equisetifolia is very similar, but the whorls of minute scale leaves are uniformly
pale, with the internodes of the needle-shaped twigs sharply ribbed.

CHENOPODIACEAE (see page 22)

3 *Salsola aphylla*   Lye ganna
SA: 103.3 Spring   Seepganna
Shrublet, shrub or small, sprawling tree with a **pale greyish** appearance; occurring
in semi-desert areas, often along dry watercourses and on associated floodplains.
Leaves **tightly packed** along the branches, **about 2 mm long**, thick and fleshy,
appearing hairless. Flowers very small, inconspicuous, greenish yellow. Fruit
enclosed in persistent perianth, the five segments of which develop into petal-like,
papery wings and are then easily mistaken for the flowers.
    The plant is heavily browsed by game and stock. Its white, fluffy, globose insect
galls may be mistaken for flowers or fruit. The ash produces a strong lye for making soap, hence the common names.
    S. arborea is restricted to Namibia and has hairier branchlets and leaves.

60

M. *muricata*: flowers

C. *cunninghamiana*: fruit

M. *muricata*: tree

S. *aphylla*: fruit

S. *aphylla*: trunk

S. *aphylla*: flowers

CUPRESSACEAE (see page 23)

1 *Widdringtonia nodiflora*   Mountain cypress
SA: 20; Z: 10   Spring   **Bergsipres**

Evergreen shrub or small tree, usually with a **column-like** shape; sexes separate on the same plant; occurring at high altitude in mountainous areas. Juvenile leaves needle-like, spirally arranged, up to 20 mm long. Adult leaves **scale-like**, **about 2 mm long**, pressed tightly against the branchlets, hairless. Male cones up to 4 mm long; female cones globose, up to 20 mm in diameter, greyish green, becoming dark brown with age; scales (valves) 4, surface **smooth or wrinkled**, **with a few warts**. Seeds blackish with a reddish wing.

The wood is used in hut construction. Often grown in gardens.

W. cedarbergensis is mainly restricted to the Cedarberg Mountains in the Western Cape. It has a more spreading crown, and the valves of the female cones are conspicuously rough and warty. Similar cones are found in *W. schwarzii*, a rare species from rocky ravines in the Eastern Cape's Baviaanskloof and Kouga Mountains.

ERICACEAE (see page 24)

2 *Erica caffra*   Water tree heath
SA: 572   Spring   **Waterboomheide**

Evergreen shrub or small tree, with strong, twisted branches; occurring in ravines and on cliffs, usually **along streams or in damp places**. Leaves **3-whorled**, **needle-like**, about 10 mm long, with short hairs; margin rolled under. Flowers axillary towards ends of branches, small (up to 7 mm long), **white**, fading through cream to pale brown, tubular with small, spreading lobes, up to 7 mm long; old flowers persist for a long time on the plant. Fruit a capsule, about 3 mm long.

E. canaliculata (found in the dry shrub forest between George and Port Elizabeth) has 3-whorled leaves, purplish pink flowers with very long, protruding styles. *E. caffrorum* (Drakensberg Escarpment) has 4-whorled leaves and pink or whitish flowers each about 3 mm long. *E. pleiotricha* (= *E. thryptomenoides*), from the Eastern Highlands of Zimbabwe, has 3-whorled leaves and pink flowers with brown to maroon anthers equalling or exceeding the tips of the corolla lobes.

3 *Philippia hexandra*   Petrolbush
Z: 823   Summer–Winter   **Petrolbos**

Evergreen shrub or small tree; occurring at high altitude on mountain slopes, often forming dense thickets among rocks or along streams. Leaves **4-whorled**, densely crowded along branches, **needle-like**, up to 2 mm long. Flowers in clusters of 4–16 at tips of branchlets, inconspicuous, greenish tinged with red, produced in profusion; anthers remaining fused after anthesis; style **protruding** from the flower, **up to 1 mm long**, with stigma **saucer-shaped**; pollen **powdery**, **released in clouds when branches are shaken**. Fruit a minute capsule.

The dry wood burns easily and rapidly, hence the common names.

Similar to *P. benguelensis*, which has joined anthers, style up to 0,3 mm long and the stigma included within the floral tube. The plant is fairly common in the Eastern Highlands of Zimbabwe. *P. mannii*, from the same area, has branchlets with very short white hairs with side branches to the tip, anthers free, and tends to flower earlier (late winter and spring). *P. simii*, from Zimbabwe, coastal Mozambique and the northeastern Drakensberg Escarpment, has branchlets with very short, white hairs, leaves in whorls of 3 and anthers that are free shortly after the buds have opened.

1

W. nodiflora: male cones

2

E. caffra: flowers

1

W. nodiflora: trees

1

W. nodiflora: female cones

3

P. hexandra: flowers

PINACEAE (see page 29)

1 •*Pinus halepensis* 'Aleppo pine
SA: X31   Spring Aleppoden
Medium to large coniferous tree, conical with a short trunk when young, old specimens with an open crown; invading fynbos and grassland. Bark silver-grey. Needles in **clusters of 2, short (40–80 mm long), slender and stiff, grey-green to yellow-green**. Cones woody, conic-ovoid, 80–100 mm long, reddish brown, glossy; cone scales **smooth** or with a slight, transverse ridge.
 A native of Europe (Mediterranean); cultivated for shelter, poles and firewood.
 P. canariensis is an invader of fynbos on the arid mountain slopes of the southwestern areas of the Western Cape; needles long (150–300 mm), slender, in clusters of three, somewhat drooping, blue-green when young, becoming bright green with age; cones light brown with cone scales sharply cross-keeled.

2 •*Pinus patula* Patula pine
SA: X35; Z: 9   Spring Treurden
Medium to large coniferous tree with **drooping foliage**, conical with a short trunk when young, mature specimens with a dense rounded crown; invading forest margins, moist grassland and road cuttings. Bark brownish grey. Needles in **clusters of 3, long (120–300 mm), slender and drooping, bright green**. Cones woody, conic-ovoid, 70–100 mm long, in clusters of 2–5, pale brown, strongly reflexed on very short stalks; cone scales with sunken centre and **minute, deciduous prickles.**
 A native of Central America; cultivated for timber in commercial plantations, particularly in the summer rainfall regions. .
 P. elliottii is an escape from commercial plantations, particularly along the northeastern Drakensberg Escarpment. Its needles are crowded towards the ends of branches, not notably drooping, 2- or 3-clustered, 180–300 mm long, dark green, course and stiff; cone scales are tipped with a blunt, greyish prickle, thus differing from *P. taedia*, which has a sharp, recurved prickle up to 7 mm long.

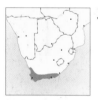

3 •*Pinus pinaster* Cluster pine
SA: X36   Spring Trosden
Medium to large coniferous tree, conical when young, becoming cylindrical with a tall, bare trunk; invading mountain and lowland fynbos. Bark reddish brown, deeply cracked into a grid-like pattern. Needles in **clusters of 2, long (80–240 mm), thick and rigid, dull grey-green**. Cones woody, conic-ovoid, 90–180 mm long, purple when young, becoming light brown when mature; cone scales with a **prominent ridge**, ending in a short, curved point.
 A native of Europe (Mediterranean); cultivated for timber in commercial plantations. This is a declared invader in South Africa.
 P. pinea has an umbrella-shaped crown and needles in clusters of two, light green, 50–150 mm long, thick and rigid; mainly found as an invader in the Western Cape and southern Drakensberg. *P. radiata* has a conical canopy in plantations, but a rounded one when in the open; needles in clusters of usually three, 60–150 mm long, slender, very densely arranged along twigs; cone scales with a fine thorn; invading predominantly fynbos and forest on the moist mountain slopes of the Western and Eastern Cape.

P. halepensis: branches with cones

P. patula: young female cones

P. patula: adult female cones

P. pinaster: male cones

P. patula: shape

P. patula: bark

P. pinaster: female cone

PORTULACACEAE (see page 29)

1 *Ceraria namaquensis* Namaqua porkbush
SA: 104.1 Summer **Wolftoon**
Shrub or small tree; occurring in semi-desert areas, usually in rocky places. Branches **silvery grey, smooth and waxy** with scattered, slightly raised, **black pustules** (extremely reduced side shoots). Leaves clustered on black pustules, almost **cylindrical**, up to 5 x 2 mm, **fleshy**. Flowers small, pink, short-lived. Fruit very small, with pinkish brown wing.
   The bark is used as cordage.

PROTEACEAE (see page 29)

2 **•***Hakea sericea* Silky hakea
SA: X352 Winter–Spring **Silwerhakea**
Evergreen shrub or small tree, much-branched and **very prickly**; invading mountain fynbos and coastal grassland. Branchlets with short hairs, becoming **hairless with age**. Leaves needle-shaped, up to 40 mm long, dark green to grey-green, hairless, **sharp-pointed**. Flowers clustered in leaf axils, small, cream. Fruit a woody capsule, unevenly rounded, with 2 apical horns, wrinkled, purplish brown with paler markings, becoming grey with age; seeds winged.
   A native of Australia; cultivated for dune reclamation, ornament and hedging. This is a declared weed in South Africa.
   H. gibbosa has densely hairy branches (both the young and older ones) as well as hairy young leaves. *H. drupaceae* has leaves which are divided into several upright, needle-shaped segments.

RHAMNACEAE (see page 30)

3 *Phylica paniculata* Common hard-leaf
SA: 453.2; Z: 625 Autumn **Gewone hardeblaar**
Much-branched shrub or small tree with **grey-green** foliage; occurring on mountain slopes and along streams. Young branchlets **grey-felted**. Leaves closely arranged along branchlets, elliptic, **10–15 x 2–6 mm**, dark green above, **white-felted below**; apex tapering, base rounded; margin rolled under; net-veining not visible. Flowers in axillary or terminal branched heads or panicles, very small, **greyish or cream**, sweetly scented. Fruit a woody capsule, more or less oval with a flat tip, about 6 mm in diameter, tipped by the remains of the calyx, reddish brown to black, dehiscent.
   P. oleifolia, from arid mountainous areas in Namaqualand and the southwestern part of the Western Cape, has larger leaves (usually more than 15 mm long) and fruit (8–10 mm in diameter). *P. purpurea* with pink flowers (occurring mainly in the mountains between Bredasdorp and Humansdorp) and *P. villosa* (Cedarberg and Piketberg areas of the Western Cape) have leaves whose margins are strongly rolled under so as to become almost needle-like; they are up to 10 x 1 mm long in the former and up to 20 x 1 mm in the latter. *P. buxifolia* (**3.1**), from the southwestern area of the Western Cape, has ovate leaves, up to 25 x 10 mm, dark green and roughly textured above, with the net-veining usually prominently raised below. The flowers are in dense stalked heads, subtended by conspicuous, fluffy, leaf-like bracts.

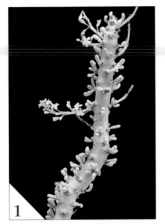

C. namaquensis: flowers

C. namaquensis: fruit

H. sericea: fruit

C. namaquensis: tree

H. sericea: fruit

P. paniculata: flowers

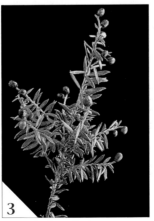

P. paniculata: fruit

P. buxifolia: fruit

67

GROUP 3

TAMARICACEAE (see page 32)

1 *Tamarix usneoides* **Wild tamarisk**
SA: 487   Summer **Abiekwasgeelhout**
Evergreen shrub or small tree, usually with an upright, cylindrical shape and somewhat drooping branches; sexes usually separate; occurring in semi-desert and arid areas, along riverbanks or in dry riverbeds and pans with subterranean, often brackish water; usually in dense stands. Leaves scale-like, very small, **closely overlapping** along branchlets, greyish green. Flowers in slender axillary sprays or racemes, very small, **pale whitish cream.** Fruit a capsule, ovate, about 6 mm long, 3-valved; seeds tipped by a tuft of hairs and a feathery awn.
The branches serve as fodder in times of drought.
T. ramosissima (**1.1**), a native of Europe and Asia, has become naturalized in the same distributional area as *T. usneoides.* It has leaves that do not overlap, and pale pink to purplish pink flowers with obovate petals. *T. chinensis,* also an alien, resembles *T. ramosissima* but has ovate petals.

THYMELAEACEAE (see page 32)

2 *Passerina filiformis* **Brown gonna**
SA: 520.1   Spring **Bruingonna**
Multistemmed, evergreen shrub or small tree; sparsely branched, often with slender, drooping stems; occurring on grassy mountainsides, coastal grassland and on streambanks. Bark **tough**, young stems difficult to break. Branchlets with **creamy-white woolly hairs.** Leaves needle-like, about 10 mm long, 1 mm wide, **bright green above**, **whitish woolly below**; apex with a minute tuft of hairs. Flowers axillary, produced in profusion towards ends of branches, small, brownish yellow, wind-pollinated. Fruit a small nut, about 2 x 1 mm, covered in fine hairs, enclosed by two bracts.
The bark is used as twine.
Similar to *P. falcifolia* (associated with montane areas in the eastern parts of the Western Cape), whose branchlets do not have creamy-white woolly hairs.

3 *Passerina rigida* **Dune gonna**
SA: 520.2   Spring **Duingonna**
Multistemmed, evergreen shrub or small tree with a somewhat **weeping** habit; occurring **mainly on coastal dunes** and in adjacent river valleys. Bark **tough**, young stems difficult to break. Branchlets **white-felted.** Leaves scale-like, up to 2 mm long, closely packed in more or less **four rows.** Flowers axillary, produced in profusion towards ends of branches, small, cream, often tinged with red, wind-pollinated. Fruit a small nut, about 3 mm in diameter, orange-yellow, enclosed by two bracts.
The bark used as twine. A suitable plant for coastal dune reclamation.

T. usneoides: bark   *P. filiformis*: flowers   *P. filiformis*: flowers

T. usneoides: trees   *P. rigida*: flowers

T. ramosissima: flowers   *T. ramosissima*: flowers

GROUP 4

Leaves simple, alternate or in tufts, not bilobed. Stipular scar prominent, encircling stem at base of petiole. Latex present.

MORACEAE (see page 27)

1 **_Cardiogyne africana_** (= *Maclura africana*)   African osage orange
SA: –; Z: 49   Autumn   Afrika-soetlemoen
Spiny, scrambling shrub or small tree; sexes separate, on different plants; occurring in hot, arid, low-altitude bushveld and riverine thicket, occasionally on coastal dunes. Branchlets often **spine-tipped**. Leaves elliptic, 30–90 x 20–40 mm, hairless. Flowers in **dense, almost spherical heads**, about 15 mm in diameter, white, sweetly scented. Fruit a head of densely packed nutlets, each surrounded by a thick and fleshy tissue, reminiscent of a globose mulberry, greyish orange when ripe.
The heartwood yields a yellow dye. Leaves and roots used medicinally.
Although distinguished by several distinct characters, the African genus *Cardiogyne* (with a single species) shares a number of similarities with *Maclura*, its generic counterpart in other parts of the world. By emphasizing the similarities rather than the differences between the two genera, one may also adopt a broader generic concept for *Maclura*, and treat our species as *M. africana*.

2 **_Ficus abutilifolia_** (= *F. soldanella*)   Large-leaved rock fig
SA: 63; Z: 62   All year   Grootblaarrotsvy
Small to medium-sized deciduous tree; occurring in bushveld, usually on rocky hills. Bark whitish yellow, rather smooth. Branchlets **hairless** or almost so. Leaves **heart-shaped, 50–150 x 50–170 mm, smooth** or slightly hairy, particularly on veins; apex rounded or broadly tapering; base heart-shaped; principal lateral veins 5–7 on either side of midrib, basal ones prominent, **yellowish**; petiole 25–180 mm long. Figs **axillary** on terminal branchlets, 10–16 mm in diameter, smooth or slightly hairy, red when ripe, sessile or with stalk up to 5 mm long.
A decoction of the leaves is used medicinally. The fallen figs are much favoured by antelope.
Leaves resemble those of *F. tettensis*, but are larger and almost hairless.

3 **_Ficus burtt-davyi_**   Veld fig
SA: 49   All year   Veldvy
Liana, shrub or small tree; occurring in coastal and inland forest, occasionally on rocky outcrops. Bark greyish, rough. Branchlets slightly hairy. Leaves **elliptic,** 15–80 x 7–35 mm, **hairless**; apex rounded or broadly tapering; base rounded; principal lateral veins 4–9 on either side of midrib, basal pair more or less prominent; petiole up to 20 mm long. Figs **axillary** on terminal branchlets, 5–7 mm in diameter, with long sparse hairs, green with white spots, turning yellowish when ripe, stalk up to 6 mm long.
The bark is pounded and woven into sleeping mats. Figs eaten by numerous birds. Resistant to salt-spray and coastal winds. A good pot-plant; suitable for bonsai.

1 C. *africana*: fruit

1 C. *africana*: flowers

1 C. *africana*: fruit

2 F. *abutilifolia*: figs

2 F. *abutilifolia*: tree

3 F. *burtt-davyi*: roots

3 F. *burtt-davyi*: tree

3 F. *burtt-davyi*: figs

1 Ficus capreifolia
Sandpaper fig
SA: 50.1; Z: 53 All year
Skurwevy

Shrub or small tree with long, slender, whip-like branches; occurring in bushveld, usually along riverbanks or in swamps, often in dense stands. Bark greenish grey, rather smooth. Branchlets hairy. Leaves oblong-ovate, 20–125 x 10–45 mm, **both surfaces rough like sandpaper**; apex **tapering or 3-lobed**; base rounded with a **minute gland (often blackish)** on either side of midrib at junction of petiole below; margin entire or slightly scalloped; principal lateral veins 5–9 on either side of midrib, basal pair prominent; petiole 3–20 mm long; stipules often subpersistent. Figs **axillary** on terminal branchlets, pear-shaped, 11–20 mm in diameter, rough, red when ripe, with stalk 9–15 mm long.

The plant is browsed by buffalo and elephant. Leaves used as a substitute for sandpaper. Fruit eaten by monkeys. Leaves and fruit often heavily parasitized by gall-forming insects. Larval food plant for the hawk moths *Pseudoclanis postica* and *Nephele accentifera.*

Closely related to *F. pygmaea*, which has oval-elliptic leaves with only the upper leaf surface sandpapery and a more distinctly toothed or scalloped margin. The plant is a low-growing shrub from moist areas in Botswana and Namibia, often growing on Kalahari sand.

2 Ficus cordata
Namaqua fig
SA: 51 All year
Namakwavy

Small to medium-sized deciduous tree with an **upright** crown, often a **rock-splitter**; occurring in arid mountainous areas, often along rivers. Bark pale grey, rather smooth. Branchlets slightly hairy. Leaves **ovate**, 25–115 x 10–50 mm, hairless; apex tapering; base heart-shaped to rounded; principal lateral veins 6–9 on either side of midrib, basal pair **prominent**; petiole up to 40 mm long. Figs **axillary** on terminal branchlets, 5–7 mm in diameter, smooth or slightly hairy, **yellowish green** when ripe, **sessile**.

The tree is a larval food plant for the butterfly *Myrina silenus.*

Closely related to *F. salicifolia*, whose ripe figs are reddish and very shortly stalked.

3 Ficus craterostoma
Forest fig
SA: 52; Z: 57/2 All year
Bosvy

Small to medium-sized deciduous tree, **often a strangler**; occurring mainly in coastal and inland forest. Bark grey, rough. Branchlets hairless. Leaves **obovate or reverse triangular**, 30–90 x 12–40 mm, hairless; apex **rounded or blunt to concave**; base broadly tapering to rounded; principal lateral veins 5–11 on either side of midrib, basal pair inconspicuous; petiole up to 25 mm long. Figs **axillary** on terminal branchlets, 5–10 mm in diameter, smooth, yellowish red when ripe, **sessile**.

The figs are much favoured by birds. Not recommended as garden tree near paved areas outside its natural range because, here, the figs, lacking pollinating wasps, will abort and drop in large numbers, and the surrounding area below will need constant clearing.

Differs from *F. natalensis* in its sessile figs, semi-persistent stipules and often blunt to concave leaf tips.

F. capreifolia: trees

F. capreifolia: figs

F. capreifolia: figs

F. cordata: figs

F. cordata: bark

F. craterostoma: figs

F. craterostoma: trunk with aerial roots

GROUP 4

1 *Ficus exasperata*   **Forest sandpaper fig**
Z: 54   All year   **Woudskurwevy**
Medium to large deciduous tree, often a strangler with the stem fluted or buttressed in large specimens; occurring in **forest**. Bark greyish green, smooth; exudes an **amber latex** when slashed. Branchlets hairless or almost so. Leaves broadly elliptic, 70–150 x 30–85 mm, **both surfaces very rough and resembling sandpaper**; apex **broadly tapering**; base rounded to square; principal lateral veins 3–5 on either side of midrib; margin entire or slightly scalloped, wavy; petiole up to 60 mm long. Figs axillary on terminal branchlets, about 10 mm in diameter, harsh to the touch, pink to red when ripe, **shortly stalked**.

The leaves are widely used as a substitute for sandpaper, not only on wood surfaces, but also in traditional medicine – for roughening inflamed or painful parts of the body until bleeding occurs. Extracts from the leaves and bark also have other medicinal applications.

2 *Ficus glumosa* (= *F. sonderi*)   **Mountain fig**
SA: 64; Z: 63   All year   **Bergvy**
Small to medium-sized deciduous tree, often a **rock-splitter**; occurring in bushveld, usually on rocky hills. Bark cream coloured, exfoliating. Branchlets are **densely covered with yellowish brown hairs**. Leaves **elliptic**, 30–120 x 20–100 mm, both surfaces initially with yellowish brown hairs, particularly on veins, becoming virtually hairless above; apex rounded or broadly tapering; base heart-shaped or rounded; principal lateral veins 4–7 on either side of midrib, basal pair prominent; petiole up to 35 mm long. Figs **axillary** on terminal branchlets, 8–15 mm in diameter, **hairy**, red when ripe, **sessile**.

The figs are much favoured by birds, bats, antelope, monkeys and baboons.

Plants from Namibia's Kaokoveld have smaller, less hairy leaves and smaller figs than those from the moister eastern parts of *F. glumosa*'s range.

Similar to *F. stuhlmannii*, which has leaves with the reticulum of smaller veins prominently raised below.

3 *Ficus ilicina*   **Laurel fig**
SA: 53   All year   **Louriervy**
Shrub or low-growing deciduous tree, often a **rock-splitter**; occurring in arid, semi-desert areas, usually on outcrops of dolomite or granite. Bark **white to whitish grey**, smooth. Branchlets hairless. Leaves **elliptic**, 30–90 x 25–45 mm, hairless; base and apex rounded or broadly tapering; principal lateral veins 7–10 on either side of midrib, basal pair **inconspicuous**; petiole up to 18 mm long. Figs **axillary** on terminal branchlets, 5–8 mm in diameter, smooth or slightly hairy, red when ripe, with stalk **up to 5 mm long**.

May be confused with *F. cordata*, which has a more upright habit.

F. exasperata: figs

F. glumosa: figs

F. glumosa: figs

F. ilicina: tree

F. ilicina: figs

1 Ficus ingens   Red-leaved fig
SA: 55; Z: 55   All year   Rooiblaarvy
Dwarf spreading shrub or small to medium-sized deciduous tree, often acting as a rock-splitter; occurring in bushveld or frost-protected sites in grassland, usually on rocky hills. Bark greyish, rather smooth. Branchlets smooth or with short hairs. Young leaves in spring strikingly **bronze-red**. Leaves **ovate to oblong-ovate**, 40–140 x 15–80 mm, hairless; apex shortly tapering to rounded; base heart-shaped or rounded; principal lateral veins usually 5–8 on either side of midrib, basal pair **more or less distinctly branched**, thus not running parallel to the margin; petiole up to 40 mm long. Figs **axillary** on terminal branchlets, **9–12 mm in diameter**, smooth or slightly hairy, pale red to pinkish or purplish when ripe, **shortly stalked**.
    The leaves are toxic to livestock, causing nervous disorders and eventual death among sheep and cattle. Figs eaten by birds, monkeys, baboons, and many other wild animals. Larval food plant for the butterfly *Myrina silenus ficedula*.
    May be confused with *F. salicifolia*, but leaves of *F. ingens* have fewer principal lateral veins (basal pair unbranched), its spring flush of new leaves is reddish, and its figs are larger.

2 Ficus lutea (= *F. vogelii*)   Giant-leaved fig
SA: 61; Z: 68   All year   Reuseblaarvy
Medium to large deciduous tree with **spreading crown**; often starting growth as a strangler (epiphyte); occurring in coastal forest and bush. Bark dark grey, smooth to rough. Branchlets hairless or almost so; apical bud sheaths **silvery**. Leaves ovate to elliptic, **very large (130–400 x 70–200 mm)**, hairless; apex rounded or broadly tapering; base rounded to broadly tapering; principal lateral veins **6–8** on either side of midrib, **yellowish**, basal pair prominent; petiole up to 75 mm long. Figs **axillary** on terminal branchlets, 18–26 mm in diameter, densely hairy to smooth, yellow or red when ripe, **sessile**.
    The bark is rich in fibres, which are woven into a good cloth. Figs eaten by birds and other wild animals. Latex used for bird lime. Decorative and fast-growing tree for frost-free coastal gardens.
    Similar to *F. trichopoda*, which has a greater number of lateral veins (7–11 pairs) and pinkish red apical bud sheaths (stipules).

3 Ficus natalensis   Natal fig
SA: 57; Z: 57   All year   Natalvy
Medium to large evergreen tree, occasionally a strangler; occurring mainly in coastal forest. Bark dark grey, rather smooth. Branchlets hairless. Leaves often sub-opposite, **elliptic or reverse triangular**, 25–75 x 12–40 mm, hairless; apex **rounded or blunt**; base broadly tapering; principal lateral veins 6–9 on either side of midrib, inconspicuous above; petiole **up to 20 mm long**. Figs **axillary** on terminal branchlets, 7–13 mm in diameter, smooth or slightly hairy, **yellow-red** when ripe, **stalk up to 7 mm long**. All material in our region belongs to subsp. *natalensis*.
    The figs are eaten by birds and many other animals.
    May be confused with *F. thonningii*, which has longer petioles (up to 45 mm) and sessile figs.

F. *ingens*: figs & young leaves

F. *ingens*: figs

F. *ingens*: figs

F. *lutea*: figs & young leaves

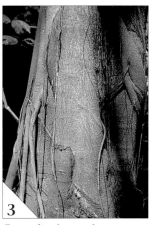

F. *natalensis*: trunk

F. *lutea*: figs

F. *natalensis*: figs

1 **Ficus salicifolia** (= *F. pretoriae*; *F. cordata* subsp. *salicifolia*)   **Wonderboom fig**
SA: 60; Z: 60   All year   **Wonderboomvy**
Shrub or medium to large evergreen tree, occasionally with a spreading crown; occurring in bushveld, usually on rocky hills or in ravines along streams. Bark dark grey, rough. Branchlets hairless. Leaves **ovate to oblong**, 25–130 x 15–60 mm, hairless; apex narrowly or broadly tapering; base heart-shaped or rounded; principal lateral veins usually **10–15** on either side of midrib, basal pair **unbranched**, usually curved and running parallel to the margin; petiole up to 50 mm long. Figs **axillary** on terminal branchlets, **5–8 mm in diameter**, smooth, red with white dots when ripe, with **stalk up to 2 mm long**.
The leaves are toxic, causing nervous disorders and even death in cattle. Figs eaten by birds and other animals. The famous 'Wonderboom' in Pretoria, established well over 1 000 years ago, is a particularly old member of the species.
Some authors consider the plant a subspecies of *F. cordata*, which has sessile yellowish figs and a different geographical distribution. Also compare *F. ingens*.

2 **Ficus sansibarica**   **Knobbly fig**
SA: 47; Z: 61   All year   **Knoppiesvy**
Medium to large evergreen tree, with a round spreading crown, often starting life as a strangler; occurring in bushveld, usually on deep sandy soil. Bark grey, rather smooth. Branchlets **hairless**. Leaves **oblong to ovate**, 40–170 x 20–105 mm, hairless; apex abruptly tapering; base rounded; principal lateral veins 7–9 on either side of midrib, basal pair conspicuous; petiole up to 60 mm long. Figs in **clusters on stout, wart-like, leafless branchlets along trunk and main branches**, 20–50 mm in diameter, warty, hairless, purplish green when ripe, with stalk **up to 25 mm long**. All material in southern Africa belongs to subsp. *sansibarica*.
F. chirindensis, a large forest tree from the far southeastern parts of Zimbabwe and adjacent areas in Mozambique, has more oval leaves and occasionally develops stilt-roots. It has stipules covered with short, appressed, white hairs, whereas *F. sansibarica* has only a marginal fringe of minute hairs.

3 **Ficus stuhlmannii**   **Lowveld fig**
SA: 65; Z: 64   All year   **Laeveldvy**
Small to medium-sized deciduous tree, often a strangler; stem often fluted; occurring in hot, low-altitude bushveld, usually on sandy soil. Bark dark grey, **rough**. Branchlets hairless or almost so. Leaves obovate, ovate or elliptic, 90–180 x 40–80 mm, **both surfaces woolly, particularly on veins**; apex rounded or broadly and abruptly tapering; base somewhat heart-shaped or rounded; venation **prominently raised below**, principal lateral veins 4–6 on either side of midrib; petiole up to 25 mm long, woolly. Figs in dense **axillary** clusters on terminal branchlets, 8–15 mm in diameter, hairy, yellowish red when ripe, **sessile**.
The figs are favoured by many birds and mammals.
May be confused with *F. glumosa*, at least some of whose twigs have yellowish hairs and leaves with the network of smaller veins almost plane below. Also reminiscent of *F. nigropunctata* (occurring in the Zimbabwe bushveld, usually on rocky outcrops), a small tree with smaller (40–100 x 25–40 mm) and thinner leaves. Its older branchlets are blackish with conspicuous whitish lenticels.

F. salicifolia: bark

F. salicifolia: figs

F. sansibarica: figs

F. salicifolia: figs

F. sansibarica: branchlet

F. stuhlmannii: figs

F. stuhlmannii: figs

1 ***Ficus sur*** (= *F. capensis*)   **Broom cluster fig**
SA: 50; Z: 52   All year   **Besemtrosvy**
Medium to large semi-deciduous tree; occurring in forest and bushveld, usually along streams and in moist ravines. Bark whitish to dark grey, rather smooth. Branchlets hairless or almost so. New growth reddish. Leaves elliptic to ovate, 40–150 x 25–120 mm, essentially **hairless**; apex usually tapering; base rounded to heart-shaped; margin **irregularly toothed**; principal lateral veins 3–6 on either side of midrib, basal pair prominent; petiole up to 60 mm long. Figs in **large (up to 1 m long), leafless clusters of branchlets on trunk and main branches**, sometimes also on the roots (even underground), rarely axillary on young branches (coastal regions of Eastern Cape and KwaZulu-Natal), **20–40 mm in diameter**, smooth or slightly hairy, orange-red to red when ripe, **stalk up to 15 mm long**.

The wood is whitish, light yet strong, used for furniture, drums, mortars and, in the past, for the brake-blocks of ox-wagons. Young leaves are cooked as a relish. Figs rather tasty and, although usually infested with insects, are eaten either fresh or sun-dried. Also much favoured by birds, bats and monkeys. Latex used for bird lime and for medicinal and veterinary purposes. Bark used in traditional medicine. Larval food plant for the butterflies *Cyrestis pantheus sublineatus*, *Myrina silenus ficedula* and *M. dermaptera*.

2 ***Ficus sycomorus***   **Common cluster fig**
SA: 66; Z: 65   All year   **Gewone trosvy**
Medium to large semi-deciduous tree with a spreading crown and buttressed trunk; occurring in bushveld, on alluvial soil along riverbanks and streams. Bark **whitish to yellow-orange, powdery or flaking off in patches**. Branchlets covered in **rough hairs**. Leaves **ovate to heart-shaped**, 45–100 x 25–90 mm, **rough** above, **both sides with short hairs**; apex rounded or bluntly tapering; base heart-shaped; principal lateral veins 5–8 on either side of midrib, basal pair prominent; petiole up to 35 mm long. Figs either axillary on terminal branchlets (in Namibia, Angola and probably parts of Botswana and Eastern Highlands of Zimbabwe), or in large leaf-less clusters of branchlets on trunk and main branches, or both, **20–50 mm** in diameter, hairy, reddish orange when ripe, **stalk up to 20 mm long**.

The young leaves are edible to humans, and cooked as a relish. Figs are also con-sumed, either in fresh or dried form, and are also favoured by birds and animals. Bark and latex used medicinally.

From a distance easily confused with *F. vallis-choudae* (occurring in riverine for-est in the Eastern Highlands of Zimbabwe), which has the figs axillary on young leafy branchlets and leaves which are essentially hairless.

3 ***Ficus tettensis*** (= *F. smutsii*)   **Small-leaved rock fig**
SA: 62; Z: 66   All year   **Kleinblaarrotsvy**
Small to medium-sized deciduous tree, often a **rock-splitter**; occurring in bushveld, usually on rocky hills. Bark **white to pale grey**, rather **smooth**. Branchlets **hairy**. Leaves **heart- to kidney-shaped, 35–90 x 30–115 mm**, rough above, **hairy on both surfaces**; apex rounded to bluntly pointed; margin **wavy**; base heart-shaped; principal lateral veins 4–6 on either side of midrib, basal pair prominent; petiole up to 30 mm long. Figs **axillary** on terminal branchlets, 7–10 mm in diameter, hairy, red when ripe, sessile or shortly stalked.

F. *sur*: figs

F. *sur*: figs

F. *sycomorus*: figs

F. *sycomorus*: figs

F. *sycomorus*: tree

F. *tettensis*: figs

F. *tettensis*: figs

1 **_Ficus thonningii_** (= _F. burkei_; _F. petersii_)   **Common wild fig**
SA: 48; Z: 57/1   All year   **Gewone wildevy**
Medium to large **evergreen** tree with dense leafy crown, often a strangler; occurring in bushveld and forest, usually on rocky hills or in ravines. Bark grey, rather smooth. Branchlets smooth to hairy. Leaves usually **elliptic to obovate**, 25–110 x 10–45 mm, smooth or slightly hairy on veins; apex rounded to tapering; base rounded to broadly tapering; principal lateral veins 6–11 on either side of midrib, basal pair inconspicuous; petiole **up to 45 mm long**. Figs **axillary** on terminal branchlets, 7–12 mm in diameter, densely covered with hairs or (rarely) smooth, red when ripe, **sessile or shortly stalked**.
   The wood is whitish, light and in appearance somewhat similar to pine; susceptible to borer attack. Fibres from bark used in mat-making. Figs eaten by birds, bats and antelope. In a remarkable symbiosis no less than 28 species of fig wasp (many species specific) are associated with the fruit of this species. Larval food plant for the butterfly _Myrina dermaptera_. Heavy infestation of the fruit by gall-forming wasps may result in abnormally large figs (up to 20 mm in diameter).
   An extremely variable species, particularly in regard to leaf shape, petiole length and whether figs are sessile or stalked.

2 **_Ficus trichopoda_** (= _F. hippopotami_)   **Swamp fig**
SA: 54   All year   **Moerasvy**
Shrub or small to medium-sized tree; main stem often **more or less horizontal** above water or marshy ground, with many **prop- ('pillar-') roots**; occurring in **swampy areas**, often in groves in swamp forest. Bark grey-green to brown, smooth. Branchlets smooth or slightly hairy; apical bud sheaths **pinkish red**. Leaves heart-shaped, **very large (80–300 x 120–230 mm)**, smooth or slightly hairy; apex rounded to broadly tapering; base heart-shaped; principal lateral veins **7–11** on either side of midrib, whitish above and reddish below; petiole up to 45 mm long, often reddish. Figs **axillary** on terminal branchlets, 10–20 mm in diameter, smooth or slightly hairy, bright red when ripe, with **stalk up to 12 mm long**.
   The figs are eaten by birds and monkeys. Latex makes a good bird lime. Bark yields a strong fibre that is used for ropes. An attractive indoor plant.
   Similar to _F. lutea_, which has fewer lateral veins (6–8 pairs) and silvery apical bud sheaths (stipules).

3 **_Trilepisium madagascariense_** (= _Bosqueia phoberos_)   **False fig**
SA: 45; Z: 51   Spring   **Bastervy**
Medium to large evergreen tree with small crown and somewhat **drooping** branchlets; occurring in forest, often along rivers. Leaves elliptic, 70–140 x 30–65 mm, very dark green and glossy, leathery; apex abruptly tapering to form a **long, narrow drip-tip**. Flowers **protruding as a puff of stamens and styles (about 10 mm in diameter) from an urn-shaped receptacle (about 15 mm long)**, somewhat resembling a fig, but with a wide opening at the apex, creamy white to mauve; male and female flowers separate in the same receptacle. Fruit fig-like, ellipsoidal, about 20 mm long, containing small nutlets.
   The wood is pinkish mauve to reddish brown, with a coarse but even texture; it works easily, and is suitable for furniture. A red dye is obtained from the sap. Larval food plant for the very attractive butterfly _Cyrestis pantheus sublineatus_.

82

F. thonningii: tree

F. thonningii: figs

F. trichopoda: figs

F. trichopoda: figs

T. madagascariense: fruit

T. madagascariense: fruit

GROUP 5

Leaves simple, alternate or in tufts, not bilobed; margin smooth.
Stipular scar absent or obscure. Latex present.

See also Group 1: *Adenium multiflorum* (p. 34).

ANACARDIACEAE (see page 19)

1 *Heeria argentea*   Rockwood
SA: 368   Summer–Winter   Kliphout
Evergreen shrub or small sturdy tree; latex **watery**; sexes separate, on different plants; occurring in mountainous areas, usually among rocks. Leaves oblong to ovate, leathery, dark green above, covered in **fine silver hairs** below; principal lateral veins **conspicuously parallel and raised below**, terminating at the margin without forming an intramarginal vein; petiole up to 5 mm long. Flowers in terminal or axillary panicles, small, white. Fruit leathery, **ellipsoid, about 25 x 20 mm**, yellowish green.

   The bark was once used for tanning and the wood for the brake-blocks of wagons and for fuel. The fallen ripe fruit is much favoured by the rock dassie (hyrax).

2 *Ozoroa concolor*   Green resin tree
SA: 369.1 Spring   Groenharpuisboom
Small tree; latex milky; sexes separate, on different plants; occurring in arid semi-desert and desert vegetation, often along dry watercourses. Leaves crowded towards ends of branches, obovate to elliptic, up to 50 x 25 mm, **glossy bright green above, slightly paler below, hairless**; margin notably **wavy**; principal lateral veins **parallel, yellowish and distinct on both surfaces**; petiole up to 5 mm long. Flowers in terminal panicles, small, creamy yellow. Fruit a drupe, oval, up to 10 mm wide, black or reddish and **wrinkled** when mature.

3 *Ozoroa crassinervia*   Namibian resin tree
SA: 369   Spring   Namibiese harpuisboom
Small to medium-sized tree; latex milky; sexes separate, on different plants; occurring in arid semi-desert vegetation, often in rocky places, particularly granite hills. Leaves crowded towards ends of branches, **broadly obovate, large (up to 110 x 80 mm),** dark green above, **densely grey-felted below**; principal lateral veins **conspicuously parallel and raised below**, terminating at the margin without forming an intramarginal vein; petiole up to 10 mm long. Flowers in terminal panicles, small, white. Fruit a drupe, oval, 5–7 x 6–9 mm, black and **wrinkled** when mature.

   O. namaensis, from southern Namibia, has smaller (13–40 x 10–13 mm) leaves that are oval, blue-green above, densely covered with velvety hairs below.

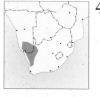

4 *Ozoroa dispar*   Namaqua resin tree
SA: 370   Autumn   Namakwaharpuisboom
Small to medium-sized tree; latex milky; sexes separate, on different plants; occurring in arid semi-desert vegetation, usually on rocky hillsides. Leaves crowded towards ends of branches, **elliptic, 20–70 x 20–30 mm**, bright green above, covered **with dense, yellowish grey hairs below**; margin rather wavy; principal lateral veins **conspicuously parallel and particularly distinct above**; petiole up to 4 mm long. Flowers in terminal panicles, small, creamy white. Fruit a drupe, kidney-shaped, up to 13 mm long, black and **wrinkled** when mature.

H. *argentea*: fruit

H. argentea: flowers

H. argentea: fruit

H. argentea: young fruit

O. crassinervia: leaves

O. concolor: flowers

O. crassinervia: flowers

O. dispar: fruit

1 *Protorhus longifolia*   **Red beech**
SA: 364   Spring   **Rooiboekenhout**
Medium to large evergreen tree, crown usually **with an occasional bright red leaf**;
latex **milky**; sexes separate, on different plants; occurring in coastal and montane
forest. Young growth reddish. Leaves **linear-oblong or narrowly elliptic**, leathery,
glossy dark green above, paler green below, hairless; apex and base tapering; principal lateral veins **conspicuously parallel and raised below**, terminating at the
margin without forming an intramarginal vein; petiole up to 25 mm long. Flowers
in terminal panicles, small, white. Fruit a drupe, oblique-oval, up to 12 mm in diameter, **purple-mauve** when ripe, single-seeded.
　　The heartwood is dark brown and suitable for furniture. Browsed by black rhino.
Bark poisonous, used medicinally. Fruit eaten by monkeys and birds.

BURSERACEAE (see page 21)

2 *Commiphora glaucescens*   **Blue-leaved corkwood**
SA: 276   Summer   **Bloublaarkanniedood**
Unarmed deciduous shrub (in southern and eastern parts of range) or small to
medium-sized tree (Kaokoveld), with trunk branching near ground level and
spreading, **bluish green** crown; sexes separate, on different plants; occurring in arid
bushveld and semi-desert areas, usually between rocks. Bark **yellowish brown to
reddish brown, peeling in papery pieces**. Leaves clustered on dwarf lateral
shoots, subsessile, elliptic to obovate, blue-green to pale green with a **powdery
bloom**, densely hairy (mainly Kaokoveld) to smooth. Flowers in axillary clusters,
small, creamy white to pinkish. Fruit a drupe, ellipsoid, up to 11 mm long, velvety;
stone partly enveloped by a bright red pseudo-aril.
　　The wood is carved into household utensils. Browsed by elephant and other game,
and by livestock.

EUPHORBIACEAE (see page 24)

3 *Croton gratissimus*   **Lavender fever-berry**
SA: 328; Z: 478   Spring   **Laventelkoorsbessie**
Shrub or small tree; crown usually **with an occasional bright orange-red leaf**;
latex **watery**; occurring in bushveld and in wooded places in grassland, often on
rocky ridges. Leaves **lanceolate to elliptic, 70–80 x 20–40 mm, shiny dark green**
above, **silvery white and dotted with scattered brownish scales** below; petiole up
to 30 mm long. Flowers in slender, often drooping spikes **up to 100 mm long**, with
1 or 2 female flowers at the base and many male ones above, small, cream to yellow. Fruit a capsule, 3-lobed, about 10 mm in diameter, yellowish brown, dehiscent.
Var. *gratissimus* has leaves with the upper surface hairless, whereas that of var. *sub-
gratissimus* is hairy (though not rough to the touch).
　　The plant is browsed by game and stock. Leaves aromatic; used by the San in
dried and powdered form as a perfume. Leaves and bark used medicinally. Larval
food plant for the butterfly *Charaxes candiope candiope*.
　　C. menyhartii is rather similar, but the upper surface of its leaves is dull green and
rough to the touch, the scales on the lower surface yellowish, and the inflorescences
usually shorter than 40 mm. *C. steenkampianus* (endemic to the Maputaland Centre,
and usually associated with sand forest) has broader leaves whose lower surface is
silvery white without prominent brownish or yellowish scales.

P. longifolia: fruit

P. longifolia: flowers

P. longifolia: fruit

C. glaucescens: bark

C. gratissimus: flowers

C. glaucescens: fruit

C. gratissimus: flowers

1 Croton pseudopulchellus —— Small lavender fever-berry
SA: –; Z: 482   Summer —— Kleinlaventelkoorsbessie
Shrub or rarely a small tree; crown usually with an occasional bright orange-red leaf; latex **watery**; occurring in hot, low-altitude bushveld, often on sandy soil. Ultimate branchlets often reddish brown due to the presence of scales. Leaves **clustered near the ends of branchlets**, lanceolate to elliptic, **up to 60 x 20 mm**, shiny dark green above, **silvery white and dotted with numerous reddish brown scales below**; petiole up to 20 mm long. Flowers in compact racemes **about 10 mm long**, with 1 or 2 female flowers at the base and many male ones above, small, cream to yellow. Fruit a capsule, 3-lobed, about 10 mm in diameter, dehiscent.
The root is used medicinally.

2 Euphorbia espinosa —— Woody milkbush
SA: –; Z: 522   Winter–Spring —— Houtmelkbos
Unarmed, softly woody, deciduous shrub or small tree, sometimes semi-scandent; latex **milky**; occurring in bushveld, usually in rocky places. Bark olive green, **peeling in yellowish brown papery pieces**. Leaves oval to elliptic, 35–40 x 20–25 mm, hairless; apex broadly tapering to rounded; base broadly tapering. 'Flowers' (cyathia) clustered on cushion-like spurs along the main branches, greenish yellow. Fruit a capsule, **3-lobed**, about 8 mm in diameter, blue-green.
Similar to *E. matabelensis* (mainly from woodland and granite outcrops in Zimbabwe), which has smooth, pale-grey bark and spine-tipped branchlets.

3 Euphorbia guerichiana —— Western woody milkbush
SA: –; Z: 525   Spring–Summer —— Westelike houtmelkbos
Unarmed, deciduous shrub or small tree, often leafless for long periods; latex **milky**; occurring in arid bushveld and semi-desert and desert areas, usually in rocky places. Bark dark brown, **peeling in yellowish brown papery pieces**. Leaves obovate or oblanceolate, **very small (3–15 x 1,5–5 mm)**, semi-succulent, hairless; petiole very short. 'Flowers' (cyathia) clustered near the ends of short lateral branchlets, yellowish. Fruit a capsule, **3-lobed**, about 6 mm in diameter.
The leaves are browsed by livestock. Dry branches once used for fire sticks.
May be mistaken for a species of *Commiphora*, but the latter's latex is watery (cloudy) rather than milky.

4 Macaranga capensis —— Wild poplar
SA: 335; Z: 496   Summer —— Wildepopulier
Medium to large tree with **long erect trunk and rounded, widely branched crown**; latex **watery**; sexes separate, on different plants; occurring in low-altitude forest, usually along streams or in marshy places. Leaves ovate to triangular-ovate, **up to 150 x 120 mm**, or even larger in juvenile trees, young leaves often pale whitish green; venation raised below with **3 or 4 prominent veins** from the base; petiole up to 160 mm long, often, especially in younger plants, **joining the blade some distance from the margin (peltate)**, sometimes tinged with pink; stipules **leaf-like, lanceolate, up to 20 x 5 mm, persisting for some time**. Flowers in branched axillary sprays (male) or few-flowered axillary spikes (females), small, yellowish green. Fruit a single-lobed capsule, up to 5 x 4 mm, **yellowish green**, dehiscent.
The wood is reddish brown and suitable for furniture. Bark is used medicinally.

C. *pseudopulchellus*: fruit

E. *guerichiana*: bark

E. *espinosa*: fruit

E. *guerichiana*: tree

M. *capensis*: fruit

E. *guerichiana*: flowers

M. *capensis*: flowers

1 *Macaranga mellifera*   Mountain poplar
Z: 497   Spring   Bergpopulier
Medium to large unarmed tree with **long erect trunk and rounded, widely-branched crown**; latex **watery**; sexes separate, on different plants; occurring in montane forest, often along streams and forest margins. Leaves ovate to oblong, up to 170 x 110 mm, or even larger in juvenile trees, lower surface with **numerous, minute, yellowish glands**, just visible to the naked eye, young leaves often pale whitish green; margin entire, occasionally with a few scattered teeth; venation raised below; petiole up to 100 mm long, **often (especially in younger plants) joining the blade some distance from the margin (peltate)**, green; stipules **small, narrow, up to 5 x 1 mm, dark-coloured, early deciduous**. Flowers in axillary spikes, small, yellowish green. Fruit a capsule, spherical, up to 5 mm in diameter, **yellowish green** with short, golden hairs, tipped by remains of the three persistent styles, dehiscent, single-seeded.
    Larval food plant for the butterfly *Neptis swynnertoni*.

2 *Uapaca kirkiana*   Mahobohobo
Z: 467   Summer   Mahobohobo
Small to medium-sized tree with a rounded crown; latex watery; sexes separate, on different plants; occurring in open woodland, often in association with species of *Brachystegia*; may form dense stands on well-drained soils. Leaves scattered or crowded near ends of branchlets, **ovate or obovate, large (about 170 x 110 mm)**, thick and leathery, shiny dark green above, with **greyish or brownish woolly hairs below**; apex rounded; base tapering, symmetric; petiole **thickset, up to 20 mm long**, velvety. Flowers axillary, often on older wood, inconspicuous, greenish yellow. Fruit fleshy with a tough skin, spherical, up to 30 mm in diameter, russet yellow, 3- or 4-seeded.
    The fruit is edible, its flesh sweet-tasting and much sought after; often fermented to make an alcoholic wine. Roots used medicinally. Wood reddish brown, suitable for furniture and as a general purpose timber, and it makes good charcoal. Larval food plant for the butterflies *Abantis arctomarginata*, *Charaxes nichetes leoninus* and *Deudorix magda* (on seed).
    U. lissopyrena, a medium to large tree from low-altitude forest along the eastern border of Zimbabwe and adjacent Mozambique, has stems with conspicuous prop- or stilt-roots and large (up to 220 x 135 mm), smooth, very thick and leathery leaves. It often grows along rivers and streams.

3 *Uapaca nitida*   Narrow-leaved mahobohobo
Z: 468   Autumn   Smalblaar-mahobohobo
Small to medium-sized tree; latex watery; sexes separate, on different plants; occurring in open *Brachystegia* woodland, usually at low altitude. Leaves crowded near ends of branchlets, **elliptic to oblong-elliptic, large (about 160 x 45 mm)**, thick and leathery, shiny dark green above, **paler green below, hairless**; apex broadly tapering to rounded; base tapering, often narrowly so, symmetric; margin often wavy; petiole slender, **up to 50 mm long**. Flowers axillary, inconspicuous, yellowish green. Fruit fleshy with a tough skin, oval, up to 20 mm long, brownish yellow.
    The fruit is edible but not very popular. Wood used as a general purpose timber. Leaves and stems often have black fruit-like insect galls. Larval food plant for the butterflies *Abantis arctomarginata* and *Charaxes nichetes leoninus*.

M. mellifera: fruit

U. kirkiana: flowers

U. kirkiana: fruit

U. nitida: fruit

1 *Uapaca sansibarica*   **Lesser mahobohobo**
Z: 469   Autumn   **Klein-mahobohobo**
Small to medium-sized tree; latex watery; sexes separate, on different plants; occurring in bushveld and woodland, usually at low altitude. Leaves scattered or crowded near ends of branchlets, **clearly obovate, large (about 145 x 70 mm)**, thick and leathery, shiny dark green above, **paler green and smooth, or with sparse hairs below**; apex rounded; base tapering, sometimes asymmetric; petiole **slender, up to 30 mm long**, with short hairs. Flowers axillary, greenish yellow or bright yellow. Fruit fleshy with a tough skin, spherical, up to 20 mm in diameter, yellow.
     Larval food plant for the butterflies *Abantis arctomarginata* and *Charaxes nichetes leoninus*.
     Distinguished from *U. kirkiana* by its generally smaller leaves, which are sometimes smooth below, and rather slender petioles.

SAPOTACEAE (see page 31)
2 *Chrysophyllum viridifolium*   **Fluted milkwood**
SA: 580; Z: 837   Summer   **Bosstamvrug**
Large evergreen tree; bole long and clear, **often deeply fluted at the base**; latex milky; occurring in evergreen subtropical forest, often as a canopy constituent. Branchlets somewhat zigzag, new growth densely covered with **short reddish brown hairs**. Leaves oblong or ovate-oblong, glossy dark-green above, paler green below, hairless when mature, except for brownish hairs on the midrib below; apex **abruptly tapering to a narrow, jutting tip**; lateral veins **numerous, closely parallel (less than 2 mm apart) and joining in a prominent marginal vein**, clearly visible on the lower surface; petiole up to 10 mm long, with brownish hairs. Flowers in axillary clusters, white. Fruit a berry, subglobose, up to 35 mm in diameter, slightly 3–5-angled, yellow, 3–5-seeded.
     The fruit is edible, with a sticky pulp and pleasant taste. Larval food plant for the butterflies *Pseudacraea lucretia* and *P. eurytus imitator*.
     C. gorungosanum is a very large tree occurring in forest in the Eastern Highlands of Zimbabwe (common in the Chirinda Forest near Mt Selinda) and adjacent Mozambique. It has leaves with dense silvery to brownish hairs below, and widely spaced secondary veins that do not join a prominent marginal vein.

3 *Englerophytum magalismontanum*
(= *Bequaertiodendron magalismontanum*)   **Transvaal milkplum**
SA: 581; Z: 838   Winter–Spring   **Stamvrug**
Small to medium-sized evergreen tree; latex **milky**; occurring on rocky outcrops or in riverine fringing forest. Branchlets densely covered in **brownish hairs**; branching not obviously subterminal. Leaves elliptic to narrowly obovate, leather, glossy dark green and hairless above, **densely covered in reddish brown to silvery hairs below, tightly folded upward** along midrib when very young. Flowers in compact clusters **on new and old wood**, including the main stems, pinkish, red or purplish brown, strongly and rather unpleasantly scented. Fruit a berry, ellipsoid, up to 25 x 28 mm, red, often borne in profusion on the old wood, single-seeded.
     The fruit is edible, pleasant tasting and rich in vitamin C; used to make wine, syrup, jelly and jam. Root used medicinally. Larval food plant for the butterfly *Pseudacraea boisduvalii trimeni*.

U. sansibarica: fruit

U. sansibarica: flowers

C. viridifolium: trunk

C. viridifolium: seeds

E. magalismontanum: flowers

E. magalismontanum: fruit

1 *Englerophytum natalense* (= *Bequaertiodendron natalense*) **Natal milkplum**
SA: 582; Z: 839   Summer **Natalmelkpruim**
Medium to large evergreen tree; latex **milky**; occurring in **forest**, particularly in subtropical areas, often in groves. Young branchlets with dense appressed brownish hairs; branching pattern **distinctly subterminal**. Leaves tend to be **clustered towards tips of branches**, oblanceolate to narrowly elliptic, leathery, glossy grey-ish green and hairless above, densely covered with **silvery hairs**, often tinged with brown below, **tightly folded upward along midrib when very young**; margin slightly wavy. Flowers solitary or in groups of 2 or 3 **in leaf axils**, white to cream. Fruit a berry, ovoid to cylindrical, up to 25 x 15 mm, red, covered with fine hairs, single-seeded.

The wood is strong and durable; suitable for general carpentry. Fruit edible.

Larval food plant for the butterflies *Euptera pluto kinugnana*, *Pseudacraea boisduvalii trimeni*, *P. eurytus imitator* and *P. lucretia*.

2 *Manilkara concolor* **Zulu milkberry**
SA: 586; Z: 842/1   Winter–Spring **Zoeloemelkbessie**
Shrub or small to medium-sized deciduous or semi-deciduous tree with a much-branched crown; latex **milky**; occurring in low-altitude bushveld, sand forest and coastal dune forest, often on termitaria. Branchlets hairless. Leaves **crowded towards branch ends but not in conspicuous rosettes, elliptic to elliptic-oblong**, leathery, hairless; apex rounded and usually slightly notched; base **bluntly tapering to rounded**. Flowers in **many-flowered** axillary clusters, greenish white; ovary with dense hairs. Fruit a berry, subglobose with persistent calyx, up to 15 mm in diameter, orange, single- or 2-seeded.

The heartwood is dark reddish brown, hard, fine grained and suitable as general purpose timber. Fruit edible, very tasty. Root used medicinally.

M. nicholsonii is a rare species restricted to forest margins in Pondoland and southern KwaZulu-Natal. It has larger (50–70 x 25–35 mm), more elliptic leaves, a more tapering lamina base, flowers in clusters of about 3, a hairless ovary and characteristic woody flower galls on the branchlets.

3 *Manilkara discolor* **Forest milkberry**
SA: 588; Z: 842   Winter–Spring **Bosmelkbessie**
Medium to large tree; latex **milky**; occurring in low-altitude evergreen forest and sand forest. Branchlets densely covered in greyish hairs, soon becoming hairless. Leaves weakly **clustered towards tips of branches, elliptic-obovate to obovate**, glossy **dark green and hairless above, densely covered with silvery hairs below**; apex **broadly tapering to rounded**; base **tapering**. Flowers in axillary clusters, small, yellowish; calyx and pedicel with rusty hairs. Fruit a berry, ovoid or ellipsoid, up to 13 x 8 mm, yellow, usually single-seeded.

The wood is hard and strong; used for xylophone keys and as a general purpose timber. Root used medicinally. Fruit edible and tasty. Larval food plant for the butterfly *Pseudacraea boisduvalii trimeni*.

Can be confused with *Englerophytum natalense*, which has the leaf tips more sharply tapering.

E. natalense: fruit

E. natalense: flowers

E. natalense: fruit

M. concolor: flowers

M. concolor: young fruit

M. concolor: fruit

M. discolor: flowers

M. discolor: fruit

1 Manilkara mochisia   Lowveld milkberry
SA: 587; Z: 843 Spring   Laeveldmelkbessie
Shrub or small deciduous or evergreen tree with somewhat drooping branches and leaves in **characteristic terminal rosettes**; latex **milky**; occurring in bushveld, often on termitaria. Branchlets heavily marked with leaf scars, hairless; branching pattern **subterminal**. Leaves densely clustered at tips of branches and on short warty branches (overtopped stem tips), **narrowly elliptic-ovate, to narrowly spatulate**, hairless when mature; apex **rounded, often notched**; base **tapering**. Flowers in dense axillary clusters among and just below the leaves, greenish yellow, **drooping**, strongly scented. Fruit a berry, ellipsoid, with persistent calyx, up to 18 mm long, yellow with red pulp, 1–3-seeded.
    The wood is pale brown to dark reddish brown (heartwood), durable, and used for fencing poles. Browsed by game. Root used medicinally. Fruit edible and tasty.

2 Mimusops caffra   Coastal red milkwood
SA: 583 Spring–Summer   Kusrooimelkhout
Evergreen shrub or small to medium-sized tree; latex **milky**; occurring in **coastal dune forest up to the high-tide mark**, also in sand forest. Branchlets covered with dense brownish hairs. Leaves **cordate or broadly to narrowly obovate, stiff and very leathery**, dark greyish green and hairless above in mature leaves, **densely covered with short silvery, yellowish or brownish hairs below**; apex **rounded**, often notched; base tapering; margin **rolled under**; petiole up to 15 mm long, with brownish hairs. Flowers in axillary groups of 1–8, white, fading to reddish brown. Fruit a berry, oval with a rounded tip and **persistent** calyx, up to 25 mm long, orange-red, single-seeded.
    The wood is reddish brown, hard, heavy and strong; used for boat-building. Fruit edible with a pleasant taste. Useful plant for the consolidation of coastal sand dunes. Larval food plant for the butterfly *Pseudacraea lucretia*.
    M. obtusifolia also occurs in coastal scrub (in Mozambique). Its leaves are usually broadest at the apex, their lower surface with short, appressed greyish hairs, or hairless, and the petiole up to 40 mm long.

3 Mimusops obovata   Red milkwood
SA: 584 Spring   Rooimelkhout
Medium to large evergreen tree; latex **milky**; occurring in forest and riverine fringes. Leaves **obovate, elliptic or oblong, thinly leathery**, shiny dark green above, dull green below, **hairless on both sides when mature**; apex broadly tapering to rounded; base tapering; margin **slightly rolled under**; petiole up to 10 mm long. Flowers axillary, solitary or in pairs, white. Fruit a berry, oval with a narrow tip and **persistent** calyx, 20–30 x 10–25 mm, shiny orange-red, single-seeded.
    The wood is pinkish white, hard and strong, and used as a general purpose timber. The fruit is edible. Bark used medicinally. Web-spinning caterpillars often defoliate the trees in autumn. Larval food plant for the butterflies *Pseudacraea boisduvalii trimeni, P. lucretia* and *P. eurytus imitator*.

M. mochisia: fruit   *M. mochisia*: flowers   *M. caffra*: fruit

M. mochisia: flowers   *M. obovata*: flowers

M. caffra: flowers   *M. obovata*: fruit

97

1 Mimusops zeyheri

Transvaal red milkwood

SA: 585; Z: 841   Spring–Summer

Moepel

Shrub or small to medium-sized evergreen tree, usually with a wide-spreading, dark-green rounded crown; latex **milky**; occurring in bushveld and along forest margins, often in rocky places and along streams. Branchlets and young leaves **often with reddish brown, appressed hairs**. Leaves oblong-elliptic or oblong-lanceolate, usually broadest at or below the middle, **thickly leathery**, shiny **dark-green** above, paler green below, **often initially with reddish brown appressed hairs**, becoming hairless with age; apex broadly tapering to rounded; base tapering; petiole up to 30 mm long. Flowers in axillary groups of 1–7, white to cream, sweetly scented. Fruit a berry, ovoid with persistent calyx, 20–30 x 10–25 mm, yellow to orange, usually single-seeded.

The wood is pale reddish-brown, suitable as a general purpose timber, but may cause sneezing when being worked. Fruit edible and rich in vitamin C; pleasantly sweet with a mealy consistency. The tall trees in the temple enclosure at Great Zimbabwe belong to this species. Larval food plant for the butterflies *Pseudacraea boisduvalii trimeni* and *P. lucretia*.

2 Sideroxylon inerme

White milkwood

SA: 579; Z: 832   Summer–Winter

Witmelkhout

Evergreen shrub or small tree, usually with a gnarled and twisted stem and branches; latex **milky**; occurring in **coastal dune thicket and forest**, also in bushveld, often on termitaria. Branchlets sometimes with short reddish brown hairs near tips and between leaves. Leaves **elliptic to obovate, thickly leathery, shiny dark green above**, paler green below, sometimes with rusty brown hairs when young, becoming **essentially hairless with age**; apex **broadly tapering to round-ed**, often notched; base tapering; margin rolled under; petiole up to 15 mm long. Flowers in few- to many-flowered axillary clusters or on older wood, small, yel-lowish or whitish green, unpleasantly scented. Fruit a berry, globose, up to 10 mm in diameter, **purple to blackish**, single-seeded. Subsp. *inerme* (occurring mainly in South Africa and southern Mozambique) tends to have hairless branchlets and young leaves with flowers mainly in axils of current season's leaves. Subsp. *diospy-roides* (mainly Zimbabwe and central Mozambique northwards) tends to have hairy branchlets and young leaves with the flowers mainly on the older growth.

The wood is yellowish brown, strong, durable and suitable as a general purpose timber. Bark and root used medicinally. Fruit favoured by birds, bats, monkeys and bushpigs. Three specimens of this species in South Africa are of considerable his-torical interest and have been proclaimed national monuments, namely the 'Post Office Tree' in Mossel Bay, estimated to be at least 600 years old; the 'Fingo Milkwood Tree' on the road to Breakfast Vlei, 13 km from Peddie and the 'Treaty Tree' in Spring Street, Woodstock, Cape Town.

M. zeyheri: flowers

M. zeyheri: fruit

M. zeyheri: fruit

S. inerme: flowers

S. inerme: fruit

1 *Vitellariopsis ferruginea*   Gourd bush milkwood
Z: 844   Summer   Kalbasbosmelkhout
Shrub or small tree with leaves crowded at tips of branches; latex **milky**; occurring in bushveld, usually among rocks on granite hills. Branchlets densely covered near tips with reddish brown hairs. Leaves in **terminal rosettes**, elliptic to obovate-elliptic, **usually less than 70 mm long**, dark green and hairless above, **densely covered with reddish hairs below**, becoming less hairy with age; apex **rounded**, often slightly notched; base tapering. Flowers in axillary groups of 1–3, white, often **tinged with pink**, sweetly scented. Fruit a berry, **ovoid-ellipsoid** (resembling miniature gourds), up to 40 x 20 mm, with reddish brown woolly hairs and **persistent calyx**, single-seeded.
2 The fruit is edible.

2 *Vitellariopsis marginata*   Natal bush milkwood
SA: 590   Winter–Summer   Natalbosmelkhout
Small to medium-sized evergreen tree with leaves crowded towards tips of branches; latex **milky**; occurring in coastal forest and in forested ravines, often along streams. Characteristic **branching pattern comprising a series of erect short stems (overtopped stem tips) with leaf rosettes, spaced along a horizontal shoot.** New growth bright red. Leaves narrowly obovate, **usually 70–100 mm**
3 **long**, glossy green above, dull and paler green below, **hairless when mature**; apex broadly tapering to rounded; base tapering; venation prominent on both surfaces. Flowers in axillary groups of 1–4, white. Fruit a berry, ovoid, up to 50 x 35 mm, purplish red, with **persistent calyx**, single-seeded.
    The wood is reddish brown, highly valued and used for carrying-sticks. The fruit is edible.
    V. dispar has leaves that are usually less than 70 mm long, and yellow, thick-skinned but thinly fleshy fruit. The tree is restricted to a small area in the upper Tugela River catchment in KwaZulu-Natal, where it occurs in bushveld, usually
4 near streams and rivers.

URTICACEAE (see page 33)
3 *Pouzolzia mixta* (= *P. hypoleuca*)   Soap-nettle
SA: 71; Z: 76   Summer   Seepnetel
Shrub or small, soft-wooded tree; latex **watery**; occurring in bushveld, particularly in rocky places, usually in dense stands. Leaves **ovate**, 25–100 x 13–75 mm, **soft-textured, dark green and somewhat rough above, silvery white-felted below**; prominently **3-veined**; margin **entire**. Flowers in axillary clusters, very small,
5 greenish-white; pollen released explosively. Fruit a nut, very small, enclosed in the persistent perianth tube.
    The leaves are cooked to provide a popular green vegetable (often mixed with *Obetia tenax*). Bark yields a strong fibre. Leaves produce a soapy lather when rubbed in water. The root used for medicinal purposes. Larval food plant for the butterfly *Hyalites obeira*.

V. ferruginea: flowers

V. marginata: flowers

V. marginata: fruit

V. ferruginea: old flowers

V. marginata: flowers

P. mixta: flowers

GROUP 6

Leaves simple, alternate or in tufts, not bilobed; margin toothed or scalloped. Stipular scar absent or obscure. Latex present.

See also Group 5: *Macaranga mellifera* (p. 90); Group 11: *Obetia carruthersiana* (p. 246) and *O. tenax* (p. 246).

ANACARDIACEAE (see page 19)

1 *Laurophyllus capensis*   **Iron Martin**

SA: 366   Summer   **Ystermartiens**

Evergreen shrub or small tree, usually slender and sparsely branched; **latex watery**; sexes separate, on different plants; occurring in fynbos and shrub forest, often in moist places or along stream banks. Leaves elliptic-oblong, leathery, glossy dark green above, **hairless**; apex broadly tapering, base tapering; margin **bluntly and roughly toothed**; principal lateral veins conspicuous above; petiole up to 20 mm long. Female flowers comprise **compact inflorescences of persistent branched antler-like structures, resembling a parasitized deformity**, male ones in terminal heads or panicles; small, cream or white. Fruit a small nutlet, flat, winged, up to 5 mm in diameter, concealed by the antler-like structures.

BURSERACEAE (see page 21)

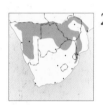

2 *Commiphora glandulosa*

(= *C. pyracanthoides* subsp. *glandulosa*)   **Tall common corkwood**

SA: 285.1; Z: 416   Spring   **Groot gewone kanniedood**

Spiny shrub or small tree, **usually with a single bole**; sexes usually separate, on different plants; occurring in dry bushveld (notably mopane woodland). Bark **yellowish green or greyish green, flaking in small yellowish papery pieces**. Young branchlets hairless, **spine-tipped**. Leaves usually simple and clustered on short branchlets, often trifoliolate on long shoots, subsessile, obovate or elliptic, **bright green above, pale green below**, essentially hairless; apex narrowly to broadly tapering. Flowers in axillary clusters, small, pink or reddish; calyx and pedicel **with large glandular hairs**. Fruit a drupe, subglobose, about 15 mm long, hairless; stone partly enveloped by a 4-lobed, **bright red pseudo-aril**.

The wood is used for household utensils. Often planted as a live fence.

Compare *C. pyracanthoides* (p. 104).

3 *Commiphora merkeri*   **Zebra-bark corkwood**

SA: 279; Z: 413   Summer   **Sebrabaskanniedood**

Spiny small to medium-sized tree, with a single trunk; sexes separate, on different plants; occurring in hot, dry bushveld, often associated with mopane woodland. Bark **grey with very characteristic, dark blackish warty horizontal (zebra-striped) bands, peeling in yellowish, papery strips. Branchlets hairless, smooth, purplish, often spine-tipped**. Leaves clustered on spine-tipped side shoots and then usually simple, occasionally 3-foliolate on long shoots, **blue-green with a greyish bloom**, hairless; apex rounded; base tapering; margin scalloped-toothed towards apex. Flowers in axillary clusters with, or just before, the new leaves, small, yellowish. Fruit a drupe, ellipsoid, up to 10 mm long, reddish brown, hairless; stone almost completely enveloped by a **yellow pseudo-aril**.

The stems often exude large quantities of resin, which is used medicinally.

L. capensis: male flowers   *L. capensis*: female flowers   *C. glandulosa*: bark

C. glandulosa: flowers   *C. glandulosa*: fruit   *C. glandulosa*: fruit

C. merkeri: flowers   *C. merkeri*: bark

1 Commiphora pyracanthoides — Common corkwood

SA: 285   Spring — Gewone kanniedood

Spiny shrub or small tree, **usually multistemmed**; sexes usually separate, on different plants; occurring in dry bushveld (notably mopaneveld), often at low altitude, on sandy soils and termitaria. Otherwise very similar to *C. glandulosa* (p. 102), but **without glandular hairs on the calyx.**

EUPHORBIACEAE (see page 24)

2 Alchornea laxiflora — Venda bead-string

SA: 334; Z: 493   Spring–Summer — Vendakralesnoer

Deciduous shrub or small tree, with attractive **purple to golden-yellow autumn colours**; latex **milky**; sexes separate, on different plants; occurring in low-altitude bushveld, often in riverine bush or thicket. Branchlets hairy when young. Leaves **ovate to elliptic, up to 200 x 90 mm**, hairy when young, becoming smoother with age; apex with an abrupt sharp tip; base rounded to narrowly lobed; margin **toothed or scalloped**; petiole 20–70 mm long, **usually with two hair-like protuberances where it joins the base of the lamina**. Male flowers are in axillary spikes with reddish bracts, female ones solitary in leaf axils, inconspicuous. Fruit a 2–4-lobed capsule, up to 7 mm in diameter, dark brown, dehiscent.

A. hirtella – which occurs in understorey of forest in the Eastern Highlands of Zimbabwe, Ngoye Forest and forest in the vicinity of Mt. Ngeli, southern KwaZulu-Natal – has elliptic to narrowly ovate leaves (up to 150 x 55 mm) with tapering base; petiole swollen at both ends, without protuberances at base of lamina; male flowers in slender sprays of about 200 x 150 mm, female ones in spikes 20–50 mm long.

3 Croton megalobotrys — Large fever-berry

SA: 329; Z: 480   Spring — Grootkoorsbessie

Small to medium-sized tree; latex **watery**; occurring in bushveld and thicket, nearly always on alluvial flats along rivers. Leaves **ovate**, usually about 80 x 50 mm, dark green above, paler green below, with **4 or 5 pairs** of principal lateral veins; apex sharply tapering; base **square to shallowly lobed**; margin **irregularly and roughly toothed**; petiole long and slender, **with two prominent, stalked glands at base of lamina**. Flowers in sturdy spikes up to 90 mm long, sexes usually separate on the same spike, small, yellowish green. Fruit a woody capsule, obscurely 3-lobed, up to 40 mm in diameter, with greyish hairs when young, becoming smoother with age, yellowish brown.

Tree browsed by game, notably elephant. Bark and seeds used medicinally.

C. leuconeurus, from the upper Zambezi River Valley, is very similar but differs in its leaves, which have 8 or more pairs of principal lateral veins, more broadly tapering apices and flowering spikes up to 220 mm long. *C. scheffleri*, from hot, low-altitude bushveld and thicket, is usually a scrambling shrub with smaller (40–70 x 15–35 mm), hairy leaves with very finely and sparsely toothed margins.

C. *pyracanthoides*: bark

C. *pyracanthoides*: flowers

C. *pyracanthoides*: fruit

A. *laxiflora*: fruit

female flowers

C. *megalobotrys*: male flowers

A. *laxiflora*: fruit

C. *megalobotrys*: fruit

1 Croton sylvaticus

Forest fever-berry
Boskoorsbessie

SA: 330; Z: 484   Spring–Summer

Shrub or medium to large deciduous tree; latex **watery**; occurring in forest or associated woodland. Leaves **ovate to broadly lanceolate**, 40–135 x 25–100 mm, both surfaces green, usually hairless when mature, with 6 or more pairs of principal lateral veins; apex **sharply tapering**; base **rounded to lobed**; margin **irregularly and roughly toothed**; petiole slender, up to 100 mm long, **with two prominent glands at base of lamina**. Flowers in sturdy spikes up to 150 mm long, sexes usually separate on the same spike, small cream or pale yellow. Fruit a capsule, obscurely 3-lobed, up to 10 mm in diameter, **bright orange** when ripe.

The bark used both as a fish poison and for medicinal purposes. Leaves used in traditional medicine. Fruit much favoured by birds. Spittle bugs (froghopper nymphs) sometimes occur in large numbers on the branches. They suck the sap and excrete excess water as a protective froth, which is produced in such quantities that it often drips from the branches, causing the host trees to 'rain'. Larval food plant for the butterfly *Charaxes candiope candiope*.

2 Excoecaria bussei

Pepper-seed tree
Pepersaadboom

SA: 341.1; Z: 514   Spring–Summer

Small to medium-sized tree; latex **milky**; occurring in bushveld and thicket, usually in hot, low-altitude areas. Leaves broadly ovate to elliptic, 45–150 x 30–80 mm, **thinly textured**, hairless; apex abruptly tapering; base tapering; margin scalloped; petiole slender, up to 10 mm long. Flowers in slender axillary spikes up to 120 mm long, small, greenish yellow. Fruit a capsule, **3-lobed**, **very large (40–50 mm in diameter)**, dark brown, thin-walled; seeds **perfectly spherical**, dark brown.

The seeds are said to produce a peppery, burning sensation when chewed; very uniform in size and can be stringed into attractive necklaces. Latex harmful to the eye. Larval food plant for the butterfly *Sallya morantii morantii*.

E. simii, from forest in KwaZulu-Natal and the Eastern Cape, is a shrub or small tree with slender branches; leaves in terminal clusters, shiny green above, paler below, with serrated margin; flowers in terminal spikes up to 25 mm long.

3 Sapium ellipticum

Jumping-seed tree
Springsaadboom

SA: 342; Z: 517   Spring–Summer

Medium to large tree with tall main stem and **somewhat drooping** branches; latex **milky**; occurring in forest and associated bush clumps, also in wooded ravines and in swamp forest. Leaves elliptic, oblong to lanceolate, dark green above, paler green below; apex sharply tapering; base **tapering to almost rounded, characteristically minutely lobed at junction with petiole**; margin **toothed to scalloped**; lateral veins close together; petiole up to 10 mm long. Flowers in axillary or terminal drooping spikes up to 50 mm long, male flowers terminal with female ones near the base, small, yellowish. Fruit a **1- or 2-lobed** capsule, about 10 x 7 mm, reddish brown, crowned by remains of the styles, reluctantly dehiscent.

Various parts of the plant are used medicinally. Fruit sometimes infested by the larvae of a moth, which causes the fruit to 'jump'. Larval food plant for the butterfly *Sallya boisduvali boisduvali*.

1 *C. sylvaticus*: flowers

1 *C. sylvaticus*: fruit

1 *C. sylvaticus*: fruit

2 *E. bussei*: fruit

3 *S. ellipticum*: fruit

3 *S. ellipticum*: fruit

3 *S. ellipticum*: flowers

1 *Sapium integerrimum*   **Duiker-berry**
SA: 343; Z: 518   Spring–Summer   **Duikerbessie**
Small to medium-sized tree, often multistemmed with rounded crown and **arching, drooping branches**; latex **milky**; occurring on forest margins and in associated wooded grassland, often as a pioneer. Leaves oblong-ovate or elliptic, shiny dark green above, **pale bluish green below**, hairless; apex tapering; base **tapering to almost rounded, characteristically minutely lobed at junction with petiole**; margin **widely scalloped**; lateral veins well spaced; petiole up to 8 mm long. Flowers in terminal spikes up to 70 mm long, male flowers terminal with female ones near the base, small, yellowish. Fruit a woody capsule, **3-lobed with 2 horns on each lobe**, up to 25 mm in diameter, **drooping**, yellowish green, splitting into 6 valves, each with a distinct horn.

The wood is hard and heavy, and can be used for hut construction. Browsed by bushbuck. Fallen fruit eaten by game and stock; also used medicinally. Fruit sometimes infested by the larvae of a moth, which causes the fruit segments to 'jump'. Larval food plant for the butterflies *Sallya boisduvali boisduvali* and *S. natalensis*.

2 *Spirostachys africana*   **Tamboti**
SA: 341; Z: 516   Spring   **Tambotie**
Medium-sized deciduous tree with a rounded crown and **yellow or reddish autumn colours**; latex **milky**; sexes separate on the same plant; occurring in low-altitude bushveld, often on heavy soils along rivers and streams. Bark dark grey to blackish, **cracked into a grid-like pattern of flakes**. Leaves ovate to elliptic, smooth or slightly hairy, **with two minute blackish glands at the junction with the petiole**; apex and base tapering to rounded; margin **finely toothed or scalloped**; petiole about 6 mm long. Flowers in slender catkin-like spikes up to 30 mm long, very small, mostly male with a few female ones at the base. Fruit a capsule, **3-lobed**, about 10 mm in diameter, splitting into three segments.

The heartwood is dark brown, hard, heavy and durable with an attractive sheen, in contrast to the sapwood, which is pale yellow, and not resistant to borers; widely used for furniture, but sawdust must be kept out of the eyes. The timber should not be used as fuel: inhalation of the smoke causes headache and nausea, and food directly exposed to the smoke is said to become poisonous. Latex toxic and may cause skin irritation; used as fish and arrow poison; also used medicinally, as is the bark. Pieces of wood can be placed among clothes as an insect repellent. Seed often infested by the larvae of a moth, which causes the fruit-segments to 'jump' into the air, particularly when heated.

S. integerrimum: fruit

S. integerrimum: flowers

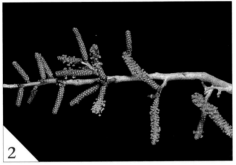

S. africana: male flowers

S. africana: fruit

S. africana: bark

GROUP 7

Leaves simple, alternate or in tufts, not bilobed; blade with single midvein from base, distinctly discolorous. Latex absent.

See also Group 9: *Maytenus undata* (p. 140) and *Salix babylonica* (p. 154); Group 10: *Bridelia cathartica* (p. 188), *Clutia pulchella* (p. 190), *Diospyros villosa* (p. 182) and *Ilex mitis* (p. 160); Group 11: *Cryptocarya latifolia* (p. 228).

ASTERACEAE (see page 20)

1 *Brachylaena discolor* Coast silver oak
SA: 724 & 731 Winter Kusvaalbos
Shrub or small tree occurring in **coastal bush and associated bushveld**; sexes separate, on different plants. Leaves **lanceolate to obovate**, usually **25–120 x 13–60 mm**, thinly leathery, dark green above, white-felted below; margin **entire or obscurely and irregularly toothed**. Flowerheads grouped in terminal panicles, creamy white. Fruit a small nutlet, tipped with tuft of bristly hairs.
  The wood is yellow, very strong, hard and durable; used for hut building and implement handles. A useful plant for stabilizing coastal dune sand.
  B. transvaalensis (**1.1**) is a large tree of montane forest.

2 *Brachylaena elliptica* Bitter-leaf
SA: 725 Spring Bitterblaar
Shrub or small tree; sexes separate, on different plants; occurring in bushveld, on rocky outcrops and along forest margins. Leaves **lanceolate, elliptic** to ovate, **20–100 x 5–30 mm**, **dark green** above, white-felted below; margin **irregularly toothed**, often with the apex **3-lobed**. Flowerheads in terminal and axillary branched clusters, creamy white. Fruit a small nutlet, tipped with tuft of bristly hairs.
  The plant is browsed by stock. Its leaves, which are extremely bitter-tasting, are used medicinally. Wood durable, used for carrying-sticks and fence posts. Sticks formerly used to start fire by friction.
  B. ilicifolia has smaller leaves (10–45 x 2–10 mm) with a distinct hair-like tip.

3 *Brachylaena huillensis* Lowveld silver oak
SA: 727; Z: 1160 Summer Laeveldvaalbos
Small to medium-sized tree, with an **untidy** appearance; sexes separate, on different plants; occurring in bushveld, often on rocky ridges. Leaves clustered towards ends of branches, **obovate to broadly elliptic, 50–70 x 20–25 mm, glossy olive green** above when mature, white-felted below; apex broadly tapering **with a bristle-like tip**; margin entire or finely toothed. Flowerheads in axillary and terminal branched clusters, creamy white. Fruit a small nutlet, tipped with tuft of bristly hairs.
  The wood is suitable as a general purpose timber.

4 *Brachylaena rotundata* Mountain silver oak
SA: 730; Z: 1161 Early Spring Bergvaalbos
Shrub or small deciduous tree, with a sparsely branched crown; sexes separate, on different plants; occurring in bushveld, usually in rocky places. Leaves **elliptic, 25–100 x 10–55 mm, greyish green** above, white-felted below; margin **irregularly toothed**. Flowerheads in globular clusters, creamy white to pale yellow, often produced before the leaves. Fruit a small nutlet, tipped with tuft of bristly hairs.

B. *discolor*: flowers

B. *discolor*: flowers

B. *transvaalensis*: flowers

B. *elliptica*: flowers

B. *huillensis*: bark

B. *rotundata*: fruit

B. *huillensis*: fruit

B. *rotundata*: flowers

1 *Oldenburgia grandis* (= *O. arbuscula*)   **Suurberg cushion bush**
SA: 737   All year   **Suurbergse kussingbos**
Shrub or small gnarled tree; occurring on rocky outcrops of **Witteberg quartzite**.
Leaves clustered towards ends of branches, oblong to ovate, **large (up to 330 x 150 mm), stiff and leathery**, glossy dark green above, **white- or creamy felted** below; margin entire. Flowerheads **large (up to 130 mm in diameter)**, in stalked, terminal clusters, purplish cream. Fruit a small nutlet, tipped by a tuft of bristly hairs.

2 *Tarchonanthus camphoratus*   **Wild camphor bush**
SA: 733; Z: 1162   Autumn   **Wildekanferbos**
Shrub or small tree, with a **grey-green** appearance; sexes separate, on different plants; occurring in a variety of habitats, including semi-desert, grassland, bushveld and forest, often on sandy soils. Leaves narrowly oblong to elliptic, 13–150 x 8–40 mm, **dull green to grey-green and minutely puckered above**, white- or greyish felted with **venation prominent below**, with **strong smell of camphor** when crushed; margin entire to finely toothed. Flowerheads in terminal panicles, creamy white. Fruit a small nutlet, covered with woolly white hairs.
    The plant is browsed by game and stock. Wood greyish brown, hard, heavy, durable, suitable for ornamental work. Leaves used medicinally and as a perfume.

3 *Tarchonanthus trilobus*   **Broad-leaved camphor bush**
SA: 733 & 734; Z: 1163   Winter–Summer   **Breëblaarkanferbos**
Shrub or small tree; occurring on forest margins and in wooded ravines. Leaves obovate to narrowly oblong-elliptic, 75–200 x 20–90 mm, **thick and leathery**, dark green and **roughly corrugated by the immersed venation above**, whitish or creamy felted below; apex **often 3-lobed** (var. *trilobus*) or rounded to broadly tapering (var. *galpinii*); margin entire, serrated or rather crinkly. Flowerheads in axillary clusters, creamy yellow. Fruit a small nutlet, thinly covered in woolly hairs.
    The plant is browsed by game. Its heartwood is yellowish brown, hard, durable, with a camphor scent.

CHRYSOBALANACEAE (see page 22)

4 *Parinari curatellifolia*   **Mobola plum**
SA: 146; Z: 166   Autumn–Spring   **Grysappel**
Medium to large evergreen tree, with rounded crown and rather **drooping** branches; occurring in bushveld, usually on deep, sandy soils. Leaves elliptic to oblong, leathery, dark green above, **greyish to brownish felted**, with many **prominent, more or less parallel principal lateral veins below**; margin entire. Flowers in axillary **rusty-haired** inflorescences, white, tinged with pink. Fruit a drupe, oval to round, up to 50 x 25 mm, brownish yellow, **greyish scaly**, usually ripening on the ground.
    The fruit is very tasty, and is eaten fresh; also made into beer. Kernels are opened and the nuts eaten, alone or mixed with green vegetables as a relish. Wood pale brown, hard, heavy, and used as a general purpose timber though it is rich in silica (which tends to blunt saw-blades and other tools). Bark used for tanning leather and medicinally; it also yields a pink-brown dye used in basketwork. Larval food plant for several butterflies of the genus *Platylesches* (hoppers).
    Very similar to *P. capensis* subsp. *incohata*, a dwarf rhizomatous shrublet which grows abundantly on the grassy coastal plains of Maputaland.

O. grandis: flowers

O. grandis: leaves

T. camphoratus: fruit

O. grandis: : tree

T. camphoratus: flowers

T. trilobus: flowers

P. curatellifolia: flowers

P. curatellifolia: fruit

DIPTEROCARPACEAE (see page 24)

1 *Monotes engleri*   **Pink-fruited monotes**

Z: 717   Summer   **Pienkmonotes**

Small to medium-sized tree; occurring in bushveld. Leaves broadly elliptic to oblong, dark green above, **whitish to grey with silvery hairs below**; apex rounded; base rounded or lobed; petiole up to 20 mm long, **with a large flat gland (extrafloral nectary) above, at junction with lamina**; stipules about 10 mm long, falling early. Flowers in short axillary heads, yellowish tinged with orange. Fruit dry, spherical, about 15 mm in diameter, **surrounded by 5 large persistent sepals** which are pink to reddish when young, drying pale brown when mature.

The wood is used in hut building and for the floor poles of granaries. Bark used medicinally.

Reminiscent of *Parinari curatellifolia*, but easily distinguished by the gland at the junction between petiole and lamina, and by the very different fruit.

FLACOURTIACEAE (see page 25)

2 *Kiggelaria africana*   **Wild peach**

SA: 494; Z: 728   Winter–Spring   **Wildeperske**

Small to medium-sized evergreen tree, crown usually with an **occasional bright-yellow leaf**; sexes separate, on different plants; occurring in forest, wooded ravines or on rocky outcrops in grassland. Leaves oblong to elliptic, 35–90 x 20–50 mm, dark green above, **bluish grey or grey-felted with domatia in axils of principal lateral veins below**, sometimes hairless below, particularly in the juvenile leaves of some forms; margin entire or toothed, particularly in juvenile or coppice leaves. Flowers axillary, in drooping many-flowered inflorescences (male) or solitary (female), yellowish green. Fruit globose, yellowish green, densely covered with hairs, **knobbly**, splitting into 5 valves; seeds black with **bright orange-red covering**.

The wood is pinkish brown, suitable as a general purpose timber and formerly used for the spokes of wagon wheels. Larval food plant for the butterflies *Acraea horta* (the plants are often completely defoliated by the caterpillars) and *Cymothoe alcimeda*.

HAMAMELIDACEAE (see page 25)

3 *Trichocladus ellipticus*   **White hazel**

SA: 143; Z: 156   Spring–Summer   **Withaselaar**

Evergreen shrub or small to medium-sized tree; occurring in the **understorey of mistbelt forest**. Branchlets with **velvety brown hairs**. Leaves lanceolate to elliptic, glossy dark green above, **cream-felted with rusty brown hairs on venation below**; margin entire. Flowers in axillary or terminal heads, creamy green. Fruit a capsule, almost spherical, about 6 mm in diameter, velvety, dehiscent. Leaves with apices narrowly tapering in subsp. *ellipticus* (South Africa), broadly tapering or rounded in subsp. *malosanus* (Zimbabwe and Mozambique).

The wood is hard, heavy, with black heartwood; makes excellent firewood.

1

M. engleri: flowers

2

K. africana: fruit

2

K. africana: fruit & seeds

1

M. engleri: fruit

2

K. africana: male flowers

3

T. ellipticus: flowers

115

LAURACEAE (see page 25)

1 *Cryptocarya myrtifolia*   **Myrtle quince**
SA: 115 Summer   **Mirtekweper**
Medium to large evergreen tree; occurring in forest. Leaves lanceolate to broadly obovate, 10–70 x 10–25 mm, glossy dark green above, **bluish below**, hairless; apex **usually tapering to a drip-tip**; margin entire, wavy. Flowers in axillary clusters, small, cream. Fruit a drupe, globose, about 12 mm in diameter, reddish purple.
The bark is used medicinally, sometimes in place of *Ocotea bullata*.
C. liebertiana (mainly found in the Northern Province and Zimbabwe) has more oval to oblong leaves with broadly tapering apices, the young growth conspicuously pinkish purple.

2 *Cryptocarya wyliei*   **Red quince**
SA: 117 Summer   **Rooikweper**
Shrub or small tree, usually **multistemmed**; occurring on forest margins or rocky outcrops in grassland, usually on sandstone. Leaves **ovate, small (10–30 x 10–20 mm)**, dull green and **minutely papillate** above, **bluish with brownish hairs** on venation below; margin entire, rolled under. Flowers solitary or in axillary clusters, very small, greenish white. Fruit a drupe, globose, up to 14 mm in diameter, red.
The fruit is edible, thinly fleshy and not very tasty.

ROSACEAE (see page 30)

3 •*Pyracantha angustifolia*   **Yellow firethorn**
SA: X425 Spring   **Geelbranddoring**
Evergreen shrub or small tree, with **stiff, spiny branches**; invading high-altitude grassland, erosion channels and rocky ridges. Leaves narrowly elongate, dull dark green above, **grey-downy below**; margin entire **rolled under**. Flowers in axillary clusters, white. Fruit a berry, subglobose, 5–8 mm in diameter, greyish-haired when green, ripening to orange-red or orange-yellow.
A native of Asia; cultivated for ornament, for security hedging and for screens on highways.
P. crenulata is an invader in more or less the same areas, also with spines and orange-red berries. It differs, however, in its leaves, which are hairless and have a shallowly toothed margin, glossy bright green above, paler green below.

SALICACEAE (see page 31)

4 *Salix mucronata* (= *S. capensis*; *S. subserrata*; *S. woodii*)   **Cape willow**
SA: 36; Z: 39 Spring   **Kaapse wilger**
Shrub or small tree with somewhat **drooping** branches; sexes separate, on different trees; occurring along streams and rivers. Branchlets often reddish. Leaves **lanceolate**, glossy green above, **pale whitish-green below**; margin entire or finely toothed. Flowers in short spikes, yellowish (male) or greenish (female). Fruit a small capsule, dehiscent; seeds covered with **woolly hairs**. A polymorphic species with at least five subspecies in southern Africa, the most characteristic being subsp. *hirsuta*, whose branches and leaves are densely covered in silvery hairs (restricted to Olifants River and its tributaries in the Western Cape); and subsp. *woodii* (drainage basins of Limpopo, Olifants and Maputo rivers, and of the KwaZulu-Natal rivers) whose leaf margin is always toothed.

116

C. myrtifolia: fruit

C. wyliei: flowers

P. angustifolia: flowers

C. wyliei: fruit

S. mucronata: male flowers

P. angustifolia: fruit

S. mucronata: fruit

S. mucronata: fruit

SOLANACEAE (see page 32)

1 *Solanum aculeastrum*　　　　　　　　　　　　　　Goat apple
SA: 669.3; Z: 1013　Summer　　　　　　　　　　　　　　Bokappel
Prickly shrub or small tree; occurring on forest margins and in grassland and bushveld, often near places of human habitation. Branchlets with **white, woolly hairs and sharp, recurved thorns up to 20 mm long**. Leaves deeply **divided into 5–7 lobes**, dark green above, **white and woolly below**, both surfaces **with spines on midrib**. Flowers in broad, flat heads, white to pale mauve. Fruit a berry, globose, **up to 50 mm in diameter**, yellow, smooth.
　　The fruit is poisonous; used medicinally and for veterinary purposes.

2 *Solanum giganteum*　　　　　　　　　　　　　　Healing-leaf tree
SA: 669.4; Z: 1014　Summer　　　　　　　　　　　　　Geneesblaarboom
Much-branched shrub or small tree; occurring in forest and bushveld, usually in shady places. Branchlets with **white woolly hairs and short straight spines up to 5 mm long**. Leaves elliptic, **large (up to 230 x 90 mm), softly textured**, dark green above, **velvety whitish below**; margin **entire**. Flowers in many-flowered, branched, terminal heads, white to purple. Fruit a berry, globose, about 10 mm in diameter, **bright red**, smooth.
　　The leaves and fruit are used medicinally.
　　Similar to the exotic *S. mauritianum*, which lacks the spines, has yellow fruit, and petioles subtended by conspicuous egg-shaped lobes.

3 •*Solanum mauritianum*　　　　　　　　　　　　　　Bug tree
SA: X961; Z: –　Spring–Summer　　　　　　　　　　　　Luisboom
Soft-wooded perennial shrub or small tree, most parts with greyish, velvety, star-shaped hairs; invading forest margins, plantations, roadsides, watercourses and urban open space. Leaves elliptic, up to 250 x 100 mm, **dull green and velvety above**, **white-felty below**, unpleasantly scented when crushed; petiole subtended by **conspicuous egg-shaped lobes**. Flowers in dense terminal clusters, purple. Fruit a berry, globose, about 10 mm in diameter, **yellow**.
　　A native of South America; cultivated for ornament. The wood is soft (stems can be nailed at the ends without splitting); used in the manufacture of cheap furniture and shelves. This is a declared weed in South Africa.

S. aculeastrum: flower

S. aculeastrum: fruit

S. giganteum: fruit

S. mauritianum: flowers

S. mauritianum: fruit

GROUP 8

Leaves simple, alternate or in tufts, not bilobed; blade
with single midvein from base, not distinctly discolorous.
Spines present. Latex absent.

See also Group 10: *Boscia foetida* (p. 164), *Securidaca longipedunculata* (p. 210)
and *Terminalia stuhlmannii* (p. 176); Group 11: *Dovyalis longispina* (p. 224) and
D. rhamnoides (p. 226).

BIGNONIACEAE (see page 21)

1 **Catophractes alexandri**   **Trumpet thorn**
SA: 676.1; Z: 1029   Spring   **Trompetdoring**
Shrub or small tree **with a grey appearance**; occurring in arid bushveld and semi-
desert vegetation, often on limestone. **Spines up to 50 mm long, arising in pairs.**
Leaves in **opposite tufts**, oblong, densely covered with grey woolly hairs; venation
prominent below; margin **toothed.** Flowers axillary, solitary, white to pinkish, with
a yellow throat. Fruit a capsule, oval, about 50 x 25 mm, greyish brown, warty,
dehiscent.
   The plant is browsed by game.

2 **Rhigozum brevispinosum**   **Short-thorn pomegranate**
SA: 674; Z: 1027   Spring   **Kortdoringgranaat**
Rigid shrub or small tree; occurring in arid bushveld and semi-desert vegetation.
Spines about 10 mm long. Leaves **in tufts on cushions below the spines**, rarely
3-foliolate, **almost stalkless**, oblanceolate, up to 25 x 4 mm; margin entire. Flowers
clustered on cushions, yellow, showy, with crinkled petals. Fruit a slender, pod-like
capsule, up to 70 mm long, thin-walled, pale brown.

CAPPARACEAE (see page 22)

3 **Capparis sepiaria**   **Wild caper-bush**
SA: 130; Z: 127   Spring   **Wildekapperbos**
Creeper, scrambling shrub or small tree; occurring in forest and bushveld. **Spines
hooked, paired at base of petiole.** Leaves lanceolate to oblong, **sparsely covered
with hairs or smooth**; margin entire. Flowers in terminal clusters, **small (up to
15 mm in diameter)**, white, cream to mauve, with many stamens. Fruit a berry, globose up to 20 mm in diameter, ripening through orange to purplish black. Branches
with hairs erect in var. *citrifolia*, appressed in var. *subglabra*.
   The flower buds, when pickled, are used as a substitute for capers. Larval food
plant for several butterflies of the family Pieridae (whites).

4 **Capparis tomentosa**   **Woolly caper-bush**
SA: 130.1; Z: 128   Spring   **Wollerige kapperbos**
Creeper, scrambling shrub or small tree; occurring in forest and bushveld, often on
termitaria. **Spines hooked, paired at base of petiole, velvety.** Leaves oblong to
broadly elliptic, **greyish green, densely covered with soft, velvety hairs**; margin
entire. Flowers in terminal clusters, **large (up to 40 mm in diameter)**, white, with
many stamens. Fruit a berry, globose **with a stout stalk**, up to 35 mm in diameter,
pinkish to bright orange.
   The plant is browsed by game. Root used medicinally. Widely used for magical
purposes. Larval food plant for many butterflies of the family Pieridae (whites).

C. *alexandri*: flowers

R. *brevispinosum*: flowers

R. *brevispinosum*: fruit

C. *sepiaria*: flowers

C. *alexandri*: fruit

C. *sepiaria*: fruit

C. *tomentosa*: flowers

C. *tomentosa*: fruit

CELASTRACEAE (see page 22)
Spiny members of *Maytenus* are treated here as belonging to the genus *Gymnosporia*. The name *Maytenus heterophylla* has in the past been uncritically applied to a heterogeneous assemblage of at least 15 different taxa of spinescent shrubs or trees, several of which are new to science and await formal description.

1 Gymnosporia buxifolia   Common spike-thorn
SA: 399; Z: 564 Autumn–Spring   Gewone pendoring
Very variable shrub or small tree, usually with somewhat drooping branches; occurring in a wide range of habitats, often as a pioneer in disturbed places or along forest fringes. Branchlets green, **never angular or striate**. Spines slender or robust, up to 100 mm long, with or without leaves. Leaves **often in tufts**, obovate, 25–45 x 10–20 mm, thinly leathery, dull green, hairless; margin **shallowly toothed, mainly in upper half**. Flowers in many-flowered axillary heads, **white**, strongly and rather unpleasantly scented. Fruit a capsule, globose, **about 5 mm in diameter, rough**, white with reddish brown patches; seeds reddish brown, partially covered by a **yellow** aril.
The wood is hard, heavy, close-grained, strong, and suitable for tool handles, engraving and turnery.
In recent years the species has usually been incorrectly referred to, in tree literature, as *Maytenus heterophylla*.

2 Gymnosporia linearis (= *Maytenus linearis*)   **Narrow-leaved spike-thorn**
SA: 399.1 Spring   **Smalblaarpendoring**
Shrub or small tree, usually with **somewhat drooping** branches; occurring in karroid and semi-desert areas. Spines slender or robust, up to 70 mm long, with or without leaves. Leaves usually **widely spaced**, rarely in tufts, **narrowly lanceolate to linear, 25–90 x 2–12 mm**, leathery, dull blue-green, hairless; margin entire or closely toothed. Flowers in many-flowered axillary heads, **yellowish green**, sweetly scented. Fruit a capsule, globose, 3–5 mm in diameter, **smooth**, brown or grey-brown; seeds dark, partially covered by a **white** aril.

3 Gymnosporia mossambicensis
(= *Maytenus mossambicensis*)   **Black forest spike-thorn**
SA: 399.2; Z: 565 Autumn–Winter   **Swartbospendoring**
Much-branched shrub or small tree; occurring in the **understorey of forest**. Branchlets reddish purple to reddish brown with pale lenticels. Spines **slender**, up to 70 mm long. Leaves **often in tufts, ovate to elliptic or subcircular**, 10–60 x 6–35 mm, thinly leathery, **glossy bright green above**, hairless; margin shallowly toothed; petiole up to 10 mm long. Flowers in many-flowered axillary heads, white. Fruit a **semi-fleshy** capsule, globose, 7–14 mm in diameter, smooth, white, pink to red; seeds reddish brown, completely enveloped by an **orange-red** aril.

G. buxifolia: flowers

G. buxifolia: fruit

G. linearis: flowers

G. mossambicensis: seed

G. mossambicensis: fruit

G. mossambicensis: flowers

1 Gymnosporia nemorosa (= *Maytenus nemorosa*)   White forest spike-thorn
SA: 399.3   Spring–Summer   Witbospendoring
Much-branched shrub or small tree, usually with somewhat drooping branches;
occurring in forest, riverine vegetation or on rocky outcrops. Branchlets greyish
brown **with numerous, small, pale yellow lenticels**. Spines **robust, up to 80 mm
long**, rarely leafy. Leaves often in tufts, obovate or elliptic, 30–65 x 15–35 mm,
thinly leathery, **glossy dark green above**, paler green below, hairless; margin **shallowly toothed**. Flowers in many-flowered axillary heads, creamy white, sweetly
scented. Fruit a capsule, ovate, about 4 mm in diameter, **smooth,** greenish yellow
to reddish; seeds blackish, partially covered by a **white** aril.

2 Gymnosporia polyacantha (= *Maytenus polyacantha*)   Kraal spike-thorn
SA: 401.2   Winter   Kraalpendoring
Shrub or small tree; branches **drooping and inflexed in the Eastern Cape form**;
occurring in bushveld, valley bushveld, karroid vegetation and grassland, often
forming impenetrable thickets. Spines slender or robust, up to 90 mm long, with or
without leaves. Leaves **often in tufts, obovate, 25–45 x 10–20 mm**, thinly leathery, **glossy green**, hairless; margin shallowly toothed or entire. Flowers in many-
flowered axillary heads, white. Fruit a capsule, weakly 3-lobed, about 5 mm in
diameter, **smooth**, red; seeds black, partially covered by a **yellow** aril.

3 Gymnosporia senegalensis (= *Maytenus senegalensis*)   Red spike-thorn
SA: 402; Z: 569   Winter   Rooipendoring
Multistemmed shrub or small tree; occurring in bushveld. Branchlets often **wine-
red**. Spines **slender**, up to 70 mm long. Leaves often in tufts, elliptic to obovate,
32–125 x 12–80 mm, leathery, **pale blue-green with a whitish bloom**, hairless;
margin **with numerous closely spaced regular rounded teeth**. Flowers in many-
flowered axillary heads, cream or greenish white, sweetly scented. Fruit a capsule,
globose, about 5 mm in diameter, **smooth, pinkish to reddish**; seeds reddish
brown, partially covered by a **white or pinkish** aril.
   The root is used for medicinal purposes. Larval food plant for the butterflies
Charaxes jasius saturnus, C. castor flavifasciatus, C. cithaeron and *Hypolycaena
philippus philippus*.

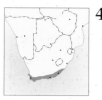

4 Putterlickia pyracantha   False spike-thorn
SA: 403.1   Summer   Basterpendoring
Scrambling shrub or small bushy tree; occurring in coastal thicket, valley bushveld
and fynbos. Branches smooth, whitish grey, with **lenticels rather obscure and not
wart-like**. Spines slender, up to 50 mm long, with or without leaves. Leaves often
in tufts, obovate, leathery, **glossy dark green**, hairless; margin entire or toothed,
wavy. Flowers in axillary heads, white. Fruit a capsule, **3-lobed, 10–20 mm long,
cream to pink or red**; seeds reddish brown, enveloped by an **orange** aril.

124

G. *nemorosa*: flowers

G. *nemorosa*: fruit

G. *nemorosa*: fruit

G. *polyacantha*: flowers

G. *senegalensis*: flowers

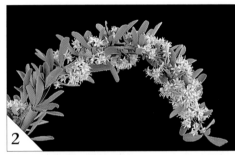

G. *senegalensis*: fruit

P. *pyracantha*: fruit

P. *pyracantha*: flowers

1 *Putterlickia verrucosa*   **False forest spike-thorn**
SA: 403.2   Winter   **Basterbospendoring**
Scrambling shrub or small bush tree; occurring in coastal forest and thicket, and in bushveld. Branches with **white, prominently raised, wart-like lenticels**. Spines slender or robust, up to 70 mm long, with or without leaves. Leaves often in tufts, ovate, obovate or oblanceolate-spathulate, 10–85 x 6–25 mm, leathery, **glossy dark green**, hairless; margin **usually toothed**. Flowers in axillary heads, white. Fruit a capsule, **3-lobed, 15–25 mm long, cream to pink or red**; seeds reddish brown, enveloped by an **orange** aril.

    P. retrospinosa is a robust creeper with backward-pointing spines and large (80–120 x 40–60 mm) leaves. It is endemic to the Pondoland Centre.

COMBRETACEAE (see page 23)

2 *Terminalia prunioides*   **Lowveld cluster-leaf**
SA: 550; Z: 788   Spring–Summer   **Sterkbos**
Shrub or small to medium-sized tree; often multistemmed with a rather untidy crown and long, **drooping** branches; occurring in hot, low-altitude bushveld. Lateral branchlets often reduced and spinescent. Leaves **clustered at ends of lateral branches**, elliptic to obovate, **20–70 x 15–30 mm**, thinly textured, dark green, hairless when mature. Flowers in slender axillary spikes, greenish white to cream, often tinged with pink, unpleasantly scented. Fruit a flattened, winged nut, **40–60 x 20–30 mm, bright red to purple red**, drying to brown.

    The plant is browsed by game. The wood is hard, tough, and used for implement handles and in hut construction.

3 *Terminalia randii*   **Thorny cluster-leaf**
SA: 550.1; Z: 789   Summer–Autumn   **Doringtrosblaar**
Rigid shrub or small tree, with a rather open crown; occurring in hot, low-altitude bushveld, often on Kalahari sand or in rocky places. Spines up to 20 mm long, **often in clusters of up to 5**. Leaves **clustered at ends of lateral branches**, narrowly obovate, **10–25 x 7–12 mm**, thinly textured, pale green to bluish green, hairless when mature. Flowers in slender axillary spikes, greenish white to cream, often tinged with pink, unpleasantly scented. Fruit a flattened, winged nut, **10–25 x 6–12 mm**, yellowish green tinged with red to purple red, drying to brown.

FLACOURTIACEAE (see page 25)

4 *Dovyalis caffra*   **Kei-apple**
SA: 507; Z: 740   Summer   **Keiappel**
Much-branched shrub or small tree; sexes separate, on different trees; occurring in coastal forest, bushveld and riverine thicket. Spines straight, prominent in young plants. Leaves **clustered on cushions, obovate to obovate-elliptic, leathery**, glossy dark green, hairless; venation **prominent on both surfaces**; margin **entire**. Flowers axillary, single or in small groups, small, creamy green. Fruit a berry, globose, **up to 40 mm** in diameter, yellow, **velvety**.

    The fruit is edible and tasty, although somewhat acidic; it makes excellent jam and jelly. Widely cultivated as a decorative hedge.

P. verrucosa: fruit

P. verrucosa: fruit and seeds

T. prunioides: flowers

T. prunioides: flowers & fruit

P. verrucosa: flowers   *T. randii*: flowers   *T. randii*: fruit   female flowers

D. caffra: male flowers

D. caffra: fruit

1 Dovyalis zeyheri — Wild apricot

SA: 511; Z: 744   Spring — Wilde-appelkoos

Small to medium-sized tree; sexes separate, on different trees; occurring on forest margins and in bushveld, often on rocky ridges and termitaria. Spines straight, up to 30 mm long, sometimes absent. Young branchlets **hairy**. Leaves obovate to broadly elliptic, **thinly textured**, glossy green above, with or without hairs; margin scalloped or almost entire. Flowers axillary, single or in small groups, small, greenish yellow. Fruit a berry, oval, up to 20 mm long, **yellow-orange, velvety**.

At certain times of year the plants (probably the leaves) emit a strong carrion smell. The fruit is edible, sour-tasting, and made into a jelly preserve.

2 Flacourtia indica — Governor's plum

SA: 506; Z: 739   Spring–Summer — Goewerneurspruim

Shrub or small deciduous tree, with **red autumn colours**; occurring in bushveld and riverine vegetation. Spines axillary or on main trunk, straight, up to 120 mm long, occasionally absent. Leaves elliptic, 15–120 x 13–75 mm, ovate to almost circular, with or without hairs; margin **scalloped**. Flowers axillary, solitary or in heads or panicles, small, greenish yellow, often flushed with red. Fruit a berry, globose, up to 25 mm in diameter, **dark red or purplish**, tipped **with persistent style**.

The leaves, bark and root are used medicinally. The fruit is edible, sour-tasting, and cooked to make jam and preserves. Larval food plant for the butterfly *Phalanta phalantha aethiopica*.

3 Oncoba spinosa — Snuff-box tree

SA: 492; Z: 726   Spring–Summer — Snuifkalbassie

Shrub or small tree; occurring in bushveld and riverine fringe forest. Branchlets **with whitish lenticels**, armed with straight axillary spines up to 50 mm long. Leaves ovate-elliptic, 30–120 x 15–60 mm, leathery, glossy dark green, hairless; margin **scallop-toothed**; petiole up to 10 mm long, channelled above. Flowers axillary or terminal, **large and showy**, up to 90 mm in diameter, white with up to 20 petals and a **central mass of yellowish stamens**. Fruit hard-shelled, globose with pointed tip, **up to 80 mm in diameter**, yellow to reddish brown, faintly ridged.

The fruit used for snuff containers and–with dry seeds left inside–as rattles. Fruit pulp edible, but not palatable. Root used medicinally. A decorative garden subject.

4 Scolopia mundii — Red pear

SA: 496; Z: 729   Autumn–Winter — Rooipeer

Small to medium-sized tree, main stem sometimes fluted; occurring in forest and on forest margins, mainly at higher altitudes. Branchlets sometimes with straight, slender spines up to 40 mm long. Leaves **ovate to narrowly ovate**, 35–70 x 20–40 mm, glossy green above, paler green below, hairless, velvety in some Pondoland forms; margin **toothed**; petiole **reddish**. Flowers in short, dense, **branched heads or racemes**, small, greenish white. Fruit a berry, globose with a persistent style, up to 10 mm in diameter, **hairless, yellow to brownish yellow**.

The wood is pale brown, hard, heavy, close-grained, suitable for furniture and formerly used in wagon making. Fruit edible but not very tasty.

S. flanaganii has smaller leaves (20–35 x 6–22 mm), flowers which are solitary or in clusters, and velvety, yellow fruit.

D. *zeyheri*: flowers

D. *zeyheri*: fruit

F. *indica*: flowers

F. *indica*: fruit

O. *spinosa*: fruit

F. *indica*: flowers

O. *spinosa*: flower

S. *mundii*: fruit

1 *Scolopia zeyheri*   Thorn pear
SA: 498; Z: 731   Winter–Spring   Doringpeer
Small to medium-sized tree; occurring in forest, on forest margins and in bushveld,
often on termitaria. Branchlets with straight, branched or unbranched, **often robust
spines** up to 200 mm long, sometimes **massed at base of main stems**. Leaves
lanceolate to almost circular, 20–80 x 10–35 mm, leathery, dull green, sometimes
with flaky, waxy covering above, **dull whitish green below**, hairless; margin entire
or bluntly toothed, mainly in upper half; petiole up to 15 mm long, **pinkish**. Flowers
in axillary, spike-like racemes, small, creamy white. Fruit a berry, globose with **persistent style**, up to 10 mm in diameter, hairless, **red**.
   The wood is very hard, and was once used in wagon making and in the manufacture of teeth for mill wheels.

OLACACEAE (see page 28)

2 *Ximenia americana*   Blue sourplum
SA: 102; Z: 92   Spring–Summer   Blousuurpruim
Much-branched shrub or small tree **with a blue-green appearance**; sexes separate
on different plants; a hemi-root parasite occurring in bushveld, often in hot, low altitude areas. Branchlets spinescent. Leaves often **in tufts**, oblong, **blue- or grey-
green**, hairless, **folded upwards along the midrib**; margin entire. Flowers clustered in axils of spines, greenish white. Fruit a drupe, oval, about 25 mm long,
orange. All the material in southern Africa belongs to var. *americana*.
   The fruit is edible, with a rather bitter-sour taste. Seeds yield an oil, used to
soften leather and for cosmetic purposes. Bark used medicinally. Larval food plant
for the butterflies *Axiocerses amanga*, *Hypolycaena phillippus phillippus* and
several members of the genus *Iolaus*.

3 *Ximenia caffra*   Sourplum
SA: 103; Z: 93   Spring   Suurpruim
Sparsely branched shrub or small tree; sexes separate, on different plants; a hemi-
root parasite occurring in bushveld and coastal bush. Branchlets spinescent. Leaves
often **in tufts**, elliptic, leathery, **dark green, often folded upwards along the
midrib**; margin entire. Flowers in axillary clusters, greenish white. Fruit a drupe,
oval, up to 40 mm long, bright red with white spots. Leaves and young branchlets
with dense brownish hairs in var. *caffra*, more or less hairless in var. *natalensis*.
   The fruit is edible, tasty but very sour near the seed; makes a good jelly. Seeds
yield an oil which is used to soften leather and for cosmetic purposes. Bark and
leaves used medicinally. Larval food plant for the butterflies *Hypolycaena phillippus phillippus*, *Mylothris agathina* and several members of the genera *Axiocerses*,
Iolaus and *Spindasis*.

S. zeyheri: flowers

S. zeyheri: flowers

S. zeyheri: fruit

X. americana: fruit

X. americana: flowers

X. caffra: flowers

X. caffra: fruit

GROUP 8

PEDALIACEAE (see page 29)

1 *Sesamothamnus guerichii*   Herero sesame-bush
SA: 679   Summer   Hererosesambos
Shrub or small tree with **swollen stems** and stiff, erect branches; occurring in semi-desert vegetation, usually in rocky places. Spines straight, alternate. Leaves **tufted**, lanceolate to ovate, **not conspicuously tapering to the base**; margin entire. Flowers in few-flowered axillary or terminal racemes, **yellow**; corolla tube up to 100 mm long, almost straight. Fruit a capsule, elliptic to ovate, up to 60 mm long, **not sharp-tipped**.
    The root is used medicinally.
    S. benguellensis occurs in the same geographical area; leaves narrowly tapering to the base; flowers white with pink or mauve flush, up to 70 mm long with a distinctly curved corolla tube; capsules up to 90 mm long, sharp-tipped.

2 *Sesamothamnus lugardii*   Transvaal sesame-bush
SA: 680; Z: 1036   Summer   Transvaalse sesambos
Shrub or small tree with **swollen, succulent stems** (like those of a miniature baobab) and stiff, erect branches; occurring in hot, low-altitude bushveld, often in rocky places and associated with mopane. Spines straight or slightly curved, alternate. Leaves **tufted**, obovate, **grey- to whitish-haired**; base **tapering**; margin entire. Flowers axillary, solitary, **white**; corolla tube up to 80 mm long, with a distinct spur at the base. Fruit a capsule, heart-shaped, up to 50 mm long.

SOLANACEAE (see page 32)

3 *Lycium hirsutum*   River honey-thorn
SA: –   Summer   Rivierkriedoring
Large, **impenetrable**, rounded shrub with **drooping** branches; occurring in arid areas, often on calcareous soils or along streams. Branches whitish, with short hairs, armed with rigid spines. Leaves usually **tufted**, narrowly oblanceolate, thinly textured, **densely covered with hairs**, with a somewhat fetid smell when crushed; margin entire. Flowers axillary, solitary, **tubular with spreading corolla lobes**, creamy white to mauve. Fruit a berry, globose, up to 8 mm in diameter, red.
    A very effective barrier plant.
    L. afrum (found mainly in the Western Cape) and *L. austrinum* (Great Karoo) occasionally grow as small trees. Both have hairless leaves, 10–25 x 1–3 mm in the former, 13–50 x 2–10 mm in the latter.

ULMACEAE (see page 32)

4 *Chaetachme aristata*   Thorny elm
SA: 43; Z: 47   Spring–Summer   Doringolm
Shrub or small to medium-sized tree, often branching low down; occurring in coastal forest and bushveld. Spines straight, single or paired, mainly on coppice shoots. Branchlets **often zigzag**. Leaves elliptic to obovate, leathery, **glossy dark green**, hairless; apex **with a conspicuous hair-like bristle**; margin entire or sharply toothed, particularly in juvenile or coppice leaves. Flowers axillary, single or in clusters, small, Fruit a drupe, globose, up to 15 mm in diameter, pinkish yellow.
    The plant is browsed by game. Larval food plant for the butterflies *Charaxes cithaeron* and *C. xiphares*.

S. guerichii: flowers

S. guerichii: fruit

S. lugardii: fruit

C. aristata: fruit

S. lugardii: flowers

L. hirsutum: flowers

C. aristata: flowers

GROUP 9

Leaves simple, alternate or in tufts, not bilobed; blade with single midvein from base; not distinctly discolorous; margin toothed or scalloped. Spines absent. Latex absent.

See also Group 7: *Kiggelaria africana* (p. 114); Group 8: *Chaetachme aristata* (p. 132), *Dovyalis zeyheri* (p. 128), *Flacourtia indica* (p. 128), *Scolopia mundii* (p. 128) and *S. zeyheri* (p. 130); Group 10: *Barringtonia racemosa* (p. 200), *Brachylaena neriifolia* (p. 162), *Drypetes gerrardii* (p. 190), *Ehretia amoena* (p. 162), *Ilex mitis* (p. 160), *Ochna pulchra* (p. 204), *Pappea capensis* (p. 222), *Terminalia gazensis* (p. 172) and *Vernonia colorata* (p. 162); Group 11: *Cordia pilosissima* (p. 224); Group 19: *Xymalos monospora* (p. 302).

ASTERACEAE (see page 20)

1 ***Chrysanthemoides monilifera***   **Bush-tick berry**
SA: 736.1; Z: 1172   Autumn–Spring   **Bietou**
Shrub or small tree; occurring **most frequently on coastal dunes**, also further inland on forest margins and rocky outcrops in mountainous regions. Branchlets brittle, often covered with **white, cobweb-like hairs**. Leaves ovate to broadly lanceolate, leathery or semi-succulent, greyish green to **shiny bright green**. Flowerheads solitary or in small groups, daisy-like, yellow. Fruit of **two types**: drupes, globose, about 6 mm in diameter, **shiny purplish black** when ripe, developing from the ray flowers and **arranged round edge of flowerhead**; also inconspicuous ellipsoid nutlets developing from disc flowers in centre of flower-head. A variable species with at least six recognized subspecies in southern Africa.
    An excellent plant for consolidating sand in coastal regions. The fleshy fruit is edible. Leaves used medicinally. A serious invader weed in many parts of Australia.

2 ***Vernonia myriantha*** (= *V. ampla*; *V. stipulacea*)   **Blue bitter-tea**
SA: 723.2; Z: 1154   Spring   **Bloubittertee**
Much-branched shrub or small tree; occurring at forest margins and in riverine bush, often weedy in disturbed places, particularly along roads in commercial plantations. Leaves **elliptic, large (up to 300 x 120 mm)**, with rough hairs above when young, becoming hairless with age, with thin layer of woolly hairs below; base narrowly rounded, asymmetric; petiole up to 40 mm long, with **prominent leaf-like lobes at base**. Flowerheads about 3 mm in diameter, in **large (300–600 mm in diameter), branched**, axillary or terminal heads, mauve to white. Fruit a nutlet, about 3 mm long, with a tuft of rough, bristly hairs.

BORAGINACEAE (see page 21)

3 ***Cordia caffra***   **Septee tree**
SA: 652   Spring   **Septeeboom**
Small to medium-sized deciduous tree; occurring in forest and riverine bush. Bark smooth, **creamy brown, often mottled with pinkish patches and with scattered, dry, flaking pieces**. Leaves **drooping, ovate to narrowly ovate**, glossy green above, paler green below; apex tapering; **base rounded to square**; petiole up to 50 mm long. Flowers in branched terminal clusters, creamy white, very short-lived. Fruit a drupe, ovoid, about 12 mm in diameter, yellow to orange, in cup-like calyx.
    The leaves are browsed by game; also used medicinally. Fruit edible but not very tasty. Wood used for hut building and carrying-sticks.

1

C. monilifera: flowers

1

C. monilifera: flowers & fruit

1

C. monilifera: tree

2

V. myriantha: flowers

3

C. caffra: flowers

3

C. caffra: fruit

1 Cordia grandicalyx
SA: 653; Z: 970 Spring–Summer

Round-leaved saucer-berry
Rondeblaarpieringbessie

Shrub or small tree with an untidy crown; occurring in hot, low-altitude bushveld, usually in rocky places. Leaves **broadly ovate to almost circular, up to 160 x 110 mm, both surfaces rough like sandpaper**; venation **prominent below**; margin obscurely toothed to entire; petiole up to 25 mm long. Flowers in loose, few-flowered terminal heads, whitish cream, fading to yellow, with conspicuous tubular calyx. Fruit a drupe, globose with a sharp tip, **up to 35 mm in diameter**, yellow, cupped by the **large, persistent calyx (reminiscent of an acorn)**.

    C. abyssinica, mainly found in riverine bush and woodland in Zimbabwe, has large leaves (up to 300 x 300 mm) which are rough on the upper surface only, showy white flowers and smaller fruit (about 10 mm in diameter).

2 Cordia monoica (= *C. ovalis*)
SA: 654; Z: 971 Spring–Autumn

Snot berry
Snotbessie

Scrambling shrub or small bushy tree; occurring in bushveld and thicket, often on floodplains and termitaria. Leaves **ovate to almost circular**, 50–80 x 40–60 mm, leathery, **very harsh to the touch (sandpapery) above**, with yellowish or brownish hairs below; midrib and lateral veins prominent below; margin obscurely toothed or entire; petiole up to 20 mm long, with rusty hairs. Flowers in terminal clusters, greenish white to white, sweetly scented. Fruit a drupe, ovoid with a sharp tip, up to 20 mm long, orange-red, cupped by the **persistent calyx**.

    The leaves are browsed by game. Fruit edible but not very tasty.

3 Cordia sinensis (= *C. gharaf*)
SA: –; Z: 973 Summer

Grey-leaved saucer-berry
Grysblaarpieringbessie

Shrub or small tree, often with slender, drooping branches; occurring in hot, low-altitude bushveld, often along rivers or on termitaria. Leaves **oblanceolate to oblong**, 30–90 x 13–45 mm, **greyish green**, with **long pale hairs on both surfaces**; petiole about 10 mm long, with long pale hairs. Flowers in **lax terminal clusters**, small, white. Fruit a drupe, ovoid with a sharp tip, up to 20 mm long, orange-red, cupped by the **persistent calyx**.

CELASTRACEAE (see page 22)

4 Cassine eucleiformis
SA: 413 Spring

White silky bark
Witsybas

Small evergreen tree; occurring in coastal and montane forest, usually on margins. Leaves **elliptic to ovate or obovate**, hairless, with **elastic (rubbery) threads evident on breaking the lamina**; apex **tapering or rounded**; margin plane; petiole, midrib and young stems more or less smooth. Flowers in axillary clusters, small, creamish green. Fruit a **drupe**, globose, about 5 mm in diameter, **yellow to pale brown** when ripe.

    C. maritima, a shrub or small tree found in coastal dune scrub in the Western and Eastern Cape, also has leaves with elastic threads. The apices, though, are usually sharp-tipped, margin rolled under and the petiole, midrib and young stems are rough-textured. The ripe fruit is white. Also compare *Maytenus acuminata*.

    Both *C. eucleiformis* and *C. maritima* are to be transferred to the new genus *Robsonodendron*.

C. grandicalyx: flowers

C. grandicalyx: fruit

C. monoica: flowers

C. sinensis: fruit

C. monoica: fruit

C. eucleiformis: fruit

Broken leaf showing elastic threads

1 Cassine transvaalensis — Transvaal saffron

SA: 416; Z: 578   Summer   **Transvaalsaffraan**

Shrub or small to medium-sized tree, much-branched with **rigid, arching** stems; occurring in bushveld, occasionally on termitaria. Leaves often clustered on reduced lateral shoots, terminal ones sometimes **apparently 3-whorled, narrowly elliptic to oblong**, leathery, green to greyish green, hairless; margin particularly **prominently toothed in juvenile growth or sucker shoots**; petiole up to 5 mm long. Flowers in stalked axillary clusters, small, greenish white. Fruit a drupe, round to oval, up to 15 mm in diameter, cream or yellowish when ripe.

The leaves are browsed by game and stock. Wood pale reddish brown, hard, fine-textured, used for household utensils. Bark extensively used in traditional medicine. Ingwavuma village in KwaZulu-Natal is named after the Zulu word for the tree.

This species is to be transferred to the genus *Elaeodendron*.

2 Maytenus acuminata — Silky bark

SA: 398; Z: 562   Summer   **Sybas**

Shrub or small tree; occurring in forest, on forest margins, often on rock outcrops in mountainous regions and along streams. Branchlets **often reddish**. Leaves **ovate to elliptic**, leathery, glossy dark green above, paler green below, with **elastic (rubbery) threads evident on breaking the lamina**; apex and base **tapering**; venation, margin and petiole **often reddish**. Flowers in axillary clusters, small creamy green, often tinged red. Fruit a **1–3-lobed capsule**, yellow, dehiscent; seed covered with an **orange** aril.

The wood is pale pinkish brown, hard, fine-grained, and is used for hut building and carrying-sticks. Bark used medicinally. Larval food plant for the butterfly *Acraea boopis*.

The species is easily confused with *Cassine eucleiformis*, but is distinguished by its more ovate leaves with tapering apices, more prominent, somewhat translucent venation and capsular fruit. Closely related to *M. cordata*, a forest species whose leaf bases are markedly rounded to lobed. *M. abbottii*, a rare species mainly from the forests of Pondoland, has relatively large (45–125 x 30–80 mm) leaves and all floral parts in whorls of four (as opposed to five in all other local members of the genus). All these species have elastic (rubber) threads in the leaves.

3 Maytenus peduncularis — Cape blackwood

SA: 401   Autumn–Winter   **Kaapse swarthout**

Medium to very large tree; occurring in forest, often along streams. Branchlets often conspicuously covered **with brownish hairs**. Leaves **lanceolate to ovate**, thinly leathery, glossy dark green above, paler green below, densely covered with **brownish hairs** when young, becoming less hairy to almost hairless with age; petiole **hairy**. Flowers axillary, solitary or in small groups, **on slender stalks up to 30 mm long**, small, yellowish green. Fruit a **1- or 2-lobed** capsule, greenish, dehiscent; seed covered with a **white** aril.

The heartwood is almost black, heavy, very hard, and used for household utensils and fighting sticks.

C. transvaalensis: fruit

M. acuminata: flowers

C. transvaalensis: flowers

M. peduncularis: flowers

M. acuminata: fruit

M. peduncularis: fruit & seed

1 Maytenus procumbens   **Dune koko tree**
SA: 401.1   Winter–Summer   **Duinekokoboom**
Scrambling shrub or small tree; occurring in **coastal forest and scrub, often directly above the high water mark**. Branchlets often reddish or pinkish orange. Leaves **oblong-elliptic or obovate, leathery**, glossy dark green or bluish green above, **yellowish green below**; margin with 3–5 teeth, rolled under. Flowers in axillary clusters, small, greenish white. Fruit a 1–3-lobed capsule, yellow-orange, dehiscent; seed covered by an **orange** aril.

Closely related to *M. lucida*, which grows on coastal dunes in the Western Cape and has almost circular leaves with entire margins.

2 Maytenus undata   **Koko tree**
SA: 403; Z: 571   Summer   **Kokoboom**
Shrub or small to large evergreen tree; occurring in forest and bushveld, often in rocky places. Leaves ovate, elliptic to almost circular, **very variable in size**, leathery, dark green to greyish green above, lower surface **yellowish green with a minute but conspicuous reticulate pattern**, or **almost white due to the presence of a powdery whitish bloom**. Flowers in dense **axillary clusters**, small, greenish white. Fruit a capsule, vaguely 3-lobed, yellow to reddish brown, dehiscent; seed covered with a yellow aril.

The heartwood is reddish brown, hard, heavy, close-grained, and was once used in wagon construction.

This is a very variable species with many different forms, some perhaps worthy of separate classification. It is closely related to *M. oleosa*, a small willow-like tree, with narrowly elliptic leaves, which is restricted to the banks of streams in the Pondoland Centre.

3 Mystroxylon aethiopicum (= *Cassine aethiopica*)   **Kooboo-berry**
SA: 410; Z: 574   Spring–Summer   **Koeboebessie**
Very variable evergreen shrub or small to medium-sized tree; occurring in bushveld and forest, often on rocky ridges and termitaria. Branchlets usually covered with **short hairs**. Leaves **leathery**; petiole up to 8 mm long. Flowers in sessile or **stalked** axillary clusters, small and yellowish green. Fruit a drupe, globose. Subsp. *aethiopica* has leaves which are elliptic to circular, usually 30–90 x 15–50 mm, greyish green and not conspicuously discolorous; with mature leaves nearly hairless; fruit yellowish to reddish brown, up to 7 mm in diameter. Subsp. *burkeanum* (= *C. burkeana*) has similar fruit, but its leaves are smaller (usually 15–25 x 8–15 mm) and notably paler green below (discolorous). Subsp. *schlechteri* (= *C. schlechteri*) has leaves which are elliptic to narrowly elliptic, usually 40–70 x 15–30 mm and bright red fruit up to 25 mm in diameter. Subsp. *macrocarpum* (= *C. velutina*) also has large red fruit, but its leaves are broadly elliptic, usually covered with dense hairs and tend to be larger (60–90 x 35–70 mm).

The leaves are browsed by game and stock. Bark used medicinally.

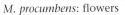

M. procumbens: flowers

M. procumbens: fruit

M. undata: fruit

M. undata: flowers

M. undata: fruit

M. aethiopicum: fruit

M. aethiopicum: flowers

M. aethiopicum: fruit

ESCALLONIACEAE (see page 24)

1 *Choristylis rhamnoides* **False dogwood**
SA: 138; Z: 154   Spring **Basterblinkblaar**
Scrambling shrub or small tree; occurring along margins of forest in **high-altitude mist-belt areas**, often on rocky outcrops in associated grassland. Leaves elliptic, shiny light green; midrib and lateral veins **prominent below**, often **with hairtuft domatia in axils**; margin toothed, each tooth with a **minute black gland**; petiole with outline of base often **3-lobed**, pinkish. Flowers axillary, in dense branched heads, small, greenish yellow. Fruit a 2-lobed capsule, brownish, dehiscent.

EUPHORBIACEAE (see page 24)

2 *Drypetes arguta* **Water ironplum**
SA: 313; Z: 458   Spring–Summer **Waterysterpruim**
Straggling shrub or small tree; sexes separate, on different plants; occurring in coastal forest, bush and sand forest. Leaves lanceolate to elliptic, leathery, glossy dark green above, paler green and dull below; apex **narrowly tapering**; base **rounded to shallowly lobed**, often **asymmetric**; margin regularly toothed. Flowers in clusters, small, yellowish green. Fruit a berry, **almost** spherical, bright orange.
   Fruit edible, used to brew beer. Wood used for carrying-sticks and in hut-building.

3 *Drypetes natalensis* **Natal ironplum**
SA: 316; Z: 461   Spring **Natalysterpruim**
Small to medium-sized tree; sexes separate, on different plants; occurring in coastal and inland forest. Branchlets somewhat angular. Leaves oblong or narrowly elliptic, **large (up to 70–170 x 50–60 mm), stiff and leathery**, glossy dark green above, paler green below; base tapering to rounded, asymmetric; margin **deeply and sharply toothed**. Flowers in **clusters on the older branches** and main trunk, yellow. Fruit a berry, globose, **up to 25 x 20 mm**, yellow-orange, velvety.

4 *Suregada africana* **Common canary-berry**
SA: 338   Spring **Gewone kanariebessie**
Small, slender tree; sexes separate, on different plants; occurring in forest and bushveld. Leaves **obovate to oblanceolate, 50–80 x 30–50 mm**, stiff and leathery, glossy dark green above, with characteristic **yellowish, micro-reticulate pattern below**; apex **rounded**; margin scalloped or obscurely toothed. Petiole up to 2 mm long. Flowers in clusters **opposite or just below** the leaves, small, yellowish green. Fruit a 3-lobed capsule, about 10 mm in diameter, yellowish when mature.

5 *Suregada procera* **Forest canary-berry**
SA: 339; Z: 512   Spring **Boskanariebessie**
Small to medium-sized tree, usually with long, slender branches; sexes separate, on different plants; occurring in forest and riverine bush. Leaves **elliptic to oblanceolate, 25–110 x 13–55 mm**, leathery, glossy dark green above, with characteristic **yellowish, micro-reticulate pattern below**; base often asymmetric; margin obscurely toothed or entire. Flowers solitary or in clusters **opposite** the leaves, small, yellowish. Fruit a 3-lobed capsule, about 10 mm in diameter, yellowish when mature.
   S. zanzibariensis, from sand and dune forest in the Maputaland Centre, has leaves with the apex abruptly tapering and the margin usually finely and sharply toothed.

1 flowers

2 *D. arguta*: fruit

2 male flowers

2 female flowers

1 *C. rhamnoides*: flowers

4 *S. africana*: fruit

3 *D. natalensis*: female flowers

3 *D. natalensis*: fruit

3 male flowers

4 female flowers

5 *S. procera*: flowers

5 *S. procera*: fruit

FLACOURTIACEAE (see page 25)

1 *Aphloia theiformis*   Mountain peach
SA: 505; Z: 738   Spring   Bergperske
Shrub or small to medium-sized tree; occurring in forest and at forest margins, often along streams. Branchlets **reddish brown, with wing-like ridges extending from stipular cushions**. Leaves tending to droop, elliptic, glossy dark green above, paler green below, hairless; margin **finely toothed**; petiole up to 3 mm long. Flowers axillary, solitary or in small groups, white, fading to creamy yellow, with numerous stamens. Fruit a berry, oval, up to 10 mm in diameter, **white with orange seeds**.

2 *Gerrardina foliosa*   Krantz berry
SA: 500   Summer–Winter   Kransbessie
Shrub or small tree with dense foliage; occurring in forest margins and on associated rocky outcrops, particularly in high-altitude, mist-belt areas. Branchlets **yellowish**, hairy towards tip. Leaves erect, elliptic, leathery, glossy bright green above; midrib raised below, **yellowish**; petiole up to 7 mm long. Flowers in **stalked (up to 40 mm long)**, axillary clusters, very small, white. Fruit a thinly fleshy capsule, roundish with persistent style, up to 8 mm in diameter, **glossy bright red**.

3 *Homalium dentatum*   Brown ironwood
SA: 501; Z: 735   Summer–Autumn   Bruinysterhout
Medium to large deciduous tree, with almost horizontal or drooping branches; occurring in forest and associated scrub. Branchlets dark brown, **lenticellate**. Leaves **broadly elliptic to almost circular, large (40–130 x 30–80 mm)**, glossy deep green on both surfaces; midrib and lateral veins prominent below, often **with hairtuft domatia in lower axils**; apex abruptly tapering to a **drip-tip**. Flowers in branched, many-flowered, axillary or terminal panicles, small, creamy green, unpleasantly scented. Fruit a capsule, obovoid, small (about 4 x 2,5 mm), surrounded by dried sepals and petals.
The wood is creamy brown, hard, and suitable as a general purpose timber.
    H. abdessammadii (a large tree, mainly found in riverine fringe forest in the Caprivi region of Namibia) and *H. chasei* (a small tree from the granite hills near Mutare, Zimbabwe) have the flowers in compact, spike-like racemes.

4 *Rawsonia lucida*   Forest peach
SA: 491; Z: 725   Spring   Bosperske
Shrub or small to medium-sized evergreen tree, with long, **drooping** branches; occurring in forest, usually as part of the understorey. Leaves **oblong, stiff, leathery**, glossy dark green above, paler green and dull below, midrib and lateral veins prominent below; margin **sharply toothed**, with **incurved** teeth. Flowers axillary, solitary or in few-flowered racemes, creamy white. Fruit a fleshy capsule, oval, **up to 40 mm in diameter**, tipped by the persistent style, yellow to yellowish brown, reluctantly splitting into 5 valves.
    The wood is pale pink to reddish brown, very hard, heavy and tough, and is used for carrying-sticks. Larval food plant for the butterflies *Acraea boopis, Cymothoe coranus, C. vumbui, Hyalites cerasa* and *Lachnoptera ayresii*.
    The tree can be confused with *Drypetes natalensis (p. 142)*, which has asymmetric leaf bases, and *Rinorea ilicifolia*, which has stipular scars encircling the twigs and a leaf margin whose teeth are not incurved.

A. *theiformis*: flowers

A. *theiformis*: fruit

G. foliosa: flowers

G. foliosa: flowers & fruit

R. lucida: flowers

R. lucida: fruit

H. dentatum: flowers

MYRICACEAE (see page 28)

1 *Myrica pilulifera*   **Broad-leaved waxberry**
SA: 37; Z: 41   Winter–Spring   **Breëblaarwasbessie**
Evergreen shrub or small tree; sexes separate on different plants; occurring in high-altitude forest regions, often along streams or on rocky outcrops in grassland. Branches lenticellate, sometimes hairy. Leaves **oval to ovate, 10–80 x 10–40 mm**, leathery, **hairy when young**, becoming glossy green and almost hairless when mature, **aromatic** when crushed; base **broadly tapering to almost rounded**. Flowers in short axillary spikes, small and inconspicuous, yellowish green or green, often tinged with red. Fruit a drupe, spherical, brown to black, covered with **white wax**.

2 *Myrica serrata*   **Lance-leaved waxberry**
SA: 38; Z: 42   Spring   **Smalblaarwasbessie**
Evergreen shrub or small tree; sexes separate, on different plants; occurring in forest areas and in high rainfall grassland regions, **usually along streams**. Leaves **narrowly elliptic, 80–150 x 5–25 mm**, leathery, lower surface dotted with **minute, yellowish glands, aromatic** when crushed; base **narrowly tapering**; margin toothed or entire. Flowers in short axillary spikes, small and inconspicuous, yellowish green or green, often tinged with red. Fruit a drupe, spherical, black, covered with **white wax**.
  The wax (fat) from the fruit was once used to make candles and soap. Leaves used medicinally. Larval food plant for the butterfly *Anthene definita*.
  M. microbracteata also has small, narrow (about 30 mm long, less than 7 mm wide), deeply toothed leaves, and is endemic to the Inyanga Mountains in the Eastern Highlands of Zimbabwe.

MYRSINACEAE (see page 28)

3 *Maesa lanceolata*   **False assegai**
SA: 577; Z: 827   Spring–Summer   **Basterassegaai**
Straggling shrub or small tree, often **multistemmed**; occurring along forest margins and in associated bushveld and grassland, often along streams. Leaves **elliptic to ovate elliptic, large (50–150 x 30–120 mm)**, leathery, glossy green and hairless above, pale green occasionally with grey or brownish hairs below; midrib and lateral veins **prominent below**; petiole up to 30 mm long. Flowers in many-flowered axillary or terminal heads, small white to cream. Fruit thinly fleshy, spherical, up to 6 mm in diameter, white when mature, crowned with persistent calyx and style.
  The root, bark, leaves and fruit are used medicinally.

4 *Myrsine africana*   **Cape myrtle**
SA: 577.1; Z: 829   Spring–Summer   **Mirting**
Evergreen shrub or small tree, with dense foliage; occurring along forest margins and in bush clumps, usually in shady situations. Leaves lanceolate, elliptic to almost circular, **very small (usually less than 20 x 10 mm)**, leathery, glossy dark green above, paler green below, hairless; petiole up to 15 mm long, often **reddish**. Flowers in axillary clusters, very small, white; petals **gland-dotted**; anthers **pink or red**. Fruit a berry, spherical, up to 4 mm in diameter, purplish red when ripe.
  Larval food plant for the butterfly *Poecilmitis lycegenes*.
  M. pillansii is a rare tree from wooded ravines. It has larger leaves (up to 50 x 25 mm), dark reddish-purple petioles and young stems, and brownish anthers.

M. *pilulifera*: fruit

M. *serrata*: male flowers

M. *serrata*: fruit

M. *serrata*: female flowers

M. *africana*: flowers

M. *lanceolata*: flowers

M. *lanceolata*: fruit

M. *africana*: fruit

OCHNACEAE (see page 28)

1 *Brackenridgea zanguebarica*   Yellow peeling plane
SA: 483.1; Z: 709 Spring   Geellekkerbreek
Deciduous shrub or small tree; occurring in bushveld or along forest margins. Bark **rough and corky with bright yellow pigment in the dead outer layers.** Leaves elliptic to obovate, glossy dark green above, paler green below, hairless, with **numerous lateral and tertiary veins prominent on both surfaces**; margin **finely toothed**, each tooth tipped by a minute gland. Flowers in terminal or axillary clusters, white to cream. Fruit 1–3 black drupes, borne on the enlarged receptacle and surrounded by reddish, persistent and enlarged sepals.
The roots are used for medicinal and magical purposes.

2 *Ochna arborea*   Cape plane
SA: 479 & 482; Z: 703   Spring   Kaapse rooihout
Small to medium-sized tree; occurring mainly in forest and on forest margins. Bark **smooth, conspicuously mottled with large patches of grey**, **cream, mauve and pink**; branchlets **without lenticels.** Leaves broadly to narrowly elliptic, leathery, glossy deep green above, paler green below; lateral veins **numerous, closely spaced**; margin distinctly toothed to almost entire. Flowers in many-flowered racemes or bunches on short lateral shoots, bright yellow. Fruit 1–5 kidney-shaped, shiny black drupes on an enlarged receptacle, surrounded by orange-red, enlarged, petal-like sepals. Leaves about 40 x 15 mm and obscurely toothed in var. *arborea*, about 80 x 25 mm and distinctly toothed in var. *oconnorii*.
The wood is pale reddish brown, hard, heavy, and used for implement handles and fence posts. Larval food plant for the butterflies *Charaxes karkloof* and *C. marieps*.

3 *Ochna barbosae*   Sand plane
SA: 479.2; Z: 694 Spring   Sandrooihout
Shrub or small deciduous tree; occurring in **sand forest and thicket**, usually on sandy soil. Bark brownish grey, slightly fissured; branchlets **with lenticels.** Leaves narrowly elliptic to elliptic, leathery, glossy deep green above, paler green below, lateral veins **numerous, closely spaced**; margin indistinctly toothed to almost entire. Flowers solitary on short lateral shoots, yellow. Fruit 1–5 oval, shiny black drupes on an enlarged receptacle, surrounded by **cream to pinkish red**, enlarged, petal-like sepals.

4 *Ochna gambleoides*   Large-leaved plane
Z: 696 Spring   Grootblaarrooihout
Small to medium-sized tree; occurring in *Brachystegia* woodland, usually on rocky hillsides. Bark grey, **deeply vertically fissured** with narrow transverse cracks; branchlets **without lenticels.** Leaves oblong elliptic to obovate, **large (85–200 x 50–100 mm), bluish green,** lateral veins **numerous,** closely spaced; margin finely toothed or scalloped. Flowers in short, 5–20-flowered clusters, yellow. Fruit comprising 1–5 ovoid, shiny black drupes on an enlarged receptacle, surrounded by **orange-red to scarlet,** enlarged, petal-like sepals.

B. *zanguebarica*: bark

B. *zanguebarica*: flowers

B. *zanguebarica*: fruit

O. *arborea*: bark

O. *arborea*: flowers

O. *arborea*: fruit

O. *barbosae*: fruit

O. *barbosae*: fruit

O. *gambleoides*: fruit

1 *Ochna inermis*   **Stunted plane**
SA: 480.1; Z: 699   Spring   **Kreupelrooihout**
Deciduous shrub or small tree; occurring in arid bushveld, particularly mopane veld, usually on rocky hillsides or sandy soil. Bark smooth, dark grey; branchlets **lenticellate**. Leaves clustered **on short spurs, elliptic to almost circular, 20–60 x 10–30 mm**, glossy fresh green, lateral veins numerous, closely spaced; margin finely and sharply toothed, wavy. Flowers 1 or 2 on spurs, yellow; stalks **recurved** in fruit. Fruit 1–5 oval, shiny black drupes on an enlarged receptacle, surrounded by crimson-red, enlarged, petal-like sepals.

Similar to *O. pretoriensis*, a shrub or small tree particularly common in bushveld on rocky ridges around Pretoria, but also extending further north. It has smaller leaves (about 35 x 10–15 mm) and flowers stalks which are not recurved in fruit.

2 *Ochna natalitia*   **Natal plane**
SA: 481; Z: 702   Spring–Summer   **Natalrooihout**
Rhizomatous shrublet, shrub or small tree; new spring leaves shiny coppery red; occurring along forest margins, in bushveld and in coastal grassland. Bark grey-brown, **rough**; branchlets **lenticellate**. Leaves oblong to elliptic-oblong, leathery, glossy dark green above, paler green below, lateral veins **numerous, closely spaced**; base often **broadly tapering to almost rounded**. Flowers in few- to many-flowered racemes or bunches on short lateral shoots, bright yellow. Fruit 1–8 oval, shiny black drupes on an enlarged receptacle, surrounded by **pink or wine red**, enlarged, petal-like sepals.

The leaves are browsed by game. Root used medicinally. Larval food plant for the butterflies *Charaxes karkloof* and *C. marieps*.

O. holstii has horizontally spreading branches, and narrowly elliptic leaves that radiate in a horizontal plane from the tips of the shoots. It occurs in forest and wooded ravines.

3 *Ochna puberula*   **Granite plane**
SA: – ; Z: 705   Spring–Summer   **Granietrooihout**
Shrub or small tree; new growth densely covered with very short hairs; occurring in bushveld, usually on rocky outcrops. Bark grey, rather smooth; branchlets with **brownish lenticels**. Leaves obovate or oblanceolate, **densely hairy** when young, becoming less hairy with age, lateral veins **numerous, closely spaced**; margin densely toothed. Flowers in few-flowered axillary clusters, bright yellow. Fruit 4–7 ovoid, shiny black drupes on an enlarged receptacle, surrounded by bright red, petal-like sepals, **at first enclosing the developing fruit, later opening back**.

4 *Ochna schweinfurthiana*   **Zambezi plane**
Z: 708   Spring   **Zambezirooihout**
Shrub or small tree; occurring in bushveld and *Brachystegia* woodland. Bark dark grey, **thick, cracked into a grid-like pattern**; branchlets **without lenticels**. Leaves elliptic, glossy olive green above, paler green below, lateral veins numerous, closely spaced; base narrowly tapering into the petiole; margin **bluntly toothed to almost scalloped**. Flowers in 4–10-flowered racemes, appearing before or with the new leaves, bright yellow. Fruit 1–5 oval, shiny black drupes on an enlarged receptacle, surrounded by **red, orange or brick-red**, enlarged, petal-like sepals.

O. inermis: flowers

O. natalitia: fruit

O. inermis: fruit

O. natalitia: flowers

O. puberula: flowers   fruit

O. schweinfurthiana: flowers

O. schweinfurthiana: fruit

1 *Ochna serrulata* **Small-leaved plane**
SA: 479.1 Spring **Fynblaarrooihout**
Densely branched shrub or small tree; occurring along forest edges, scrub forest, coastal grassland, bushveld and fynbos. Bark brown, smooth; branchlets densely covered **with greyish white lenticels**. Leaves **narrowly elliptic**, leathery, glossy deep green above, paler green below, lateral veins **numerous, closely spaced**; margin **distinctly and sharply toothed**, often wavy; petiole up to 1 mm long. Flowers usually **solitary** on short lateral spurs, bright yellow. Fruit 1–6 oval, shiny black drupes on an enlarged receptacle, surrounded by **red to deep wine red**, enlarged sepals.
  A decorative garden ornamental. Root used medicinally. Larval food plant for the butterflies *Charaxes karkloof* and *C. marieps*.

RHAMNACEAE (see page 30)

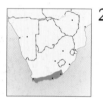

2 *Noltea africana* **Soap dogwood**
SA: 453 Spring **Seepblinkblaar**
Shrub or small bushy tree, with **spreading** branches; occurring on forest margins and in scrub, usually along streams. Branches **purplish red**. Leaves **oblong-lanceolate**, 40–70 x 10–18 mm, leathery, glossy dark green above, paler green below; apex **somewhat rounded**; stipules small, greenish. Flowers in many-flowered terminal or axillary panicles, small, white, short-lived. Fruit a 3-lobed capsule, up to 10 mm in diameter, brownish, dehiscent.
  The crushed twigs and leaves produce a soapy lather when rubbed in water; used as a soap substitute.

3 *Rhamnus prinoides* **Dogwood**
SA: 452; Z: 623 Spring–Summer **Blinkblaar**
Scrambling shrub or small tree; occurring in forest margins, scrub forest and grassland, usually along stream banks. Leaves **elliptic to oblong-elliptic, very glossy dark green above**, paler green below, hairless; net-veining very distinct when held against the light, **forming small rectangular areolae**, usually **with hairtuft domatia** in axils of principal lateral veins. Flowers in axillary groups, inconspicuous, greenish. Fruit a drupe, roundish, up to 8 mm in diameter, reddish to purple-black.
  The root and leaves are used medicinally. A decorative garden plant, fairly frost resistant. Larval food plant for the butterfly *Charaxes xiphares*.
  R. staddo, a rare bushveld species from rocky outcrops and termitaria in Zimbabwe, has smaller leaves (12–25 x 7–15 mm) and some of its branches are often spine-tipped.

ROSACEAE (see page 30)

4 *Prunus africana* (= *Laurocerasus africana*) **Red stinkwood**
SA: 147; Z: 163 Spring–Autumn **Rooistinkhout**
Small to large evergreen tree; occurring in montane forest, usually in mist-belt areas. Bark **thick, rough, dark brown to almost black**. Leaves elliptic, 50–150 x 20–60 mm, glossy dark green above, paler green below, hairless; petiole **pinkish**. Flowers in long, branched, axillary racemes, small, white. Fruit a drupe, spherical, about 10 mm in diameter, purplish brown.
  The reddish brown wood is occasionally used for furniture. Bark extensively used in traditional medicine (many old trees are killed by ring-barking).

1

O. serrulata: flowers

2

N. africana: flowers

1

O. serrulata: fruit

2

N. africana: flowers

2

N. africana: fruit

3

R. prinoides: flowers

3

R. prinoides: fruit

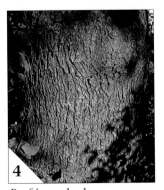

4

P. africana: bark

4

P. africana: flowers

4

P. africana: fruit

SALICACEAE (see page 31)

1 •*Salix babylonica* Weeping willow
SA: X258; Z: 38 Spring Treurwilger
Medium to large deciduous tree, with **long, slender, drooping** branches; invading watercourses. Leaves **drooping**, narrowly lanceolate, up to 160 x 15 mm, bright green above, **paler green below**, spring leaves slightly silky, summer leaves hairless; apex tapering to a long, narrow point; margin finely toothed. Flowers in drooping axillary spikes about 20 mm long, greenish. Fruit a greenish capsule, sterile, reproduces vegetatively by the spreading of detached branches which easily strike root.
   A native of Asia; cultivated for ornament, shade, fodder and erosion control.

SAPINDACEAE (see page 31)

2 *Allophylus dregeanus* Forest false currant
SA: 424 Autumn Bosbastertaaibos
Evergreen shrub or small tree; occurring in forest and along forest margins, in both coastal and mist-belt regions. Leaves **broadly ovate to elliptic**, dark green above, pale green below, hairless except for **domatia** in the axils of the principal lateral veins below; margin usually **wavy**; petiole up to 25 mm long, **conspicuously swollen at base of leaf blade**. Flowers in spike-like racemes, very small, whitish. Fruit fleshy, ovoid, up to 10 mm long, red, indehiscent.
   Larval food plant for the butterfly *Charaxes varanes*.

VIOLACEAE (see page 33)

3 *Rinorea angustifolia* White violet-bush
SA: 489 Spring Witviooltjiebos
Shrub or small slender tree; occurring in the **understorey of evergreen forest**. Leaves narrowly elliptic to oblong, thinly textured, glossy dark green above, **paler green below**, hairless or slightly hairy along midrib; **venation prominent above and below**; stipules **narrow, up to 3 mm long**, early deciduous. Flowers in short, 1–8-flowered, axillary racemes, **drooping**, white, fading to cream; **stamens joined** to form a tube. Fruit a capsule, ovoid, up to 15 mm long, tipped by persistent style.
   R. convallarioides (mainly from Eastern Highlands of Zimbabwe and adjacent parts of Mozambique) is more floriferous and has free stamens. *R. domatiosa*, from Pondoland, has leaves with rusty brown hairtuft domatia in the axils of lateral veins below.

4 *Rinorea ferruginea* Hairy violet-bush
Z: 723 Spring–Summer Harige viooltjiebos
Shrub or small tree; occurring in the **understorey of evergreen forest**. Leaves narrowly elliptic to oblanceolate, large **(120–200 x 45–80 mm), leathery**, glossy dark green above, paler green below, midrib and lateral veins **covered with brown woolly hairs below**; apex abruptly tapering into a **slender drip-tip**; stipules early deciduous. Flowers in **erect terminal racemes**, inconspicuous, pale yellow. Fruit a capsule, spherical, up to 15 mm in diameter, dehiscent.
   Similar to, and often associated with, *Argomuellera macrophylla* (Euphorbiaceae), which has leaves up to 310 x 85 mm and unisexual flowers in fluffy racemes up to 130 mm long.

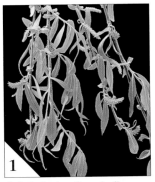

S. babylonica: female flowers   *A. dregeanus*: fruit   *R. angustifolia*: fruit

A. dregeanus: flowers   *A. dregeanus*: fruit

R. angustifolia: flowers   *R. ferruginea*: flowers

R. ferruginea: fruit

GROUP 10

Leaves simple, alternate or in tufts, not bilobed; blade with
single midvein from base, not distinctly discolorous; margin smooth.
Spines absent. Latex absent.

See also Group 3: *Phylica paniculata* (p. 66); Group 7: *Kiggelaria africana* (p. 114);
Group 8: *Chaetachme aristata* (p. 132) and *Terminalia prunioides* (p. 126); Group 9:
Cassine eucleiformis (p. 136), *Cordia grandicalyx* (p. 136), *C. monoica* (p. 136),
C. sinensis (p. 136), *Myrica pilulifera* (p. 146) and *M. serrata* (p. 146); Group 11:
Cordia pilosissima (p. 224); Group 23: *Berchemia discolor* (p. 350); Group 38:
Heteromorpha trifoliata (p. 450).

ANNONACEAE (see page 19)

1 *Annona senegalensis*   Wild custard-apple
SA: 105; Z: 118   Spring–Summer   Wildesuikerappel
Shrub or small deciduous tree; occurring in bushveld, usually on sandy soils or
along rivers. Leaves **oval or almost circular, large (60–180 x 15–115 mm)**, green
to bluish green, almost hairless, venation **prominent below**; apex **rounded**; base
square to slightly lobed; petiole short, thickset. Flowers axillary, cream to yellow,
often tinged with red or maroon, up to 30 mm in diameter. Fruit fleshy, ovate, comprising many fused ovaries, up to 40 mm in diameter, yellow to orange when ripe.
     The leaves are browsed by game. Fruit edible and pleasantly flavoured; best
picked when green and stored in dark, warm place to ripen. Bark, leaves and root
used medicinally. Larval food plant for several swordtail butterflies (*Graphium*
spp.). Bark yields a yellow or brown dye.
     A. stenophylla subsp. *nana* is a dwarf rhizomatous shrublet from northern
Botswana and Namibia.

2 *Artabotrys monteiroae*   Red hook-berry
SA:–; Z: –   Spring   Rooi-haakbessie
Climber, scrambling shrub or small tree; **climbing by means of hooked, flattened
inflorescence stalks**; occurring in low-altitude, bushveld, riverine fringe forest and
sand forest. Branchlets **reddish brown to blackish**, with reddish brown hairs.
Leaves ovate to elliptic-oblong, glossy dark **bluish green above**, paler green below,
more or less hairless; apex **abruptly tapering**. Flowers clustered on **hooked stalks,
small (about 10 mm in diameter),** creamy yellow with narrow petals. Fruit a cluster of oval berries, each up to 15 x 10 mm, **glossy bright red**.
     Larval food plant for several swordtail butterflies (*Graphium* spp.).
     A. brachypetalus has more rounded leaf apices, the flowers are bigger (about
20 mm in diameter) with broad petals, and the fruits ripen purplish black.

3 *Cleistochlamys kirkii*   Purple cluster-pear
Z: 109   Spring   Pers-trospeer
Much-branched shrub or small straggling tree; occurring in hot, arid bushveld, usually in riverine thicket. Leaves arranged in **two rows in a single plane,** narrowly
oblong to ovate, **thinly textured**, glossy dark green above, paler green below; apex
rounded, base broadly tapering to rounded. Flowers axillary, creamy yellow with
reddish brown bracts below, **appearing when trees are leafless** in spring. Fruit a
cluster of fleshy oval berries, each about 25 x 10 mm, purplish black.
     The fruit is eaten fresh, or left to stand in water to make a pleasant fruit drink.

A. *senegalensis*: fruit

A. *senegalensis*: flowers

A. *monteiroae*: fruit

A. *monteiroae*: flower

A. *monteiroae*: fruit

C. *kirkii*: flower buds

C. *kirkii*: fruit

157

1 Friesodielsia obovata Savanna dwaba-berry
SA: 108; Z: 110   Spring–Summer Savannedwabbabessie
Evergreen, scrambling shrub or small tree, often with **arcuate branches**; occurring in bushveld, sometimes subdominant in drier *Brachystegia-Julbernardia* (miombo) woodland on Kalahari sand, often on termitaria. Leaves tending to **droop**, inserted on the stem in **two opposite rows, in the same plane**, obovate to obovate-oblong, bright green above, pale grey- or blue-green and slightly hairy below, venation **prominently raised below**, with lateral veins gradually diminishing towards the margin without forming prominent marginal loops; base **rounded to lobed**, the latter often thickened and yellowish. Flowers solitary, borne **leaf-opposed**, greenish yellow. Fruit a cluster of 3–12 cylindrical berries, constricted between seeds, bright scarlet when ripe.

The fruit walls are edible, either fresh or stewed, but sour-tasting. Wood termite-resistant and used for hut and fence construction. Thin stems used for binding. The root is used medicinally. Larval food plant for several swordtail butterflies (*Graphium* spp.).

2 Hexalobus monopetalus Shakama plum
SA: 106; Z: 112   Spring Shakamapruim
Deciduous shrub or small crooked tree; occurring in bushveld, usually in rocky places and riverine thicket. Older branchlets with **prominent persistent petiole bases**, each about 3 mm long. Leaves leathery, with **brownish hairs**, at least along the midrib, oblong-elliptic with lateral veins rather obscure (var. *monopetalus*), or obovate with venation prominent on both surfaces (var. *obovatus*; confined to Eastern Highlands of Zimbabwe and adjacent Mozambique); apex **broadly tapering to rounded**; petiole up to 4 mm long. Flowers axillary, spidery, cream to pale yellow; buds **brown velvety**. Fruit 1–3 irregular berries, cylindrical or oval, often constricted between seeds, up to 35 mm long, finely velvety, bright orange to red when ripe.

The fruit is edible with a pleasant flavour, although often infested with insects; also made into an excellent jam. Larval food plant for several swordtail butterflies (*Graphium* spp.).

3 Monodora junodii Green-apple
SA: 107; Z: 119   Spring Groenappel
Deciduous shrub or small tree; occurring in hot, dry bushveld and sand forest, often in rocky places. Leaves **drooping**, oblanceolate to elliptic oblong, **large (65–160 x 30–35 mm), thinly textured**, glossy (particularly when young) pale green, hairless. Flowers solitary, **drooping**, large and attractive, lime green tinged with maroon, reddish brown to wine red, faintly scented. Fruit a berry with a hard woody shell, roundish, **up to 40 mm in diameter**, mottled grey-green, becoming wrinkled and blackish, many-seeded.

The seeds are somewhat flattened, brown, and when strung together make attractive necklaces. Fruit pulp edible, sweet-tasting but very dry.

F. obovata: flowers

F. obovata: fruit

flowers

fruit

M. junodii: flowers

M. junodii: flowers

M. junodii: flowers

M. junodii: fruit

1 Uvaria caffra   **Small cluster-pear**
SA: 108.1   Spring–Autumn   **Kleintrospeer**
Climber, scrambling shrub or small tree; occurring at coastal forest margins, and in sand forest. Young stems with **velvety hairs**. Leaves **elliptic to oblong, up to 110 x 40 mm, glossy dark green above**, paler green below; apex tapering with tip often slightly twisted; margin **wavy**. Flowers solitary, **leaf-opposed**, yellowish green. Fruit a cluster of **up to 6 berries** developing from the same flower, **each up to 20 x 10 mm**, often constricted between seeds, reddish orange and with fine hairs.
   The fruit is edible, sweet-tasting. Stems used for binding. Larval food plant for several swordtail butterflies (*Graphium* spp.).
   U. gracilipes (found in southern Mozambique and southeast Zimbabwe) is very similar but its leaves are ovate-lanceolate and smaller, up to 75 x 25 mm. *U. lucida* (Maputaland and further north) has 10–20 berries per flower, each up to 50 mm long, and leaves which are rather dull grey-green with venation prominent below.

2 Xylopia parviflora   **Bush bitterwood**
SA: 109; Z: 115   Spring   **Bosbitterhout**
Medium to large tree with a sparingly branched crown; occurring in low-altitude evergreen forest, riverine fringe forest and high-rainfall bushveld on sandy soils. Branchlets sparsely covered with hairs. Leaves **narrowly oblong to narrowly elliptic**, 45–110 x 10–47 mm; **velvety below**, apex **narrowly tapering**. Flowers axillary, solitary or in few-flowered clusters, **drooping, up to 25 mm long**, greenish yellow. Fruit a **cluster of 1–8 cylindrical berries**, each up to 30 x 10 mm, often slightly constricted between seeds, red.
   Very similar to *X. odoratissima*, a smaller tree found in hot dry bushveld in western Zimbabwe and adjacent Namibia and Botswana, probably also in southeastern Zimbabwe and adjacent South Africa; usually associated with Kalahari sand; leaves oblong to elliptic with broadly tapering to rounded apices. *X. aethiopica*, a large forest tree from the Eastern Highlands of Zimbabwe and adjacent Mozambique, has clusters of more than 10 berries per flower, each up to 60 mm long.

AQUIFOLIACEAE (see page 20)
3 Ilex mitis   **Cape holly**
SA: 397; Z: 561   Spring–Summer   **Without**
Medium to large evergreen tree with a dense crown; occurring in forest and bushveld, usually **beside rivers and streams**. Young branchlets usually **purplish, becoming whitish with age**. Leaves elliptic to elliptic-lanceolate, dark green above, paler green to whitish green below, hairless, midrib **conspicuously sunken above**; margin usually entire, rarely with a few teeth towards apex, toothed in juvenile leaves; petiole up to 2 mm long, usually **reddish purple**, channelled above; stipules small, semi-persistent. Flowers in bunches in axillary clusters, small, white, sweet-scented, often **produced in profusion**. Fruit a berry, spherical, up to 6 mm in diameter, shiny, ripening through pink to dark crimson. All the material in southern Africa belongs to subsp. *mitis*.
   The leaves, when rubbed in water, yield a soap-like lather which is used medicinally. Bark also used in traditional medicine. Wood whitish, hard, fine-grained, and suitable as a general purpose timber. Fruit much favoured by birds.

160

U. caffra: flowers

U. caffra: fruit

I. mitis: fruit

X. parviflora: flowers

X. parviflora: fruit

I. mitis: flowers

I. mitis: fruit

ASTERACEAE (see page 20)

1 *Brachylaena neriifolia*   **Water white alder**
SA: 729   Summer   **Waterwitels**
Shrub or small tree, young growth often with reddish brown hairs; sexes separate, on different trees; occurring in forest and fynbos, **usually along streams**. Leaves **lanceolate, 5–25 mm wide, leathery**, glossy dark green above, paler green below, hairless, or with sparse rusty hairs below; margin **rolled under**, occasionally with a few coarse teeth; petiole up to 10 mm long. Flowerheads in terminal or axillary pyramidal panicles, whitish, fading to cream. Fruit a slender nutlet, up to 5 mm long, tipped with a tuft of long, creamy hairs.

2 *Vernonia colorata*   **Lowveld bitter-tea**
SA: 723.4; Z: 1150   Autumn–Winter   **Laeveldbittertee**
Much-branched shrub or small tree with brittle branches; occurring in bushveld, often in riverine fringes. Young stems **velvety**. Leaves **elliptic, up to 150 x 75 mm**, leathery, medium to dark green and sparsely covered with hairs above, with sparse star-shaped hairs below, net-veining obscure; apex tapering; base **broadly tapering to rounded**; margin finely and obscurely toothed, **wavy**. Flowerheads in small dense heads grouped in a wide panicle, white or pale mauve, **about 10 mm in diameter**. Fruit dry, about 2 mm long, **hairless**, plumed with rough bristles.

    The root and bark are used medicinally.

    V. amygdalina has smaller flowerheads (less than 5 mm in diameter), narrower leaves and hairy fruit.

BORAGINACEAE (see page 21)

3 *Ehretia amoena*   **Sandpaper bush**
SA: 656; Z: 974   Spring–Summer   **Skurweblaarbos**
Shrub or small tree with somewhat **arching branches**; occurring in bushveld. Leaves **obovate, 40–110 x 25–65 mm**, dark green above, paler green with venation **prominent below**, both surfaces **roughly hairy (like sand paper)**; apex **rounded with a short, sharp, tip**; margin entire or widely toothed in upper third, slightly wavy; petiole up to 8 mm long. Flowers in terminal panicles, small, white to pale mauve. Fruit a berry, spherical, up to 8 mm in diameter, red.

    The leaves are browsed by game. Fruit edible but not very tasty.

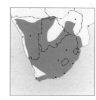

4 *Ehretia rigida*   **Puzzle bush**
SA: 657; Z: 976   Spring–Summer   **Deurmekaarbos**
Deciduous shrub or small tree; branches rigid, often drooping; occurring in a wide variety of habitats, including wooded grassland, karroid vegetation and bushveld. Leaves sometimes **clustered** on reduced shoots, **obovate, up to 25–30 x 10–20 mm**, pale or dark green above, **more or less hairless**; venation rather obscure, often with **minute domatia in the axils** of principal lateral veins; apex **broadly tapering to rounded**; base narrowly tapering; petiole **up to 2 mm long**. Flowers in terminal heads, small, pale mauve, blue or white. Fruit a berry, spherical, up to 8 mm in diameter, ripening yellow through to bright orange red and eventually black.

    The leaves are browsed by stock and game. Root used medicinally. Fruit edible but not very tasty. Often parasitized by the mistletoe *Viscum rotundifolium*.

    Very similar to *E. obtusifolia* (also with blue to mauve flowers), which has leaves without domatia and petioles more than 4 mm long.

B. neriifolia: flowers

V. colorata: flowers

V. colorata: flowers

E. amoena: flowers

E. rigida: flowers

E. amoena: fruit

E. rigida: fruit

CAPPARACEAE (see page 22)

1 *Boscia albitrunca*   Shepherd's tree
SA: 122; Z: 130   Spring   Witgat
Small tree with a rounded, much-branched crown and rigid branchlets; occurring in
semi-desert areas and bushveld, often on termitaria. Bark **smooth, grey to whitish
grey**. Leaves often clustered on reduced shoots, oblanceolate to elliptic, 15–80 x
4–20 mm, stiff and leathery, grey-green to green above and below, secondary veins
obscure; apex **rounded or abruptly tapering**, often **bristle-tipped**. Flowers in
dense clusters on short lateral shoots, small, yellowish green, **without petals**. Fruit
a berry, round, about 10 mm in diameter, hairless, yellowish.
   The tree is heavily browsed by game and stock. Roots edible, pounded and made
into a porridge, or roasted and used as a substitute for coffee or chicory. Leaves and
roots used medicinally. Flower buds may be pickled in vinegar and used as capers.
Fruit pulp mixed with milk and used as side dish. Larval food plant for butterflies
of the family Pieridae (whites).

2 *Boscia angustifolia*   Rough-leaved shepherd's tree
SA: 123; Z: 131   All year   Skurweblaarwitgat
Small evergreen tree with rigid branches; occurring in dry bushveld, often on termitaria. Bark pale grey, often fluted. Leaves alternate or in clusters, elliptic to
oblanceolate, 20–70 x 7–20 mm, leathery, dark green above, pale grey-green or
bluish green and **densely covered with fine hairs below**; venation **clearly visible**;
apex **rounded or broadly tapering with a spiny tip**. Flowers in dense clusters,
small, yellowish green. Fruit a berry, round, about 10 mm in diameter, hairless, yellow to almost black. All the material in southern Africa belongs to var. *corymbosa*.
   Similar to *B. mossambicensis*, whose leaves are more or less evenly hairless or
hairy on both surfaces.

3 *Boscia foetida* subsp. *foetida*   Stink-bush
SA: 124   Spring   Stinkbos
Shrub or small tree, **branched from the base**; occurring in karroid and semi-desert
areas, usually on rocky ridges. Bark smooth, pale grey to grey. Branchlets often
spine-tipped. Leaves small, in **tight clusters** along branches, oblanceolate, elliptic
or linear, **4–10 x 1–5 mm**, leathery, grey-green to green on both surfaces, secondary
veins **obscure**. Flowers in clusters along stems, small, yellowish green, unpleasantly scented. Fruit a berry, round, about 10 mm in diameter, densely covered with
hairs, yellowish.
   The freshly cut wood emits an unpleasant odour.

4 *Boscia foetida* subsp. *rehmanniana*   Stink shepherd's tree
SA: 125; Z: 132   Spring   Stinkwitgat
Small tree **with a single stem**, usually starting to branch at least 1 m above the
ground; occurring in dry bushveld. Bark **smooth, pale grey to grey**. Branchlets
often spine-tipped. Leaves small, in **tight clusters** along branches, oblanceolate,
rarely elliptic, **5–25 x 3–6 mm**, leathery, usually discolorous with reticulate venation **prominent below**. Flowers in clusters along stems, small, yellowish green,
unpleasantly scented. Fruit a berry, round, about 10 mm in diameter, densely covered with hairs, yellowish.
   The freshly cut wood emits an unpleasant odour.

B. albitrunca: tree

B. albitrunca: fruit

flowers & fruit

B. albitrunca: flowers

B. angustifolia: flowers

B. foetida subsp. *foetida*: flowers

B. foetida subsp. *foetida*: fruit

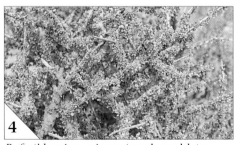

B. foetida subsp. *rehmanniana*: branchlets

B. foetida subsp. *rehmanniana*: flowers

1 *Boscia mossambicensis*   Broad-leaved shepherd's tree
SA: 127; Z: 134   Autumn–Winter   Breëblaarwitgat
Shrub or small tree, usually with several, rigid branches from the base; occurring in dry low-altitude bushveld. Bark dark **grey, rough and flaky**. Leaves usually in **clusters**, broadly elliptic to obovate, **40–70 x 15–45 mm**, leathery, **brittle**, dark green above, paler green below, slightly hairy, becoming hairless with age; venation **clearly visible**; apex broadly tapering or rounded, with a **bristle tip**. Flowers in axillary racemes, small, whitish green. Fruit a berry, round, about 20 mm in diameter, hairless, yellowish to red.
   Similar to *B. angustifolia*, whose leaves below are covered in denser hairs.

2 *Boscia oleoides*   Karroo shepherd's tree
SA: 128   Spring   Karoowitgat
Shrub or small tree with a rounded, much-branched crown and **rigid, yellowish branchlets**; occurring in karroid vegetation and valley bushveld. Bark **smooth, whitish grey to white**. Leaves **not clustered**, oblanceolate to elliptic, 25–60 x 6–15 mm, **stiff and leathery**, slightly shiny; petiole up to 5 mm long, grooved above. Flowers in **terminal** racemes, small, yellowish green, **with 2–4 petals**, sweetly scented. Fruit a berry, round, up to 13 mm in diameter, hairless, yellowish.
   The leaves are rich in crude protein and heavily browsed by stock and game. Root once roasted and used as a coffee substitute. Flower buds may be pickled and used as capers. Larval food plant for butterflies of the family Pieridae (whites).
   Similar to *B. albitrunca*, but distinguished by its terminal inflorescences, flowers with petals, and leaves which are not clustered.

3 *Boscia salicifolia*   Willow-leaved shepherd's tree
Z: 135   Spring   Wilgerblaarwitgat
Small to medium-sized deciduous tree; occurring in *Brachystegia-Julbernardia* woodland, often on termitaria. Bark dark grey, rough and flaky. Leaves alternate, **not in clusters, long and narrow, 70–150 x 15–25 mm**, leathery, dull green above and below, **fine-haired below** when mature; apex **tapering, bristle-tipped**. Flowers in axillary racemes or panicles, small, yellowish green. Fruit a berry, round, about 20 mm in diameter, hairless, yellow.
   The wood is used as a general purpose timber. Roots eaten in times of famine.

4 *Cadaba kirkii*   Large-flowered worm-bush
Z: 138   Autumn–Spring   Grootblomwurmbos
Shrub or small tree; occurring in hot, low-altitude bushveld, often in riverine thicket. Branchlets with **sticky yellowish glands**. Leaves ovate to broadly elliptic, hairless or with fine glandular-hairs on both surfaces, midrib raised below, pale coloured;· apex **rounded, bristle-tipped**; base **rounded to shallowly lobed**. Flowers in large, showy, **terminal racemes** up to 150 mm long, **large (up to 40 mm in diameter)**, cream to yellow. Fruit narrowly cylindrical, about 60 x 5 mm, dark green to dark brown, **sticky**, splitting into 2 valves.
   C. natalensis and *C. termitaria* have flowers that are solitary or clustered on short lateral shoots; all parts hairless or with very short hairs in the former, most parts with grey hoary hairs in the latter. In both species the seeds are embedded in an orange to scarlet, powdery pulp.

flowers & fruit

B. oleoides: tree

B. oleoides: flowers

B. mossambicensis: fruit

C. kirkii: fruit

B. salicifolia: fruit

C. kirkii: flowers

1 *Maerua angolensis*   **Bead-bean tree**
SA: 132; Z: 141   Winter–Summer   **Knoppiesboontjieboom**
Small to medium-sized tree; occurring in bushveld, usually at low altitude. Branchlets with **numerous whitish lenticels.** Leaves elliptic to lanceolate, **thinly textured**, shiny dark green above, paler green below; midrib **whitish**; apex **rounded, bristle-tipped**; base broadly tapering to rounded; petiole up to 30 mm long, sometimes swollen and channelled in upper half. Flowers axillary, creamy white **with many long stamens**, fading to yellow, sweetly scented. Fruit a long slender pod up to 160 mm long, **irregularly constricted** between seeds.
    Larval food plant for butterflies of the family Pieridae (whites).
    Compare *M. schinzii (below).*

2 *Maerua kirkii*   **Large-flowered bush-cherry**
Z: 146   Spring   **Grootblomwitbos**
Evergreen shrub or small tree; occurring in dry, low-altitude bushveld, usually in rocky places, or on termitaria in *Brachystegia* woodland. Leaves oblong-obovate to oblanceolate, **thickly leathery and brittle**, glossy dark green above, dull green with **conspicuous net-veining below**; apex broadly tapering, bristle-tipped. Flowers in terminal clusters, greenish cream with stamens **up to 30 mm long**. Fruit a berry, round, up to 20 mm in diameter, shiny red.

3 *Maerua schinzii*   **Ringwood tree**
SA: 136   Spring   **Kringboom**
Small to medium-sized tree, much-branched with a rounded crown; occurring in arid bushveld and semi-desert areas, usually along watercourses and at base of mountains. Branchlets with **numerous whitish lenticels**. Leaves elliptic to ovate, leathery, **yellowish green**, usually **velvety**; apex **rounded, bristle-tipped**; base broadly tapering to rounded. Petiole up to 30 mm long, sometimes swollen and channelled in upper half. Flowers in terminal racemes, creamy white **with many long stamens**, fading to yellow. Fruit a long slender pod up to 120 mm long, **irregularly constricted** between seeds.
    The tree is browsed by stock. Larval food plant for butterflies of the family Pieridae (whites).
    Similar to *M. angolensis*, but *M. schinzii's* leaves are yellowish green and more hairy, and it has a different geographical distribution.

CELASTRACEAE (see page 22)

4 *Maytenus oleoides*   **Rock candlewood**
SA: 400   Spring   **Klipkershout**
Shrub or small tree; occurring on rocky mountain slopes. Leaves elliptic or obovate, **thick and leathery**, bright green above, paler green below, often with a bluish bloom, **hairless**, lateral veins **obscure**; margin rolled under. Flowers in tight axillary clusters, small, creamy white. Fruit a **2-lobed capsule**, about 10 mm in diameter, somewhat fleshy when young, becoming orange and dry when mature, dehiscent; seeds enveloped by a **yellow** aril.
    Sterile material easily confused with *Pterocelastrus tricuspidatus* (p. 170).

M. angolensis: flowers

M. angolensis: flowers

M. angolensis: fruit

M. kirkii: fruit

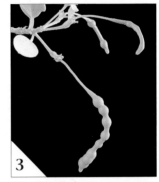

M. schinzii: fruit

M. kirkii: flowers

M. schinzii: flowers

M. oleoides: fruit

M. oleoides: flowers

1 *Pterocelastrus echinatus*   White candlewood
SA: 405; Z: 573 All year   Witkershout
Shrub or small evergreen tree; occurring in forest, on forest margins and moist mountain slopes. Bark usually with a yellow pigment when lightly scraped. Young branchlets often **reddish**. Leaves **lanceolate, elliptic or ovate**, 30–90 x 10–40 mm, **leathery**, glossy dark green above, paler green below, hairless; apex tapering to a blunt tip; margin often slightly rolled under; petiole up to 8 mm long. Flowers in compact axillary clusters, small, white to cream. Fruit a **3-lobed** capsule, about 10 mm in diameter, each lobe with **sharp horns**, orange-yellow when mature, dehiscent.
The bark is used medicinally.

2 *Pterocelastrus rostratus*   Red candlewood
SA: 408 Spring–Autumn   Rooikershout
Small to medium-sized evergreen tree; occurring in moist mountain and ravine forest, often in mistbelt areas. Young branchlets 4-angled, often **pinkish to red**. Leaves **oblong-lanceolate**, 20–90 x 13–50 mm, leathery, shiny dark green above, paler green below, hairless; apex tapering to a blunt tip; margin **wavy**; petiole up to 8 mm long. Flowers in compact axillary clusters, small, white. Fruit a **3-lobed** capsule, about 10 mm in diameter, each lobe with **many curly horns**, orange-yellow when mature, dehiscent.
The bark is used medicinally.

3 *Pterocelastrus tricuspidatus*   Candlewood
SA: 409 Winter–Spring   Kershout
Shrub or small to medium-sized evergreen tree; occurring along forest margins, in drier forest, dune scrub and on rocky outcrops. Young branchlets often **pinkish to red**. Leaves **lanceolate, obovate or broadly oval**, 30–80 x 10–40 mm, **thick and brittle**, shiny dark green to yellowish green above, paler green below, hairless; apex broadly tapering or rounded; margin rolled under; petiole **stout, pinkish to red**. Flowers in branched axillary clusters, small, creamy white. Fruit a **3-lobed** capsule, about 10 mm in diameter, each lobe with **one or two wing-like horns**, orange-yellow when mature, dehiscent.
The wood is pinkish red to reddish brown, hard, heavy, and suitable for furniture. Bark used medicinally; is also rich in tannin and once used in the tanning of leather.
Sterile material easily confused with *Maytenus oleoides* (p. 168).

CHENOPODIACEAE (see page 22)

4 •*Atriplex nummularia* subsp. *nummularia*   Old man's salt bush
SA: X370 Spring   Oumansoutbos
Evergreen shrub or small tree with **grey foliage** and **creamy white stems**; invading semi-desert areas, usually sandy riverbeds, coastal dunes, edges of pans and roadsides. Leaves **broadly elliptic to almost circular**, greyish or blue-green, covered with tiny scales, surface with a **salty taste** when licked; margin entire or toothed. Flowers in compact, terminal, drooping clusters, very small, greyish or yellowish. Fruit bladdery and inflated, small (about 5 mm in diameter), papery or corky, single-seeded, grey-green, becoming pinkish or light brown.
A native of Australia; cultivated for fodder.

P. echinatus: fruit

P. rostratus: flowers

P. echinatus: flowers

P. rostratus: fruit

P. tricuspidatus: flowers

P. tricuspidatus: fruit

A. nummularia: flowers

COMBRETACEAE (see page 23)

1 *Terminalia brachystemma* — Green cluster-leaf
SA: 548; Z: 785   Spring–Summer — Groenvaalboom

Semi-deciduous shrub or small tree with a rounded, spreading crown; occurring in bushveld, usually on Kalahari sand and in places with a shallow water table. Branchlets with **plum-coloured, peeling bark**, often zigzag between lateral branching points and in the vertical plane. Leaves **clustered** near ends of branches, sessile or shortly stalked, elliptic to obovate, 90–150 x 50–70 mm, leathery, **green above**, **bluish green** below, with or without sparse hairs; margin entire; petiole often with decurrent leaf base, up to 4 mm long. Flowers in axillary spikes, small, cream to pale yellow. Fruit with an almost circular wing, **up to 50 x 35 mm**, bright crimson when mature, drying to reddish or purplish brown, indehiscent.

The wood is used for axe handles. Root used medicinally.
Compare *T. sericea* (p. 174).

2 *Terminalia gazensis* — Fringed cluster-leaf
Z: 786   Summer — Maanhaarvaalboom

Evergreen or semi-deciduous medium-sized tree; crown rounded with a tendency to stratification; occurring in bushveld and evergreen forest, often along rivers. Leaves **in rosettes**, elliptic to obovate, 50–80 x 30–50 mm, **thinly textured**, velvety when young, becoming hairless with age; margin **finely scalloped** or rarely entire, occasionally **with a fringe of hairs**; petiole slender, about 3 mm long. Flowers in loose axillary spikes, small, white to pale yellow. Fruit surrounded by a wing, up to 30 x 15–20 mm, yellowish green tinged with red, indehiscent.

3 *Terminalia mollis* — Hairy cluster-leaf
Z: 787   Spring–Summer — Harige vaalboom

Deciduous medium-sized tree with a dense, rounded crown; autumn colours yellow to bright red; occurring in bushveld, often in association with mopane and *Brachystegia*, and especially on alluvial flats near rivers and the edges of vleis. Branchlets **corky**. Leaves elliptic to oblong, **large (160–320 x 70–130 mm)**, hairless above with age, **densely covered in hairs below**; margin entire, often with a fringe of long hairs; petiole **thickset, up to 40 mm long**. Flowers in axillary spikes, relatively large (up to 12 mm in diameter), greenish white, strongly scented. Fruit surrounded by a stout, hairy wing, **large (up to 80 x 55 mm)**, green, often slightly tinged with pink, becoming pale brown when dry, indehiscent.

Similar to *T. stenostachya*, whose leaves are arranged in distinct terminal rosettes, their upper surfaces puckered.

4 *Terminalia phanerophlebia* — Lebombo cluster-leaf
SA: 549   Spring–Summer — Lebombotrosblaar

Shrub or small evergreen to semi-deciduous tree; occurring in bushveld, often in rocky places or along watercourses. Leaves **broadly obovate**, 30–100 x 15–45 mm, pale to dark green, sparsely covered **with hairs when young**, becoming hairless with age; margin entire. or finely scalloped towards apex; venation **immersed above, prominent below**; petiole up to 20 mm long. Flowers in axillary spikes, small, cream to pale yellow, faintly but sweetly scented. Fruit surrounded by a wing, usually about 30 x 15–25 mm, greenish yellow, often tinged dull reddish brown when mature, covered with minute hairs, indehiscent.

T. *brachystemma*: fruit

T. *gazensis*: flowers

T. *gazensis*: fruit

T. *mollis*: fruit

T. *mollis*: bark

flowers & fruit

T. *phanerophlebia*: flowers

1 *Terminalia sambesiaca*   River cluster-leaf
Z: 790   Summer   Riviervaalboom
Medium to large evergreen or semi-deciduous tree; occurring in low-altitude bushveld, usually in riverine fringes or on rocky hills. Leaves **in rosettes** near ends of branches, elliptic to broadly obovate, usually about 70 x 30 mm, **thinly textured**, green, with soft hairs on veins below; margin entire or obscurely scalloped; petiole **up to 30 mm long**. Flowers in axillary spikes, small, creamy white, unpleasantly scented. Fruit surrounded by a wing, **large (up to 90 x 50 mm)**, green tinged with pink, drying to reddish brown, indehiscent.

2 *Terminalia sericea*   Silver cluster-leaf
SA: 551; Z: 791   Spring–Summer   Vaalboom
Small to medium-sized deciduous tree; crown rounded to flattish, characteristically layered as in most other members of the genus; foliage **silvery grey**, rarely green; occurring in bushveld, almost invariably on **sandy soils**. Branchlets dark brown or purplish, **peeling in rings and strips**. Leaves **clustered** towards tips of branches, narrowly obovate-elliptic, 55–120 x 15–45 mm, thinly textured, **densely covered with silvery silky hairs** which give a characteristic sheen (almost absent in some local variants), lateral veins **obscure**; margin entire; petiole up to 10 mm long. Flowers in axillary spikes, small, cream to pale yellow, strongly and rather unpleasantly scented. Fruit surrounded by a wing, **25–35 x 15–45 mm**, pink to purplish red when mature, drying to reddish brown, with short hairs, indehiscent.

The wood is yellow and hard, suitable as a general purpose timber. Root widely used medicinally. Fruit often parasitised by insects and deformed into long, slender, rusty-haired structures. Larval food plant for the butterfly *Hamanumida daedalus*.

3 *Terminalia stenostachya*   Rosette cluster-leaf
Z: 792   Spring–Summer   Rosetvaalboom
Small to medium-sized evergreen or semi-deciduous tree; crown often rounded; occurring in mixed bushveld and *Brachystegia* woodland. Leaves in terminal **rosettes**, oval to broadly elliptic, **110–180 x 45–75 mm**, dark green, hairless and **conspicuously net-veined (recessed) and puckered above, heavily net-veined (raised)** with greyish to brownish hairs below; base broadly tapering to rounded; midrib **with 2 minute glands (extrafloral nectaries) at the junction with the petiole** below; margin entire, slightly wavy; petiole up to 30 mm long. Flowers in slender axillary spikes, small, cream to pale yellow, strongly and unpleasantly scented. Fruit surrounded by a wing, usually somewhat concealed by the leaves, 30–50 x 20–30 mm, bright red when mature, drying to reddish brown, with short hairs, indehiscent.

The wood is yellowish grey, compact, strong, lustrous, and suitable as a general purpose timber.

Similar to *T. trichopoda*, a bushveld species found mainly in Zimbabwe and eastern Botswana. The leaves of the latter species have the venation obscure above and lack the two extrafloral nectaries at the base of the lamina. Fruit dull pink or red and produced in dense clusters, resembling *T. mollis*, a species distinguished by its corky branchlets, very large leaves and yellowish green mature fruit.

T. sambesiaca: fruit

T. sericea: fruit

T. sambesiaca: flowers

T. sericea: flowers

T. stenostachya: flowers

T. stenostachya: fruit

T. stenostachya: fruit

GROUP 10

1 *Terminalia stuhlmannii*   **Resin cluster-leaf**
SA: 551.1; Z: 793 Autumn   **Harpuistrosblaar**

Small to medium-sized deciduous tree; crown rather open, **flat-topped**, spreading and usually stratified; occurring at low altitudes in hot, arid bushveld, often on Kalahari sand. Lateral shoots occasionally spiny. Leaves in **rosettes** on short lateral shoots, **narrowly obovate, 15–60 x 10–20 mm**, leathery, **bluish green** with lateral veins **prominent above**, yellowish green below, almost hairless when mature; margin entire, slightly and very tightly rolled under; petiole **slender, up to 30 mm long**. Flowers in rather sparse axillary spikes, small, white to cream. Fruit surrounded by a wing, 20–30 x 15–18 mm, reddish purple, drying to pale brown, indehiscent.

Poles from the wood are used in hut construction.

Resembles *T. randii* (Group 8, page 126), which has smaller leaves (up to 25 x 12 mm) with lateral veins not prominent on the upper surface.

DIPTEROCARPACEAE (see page 24)

2 *Monotes glaber*   **Pale-fruited monotes**
Z: 718 Spring–Summer   **Vaalmonotes**

Small to medium-sized tree with a rounded crown and **brittle** branches; occurring in open woodland, often on sandy soils. Leaves broadly elliptic to oblong, glossy yellowish green above, dull green or brownish below, especially along the veins, with a **large flat gland (extrafloral nectary) at the base of the upper surface of the leaf blade**; new leaves rather **sticky**; stipule **about 10 mm long**, fairly persistent. Flowers in lax axillary heads, greenish yellow. Fruit dry, almost spherical, ridged, about 10 mm in diameter, **surrounded by 5 large persistent sepals** which are greenish yellow or pinkish when young, drying pale brown when mature.

The heartwood is reddish brown with pale streaks, suitable for furniture but difficult to work. Root used medicinally.

M. katangensis from *Brachystegia* woodland in the Zambezi Valley has leaves which are rather harsh to the touch above, and yellowish and velvety below. Compare also *M. engleri* (Group 7, page 114).

EBENACEAE (see page 24)

Leaf arrangement in some species of the genus *Euclea* is very variable: it may be opposite to subopposite, alternate or whorled, even on the same plant. Therefore also compare those members of the genus included in Group 23.

3 *Diospyros dichrophylla*   **Common star-apple**
SA: 603 Spring–Summer   **Gewone sterappel**

Shrub or small to medium-sized tree with **ascending** branches; sexes separate, on different plants; occurring in coastal scrub, open grassland, wooded ravines and along forest margins. Leaves oblanceolate to narrowly ovate, 15–60 x 6–15 mm, **leathery**, glossy dark green and hairless above, pale green and **sparsely to densely covered with hairs below**; apex broadly tapering to rounded; base tapering; margin tightly rolled under; petiole up to 6 mm long. Flowers axillary, solitary, drooping, creamy white. Fruit a berry, depressed-spherical, up to 25 mm in diameter, densely **covered with golden hairs**; calyx **persistent**, reflexed or clasping the fruit.

D. simii tends to be scandent with branches spreading at about right angles or reflexed, and has thinly textured leaves.

T. *stuhlmannii*: flowers

T. *stuhlmannii*: fruit

M. *glaber*: bark

M. *glaber*: fruit

D. *dichrophylla*: flowers

D. *dichrophylla*: fruit

177

1 *Diospyros glabra*   Blueberry bush
SA: 603.1 Spring–Summer   Bloubessiebos
Much-branched, dense, evergreen shrub or small tree; sexes separate, on different plants; occurring in **fynbos**, on mountain slopes or sandy flats. Leaves **narrowly to broadly elliptic, small (15–30 x 4–10 mm)**, leathery, **glossy dark green above**, pale green and glossy below, hairless; apex and base tapering; petiole **about 1 mm long**. Flowers axillary, solitary or in 2–5-flowered racemes, drooping, white. Fruit a berry, ovoid to almost spherical, up to 10 mm in diameter, **purple or reddish** when mature; calyx **persistent**, not notably enlarged, mostly reflexed.

2 *Diospyros kirkii*   Pink jackal-berry
Z: 855 Spring   Pienkjakkalsbessie
Shrub or small tree; sexes separate, on different plants; occurring in bushveld, often in dense stands on rocky ridges. Leaves **broadly elliptic to almost circular, up to 150 x 85 mm**, young growth densely covered with **woolly creamy-pink hairs**, becoming less hairy with age; apex **rounded**; base tapering to square; petiole **thick-set**, up to 12 mm long. Flowers in few-flowered axillary heads, **pinkish**, densely covered with creamy-pink woolly hairs. Fruit a berry, depressed-spherical, up to 40 mm in diameter, yellowish when mature; calyx **persistent**, tightly **clasping** the fruit.
     The fruit is edible and much sought after.

3 *Diospyros lycioides*   Bluebush
SA: 605; Z: 856 Spring–Summer   Bloubos
Shrub or small to medium-sized tree with ascending branches; sexes separate, on different plants; occurring in a wide variety of habitats. Bark **dark grey, rather smooth**. Leaves clustered towards ends of branches, oblanceolate, 15–80 x 5–30 mm, dull or grey green, with **silky** hairs when young, becoming more or less hairless with age; apex broadly tapering to rounded; base tapering; margin tightly rolled under; petiole 3–15 mm long. Flowers axillary, solitary, **drooping, creamy yellow**, sweetly scented. Fruit a berry, broadly ovoid, up to 20 mm long, hairy, particularly when young, orange red to dark red when ripe; calyx **persistent**, strongly **reflexed**. Mature leaves almost hairless with venation **not prominently raised** in subsp. *lycioides*; secondary and tertiary veins **conspicuously raised below** in subsp. *guerkei*. Mature leaves up to 20 x 10 mm, **dense with silvery hairs** in subsp. *nitens*; up to 80 x 30 mm, **sparsely** covered with **appressed hairs** in subsp. *sericea*.
     The roots, chewed to fray the ends, are used as toothbrushes. Larval food plant for the butterfly *Poecilmitis lycegenes*.
     D. austro-africana (**3.1**), a much-branched shrub or small tree with greyish green foliage, is widespread, particularly in the central grassland, bushveld and karroid areas of South Africa. It has narrowly obovate, small (4–30 x 2–5 mm), stiff and leathery leaves, which are densely grey-felted, at least below. The flowers are axillary, solitary, drooping, creamy white, pink or red. Leaves almost hairless and wrinkled above in var. *rugosa* (winter-rainfall regions), with dark-coloured hairs in var. *microphylla* (dry summer-rainfall areas), with soft pale grey hairs above and deep pink to red flowers in var. *rubiflora* (highlands of Free State, Lesotho and KwaZulu-Natal), with short, soft pale grey hairs above and cream to white flowers in var. *austro-africana* (Namaqualand and western parts of winter-rainfall region).

D. glabra: fruit

D. kirkii: young fruit

D. glabra: flowers

D. kirkii: flowers

D. lycioides: fruit

D. lycioides: flowers

D. lycioides: fruit

D. austro-africana: fruit

flowers

179

1 *Diospyros mespiliformis*   Jackal-berry
SA: 606; Z: 857   Spring   Jakkalsbessie

Medium to **large** evergreen to deciduous tree; autumn colours **dark yellow**; sexes separate, on different plants; occurring in bushveld, often along rivers or on termitaria. Leaves **elliptic to obovate-oblong**, 45–140 x 10–30 mm, glossy dark green above, pale green below, virtually hairless, autumn leaves yellow, spring flush red; apex broadly tapering to rounded; base tapering; margin **often wavy**; petiole up to 10 mm long. Flowers axillary, solitary or in few-flowered clusters, creamy white. Fruit a berry, ovoid to almost spherical **with a bristle-like tip**, up to 25 mm in diameter, yellow to purplish when ripe; calyx **persistent**, clasping the fruit but with tips of lobes reflexed.

The heartwood is pale reddish brown, dark brown to almost black, close-grained, hard, strong and suitable as a general purpose timber. Fruit edible and much sought after, either eaten fresh, used to brew a beer or stored as a fruit preserve; also eaten by jackals, hence the common names. Leaves, twigs and bark used medicinally. Larval food plant for the butterfly *Charaxes achaemenes achaemenes*.

2 *Diospyros natalensis*   Small-leaved jackal-berry
SA: 607; Z: 858   Winter–Spring   Fynblaarjakkalsbessie

Much-branched shrub or small to medium-sized evergreen tree; sexes separate, on different plants; occurring in coastal dune forest, along riverine fringes or at the edge of inland evergreen forest margins, occasionally on rocky outcrops. Leaves borne **horizontally (in one plane)** along stems, **elliptic to ovate, relatively small (10–36 x 5–20 mm)**, glossy dark green above, pale green below, hairy at first, becoming hairless with age; apex broadly tapering to rounded; base broadly tapering to almost square; petiole up to 2 mm long. Flowers axillary, solitary or in few-flowered clusters, white. Fruit **resembling small acorns, up to 12 x 6 mm**, sharply tipped, yellowish orange to red when ripe; calyx **persistent, cup-like**, covering almost half the fruit at base.

The wood is dark brown, hard, used for hut building and carrying-sticks. Larval food plant for the butterfly *Charaxes gallagheri*.

3 *Diospyros quiloensis*   Crocodile-bark jackal-berry
Z: 859   Spring–Summer   Krokodilbasjakkalsbessie

Small to medium-sized tree with a rounded crown; sexes separate, on different plants; occurring in hot, arid, low-altitude bushveld. Bark **deeply fissured into a grid-like pattern** (hence common names). Leaves oblanceolate, narrowly obovate or spathulate, usually about 40–50 x 15 mm, dark green and **very glossy** above, pale green and sometimes slightly hairy below; apex broadly tapering; base narrowly tapering; margin **wavy**; petiole up to 5 mm long. Flowers in few-flowered axillary groups, creamy white to pale yellow. Fruit **resembling small acorns, up to 25 x 10 mm**, yellowish when mature; calyx **persistent, cup-like**, covering the basal portion (about one quarter) of the fruit.

The heartwood is black with yellow sapwood; a very durable general purpose timber and widely used for carving. Fruit edible but not very tasty.

D. mespiliformis: flowers

D. mespiliformis: fruit

D. natalensis: flowers

D. natalensis: fruit

D. quiloensis: flowers

D. quiloensis: fruit

1 *Diospyros rotundifolia*   **Dune jackal-berry**
SA: 608   Spring   **Duinjakkalsbessie**
Shrub or small tree with stout twigs; sexes separate, on different plants; occurring in **coastal dune scrub and forest**, often in dense stands just above the high-water mark. Leaves **obovate to almost circular**, 30–60 x 20–60 mm, **very thick and leathery**, glossy dark green above, pale green below; apex rounded, often notched; base broadly tapering to square; margin often **rolled under**, petiole up to 5 mm long. Flowers axillary, solitary, creamy white. Fruit a berry, ovoid, up to 25 x 15 mm, glossy red to purplish when mature; calyx persistent, with **basal cup-shaped part and reflexed lobes**.
    Easily confused with *Eugenia capensis* (Group 22, p. 318), a species with opposite leaves containing secretory cavities (leaves are aromatic when crushed).

2 *Diospyros scabrida*   **False blackbark**
SA: 608.1   Summer–Autumn   **Vals-swartbas**
Evergreen shrub or small tree; sexes separate, on different plants; occurring in scrub on rocky outcrops in grassland, rarely along forest margins. Leaves **elliptic** and **broadly oblong to almost circular**, 10–70 x 12–30 mm, **very glossy** dark green; base **square to lobed**. Otherwise very similar to *D. whyteana*, but easily recognized by its calyx lobes, which are **free** and completely envelope the fruit. Leaves elliptic, 30–80 mm long in var. *scabrida* (found mainly in KwaZulu-Natal), broadly ovate to almost circular and usually shorter than 40 mm in var. *cordata* (found mainly in the Eastern Cape).

3 *Diospyros usambarensis*   **Black star-apple**
Z: 862   Spring–Summer   **Swartsterappel**
Shrub or small tree; sexes separate, on different plants; occurring in low altitude bushveld, often along rivers on rocky hill slopes. Bark rough, grey to blackish. Leaves crowded towards ends of branches, **obovate to elliptic, 50–100 x 25–50 mm**, glossy dark green above, pale green below; apex broadly tapering; base tapering; margin sometimes finely wavy; petiole **slender, up to 10 mm long**. Flowers in 3- or 4-flowered axillary clusters, white. Fruit a berry, ovoid, up to 20 mm long, yellowish when mature, with short golden hairs; calyx persistent, with 4 or 5 **leaf-like lobes**, up to 30 mm long, **conspicuously veined** and **clasping** the fruit.

4 *Diospyros villosa*   **Hairy star-apple**
SA: 610   Autumn   **Harige sterappel**
Scandent shrub or small straggling tree, branches often **at about right angles** to the main stem; sexes separate, on different plants; occurring along forest margins and in wooded ravines, rarely in bushveld (var. *parviflora*). Leaves obovate-oblong to broadly oblong, 10–130 x 5–60 mm, **stiff and leathery**, both surfaces **hairy** when young, becoming almost hairless above, **lower surface remaining densely covered with whitish or brownish woolly hairs**; apex broadly tapering to rounded; base square to lobed; margin rolled under; petiole up to 20 mm long. Flowers axillary, solitary or in few-flowered spikes, **yellow**, fragrant. Fruit a **dehiscent** berry (splits into 5 woody valves), depressed-spherical, markedly **5-angled**, 15–25 x 30 mm, densely covered with **golden hairs**; calyx persistent with 5 wing-like lobes clasping the fruit. Leaves longer than 35 mm in var. *villosa*, shorter in var. *parvifolia*.

1

D. rotundifolia: fruit

2

D. scabrida: flowers

1

D. rotundifolia: fruit

2

D. scabrida: fruit

2

D. scabrida: fruit

3

D. usambarensis: fruit

4

D. villosa: flowers

4

D. villosa: fruit

3

D. usambarensis: fruit

4

D. villosa: young leaves & fruit

1 *Diospyros whyteana*   Bladder-nut
SA: 611; Z: 863   Autumn   Swartbas

Evergreen shrub or small tree; crown usually with an **occasional bright orange or red leaf**; sexes separate, on different plants; occurring in scrub and forest, often in rocky places. Bark rather **smooth, grey to almost black**. Leaves arranged in 2 ranks, **narrowly elliptic to ovate-oblong**, 25–45 x 10–20 mm, **very glossy** dark green above, pale green and sparsely covered with hairs below; apex narrowly tapering; base **tapering to almost rounded**; margin with a **fringe of hairs**, rather wavy; petiole up to 2 mm long. Flowers in short axillary racemes, white to cream. Fruit a berry, ovoid to almost spherical, 10–20 mm long; calyx **persistent**, with four or five lobes **joined to form an inflated, bladder-like structure completely enveloping the fruit**, often tinged reddish brown.

The leaves are browsed by stock. An attractive garden subject, especially suitable as a hedging plant.

Similar to *D. scabrida*, whose fruit is surrounded by free calyx lobes.

2 *Euclea natalensis*   Natal guarri
SA: 597   Winter–Summer   Natalghwarrie

Shrub or small to medium-sized tree with a somewhat spreading crown; occurring in a variety of habitats, including coastal and inland forest as well as bushveld. Leaves **elliptic to obovate-oblong, tough and leathery**, glossy dark green above, densely covered **with pale rusty woolly hairs below**; margin **wavy**; petiole up to 10 mm long. Flowers in dense, branched, axillary heads, small greenish white to cream, sweetly scented. Fruit a berry, spherical, 7–10 mm in diameter, red becoming black when mature. Leaves **rounded** with margin strongly **rolled under** in subsp. *rotundifolia* (confined to coastal dune forest in the Maputaland Centre); leaves broadest in upper half and **relatively narrow (45–130 x 15–35 mm)** in subsp. *natalensis* (coastal forest and scrub), and leaves with **sparse hairs** below, 25–110 x 45 mm, with tip **broadly rounded** in subsp. *obovata* (southern KwaZulu-Natal and Eastern Cape).

Juice from the boiled roots is used for dyeing palm-mats black; also used medicinally. Twigs used for toothbrushes. Fruit edible.

3 *Euclea pseudobenus*   Ebony tree
SA: 598   Spring   Ebbeboom

Shrub or small to medium-sized tree with **slender, drooping** branches; sexes separate, on different plants; occurring in semi-desert and desert areas, usually along **watercourses** and in depressions. Branchlets with fine hairs. Leaves **very narrow and slender**, slightly curved, leathery, **bluish green**; petiole up to 2 mm long. Flowers in axillary clusters, small, greenish yellow. Fruit a berry, ovoid, 5–8 mm in diameter, black when mature.

The heartwood is pitch black (hence common names), hard and durable, used in construction and as fuelwood. Twigs used for toothbrushes. Browsed by stock. Fruit edible but not very palatable; also fed to chickens to harden eggshells.

E. linearis, which also has very narrow leaves (2–4 mm wide), occurs in areas of higher rainfall, usually in dense stands on rocky ridges or heavy mineralized soils; all parts are hairless.

D. whyteana: flowers

D. whyteana: fruit

D. whyteana: fruit

E. natalensis: flowers

E. natalensis: flowers

E. natalensis: fruit

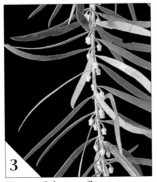

E. pseudobenus: flowers

E. pseudobenus: fruit

1 Euclea racemosa   Sea guarri
SA: 599   Summer   Seeghwarrie
Evergreen shrub or small tree; sexes separate, on different plants; occurring in coastal dune scrub and forest. Leaves alternate, subopposite or opposite, **oblanceolate to obovate**, **thickly leathery, glossy dark green** above, paler green below, **hairless**; margin **rolled under**; petiole up to 4 mm long, wrinkled. Flowers in short axillary spikes, small, drooping, creamy white. Fruit a berry, globose, up to 7 mm in diameter, black when mature.

2 Euclea tomentosa   Honey guarri
SA: 600.2   Spring   Heuningghwarrie
Evergreen shrub or small tree; sexes separate, on different plants; occurring in arid semi-desert areas, usually on rocky mountain slopes or in ravines. Branchlets **greyish-haired**. Leaves **obovate to ovate-oblong, stiffly leathery, dull green** to grey above and below, **thinly covered with crisped white hairs**, at least below; margin flat, **not rolled under**; petiole very short. Flowers small, in few-flowered axillary racemes, covered with crisped white hairs. Fruit a berry, subglobose, up to 9 mm in diameter, red to purplish black when mature.

ERYTHROXYLACEAE (see page 24)

3 Erythroxylum delagoense   Small-leaved coca tree
SA: 248   Spring   Fynblaarkokaboom
Shrub or small tree; occurring in bushveld and coastal grassland, notably in the Maputaland Centre. Branchlets **flattened** towards tip. Leaves elliptic or rather **rounded, small (10–30 x 7–15 mm), thinly textured, pale blue-green** above, paler below; petiole up to 3 mm long; stipules intrapetiolar. Flowers axillary, small, white to yellowish green. Fruit fleshy, oval, up to 10 mm long, **bright red**.
    E. zambesiacum (**3.1**) (from upper Zambezi River Valley) has larger (18–70 x 12–40 mm) leaves with more distinct venation.

4 Erythroxylum emarginatum   Common coca tree
SA: 249; Z: 378   Spring–Summer   Gewone kokaboom
Shrub or small tree; occurring in coastal and inland forest, also on rocky hillsides in bushveld. Branchlets **flattened** towards tip. Leaves **oblanceolate to elliptic, 20–125 x 10–45 mm**, leathery, dark green above, paler green below; venation prominent; petiole up to 6 mm long; stipules intrapetiolar. Flowers axillary, small, white, scented. Fruit fleshy, oval, up to 14 mm long, red.
    Fruit edible but not tasty. Larval food plant for the butterfly *Euriphene achlys*.

5 Erythroxylum pictum   Forest coca tree
SA: 250   Summer   Boskokaboom
Small to medium-sized tree; crown well-branched and spreading, often with a few **bright yellow leaves**; occurring in forest and at forest margins, often along streams or on rocky outcrops. Branchlets **flattened** towards tip. Leaves **oval to ovate**, 30–60 x 15–35 mm, **thinly textured, bluish green** above, paler below; venation **obscure**; margin slightly wavy; petiole up to 5 mm long; stipules intrapetiolar. Flowers axillary, small, creamy green. Fruit fleshy, oval, up to 10 mm long, bright, **shiny red**.
    The fruit is edible but not very tasty. Wood used for carvings.

E. racemosa: flowers

E. racemosa: fruit

E. delagoense: flowers

E. delagoense: fruit

E. zambesiacum: fruit

E. emarginatum: flowers

E. emarginatum: fruit

E. tomentosa: fruit

E. pictum: flowers & fruit

1 *Nectaropetalum zuluense*   Natal coca tree
SA: 247   Winter   Natalkokaboom
Small to medium-sized tree; occurring in deep shade in the understorey of forest.
Apical buds are conspicuous, **long and narrow** (enclosed by spike-like stipule).
Leaves oblong, glossy dark green above, hairless; tertiary veins **obscure** when held
against the light; margin wavy. Flowers axillary, solitary or in small clusters, white.
Fruit fleshy, oval, up to 10 mm long, green, turning yellow after falling.
    The wood is reddish brown, tough, and used for yokes and carrying-sticks.
    Similar to *N. capense* (**1.1**) (found in southern KwaZulu-Natal and the Eastern
Cape), whose leaves, when viewed against the light, have translucent, tertiary venation.

EUPHORBIACEAE (see page 24)

2 *Antidesma venosum*   Tassel berry
SA: 318; Z: 465   Summer   Voëlsitboom
Shrub or small tree with somewhat spreading and arching branches; sexes separate,
on different trees; occurring in moist bushveld and wooded grassland, sand forest
and along forest margins. Leaves **oval to elliptic**, leathery, glossy bright green
above, paler green and **hairy** below, with **conspicuous lateral veins** looping along
the margin below; stipules **large and conspicuous** with **narrowly tapering** apices.
Flowers in **drooping** spikes (often parasitized by insects and transformed into large,
tangled, sterile growths), very small, greenish yellow. Fruit a berry, almost spherical, about 10 x 8 mm, white to red, ripening purplish black.
    The leaves are browsed by game. Various parts are used medicinally; root extract
has proven physiological effects on the heart. Fruit edible.

3 *Bridelia cathartica*   Blue sweetberry
SA: 322; Z: 474   Summer   Blousoetbessie
Scrambling shrub or small multistemmed tree occurring on forest margins, in sand
forest and in riverine fringe thicket. Leaves **elliptic to broadly oblanceolate**,
glossy dark green above, pale **grey-green to bluish green** below. Flowers in axillary clusters, very small, greenish to yellowish. Fruit a berry, globose or somewhat
2-lobed, up to 9 x 7 mm, **purplish red ripening to black**, produced in profusion.
Subsp. *cathartica* has **straight** branches and leaves with lateral veins which tend to
end at the margin; subsp. *melanthesoides* has somewhat **zigzag** branchlets and
leaves with lateral veins that **break up before reaching the margin**.
    The leaves are browsed by game. Fruit used medicinally.

4 *Bridelia micrantha*   Mitzeeri
SA: 324; Z: 475   Spring–Summer   Mitseeri
Medium to large deciduous tree; crown spreading, usually with **scattered bright red
leaves**; occurring in coastal, riverine and swamp forest, usually in moist places.
Leaves **elliptic to obovate**, glossy dark green above, paler green below, more or less
hairless, lateral veins **prominent below** and **terminating at the margin** to form a
'herringbone' pattern; petiole short, thickset. Flowers in axillary clusters, very small,
yellowish green. Fruit a berry, **oval**, about 8 x 4 mm, **black** when mature.
    Root and bark used medicinally. Heartwood used for furniture and ornaments.
Fruit edible. Larval food plant for the butterflies *Abantis paradisea*, *Charaxes castor flavifasciatus* and *Parosmodes morantii morantii*.

N. zuluense: flowers

N. capense: flowers

A. venosum: fruit

A. venosum: flowers

A. venosum: fruit

B. cathartica: flowers

B. cathartica: fruit

B. micrantha: fruit

B. micrantha: flowers

B. micrantha: fruit

1 *Bridelia mollis* Velvet sweetberry
SA: 325; Z: 476 Summer Fluweelsoetbessie
Deciduous shrub or small tree; occurring in bushveld, often in rocky places. Young growth **densely furry**. Leaves **ovate to obovate**, both surfaces with **dense velvety hairs**, lateral veins **prominent below** and **terminating at the margin** to form a 'herringbone' pattern; apex broadly tapering, often notched; petiole short, thickset, **densely velvety**. Flowers in tight axillary clusters, very small, greenish yellow. Fruit a berry, almost spherical, about 10 mm in diameter, black when mature. The fruit is edible, and is made into a jam.

2 *Cleistanthus schlechteri* False tamboti
SA: 320; Z: 472 Spring Bastertambotie
Medium to large deciduous tree with somewhat drooping branches and reddish brown autumn colours; sexes separate, on different trees; occurring in sand forest and bushveld, often in riverine vegetation. Bark **cracked into a grid-like pattern**. Leaves **elliptic, glossy** dark green above, paler green below, hairless, except for **minute hairtuft domatia** usually present in the axils of lateral veins below; base **rounded to lobed**. Flowers in axillary clusters, small, greenish yellow, sweetly scented. Fruit a **3-lobed** capsule, about 10 mm in diameter, splitting into 3 segments.
The tree is browsed by elephant and other game. Wood dark brown, very hard and termite resistant; used for carvings, hut building and fuel. Bark used medicinally.

3 *Clutia pulchella* Common lightning bush
SA: 336.1; Z: 509 Summer Gewone bliksembos
Shrub or small deciduous tree, usually with an **occasional bright orange or red leaf** among the foliage; sexes separate, on different plants; occurring in karroid areas, wooded grassland, bushveld and in forest margins. Leaves ovate to elliptic or almost circular, **thinly textured, pale green to greyish green** above, **bluish green** below; venation more or less **translucent**; petiole **slender, up to 25 mm long**. Flowers axillary, very small, greenish white. Fruit a capsule, round, about 5 mm in diameter, slightly warty, dehiscent.
Larval food plant for the butterfly *Poecilmitis aureus*. Also used medicinally.
Andrachne ovalis, from forest margins, is very similar, but it has thicker, dark green leaves with obscure venation.

4 *Drypetes gerrardii* Forest ironplum
SA: 314; Z: 459 Spring Bosysterpruim
Small to medium-sized tree with a dense crown; branches spread out **horizontally at right angles** to the trunk; sexes separate, on different trees; occurring in evergreen forest, often along streams. Branchlets and buds with fine, **yellowish or brownish hairs**. Leaves arranged in a **horizontal plane, ovate to elliptic**, glossy dark green above, paler green below, midrib with **brownish hairs** towards base below; apex narrowly tapering; base broadly tapering, usually **unequal**; margin entire or broadly and shallowly toothed. Flowers in axillary clusters, small, greenish yellow. Fruit fleshy, oval, up to 10 mm in diameter, hairy, yellowish orange.
Larval food plant for the butterflies *Appias sabina phoebe* and *Coeliades libeon*.
D. reticulata, an understorey tree found in coastal dune forest along the east coast, is very similar, but lacks the yellowish brown hairs on the stem and petioles.

B. mollis: flowers

C. schlechteri: flowers

B. mollis: fruit

C. schlechteri: fruit

C. pulchella: flowers

C. pulchella: fruit

D. gerrardii: female flowers

D. gerrardii: fruit

1 Flueggea virosa (= *Securinega virosa*) White-berry bush
SA: 309; Z: 446   Spring–Summer Witbessiebos
Many-stemmed shrub or small tree; sexes separate, on different trees; occurring in bushveld and at forest margins, often in rocky places. Branches **stiff and angular**. Leaves elliptic to obovate, usually **about 25 x 15 mm, thinly textured**, fresh green; apex **tapering to rounded**; petiole slender, up to 3 mm long. Flowers axillary, very small, greenish yellow. Fruit fleshy, spherical, about 5 mm in diameter, **white**.
   The leaves are browsed by game. Wood strong and supple, used for fish traps. Root and bark used medicinally. Larval food plant for some *Charaxes* butterflies.
   Similar to *Phyllanthus reticulatus*, but easily distinguished by the angular young twigs. Stems of *Flueggea verrucosa*, found mainly in valley bushveld in the Eastern Cape, are conspicuously warty.

2 Heywoodia lucens Stink ebony
SA: 306   Spring Stinkebbehout
Large evergreen tree with **dark green** foliage; sexes separate, on different trees; occurring in evergreen forest, often in groups. Leaves ovate to lanceolate, **leathery**, dark green, **hairless**, venation somewhat translucent and visible on both surfaces; apex tapering; base **broadly tapering to rounded**; petiole up to 2 mm long, often **attached within the blade (leaves peltate)** in juvenile plants and sucker shoots. Flowers in axillary heads, small, greenish yellow. Fruit a 4- or 5-ridged capsule, roundish, about 20 mm wide, wrinkled, dehiscing explosively.
   The heartwood is almost black, hard and heavy with a coarse grain and unpleasant smell; used for carrying-sticks.

3 Hymenocardia acida Heart tree
Z: 462   Summer Hartboom
Shrub or small tree; sexes separate on different plants; occurring in *Brachystegia* woodland and wooded mountain slopes. Branchlets **orange to reddish brown**. Leaves **elliptic-oblong**, dark green, hairy when young, becoming almost hairless with age, with **minute orange dots** below (use hand lens); venation slightly immersed above, usually with **minute domatia** in axils of lateral veins below. Flowers in drooping spikes (male) or axillary (female), small, reddish. Fruit a flattened capsule with **2 large, diverging wings, reddish** and conspicuous when mature.
   The bark and root are used medicinally.

4 Hymenocardia ulmoides Red-heart tree
SA: 317; Z: 463   Summer Rooihartboom
Small to medium-sized deciduous tree; sexes separate, on different plants; occurring in sand forest and bushveld, usually on sandy soils. Leaves ovate, elliptic to lanceolate, **25–30 x 18 mm**, glossy dark green above, paler green below; midrib often **reddish** and hairy; apex tapering, often **bent downwards**. Flowers in drooping spikes (male) or axillary (female), small, pinkish to reddish. Fruit a flattened capsule surrounded by a **papery wing** with an apical notch, **yellowish green**, usually **tinged with red**, produced in abundance.
   The tree is browsed by game. Wood strong, straight and elastic; used in hut construction, fish kraals (notably in the Kosi Bay area) and for fishing baskets.
   Pteleopsis myrtifolia (p. 338), has fruit with 2–4 wings, and opposite leaves.

F. virosa: flowers

H. acida: female flowers

F. virosa: fruit

H. lucens: fruit

H. acida: fruit

H. acida: male flowers

H. acida: fruit

H. ulmoides: fruit

H. ulmoides: fruit

GROUP 10

1 *Margaritaria discoidea* (= *Phyllanthus discoideus*)   **Pheasant-berry**
SA: 310; Z: 447   Spring   **Fisantebessie**
Small to medium-sized (in bushveld) or very large (in forest) deciduous tree; sexes
separate, on different trees; occurring in forest, bushveld and thicket. Bark in large
trees **rough and flaky**, the deeper layers **reddish brown**. Leaves arranged in **one
plane**, ovate or obovate to elliptic, **thinly textured**, bright green, **hairless**; venation
prominent below. Flowers axillary, small, greenish yellow. Fruit a **3-lobed** capsule,
about 10 mm in diameter, golden brown to semi-transparent, dehiscent; seed globose, often with an unusual **metallic blue-green lustre**.
    The heartwood is reddish brown, hard and durable. Bark used medicinally. Larval
food plant for the butterfly *Charaxes etesipe tavetensis*.

2 *Phyllanthus reticulatus*   **Potato bush**
SA: 311; Z: 455   Winter–Spring   **Aartappelbos**
Multi-stemmed shrub or small tree; occurring in bushveld, particularly riverine
thicket and in the shade of bush clumps. Leaves **oval to elliptic**, arranged on **short,
slender side shoots which are strongly reminiscent of compound leaves, thinly
textured**; venation conspicuous and often tinged reddish below; petiole short.
Flowers in axillary clusters, very small, yellowish, often tinged pinkish red. Fruit
berry-like, globose, up to 6 mm in diameter, **black** when mature, dehiscent.
    The plants emit a strong scent of potatoes during certain times of the year, partic-
ularly on spring and summer evenings. Browsed by game and stock. Leaves and
fruit used medicinally. The fruit produces a black dye.

3 *Pseudolachnostylis maprouneifolia*   **Kudu-berry**
SA: 308; Z: 445   Winter–Spring   **Koedoebessie**
Small to large deciduous tree with a rounded crown and dark red and yellow autumn
colours; sexes separate, on different trees; occurring in bushveld, often on rocky
ridges. Leaves **ovate, ovate-elliptic to almost circular, thinly textured**, rather dull
fresh green to bluish green above, paler green below, **hairless**; apex broadly tapering to rounded; base tapering to rounded; petiole up to 15 mm long, **yellowish**.
Flowers in axillary clusters, small, greenish white. Fruit **somewhat fleshy**, spherical, about 20 mm in diameter, **faintly 6-segmented**, yellowish brown and wrinkled
when mature, indehiscent.
    The leaves and fruit are eaten by antelope and elephant. Bark, root and leaves used
medicinally. Larval food plant for the butterflies *Abantis paradisea* and *Deudorix
dinochares*.

FABACEAE (see page 25)

4 *Baphia massaiensis*   **Sand camwood**
SA: 223; Z: 288   Spring–Summer   **Sandkamhout**
Shrub or small tree, occurring in bushveld, usually in dense stands on deep Kalahari
sand. Leaves **obovate**, often **folded upward** along the midrib, dull green above,
paler green with 6–10 pairs of **conspicuous lateral veins** below, hairless; apex
broadly tapering to rounded; base tapering; petiole **swollen at both ends**.
Flowers in short racemes; petals crinkled, white with **golden yellow spot** in centre
of upper petal, jasmine-scented. Pods up to 120 mm long, dark brown to reddish
brown, dehiscent. All the material in southern Africa belongs to subsp. *obovata*.

M. discoidea: flowers

M. discoidea: fruit

M. discoidea: fruit & seeds

P. reticulatus: flowers

B. massaiensis: fruit

P. maprouneifolia: female flowers

P. maprouneifolia: fruit

B. massaiensis: flowers

1 *Baphia racemosa* — Natal camwood
SA: 224   Summer — Natalse kamhout
Shrub or small to medium-sized tree, occurring in coastal forest, usually along streams and rivers. Leaves **ovate**, **dark green** above, paler green below, **hairless**; apex **narrowly tapering**; base tapering; petiole **swollen at both ends**; stipules fall early. Flowers produced in profusion, white with **golden yellow spot** in centre of upper petal, violet-scented. Pod flat, up to 120 mm long, brown, dehiscent.

The wood was once used in wagon building and for hoe handles. Larval food plant for the butterflies *Charaxes cithaeron joanae* and *Deudorix diocles*.

2 *Lonchocarpus nelsii* — Kalahari apple-leaf
SA: 239; Z: 359   Spring — Kalahari-appelblaar
Small to medium-sized deciduous tree with yellow autumn colours; occurring in hot, dry bushveld, often on deep Kalahari sand. Leaves compound with 1 or 2 pairs of leaflets plus a terminal one, or reduced to a single leaflet; leaflets **oval to ovate**, **up to 120 x 60 mm**, densely velvety when young, becoming less hairy with age, **leathery and puckered** above, net-veining **conspicuously raised** below; apex and base **rounded**. Flowers in panicles, mauve to purplish, usually produced before the new leaves. Pods flat, 5–9 x 10 mm, pale brown, finely velvety, indehiscent.

The leaves are browsed by stock and game. Larval food plant for the butterfly *Charaxes bohemani*.

The hairy leaves resemble those of *Combretum molle* (p. 334) and *C. zeyheri* (p. 338). However, both these species have opposite leaves and lack stipules.

3 *Podalyria calyptrata* — Water blossom pea
SA: 225   Winter–Spring — Waterkeurtjie
Much-branched shrub or small slender tree with **silvery grey** foliage; occurring in fynbos, usually in mountainous areas and along streams. Branchlets **velvety**. Leaves **obovate-elliptic to obovate**, greyish green and with sparse hairs above, dense with **silky hairs below**; margin entire, rolled under. Flowers axillary, solitary or in clusters, mauve to pink, sweetly scented; floral buds **enclosed by a hood** of two united, silky bracts. Pods **inflated**, hard, up to 40 x 15 mm, with brown woolly hairs.

FLACOURTIACEAE (see page 25)
4 *Xylotheca kraussiana* — African dog-rose
SA: 493   Spring — Afrikaanse hondsroos
Multi-stemmed shrub or small tree; occurring in coastal bush and forest, also in sand forest and bushveld. Leaves **elliptic**, dark green above, paler green below, with or without soft hairs on both surfaces; apex tapering, base broadly tapering to rounded; petiole up to 10 mm long. Flowers in axillary or terminal groups, **up to 70 mm in diameter**, white with **bright yellow anthers**, sweet-scented. Fruit a woody capsule, ovoid with **8 longitudinal ridges**, up to 40 mm long, ripening to yellow and splitting into 4–8 valves; seeds **reddish black**, covered by a **bright red**, hairy aril.

The aril is edible. Root used medicinally. Larval food plant for the butterflies *Acraea oncaea* and *A. petraea*.

X. tettensis (found in eastern Zimbabwe and Mozambique) has obovate to broadly oblong leaves and seeds embedded in a yellowish or scarlet pulp (no aril).

196

B. *racemosa*: flowers

B. *racemosa*: fruit

L. *nelsii*: fruit

P. *calyptrata*: flowers

P. *calyptrata*: fruit

L. *nelsii*: flowers

X. *kraussiana*: flowers

X. *kraussiana*: fruit

X. *kraussiana*: dehisced fruit

197

HETEROPYXIDACEAE (see page 25)

1 Heteropyxis natalensis (= *H. dehniae*)   Lavender tree
SA: 455; Z: 805   Summer   Laventelboom

Small deciduous to semi-deciduous tree with **drooping** foliage; occurring in bushveld and along forest margins, often in rocky places. Bark **pale grey to almost white, flaking**. Leaves narrowly elliptic, ovate to obovate, **shiny dark green** above, paler green below, **slightly hairy to hairless** when mature, **pleasantly aromatic** (lavender scent) when crushed (**secretory cavities present** in blade), at least one pair of principal lateral veins **more strongly developed** with **hairtuft domatia** in their axils below. Flowers in branched terminal clusters, very small, yellowish green. Fruit a capsule, oval, up to 4 x 2,5 mm, brownish when mature, dehiscent.

The leaves and root are used medicinally. Browsed by game. A decorative tree for small gardens.

H. canescens is a rare species restricted to a small area in Mpumalanga and adjacent Swaziland. The lateral veins of the leaves are prominent below, the lower surface usually covered in greyish hairs.

ICACINACEAE (see page 25)

2 Apodytes dimidiata   White pear
SA: 422; Z: 593   Spring–Summer   Witpeer

Small to large evergreen tree; occurring in coastal and inland forest and in bushveld. Bark pale **grey, more or less smooth**. Leaves **ovate-elliptic**, usually **50–80 x 25–40 mm**, usually **softly-leathery**, glossy dark green above, paler green below, usually hairless but sometimes hairy, **mainly along the basal portion of the midrib below**; margin **wavy**; petiole often **pinkish red**. Flowers in many-flowered terminal panicles, small, white. Fruit a **black** nut with a fleshy appendage that ripens from green through **scarlet to black, or directly to black**. All the material in southern Africa belongs to subsp. *dimidiata*.

The wood is pale pinkish brown, very hard and once used in wagon construction. Root and leaves used medicinally; the latter also have snail-killing properties.

A. abbottii (endemic to the Pondoland Centre) has blue-green leaves which are thick, stiff and brittle (they snap, audibly, into two when bent). *A. geldenhuysii* (found in the mountains of the southwestern part of the Western Cape) has small leaves (usually 25–40 x 10–15 mm), axillary, few-flowered inflorescences and fruit whose fleshy appendage ripens through translucent green to black.

LAURACEAE (see page 25)

3 Cryptocarya woodii   Cape quince
SA: 116   Spring–Summer   Kaapse kweper

Small to medium-sized evergreen tree; crown often **with an occasional bright yellow leaf**; occurring in forest, often along streams. Leaves **ovate to broadly ovate**, 15–80 x 15–40 mm, thinly leathery, shiny bright green above, slightly paler green below, hairless, tertiary venation well developed, consisting of **minute squarish areolae when viewed against the light**; apex tapering to a pronounced **drip-tip**. Flowers axillary, very small, greenish white. Fruit a drupe, spherical, up to 20 mm in diameter, dark purplish black.

Various parts of the tree are used medicinally. Larval food plant for the butterflies *Charaxes xiphanes* and *Papilio euphranor*. A decorative tree for small gardens.

H. natalensis: bark

H. natalensis: flowers

H. natalensis: fruit

A. dimidiata: flowers

A. dimidiata: fruit

A. dimidiata: fruit

C. woodii: flowers

C. woodii: fruit

1 *Ocotea bullata*   **Stinkwood**
SA: 118   Summer–Autumn   **Stinkhout**
Medium to large evergreen tree; older specimens often with hollow trunks and coppicing from the base; occurring in montane forest. Leaves oblong, **large (70–120 x 25–50 mm)**, glossy dark green above, paler green below, with **conspicuous large domatia in axils of some of the lower principal lateral veins below,** visible as raised 'bubbles' on the upper surface; margin **wavy.** Flowers in axillary clusters, very small, yellowish green. Fruit **acorn-like,** oval, about 20 mm long, lower part enveloped by the cup-shaped receptacle, purple when ripe.
    The wood ranges from cream to dark brown to almost black, fine-textured with a satiny lustre, very attractive and used for high quality furniture. Freshly cut timber emits an unpleasant smell, hence the common names. Bark extensively used in traditional medicine; indiscriminate ringbarking kills many trees.

LECYTHIDACEAE (see page 26)

2 *Barringtonia racemosa*   **Powder-puff tree**
SA: 524   Summer–Autumn   **Poeierkwasboom**
Small to medium-sized tree; occurring **along estuaries and in swamp forest** along the coast, always in or near water. Leaves clustered at ends of branches, obovate-oblong to oblanceolate, **very large (80–350 x 40–130 mm)**, leathery, midrib purplish at base; petiole very short, **purple.** Flowers in many-flowered **pendulous** racemes, large, white, with mass of stamens, often tinged with pink; buds shiny pinkish red, opening at night and fading the next morning. Fruit hard and fibrous, conical to ovate, about 40 x 30 mm, yellowish brown, buoyant, dispersed by water.
    The bark is used as a fish poison; it also has insecticidal properties. Fruit used medicinally. Larval food plant for the butterfly *Coeliades keithloa.*

MELIACEAE (see page 26)

3 *Nymania capensis*   **Chinese lanterns**
SA: 295   Winter–Spring   **Klapperbos**
Rigid shrub or small tree; occurring in hot, semi-desert areas, often along watercourses. Leaves alternate or clustered on short lateral shoots, linear to **linear lanceo-late, 8–40 x 2–6 mm**, leathery, densely hairy to hairless; petiole very short. Flowers axillary, solitary, greenish pink to dark pink or scarlet, tubular at first, becoming bell-shaped with age. Fruit an **inflated capsule**, papery, 30–40 x 30–40 mm, creamy-pink to bright reddish pink with a silky sheen, very attractive.
    Larval food plant for the butterfly *Deudorix antalis.*

4 *Turraea floribunda*   **Wild honeysuckle tree**
SA: 296; Z: 426   Spring–Summer   **Wildekamperfoelieboom**
Small to medium-sized deciduous tree, with horizontally spreading branches; occurring in coastal forest and bushveld. Leaves **ovate to lanceolate**, dark green above, paler green below, almost hairless with age, **lateral veins sunken above, prominently raised below**; apex tapering to a **slender tip.** Flowers axillary, appearing with the new leaves, greenish white, **fading to greenish yellow**; petals long, narrow and recurved; central staminal tube conspicuous. Fruit a capsule, subspherical, up to 25 mm wide, segmented, splitting to reveal **orange-red** seeds.
    The root and bark are used medicinally.

O. *bullata*: fruit

B. *racemosa*: flowers

B. *racemosa*: flowers

B. *racemosa*: fruit

N. *capensis*: flowers & fruit

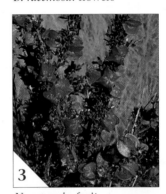

N. *capensis*: fruit

O. *bullata*: flowers

T. *floribunda*: flowers

T. *floribunda*: fruit

T. *floribunda*: fruit – one dehisced

1 Turraea nilotica   Lowveld honeysuckle tree

SA: 297; Z: 427   Winter–Spring   Laeveldse kamperfoelieboom

Shrub or small to medium-sized deciduous tree; occurring in bushveld, often in *Brachystegia* woodland. Leaves **elliptic, large (up to 160 x 100 mm)**, densely to sparsely hairy above, **densely hairy below**; apex **broadly tapering to rounded**; petiole very short. Flowers in dense, tight clusters along stems, **appearing before the new leaves in spring**, greenish white turning yellowish with age. Fruit a capsule, almost spherical, up to 10 mm in diameter, **segmented**, splitting to reveal the black shiny seeds partly covered by a red aril.

The root is used medicinally.

MIMOSACEAE (see page 27)

2 •Acacia saligna (= *A. cyanophylla*)   Port Jackson willow

SA: X499   Spring   Goudwilger

Evergreen shrub or small to medium-sized tree, with a sparse, **willow-like** appearance; invading fynbos, coastal dunes, roadsides and watercourses. Leaves (phyllodes) **more or less drooping**, straight or slightly sickle-shaped, **up to 200 x 10–60 mm**, blue-green when young, bright green when mature, **hairless**; apex **tapering**. Flowers clustered in **globose** heads borne in short axillary clusters, bright yellow. Pods straight, 50–100 mm long, flattened, slightly constricted between the seeds, brown with a hardened, whitish margin.

A native of Australia; cultivated for dune reclamation, shelter, and tanbark; also used as fodder for stock. This is a declared invader in South Africa.

A. podalyriifolia (a native of Australia) is an invader of roadsides, urban open spaces and watercourses. Its leaves (phyllodes) are ovate or elliptic (20–40 mm long), with a hair-like tip, and densely covered with greyish hairs. *A. pycnantha* (also from Australia) invades coastal and mountain fynbos and roadsides. Its 'leaves' are distinctly sickle-shaped, up to 200 mm long, hairless, with a blunt or rounded apex, and a large gland at the base of the blade.

MYRSINACEAE (see page 28)

3 Rapanea melanophloeos   Cape beech

SA: 578; Z: 830   Winter–Summer   Kaapse boekenhout

Medium to large evergreen tree; occurring in forest and bush clumps, usually in damp areas. Leaves clustered near ends of branches, oblong or oblong-lanceolate, **50–130 mm long, thick and leathery**, dull dark green above, paler green below, hairless, young leaves often bright pinkish red; petiole up to 15 mm long, usually **reddish purple**, with a **brownish secretion** oozing from the broken base. Flowers in clusters mainly below the leaves **on the older wood**, small, greenish white. Fruit fleshy, round, **up to 5 mm in diameter**, purple.

The wood is pinkish brown, hard, heavy, fine-grained, very attractive and durable; used for superior furniture and for making violins. Bark used medicinally.

R. gilliana is a shrub or small tree from coastal dune scrub in the Eastern Cape. It has smaller (30–40 mm long) oblanceolate leaves with the margin rolled under, and larger (up to 10 mm long), oval fruit.

T. nilotica: flowers

T. nilotica: fruit

R. melanophloeos: fruit

A. saligna: flowers

A. saligna: fruit

R. melanophloeos: flowers

MYRTACEAE (see page 28)

1 •*Callistemon viminales*   **Weeping bottlebrush**
SA: X856; Z: 806   Spring   **Treurperdestert**
Evergreen shrub or small tree, with a sparse crown and **drooping** branches; invading bushveld and roadsides. Leaves **narrowly elliptic**, up to 80 mm long, leathery, with **numerous minute secretory cavities** when held against the light, aromatic when crushed. Flowers in showy, **drooping**, cylindrical terminal spikes, with numerous **bright red stamens**. Fruit a small woody capsule, in dense clusters, persisting on the tree for many months.
A native of Australia; cultivated for ornament.

2 •*Eucalyptus camaldulensis*   **Red gum**
SA: X799; Z: –   Spring   **Rooibloekom**
Large evergreen tree with a short, thick stem and large, spreading crown; invading watercourses. Bark shed in **long, thin strips, exposing smooth, white and reddish patches**. Branchlets reddish. Adult leaves **drooping, lanceolate to narrowly lanceolate**, 80–300 x 7–20 mm, pale grey-green, hairless, **aromatic** when crushed; juvenile leaves 130–260 x 45–80 mm; petiole **reddish**. Flowers in stalked, axillary, 7–11-flowered clusters, **cream to whitish**, with numerous, exerted stamens; buds spherical, with a hemispherical lid narrowing into a slender tip. Fruit a capsule, subglobose, up to 8 mm long, reddish brown to brown, with prominent rims and protruding valves.
A native of Australia; cultivated for shelter, timber, firewood and ornament. Bees produce a good honey from the floral nectar.
At least three other eucalypts also occur as invaders in the Western Cape. *E. cladocalyx* is a tall, slender tree with smooth bark (except at base) which is quite colourful, with patches of grey, cream, yellowish and bluish grey. *E. diversicolor* is a tall, dense, massively branched tree with bark that is smooth to ground level, bronze or yellowish white. *E. lehmannii* (**2.1**) is a small to medium-sized tree which tends to branch near ground level. Its flowers are greenish yellow and fused into large globose clusters; the buds are capped with elongated, curved, finger-like lids, up to 50 mm long.

OCHNACEAE (see page 28)

3 *Ochna pulchra*   **Peeling plane**
SA: 483; Z: 706   Spring   **Lekkerbreek**
Small deciduous tree, sometimes a dwarf shrublet; occurring in bushveld, often on sandy soil. Bark pale grey, **peeling to reveal smooth, cream patches**; branchlets **brittle** and **without lenticels**. Leaves elliptic to oblanceolate, fresh light green to yellowish green, shiny, **hairless, many-veined**; apex **broadly tapering to almost rounded**; margin may be very slightly toothed towards apex. Flowers in terminal racemes, **pale yellow or greenish yellow**, sweetly scented, falling very early, appearing with the new leaves in spring. Fruit flower-like, comprising 1–3 separate kidney-shaped carpels which ripen shiny black, surrounded by the **pink to reddish, persistent and enlarged sepals**.
The wood is pale brown with a curious papery feel when planed smooth (said to rustle faintly when slightly touched); suitable for small ornaments. Seeds yield an unpleasant-smelling greenish brown oil which is used to make soap.

C. viminales: flowers

E. camaldulensis: bark

E. camaldulensis: flowers

O. pulchra: bark

O. pulchra: flowers

E. lehmannii: flowers & buds

O. pulchra: fruit

OLACACEAE (see page 28)

1 Olax dissitiflora — Small sourplum
SA: 101; Z: 90   Spring — Kleinsuurpruim
Deciduous scrambling shrub or small tree with **lax drooping** branches; occurring in low-altitude bushveld, often along streams and on rocky outcrops. Branches **green**, somewhat **4-angled**. Leaves **ovate to narrowly ovate, 15–50 x 5–25 mm**, glossy fresh green above, paler green below, hairless, usually **folded upwards** along midrib; apex **sharply tapering**; base **rounded**; petiole slender, **3–8 mm long**. Flowers solitary or in axillary clusters or racemes, small, white. Fruit a drupe, round or oval, **up to 10 mm long**, orange to red when ripe, the base enveloped by the persistent calyx.

The plant is browsed by game. Leaves used medicinally. Larval food plant for the butterfly *Hypolycaena caeculus*.

2 Olax obtusifolia — Large-fruited sourplum
Z: 91   Spring — Grootvrugsuurpruim
Shrub or small tree; occurring in hot, low-altitude bushveld, particularly in the Zambezi Valley. Branches **rust-coloured**. Leaves ovate to elliptic, **40–80 x 20–40 mm**, thinly textured, dull green above, paler green below, hairless; apex **broadly tapering**; base rounded; petiole very short, **up to 2 mm long**. Flowers axillary, solitary or in clusters, small, creamy white. Fruit a drupe, round or oval, **about 25 mm in diameter**, yellowish orange when ripe, base enveloped by the persistent calyx.

Larval food plant for the butterfly *Hypolycaena caeculus*.

PITTOSPORACEAE (see page 29)

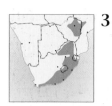

3 Pittosporum viridiflorum — Cheesewood
SA: 139; Z: 155   Summer — Kasuur
Small to medium-sized tree, deciduous or evergreen; occurring along forest margins, in bush clumps and in bushveld, often on rocky outcrops. Leaves usually ovate to broadly oblanceolate, very variable in size, **shiny dark green** above, paler green below, more or less hairless, with a **resinous smell** when crushed; apex **rounded to shortly tapering**; base tapering; margin usually **wavy**. Flowers in branched terminal heads or panicles, small, creamy yellow, sweetly scented. Fruit a capsule, 5–10 mm in diameter, yellowish brown, dehiscent; seeds covered by a **sticky, bright orange-red** covering.

The bark smells of liquorice, bitter-tasting, used medicinally. Seeds much favoured by birds.

PODOCARPACEAE (see page 29)

4 Podocarpus falcatus (= *Afrocarpus falcatus*) — Outeniqua yellowwood
SA: 16   Spring–Summer — Outeniekwageelhout
Medium to large evergreen tree; occurring mainly in afromontane forest, occasionally in coastal and sand forest. Bark **flaking in round or rectangular patches**. Leaves twisted at the base, **narrow**, somewhat **sickle-shaped, 30–50 x 3–5 mm**, bluish to yellowish green. Male cones axillary, about 10 x 3 mm. Female cones **without a fleshy receptacle**; seed spherical, about 15 mm in diameter, **yellow**.

The wood is pale yellow and highly prized for furniture. This species is the tallest indigenous South African forest tree, reaching up to 60 m in height.

O. dissitiflora: flowers

O. dissitiflora: fruit

O. obtusifolia: fruit

P. viridiflorum: flowers

P. viridiflorum: fruit & seeds

P. falcatus: male cones

P. falcatus: seed

207

1 *Podocarpus henkelii*   Henkel's yellowwood
SA: 17   Spring–Summer   Henkel-se-geelhout
Medium to large evergreen tree; occurring mainly in afromontane forest. Bark **flaking in long strips**. Leaves held horizontally, **drooping, narrowly lanceolate-elliptic**, long and slender with lamina **tapering from about the middle to the apex, up to 60–300 x 10–13 mm**, glossy dark green above. Male cones axillary, about 30 x 4 mm. Female cones with greenish receptacle, not well developed; seeds spherical, about 25 mm in diameter, olive green.

The wood is yellow, of excellent quality but not widely utilized because of the limited supply. A decorative garden tree.

Easily confused with the juvenile plants and coppice shoots of *P. latifolius*, the middle portion of whose leaves tend to be more or less parallel-sided before abruptly tapering at the end.

2 *Podocarpus latifolius*   Real yellowwood
SA: 18; Z: 8   Winter–Spring   Opregte geelhout
Medium to large evergreen tree; occurring in afromontane and coastal forest. Bark **longitudinally fissured and peeling in strips**. Leaves held horizontally, spreading or somewhat drooping, **narrowly elliptic, 60–150 x 5–13 mm**, glossy dark green, dull bluish green in some areas. Male cones axillary, up to 50 x 5 mm. Female cones with a **fleshy, bright red, pink or reddish purple receptacle**, about 10 mm long; 1 or 2 seeds, spherical, about 15 mm in diameter, blue green, sometimes tinged purplish.

The wood is pale yellow and fine-grained, becoming deep yellow with age, and highly valued for furniture.

Similar to *P. elongatus* (**2.1**) (found in the mountains of the Western Cape, often along streams), a shrub or small tree, generally with smaller (usually 40–60 x 3–5 mm), greyish or bluish green leaves.

POLYGALACEAE (see page 29)
3 *Polygala myrtifolia*   September bush
SA: 302.1   All year   Septemberbossie
Shrub or small tree with a much-branched, rounded crown; occurring in coastal dune bush and along forest margins, often along streams. Leaves **almost sessile**, closely arranged along branches, **narrowly oblong, thinly textured**, bright green, hairless; apex rounded, **bristle-tipped**; base broadly tapering. Flowers in short terminal clusters, showy, mauve to bright purple; lower petal with a **brush-like appendage**. Fruit a flattened capsule, oval, brown.

A decorative garden subject; widely cultivated.

P. henkelii: male cones

P. henkelii: female cones

P. latifolius: male cones

P. elongatus: female cones

P. myrtifolia: flowers

P. latifolius: female cones

P. myrtifolia: flowers

1 *Securidaca longipedunculata* Violet tree
SA: 303; Z: 442 Spring Krinkhout
Small to medium-sized deciduous tree with a rather **sparse upright** crown; occurring in bushveld. Bark pale grey, smooth. Branchlets sometimes spine-tipped. Leaves often in clusters on abbreviated shoots, broadly **oblong to narrowly elliptic**, leathery, grey-green, more or less hairless when mature; apex **rounded**; base narrowly tapering. Flowers in terminal or axillary racemes, pink to lilac or purple, violet-scented, produced with the new leaves. Fruit a round nut with a **distinct membranous wing** up to 40 mm long, purplish green, drying pale brown.
  Roots extremely poisonous; they also contain methyl salicylate, and have the smell of oil of wintergreen; widely used medicinally, as are the leaves. Bark used to make soap, and it yields a durable fibre.

PROTEACEAE (see page 29)

2 *Faurea rochetiana* (= *F. speciosa*) Broad-leaved beech
SA: 76; Z: 79 Autumn–Winter Breëblaarboekenhout
Small to medium-sized deciduous tree with a crooked trunk, greyish crown and reddish autumn colours; occurring in high-altitude grassland and woodland, usually in mistbelt areas. Branchlets **velvety**. Leaves oblong to elliptic, **up to 170 x 60 mm**, green above, densely covered **with greyish velvety hairs** below; margin **wavy**; petiole up to 12 mm long, thick and hairy. Flowers in **pendulous spikes** up to 250 mm long, cream, often tinged with pink. Fruit a nutlet, hairy, tipped with persistent style.
  The root is used medicinally.

3 *Faurea rubriflora* Manica beechwood
Z: 77 Autumn Manicaboekenhout
Medium to large tree; occurring in forest and along forest margins in mountainous areas, often along streams. Branchlets often **reddish**. Leaves narrowly elliptic, **up to 125 x 20 mm**, **hairless**; margin **wavy**; venation often **reddish**; petiole often dark maroon. Flowers in **pendulous spikes** up to 200 mm long, **pink to pale red**, very attractive. Fruit a nutlet, hairy and with short wings, tipped with persistent style.
  Previously referred to as *F. forficuliflora*.

4 *Faurea saligna* Transvaal beech
SA: 75; Z: 78 Spring–Summer Transvaalboekenhout
Small to medium-sized semi-deciduous tree with an erect trunk and narrow crown with somewhat **drooping** foliage (resembles a eucalypt); occurring in bushveld, often on sandy soils. Bark dark grey-brown to almost black, deeply longitudinally fissured. Leaves narrowly elliptic, **slightly sickle-shaped, up to 125 x 20 mm**, drooping, almost **hairless**; margin **wavy**; petiole **up to 20 mm long, reddish**. Flowers in **pendulous spikes** up to 150 mm long, **sessile**, greenish to cream white. Fruit a nutlet, hairy, tipped with persistent style.
  The wood is reddish brown, attractively figured and suitable as a general purpose timber; makes beautiful furniture. Bark used for tanning leather.
  F. delevoyi, a woodland species from Zimbabwe, has a more spreading crown and very short-stalked or sessile leaves which are up to 50 mm wide. *F. galpinii*, a small tree found in high-altitude mistbelt areas, has erect flowering spikes and short-stalked flowers.

S. *longipedunculata*: flowers

S. *longipedunculata*: fruit

S. *longipedunculata*: bark

F. *rochetiana*: flowers

F. *rochetiana*: fruit

F. *rubriflora*: flowers

F. *saligna*: tree

F. *saligna*: fruit

1 *Leucadendron eucalyptifolium*   Tall yellowbush
SA: 81   Winter–Spring   Grootgeelbos
Shrub or small tree; sexes separate, on different plants; occurring in mountainous fynbos and at forest margins, often in dense, extensive stands on sandy soils. Leaves **stalkless, linear-lanceolate, up to 105 x 8 mm**, with soft hairs at first, becoming hairless with age; base often **twisted**. Male flowers in conical heads surrounded by a cup of **yellow** bracts; female flowers in silvery green, ovoid heads, surrounded by **yellow** bracts. Fruit a winged nutlet, produced in cones up to 45 x 20 mm.

2 *Leucospermum conocarpodendron*   Tree pincushion
SA: 84   Spring–Summer   Kreupelhout
Rounded shrub or small tree; occurring in mountainous areas and coastal dunes, often in dense stands. Branches often somewhat **crooked and interlocking** (hence Afrikaans common name). Leaves stalkless, **oblong to obovate**, greyish silver and densely covered with minute woolly hairs (subsp. *conocarpodendron*), or deep green and more or less smooth when mature (subsp. *viridum*); apex **rounded** with 3–10 often **reddish glandular teeth**; base tapering. Flowerhead globose to ovoid, usually borne in groups of 3. Flowers yellow; styles up to 55 mm long. Fruit a small nut, brownish, released 1–2 months after flowering.
The bark was once used in the tanning of leather. An attractive cut flower.

3 *Leucospermum reflexum*   Rocket pincushion
SA: –   Spring–Summer   Perdekop
Rounded shrub or small tree; occurring in mountain fynbos, usually on sandstone and near streams, often in dense stands. Branchlets conspicuously **hairy**. Leaves **stalkless, elliptic to oblanceolate, grey, densely covered with crispy hairs**; apex **broadly tapering to rounded**, with 2 or 3 **glandular teeth**. Flowerhead terminal, solitary. Flowers deep orange to crimson (var. *reflexum*), rarely pale yellow (var. *luteum*); styles and flowers initially erect or spreading, **sharply reflexing backwards and downwards** with age. Fruit a small nut, brownish, released 1–2 months after flowering.
Widely cultivated in gardens and for the cut-flower trade.

4 *Protea angolensis*   Northern sugarbush
Z: 80   Autumn–Winter   Noordelike suikerbos
Dwarf, multistemmed shrub or small straggling tree; occurring in open wooded grassland and *Brachystegia* woodland. Leaves **oblanceolate to elliptic, up to 160 x 80 mm**, green to bluish green, **leathery, hairless**. Flowerhead solitary, up to 100 x 120 mm; involucral bracts pale green to bright pink or red, inner series sparsely to densely covered with silk hairs; flowers white to dark pink. Fruit a nut, densely hairy. Var. *angolensis* is a dwarf plant usually less than 1 m high, whereas var. *divaricata* is usually a small tree that grows up to about 4 m.
Larval food plant for the butterflies *Capys disjunctus* and *C. connexivus*.

L. eucalyptifolium: male flowerheads

L. conocarpodendron: tree

L. conocarpodendron: flowerhead

L. reflexum: flowerheads

P. angolensis: flowerheads

1 Protea aurea   Long-bud sugarbush
SA: 90.3 All year   Geelsuikerkan
Shrub or small tree with a single trunk; occurring in mountain fynbos, usually in
dense stands on cool, moist, southern slopes. Leaves **oblong to ovate**, up to 90 x
40 mm; base **cordate**. Flowerhead solitary, **up to 120 mm long**, resembling a
shuttlecock on opening; involucral bracts creamy green to bright red, inner series
oblong, up to 90 x 14 mm. Fruit a nut, densely hairy. Most material belongs to
subsp. *aurea*. Subsp. *potbergensis* has large ovate leaves which, when young, are
markedly hairy; the subspecies is rare, restricted to the Potberg.
    A fast growing and adaptable plant in cultivation, although rather short-lived
(about 8 years).

2 Protea caffra (= *P. multibracteata*)   **Common sugarbush**
SA: 87; Z: 83   Spring–Summer   **Gewone suikerbos**
Shrub or small tree; occurring in open or wooded grassland, usually in large
colonies on rocky ridges. Leaves **narrowly oblong**, up to 250 x 45 mm, pale green
to bluish green, **leathery, hairless**. Flowerhead solitary or in clusters of 3 or 4, up
to 80 mm in diameter; involucral bracts pale red, pink or cream, inner series **oblong
to oblong-spatulate** up to 50 x 20 mm. Fruit a nut, densely hairy. A very variable
species, with several subspecies.
    The bark is used medicinally. Larval food plant for the butterflies *Capys disjunctus* and *C. penningtoni*.

3 Protea eximia   Broad-leaved sugarbush
SA: 88.3 Winter–Summer   Breëblaarsuikerbos
Shrub or small tree; occurring in mountain fynbos, often in extensive stands on
sandy soils. Leaves spreading, **oblong to broadly ovate**, **up to 100 x 65 mm**, green
to bluish green, **hairless** when mature; base **cordate**. Flowerhead solitary, obconic,
up to 140 x 120 mm; involucral bracts orange brown to dark pink, outer series with
margin brown, inner series spoon- or tongue-shaped, **widely spaced**, up to 100 x
15 mm; flowers with awns covered in **purple-black**, velvety hairs. Fruit a nut,
densely covered with hairs.
    A commonly cultivated garden plant.
    Similar to *P. compacta* (Kleinmond to Bredasdorp Mountains), one of the best
known proteas in the cut-flower trade; its leaves are curved upward; the outer
involucral bracts are usually without a broad brown margin.

4 Protea magnifica (= *P. barbigera*)   Bearded sugarbush
SA: 86.1 Winter–Summer   Baardsuikerbos
Shrub or small tree; occurring in high-altitude mountain fynbos, usually in dense
stands on steep, rocky, hot and arid slopes, often covered with snow in early spring.
Stems blue-green and hairless when mature. Leaves variable, oblong to oblanceolate, up to 210 x 60 mm, **blue-green**, hairless when mature; margin **horny, wavy,
red to yellow**. Flowerhead solitary, cup-shaped, up to 150 mm in diameter; involucral bracts with **silky hairs**, variable in colour, greenish cream, cream, pink to deep
carmine, tipped with **dense white, pinkish, black, tawny brown or purple-black
beard**. Fruit a nut, densely covered with hairs.

P. aurea: flowerhead

P. aurea: flowerhead

P. eximia: flowerhead

P. caffra: tree

P. caffra: flowerheads

P. caffra: flowerhead

P. magnifica: flowerhead

1 Protea mundii   White sugarbush
SA: 93   Summer–Autumn   Witsuikerbos
Shrub or small to medium-sized tree; occurring in mountain fynbos and as a pioneer along evergreen forest margins, usually in dense stands in permanently moist places. Leaves elliptic to elliptic-lanceolate, up to 120 x 40 mm, **bright green**, hairless when mature. Flowerhead solitary, **small (up to 80 x 65 mm)**, oblong to narrowly obconic; involucral bracts usually creamy white, rarely pink, inner series oblong, up to 40 x 15 mm, with **white to tawny silky fringes**. Fruit a nut, densely covered with hairs.

2 Protea neriifolia   Blue sugarbush
SA: 93.1   Summer–Spring   Blousuikerbos
Shrub or small tree; occurring on sandy soils in fynbos, usually in dense stands on south-facing slopes. Stems hairless when mature. Leaves sessile, **curved upwards**, elliptic with parallel margins, green or blue-grey, hairless when mature. Flowerhead solitary, **oblong to obconic**, up to 130 x 80 mm; involucral bracts cream to pink or carmine, inner series oblong to spatulate, tips **incurved**, rounded with **white or black beard**. Fruit a nut, densely covered with hairs.
    A highly adaptable garden ornamental with many cultivars; extensively grown for cut flowers.
    Similar to *P. laurifolia* **(2.1)** , which has a more westerly distribution and leaves typically grey to bluish green, elliptic, shortly stalked, with heavy horny margins.

3 Protea nitida (= *P. arborea*)   Wagon tree
SA: 86   All year   Waboom
Shrub or small to medium-sized gnarled tree with a whitish trunk; new growth flushes brilliant crimson; occurring in fynbos, usually in rocky places, often forming an open woodland. Leaves **oblong to elliptic**, up to 180 x 60 mm, **olive-green to bluish green**, leathery, **hairless**. Flowerhead solitary, **globose**, up to 160 mm in diameter; involucral bracts creamy white, rarely pink, inner series oblong, up to 45 x 20 mm; flowers **projecting beyond involucral bracts** in bud. Fruit a nut, densely covered with hairs.
    The leaves are used to make ink. Bark used medicinally and for tanning leather. Wood red-brown with an attractive grain, once extensively used for wagon wheel-rim pieces and brake blocks, and for furniture. It produces excellent firewood.

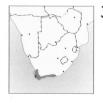

4 Protea obtusifolia   Bredasdorp sugarbush
SA: 94   Autumn–Spring   Bredasdorpsuikerbos
Rounded shrub or small tree; occurring in coastal fynbos, usually in dense stands on limestone hills and flats. Leaves **curved upwards**, oblanceolate to elliptic, up to 150 x 40 mm, leathery, hairless when mature. Flowerhead solitary, oblong-obconic, up to 120 x 80 mm; involucral bracts creamy white to deep carmine, inner series **lanceolate to spatulate**, hairless except for a margin **densely fringed with whitish hairs**. Fruit a nut, densely covered with hairs.
    An attractive garden species; tolerates alkaline soils, but sensitive to frost.
    Often associated with *P. susannae* **(4.1)**. Its crushed leaves have a distinctive sulphurous odour and the outer involucral bracts a slightly sticky, dark brown, varnish-like coating.

P. mundii: tree

P. neriifolia: flowerhead

P. mundii: flowerheads

P. laurifolia: flowerheads

P. nitida: flowerhead

P. obtusifolia: flowerhead

P. susannae: flowerhead

217

1 **Protea petiolaris**   Sickle-leaf sugarbush
Z: 84   Spring–Summer   **Sekelblaarsuikerbos**
Small to medium-sized straggling tree; occurring in mountain grassland and high-altitude *Brachystegia* woodland, usually in wet and rocky places. Leaves crowded at ends of branches, **distinctly stalked and drooping**, broadly lanceolate and **markedly sickle-shaped, up to 160 x 30 mm**, green, leathery, **hairless**; petiole **up to 20 mm long**. Flowerhead solitary, up to 120 mm in diameter; involucral bracts green to red, outer series with a white, powdery coating, inner series **widely spaced**, up to 50 mm long, fringed with **white hairs**. Fruit a nut, densely covered with hairs. All the southern African material belongs to subsp. *elegans*.
Larval food plant for the butterfly *Capys disjunctus*.

2 **Protea repens** (= *P. mellifera*)   **Real sugarbush**
SA: 94.2   All year   **Opregte suikerbos**
Much-branched shrub or small tree; occurring in fynbos, often in dense stands. Branchlets hairless. Leaves **upright, linear-spatulate to oblanceolate**, up to 150 x 18 mm, green, **hairless**. Flowerhead solitary, **oblong to obconic**, up to 160 x 90 mm; involucral bracts **tightly overlapping**, creamy white, white tipped with pink or red, or bright red to deep plum-coloured, often with a **sticky gum-like coating**, inner series lanceolate. Fruit a nut, densely covered with hairs, retained in a compact, brown seedhead.
Widely cultivated as a garden ornamental and for the cut-flower trade. Flowerheads produce abundant nectar, which was once collected and cooked to produce a thick brown or amber-coloured syrup known as *bossiestroop*. The syrup has been used as a sweetening agent and for curing coughs and other chest complaints. Larval food plant for the butterfly *Capys alphaeus*.

3 **Protea roupelliae** subsp. *roupelliae*   **Silver sugarbush**
SA: 96   All year   **Silwersuikerbos**
Small to medium-sized tree, often with **silvery** foliage; occurring on grassy hills and mountain slopes, often forming an open woodland. Leaves **curved upwards**, linear-lanceolate to obovate, up to 170 x 50 mm, **silvery-haired** to hairless. Flowerhead **goblet-shaped**, solitary, up to 120 x 100 mm; involucral bracts pink, creamy yellow or brownish, sparsely to densely covered with silvery, silky hairs, outer series with the tips **brown, recurved, with splitting margins**, inner series **spoon-shaped**. Fruit a nut, densely covered with hairs. Subsp. *hamiltonii*, a low, sprawling shrublet, is extremely localized at Nelshoogte near Barberton.
A much-favoured source of nectar for Gurney's sugarbird and the malachite sunbird. Larval food plant for the butterfly *Capys alphaeus*.

4 **Protea rubropilosa**   **Transvaal mountain sugarbush**
SA: 97   Spring   **Transvaalse bergsuikerbos**
Small tree with **thick, stout** stems; occurring in open and wooded montane grassland, usually on sandy quartzitic soils in mistbelt areas. Leaves sessile, elliptic-oblanceolate, up to 220 x 65 mm, **dark green with red midrib**, leathery, **hairless**. Flowerhead solitary, up to 90 mm in diameter; involucral bracts with outer surface densely covered with **thick, brown, velvety hairs**, inner surface dark pink to red. Fruit a nut, densely covered with hairs.

P. petiolaris: flowerheads

P. repens: flowerheads

P. roupelliae: flowerhead

P. roupelliae: tree

P. rubropilosa: flowerhead

GROUP 10

1 Protea subvestita SA: 98   Summer–Autumn
Lip-flower sugarbush
Lippeblomsuikerbos

1 **Protea subvestita**   **Lip-flower sugarbush**
SA: 98   Summer–Autumn   **Lippeblomsuikerbos**
Shrub or small tree; occurring in montane grassland, usually gregarious. Leaves **curved upwards**, elliptic to lanceolate, **up to 110 x 35 mm**, densely covered with **shaggy to woolly hairs**, becoming hairless when mature. Flowerhead solitary, **up to 70 x 40 mm**; involucral bracts carmine, pink or creamy white, inner series with tips **bending outwards and even downwards**, margin fringed with long, white, silky hairs. Fruit a nut, densely covered with hairs.

Unlike other grassland proteas, the species does not survive burning, and has to regenerate from seed. Larval food plant for the butterfly *Capys alphaeus*.

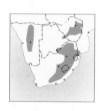

2 **Protea welwitschii**   **Cluster-head sugarbush**
SA: 98.2; Z: 85   Summer–Autumn   **Troshofiesuikerbos**
Spreading multistemmed shrub or small gnarled tree; occurring in grassland and bushveld, often in rocky places. Leaves elliptic to broadly oblanceolate, up to 120 x 95 mm, **bluish green**, densely covered with white or brown hairs, tending to be **hairless when mature except at the base**. Flowerheads usually in **clusters of 3 to 4**, up to 60 mm in diameter; involucral bracts white to pale cream, with silky hairs, inner series oblong, up to 50 x 15 mm. Fruit a nut, densely covered with hairs.

P. gaguedi (**2.1**) has hairless mature leaves and flowerheads which are usually solitary, up to 110 mm in diameter.

SANTALACEAE (see page 31)

3 **Osyris quadripartita** (= *O. lanceolata*)   **Transvaal sumach**
SA: 100; Z: 87   Summer–Winter   **Bergbas**
Evergreen shrub or small slender tree with sparse blue-green foliage; probably a root parasite; occurring in bushveld and wooded grassland, often on rocky hill slopes. Bark grey, **smooth**. Leaves **oval**, up to 35 x 17–27 mm, **thick and leathery**, **blue green with a grey bloom**, hairless; petiole about 2 mm long. Flowers in axillary clusters, small, yellowish green. Fruit a drupe, oval, about 15 x 10 mm, **crowned with the persistent calyx**, ripening bright red to purplish black.

Similar to *Osyris compressa* (Group 23), a coastal species with opposite leaves and terminal flowerheads. Larval food plant for the butterfly *Mylothris agathina*.

SAPINDACEAE (see page 31)

4 **Dodonaea angustifolia** (= *D. viscosa*)   **Sand olive**
SA: 437; Z: 609   Autumn–Winter   **Sandolien**
Shrub or small tree, usually **multistemmed**; occurring in open areas associated with forest, bushveld, wooded grassland, karroid vegetation and fynbos. Leaves **narrowly elliptic**, shiny light green above, paler green below, often **sticky and resinous**, somewhat rough to the touch; petiole up to 10 mm long. Flowers in axillary or terminal groups, small, greenish yellow. Fruit a capsule with **2 or 3 membranous, papery wings**, about 20 mm in diameter, yellowish green, often tinged with pink or red.

The leaves and root are used medicinally. Widely used to consolidate sandy areas.

220

P. subvestita: flowerhead

P. gaguedi: flowerheads

P. welwitschii: flowerheads

O. quadripartita: flowers

D. angustifolia: flowers

O. quadripartita: fruit

D. angustifolia: fruit

1 *Pappea capensis*   Jacket-plum
SA: 433; Z: 605   Summer–Autumn   Doppruim
Small to medium-sized deciduous tree with a spreading, often intricately branched crown; sexes separate, on different plants; occurring in bushveld, wooded grassland, valley bushveld and karroid vegetation. Branchlets with **short brownish hairs**. Leaves often crowded near ends of branches, oblong to rounded, leathery, rough to the touch, dull green above, paler green below; venation **yellowish, raised below**; apex and base **rounded**; margin entire or closely spine-toothed, particularly in juvenile growth. Flowers in axillary and terminal drooping spikes, greenish yellow. Fruit a capsule, up to 3-lobed, up to 20 mm in diameter, **furry-green**, splitting to reveal a shiny black seed enclosed by a **fleshy, orange-red appendage**.
   The tree is heavily browsed by game and stock. Fleshy cover of seeds edible and makes a delicious jam. Seeds yield an oil which is edible, and is also used medicinally and for soap-making. Bark used medicinally.

SOLANACEAE (see page 32)

2 •*Nicotiana glauca*   Wild tobacco
SA: X967; Z: 1022   All year   Wildetabak
Slender evergreen shrub or small tree, with a sparse crown and **blue-green** appearance; invading roadsides, road cuttings, waste places, riverbanks and riverbeds. Leaves **ovate to elliptic**, up to 200 x 120 mm, **leathery**, blue-green, **hairless**; base **asymmetric**. Flowers in terminal **drooping** clusters, tubular, 30–50 mm long, yellow. Fruit a capsule, oval, about 15 mm long, dehiscing with 4 valves.
   A native of South America; cultivated for ornament.

STERCULIACEAE (see page 32)

3 *Cola natalensis*   Coshwood
SA: 478   Spring   Knuppelhout
Small to medium-sized tree with rather **drooping** leaves; occurring in evergreen coastal forest. Branchlets **more or less hairless** when mature. Leaves elliptic, dark green above, pale green below; petiole **up to 50 mm long**, with conspicuous **hairless swelling just below the leaf blade**. Flowers in axillary clusters, small, yellowish with reddish brown hairs on the outside. Fruit fleshy, comprising 2–5 carpels joined in a ring, warty, with short hairs and orange when ripe.
   In *C. greenwayi* (**3.1**) (from Maputaland northwards) the branchlets and swelling below the leaf blade are covered with brownish hairs.

THYMELAEACEAE (see page 32)

4 *Peddiea africana*   Poison olive
SA: 517; Z: 757   Spring–Summer   Gifolyf
Shrub or small tree, with very shiny, pale green new growth; occurring in forest and on forest margins, often **in deep shade**. Stems with very **tough, fibrous bark**. Leaves **clustered near ends** of branches, elliptic, obovate to lanceolate, glossy dark green above, paler glossy green below, hairless; petiole **very short** with decurrent leaf base, **purplish red**. Flowers in stalked axillary clusters of 3–10, tubular, green to yellowish green, often tinged reddish or maroon. Fruit a berry, **ovoid**, about 10 x 7 mm, sometimes tipped with a small tuft of creamy hairs, reddish purple to black.
   The bark yields a strong fibre which is used as cordage.

P. capensis: flowers

P. capensis: fruit & seed

N. glauca: flowers

C. natalensis: flowers

P. africana: fruit

C. natalensis: fruit

P. africana: flowers

C. greenwayi: flowers

C. greenwayi: fruit

GROUP 11

Leaves simple, alternate or in tufts, not bilobed; blade prominently
2–7- veined from base. Latex absent.

See also Group 8: *Dovyalis zeyheri* (p. 128).

ARALIACEAE (see page 20)

1 *Cussonia natalensis*   **Rock cabbage tree**
SA: 562; Z: 814   Autumn–Spring   **Rotskiepersol**
Sturdy, small to medium-sized deciduous tree with a rounded crown and yellow
autumn colours; occurring in bushveld, usually in rocky places. Leaves deeply **3–5-
lobed, 50–150 mm wide**, glossy green, hairless; margin **bluntly toothed**. Flowers
in terminal heads of radiating **cylindrical spikes**, each up to 150 mm long, greenish yellow. Fruit fleshy, about 4 mm in diameter, crowded on spikes, purplish.
The leaves are used medicinally.

BORAGINACEAE (see page 21)

2 *Cordia pilosissima*   **Woolly saucer-berry**
SA: –; Z: 972   Summer   **Wollerige pieringbessie**
Scandent shrub or small tree; occurring in hot, low-altitude bushveld, mainly confined to the Zambezi Valley. Branchlets densely **covered with hairs**. Leaves **ovate
to almost circular, 80–160 x 70–160 mm**, densely covered **with soft hairs**; venation **prominently raised below**; margin entire or obscurely scalloped. Flowers in
terminal heads, white, cream or pale yellow. Fruit a berry, ovoid and sharp-tipped,
up to 25 mm long, yellow-orange, surrounded by the **enlarged, persistent calyx**.
The plant is heavily browsed by elephant.
C. grandicalyx (Group 9, p. 136) has leaves with harsh hairs.

EUPHORBIACEAE (see page 24)

3 *Acalypha glabrata*   **Forest false-nettle**
SA: 335.1; Z: 500   Spring–Summer   **Bosvalsnetel**
Shrub or small tree with long slender branches, usually **multistemmed**; occurring in
forest and bushveld, often in dense stands. Branchlets **velvety**. Leaves **ovate, 20–80
x 12–45 mm, thinly textured**, hairless or velvety; margin roughly **toothed to scalloped**. Flowers in axillary spikes up to 40 mm long, male ones terminal, female ones
towards base, yellowish green. Fruit a **3-lobed** capsule, about 7 mm in diameter.
The plant is browsed by game and stock. Its branches are used to make fish traps.
Larval food plant for the butterfly *Neptis scalava marpessa*.

FLACOURTIACEAE (see page 25)

4 *Dovyalis longispina*   **Natal apricot**
SA: 510.1   Spring   **Natalappelkoos**
Small to medium-sized tree; sexes separate, on different plants; occurring in coastal
dune forest. Branches with **slender straight spines up to 80 mm long**. Leaves elliptic to obovate, 20–90 x 13–60 mm, **3–5-veined** from base; margin entire, **rolled
under**. Flowers in axillary clusters, small, yellowish white. Fruit a berry, oval, up to
15 mm long, bright orange to red, **flecked with white**, with **persistent calyx**.
The fruit is edible, tasty but slightly acid.
D. caffra (Group 8, p. 126) has rounder leaves in clusters and yellow fruit.

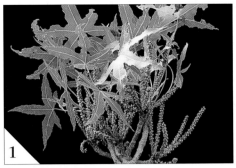

C. natalensis: flowers

C. natalensis: fruit

C. pilosissima: flowers

A. glabrata: male flowers

male & female flowers

D. longispina: flowers

D. longispina: fruit

1 *Dovyalis rhamnoides*   Common sourberry
SA: 509   Winter   Gewone suurbessie
Small to medium-sized tree; occurring in coastal and inland forest. Branches hairy when young, armed with **slender straight spines up to 70 mm long**. Leaves arranged **horizontally, ovate**, 13–30 x 13–20 mm, usually **3–5-veined** from base, **thinly textured**, covered **with rough hairs when young**; margin entire or obscurely toothed, wavy. Flowers solitary or in axillary clusters, small, yellowish white. Fruit a berry, oval, up to 13 mm long, bright red, with **persistent calyx** at base.
The fruit is edible, tasty, and used to make a jelly preserve, brandy and vinegar. Wood formerly used for ox-yokes, wagons and agricultural implements. Various parts used medicinally. Larval food plant for the butterfly *Phalanta eurytis*.

2 *Trimeria grandifolia*   Wild mulberry
SA: 503; Z: 737   Summer   Wildemoerbei
Scandent shrub or small tree; occurring in forest and on forest margins. Leaves **obovate to almost round, 40–130 x 40–130 mm, 5–9-veined** from base, more or less hairless; margin **finely toothed**; petiole up to 30 mm long, moved by the slightest breeze. Flowers in axillary clusters (male) or in spike-like racemes (female), very small, greenish white. Fruit a capsule, oval, about 5 mm long, yellow, splitting into 3 segments.
Various parts of the plant are used medicinally. Larval food plant for the butterfly *Phalanta phalantha aethiopica*.
T. trinervis (**2.1**), a small forest tree from KwaZulu-Natal and the Eastern Cape, has small (20–50 x 13–25 mm) ovate to lanceolate leaves which are conspicuously 3-veined from the base, and pinkish petioles.

GREYIACEAE (see page 25)
3 *Greyia radlkoferi*   Transvaal bottlebrush
SA: 445   Winter–Spring   Transvaalse baakhout
Shrub or small **deciduous** tree; occurring in wooded grassland in forest areas, often in rocky places. Leaves ovate, **up to 100 x 90 mm**, more or less hairless above, **densely covered with yellowish white woolly hairs below**; base tapering; margin **toothed**; petiole with base **clasping** the stem. Flowers in terminal racemes, red, more or less **horizontal**, with **spreading petals**. Fruit a capsule, cylindrical.
The plant is occasionally cultivated by gardeners.
G. flanaganii (**3.1**) is a rare evergreen shrub or small tree restricted to the Eastern Cape. It has smaller leaves (50–80 x 50–80 mm), drooping pinkish red flowers, and petals which are not spreading.

4 *Greyia sutherlandii*   Natal bottlebrush
SA: 446   Spring   Natalse baakhout
Shrub or small **deciduous** tree; occurring in montane grassland, often in rocky places and associated with forest patches. Leaves ovate-oblong to almost circular, **up to 100 x 110 mm**, with **sparse hairs or smooth**; margin **toothed**; petiole with base **clasping** the stem. Flowers in terminal racemes, red, more or less **horizontal**, with **spreading** petals. Fruit a capsule, cylindrical.
The wood is pale brown, light, used for carvings and household utensils. Widely cultivated in gardens.

D. rhamnoides: flowers

T. trinervis: male flowers

T. grandifolia: female flowers

T. grandifolia: fruit

G. radlkoferi: flowers

G. radlkoferi: leaves

G. flanaganii: flowers

G. radlkoferi: fruit

G. sutherlandii: flowers

G. sutherlandii: fruit

227

HERNANDIACEAE (see page 25)

1 *Gyrocarpus americanus*   **Propeller tree**
SA: 120; Z: 122   Autumn   **Helikopterboom**
Small to medium-sized deciduous tree; occurring in hot, arid, low-altitude bushveld, usually on rocky ridges. Bark **grey to whitish, smooth.** Leaves **almost circular** in outline, usually **3-lobed,** about 100 x 100 mm, **soft-textured,** dark green above, **pale greyish below;** margin entire. Flowers in dense heads or racemes, small, yellowish green, unpleasantly scented. Fruit a nut, with **2 long, thin wings, drooping,** spinning like a helicopter when falling to the ground.
The bark and root are used medicinally.

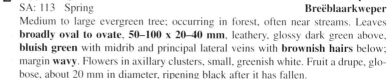

LAURACEAE (see page 25)

2 *Cryptocarya latifolia*   **Broad-leaved quince**
SA: 113   Spring   **Breëblaarkweper**
Medium to large evergreen tree; occurring in forest, often near streams. Leaves **broadly oval to ovate, 50–100 x 20–40 mm,** leathery, glossy dark green above, **bluish green** with midrib and principal lateral veins with **brownish hairs** below; margin **wavy.** Flowers in axillary clusters, small, greenish white. Fruit a drupe, globose, about 20 mm in diameter, ripening black after it has fallen.
The bark is used medicinally and for magical purposes, often as an alternative to *Ocotea bullata.* Fast-growing tree for inland gardens; tolerates mild frost.

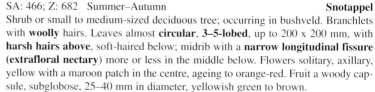

MALVACEAE (see page 26)

3 *Azanza garckeana*   **Snot apple**
SA: 466; Z: 682   Summer–Autumn   **Snotappel**
Shrub or small to medium-sized deciduous tree; occurring in bushveld. Branchlets with **woolly** hairs. Leaves almost **circular, 3–5-lobed,** up to 200 x 200 mm, with **harsh hairs above,** soft-haired below; midrib with a **narrow longitudinal fissure (extrafloral nectary)** more or less in the middle below. Flowers solitary, axillary, yellow with a maroon patch in the centre, ageing to orange-red. Fruit a woody capsule, subglobose, 25–40 mm in diameter, yellowish green to brown.
The fruit is edible while still green and juicy; the seeds and rind are discarded. When chewed the flesh is sweet and glutinous. Bark provides fibre. The wood is attractive, fine-grained, with yellow sapwood and deep brown heartwood.

4 *Hibiscus tiliaceus*   **Wild cotton tree**
SA: 464   Spring–Summer   **Wildekatoenboom**
Shrub or small tree; occurring **along the coast,** fringing lagoons and rivers. Branchlets densely covered in hairs. Leaves almost **circular, up to 150 x 150 mm,** olive green above, **velvety white to greyish below;** venation **prominent below,** each of the principal veins with a narrow, **elongated gland (extrafloral nectary)** near the base. Flowers large, yellow with a dark maroon centre, ageing to orange-red, dropping after one day. Fruit a capsule, ovoid, up to 25 mm long, covered with golden hairs.
The bark yields a fibre. Larval food plant for the butterfly *Abantis paradisea.*
H. diversifolius is a scrambling shrub or small tree from coastal and riverine vegetation along the eastern seaboard and from the western Zambezi River Valley. It has young branches densely covered with prickles, leaves with 3–7 distinct lobes, and yellow, reddish or purple flowers with a deep reddish purple centre.

228

G. americanus: flowers

C. latifolia: flowers

G. americanus: fruit

A. garckeana: flower

A. garckeana: fruit

H. tiliaceus: fruit

H. tiliaceus: flower (old)

H. tiliaceus: flower

1 *Thespesia acutiloba* Wild tulip tree
SA: 465 Summer–Autumn Wildetulpboom
Shrub or small tree; occurring in bushveld and coastal dune forest. Leaves almost circular in outline, usually **3-lobed and ivy-like, up to 70 x 60 mm**, dark green above, paler green below, **fine-haired**, with **small domatia** in the axils of the principal lateral veins below. Flowers yellow, **not opening fully**. Fruit a capsule, roundish, up to 20 mm in diameter, bright red.

The heartwood is dark brown, hard and durable when seasoned, and is used for carving, for carrying-sticks and for musical instruments.

T. populnea, from coastal areas in Mozambique, has larger (up to 150 x 120 mm) leaves, without fine hairs.

MIMOSACEAE (see page 27)

2 •*Acacia cyclops* Red eye
SA: X489 All year Rooikrans
Evergreen shrub or small tree, with a rounded or wind-clipped crown; invading fynbos, forest gaps, coastal dunes, roadsides and watercourses. Mature leaves (phyllodes) **narrowly elliptic**, 30–90 x 8–15 mm, more or less **straight, 3–5-veined** from the base, bright green. Flowers clustered in globose, axillary **heads**, bright yellow. Pods 8–12 mm wide, not constricted, **curved and finally twisted**, brown, persisting after dehiscence; seeds **black**, encircled by **fleshy, bright red or orange** stalks.

A native of Australia; cultivated for dune reclamation and shelter; provides excellent firewood. This is a declared invader in South Africa.

3 •*Acacia longifolia* Sallow wattle
SA: X493 Winter–Spring Bleekwattel
Evergreen shrub or small, spreading tree; branches usually (at least in the Western and Eastern Cape) with **spherical galls** caused by an introduced wasp (biocontrol); invading fynbos, bushveld and watercourses. Leaves (phyllodes) **linear-lanceolate or narrowly oblong, straight**, 40–180 x 7–20 mm, bright green and hairless, **2–5-veined** from the base; margin with a **small gland on one side** towards base of the blade. Flowers in **cylindrical**, axillary, flowerheads (spikes) up to 50 mm long, bright yellow. Pods constricted between the seeds, sharply pointed, pale brown.

A native of Australia; cultivated for dune reclamation, shade and ornament. This is a declared invader in South Africa.

4 •*Acacia melanoxylon* Blackwood
SA: X495; Z: 212/1 Spring Swarthout
Medium-sized to large evergreen tree, with a straight trunk and dense pyramidal to cylindrical crown; invading forest edges or gaps, wooded ravines, grassland and watercourses. Leaves (phyllodes) linear-lanceolate to oblanceolate, straight to slightly curved, 60–120 x 6–12 mm, **dark dull-green**, hairless, **3–7-veined** from the base; young plants and coppice shoots **often with twice-divided leaves at apex of phyllodes**. Flowers in **globose** flowerheads borne in axillary clusters, pale yellow. Pods slightly constricted between the seeds, reddish brown; seeds brownish black, almost encircled by **pinkish red** seed stalks.

A native of Australia; cultivated for timber, shelter and ornament. This is a declared invader in South Africa.

T. acutiloba: flowers

T. acutiloba: fruit

A. cyclops: fruit

A. cyclops: flowers

A. longifolia: flowers

A. cyclops: seeds

A. longifolia: insect galls

A. melanoxylon: flowers

RHAMNACEAE (see page 30)

1 *Ziziphus abyssinica*   Jujube
Z: 616   Summer   Jujube
Spiny shrub or small tree; occurring in low-altitude bushveld, often along river-banks. Leaves ovate to broadly ovate, up to 80 x 50 mm, **dark green** above, pale green and densely covered **with rusty, grey or yellowish hairs** below; base **markedly asymmetric**; margin **finely toothed**; stipules spinescent, one sharply **hooked downwards**, the other slightly **curved upwards**. Flowers in axillary clusters, small, yellowish green. Fruit a drupe, subglobose, up to 30 mm in diameter, shiny red to reddish brown.
The leaves are used medicinally.

2 *Ziziphus mucronata*   Buffalo-thorn
SA: 447; Z: 618   Summer   Blinkblaarwag-'n-bietjie
Shrub or small to medium-sized tree; occurring in a wide variety of habitats. Leaves **ovate to broadly ovate**, 30–80 x 20–50 mm, **glossy dark green** above, lower surface slightly hairy (subsp. *mucronata*), or with coarse brownish hairs, at least when young (subsp. *rhodesica*); base **markedly asymmetric**; margin **finely toothed over upper two-thirds**; stipules spinescent, one **hooked**, the other **straight**, or plants unarmed. Flowers in axillary clusters, small, yellowish green. Fruit a drupe, subglobose, up to 30 mm in diameter, shiny reddish to yellowish brown.
The leaves are browsed by game and stock. Widely used for magical and medicinal purposes and in traditional religious rituals. Juice from the tree is used by the San as a mixing agent for arrow poison obtained from the larvae of *Diamhidia nigroornata*, a beetle that feeds on the leaves of *Commiphora africana* (Group 28). The fruit is edible but not tasty. Wood hard, heavy and fine-textured, suitable for tool handles, spoons and as a general purpose timber. Larval food plant for the butterflies *Tuxentius calice*, *T. melaena*, *T. hesperis* and *Tarucus sybaris*.
A very variable species; some large-fruited forms are almost spineless when mature.

3 *Ziziphus rivularis*   False buffalo-thorn
SA: 448   Spring–Summer   Valswag-'n-bietjie
Shrub or small **unarmed** tree; occurring in bushveld, usually among rocks along streams. Leaves **lanceolate to ovate-lanceolate**, up to 65 x 35 mm, dark green above, pale green below, **hairless** when mature; base rather **asymmetric**; margin **finely toothed**. Flowers in unstalked axillary clusters, small, yellowish green. Fruit a drupe, globose, about 8 mm in diameter, yellowish brown.

STERCULIACEAE (see page 32)

4 *Dombeya burgessiae*   Pink wild pear
SA: 468.1; Z: 685   Autumn–Winter   Persdrolpeer
Shrub or small tree; occurring along forest margins and in rocky places in high-rainfall regions. Leaves **ovate, large (50–180 x 50–180 mm)**, bluntly 3–5-lobed; **lower surface hairy but not conspicuously pale**. Flowers in many-flowered axillary heads, **pink to white**. Fruit a capsule, velvety, enclosed within dry reddish remains of the perianth, dehiscent.
The bark is used for fibre. An attractive garden plant.
D. pulchra (**4.1**) (mainly from northeastern Drakensberg) has leaves which are silvery or greyish white below, and white flowers, often with a deep pink centre.

1

Z. abyssinica: flowers

2

Z. mucronata: flowers

2

Z. mucronata: fruit

3

Z. rivularis: flowers

3

Z. rivularis: fruit

4

D. burgessiae: flowers

4.1

D. pulchra: flowers

233

1 *Dombeya cymosa* Natal wild pear
SA: 469   Autumn–Spring Nataldrolpeer
Shrub or small deciduous tree; occurring on forest margins and in valley bushveld, often along streams. Bark pale **whitish grey, smooth**. Leaves **ovate, 30–100 x 20–75 mm**, almost hairless; apex tapering to a long sharp tip. Flowers in axillary heads, white, usually **less than 13 mm in diameter**. Fruit a capsule, up to 4 mm in diameter, hairy.

The wood is dark brown, hard, fine-grained, and suitable for small ornaments. Larval food plant for the butterflies *Eagris nottoana* and *Netrobalane canopus*.

D. tiliacea has larger leaves (35–80 x 25–60 mm) and flowers (30–45 mm in diameter), and its bark is darker and rougher.

2 *Dombeya kirkii* River wild pear
SA: 470; Z: 686   Autumn–Winter Rivierdrolpeer
Shrub or small tree; occurring in low-altitude bushveld, usually in riverine thicket. Leaves **broadly ovate, 50–130 x 40–100 mm**, occasionally **shallowly 3-lobed**, with **harsh hairs above**, with sparse and soft hairs below; apex sharply tapering. Flowers in axillary heads towards tips of branches, white, about 13 mm in diameter, produced in profusion. Fruit a capsule, about 5 mm in diameter, silky-haired.

3 *Dombeya rotundifolia* Common wild pear
SA: 471; Z: 687   Winter–Spring Gewone drolpeer
Small deciduous tree; occurring in bushveld. Bark **dark grey-brown, rough and fissured**. Leaves **broadly ovate to almost circular**, 30–150 mm in diameter, dark green and **rough** above, pale green and hairy with **prominent net veins** below. Flowers in axillary clusters before the appearance of the new leaves in early spring, white or pale pink, fading to brown, produced in profusion; ovary **hairy**. Fruit a capsule, about 6 mm in diameter, silky-haired.

The wood is heavy, tough, fine-textured, and used for implement handles and ornaments. Bark, root and wood used medicinally. The bark provides a strong fibre. Flowering period widely used as a seasonal indicator (beginning of spring) in southern Africa. Larval food plant for the butterfly *Caprona pillaana*.

D. autumnalis has smaller leaves, flowers in autumn, and is more or less restricted to the Lydenburg-Ohrigstad area, usually on dolomite. *D. shupangae*, from central Mozambique, has larger leaves (often 80–200 x 80–200 mm) and an ovary covered with minute brown protuberances.

4 *Sterculia africana* African star-chestnut
SA: 474; Z: 689   Spring Afrikaanse sterkastaiing
Small to medium-sized tree, usually **thick-stemmed**; occurring in hot, low-altitude bushveld and semi-desert areas, often on rocky outcrops in mopane veld. Bark **smooth, silvery white or marbled**. Leaves **crowded** near ends of branches, almost **circular** or **3–5-lobed, large (60–150 x 40–130 mm)**; margin entire. Flowers in compact, terminal, spike-like racemes, greenish yellow with **reddish lines**, appearing before the new leaves in spring. Fruit 1–5 boat-shaped carpels, each up to 150 mm long and with a tapering tip, **golden velvety**; seeds blue-grey, tick-like, attached among hairs which are extremely irritating to the skin.

The bark is fibrous, used for mats and ropes.

D. cymosa: flowers

D. rotundifolia: flowers

S. africana: fruit

D. kirkii: flowers

D. rotundifolia: flowers

S. africana: flowers

S. africana: fruit

1 *Sterculia quinqueloba*　　　　　　　Large-leaved star-chestnut
SA: 476; Z: 691　Summer–Autumn　　　　Grootblaarsterkastaiing
Small to medium-sized deciduous tree with yellow autumn colours, usually **thick-stemmed**; occurring in hot, low-altitude bushveld, often on rocky granite hills. Bark rather smooth, cream to pinkish brown. Leaves crowded near ends of branches, broadly ovate and **5-lobed, large (150–400 x 150–400 mm)**; margin entire. Flowers in terminal, many-flowered, branched heads, yellow, appearing with the new leaves in spring. Fruit 5 boat-shaped carpels, each up to 60 mm long and **with a tapering tip**, golden velvety; seeds black, attached among hairs which are irritating to the skin.
　　The wood is reddish brown, suitable for furniture and as a general purpose timber.
　　S. appendiculata (lower Zambezi Valley) has a tall straight trunk with no side branches for 15–20 m. The fruits are bluntly tipped; the seeds are brown with a yellow aril.

2 *Sterculia rogersii*　　　　　　　　Common star-chestnut
SA: 477; Z: 692　Winter–Summer　　　　Gewone sterkastaiing
Small tree, usually **thick-stemmed and branching from low down**; occurring in hot, low-altitude bushveld. Bark grey, **peeling to reveal pink, purplish or creamy yellow patches**. Leaves broadly ovate, more or less **3-lobed, small (30–60 x 20–50 mm)**, softly **velvety** below; margin entire. Flowers solitary or in clusters on the old wood and young branches, greenish yellow with reddish lines, often flushed with pink. Fruit 3–5 boat-shaped carpels, each up to 80 mm long and with a tapering tip, golden velvety; seeds dark grey, inserted among hairs which are irritating to the skin.
　　The tree is browsed by game and stock. The bark yields a good quality fibre. The seeds are edible.

3 *Triplochiton zambesiacus*　　　　　Wine-cup
Z: 688　Summer–Autumn　　　　　　　Wynkelk
Medium to large tree with a rather short bole and leafy crown; occurring on alluvial floodplains in the Zambezi Valley, often associated with termitaria. Leaves almost **circular, 5–9-lobed**, up to 170 x 200 mm, hairless. Flowers axillary or terminal, solitary or in small groups, **large (up to 70 mm in diameter)**, white or yellowish, with a **dark red centre**, showy, opening only in the mornings. Fruit a cluster of 4 or 5 carpels, each with a **large wing**, up to 80 x 35 mm, fine-haired.
　　Leaves are cooked as a green vegetable. Wood once used as yokes for oxen.

TILIACEAE (see page 32)

4 *Grewia bicolor*　　　　　　　　　White raisin
SA: 458; Z: 464　Spring–Summer　　　　Witrosyntjie
Multistemmed shrub or small tree; occurring in bushveld, mainly at low altitude and often associated with mopane. Older stems **roundish**. Leaves elliptic to lanceolate, 15–70 x 13–20 mm, green and more or less hairless above, **silvery white with fine hairs** below; apex tapering to rounded; base broadly tapering to rounded, asymmetric; margin finely toothed. Flowers in axillary clusters, **bright yellow**. Fruit a drupe, **1- or 2-lobed**, each about 6 mm in diameter, reddish brown to purple black.
　　The plant is browsed by game. Bark used medicinally and for fibre. Fresh leaves used to make a a kind of tea. The fruit is edible.

S. quinqueloba: flowers

S. quinqueloba: young fruit

S. rogersii: bark

S. rogersii: flowers & fruit

S. rogersii: fruit

T. zambesiacus: fruit

G. bicolor: flowers

G. bicolor: fruit

1 *Grewia caffra*   Climbing raisin

SA: 459; Z: 647   Summer–Autumn   Rankrosyntjie

Robust climber, scandent multistemmed shrub or small tree; occurring in low-altitude bushveld and thicket, often along the banks of rivers. Older stems **4-angled**. Leaves oblong-ovate to lanceolate, 20–50 x 10–25 mm, green, hairless or very sparsely stellate on both sides; apex tapering; base broadly tapering to rounded; margin finely toothed. Flowers in axillary clusters, **yellow**. Fruit a drupe, **globose**, 7–10 mm in diameter, yellowish brown to reddish.

The plant is browsed by game and stock. Stems used for hut construction, and to make traps (for monkeys and crocodiles).

2 *Grewia flava*   Velvet raisin

SA: 459.1; Z: 649   Spring–Summer   Fluweelrosyntjie

Multistemmed shrub or small tree; occurring in bushveld and wooded grassland, often in drier areas and on Kalahari sand. Older stems **roundish**. Leaves elliptic to oblanceolate, 14–70 x 7–25 mm, **greyish green**, densely covered with hairs and paler green below, with prominently **raised** venation; apex **rounded**; base broadly tapering, symmetric; margin finely toothed. Flowers in axillary clusters, **yellow**. Fruit a drupe, **globose or faintly 2-lobed**, about 8 mm in diameter, reddish brown.

The stems are strong, elastic, and used for bows. Heavily browsed by game and stock. The bark provides a strong fibre. Fruit edible, and used in making beer. Frayed ends of twigs used as toothbrushes. Larval food plant for the butterflies *Caprona pillaana*, *Leucochitonia levubu* and *Abantis tettensis*.

3 *Grewia flavescens*   Sandpaper raisin

SA: 459.2; Z: 650   Summer–Autumn   Skurwerosyntjie

Scrambling multistemmed shrub or small tree; occurring in bushveld. Older stems **4-angled**. Leaves oblanceolate to obovate, 40–120 x 20–85 mm, green, **harshly covered with hairs**, particularly below; margin **irregularly** toothed. Flowers in **stalked** (the stalks usually longer than 10 mm in var. *olukondae*, shorter than 10 mm in var. *flavescens*) axillary clusters, **yellow**. Fruit a drupe, globose, usually **shallowly 2–4-lobed**, 8–14 x 14–15 mm in diameter, yellowish brown.

The leaves are browsed by game and stock.

Easily confused with *G. retinervis*, a multistemmed shrub or small tree from arid bushveld, usually on Kalahari sand. It has somewhat compressed (but not 4-angled) older stems, unlobed drupes, and leaves with both surfaces slightly rough .

4 *Grewia hexamita*   Giant raisin

SA: 460; Z: 652   Spring   Reuserosyntjie

Shrub or small tree; occurring in bushveld. Older stems **roundish**, young ones with **woolly, reddish brown hair**. Leaves elliptic to oblong-elliptic, 30–100 x 25–60 mm, glossy green, hairless and slightly rough above, densely covered with yellowish hairs below; apex rounded or tapering; base **cordate, strongly asymmetric**; margin finely toothed. Flowers in axillary clusters, **yellow**. Fruit a drupe, **1- or deeply 2-lobed**, each **up to 20 mm diameter**, reddish.

The leaves are browsed by game and stock. Fruit edible but not very popular.

G. *caffra*: flowers

G. *caffra*: fruit

G. *flava*: flowers

G. *flavescens*: stems

G. *flavescens*: fruit

G. *flava*: fruit

G. *hexamita*: flowers

G. *hexamita*: fruit

1 *Grewia lasiocarpa*   Forest raisin
SA: 461   Summer   Bosrosyntjie
Scrambling shrub or small tree; occurring along forest margins and on associated
rocky outcrops. Leaves **broadly ovate to almost circular, large (up to 150 x
150 mm)**, slightly rough-haired above, densely covered with **soft hairs below**,
strongly 3-veined from base; margin **coarsely scalloped-toothed**; petiole up to
20 mm long, coarsely hairy. Flowers in **stalked** clusters **opposite** leaves, **pink**. Fruit
a drupe, **4-lobed**, up to 20 mm in diameter, reddish.
  Sterile material very similar to *Trimeria grandifolia (p. 226)*, which has leaves
with 5–7 veins from the base.

2 *Grewia microthyrsa*   Lebombo raisin
SA: 461.1   Spring–Summer   Lebomborosyntjie
Multistemmed shrub or small tree; occurring in bushveld and sand forest, particularly in the Maputaland Centre. Older stems **roundish**. Leaves oblong to oblong-
elliptic, 20–55 x 12–25 mm, glossy dark green above, paler green below, slightly
rough to the touch; margin **entire** or **finely toothed in upper half**. Flowers in **terminal** clusters, **cream to pale yellow**. Fruit a drupe, **pear-shaped**, about 13 x
7 mm, **drooping**, with long, **curved** stalks, reddish brown.
  The plant is browsed by game and stock. Stems used for spear shafts, in hut building, and in the construction of courtyard fences. Fruit edible.

3 *Grewia monticola*   Silver raisin
SA: 462; Z: 658   Spring–Summer   Vaalrosyntjie
Shrub or small tree, usually with somewhat **drooping** branches; occurring in
bushveld, often on sandy soils. Older stems **roundish**. Branchlets densely covered
with **brownish hairs**. Leaves **obliquely elliptic-oblong**, 25–90 x 10–50 mm, rough
and slightly hairy above, densely covered with whitish or greyish hairs below; base
cordate to rounded, asymmetric; margin **irregularly** toothed. Flowers in axillary
clusters, bright **yellow**. Fruit a drupe, **1- or deeply 2-lobed**, each about 8 mm in
diameter, yellowish or reddish.
  The leaves are browsed by game and stock. The heartwood is dark brown, attractive, and used for ornaments. Fruit edible, and much sought after.
  G. hornbyi has smaller leaves (15–35 x 8–20 mm) and fruit (about 4 mm in diameter), and is endemic to the Maputaland Centre.

4 *Grewia occidentalis*   Cross-berry
SA: 463; Z: 659   Spring–Summer   Kruisbessie
Scrambling shrub or small tree; occurring on forest margins, in bushveld, thicket
and wooded grassland. Older stems **roundish**. Leaves lanceolate to ovate, 20–50 x
10–30 mm, **thinly textured**, with or without sparse hairs above and below; margin
finely toothed to scalloped. Flowers in 1–3-flowered, **leaf-opposed clusters,
purple, pink or mauve**. Fruit a drupe, **4-lobed**, up to 25 mm in diameter, reddish
brown to purple.
  The bark and leaves are used medicinally. Browsed by game and stock. Larval
food plant for the butterflies *Eagris nottoana* and *Netrobalane canopus*.
  G. pondoensis has leaves which are thick and leathery, more glossy dark green,
with sub-entire margins, and is restricted to the Pondoland Centre.

G. lasiocarpa: fruit

G. lasiocarpa: flowers

G. microthyrsa: flowers

G. microthyrsa: fruit

G. monticola: flowers

G. monticola: fruit

G. occidentalis: flowers

G. occidentalis: fruit

1 *Grewia pachycalyx*   **White cross-berry**
SA: –; Z: 660   Summer–Autumn   **Witkruisbessie**
Scandent shrub or small tree, often with **drooping** branches; occurring in low altitude bushveld, often thicket-forming along rivers. Older stems **roundish**. Leaves
oblong-lanceolate, 60–190 x 25–90 mm, **thinly textured**, both surfaces bright
green; base tapering to rounded, **almost symmetric**; margin finely toothed. Flowers
in **stalked, leaf-opposed clusters of 1–9, white**. Fruit a drupe, **deeply 4-lobed**,
each lobe about 10 mm in diameter, shiny orange-red.
    G. sulcata (from Northern Province, Mozambique and southeastern Zimbabwe)
has white or cream flowers and deeply 4-lobed fruit. It is a scandent multistemmed
shrub or small tree from low-altitude bushveld, occurring particularly on sandy
riverbanks. The leaves are obovate to oblong, 20–70 x 15–45 mm, and roughly
hairy on both surfaces. *G. praecox* is a white-flowered scandent shrub or small tree
from the Zambezi Valley. Its leaves are slightly velvety and still incompletely
expanded at flowering time.

2 *Grewia robusta*   **Karoo cross-berry**
SA: –   Winter–Summer   **Karookruisbessie**
Multistemmed shrub or small tree, with rather stiff (occasionally spine-tipped)
branches; occurring in karroid vegetation and valley bushveld. Older stems
roundish. Leaves often **clustered** on abbreviated side-shoots, broadly elliptic to
ovate, up to 20 x 16 mm, glossy dark green above, pale greyish green and with short
hairs below; margin finely scalloped or almost entire. Flowers **solitary, leaf-
opposed, pink**. Fruit a drupe, **deeply 2–4-lobed**, up to 20 mm in diameter, and
reddish brown in colour.
    The plant is heavily browsed by game and stock.

3 *Grewia tenax*   **Small-leaved cross-berry**
SA: –; Z: 667   Summer–Autumn   **Kleinblaarkruisbessie**
Shrub or small tree; occurring in low-altitude arid bushveld and semi-desert vegetation. Older stems **roundish**. Leaves broadly **oval to circular**, 15–30 x 10–30 mm,
leathery, grey-green, hairless or with a few rough hairs, particularly below; margin
coarsely toothed. Flowers **solitary, leaf-opposed, white**. Fruit a drupe, **deeply
4-lobed**, each about 10 mm in diameter, shiny orange-red.

4 *Grewia villosa*   **Mallow raisin**
SA: 463.3; Z: 668   Summer   **Malvarosyntjie**
Much-branched shrub or small tree; occurring in low-altitude bushveld, often on
rocky ridges or sandy soil. Older stems **roundish**, younger ones with yellowish
silky hairs. Leaves **broadly elliptic to almost circular**, 60–120 x 60–120 mm,
green and finely reticulate above, paler with rough, grey or whitish hairs and
prominently reticulate below; base slightly lobed, almost symmetric; margin
toothed. Flowers in tight **leaf-opposed clusters, yellow**. Fruit a drupe, **shallowly
4-lobed**, about 15 mm in diameter, reddish.
    The fruit is edible. Root used medicinally.

G. pachycalyx: flowers

G. robusta: flowers

G. robusta: fruit

G. tenax: flowers

G. tenax: fruit

G. villosa: fruit

1 *Sparrmannia africana* .... Cape stock-rose
SA: 457   Winter–Spring .... Kaapse stokroos
Shrub or small tree; occurring in forest, usually in wet places and along forest margins. Leaves broadly ovate, **large (up to 270 x 210 mm)**, usually **5–9-lobed, softly textured, pale green, hairy**; margin toothed; petiole up to 150 mm long. Flowers in stalked heads towards ends of branches, white; stamens numerous, outer sterile ones **beaded**, yellow, often tinged with purple, inner fertile ones purple. Fruit a capsule, covered with rigid bristles.
  The fibre from the bark was once commercially exploited. Stamens from newly opened flowers spread outwards when touched. An attractive flowering shrub for shady gardens; tolerates moderate frost.

ULMACEAE (see page 32)

2 *Celtis africana* .... White stinkwood
SA: 39; Z: 43   Spring .... Witstinkhout
Medium to large deciduous tree; occurring in forest, bushveld and grassland, often on dolomite. Bark **pale grey, smooth**. Leaves **ovate**, 15–100 x 10–50 mm, dull green, sparsely to densely **covered with hairs**; apex shortly and abruptly tapering; base clearly **asymmetric**; margin **toothed over upper half or two-thirds**. Flowers axillary, small, greenish, appearing with the new leaves. Fruit a drupe, ovoid, about 6 mm in diameter, yellow or brownish.
  Widely planted as a shade tree in gardens, parks and along streets. Larval food plant for the butterflies *Charaxes cithaeron* and *Libythea labdaca*.
  In cultivation the tree is often confused with the alien species *C. australis* and *C. sinensis*. The former has glossy green and hairless leaves and the latter coarse-haired leaves with a more tapering tip and larger marginal teeth.

3 *Celtis durandii* (= *C. gomphophylla*) .... False white stinkwood
SA: 40; Z: 44   Winter–Spring .... Basterwitstinkhout
Medium to large tree, often with a **fluted** trunk; occurring in forest. Leaves **ovate to oblong, 80–190 x 25–90 mm**, covered in short, rough hairs; apex tapering to a **long drip-tip**; base **weakly asymmetric**; margin obscurely **toothed in upper half**. Flowers in axillary clusters, small, inconspicuous. Fruit a drupe, oval, about 10 x 6 mm, yellow.
  The wood is unpleasantly scented, even when decaying in the forest.

4 *Trema orientalis* .... Pigeonwood
SA: 42; Z: 46   Spring–Summer .... Hophout
Small to medium-sized deciduous tree; occurring as a pioneer in forest areas, also in bushveld along rivers. Leaves **ovate**, 40–200 x 25–50 mm, glossy dark green above, paler green below; base **rounded to lobed, asymmetric**; margin finely **toothed along the entire length**. Flowers in axillary clusters, small and inconspicuous, yellowish green. Fruit a drupe, round, up to 6 mm in diameter, black.
  The leaves are cooked as a green vegetable. Browsed by game. Larval food plant for the butterflies *Charaxes castor flavifasciatus* and *C. cithaeron*.

S. africana: flowers & fruit

T. orientalis: fruit

S. africana: flowers

C. africana: flowers

C. africana: fruit

C. durandii: flowers

C. durandii: fruit

T. orientalis: flowers

URTICACEAE (see page 33)

1 *Obetia carruthersiana*   Angola nettle
SA: 69   Spring   Angolabrandnetel
Shrub or small deciduous tree; **latex present, watery**; occurring in semi-desert vegetation, usually in rocky places. Young branchlets **bright red**. Leaves **ovate**, usually about 70 x 100 mm, densely **covered with stinging hairs**; margin **coarsely toothed**; petiole **up to 90 mm** long. Flowers in much-branched clusters, very small, greenish yellow, produced before the leaves. Fruit a nut, oval, very small, surrounded by the persistent floral remains.
Contact with the hairs causes intense itching.

2 *Obetia tenax* *(= Urera tenax)*   Mountain nettle
SA: 70; Z: 74   Spring   Bergbrandnetel
Shrub or small deciduous tree, soft-wooded; **latex present, watery**; occurring in bushveld, often on hot, dry, rocky hillsides. Branchlets with **long stinging hairs**. Leaves **round to ovate**, usually about 70 x 100 mm, densely **covered with stinging hairs**; margin **coarsely toothed**; petiole **up to 140 mm long**. Flowers in much-branched clusters, very small, greenish yellow, produced before the leaves. Fruit a nut, oval, very small (up to 3 mm in diameter), and surrounded by the persistent floral remains.
Contact with the hairs causes intense itching. Bark yields a strong fibre. The leaves are cooked as a green vegetable (often mixed with *Pouzolzia mixta*) and eaten as a relish with porridge. The plant is browsed by black rhino. Larval food plant for the butterflies *Hyalites obeira* and *H. esebria*.

VITACEAE (see page 33)

3 *Rhoicissus tomentosa*   Common forest grape
SA: 456.5; Z: 633   Spring–Summer   Gewone bosdruif
Robust canopy **climber** or small scrambling tree, with **leaf-opposed tendrils**; occurring mainly in forest and riverine bush. Young branchlets with **reddish brown, velvety hairs**. Leaves almost **circular to kidney-shaped, slightly 3-lobed**, 80–200 x 60–160 mm, dark green above, dense with **brownish hairs** below; margin entire or toothed, **wavy**. Flowers in dense axillary heads, small, yellowish green. Fruit a berry, globose, about 20 mm in diameter, red to purplish black.
The fruit is edible, made into jam or jelly. Root used medicinally and for veterinary purposes. Underground tubers eaten by bushpig and porcupine.

O. carruthersiana: trunk

O. carruthersiana: tree

O. tenax: flowers

O. tenax: flowers

O. tenax: flowers

R. tomentosa: flowers

R. tomentosa: fruit

GROUP 12

Leaves simple, opposite; blade prominently 3–5-veined from or near the base

LOGANIACEAE (see page 26)

Although the fruit pulp of all large-fruited *Strychnos* species in southern Africa is edible, the seeds, which can be sucked for quite some time to remove the pulp, should never be swallowed as they may be poisonous. The well-known drug strychnine is obtained from the seeds of an Indian species.

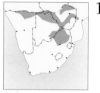

1 *Strychnos cocculoides*   Corky monkey orange
SA: 623; Z: 881   Spring   Kurkbasklapper
Armed deciduous shrub or small tree with a compact, rounded crown; occurring in bushveld, usually on sandy soils or in rocky places. Stems **thickly and persistently corky, longitudinally fissured**. Branchlets rather thick, purplish or brownish, with **longish hairs**, often ending in a **terminal spine**, also armed with strong, **curved, axillary spines**. Leaves broadly ovate-oblong to almost circular, with or without rough hairs; shiny dark green above, dull and paler below, conspicuously **5-veined** from base; petiole up to 6 mm long. Flowers in dense compact heads, terminal on the main branches or on short lateral shoots, greenish white. Fruit **large (up to 70 mm in diameter)**, globose; rind thick and woody, dark green speckled with white, ripening to pale yellow; seeds many, embedded in pulp.

The wood is whitish, tough, pliable, suitable for implement handles and other small items. Fruit pulp edible and much sought after, considered the most delicious of all the local members of the genus. The fruit is sometimes buried in the sand to allow the pulp to liquefy.

Similar to *S. spinosa*, which lacks the thick corky bark, has branchlets which are smooth or covered with very short hairs, and less tasty fruit.

2 *Strychnos decussata*   Cape teak
SA: 624; Z: 882   Spring–Summer   Kaapse kiaat
Small to medium-sized slender tree, often with a dense, somewhat drooping crown; occurring in coastal thicket and bushveld, often along dry watercourses or on termitaria. Branchlets with conspicuous, **pale brown lenticels**. Leaves obovate to elliptic, **broadest at or above the middle**, up to 50 mm long, leathery, glossy dark green above, hairless, **rather obscurely 3–5-veined** from the base, with netveining not visible; apex rounded; base broadly tapering; petiole up to 3 mm long. Flowers in small, loose, branched heads, axillary, on twigs or old stems, greenish white. Fruit **small (up to 15 mm in diameter)**, globose; rind thin and soft, with very short hairs, **orange or red** when mature; 1 or 2 seeds, **not grooved**.

The heartwood is dark brown, heavy and attractive, and has been fashioned into musical instruments. Bark and root used medicinally. Yields tough sticks which are believed to provide protection against lightning; used for ceremonial purposes and as laths in hut construction. Browsed by game.

S. cocculoides: bark

S. cocculoides: fruit

S. decussata: flowers

S. decussata: fruit

1 Strychnos gerrardii   False black monkey orange
SA: – Summer   Basterswartklapper
Medium to large tree with upright branches and an **open, spreading crown**; occurring in coastal and dune forest. Branchlets rather slender, hairless, with whitish lenticels. Leaves **not conspicuously clustered** on short side-shoots, elliptic or elliptic-oblong, shiny dark green above, paler green below, **hairless**, 3–5-veined from base; apex **tapering**; petiole up to 5 mm long. Flowers in axillary clusters, greenish yellow. Fruit **large (50–70 mm in diameter)**, globose; rind thick and woody, bluish green when young, orange yellow when mature; seeds many, embedded in pulp.
     The fruit pulp is edible and quite tasty.
     Similar to *S. madagascariensis*, a rather stunted, multistemmed tree found in open bushveld, whose leaves are usually hairy and clustered on abbreviated side-shoots, and which has a much larger fruit (80–100 mm in diameter).

2 Strychnos henningsii   Red bitterberry
SA: 625; Z: 883 Winter–Spring   Rooibitterbessie
Shrub or medium-sized tree, often with a single trunk and spreading rounded crown; occurring in forest and bushveld, in dryer areas usually along rivers and on termitaria. Branchlets **4-angled**, without conspicuous lenticels, **hairless**. Leaves elliptic to broadly ovate, **broadest at or above the middle**, up to 65 mm long, leathery, glossy dark green above, hairless, **3-veined** from the base, **net-veining raised on both sides**, especially when old; apex and base broadly tapering. Flowers in dense axillary heads on leafy shoots, greenish white to cream. Fruit **small (up to 12 mm in diameter)**, globose; rind fleshy, ripening through yellow-orange to purplish black; seed solitary, **deeply grooved down one side** (like a coffee bean).
     The heartwood is pale to dark brown, heavy, very durable, used for implement handles and as fencing posts. Bark and root used medicinally (they contain poisonous alkaloids), as is the fruit.

3 Strychnos madagascariensis   Black monkey orange
SA: 626; Z: 886 Spring   Swartklapper
Deciduous shrub or small tree, often **many-stemmed** with a much-branched, spreading canopy; occurring in bushveld, sand forest and coastal bush. Stems unarmed, often with **sturdy abbreviated side shoots**. Leaves **clustered towards ends of twigs**, **elliptic to almost circular**, leathery, shiny dark green above, paler green below, **usually hairy, at least on the veins below**, rarely smooth, **3–5-veined** from base; apex rounded or broadly tapering; margin entire, **often with a fringe of hairs**; petiole up to 5 mm long. Flowers in axillary clusters and on the old wood, greenish yellow. Fruit **large (80–100 mm in diameter)**, globose; rind thick and woody, bluish green when young, yellow when mature; seeds many, embedded in pulp.
     The leaves are browsed by game and stock. Fruit pulp edible but not very tasty; usually dried, powdered and stored for later use. Sold at markets in Maputaland.
     Strychnos innocua, from the Zambezi River Valley, is very similar but lacks dwarf lateral shoots, and its leaves are dull blue-green with conspicuous pale net-veining on both surfaces. *S. madagascariensis* is sometimes confused with *S. gerrardii*, a species mainly confined to coastal dune forest. It is a taller tree with a more upright and open crown, hairless leaves and slightly smaller fruit (50–70 mm in diameter).

S. gerrardii: flowers

S. henningsii: fruit

S. gerrardii: fruit

S. henningsii: flowers

S. madagascariensis: flowers

S. madagascariensis: fruit

S. madagascariensis: fruit

1 *Strychnos mitis*   Yellow bitterberry
SA: 627; Z: 889   Summer–Autumn   Geelbitterbessie
Medium to large evergreen tree with a rounded crown; occurring in coastal bush and forest, usually in moist places. Branchlets **slender, lenticellate**, often with a **pair of persistent, reduced leaves at the base of the current season's growth.** Leaves elliptic to ovate, mostly over 60 mm long, rather **thin-textured**, glossy dark green above, paler green below, **hairless, 3–5-veined** from base; apex tapering; base tapering to rounded; principal lateral veins **often with domatia in their axils below**; petiole up to 7 mm long. Flowers in dense, branched, axillary heads, yellowish white, often produced in profusion. Fruit **small (up to 15 mm in diameter)**, subglobose; rind rather thin, **yellow to orange** when mature, 1- or 2-seeded.

The wood is whitish to pale brown, hard, heavy, and used for implement handles and fighting sticks. Fruit eaten by birds, squirrels and monkeys.

2 *Strychnos potatorum* (= *S. stuhlmannii*)   Black bitterberry
SA: 630; Z: 890   Spring–Summer   Swartbitterbessie
Small to medium-sized deciduous tree, crown densely foliate; occurring in riverine forest and bushveld, often along watercourses or on termitaria. Branchlets often **dichotomously branched, with a ring-like scar** left by the first pair of deciduous, reduced leaves on the new season's growth, sometimes with **spinescent** tips; old leaf scars prominent. Leaves elliptic to ovate, **60–150 mm long, thinly textured**, glossy dark green above, paler green below, **hairless**, with **3–5 prominent pale green or yellowish veins** from the base, or more usually **some distance above the base**; apex narrowly tapering; base rounded to shallowly lobed; petiole up to 7 mm long. Flowers in stalked heads near the base of the branchlets in axils of reduced leaves; yellowish green. Fruit **small (up to 20 mm in diameter)**, subglobose; rind soft, **blue-black** when mature, single-seeded.

Bark and root used as fish poison. The seeds are reputed to purify drinking water.

3 *Strychnos pungens*   Spine-leaved monkey orange
SA: 628; Z: 891   Spring   Stekelblaarklapper
Small deciduous to evergreen tree; occurring in bushveld, often in rocky places. Bark thick and fissured. Branchlets **thick, rough and corky**, with **swollen nodes** and conspicuous lenticels. Leaves usually elliptic, **hard and rigid, hairless**, 3–5-veined from base; apex ending in a **hard, sharp spine**; petiole sturdy, up to 4 mm long. Flowers in axillary clusters, greenish white. Fruit large **(up to 120 mm in diameter)**, globose; rind thick and woody, bluish green, ripening to yellow to golden brown; seeds many, embedded in pulp.

The leaves and root are used medicinally. Fruit pulp edible, but not as tasty as those of the other large-fruited species.

S. mitis: fruit

S. potatorum: flowers

S. potatorum: fruit

S. pungens: flowers

S. pungens: fruit

S. pungens: fruit

1 *Strychnos spinosa*   Green monkey orange
SA: 629; Z: 892   Spring–Summer   Groenklapper

Armed deciduous shrub or small tree; occurring in bushveld, riverine fringes, sand forest and in coastal bush. Stems **not very thickly corky**, often flaking in elongated pieces, but not deeply fissured. Branchlets rather pale coloured, **usually hairless**, often ending in a **terminal spine**, also armed with **axillary curved or straight spines**. Leaves elliptic, ovate to almost circular, with or without short hairs; shiny dark green above, dull and paler below, conspicuously 3–5-veined from base; margin often somewhat wavy; petiole up to 10 mm long. Flowers in dense compact heads, terminal on the main branches or on short lateral shoots, greenish white. Fruit **large (up to 120 mm in diameter)**, globose; rind thick and woody, yellow to yellow-brown when mature, usually warty; seeds numerous, embedded in pulp.

The wood is off-white, straight-grained and suitable for general carpentry. Browsed by game and stock. Leaves and root used medicinally. The shells of dried fruit are sometimes used as sounding-boxes in musical instruments such as the *marimba*; also, when painted, as ornaments. Fruit pulp edible and delicious; may be sundried as a food preserve.

2 *Strychnos usambarensis*   Blue bitterberry
SA: 631; Z: 893   Summer–Autumn   Bloubitterbessie

Small to medium-sized tree with a spreading crown; occurring in forest, wooded ravines and moist bushveld, often along streams and in rocky places. Branchlets **slender**, very **dark brown, with whitish lenticels**. Leaves **borne horizontally in one plane** along branches, **ovate-lanceolate**, usually under 60 mm long, **broadest below the middle**, often folded upward along midrib, glossy dark green above, dull and paler green below, **hairless**, rather **obscurely 3–5-veined** from the base; apex narrowly tapering, **often forming a drip-tip**; base tapering to rounded; petiole up to 6 mm long. Flowers in compact axillary clusters, greenish white. Fruit **small (up to 15 mm in diameter)**, globose, **narrowed at the base into a short (1 mm long) neck** before joining the stalk; rind soft, **yellow or orange** in colour when mature; single-seeded.

The leaves are browsed by game. Parts of the plant are used medicinally.

MELASTOMATACEAE (see page 26)

3 *Memecylon sousae*   Tonga rose-apple
SA: 560.2   Spring–Summer   Tongaroosappel

Evergreen shrub or small tree, usually multistemmed; occurring in sand forest; endemic to the Maputaland Centre. Branchlets **4-angled**. Leaves elliptic or ovate, **thick and leathery**, glossy dark green above, paler green below, **hairless, 3-veined** from base; apex broadly tapering to rounded; base rounded. Flowers in axillary clusters, usually **on older stems**; small, greenish yellow. Fruit a berry, oval, up to 10 mm long, **tipped by the persistent calyx**, purplish black, single-seeded.

If not in fruit, easily mistaken for a species of *Strychnos*.

S. spinosa: fruit

S. usambarensis: flowers

S. spinosa: flowers

S. usambarensis: fruit

M. sousae: flowers

M. sousae: fruit

GROUP 13

Leaves simple, opposite; blade single- or pinnately veined, distinctly discolorous, white or silvery grey beneath. Interpetiolar stipules, scar or ridge present.

See also Group 18: *Curtisia dentata* (p. 292) and Group 23: *Buddleja saligna* (p. 324).

BUDDLEJACEAE (see page 21)

1 *Buddleja auriculata* — Weeping sage
SA: 636.5; Z: 899   Autumn–Winter — Treursalie

Evergreen, semi-scandent shrub or small tree; branches **drooping**; occurring in montane forest and thicket, usually along forest margins or streams. Branchlets densely covered with **whitish hairs**. Leaves elliptic or ovate, **drooping**, shiny dark green and **slightly wrinkled and puckered above**, densely covered with **whitish hairs below**; apex tapering; base broadly tapering to rounded; margin toothed or entire; venation **impressed** above, **prominent** below; petiole up to 11 mm long; stipules **leafy, often recurved**, sometimes reduced to a line. Flowers in large terminal or axillary panicles, creamy white to orange-yellow or lilac, with orange throat, sweetly scented. Fruit a capsule, ellipsoid, dehiscent.

B. pulchella (a scrambling shrub or small tree of forest margins) also has cylindrical cream to yellowish flowers, often with an orange throat, but the interpetiolar stipules are absent or reduced to a faint ridge.

2 *Buddleja dysophylla* — White climbing sage
SA: 636.3   Winter — Witranksalie

Scandent shrub or small, straggling tree; occurring in forest margins. Branchlets densely covered with **brownish hairs**. Leaves **deltoid or almost triangular**, green, sparsely covered with hairs and not conspicuously **wrinkled above**, densely covered with **greyish to creamy or rusty hairs below**; apex tapering to rounded; base square to shallowly lobed, often decurrent into petiole; margin irregularly scalloped or toothed; petiole **up to 30 mm long**; stipules represented by an **interpetiolar ridge**. Flowers in lax terminal panicles, white or cream, sometimes with a maroon throat, sweetly scented. Fruit a capsule, ovoid or ellipsoid, dehiscent.

3 *Buddleja glomerata* — Karoo sage
SA: 636.1   Spring–Summer — Karoosalie

Straggling shrub or small bushy tree; occurring in arid karroid areas, usually among rocks on hills and mountains. Branchlets densely covered with **whitish hairs**. Leaves oblong to broadly oblong, upper surface **bluish green**, sparsely hairy, **wrinkled and puckered**; lower surface densely covered with **white or brownish hairs**; apex broadly tapering; base broadly tapering to rounded; margin **deeply lobed**, with the **lobes again minutely scalloped**; petiole up to 15 mm long; stipules present in the form of a prominent **interpetiolar ridge**. Flowers in terminal panicles, yellow, cup-shaped, reported to be foul-smelling. Fruit a capsule, obovoid, laterally compressed, dehiscent.

An attractive garden plant; drought and frost resistant.

B. *auriculata*: flowers

B. *glomerata*: flowers

B. *auriculata*: flowers

B. *auriculata*: fruit

B. *dysophylla*: flowers

B. *dysophylla*: flowers

1 *Buddleja salviifolia*   Sagewood
SA: 637; Z: 902   Spring   Saliehout

Shrub or small tree with a **greyish** appearance; occurring along forest margins and in high-altitude grassland, usually along watercourses and in rocky places. Branchlets densely covered with grey or white woolly hairs. Leaves narrowly ovate to narrowly oblong, dark green to grey green and **conspicuously wrinkled and puckered above**, densely covered with **whitish or brownish hairs below**; apex narrowly tapering; base deeply lobed; margin **finely scalloped**; petiole absent or up to 7 mm long; stipules **leafy, interpetiolar**. Flowers in terminal panicles, white to lilac or purple, with a dark orange throat, tubular, sweetly scented. Fruit a capsule, ellipsoid, dehiscent.

The leaves are browsed by game. Heartwood brown, compact, hard, heavy, and once used for the shafts of assegais; also suitable for fishing rods. Leaf and root used medicinally. Fresh or dried leaves make an aromatic herbal tea. An attractive garden subject, frost-hardy and suitable as a hedge.

B. loricata (= *B. corrugata*), from the high Drakensberg (mainly in and around Lesotho) is usually a shrub with leaves narrowly elliptic, stiff and densely covered with both whitish and brownish hairs below, and stipules reduced to an interpetiolar ridge. It has cup-shaped cream flowers, sometimes with an orange throat.

EUPHORBIACEAE (see page 24)

2 *Androstachys johnsonii*   Lebombo ironwood
SA: 327; Z: 477   Spring   Lebombo-ysterhout

Medium to large deciduous to semi-deciduous tree with an upright habit; sexes separate, on different plants; occurring in hot, low-altitude bushveld, usually in **almost pure stands** on rocky hillsides. Branchlets **4-angled**, densely covered with **white, woolly hairs**. Leaves **heart-shaped**, leathery, shiny dark green above, white-felted below; margin entire, rolled under; petiole up to 20 mm long; stipules very distinctive, **large, elliptic, with a pair enclosing the apical bud**, early deciduous. Flowers axillary, in drooping catkins (male) or solitary (female), inconspicuous, without petals, wind-pollinated. Fruit a capsule, conspicuously **3-lobed**, up to 12 mm in diameter, splitting into 3 segments.

The wood is extremely hard, durable and termite proof, hence the common names; used in hut construction and as fence poles. Several plant species are consistently associated with *Androstachys* groves (forests), notably in the Soutpansberg and Lebombo mountains, thus comprising a unique plant community.

B. *salviifolia*: flowers

A. *johnsonii*: male flowers

B. *salviifolia*: flowers

A. *johnsonii*: female flowers

A. *johnsonii*: fruit

A. *johnsonii*: fruit

GROUP 14

Leaves simple, opposite; blade single- or pinnately veined, not distinctly discolorous; margin smooth. Interpetiolar stipules, scar or ridge present. Spines present.

RUBIACEAE (see page 30)

1 Canthium ciliatum   Hairy turkey-berry
SA: 709   Spring–Summer   Harige bokdrol
Shrub or small tree; occurring in the **understorey of forest** or on rocky outcrops in montane grassland. Branches with paired, slender, straight spines. Leaves opposite or clustered on reduced lateral shoots, ovate to elliptic, 6–30 x 4–18 mm, dark green above, **soft textured, shortly haired**; apex **tapering**; margin entire, **fringed with hairs**. Flowers **1 or 2**, on a long, slender stalk, cream; corolla tube **about 4 mm long, notably constricted** below the mouth. Fruit a drupe, 1- or 2-lobed, asymmetric about 13 mm long, dark brown to blackish.
The leaves are used medicinally.

2 Canthium glaucum subsp. *frangula* (= *C. frangula*)   **Pink-fruited rock elder**
Z: 1105   Summer   Pienkvrugklipels
Shrub or small deciduous tree; occurring in hot, low-altitude bushveld, often in riverine thicket and on Kalahari sand. Branchlets with paired, straight spines up to 20 mm long. Leaves clustered on **short lateral shoots**, ovate, up to 30 x 17 mm, **thinly textured**, with **hairtuft domatia** in axils of principal lateral veins; base tapering and running into the petiole. Flowers in **3-flowered** axillary clusters, very small, whitish. Fruit a drupe, 2-lobed, 5–10 mm long, **pink**, on a slender stalk. Leaves hairless (at least above) in var. *frangula*, densely hairy on both sides in var. *pubescens*.

3 Canthium inerme (= *C. ventosum*)   Common turkey-berry
SA: 708; Z: 1109   Spring   Gewone bokdrol
Small to medium-sized tree; occurring in coastal or montane forest, or on rocky outcrops in associated grassland. Branchlets occasionally with paired, **robust**, straight spines, particularly on sucker shoots. Leaves **elliptic**, 25–75 x 10–38 mm, rather **fleshy and softly leathery**, glossy light green above, paler green below, **hairless**; margin **wavy**; petiole up to 12 mm long. Flowers in **many-flowered** axillary heads, small, greenish. Fruit a drupe, oblong-ovate, about 15 x 9–10 mm, 1- or weakly 2-lobed, dark brown.
The wood is hard, heavy and tough but available, usually, only in small pieces. Leaves used medicinally. Larval food plant for the butterfly *Spindasis natalensis*.

4 Canthium vanwykii   Pondo turkey-berry
SA: –   Summer   Pondo-klipels
Shrub or small tree; occurring on forest margins or rocky outcrops in grassland, **always on sandstone**; endemic to the Pondoland Centre. Branches with or without paired, straight spines. Leaves widely ovate to widely elliptic, usually 22–30 x 13–20 mm, **leathery**, glossy dark green to yellowish green, **essentially hairless**; apex **broadly tapering to rounded**; margin entire, **hairless**. Flowers in branched axillary clusters of **8–50**, yellow to greenish yellow; corolla tube about **1,5 mm long, not constricted** at the mouth. Fruit a drupe, 1- or 2-lobed, about 10 mm long, dark brown to blackish.

C. *ciliatum*: flowers

C. *glaucum*: flowers

C. *inerme*: flowers

C. *vanwykii*: flowers

C. *inerme*: fruit

C. *inerme*: fruit

C. *vanwykii*: fruit

1 *Catunaregam spinosa* (= *Xeromphis obovata*)   **Thorny bone-apple**
SA: 689; Z: 1067   Spring   **Doringbeenappel**
Shrub or small tree with sparse foliage; occurring in coastal bush and bushveld, often in dense stands. Branchlets with paired, straight spines. Leaves opposite or clustered on **reduced lateral shoots, oval to obovate**, up to 38 x 25 mm, densely **hairy on both surfaces**, or almost hairless, dark green; venation **whitish, translucent** when viewed against the light; apex **rounded**; petiole up to 3 mm long. Flowers in axillary groups of 2 or 3, up to 20 mm in diameter, white fading cream to yellow. Fruit hard, oval, up to 25 mm long, **crowned with the persistent remains of the calyx**, greenish brown.
    The plant is browsed by game and stock. Fruit edible, and used medicinally. Stems used as laths in hut construction.

2 *Hyperacanthus amoenus* (= *Gardenia amoena*)   **Thorny gardenia**
SA: 690   Summer–Autumn   **Doringkatjiepiering**
Multistemmed shrub or small tree, with **short, rigid lateral branches** and pinkish red young growth; occurring in bushveld, forest, rarely in sand forest. Lateral branchlets frequently reduced to stout, opposite spines. Leaves opposite or **clustered** on reduced lateral shoots, **obovate to elliptic, 15–70 x 8–23 mm**, glossy dark green, paler green below, hairless; venation **obscure** when held up to the light; margin wavy; petiole up to 2 mm long. Flowers axillary, **solitary**, large and attractive, white inside, pink to reddish on the outside, sweetly scented. Fruit tough and leathery, **subglobose, 14–20 x 14–16 mm**, dark brown to blackish, tipped by the tubular remains of the calyx.
    The leaves are browsed by game. Fruit and root used medicinally. Branches used in Maputaland for fences and the frameworks of fishing baskets. Larval food plant for the butterflies *Deudorix dariaves* and *D. dinochares*.
    Easily confused with *H. microphyllus* (**2.1**), a multistemmed shrub or small tree endemic to sandforest in the Maputaland Centre; often growing with *H. amoenus*. It has elliptic to broadly elliptic leaves (35–90 x 18–45 mm) with the venation distinct when held up to the light and often slightly immersed above. The flowers are solitary or in clusters or 2 or 3, and the fruit characteristically oval or spindle-shaped (25 x 11–12 mm).

3 *Plectroniella armata*   **False turkey-berry**
SA: 715   Summer   **Basterbokdrol**
Shrub or small tree; occurring in hot, low-altitude bushveld, often on rocky hillsides or in association with mopane. Branchlets with paired, straight spines up to 40 mm long. Leaves opposite or clustered on reduced lateral shoots, **obovate**, 20–50 x 15–30 mm, glossy dark green above, paler green below, usually hairless, at least above; apex **broadly tapering to rounded**; petiole **up to 13 mm long**. Flowers in **many-flowered**, branched, axillary heads, white. Fruit a drupe, oval, asymmetric, about 12 x 8 mm, **yellow-orange to red**, in **drooping clusters**.
    The fruit is edible; also eaten by birds.

C. spinosa: flowers

C. spinosa: fruit

H. microphyllus: flower

H. amoenus: fruit

P. armata: fruit

H. amoenus: flowers

H. microphyllus: fruit

P. armata: fruit

GROUP 15

Leaves simple, opposite; blade single- or pinnately veined, not distinctly discolorous, with blackish bacterial nodules; margin smooth. Interpetiolar stipules, scar or ridge present. Spines absent.

See also Group 16: *Sericanthe andongensis* (p. 272); Group 17: *Psychotria zombamontana* (p. 284).

RUBIACEAE (see page 30)
Members of the genus *Pavetta* have very similar flowers and fruit, and the approximately 30 southern African species are easily confused. Of particular importance for correct identification is the shape of the calyx lobes, established either in flowering or fruiting material.

1 **Pavetta bowkeri**   Pondo bride's bush
SA: –   Summer   Pondobruidsbos
Shrub or small tree; occurring on forest margins and in the understorey of forest, particularly on **sandstone**. Leaves elliptic, **50–140 x 20–40 mm, leathery**, glossy dark green and hairless above, **densely velvety below**; bacterial nodules **elliptic to linear, aligned adjacent to the midrib**; petiole up to 15 mm long. Flowers in terminal and axillary clusters, white; calyx lobes **very narrow, needle-shaped**. Fruit fleshy, globose, up to 5 mm in diameter, black, and crowned with the remains of the calyx.
  P. natalensis, from coastal areas of KwaZulu-Natal and Pondoland, also has elliptic to linear bacterial nodules restricted to the midrib region, but the leaves are hairless.

2 **Pavetta catophylla**   Sand bride's bush
SA: – ; Z: –   Summer–Autumn   Sandbruidsbos
Shrub or small tree; occurring in bushveld and sand forest, particularly in Maputaland. Leaves **sessile or shortly stalked**, obovate to spathulate, usually 50–120 x 15–30 mm, semi-leathery, hairy or hairless, **usually without domatia**; bacterial nodules more or less **circular, scattered over the lamina**; petiole 2–6 mm long. Flowers in terminal and axillary clusters, white; calyx lobes **lanceolate, large and leafy, 7–12 x 1,5–4 mm**. Fruit fleshy, globose, up to 10 mm in diameter, black, crowned with the enlarged remains of the calyx.
  P. cataractarum (occurring in northern Namibia and Zimbabwe) and *P. gerstneri* (along the Maputaland coast) have distinctly stalked leaves, hairy in the former, hairless in the latter.

3 **Pavetta edentula**   Gland-leaf tree
SA: 717   Summer   Kliertjiesboom
Shrub or small deciduous tree, with **thick, rigid** branches and sparse crown; occurring in bushveld, usually on rocky hillsides. Leaves **clustered** towards ends of branches, **lanceolate, up to 200 x 50 mm**, leathery and rather fleshy, bright green, hairless, bacterial nodules **circular to elliptic, scattered over the lamina**; petiole up to 25 mm long. Flowers in compact axillary clusters, white; calyx lobes **reduced to minute, sharp tips**. Fruit fleshy, globose, up to 8 mm in diameter, black, crowned with the remains of the calyx.

P. bowkeri: flowers

P. catophylla: flowers

P. bowkeri: fruit

P. edentula: fruit

P. edentula: flowers

P. catophylla: fruit

P. edentula: tree

1 *Pavetta eylesii*   Large-leaved bride's bush
SA: 717.1; Z: 1126   Summer   Grootblaarbruidsbos
Shrub or small tree; occurring in bushveld, often in bush clumps and rocky places.
Leaves **broadly elliptic to almost circular, large (up to 160 x 90 mm),** semi-leathery, with or without hairs above, **velvety below**; bacterial nodules more or less **circular, scattered over the lamina**; petiole up to 15 mm long. Flowers in axillary clusters, white; calyx lobes **reduced to minute, sharp tips.** Fruit fleshy, globose, up to 10 mm in diameter, black, crowned with the remains of the calyx.

2 *Pavetta gardeniifolia*   Common bride's bush
SA: 716 & 716.1; Z: 1125   Summer   Gewone bruidsbos
Shrub or small tree; occurring in bushveld, often on rocky hillsides. Leaves often clustered on reduced lateral branchlets, **obovate to oblong,** 25–60 x 15–40 mm, semi-leathery, hairless (var. *gardeniifolia*), or densely hairy (var. *subtomentosa*); bacterial nodules more or less **circular, scattered over the lamina**; apex **broadly tapering to rounded**; petiole **up to 3 mm long**. Flowers in axillary clusters, white; calyx lobes **reduced to minute, sharp tips.** Fruit fleshy, globose, about 5 mm in diameter, black, crowned with the remains of the calyx.

3 *Pavetta gracilifolia*   Dwarf bride's bush
SA: –   Summer   Dwergbruidsbos
Shrub or small tree; occurring on forest margins and in associated grassland and bushveld, usually in rocky places. Leaves **narrowly elliptic**, usually 15–50 x 5–15 mm, semi-leathery, hairy or hairless, **usually without domatia**; bacterial nodules more or less **circular, scattered over the lamina**, particularly towards the midrib; petiole 3-6 mm long. Flowers in terminal and axillary clusters, white; calyx lobes **very narrow, needle-shaped, 3–6 x 0,5 mm**. Fruit fleshy, globose, up to 7 mm in diameter, black, crowned with the remains of the calyx.

4 *Pavetta lanceolata* (= *P. tristis*)   Weeping bride's bush
SA: 718.1   Summer   Treurbruidsbos
Shrub or small tree; occurring on forest **margins** and in **bushveld**. Leaves **elliptic**, usually **50–70 x 9–15 mm**, semi-leathery, hairless, with **hairtuft domatia in axils of principal lateral veins**; bacterial nodules more or less **circular, scattered over the lamina**; petiole **2–6 mm long**. Flowers in terminal and axillary clusters, white; calyx lobes **reduced to minute, sharp tips, 0,2–0,4 x 0.3–0,6 mm**; corolla tube 5,2–6,5 mm long. Fruit fleshy, globose, up to 7 mm in diameter, black, crowned with the remains of the calyx.

     P. inandensis, a small, upright tree found in shady places inside forest, has larger (45–95 x 13–24 mm) leaves, with a longer (5–15 mm) petiole. *P. kotzei*, an often decumbent shrub from the understorey in mistbelt forest, has oblanceolate leaves, larger flowers, with the calyx lobes broadly tapering to rounded, 0,8–1,5 mm long and the corolla tube 8–11 mm long.

P. eylesii: flowers

P. eylesii: fruit

P. gardeniifolia: fruit

P. gracilifolia: flowers

P. gardeniifolia: flowers

P. lanceolata: flowers

P. lanceolata: fruit

1 Pavetta revoluta   Dune bride's bush
SA: 720   Summer   Duinebruidsbos
Shrub or small tree; occurring in dune bush and forest along the coast. Leaves **elliptic to obovate**, 25–80 x 18–40 mm, **thick and leathery, hairless,** with **domatia in axils of principal lateral veins**; bacterial nodules **elliptic**, occurring **mainly next to the midrib**; apex **broadly tapering to rounded**; margin **rolled under**, petiole up to 10 mm long. Flowers in terminal and axillary clusters, white; calyx lobes **toothed, with sharp tips**. Fruit fleshy, globose, up to 10 mm in diameter, black, crowned with the remains of the calyx.

2 Pavetta schumanniana   Poison bride's bush
SA: 721; Z: 1130   Summer   Gifbruidsbos
Shrub or small tree; occurring in bushveld. Leaves **obovate, 70–150 x 25–75 mm**, leathery, **shortly hairy**; bacterial nodules more or less **circular, scattered over the lamina**; venation **raised below**; petiole up to 15 mm long. Flowers in **compact** axillary clusters, white; calyx lobes **toothed, with sharp tips**. Fruit fleshy, globose, up to 8 mm in diameter, black, crowned with the remains of the calyx.

The plant is poisonous to stock, causing gousiekte, a disease of domestic ruminants characterized by acute heart failure. Root used medicinally.

P. harborii, from the northwestern parts of the Northern Province and adjacent Botswana, also has compact inflorescences and is poisonous to stock, but it differs in that it is a low-growing shrub with sessile leaves.

3 Pavetta trichardtensis (= *P. zoutpansbergensis*)   Soutpansberg bride's bush
SA: –   Summer   Soutpansbergbruidsbos
Shrub or small tree; occurring on forest margins and on rocky outcrops in montane grassland. Leaves **elliptic**, 20–80 x 12–35 mm, **semi-leathery and somewhat fleshy, glossy** green above, hairy or hairless, **without domatia**; bacterial nodules **circular, scattered over the lamina, prominently raised** above and below; principal lateral veins notably **immersed above**, slightly raised below; petiole up to 15 mm long. Flowers in terminal and axillary clusters, white; calyx lobes **very narrow, needle-shaped, 6 x 0,5 mm**. Fruit fleshy, globose, up to 10 mm in diameter, black, crowned with the remains of the calyx.

A very decorative garden plant for areas of semi-shade; flowers profusely.

4 Pavetta zeyheri   Small-leaved bride's bush
SA: 722   Spring–Summer   Fynblaarbruidsbos
Shrub or small tree; occurring in bushveld and grassland, usually on rocky ridges. Leaves **narrowly lanceolate, 15–75 x 5–12 mm**, **leathery**, dark green to bluish green, **hairless**, usually **without domatia** in axils of principal lateral veins; bacterial nodules **more or less circular, scattered over the lamina**; apex **tapering**; petiole **very short**. Flowers in axillary clusters, white; calyx lobes **toothed, with sharp tips**. Fruit fleshy, globose, up to 10 mm in diameter, black, crowned with the remains of the calyx.

P. revoluta: fruit   P. trichardtensis: flowers

P. schumanniana: flowers   P. schumanniana: fruit

P. trichardtensis: flowers   P. zeyheri: flowers   P. zeyheri: fruit

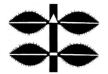

GROUP 16

Leaves simple, opposite; blade single- or pinnately veined, not distinctly discolorous, without bacterial nodules, densely hairy, at least below; margin smooth. Interpetiolar stipules, scar or ridge present. Spines absent.

See also Group 15: *Pavetta bowkerii* (p. 264); Group 17: *Burchellia bubalina* (p. 278), *Keetia gueinzii* (p. 280) and *Rothmannia capensis* (p. 286); Group 25: *Gardenia resiniflua* (p. 366).

RUBIACEAE (see page 30)

1 *Canthium gilfillanii*   **Velvet rock alder**
SA: 706   Spring   **Fluweelklipels**
Shrub or small tree; occurring on rocky ridges in bushveld and grassland. Leaves elliptic, ovate to almost circular, rather **thinly textured**, **velvety**, with **domatia often present** in axils of principal lateral veins below; margin **wavy**. Flowers in axillary clusters, small, greenish white. Fruit a drupe, oval, asymmetric, black.
   The stems of young shoots are often attractively grooved longitudinally when debarked, and are used for walking sticks and ornaments.
   Very similar to *C. mundianum* (Group 17, p. 278), which has more or less hairless leaves. *C. setiflorum* (**1.1**) is a scrambling shrub or small tree from hot, low-altitude bushveld; particularly common in Maputaland. The leaves, which are often clustered on reduced lateral shoots, are elliptic to oblong-elliptic, 12–45 x 5–12 mm, with or without rather rough hairs, and a very short (up to 2 mm long) petiole. Diagnostic is the very small (up to 3 mm long) pale yellow flowers and the single or 2-lobed fruits which are laterally flattened.

2 *Crossopteryx febrifuga*   **Sand crown-berry**
SA: 683; Z: 1056   Summer   **Sandkroonbessie**
Shrub or small deciduous tree; occurring in hot, dry bushveld, usually on sandy soil. Leaves **elliptic to ovate**, 40–130 x 20–60 mm, **leathery**, glossy dark green and **rough-haired** above, soft-haired below; venation **prominently raised** below. Flowers in dense, branched, terminal heads, creamy white, often flushed with pink; corolla lobes recurved. Fruit a **capsule**, oval, about 10 x 7 mm, tipped by a **circular scar** left by the calyx, dehiscent.
   The plant is browsed by game. The wood is pale brown with a reddish tinge, hard, durable, and suitable for woodwork and carving. Bark used medicinally.
   Vegetative material can be confused with *Combretum molle* (Group 23, p. 334), which lacks interpetiolar stipules.

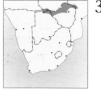

3 *Feretia aeruginescens*   **Red-leaved medlar**
Z: 1082   Spring   **Rooiblaarmispel**
Scrambling shrub or small tree; occurring in low-altitude bushveld, usually along rivers or at the edges of springs and pans. Branchlets soft-haired. Leaves on new growth towards ends of stems, **obovate to oblanceolate**, usually about 30–125 x 20–60 mm, glossy dark green and hairy above, **reddish brown with soft hairs below**; lateral veins almost parallel, **immersed above**, **raised below**; petiole up to 3 mm long. Flowers axillary, solitary or in few-flowered clusters, white, often flushed with pink, appearing **before** the new leaves. Fruit a drupe, almost globose, up to 20 mm in diameter, **pink to bright red**, crowned with the persistent calyx, or a scar after it has been shed.

1

C. gilfillanii: flowers

1

C. gilfillanii: fruit

2

C. febrifuga: flowers

1.1

C. setiflorum: flower & fruit

2

C. febrifuga: fruit

3

F. aeruginescens: flowers

3

F. aeruginescens: fruit

1 *Heinsia crinita*   **False gardenia**
SA: –; Z: 1091   Summer   **Valskatjiepiering**
Compact shrub or small tree; occurring in hot, low-altitude bushveld, thicket and riverine fringe forest. Leaves elliptic to oblong or lanceolate, 20–80 x 10–50 mm, **light green**, hairless or with rough hairs above, **velvety, at least on principal veins below**; petiole up to 8 mm long. Flowers axillary or terminal, solitary or in few-flowered clusters, white, **up to 40 mm in diameter**, with corolla **tube up to 30 mm long**, sweetly scented. Fruit a drupe, oval, up to 12 mm long, **orange**, crowned with the calyx. All the southern African material belongs to subsp. *parviflora*.

2 *Lagynias dryadum*   **Lagynias**
SA: –; Z: 1102   Summer   **Lagynias**
Scrambling shrub or small tree; occurring in bushveld, often in rocky places. Leaves **narrowly ovate to elliptic, up to 40 x 20 mm**, yellowish green to grey-green, both surfaces **velvety**; apex tapering; base broadly tapering to rounded, petiole about 5 mm long. Flowers in axillary **clusters, pale yellow to cream**, often produced in profusion; calyx lobes **conspicuous, 7–10 mm long**, with apices **broadly tapering to rounded**. Fruit a drupe, globose, about 25 mm in diameter, **drooping** on slender stalks, brown, crowned with persistent remains of the calyx.
    Strongly resembles *Pachystigma triflorum* (found mainly in the Waterberg range, Northern Province), which has smaller (less than 20 mm long) leaves and flowers produced in 3-flowered clusters, with more tapering calyx lobes.

3 *Lagynias monteiroi* (= *Ancylanthos monteiroi*)   **Dune medlar**
SA: 714.3   Summer   **Duinemispel**
Scrambling shrub or small tree, usually **multistemmed**; occurring in coastal and sand forest, endemic to the Maputaland Centre. Leaves opposite or clustered on reduced lateral branches, **ovate**, up to 30 x 20 mm, **leathery**, both surfaces **densely covered in hairs**, paler below. Flowers axillary, solitary, cream or yellowish, with a **long, slightly curved corolla tube up to 20 mm long, velvety** on the outside. Fruit a drupe, subglobose, about 15 mm in diameter, with sparse hairs, orange or brownish, crowned with the persistent calyx lobes.
    The fruit is edible.

4 *Sericanthe andongensis* (= *Neorosea andongensis*)   **Venda coffee**
SA: 697; Z: 1089   Winter–Spring   **Vendakoffie**
Deciduous shrub or small tree, occurring in bushveld, usually along rocky ridges or streams. Leaves obovate to oblanceolate, 30–90 x 10–50 mm, **thinly textured**, both surfaces **with silky hairs when young**, becoming almost hairless with age (var. *andongensis*), or with lower surface remaining soft-haired (var. *mollis*); venation **prominent below**, with **linear bacterial 'nodules' next to midrib along basal portion** (appearing as darker protuberances along midrib, visible only from below); petiole up to 8 mm long. Flowers axillary, solitary, white, up to 30 mm in diameter, with corolla lobes **slender and slightly twisted**. Fruit a drupe, globose, about 10 mm in diameter, orange to bright red; persistent tubular calyx up to 4 mm long.
    S. odoratissima var. *uluguru*, an understorey forest component (found in south-eastern Zimbabwe and adjacent Mozambique), also has elongated bacterial nodules along the midrib.

H. crinita: flowers

L. dryadum: flowers

L. dryadum: fruit

S. andongensis: flowers

H. crinita: fruit

L. monteiroi: flowers

S. andongensis: fruit

1 *Tapiphyllum parvifolium*   Mountain medlar

SA: 703   Spring–Summer   **Bergmispel**

Shrub or small, much-branched tree; occurring in bushveld, usually on rocky ridges. Leaves opposite or clustered on reduced lateral shoots, **broadly elliptic to almost circular, small (usually about 15 mm long)**, both surfaces densely covered with **fine soft hairs**; midrib and lateral veins **raised below**; apex broadly tapering to rounded; base square or lobed; margin slightly wavy; petiole **almost absent**. Flowers in dense axillary clusters, small, greenish. Fruit a drupe, globose, up to 15 mm in diameter, brown or reddish, crowned by a circular scar left by the calyx. The wood has been used to make arrowheads. Fruit edible.

T. velutinum (from Zimbabwe) has leaves which are usually about 40 mm long, with thick woolly hairs and prominently raised venation on both surfaces. *Pachystigma macrocalyx* (mainly from the Eastern Cape and KwaZulu-Natal) is a shrub or small tree from rocky outcrops in high-rainfall grassland and bushveld. It has larger (25–45 x 18–25 mm) ovate to elliptic leaves, with a longer (up to 10 mm) petiole. The calyx has well-developed lobes, up to 5 mm long; these persist and enlarge to become strap-shaped and about 10 mm long in the fruit.

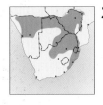

2 *Vangueria infausta*   Wild medlar

SA: 702; Z: 1096   Spring   **Wildemispel**

Shrub or small deciduous tree; occurring in wooded grassland, bushveld and coastal forest, often in rocky places. Branchlets shortly hairy. Leaves elliptic to ovate, **large (50–240 x 38–150 mm)**, dull green, **densely covered with short, soft, hairs**, particularly when young. Flowers in axillary clusters, greenish white, often produced before the leaves. Fruit a drupe, subglobose, up to 35 mm in diameter, yellowish to brown, crowned with a circular scar left by the calyx.

The plant is browsed by game. The fruit is edible, with a rather dry sweet-sour flesh. Often found with elongated, papillate galls on the leaves, caused by an insect. Root used medicinally.

V. cyanescens (Group 17, p. 290) is very similar but has hairless leaves. Also compare *Vangueriopsis lanciflora* (below).

3 *Vangueriopsis lanciflora*   False medlar

SA: 704; Z: 1101   Spring   **Valsmispel**

Shrub or small deciduous tree, with spreading, more or less horizontal branches; occurring in bushveld, often on rocky outcrops or sandy soil. Branchlets often **powdery reddish brown**. Leaves oblong to oblanceolate, up to 139 x 60 mm, **dark green** and rough-haired to smooth above, with a dense **yellowish-white** cover of **woolly hairs** below; margin **wavy**; petiole thickset, up to 10 mm long. Flowers in axillary heads, cream; corolla lobes **up to 15 mm long, curved backwards**, appearing before the leaves. Fruit a drupe, ovoid, often asymmetric, about 25 x 20 mm, yellowish brown, crowned with the persistent calyx lobes.

The fruit is edible. Easily grown from truncheons.

Rather similar to *Vangueria infausta*, whose leaves are densely covered in hairs on both surfaces, and which has smaller flowers without the strongly recurved corolla lobes.

T. parvifolium: flowers

T. parvifolium: fruit

V. infausta: flowers

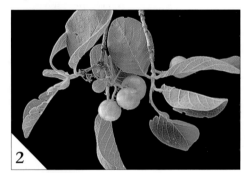

V. infausta: fruit

V. lanciflora: fruit

GROUP 17

Leaves simple, opposite; blade single- or pinnately veined, not distinctly discolorous, without bacterial nodules, smooth or sparsely hairy; margin smooth. Interpetiolar stipules, scar or ridge present. Spines absent.

See also Group 12: *Strychnos potatorum* (p. 252); Group 14: *Canthium inerme* (p. 260) and *Hyperacanthus amoenus* (p. 262); Group 16: *Sericanthe andongensis* (p. 272); Group 18: *Cassipourea mossambicensis* (p. 294); Group 23: *Duvernoia adhatodoides* (p. 324); Group 25: *Cassipourea gummiflua* (p. 364), *Gardenia cornuta* (p. 366), *G. resiniflua* (p. 366), *G. ternifolia* (p. 366), *G. thunbergia* (p. 366) and *G. volkensii* (p. 368).

ICACINACEAE (see page 25)

1 Cassinopsis tinifolia   False lemon thorn
SA: 421; Z: 592   Winter–Spring   Valslemoentjiedoring
Evergreen scrambling shrub or small tree; occurring on forest margins, often along streams. Young branchlets more or less **4-angled**, **green**. Leaves **oval, thick, leathery**, dark green above, dull pale green (whitish bloom in Zimbabwe) below; margin **rolled under**. Flowers in branched axillary heads, small, white to cream. Fruit fleshy, **ovoid, subcompressed**, up to 8 mm long; 1 seed, longitudinally ridged.

LOGANIACEAE (see page 26)

2 Anthocleista grandiflora   Forest fever tree
SA: 632; Z: 894   Spring–Summer   Boskoorsboom
Tall deciduous tree with a **straight, clean bole** and a compact, rather sparsely branched crown; occurring in forest, usually in moist places. Leaves clustered at ends of branches, **very large (up to 1 000 x 300 mm)**, hairless; petiole **absent** or very short. Flowers in large, branched, terminal heads or panicles, creamy white; corolla tube **up to 40 mm long**. Fruit fleshy, oval, about 35 mm in diameter.

The wood is pale white, soft and brittle. Bark and leaves used medicinally. An interesting accent plant for frost-free gardens.

This is the southern African dicotyledonous tree with the largest simple leaves.

RHIZOPHORACEAE (see page 30)

3 Bruguieria gymnorrhiza   Black mangrove
SA: 527   Winter–Summer   Swartwortelboom
Small to medium-sized evergreen tree, with numerous **knee-like aerial breathing roots** (pneumatophores) arising from the mud around the tree; occurring **along tidal estuaries and lagoons** as a constituent of mangrove swamp thicket and forest, mainly towards the seaward side. Leaves **elliptic, thick and leathery**, lower surface usually with small black dots; apex with a **broad, sharp tip**. Flowers axillary, solitary, creamy-white, soon fading to brown; pollen released explosively on touching; calyx **persistent**. Fruit a single-seeded berry, **up to 25 mm** long, germinating while still on the tree; emerging hypocotyl ('root') **up to 150 x 12 mm**, **cigar-shaped**, with **shallow and blunt longitudinal ridges**.

The poles are used in the construction of huts and fish kraals. The bark is rich in tannin, and yields a black dye. Leaves shed continually throughout the year: an important food source for large mangrove crabs.

Often grows with *Rhizophora mucronata* (p. 278), which has distinct stilt-roots and leaves with a bristle-like tip.

C. tinifolia: flowers   *A. grandiflora*: flowers   *A. grandiflora*: fruit

C. tinifolia: flowers & fruit   *A. grandiflora*: flowers

B. gymnorrhiza: tree   *B. gymnorrhiza*: flowers   *B. gymnorrhiza*: fruit

1 *Rhizophora mucronata*   Red mangrove
SA: 526   Summer–Spring   Rooiwortelboom
Small to medium-sized evergreen tree, with numerous **arching, branched, aerial stilt-roots up to 2 m long**; occurring along **tidal estuaries and lagoons** as a constituent of mangrove swamp thicket and forest. Branchlets rather **thick and brittle**. Leaves **elliptic, thick and leathery**, lower surface usually with small black dots; apex with a **slender bristle-like tip up to 5 mm long**. Flowers in few-flowered axillary heads, creamy white; calyx persistent. Fruit a single-seeded berry, **up to 70 mm long**, germinating while still on the tree; emerging hypocotyl ('root') **up to 450 x 20 mm, not ridged**.
Stems are used in the construction of huts and fish traps. The bark is rich in tannin, and yields a deep brown dye.
Rather similar to *Ceriops tagal*, a mangrove whose leaf apices are rounded and without a bristle-like tip, and a hypocotyl that is shorter (up to 260 mm long) and sharply ridged longitudinally.

RUBIACEAE (see page 30)
2 *Alberta magna*   Natal flame bush
SA: 701   Summer–Autumn   Breekhout
Sturdy small to medium-sized evergreen tree; occurring along forest margins and on rocky outcrops, often at the **upper end of forested gullies**. Leaves **elliptic to elliptic obovate**, leathery, **hairless**; base narrowly tapering; margin **rolled under**. Flowers in opposite panicles, bright red, tubular, showy. Fruit a nut, with two **bright red, papery wings** (enlarged calyx lobes).
A spectacular sight when in flower and fruit, but unfortunately slow growing and difficult to maintain in gardens. Bark used medicinally.

3 *Burchellia bubalina*   Wild pomegranate
SA: 688   Spring–Summer   Wildegranaat
Shrub or small evergreen tree; occurring in forest or on rocky outcrops in grassland. Branchlets **hairy** when young. Leaves **broadly ovate, 50–180 x 25–80 mm**, glossy dark green, hairless, or fine-haired above, dull green and soft-haired below; petiole **thickset, hairy**. Flowers in **dense terminal clusters**, orange to dark red, tubular, hairy. Fruit urn-shaped, crowned by **persistent calyx lobes**.
The bark and root are used medicinally. An ornamental garden subject and extended bloomer, grown in semi-shade or full sun.

4 *Canthium mundianum*   Rock alder
SA: 710; Z: 1113   Spring   Klipels
Shrub or small tree; occurring in forest or on rocky ridges in bushveld and grassland. Leaves elliptic, ovate to almost circular, rather **thinly textured**, sparsely haired or **smooth**, with **domatia often present in axils of principal lateral veins below**; margin **wavy**. Flowers in axillary clusters, small, greenish white. Fruit a drupe, oval, asymmetric, black.
The wood is hard, insect-resistant, and used for fence posts, furniture and implements. The fruit is edible, but not very tasty.
Very similar to *C. gilfillanii* (Group 16, p. 270), the leaves of which are densely covered in hairs, and which may merely be a hairy variant of *C. mundianum*.

R. mucronata: flowers

R. mucronata: fruit

C. mundianum: fruit

A. magna: flowers

A. magna: fruit

B. bubalina: flowers

B. bubalina: flowers

B. bubalina: fruit

C. mundianum: flowers

GROUP 17

1 ***Cephalanthus natalensis***   **Strawberry bush**
SA: 685; Z: 1058   Spring–Summer   **Witaarbeibos**
Scrambling shrub, canopy climber or small **bushy tree**; occurring along forest margins and on rocky outcrops in high-rainfall montane grassland. Leaves **ovate, glossy dark green** above, paler green below, often **tinged with red**, with **domatia in axils of lateral veins**; margin wavy. Flowers in dense spherical heads, greenish white or yellowish. Fruit fleshy, comprising several small fruits clustered together in a round, **strawberry-like** head, whitish or reddish.
    The leaves are browsed by game and stock. The fruit is edible, either eaten fresh or made into a preserve; also used medicinally.

2 ***Coddia rudis*** (= *Xeromphis rudis*)   **Small bone-apple**
SA: 689.1; Z: 1068   Spring   **Kleinbeenappel**
Shrub or small tree, usually **multistemmed** with arching branches; occurring in bushveld and on forest margins. Leaves opposite or **clustered on short lateral shoots, broadly obovate, small (rarely more than 20 x 15 mm), hairless**; margin **wavy**. Flowers in axillary clusters, white, fading to cream. Fruit spherical, up to 8 mm in diameter, greenish brown, **tipped with persistent calyx**.
    The plant is browsed by game and stock.

3 ***Hymenodictyon floribundum***   **Firebush**
Z: 1054   Spring–Summer   **Brandbos**
Shrub or small deciduous tree, with **bright red or crimson autumn colours**; occurring in bushveld and forest areas, associated with rocky outcrops of granite or quartzite. Leaves **crowded** near ends of branches, obovate to oblong-elliptic, **large (up to 240 x 180 mm), thick** and **rather fleshy**; margin **wavy**; petiole **thickset**, up to 20 mm long, grooved. Flowers in erect, spike-like racemes, up to 150 mm long, small, greenish white. Fruit a capsule, reddish brown, densely clustered along the inflorescence.

4 ***Hymenodictyon parvifolium***   **Yellow firebush**
SA: 682; Z: 1055   Spring–Summer   **Geelbrandbos**
Shrub, climber or small deciduous tree, with **bright yellow autumn colours**; occurring in bushveld, usually on sandy soil or rocky ridges. Leaves ovate, **up to 50 x 20 mm, thick** and **rather fleshy**, hairless; margin **wavy**; petiole **slender**, about 5 mm long. Flowers in terminal, branched, spike-like racemes about 120 mm long, small, yellow, ageing through white to dark brown. Fruit a capsule, oval, **up to 25 x 10 mm**, greyish or reddish brown with **large whitish lenticels**, dehiscent.
    The root is used medicinally.

5 ***Keetia gueinzii*** (= *Canthium gueinzii*)   **Climbing turkey-berry**
SA: 714; Z: 1106   All year   **Rankbokdrol**
Robust evergreen climber, scrambling shrub or small tree; occurring on forest margins. Branchlets and young growth usually covered in **brownish hairs**. Leaves ovate to oblong-lanceolate, **glossy dark green** and hairless above, paler green and rough-haired, often with domatia, below; base **lobed**; stipules **conspicuous**. Flowers in dense axillary heads, cream to pale yellow, sweetly scented. Fruit a drupe, 1- or 2-lobed, black.

280

C. *natalensis*: fruit

C. *rudis*: fruit

H. *floribundum*: flowers

C. *natalensis*: flowers

C. *rudis*: flowers

H. *floribundum*: fruit (old)

H. *parvifolium*: flowers

H. *parvifolium*: fruit

K. *gueinzii*: flowers

K. *gueinzii*: fruit

1 *Kraussia floribunda* Rhino-coffee
SA: 700.1 Summer Renosterkoffie
Shrub or small tree; occurring in bushveld, dune forest, swamp forest and riverine vegetation. Leaves **elliptic**, 40–90 x 25–40 mm, **glossy** dark green, **hairless**, with **domatia in axils of lateral veins**; margin **wavy**. Flowers in **loose, few-flowered, branched and rather drooping** heads, white. Fruit a drupe, spherical, up to 8 mm in diameter, black, tipped by the remains of the calyx.
The plant is browsed by game. Fruit edible, sweet-tasting.

2 *Lagynias lasiantha* Natal medlar
SA: 705 Summer Natalmispel
Scrambling shrub or small tree; occurring in bushveld, sand forest and along forest margins. Leaves ovate to lanceolate, glossy green above, **pale blue- to grey-green below, hairless**; margin entire, **wavy**. Flowers in axillary clusters, greenish yellow, ageing to orange; petals **pointing backwards**. Fruit a drupe, spherical, 25–45 mm in diameter, **drooping on twisted stalks**, yellowish brown.

3 *Oxyanthus latifolius* Zulu loquat
SA: 696.1 Summer Zoeloelukwart
Evergreen shrub or small tree, usually multistemmed; occurring in **sand forest**. Leaves elliptic, **large (50–200 x 40–130 mm)**, leathery, with **domatia** in axils of lateral veins; base **lobed, asymmetric**. Flowers in axillary clusters, white; floral tube **very slender, up to 60 mm long**, pollinated by hawk moths. Fruit fleshy, oval with slender neck, yellowish orange.

4 *Oxyanthus speciosus* (= *O. gerrardii*) Wild loquat
SA: 696; Z: 1080 Summer Wildelukwart
Evergreen shrub or small tree, usually with **horizontal** branches; occurring in the **understorey** of forest. Leaves with a tendency to droop, elliptic to narrowly ovate, very large (75–300 x 37–150 mm), **glossy** dark green, hairless except for domatia in axils of lateral veins below; apex **tapering to a drip-tip**; base **tapering or rounded, symmetric**. Flowers in axillary clusters, white; floral tube **very slender, up to 35 mm long**, pollinated by hawk moths. Fruit fleshy, oval with slender neck, yellow. All material in southern Africa belongs to subsp. *gerrardii*.
Similar to *O. pyriformis* (= *O. natalensis*), a rare shrub or small tree confined to the understorey of forest in KwaZulu-Natal. It has leaf bases that are markedly asymmetric, and floral tubes up to 80 mm long.

5 *Psychotria capensis* Black bird-berry
SA: 723; Z: 1137 Spring–Summer Swartvoëlbessie
Shrub or small tree; occurring in forest in bush clumps, on rocky outcrops in high-rainfall grassland. Leaves elliptic to obovate, **stiffly leathery, glossy** dark green above, paler green below, **hairless**; principal lateral veins **4–6 pairs**, prominent below, with **domatia** in their axils. Flowers in branched, **rather flat-topped**, terminal heads, yellow. Fruit fleshy, oval, ripening through yellow to red or black.
P. mahonii, from forest in the Eastern Highlands of Zimbabwe and adjacent Mozambique, has leaves with 7–10 pairs of principal lateral veins, and smooth fruit.
P. zombamontana has 10–16 pairs of principal lateral veins, and ribbed fruit.

K. floribunda: flowers

K. floribunda: fruit

L. lasiantha: flowers

L. lasiantha: fruit

O. latifolius: flowers

O. latifolius: fruit

O. speciosus: flowers

O. speciosus: fruit

P. capensis: flowers

P. capensis: fruit

1 Psychotria zombamontana　　　　　　　　　　**Red bird-berry**
SA: 723.1; Z: 1140　Summer　　　　　　　　　　**Rooivoëlbessie**
Shrub or small tree; occurring as an **understorey** constituent in forest. Leaves elliptic to oblanceolate, 75–150 x 13–60 mm, leathery, reportedly with scattered bacterial nodules, but these were not noticed by the authors; principal lateral veins **10–16 pairs**, with **domatia** in their axils below; margin slightly rolled under; petiole up to 15 mm long. Flowers in rather lax, branched, terminal heads up to 30 mm long, small, **greenish white**. Fruit fleshy, oval, about 5 mm long, **strongly ribbed longitudinally** (most noticeable when dry), pink, yellow-orange to red.

2 Psydrax livida (= *Canthium huillense*)　　　　　　　**Green tree**
SA: 713; Z: 1108　Summer　　　　　　　　　　　**Groenboom**
Shrub or small tree with rather horizontally spreading branches; occurring in bushveld, often on rocky ridges or Kalahari sand. Leaves **ovate**, rather leathery, glossy dark green above, paler green below, usually **hairless**; base tapering to **rounded** or **square**. Flowers in branched axillary heads, small, creamy yellow. Fruit a drupe, 1- or 2-lobed, brownish to black.
　　The plant is browsed by cattle.

3 Psydrax locuples (= *Canthium locuples*)　　　　　　**Krantz quar**
SA: 712; Z: 1111　Spring–Summer　　　　　　　　**Kranskwar**
Shrub or small tree; occurring in bushveld and sand forest, often on sandy soil. Leaves **ovate to elliptic, up to 50 x 25 mm**, glossy dark green above, paler green below, **hairless**; apex **tapering**, base **tapering and running into the short petiole**; margin **wavy**. Flowers in branched axillary heads, small, greenish white. Fruit a drupe, 1- or 2-lobed, about 5 x 7 mm, black.
　　Often associated with *P. fragrantissima*, whose leaf apices are rounded or broadly tapering.

4 Psydrax obovata (= *Canthium obovatum*)　　　　　　**Quar**
SA: 711; Z: 1114　Summer–Autumn　　　　　　　　**Kwar**
Medium to large tree; occurring in coastal and inland forest. Leaves **elliptic or obovate, up to 20–50 x 15–30 mm** (very small in juveniles), **leathery**, glossy dark green above, paler green below, **hairless**, often **with domatia in axils of lateral veins** below; apex **rounded or broadly tapering**, base tapering; margin **rolled under**. Flowers in branched axillary heads, creamy green; corolla tube **2–3,5 mm long**. Fruit a drupe, 1- or 2-lobed, about 6 x 8 mm, black. Leaves obovate or rounded with hairless domatia in subsp. *obovata* (found in coastal areas), more elliptic with hairy domatia in subsp. *elliptica* (inland areas).
　　The wood is yellow or reddish brown, hard, heavy, close-grained, used for fencing, hut building and suitable as a general purpose timber.
　　P. fragrantissima (**4.1**) has smaller leaves (13–35 mm long) and flowers (corolla 1,5–2,5 mm long). It is endemic to the Maputaland Centre and is associated with sand forest, often growing with *P. locuples*.

1

P. zombamontana: flowers

1

P. zombamontana: fruit

2

P. livida: flowers

3

P. locuples: flowers

3

P. locuples: fruit

4

P. obovata: flowers

4.1

P. fragrantissima: fruit

1 *Rothmannia capensis*   Cape gardenia
SA: 693   Summer   Kaapse katjiepiering
Small to medium-sized evergreen tree; occurring in forest and on rocky hillsides in bushveld. Leaves **crowded** towards ends of branches, opposite with the odd third leaf, **elliptic, leathery**, hairless in mature plants, velvety in juveniles, with **distinct pit-domatia** in axils of principal lateral veins below; margin wavy. Flowers axillary, solitary, white with **maroon streaks inside throat of corolla tube**, fading to cream. Fruit spherical, about 70 mm in diameter, green.
Wood hard and strong, suitable for implement handles. Fruit used medicinally.
R. urcelliformis is a large forest tree (from the Eastern Highlands of Zimbabwe) with short-haired stems and leaves. *R. manganjae* is a shrub or small tree from more open habitats in the same region. It has hairless leaves and flowers with corolla lobes overlapping to the left (overlapping to the right in all the other southern African members of the genus).

2 *Rothmannia fischeri*   Rhodesian gardenia
SA: 694; Z: 1075   Spring–Summer   Rhodesiese katjiepiering
Small to medium-sized evergreen tree; occurring in bushveld and sand forest. Leaves **somewhat drooping, crowded** towards ends of branches, opposite with the odd third leaf, **lanceolate to elliptic, leathery**, hairless, with **distinct pit domatia** in axils of principal lateral veins below; margin wavy. Flowers axillary, solitary, white to cream with **maroon markings outside throat of corolla tube**. Fruit spherical, about 50 mm in diameter, green, ripening dark brown.
Larval food plant for the butterfly *Deudorix lorisona coffea*.

3 *Rothmannia globosa*   Bell gardenia
SA: 695   Spring   Klokkieskatjiepiering
Small slender evergreen tree; occurring along forest margins and in riverine fringe forest. Leaves **elliptic to lanceolate**, leathery, hairless, with **domatia** in axils of principal lateral veins below; margin wavy; venation pale green and **translucent when viewed against the light**, characteristically **tinged pink or reddish**. Flowers axillary, in groups of 2–4, white with inside of tube yellowish, often flecked with pink in the throat, produced in **profusion**. Fruit spherical, about 25 mm in diameter, brown.
A decorative tree for small gardens, although flowering is very brief.

4 *Tarenna littoralis* (= *Enterospermum littorale*)   **Dune butterspoon bush**
SA: 687; Z: 1065   Spring   **Duinebotterlepelbos**
Evergreen shrub or small tree; occurring in coastal bush and sand forest. Branchlets **4-angled**. Leaves **elliptic to obovate, leathery**, hairless, with **domatia** in axils of lateral veins below; apex broadly tapering to **rounded**; margin **rolled under**; petiole 4–14 mm long; stipules **large**, triangular, **tightly enclosing the growing tip of shoots and appearing spoon-like** (hence common names). Flowers in dense terminal and axillary heads, small, white to cream. Fruit a drupe, spherical, about 8 mm in diameter, ripening through yellow to brown.
T. zimbabwensis (= *Enterospermum rhodesiacum*) is an inland species (from southeastern Zimbabwe and adjacent areas) with leaf apices tapering and margin flat. The stipules are also leaf-like and conspicuously sheathing the growing tips, but the petioles are longer (12–25 mm).

R. capensis: flower

R. capensis: flower & fruit

R. fischeri: flowers

R. fischeri: fruit

R. globosa: flowers

R. globosa: flowers

R. globosa: fruit

T. littoralis: flowers

T. littoralis: fruit

1 Tarenna pavettoides — False bride's bush
SA: 686; Z: 1064 Spring–Summer — Basterbruidsbos
Small to medium-sized tree with a leafy crown; occurring along forest margins and in swamp forest. Branchlets **4-angled**. Leaves **oblanceolate, 38–200 x 20–50 mm**, thinly textured, more or less hairless; apex tapering to a **drip-tip**; margin **wavy**. Flowers in many-flowered, branched, axillary heads, small, white. Fruit a drupe, spherical, about 8 mm in diameter, black, tipped by the persistent calyx.
Superficially rather similar to *Nuxia floribunda* (Group 25, p. 362), which has 3-whorled leaves.

2 Tarenna supra-axillaris
(= *T. barbertonensis*) — Narrow-leaved false bride's bush
SA: 686.1; Z: 1064/1 Spring — Smalblaarbasterbruidsbos
Much-branched shrub or small tree; occurring on rocky outcrops in forest and bushveld, and in sand forest. Leaves **widely spaced** along stems, **lanceolate**, 30–90 x 7–40 mm, **leathery**, glossy green with venation **prominent** above, hairless; apex broadly tapering; margin **wavy**. Flowers in axillary clusters, white. Fruit a drupe, spherical, about 8 mm in diameter, black, tipped by the persistent calyx. Very young branches with reddish brown bark and leaves 11–42 mm wide in subsp. *supra-axillaris* (found in Zimbabwe and further north), pale grey or fawn and 7–20 mm wide in subsp. *barbertonensis* (South Africa and Swaziland).

3 Tricalysia capensis — Cape coffee
SA: 698; Z: 1085 Spring — Kaapse koffie
Shrub or small tree, usually multistemmed; occurring in forest, on forest margins and in riverine vegetation. Leaves **ovate to lanceolate**, 30–100 x 10–35 mm, sparsely haired on veins, with **hairtuft domatia** in axils of principal lateral veins below; apex tapering to a drip-tip; venation **not translucent below**; margin rolled under; petiole **hairy**. Flowers in axillary clusters, white. Fruit a drupe, oval, about 8 mm long, red to black, tipped with persistent calyx.
T. delagoensis, from coastal bush in Maputaland and northwards, is very similar but differs in its leaves, which have very small pit-domatia and more or less hairless petioles.

4 Tricalysia lanceolata — Jackal-coffee
SA: 699 Spring — Jakkalskoffie
Shrub or small tree, usually multistemmed; occurring in forest, on forest margins, in riverine vegetation and wooded ravines in bushveld. Leaves **elliptic to lanceolate**, 25–100 x 10–30 mm, thinly leathery, **hairless**; apex tapering; venation **more or less translucent below**; margin rather **wavy**. Flowers in axillary clusters, white. Fruit a drupe, oval, about 8 mm long, red to black, tipped with persistent calyx.
T. sonderiana, from coastal dune forest in KwaZulu-Natal and southern Mozambique, has thickly leathery, dull green leaves, with the venation conspicuous above and margin rolled under.

T. pavettoides: flowers

T. pavettoides: fruit

T. capensis: flowers

T. capensis: fruit

T. supra-axillaris: flowers

T. supra-axillaris: fruit

T. lanceolata: flowers

T. lanceolata: fruit

1 *Vangueria cyanescens*   **Bush medlar**
SA: 702.1; Z: 1095   Spring   **Bosmispel**
Deciduous shrub or small tree; occurring in bushveld, sand forest and coastal bush.
Leaves **elliptic to ovate, large (80–150 x 40–90)**, rather thinly leathery, **hairless**;
apex broadly tapering; base lobed or tapering; margin **wavy**. Flowers in axillary
clusters, yellowish green, with **short, tapering calyx lobes**. Fruit a drupe, spher-
ical, about 25 mm in diameter, yellowish to orange brown, tipped by a **circular scar**
(remains of calyx).
  The fruit is edible.
  Similar to, and often associated with, *V. infausta* (Group 16), which has densely-
haired leaves. Also resembles *Pachystigma bowkeri*, a forest species with large,
hairless leaves and flowers with long (up to 10 mm), strap-shaped, calyx lobes.
  The species which appears here as *Vangueria cyanescens* has been referred to as
V. esculenta by some authors. The correct application of these two names is
uncertain at present.

2 *Vangueria randii* (= *V. chartacea*)   **Natal bush medlar**
SA: 702.2; Z: 1097   Summer   **Natalbosmispel**
Deciduous shrub or small tree with somewhat horizontal branchlets; occurring
in coastal forest and bushveld. Leaves **ovate to elliptic, 60–150 x 10–70 mm**,
thinly textured, glossy bright green above, **bluish green** below, usually **hairless**;
apex narrowly tapering; base rounded or tapering. Flowers in axillary clusters,
greenish white. Fruit a drupe, spherical, up to 20 mm in diameter, yellow, tipped by
a **circular scar** (remains of the calyx). Calyx tube hairy in subsp. *randii* (found in
Zimbabwe), hairless in subsp. *chartacea* (South Africa).
  The fruit is edible. Larval food plant for the butterfly *Hypolycaena philippus*.

V. cyanescens: flowers

V. cyanescens: fruit

V. randii: flowers

V. randii: flowers

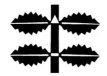

GROUP 18

Leaves simple, opposite; blade single- or pinnately veined, not distinctly discolorous; margin toothed. Interpetiolar stipules, scar or ridge present.

See also Group 19: *Mackaya bella* (p. 296) and *Pseudoscolopia polyantha* (p. 302).

CELASTRACEAE (see page 22)

1 *Catha edulis*   Bushman's tea
SA: 404; Z: 572   Summer–Spring   Boesmanstee
Small to medium-sized deciduous tree (attractive yellowish autumn colours) with a sparse **upright crown** and somewhat **drooping** branches (resembling a eucalypt from a distance); occurring in bushveld and associated with evergreen forest, often in rocky places. Bark with **yellow pigment.** Leaves **elliptic to oblong, pendulous,** leathery, shiny bright green above, dull and pale green below; margin **finely and evenly** toothed, each tooth **tipped by a minute gland**; venation **distinct on both surfaces.** Flowers in **dense** axillary clusters, small, white. Fruit a capsule, **oblong,** about 10 mm long, dehiscent; seeds with a small narrow **wing.**

The leaves contain a habit-forming stimulant with an amphetamine-like action; commonly known as 'khat', the tree is extensively cultivated and the leaves chewed in certain North African and Arabian countries. Local wild forms do not appear to be as potent as some of the cultivated selections.

2 *Catha transvaalensis*   Sekhukhune Bushman's tea
SA: 404.1   Autumn–Spring   Sekhukhuneboesmanstee
Small to medium-sized deciduous tree with spreading branches; occurring in bushveld, usually in groves, clearly associated with specific geological features (the exact nature of the association remains obscure). Bark **rough and corky,** cracked in a more or less grid-like pattern, with yellow pigment. Leaves usually **widely elliptic to elliptic,** spreading or erect, **thick and leathery,** shiny bright green above, dull and pale green below; margin **finely and evenly toothed,** each tooth **tipped by a minute gland**; principal lateral veins **4–6 pairs.** Flowers in axillary panicles towards ends of branches, small, white. Fruit a capsule, **ovate,** with a **sharply tapering** tip, about 10 mm long, dehiscent; seeds **wingless.**

C. abbottii, an extremely rare tree from Pondoland, has leaves with more than 10 pairs of principal lateral veins, and capsules that are oblong with a blunt tip.

CORNACEAE (see page 23)

3 *Curtisia dentata*   Assegai
SA: 570; Z: 819   Spring–Autumn   Assegaai
Medium to large evergreen tree; occurring in coastal and montane forest. Young growth densely covered with **woolly grey or brownish hairs.** Leaves leathery, shiny dark green above, lower surface with **prominent venation** and densely covered with **woolly grey or brownish hairs**; margin **strongly and sharply** toothed. Flowers in branched terminal sprays, small, cream. Fruit fleshy, roundish, about 10 mm in diameter, **crowned with remains of persistent calyx,** white or reddish, 4-seeded.

The fruit is eaten by animals; bitter-tasting and used medicinally. Wood reddish brown, hard, heavy, strong and elastic; suitable for general carpentry and once extensively used for wagon-making. Bark used for tanning. A decorative foliage plant (usually shrubby) for gardens; makes an excellent hedge; frost tender.

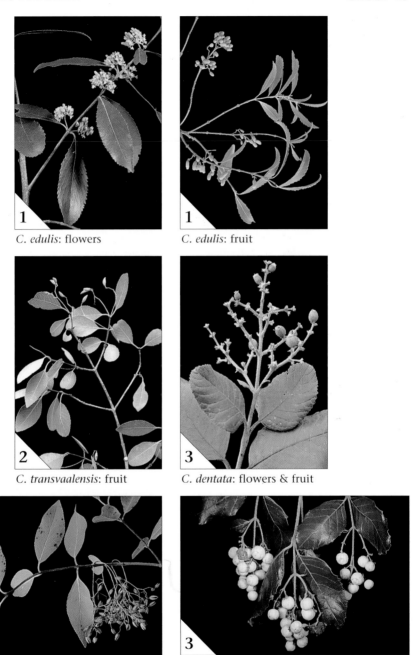

1 *C. edulis*: flowers

1 *C. edulis*: fruit

2 *C. transvaalensis*: fruit

3 *C. dentata*: flowers & fruit

2 *C. transvaalensis*: fruit

3 *C. dentata*: fruit

ICACINACEAE (see page 25)

1 *Cassinopsis ilicifolia*   Lemon thorn
SA: 420; Z: 591   Spring   Lemoentjiedoring

Evergreen **scrambling** shrub or small tree; occurring in montane forest margins and wooded ravines, often along streams. Branchlets **green** with a sharp straight spine **between the petioles of opposite leaves**, often somewhat zigzag. Leaves shiny green above, dull green below; margin with **sharp-tipped** teeth, rolled under. Flowers in stalk clusters inserted **on the side of the branch, between the opposite petioles**, small, white or cream. Fruit a drupe, ovoid, about 10 mm long, slightly flattened, bright orange.

An attractive foliage plant, occasionally cultivated in gardens, even in areas with fairly heavy frost. It prefers temperate summers and plenty of moisture. Fruit relished by birds; fruiting very erratic in cultivation.

RHIZOPHORACEAE (see page 30)

2 *Cassipourea malosana*
(= *C. gerrardii; C. congoensis* var. *gerrardii*)   Common onionwood
SA: 529; Z: 762.1   Spring–Summer   Gewone uiehout

Shrub or small to medium-sized tree with a straight, slender stem, **horizontally spreading** branches and rather small crown; occurring in the **understorey** of evergreen forest. Twigs **purplish black** with **swollen** nodes, hairy when young. Leaves variously elliptic, lanceolate to oblanceolate, **stiff and leathery**, shiny dark green above, dull green below, hairless; apex broadly tapering; margin with hooked serrations; lower third often untoothed; stipules between petioles, falling early. Flowers in small axillary clusters, inconspicuous, greenish white. Fruit a capsule, initially thinly fleshy, oval, up to 10 mm long, sparsely hairy to smooth, orange drying black, surrounded at the base by the **persistent remains of the calyx**; seeds dark brown to black with a reddish aril.

The bark is heavily utilized in traditional medicine. Plants have already been eradicated or are under threat in many places.

Similar to C. *flanaganii*, whose leaves are usually less than 40 mm long, the venation translucent green and distinct below; confined to the Eastern Cape. Also resembles *C. swaziensis*, a species with a restricted distribution in northern KwaZulu-Natal and Swaziland, usually found on quartzite rock outcrops. It is usually a shrub which has leaves with the venation raised on the lower surface, often with an entire margin and densely hairy petioles.

3 *Cassipourea mossambicensis*   Sand onionwood
SA: 531   Summer   Sanduiehout

Shrub or small evergreen tree; occurring in sand forest and rocky places in the Lebombo Mountains; **restricted to Maputaland**. Stems hairy. Leaves usually **ovate to nearly round, stiff and leathery**, shiny dark green above, pale green below; margin with a **few teeth towards tip, or entire**, conspicuously **rolled under**; lateral veins and reticulation **conspicuous** on both surfaces; stipules interpetiolar, small, hairy, early deciduous. Flowers in axillary groups of 1–3, green. Fruit a capsule, greenish white to yellowish, hairless, dehiscent, surrounded at the base by the persistent remains of the calyx; seeds with bright orange aril.

The freshly cut wood smells of onions.

C. ilicifolia: flowers

C. ilicifolia: fruit

C. malosana: fruit

C. mossambicensis: fruit

C. malosana: flowers

C. mossambicensis: flowers

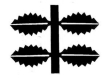

GROUP 19

Leaves simple, opposite; blade single- or pinnately veined, margin toothed or lobed. Interpetiolar stipules, scar or ridge absent.

See also Group 8: *Catophractes alexandri* (p. 120); Group 18: *Curtisia dentata* (p. 292); Group 23: *Anastrabe integerrima* (p. 352); Group 25: *Clerodendrum myricoides* (p. 370).

ACANTHACEAE (see page 19)

1 Mackaya bella   River bells
SA: 681.1 Spring   Blouklokkiesbos
Shrub or small semi-deciduous tree, usually **multistemmed**; occurring in the understorey of evergreen forest, often along stream banks. Leaves elliptic, shiny dark green above, dull green below, tapering to a **drip tip**; margin **irregularly scalloped** or widely and coarsely toothed; midrib and side veins raised below, the latter with **reddish purple hair-tuft domatia** in their axils. Flowers in lax terminal racemes, large and attractive, mauve to white, usually marked with **fine purple-pink lines**. Fruit a capsule, narrowly club-shaped, splitting into two valves to explosively eject the seed.
The wood was once used to kindle fire by friction. A decorative garden plant suitable for shady areas, but sensitive to heavy frost. Larval food plant for the butterfly *Presis oenone oenone*.

2 Sclerochiton harveyanus   Blue-lips
SA: – ; Z: 1045 Summer   Bloulipbos
Shrub or small tree, usually **multistemmed**; occurring in the understorey and at the margins of evergreen forest, often gregarious. Leaves elliptic to oblanceolate, **25–60 x 15–25 mm, glossy dark green** above, dull green below; margin **bluntly and irregularly toothed**. Flowers in short racemes, bluish mauve to violet-blue; stamens 4, protruding from the mouth of the corolla tube. Fruit a capsule, ellipsoidal with a tapering tip, splitting into 5 valves to explosively eject the seed.
S. odoratissimus, a shrub or small understorey tree found in the forests of KwaZulu-Natal and the Eastern Cape, has similar foliage but is more floriferous with white, strongly scented flowers.

ASTERACEAE (see page 20)

3 Didelta spinosa   Thorny salad bush
SA: 736.2 Spring   Doringslaaibos
Shrub or small, slender tree with a small though dense and well-defined crown; occurring in semi-desert areas, often in stony places. Leaves **sessile**, thick and **rather succulent**, often with a dense covering of **cobweb-like hairs**; apex often **spine-tipped**; margin usually with irregularly spaced, **spine-tipped teeth**. Flower heads radiate, at ends of branches, yellow, about 60 mm in diameter. Fruit a small nutlet, one end with hairy scales.
Heavily browsed by livestock, notably horses. The leaves are used in salads.

1

M. bella: fruit

2

S. harveyanus: flowers

1

M. bella: flowers

1

M. bella: flowers

3

D. spinosa: tree

3

D. spinosa: tree

3

D. spinosa: flowerheads

CELASTRACEAE (see page 22)

1 Cassine peragua   **Cape saffron**
SA: 414   Summer–Autumn   **Bastersaffraan**
Small to medium-sized evergreen tree; occurring in evergreen forest, often on forest margins; some forms on coastal dunes in the Western Cape are rhizomatous. Bark with yellow pigment. Leaves **broadly elliptic to almost circular**, thick, leathery, shiny dark green above, paler below; margin **toothed along the upper half**; venation **distinct on both surfaces, translucent when viewed against the light**; stipules **minute, dry, not connected** between the petioles. Flowers in axillary clusters towards ends of branches, small, white. Fruit **fleshy**, round, 5–15 mm in diameter, green ripening orange yellow, red, reddish brown to purplish black; seed 1–6 per fruit.
   The leaves are reported to be toxic. Wood reddish brown, hard, heavy, suitable for furniture. Fruit eaten by birds.
   Often confused with *Hartogiella schinoides* (p. 300), whose leaf venation is obscure when held against the light. Sterile material may also be confused with the capsular-fruited *Catha abbottii*, a rare species with a restricted distribution in southern KwaZulu-Natal and Pondoland. Stipules in *C. abbottii* are large and free with their bases united between the petioles; they are shed at an early stage and leave a conspicuous scar on the stem.

2 Cassine tetragona   **Climbing saffron**
SA: 411.1   Spring   **Ranksaffraan**
Woody climber, scrambling shrub or a small tree; occurring in evergreen forest, on forest margins and in wooded grassland. Branchlets **4-angled**, short side shoots often pointing backwards to assist in climbing. Young growth reddish brown. Leaves **elliptic, thick and leathery, shiny** dark green above, dull and pale green below; margin toothed; petiole **very short (rarely more than 3 mm)**. Flowers in branched axillary clusters, small, creamy white. Fruit fleshy, globose, about 8 mm in diameter, green ripening red to purplish black, seed 1 or 2.
   Leaves browsed by stock. Fruit edible (eaten by children) and favoured by birds. Attractive container plant, especially when fruiting. Larval food plant for the butterfly *Acraea boopis*.

3 Elaeodendron croceum (= *Cassine papillosa*)   **Common saffron**
SA: 415; Z: 576   Spring–Summer   **Gewone saffraan**
Shrub or small to medium-sized evergreen tree; occurring in evergreen forest, often on forest margins. Bark often with yellow pigment. Branchlets with **raised brown or black dots**. Leaves opposite to subopposite, **oblong to elliptic, thick and leathery, dark green** above, paler below; apex usually **tapering**; margin with widely spaced teeth. Flowers in axillary clusters, small, greenish, **4-merous**. Fruit fleshy, **oval**, up to 25 mm long, **cream to pale yellow**, with a single stone.
   Wood hard, yellowish white, durable. Bark widely used for medicinal and magical purposes. Most parts of the plant are poisonous. Seed dispersed by elephants, fruit bats and rameron pigeons.
   This species was until recently known as *Cassine papillosa*. Note that *Elaeodendron zeyheri* is the correct name for the tree, hitherto incorrectly referred to in southern African tree literature as *Cassine crocea*.

C. *peragua*: flowers

C. *peragua*: fruit

C. *tetragona*: fruit

C. *tetragona*: fruit

E. *croceum*: flowers

E. *croceum*: fruit

1 *Elaeodendron matabelicum* (= *Cassine matabelicum*)   Condiment saffron
Z: 575   Spring–Autumn   Speserysafraan
Medium to tall tree with somewhat **drooping** branchlets; occurring in bushveld and wooded grassland, often on termitaria or rocky hillsides. Leaves opposite or subopposite, occasionally alternate on the same shoot, **oblong to elliptic**, shiny yellowish green above, dull pale green below; apex tapering or rounded; margin finely toothed or more or less entire. Flowers in dense axillary heads, small, cream to greenish. Fruit **fleshy**, more or less globose, up to 18 mm in diameter, **cream or yellow**, with a single stone.
    Wood used for carved items (notably spoons). Bark extensively used medicinally. Root bark yields a yellow dye. Parts of the plant are said to have been used to flavour meats and stews (hence the common names), but this application is not recommended because the plant may have toxic properties.

2 *Elaeodendron zeyheri*   Small-leaved saffron
SA: 412   Summer–Winter   Fynblaarsaffraan
Small to medium-sized evergreen tree; occurring in forest and mesic bushveld, on forest margins or rocky outcrops; rather rare. Bark often with yellow pigment. Leaves **oval, thick and leathery, greyish green** above, paler below; apex often **rounded**; margin with widely spaced teeth. Flowers in axillary clusters, small, greenish, **5-merous**. Fruit fleshy, **spheroid or ovoid, up to 25 mm long, yellowish**, with 1 or 2 stones.
    Wood reddish brown, fine-grained, hard and tough, serves as a general purpose timber. The bark is used medicinally and for tanning and dying. Root believed to be poisonous.
    Until recently incorrectly referred to in the literature as *Cassine crocea* or *Crocoxylon croceum*.

3 *Hartogiella schinoides*   Spoonwood
SA: 418   Spring–Summer   Lepelhout
Small to medium-sized evergreen tree; occurring in wooded areas in fynbos, often on the edge of forest and along streams; bark often with layers of powdery yellow pigment. Leaves **narrowly elliptic to lanceolate, leathery, dark green** above, grey-green below; margin slightly or deeply bluntly toothed; venation **obscure when held against the light**. Flowers in lax axillary clusters, small, white or cream. Fruit with the fleshy part rather tough and hard, spheroid to ellipsoid, yellow to brown, indehiscent, with 1 or 2 seeds.
    Wood pale brown, hard and fine-grained, and makes attractive furniture. Leaves were chewed as a thirst quencher.
    Similar to *Cassine peragua*, whose leaves have a translucent and clearly visible venation when held up against the light.

E. matabelicum: flowers   *E. zeyheri*: fruit

H. schinoides: fruit   *H. schinoides*: fruit

FLACOURTIACEAE (see page 25)

1 *Pseudoscolopia polyantha*   **False red pear**
SA: 499   Spring–Summer   **Valsrooipeer**
Shrub or small evergreen tree; occurring on forest margins, **always on sandstone**; locally common, although with a very restricted geographical distribution. Branchlets angled, usually **reddish**. Leaves **narrowly elliptic to elliptic, leathery**, dark green; margin bluntly toothed or almost entire; petiole 3–8 mm long, **reddish**. Flowers in axillary clusters of 4–6, **white**; petals **4**, rather similar to the 4 sepals; stamens **many**. Fruit a capsule, ovoid, splitting into 2 or 3 valves; seeds small, ellipsoid, covered with minute star-shaped hairs.
Resembles *Cassipourea flanaganii* and *C. malosana* (Group 18), both of which have greenish flowers and lack the reddish tinge to the branchlets and petioles.

LOGANIACEAE (see page 26)

2 *Nuxia oppositifolia*   **Water elder**
SA: 635; Z: 897   Spring–Summer   **Watervlier**
Shrub or small, slender tree with thin, **drooping** branches, often multistemmed; occurring **along rivers and streams**, often growing between rocks in the riverbed. Branchlets **angled**. Leaves **long and narrow, 45–90 x 4–15 mm**, shiny pale green above, slightly sticky; margin **shallowly toothed** or entire. Flowers in dense, much branched axillary heads towards ends of branches, small, white; calyx **shiny green**. Fruit a capsule, about 5 mm long, enclosed by the persistent calyx tube.
Wood pale to dark brown, suitable for carved ornaments. Browsed by game.

MONIMIACEAE (see page 27)

3 *Xymalos monospora*   **Lemon wood**
SA: 111; Z: 120   Winter–Spring   **Lemoenhout**
Medium to large evergreen tree, frequently coppicing from old stumps; sexes separate, on different trees; occurring in coastal and montane forest, usually in **wet places**. Bark flaking to leave **circular or whirling concentric markings**. Leaves opposite or subopposite, occasionally alternate, shiny dark green with midrib and lateral veins **conspicuously sunk above**, creating an embossed effect; margin **irregularly toothed**, rarely entire, pleasantly scented when crushed. Flowers in short axillary spikes, inconspicuous, greenish. Fruit fleshy, oval, about 15 mm long, red.
Fruit eaten by birds. The wood is yellow (hence the common names), durable and suitable for furniture. Bark used medicinally.

SCROPHULARIACEAE (see page 31)

4 *Halleria lucida*   **Tree fuchsia**
SA: 670; Z: 1023   Winter–Summer   **Notsung**
Shrub or small evergreen tree with a spreading and drooping crown; occurring in forest, forested ravines and grassland, often along streams or in rocky places. Leaves **drooping, ovate**, thinly leathery, shiny bright green above, hairless; base very **broadly tapering to square**, often **asymmetrical**; margin **finely toothed to scalloped**. Flowers in small axillary clusters on new growth, or characteristically **in dense clusters on old wood**, orange or bright red, tubular, curved, rich in nectar. Fruit fleshy, ovoid, black when ripe, crowned by the dry remains of the style.
Fruit edible but not tasty. Various parts used in traditional medicine. Flowers attract nectar-feeding birds who also act as pollinators; easily grown in gardens.

P. polyantha: fruit

X. monospora: fruit

P. polyantha: flowers

N. oppositifolia: flowers

N. oppositifolia: flowers

X. monospora: flowers

H. lucida: flowers

H. lucida: fruit

VERBENACEAE (see page 33)

1 •*Duranta erecta* (= *D. repens*)   **Forget-me-not tree**
SA: X949; Z: 981   Spring–Summer   **Vergeet-my-nie-boom**
Evergreen to semi-deciduous shrub or small tree, with somewhat **drooping** branches; invading bushveld and urban open space. Branchlets **4-angled**, often with straight axillary **spines** up to 30 mm long. Leaves **ovate to obovate**, 25–45 x 10–25 mm, soft-textured; margin toothed, mainly in the upper half. Flowers in **drooping** terminal racemes, small and trumpet-shaped, pale mauve, blue or white. Fruit a berry, ovate, up to 10 mm in diameter, with an **elongated beak at the tip** (persistent calyx which tightly encloses the fruit), **shiny orange**, in **dense, drooping clusters**.
    A native of Central America; cultivated for ornament. The berries are poisonous.

2 *Karomia speciosa* (= *Holmskioldia speciosa*)   **Wild parasol flower**
SA: 668   All year   **Wildesambreelblom**
Deciduous, sparsely branched shrub or small tree; occurring in bushveld, usually on hot, dry, rocky mountain slopes. Leaves small (20–50 x 15–30 mm), **softly textured**, both surfaces **finely hairy**; margin **coarsely toothed**, mainly in upper half; petiole **about 10 mm long**. Flowers in small axillary clusters towards ends of branches, bicoloured; calyx **plate-like, 20–25 mm in diameter, distinctly 5-lobed**, papery, mauve to pink; corolla 2-lipped, with slightly curved cylindrical tube, deep blue. Fruit thinly fleshy, 4-lobed, enclosed within the persistent calyx.
    Similar to *K. tettensis* (**2.1**) from the Zambezi River Valley and adjacent areas, which has the petiole obscured by the decurrent leaf base and the calyx larger (30–40 mm in diameter) and scarcely lobed.

3 •*Lantana camara*   **Lantana**
SA: – ; Z: –   All year   **Lantana**
Much-branched scrambling shrub; invading bushveld, forest and plantation margins, watercourses, roadsides and degraded land. Stems **4-angled**, with scattered **recurved prickles**. Leaves ovate, covered with **rough hairs**, foul-smelling when crushed. Flowers in compact, flat-topped heads, with those in the centre opening first and usually changing colour as they fade; **colour very variable**, pink, yellow, orange or orange-brown. Fruits fleshy, globose, **glossy purplish black**.
    A native of Central and South America; cultivated for ornament and hedging. This is a declared weed in South Africa.

4 *Premna mooiensis*   **Small skunk bush**
SA: 658   Spring   **Kleinmuishondbos**
Shrub or small tree; occurring in bushveld and thicket, often in rocky places. Leaves **ovate to elliptic**, bright green, **soft**, hairless, with a **pungent, unpleasant scent** when crushed; margin entire or with a few coarse teeth in upper half; petiole **slender**, up to 12 mm long. Flowers in sparse terminal clusters, small (up to 5 mm long), white, 2-lipped. Fruit more or less globose, fleshy, about 8 mm in diameter, **shiny purple-black** when ripe, held in the **persistent calyx**.
    The wood is yellowish brown, hard, brittle, fine-grained, prone to attack by wood borers, used for fence posts. Fruit eaten by birds.
    P. senensis is a shrub or small bushy tree from northern Botswana, the Caprivi region of Namibia and the Zambezi River Valley. It has a somewhat drooping crown, leaves with both surfaces softly hairy and flowers up to 25 mm long.

D. erecta: flowers

D. erecta: fruit

K. speciosa: flowers

K. tettensis: old flowers

L. camara: flowers

L. camara: flowers

P. mooiensis: flowers

P. mooiensis: fruit

GROUP 20

Leaves simple, opposite; blade single- or pinnately veined, margin smooth. Interpetiolar stipules, scar or ridge absent. Spines present. Latex present.

APOCYNACEAE (see page 20)

1 *Carissa bispinosa*   Forest num-num
SA: 640.1; Z: 905   Spring–Summer   **Bosnoemnoem**

Much-branched spiny evergreen shrub or small tree, usually **multistemmed**, often scrambling; occurring in forest, bushveld and wooded places in a wide range of habitats. Latex white. Spines opposite, either **robust**, simple, once or twice forked and **up to 50 mm long** (subsp. *bispinosa*; usually in relatively hot, dry areas) or **slender**, once forked or nearly absent and **rarely more than 25 mm long** (subsp. *zambesiensis*; usually in shady forest habitats). Flowers in terminal clusters, **small**, white; corolla lobes **3,5–5 mm long, longer than broad, overlapping to the left.** Fruit fleshy, oval, **4–6 mm in diameter, bright red**, 1- or 2-seeded.

Fruit edible to humans, also eaten by monkeys and birds. Root used medicinally.

A heterogeneous species in need of more taxonomic study. Closely resembles *C. edulis*, which has unbranched spines and corolla lobes overlapping to the right. Large-leaved forms of *C. bispinosa* subsp. *zambesiensis* resemble *C. wyliei*, a rather rare forest understorey species with much larger flowers (corolla lobes 9–12 mm long). *C. tetramera* has flowers with 4 instead of 5 petals and purplish black fruit, and is particularly common in Maputaland (northern KwaZulu-Natal), often in association with sand forest.

2 *Carissa edulis*   Simple-spined num-num
SA: 640.4; Z: 906   Spring–Summer   **Enkeldoringnoemnoem**

Much-branched spiny evergreen shrub or small tree, usually **multistemmed**, often **scrambling**; occurring in bushveld. Latex white. Spines **nearly always single, straight (not forked)**, up to 40 mm long. Leaves with or without hairs. Flowers in terminal clusters, small, white, often **tinged with pink or purple**; corolla lobes **4–9 mm long, longer that broad, overlapping to the right**. Fruit fleshy, oval, **6–11 mm in diameter, purplish black**, 2–4-seeded.

The fruit is edible, sweet and juicy, makes a good jam or jelly, and is used to kill intestinal worms in man and cattle. Crushed roots have the characteristic smell of oil of wintergreen and are widely used in traditional medicine.

C. bispinosa: flowers

C. bispinosa: fruit

C. edulis: flowers

C. edulis: fruit

C. edulis: fruit

1 Carissa haematocarpa
SA: 640.2   Spring–Summer

Karoo num-num
Karoonoemnoem

Robust, **intricately-branched** and very spiny evergreen shrub or small tree, usually multistemmed; occurring in arid karroid bush. Latex white. Spines opposite, usually **once or twice forked**, up to 45 mm long, persistent, green, becoming **stout and woody**. Leaves glossy dark green above, pale green and often wrinkled below, with or without hairs. Flowers in few-flowered terminal clusters, small, white; corolla lobes **2 mm long, broader than long, overlapping to the left**. Fruit fleshy, oval, **4–5 mm in diameter, black to bluish-purple**, 1- or 2-seeded.

The fruit is edible, but stains the teeth pale blue to black. Browsed by domestic stock and game in times of drought.

Differs from *C. bispinosa (p. 306)* in its more robust habit, small flowers with rounded corolla lobes and black mature fruits.

2 Carissa macrocarpa
SA: 640.3   Winter–Spring

Big num-num
Grootnoemnoem

Much-branched spiny evergreen shrub or small tree, usually **multistemmed**; occurring in coastal bush **never far from the sea**, usually on sand dunes. Latex white. Spines opposite, **once or twice forked**, up to 45 mm long, **rigid**, persistent. Leaves **glossy dark green** above, paler below, hairless. Flowers solitary or in few-flowered groups at the ends of branchlets, sometimes in the fork of a spine, large, white, often tinged with pink, **5-merous**, corolla lobes **15–35 mm long, overlapping to the left**. Fruit fleshy, oval, **relatively large (up to 50 mm long, 35 mm in diameter), bright red**; many-seeded.

Whole fruit (including skin and seeds) is edible, delicious and rich in vitamin C, calcium, magnesium and phosphorus; it is also made into a jam. Unlike that of many other members of the family, the latex is harmless. Makes an excellent evergreen hedge resistant to saltspray, although rather frost-tender. The prostrate cultivar, 'Green Carpet', is widely grown as a ground cover and for flower boxes.

Resembles *C. wyliei*, which also has fairly large flowers (corolla lobes 9–14 mm long), but with spines absent or very small (about 4 mm long). This plant is an understorey shrub of evergreen forest with a localized distribution in KwaZulu-Natal and Pondoland.

3 Carissa tetramera
SA: – ; Z: –   Summer

Sand Forest num-num
Sandwoudnoemnoem

Much-branched spiny evergreen shrub or small tree, usually multistemmed; occurring in sand forest, bushveld and coastal bush. Latex white. Spines opposite, usually **twice-forked**, rarely simple, up to 50 mm long, **slender**. Flowers in terminal clusters or the spine-forms, white, often tinged with red, **4-merous**; corolla lobes **4,3–5 mm long, oval to round, overlapping to the left**. Fruit fleshy, oval, **7–10 mm in diameter, purplish black**, 4–8-seeded.

The plants are browsed by game. Fruit eaten by people, monkeys and birds.

C. haematocarpa: fruit

C. haematocarpa: fruit

C. macrocarpa: flowers

C. tetramera: fruit

C. macrocarpa: fruit

C. tetramera: flowers

GROUP 21

Leaves simple, opposite; blade single- or pinnately veined, margin smooth. Interpetiolar stipules, scar or ridge absent. Spines absent. Latex present.

See also Group 5: *Protorhus longifolia* (p. 86); Group 24: *Ozoroa engleri* (p. 356), *O. insignis* (p. 356), *O. obovata* (p. 356), *O. paniculosa* (p. 358) and *O. sphaerocarpa* (p. 358).

APOCYNACEAE (see page 20)

1 *Acokanthera oblongifolia*   Dune poison-bush
SA: 638   Spring   **Duinegifboom**
Small to medium-sized evergreen tree; occurring in coastal dune forest and bush, on sand dunes **rarely far from the sea**. Latex white. Leaves **broadly elliptic to lanceolate, thick and leathery**, often tinged with red or purple; apex **rounded** with a **hair-like tip**; principal side veins **obscure**; petiole thick, wrinkled. Flowers in axillary groups, forming dense masses of flowers along the young shoots, white or tinged with pink; corolla tube **longer than 13 mm**. Fruit fleshy, ovoid to almost globose, **more than 20 mm long**, red to purplish black, 1- or 2-seeded.

Highly toxic, and has been used in the preparation of arrow poison; the plant has featured in suicides and murders; various parts are used in traditional medicine. A decorative garden subject and good container plant, but potentially dangerous because of its toxic properties.

Similar to *A. oppositifolia*, which has leaves whose secondary and often tertiary side veins are very distinct, flowers with the corolla tube shorter (8–11 mm), and fruit less than 20 mm long.

2 *Acokanthera oppositifolia*   Common poison-bush
SA: 639; Z: 903   Autumn–Summer   **Gewone gifboom**
Shrub to small evergreen to semi-deciduous tree; occurring in wooded places in a variety of habitats. Latex white. Young growth often reddish. Leaves **ovate-elliptic, oblong or lanceolate, thick and leathery**, often tinged with red or purple; apex tapering to a **sharp, spine-like point**; principal side veins **very distinct**; petiole thick, wrinkled. Flowers in dense axillary clusters; white, often tinged with pink, particularly on the outside; corolla tube **8–11 mm long**. Fruit fleshy, usually ovoid, **10–20 mm long**, red ripening purplish black, 1- or 2-seeded.

With the possible exception of the ripe fruit, all parts of the plant are highly toxic; even meat grilled on a fire made from the wood has proved fatal. Various parts are employed in traditional medicine. Bark and wood are used to prepare a very potent arrow poison.

This is a heterogeneous species, particularly in regard to the upper leaf surface sculpture (rough to the touch in Eastern Cape coastal forms) and in fruit size. Easily confused with *A. oblongifolia*.

A. *oblongifolia*: flowers

A. *oppositifolia*: flowers

A. *oblongifolia*: fruit

A. *oppositifolia*: fruit

1 *Acokanthera rotundata* (= *A. schimperi*)   **Round-leaved poison-bush**
SA: 640; Z: 904 Spring   **Rondeblaargifboom**
Shrub or small evergreen tree with a sparse crown; occurring in bushveld, often on rocky outcrops. Latex white. Leaves **broadly elliptic to almost round, thick and leathery**, usually **rough to the touch (sandpapery) above**; apex **rounded**; margin rolled under; principal side veins **obscure**. Flowers in many-flowered axillary clusters, white, often tinged with pink or red; corolla tube **8–10 mm long**. Fruit fleshy, round to oval, 15–20 mm in diameter; red ripening purple-black, 1- or 2-seeded.

Ripe fruit said to be edible (with a bitter taste) but best avoided because of the poisonous properties of the tree group.

2 *Diplorhynchus condylocarpon*   **Horn-pod tree**
SA: 643; Z: 915 Spring–Summer   **Horingpeultjieboom**
Shrub or small deciduous tree, usually **multistemmed** with a sparse crown and long, **slender, drooping** branches; occurring in bushveld, often on rocky ridges and in sandy soil. Latex white. Leaves more or less **drooping**, elliptic, **shiny yellowish green** above, paler below; margin often wavy; principal side veins 8–16 pairs, **parallel, yellowish**; petiole **slender, 10–23 mm long**. Flowers in terminal sprays, small, white, sweetly scented. Fruit of paired follicular carpels **standing away at an angle**, hard, dark reddish brown with **small whitish dots (lenticels)** when mature.

The latex is used as a bird lime, also applied to the hides of drums to improve their quality and tone. Leaves and root used in traditional medicine. Wood pale brown, fine-grained and suitable for small carved ornaments. Heavily browsed by elephant.

3 *Holarrhena pubescens*   **Fever pod**
SA: 642; Z: 914 Summer   **Koorspeulboom**
Shrub or small, sparsely branched deciduous tree; occurring in low-altitude bushveld, often on rocky outcrops and in sandy soil. Bark **rough and corky** with longitudinal fissures. Latex white. Branchlets with **white dots (lenticels)**. Leaves sparsely to densely **hairy**; margin **wavy**. Flowers in many-flowered heads **opposite or close to** a leaf axil, large (up to 20 mm in diameter), white, jasmine-scented. Fruit of paired and **drooping** follicles, **slender, 200–300 mm long**; seeds numerous, each crowned by a dense tuft of silky hairs.

Contains toxic alkaloids. Bark used medicinally.

4 *Tabernaemontana elegans*   **Toad tree**
SA: 644; Z: 917 Spring–Autumn   **Paddaboom**
Shrub or small deciduous to semi-deciduous tree with a single upright trunk; occurring in bushveld and coastal forest, often along rivers or in rocky places. Bark **thick and corky, longitudinally fissured**. Latex white. Leaves crowded towards ends of branches, **glossy dark green** above, **rather large (90–200 x 50–70 mm)**, hairless; lateral veins up to 22 pairs, prominently raised below. Flowers in branched clusters towards ends of branches, white, fragrant; corolla lobes about 10 mm long, **twisted to the left**. Fruit **paired** on pendulous stalks, joined at the base, each half roundish, beaked, with **two lateral and one dorsal ridge**, grey-green dotted with numerous **pale grey corky warts**, dehiscent; seeds embedded in a bright orange pulp.

The leaves are browsed by game. Pulp of ripe fruit edible; also used to curdle milk. Latex used for bird lime and to stop bleeding. Root used medicinally.

A. rotundata: flowers

A. rotundata: fruit

D. condylocarpon: flowers

H. pubescens: flowers

D. condylocarpon: fruit

H. pubescens: fruit

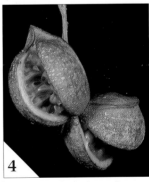

T. elegans: fruit & seeds

T. elegans: flowers

T. elegans: fruit

1 *Tabernaemontana ventricosa*   **Forest toad tree**
SA: 645; Z: 918 Spring–Summer   **Bospaddaboom**
Small to medium-sized tree, usually with a single upright trunk; occurring in the understorey or along the margins of coastal and montane forest, often in dense shade. Bark **rather smooth**. Leaves crowded towards ends of branches, **rather large (90–170 x 35–60 mm)**, apex **sharply tapering**, lateral veins **up to 22 pairs**, prominently **raised below**. Flowers in branched clusters towards ends of branches, white, fragrant; corolla lobes twisted to the left. Fruit **paired on pendulous stalks**, joined at the base, each half **roundish**, dark green, **mottled paler green, surface not warty**, dehiscent on the tree; seeds embedded in a bright orange pulp.
   The pulp of the ripe fruit is edible. Latex used for bird lime.
   Easily confused with *Voacanga thouarsii*, which has leaves with more or less rounded leaf apices, indistinct side veins, often with domatia in their axils, petioles united at the base into a rim or short sheath, and flowers with a distinct calyx tube which breaks off along a transverse circular line at the base (divided almost to the base in *Tabernaemontana*). *T. stapfiana* (= *T. angolensis*), a forest species from the Eastern Highlands of Zimbabwe, has large (up to 40 mm in diameter) white flowers with a yellow throat. The twin fruits are very large (each up to 200 mm in diameter), indehiscent, and fall to the ground to rot.

2 *Voacanga thouarsii*   **Wild frangipani**
SA: 646; Z: 919 Spring–Summer   **Wildefrangipani**
Medium to large tree with a spreading crown, sometimes–in swampy habitats–with thin, cylindrical air roots which emerge above the water level; occurring in coastal forest, usually associated with forest margins, **swampy places or stream banks**. Bark **more or less smooth**. Latex white. Leaves crowded towards ends of branches, leathery, glossy dark green above, **rather large (80–160 x 22–55 mm)**; apex usually **broadly rounded**; lateral veins **up to 12 pairs**, **indistinct**, usually with **domatia** in their axils below; stipules united into an interpetiolar rim. Flowers in clusters towards ends of branches, white turning creamy yellow; corolla lobes about 22 mm long, overlapping to the left. Fruit **paired on pendulous stalks**, joined at the base, each half **roundish**, dark green, **mottled with whitish or yellowish spots**, dehiscent on the tree; seeds embedded in a bright orange pulp.
   The latex is used for bird lime. Fruit edible.
   The fruit is reminiscent of *Tabernaemontana ventricosa* (above).

3 *Wrightia natalensis*   **Saddle pod**
SA: 650; Z:933 Spring   **Saalpeultjieboom**
Small to medium-sized deciduous tree with a sparse, spreading and rather **weeping crown**; occurring in hot, arid bushveld and sand forest, often on hillsides. Latex white. Leaves **drooping, lanceolate, 15–20 mm wide**, tapering to a **pointed tip**. Flowers in clusters towards ends of branches, small, **pale yellow**, sweetly scented. Fruit **paired**, pod-like, **long and slender (200–260 x 8–10 mm)**, **pendulous**, dark green with **minute white dots**, dehiscent; seeds with a tuft of silky hairs at one end.
   The wood is pale brown, very light and buoyant, soft but tough and insect proof, used for fishing-net floats, flat-bottomed punts, oars, carved spoons, plates and small items of furniture. Various parts used medicinally.

T. *ventricosa*: flowers

T. *ventricosa*: fruit

V. *thouarsii*: flowers

W. *natalensis*: flowers

V. *thouarsii*: fruit

W. *natalensis*: fruit

W. *natalensis*: fruit & seeds

CLUSIACEAE (see page 23)

1 *Garcinia buchananii* (= *G. huillensis*)   **Granite garcinia**
Z: 714   Spring   **Granietgeelmelkhout**
Small to medium-sized evergreen tree, often multistemmed; occurring in open woodland and along forest margins, often **on outcrops of granite**. Latex **yellow**, thick and sticky. Leaves 50–110 mm long, **thick and leathery**, sharply tapering, hairless; margin **wavy**; lateral veins very distinctive, **numerous, leaving the midrib at an acute angle and clearly etched on both leaf surfaces**; petiole and midrib often tinged with red. Flowers solitary or in few-flowered axillary clusters, greenish yellow, male, female or bisexual. Fruit fleshy, globose, up to 25 mm in diameter, yellow to orange, 1–3-seeded.

The wood is yellow to orange-brown, dense and hard, suitable for carving and as a general purpose timber. Fruit edible and rich in vitamin C; also used to prepare sour milk. Bark used in traditional medicine.

G. kingaensis is a slender understorey tree from evergreen forests in the Eastern Highlands of Zimbabwe. It has numerous regularly formed horizontal branches; leaves dull bluish to grey-green, usually 100–130 mm long, with numerous fine lateral veins leaving the midrib at almost right angles.

2 *Garcinia gerrardii*   **Forest mangosteen**
SA: 485   Spring–Summer   **Bosgeelmelkhout**
Shrub or small to medium-sized evergreen tree; sexes separate, on different plants; occurring in coastal and montane forest, **often in deep shade** or among stream banks. Latex **pale yellow** (rarely tinged reddish brown). Branchlets **angled by decurrent** petioles. Leaves elliptic, leathery, glossy on both surfaces, hairless; apex **sharply pointed**; petiole **clasping** the stem. Flowers at ends of branches, yellowish green. Fruit fleshy, **subglobose**, orange when ripe, 1- or 2-seeded.

The fruit is edible. Saplings used as whipsticks. Latex from roots effective in killing snails. Various parts used medicinally. Good container plant, particularly for areas of deep shade.

Superficially similar to, and often growing together with, *Buxus natalensis*. The latter, however, does not have latex.

3 *Harungana madagascariensis*   **Orange-milk tree**
Z: 713   Summer–Autumn   **Oranjemelkhout**
Shrub or small to medium-sized bushy tree with a **browny-yellow appearance**; occurring in forest areas, usually on forest margins or as a pioneer in cleared areas. Latex **thick, bright orange**. Stems densely covered with **rusty hairs**. Leaves glossy dark green above, densely **rusty-hairy below**; pair of **youngest leaves at ends of branches remain tightly pressed together until fairly large**. Flowers in many-flowered terminal sprays, small (about 5 mm in diameter), cream, sweetly almond scented. Fruit fleshy, globose, 2–4 mm in diameter, produced in abundance.

The latex is used as a dye and (as are various other parts) in traditional medicine.

316

G. *buchananii*: flower

G. *buchananii*: fruit

G. *gerrardii*: flowers

G. *gerrardii*: fruit

H. *madagascariensis*: fruit

H. *madagascariensis*: flowers

H. *madagascariensis*: fruit

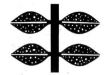

GROUP 22

Leaves simple, opposite; blade single- or pinnately veined, with secretory cavities; margin smooth. Interpetiolar stipules, scar or ridge absent. Latex absent.

MYRTACEAE (see page 28)

1 *Eugenia capensis*   **Dune myrtle**
SA: 553.1   Summer   **Duinemirt**
Shrub to small evergreen tree; sexes separate, on different plants; occurring as a pioneer on **coastal dunes**, usually fully exposed to the salt-spray. Leaves **round to oval, thick and leathery**, dark shiny green above, pale green below, **hairless**; margin strongly **rolled under**. Flowers in axillary clusters **on twigs of previous season and older**, white, sweetly scented, with numerous stamens. Fruit a berry, ellipsoid, up to 10 mm long, **purplish black**, tipped by the persistent calyx, usually single-seeded.
In northern KwaZulu-Natal and southern Mozambique the plant is easily confused with the associated *Diospyros rotundifolia* (Group 10, p. 182) and *Euclea natalensis* subsp. *rotundifolia* (Group 10, p. 184), both of which have alternate leaves.

2 *Eugenia natalitia*   **Common forest myrtle**
SA: 553.2; Z: 796   Spring–Summer   **Gewone bosmirt**
Small or medium-sized evergreen tree; sexes separate, on different plants; occurring in coastal and montane forest; bark **more or less smooth.** Leaves widely elliptic, shiny dark green above, dull green below, **hairless**; apex narrowly tapering, often **slightly twisted**. Flowers solitary or in short, few-flowered axillary racemes, predominantly **on the previous season's growth**, white, hairless; stamens usually more than 30. Fruit a berry, more or less globose, **red to purplish black**, tipped by the remains of the calyx; seed usually solitary, more or less **kidney-shaped**.
Similar to *E. simii*, a shrub with narrowly elliptic leaves that is confined to banks and islands of rivers in southern KwaZulu-Natal and Pondoland, as well as *E. umtamvunensis*, a rare and more robust plant with thick leathery leaves from the same region. Often confused, too, with *E. woodii*, whose young leaves are usually densely hairy and has flowers that are hairy towards the base and borne in stalked groups of 3 on new growth, and more or less globose seeds. *E. zuluensis* occurs in the mistbelt forest of KwaZulu-Natal, Transkei and the northeastern Drakensberg Escarpment, usually in the understorey. Its leaves are elliptic to obovate with a tapering tip, hairless, with midrib markedly raised into a narrow median ridge on the upper surface. *Memecylon natalense* (Group 23, p. 342) has leaves without secretory cavities, and branchlets that tend to be 4-angled.

3 *Eugenia zeyheri*   **Wild myrtle**
SA: 553   Spring   **Wildemirt**
Shrub to small evergreen tree; sexes separate, on different plants; occurring along margins of relatively dry forest and bush clumps. Leaves **narrowly elliptic, glossy dark green above, pale whitish green below**. Flowers axillary, **mainly on new growth**, white. Fruit a berry, more or less globose, ripening **yellow through orange to red**, tipped by the persistent calyx, single-seeded.
E. verdoorniae **(3.1)** is a rare ornamental shrub or small tree, restricted to southern KwaZulu-Natal and Pondoland, which has very narrow leaves (4–8 mm wide) that are often dark red to pinkish when young.

318

E. capensis: flowers

E. natalitia: flowers

E. capensis: fruit

E. natalitia: fruit

E. verdoorniae: flowers

E. zeyheri: fruit

E. verdoorniae: fruit

1 *Metrosideros angustifolia*   Lance-leaved myrtle
SA: 559   Spring–Summer   Smalblad
Shrub to small evergreen tree, occurring **along rivers and watercourses** in the
mountains of the Western Cape. Leaves **long and narrow, 35–80 x 4–10 mm**, hairless. Flowers in axillary, branched heads near the ends of branches, white to cream;
stamens **conspicuous, usually more than 30**. Fruit a capsule, brown, about 3 x
4 mm, many-seeded.

2 •*Psidium guajava*   Guava
SA: X778; Z: 795   Spring–Summer   Koejawel
Evergreen shrub or small tree; invading forest margins, bushveld, watercourses and
roadsides. Bark **smooth, mottled with reddish brown, grey and whitish patches**.
Branchlets **4-angled**, hairy. Leaves ovate to oblong-elliptic, 40–80 mm long, thick,
stiff, hairy below; venation **impressed** above, **raised** below. Flowers in axillary
clusters, white. Fruit a berry, oval, 50–100 mm long, green turning yellow, crowned
with the persistent calyx, many-seeded; flesh white, yellow, or pink, with a penetrating odour.
    A native of tropical America; cultivated for its edible fruit and for shade.
    P. littorale var. *longipes* invades subtropical coastal bush and forest margins;
leaves glossy dark green, veins not conspicuously impressed above, base long-
tapering; fruit globose, 20–30 mm in diameter, purplish red, with white, sweet-
tasting flesh.

3 *Syzygium cordatum*   Water berry
SA: 555; Z: 798   Spring   Waterbessie
Medium to large evergreen tree, often with a somewhat crooked stem and a
rounded crown; occurring in wooded areas and in forest, nearly always near water
or along watercourses, sometimes dominant in swamp forest. Branchlets **4-angled**.
Leaves **elliptic to almost circular, bluish green**, leathery; base often **deeply
lobed**; petiole **absent or very short**. Flowers in branched terminal heads, white to
pinkish, with **numerous fluffy stamens**, fragrant. Fruit a berry, oval, deep purple
when ripe, **tipped by the remains of the calyx**, usually single-seeded.
    The wood is pale reddish brown to greyish, hard, heavy, fine-grained and very
durable, particularly in water. Bark provides a reddish brown dye. Flowers nectar-
rich and visited by numerous insects. The fruit is edible but not very tasty, and is
also used medicinally and magically. Host plant for the emperor moth *Micragone
cana*, whose caterpillars are collected for food. Also a larval food plant for the butterflies *Charaxes druceanus* (at least some of its races), *Deudorix dinochares* and
Parosmodes morantii morantii.

M. angustifolia: flowers

M. angustifolia: fruit

P. guajava: fruit

P. guajava: flower

P. guajava: bark

S. cordatum: flowers

S. cordatum: fruit

1 Syzygium gerrardii

Forest waterwood
Boswaterhout

SA: 556; Z: 800   Winter–Spring

Medium to large evergreen tree with a dense crown, main stem **often buttressed**; occurring in coastal and montane forest, often as a **canopy constituent**. Young growth pinkish red to yellowish green. Leaves elliptic, thinly leathery, shiny dark green above, paler below, blade usually **somewhat folded upwards along the midrib, distinctly stalked**; base narrow; apex abruptly tapering to a **long narrow tip**; margin often somewhat **wavy**. Flowers in branched terminal heads, white, with numerous fluffy stamens, fragrant. Fruit a berry, **globose, dark red to purplish black**, tipped by the persistent calyx, usually single-seeded.

The wood is pinkish brown, hard, durable, and suitable for furniture. Bark used medicinally. Flowers rich in nectar, attracting bees and numerous other insects. Fruit edible but not very tasty.

Related to *S. legatii*, a smaller tree from more open areas and with rather stiff, flat leaves. The plant is very common in the mistbelt of the Soutpansberg range, from where it extends further south along the adjacent Drakensberg Escarpment. *S. pondoense*, a rare shrub or small bushy tree restricted to rocky stream banks in Pondoland, has very narrow leaves (3–10 mm wide), often with reddish tinged venation.

2 Syzygium guineense

Water pear
Waterpeer

SA: 557; Z: 801   Spring–Summer

Medium to tall evergreen tree with a somewhat **drooping** habit (resembling a eucalypt from a distance); occurring in open woodland, often in sandy soil or near water. Branchlets **4-angled**. Leaves **elliptic**, leathery, shiny dark green above, pale green below; base and apex **tapering**; petiole **distinct, 6–25 mm long**. Flowers in branched terminal heads, white, with numerous fluffy stamens, fragrant. Fruit a berry, **oval, purplish black**, tipped by the persistent calyx, usually single-seeded.

The wood is reddish brown, hard, strong and durable. Root and bark used in traditional medicine. Fruit edible but not very tasty. Larval food plant for the butterflies *Charaxes druceanus* (at least some of its races) and *Deudorix antalus*.

An extremely variable species with a complex taxonomy.

RUTACEAE (see page 30)

3 Calodendrum capense

Cape chestnut
Wildekastaiing

SA: 256; Z: 391   Spring–Summer

Medium to large deciduous to semi-deciduous tree; occurring mainly in evergreen afromontane forest and in riverine thicket. Bark more or less **smooth**. Leaves **elliptic**, hairless; margin entire, rather wavy. Flowers in terminal, branched heads, spectacular, large and pink, with long narrow curved petals **dotted with dark maroon glands**, usually covering the tree in mid-summer, readily identifying it, even from a distance, in the forest canopy. Fruit a **large woody capsule** with a **knobby** texture, 5-lobed.

The wood is pale yellow, suitable for furniture and turnery. Seeds eaten by samango monkeys, rameron pigeons and Cape parrots. Easily grown from seed and widely planted in gardens, but flowering is often disappointing; tolerates slight frost. Knobby surface of fruit reminiscent of the edible chestnut, hence the common names. Several swallowtail butterflies (*Papilio* spp.) breed on the tree.

S. gerrardii: flowers

S. gerrardii: fruit

S. gerrardii: young leaves

S. guineense: flowers

S. guineense: fruit

C. capense: flowers

C. capense: fruit

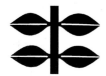

GROUP 23

Leaves simple, opposite; blade single- or pinnately veined, without secretory cavities; margin smooth. Interpetiolar stipules, scar or ridge absent. Latex absent.

See also Group 8: *Rhigozum brevispinosum* (p. 120); Group 9: *Cordia sinensis* (p. 136); Group 19: *Premna mooiensis* (p. 304).

ACANTHACEAE (see page 19)

1 *Duvernoia adhatodoides*   **Pistol bush**
SA: 681   Summer–Winter   **Pistoolbos**

Evergreen shrub to small tree with a dense, dark green crown; occurring in and at the margins of evergreen forest, often along streams or on rock outcrops. Branchlets **square** in transverse section, **brittle**. Leaves broadly lanceolate, **large (150–230 x 70–150 mm)**, dark green above, midrib and side veins raised above; margin wavy, conspicuously **rolled under and shrivelled at the very base** (a kind of domatium). Flowers in short, compact axillary racemes, white, 2-lipped, marked with purple in the throat. Fruit a capsule, **club-shaped**, about 30 x 10 mm, green, and dehiscing explosively (hence the common names) to eject the rough, disc-shaped seeds.

The heartwood is yellow, close-grained, heavy, attractive and can be fashioned into small ornaments. Decorative garden plant, frost-sensitive.

BUDDLEJACEAE (see page 21)

2 *Buddleja saligna*   **False olive**
SA: 636; Z: 901   Spring–Summer   **Witolienhout**

Evergreen shrub or small tree with **greyish green**, somewhat drooping crown; occurring in bushveld, grassland and forest, usually in wooded ravines or on rocky outcrops. Bark **longitudinally furrowed**. Branchlets **4-angled**. Leaves **linear to oblong, 15–100 x 2–15 mm**, shiny dark to greyish green and hairless above, **whitish with prominently raised venation** below. Flowers in dense, many-flowered terminal and axillary panicles, small, white; stamens **4**. Fruit a capsule, about 2 mm long.

The heartwood is dark brown, tough, hard, heavy and very durable. Leaves and root used medicinally. An attractive, frost-hardy garden plant.

B. loricata, from the high Drakensberg range centred on Lesotho, is usually a shrub which has narrowly elliptic leaves that are densely covered with hairs below, and stipules reduced to an interpetiolar ridge.

BUXACEAE (see page 21)

3 *Buxus natalensis*   **Natal box**
SA: 359   Spring   **Natalse buksboom**

Evergreen shrub or small tree; occurring in the **understorey** of evergreen forest. Leaves ovate-lanceolate, **60–110 x 20–50 mm**, leathery, **shiny dark green**, hairless; petiole short and thickset. Flowers in short axillary clusters, sexes separate in the same cluster; small, greenish. Fruit a **woody capsule**, about 20 mm long, crowned with **three horns (persistent styles)**, dehiscent.

Young stems used as laths and poles in hut construction. Decorative garden and container plant, suitable for shady areas.

Resembles *Garcinia gerrardii* (Group 21, p. 316), a species with yellowish milky latex. *B. macowanii* (**3.1**), mainly from Eastern Cape forest, has ovate to ovate-oblong leaves which are much smaller (15–30 x 7–18 mm; even smaller on younger plants).

324

D. adhatodoides: flowers

B. macowanii: fruit

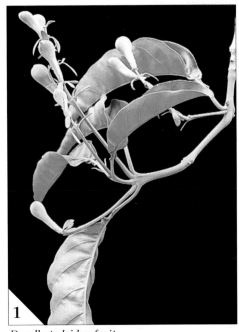

D. adhatodoides: fruit

B. saligna: flowers

B. natalensis: flowers

325

CELASTRACEAE (see page 22)

1 Maurocenia frangula Hottentot's cherry
SA: 417 Winter Hotnotskersie
Evergreen shrub or small tree; occurring in mountain ravines and in coastal bush on rocky seashores. Bark with layers of powdery **yellow pigment**. Leaves **widely elliptic to circular**, dark green above, paler below, **leathery and rigid**; apex rounded or slightly indented; margin **rolled under**; petiole up to 3 mm long. Flowers in axillary clusters, often unisexual, inconspicuous, white to yellowish. Fruit a berry, spheroid, 7–10 mm in diameter, pale red, usually 1- or 2-seeded. The specific epithet is sometimes incorrectly spelled '*frangularia*'.

The wood is yellowish brown, hard, fine-grained, and was once used to fashion musical instruments. The fruit is edible, hence the common names.

2 Pleurostylia capensis (= *P. africana*) Coffee pear
SA: 419; Z: 580 Spring Koffiepeer
Small to large evergreen tree; young leaves tend to **droop**; occurring in forest and wooded ravines. Bark with layers of **powdery orange pigment**. Branchlets more or less 4-angled. Leaves **lanceolate to elliptic**, leathery, glossy green above; apex and base **tapering**; venation **raised on both sides**; petiole up to 8 mm long. Flowers in axillary clusters, small, greenish yellow. Fruit leathery, ellipsoid, dark brown, scar of style **off-centre** due to the development of only 1 of the 2 locules.

The wood is pale brown with a pinkish tinge, hard, strong, and once used in wagon-making.

CLUSIACEAE (see page 23)

3 Hypericum revolutum Curry bush
SA: 484; Z: 710 All year Kerriebos
Shrub or small tree, often **multistemmed**; occurring in montane forest areas, usually along streams or forest margins, and on rocky outcrops. Bark scaly, reddish brown. Branchlets **angular**. Leaves **sessile, closely spaced, small, about 20 x 5 mm**, soft-textured; base **clasping** the stem. Flowers solitary, terminal, large, bright yellow with **numerous stamens in 5 clusters**. Fruit a capsule, reddish brown, dehiscent.

A widely cultivated garden plant.

The leaves of *H. roeperianum*, which also occurs in high-altitude montane areas, are larger (30–80 x 10–30 mm) and more widely spaced along the stems.

COMBRETACEAE (see page 23)

4 Combretum adenogonium (= *C. fragrans*) Four-leaved bushwillow
Z: 771 Spring Vierblaarboswilg
Deciduous shrub or small tree, with reddish and yellowish autumn colours; occurring in low-altitude bushveld, often at edges of seasonal swamps and on termitaria. Leaves **opposite or, more usually, 3- or 4-whorled, ovate or ovate-elliptic, up to 200 x 90 mm**, shiny and glutinous when very young, golden brown-haired to almost smooth when mature; apex tapering to rounded; base broadly tapering; principal lateral veins **7–10 pairs**, with hairtuft domatia in axils; petiole up to 8 mm long. Flowers in axillary spikes up to 70 mm long, often appearing before the leaves, greenish or whitish yellow, fragrant, particularly at night. Fruit 4-winged, **25–35 x 25–30 mm** with wings up to 12 mm wide, glutinous when young, brown or reddish yellow.

326

1

M. frangula: fruit

2

P. capensis: flowers

2

P. capensis: fruit

4

C. adenogonium: fruit

3

H. revolutum: flower

4

C. adenogonium: fruit

1 **_Combretum apiculatum_** subsp. *apiculatum*   **Red bushwillow**
SA: 532; Z: 766   Spring–Summer   **Rooibos**
Small to medium-sized deciduous tree, with brownish red or golden yellow autumn colours; occurring in bushveld, often at low altitudes and in rocky places, **on well-drained soils.** Leaves opposite or occasionally alternate or 3-whorled, **elliptic to broadly obovate**, up to 140 x 75 mm, **hairless** and **often glutinous**; apex **sharply tapering and usually conspicuously twisted**; base tapering to rounded; principal lateral veins 4–7 pairs, with **hairtuft domatia** in axils; petiole up to 10 mm long. Flowers in axillary spikes up to 35 mm long, creamy yellow. Fruit 4-winged, **20–30 x 15–25 mm** with wings up to 7 mm wide, **glutinous when young,** yellowish green, often tinged with red. Subsp. *leutweinii*, which occurs mainly in mopane veld, has leaves that are **sparsely or densely hairy** above and below.

Heartwood dark brown to black, hard, heavy, fine-grained and termite resistant, used for fencing posts and fuel (the coals can last up to 12 hours). Bark used for tanning leather. Leaves browsed by game, the fallen ones by cattle; also used medicinally. Seeds eaten by brownheaded parrots, but apparently poisonous to humans (hiccups are symptomatic). Typical subspecies recorded as larval food plant for the butterfly *Coeliades forestan forestan.*

Subsp. *apiculatum* may be confused with *C. nelsonii,* whose leaf apex is plane or only slightly twisted. From a distance the trees of subsp. *leutweinii* may be confused with *Lonchocarpus nelsii* (Group 10, p. 196), particularly when clothed in their yellow autumn colours.

2 **_Combretum collinum_**   **Variable bushwillow**
SA: 541; Z: 768   Spring   **Variërende boswilg**
A very variable aggregate of semi-deciduous shrubs or small to medium-sized trees; occurring in bushveld, usually at low altitude. Leaves **narrowly elliptic to broadly ovate or obovate, dark green above**, paler green to silvery below, with or without a dense covering of hairs below; apex and base usually **broadly tapering**; apex up to 30 mm long. Flowers in axillary spikes **up to 100 mm long**, often appearing with the old leaves, cream to yellow. Fruit 4-winged, **25–55 x 20–55 mm,** dark reddish brown when young, drying **dark brown**, usually with a distinctive **metallic sheen.** Four subspecies are distinguished in southern Africa:

Subsp. *gazense* has the leaves distinctly **greyish-hairy below**; venation, including reticulum, **prominent below**. Fruit usually **more than 36 mm long**, densely covered with conspicuous **reddish** scales. Vegetatively rather similar to *C. vendae*, but the hair-cover is more woolly.

Subsp. *ondongense* has the leaves **hairless below**, or almost so; apex **rounded to broadly tapering**; lower surface **yellowish green.** Fruit usually **more than 38 mm long, hairless,** pale reddish brown.

Subsp. *suluense* has the leaves **hairless below**, or almost so. Fruit **usually 38–50 mm long, densely hairy,** reddish brown.

Subsp. *taborense* has the leaves **hairless below**, or almost so; apex usually **tapers gradually**; lower surface **silvery-white.** Fruit usually **more than 38 mm long, hairless,** dark reddish brown.

The leaves of all the subspecies are browsed by game.

C. apiculatum: flowers

C. apiculatum: fruit

C. collinum: fruit

C. collinum: flowers

C. collinum: flowers and fruit

C. collinum: fruit

GROUP 23

1 *Combretum elaeagnoides*   Oleaster bushwillow
SA: 534.3; Z: 769 Spring–Summer   Oleasterboswilg
Deciduous, multistemmed shrub or small tree; occurring in hot, low-altitude bushveld and thicket, mainly along the Zambezi Valley, often dominant on seasonally inundated drainage lines. New growth grey-green. Leaves **narrowly elliptic to oblong-elliptic, usually 70–110 x 18–30 mm, hairless**; apex broadly tapering; base **rounded to shallowly lobed**; principal lateral veins 8–13 pairs, occasionally with axillary hairtuft domatia, midrib **grooved above**; margin **wavy**; petiole up to 10 mm long. Flowers in axillary spikes up to 25 mm long, appearing before or with the new leaves, greenish yellow. Fruit 4-winged, **20–35 x 10–35 mm**, wings about 12 mm wide, whitish green, drying brown with the central portion tinged greyish.

The plant often invades old cultivated fields as a pioneer. Wood used for the handles of fish spears and in hut construction.

2 *Combretum erythrophyllum*   River bushwillow
SA: 536; Z: 770 Spring   Vaderlandswilg
Small to large deciduous tree, with reddish autumn and sometimes whitish spring colours; occurring **mainly along the banks of rivers**. Leaves opposite, alternate or 3-whorled, **elliptic to oblong-elliptic**, usually about **50 x 20 mm**, distinctly **hairy**, at least on the midrib and principal lateral veins; apex **tapering**, occasionally slightly twisted; base **tapering**; principal lateral veins 6–10 pairs; petiole up to 4 mm long. Flowers in axillary **subcapitate** spikes up to 20 mm long, greenish yellow. Fruit 4-winged, about **15 x 12 mm** with wings up to 6 mm wide, greenish brown, ripening to yellowish brown.

The wood is pale yellowish brown, soft with a coarse and rather featureless grain; suitable as a general purpose timber and for carved household utensils. Damaged stems yield a gum that can be used as a varnish. Browsed by giraffe and elephant. The seeds are apparently poisonous, used to purge dogs of intestinal worms; eaten by pied barbets. A popular shade tree for gardens; fast growing and frost resistant.

Similar to *C. caffrum* (**2.1**), which prefers a similar habitat but occurs further south (mainly in the Eastern Cape). The plant has narrowly elliptic to lanceolate leaves (usually less than 18 mm wide) which are hairless, and fruit which is usually tinged pink when ripening.

C. elaeagnoides: fruit

C. erythrophyllum: flowers

C. erythrophyllum: fruit

C. caffrum: flowers

C. elaeagnoides: flowers

C. caffrum: bark

1 Combretum hereroense   **Russet bushwillow**
SA: 538; Z: 772   Spring   **Kierieklapper**
Deciduous or semi-deciduous shrub or small tree, often with **arching stems**; occurring in bushveld, often on sandy soil and termitaria. Leaves often on short shoots, **elliptic to broadly elliptic or obovate** to broadly obovate, usually **20–70 x 10–45 mm**, usually dense with **brownish hairs (particularly below)**; apex and base **broadly tapering to rounded**; tertiary veins notably **raised** below. Flowers in axillary **subcapitate** spikes up to 30 mm long, often appearing before the leaves, greenish yellow. Fruit 4-winged, about 20 x 20 mm, **dark reddish brown, at least on the central seed-containing part.**

Plants are browsed by game and cattle. Gum from wounds much favoured by bushbabies. Root used medicinally. In parts of Zimbabwe the fruit is made into a traditional tea; the seeds, however, should be considered poisonous.

C. edwardsii, a robust forest creeper, also has leaves with brownish hairs, particularly when young. It has larger leaves (up to 90 x 50 mm) and the fruits are yellowish green with a pinkish tinge, drying pale brown.

2 Combretum imberbe   **Leadwood**
SA: 539; Z: 773 Spring–Summer   **Hardekool**
Medium to large semi-deciduous tree with a **greyish** appearance; occurring in bushveld, often on alluvial soils along rivers or dry watercourses. Bark pale grey, with deep longitudinal and irregular transverse cracks, which produce a **mesh of closely packed rectangular flakes**. Leaves **obovate to oval**, 25–80 x 10–30 mm, both surfaces **greyish green with minute silvery and occasionally brownish scales**. Flowers in axillary **spikes** up to 100 mm long, often forming terminal heads, whitish yellow, sweetly scented. Fruit 4-winged, usually about **15 x 15 mm**, pale yellowish green, covered with **minute silvery scales.**

The heartwood is dark brown, exceptionally hard and heavy, and in former times (before the introduction of metals) was fashioned into blades for hoes; an outstanding fuel-wood. Gum edible. Ash used as toothpaste and as substitute for whitewash. Of considerable religious importance to the Herero and Ovambo people of Namibia. Browsed by game. Leaves and root used medicinally. The trees are long-lived, the larger specimens estimated to be well over 1 000 years old.

3 Combretum kraussii   **Forest bushwillow**
SA: 540   Spring   **Bosvaderlandswilg**
Medium to large deciduous or semi-deciduous tree, with reddish autumn and sometimes **whitish spring colours**; occurring mainly **in or near forest**. Leaves **elliptic to obovate-elliptic**, up to **90–50 mm, hairless**, glossy **dark green** above, dull pale green below; intersecondary veins **more or less plane below**. Flowers in **elongated axillary spikes up to 85 mm long**, creamy-white. Fruit 4-winged, about 16 x 15 mm, ripening ones greenish brown, usually **tinged pink to dark red.**

Young stems pliable and used in basket-making. Sawdust can cause skin irritation.

Related to *C. nelsonii* (p. 334), a shrub or small tree from rocky bushveld habitats. It has medium green leaves and flowers in subcapitate spikes. *C. woodii*, a bushveld species from northern KwaZulu-Natal, Swaziland and Mpumalanga, also has flowers in elongated spikes, but differs in its much larger leaves, with leaf margins conspicuously wavy, and secondary and intersecondary veins raised below.

C. hereroense: flowers & fruit

C. hereroense: fruit

C. imberbe: bark

C. imberbe: flowers

C. imberbe: fruit

C. kraussii: trees with young leaves (white)

C. kraussii: young leaves and flowers

C. kraussii: fruit

1 **Combretum molle** — Velvet bushwillow

SA: 537; Z: 775   Spring — Fluweelboswilg

Small to medium-sized semi-deciduous to deciduous tree with autumn leaves tinged reddish or purplish; occurring in bushveld or in sheltered, rocky places in grassland. Branchlets with bark exfoliating in **untidy, irregular, fibrous strips or threads.** Leaves narrowly elliptic, ovate-elliptic to almost circular, usually about 60–100 x 40–60 mm, **dense with velvety hairs**, particularly below, almost hairless in some forms; apex tapering; base rounded to shallowly lobed; net-veining **conspicuously raised below.** Flowers in **axillary spikes** up to 90 mm long, often appearing before or with the new leaves, greenish yellow. Fruit 4-winged, usually **15–20 x 15–20 mm, yellowish green flushed with red**, drying to golden reddish brown.

The wood is yellowish brown, hard and termite resistant, suitable for household utensils, implement handles, hut-building and fencing posts. Browsed by game. Leaves and root used medicinally; the former yield a red, the latter a yellow-brown dye, both of which are used in woven fabrics. Larval food plant for the butterflies *Hamanumida daedalus* and *Parosmodes morantii morantii*.

Similar to *C. psidioides*, whose branchlets have bark that peels off in large, more or less cylindrical or hemicylindrical pieces to expose a reddish brown surface.

2 **Combretum mossambicense** — Knobbly creeper

SA: 545.1; Z: 776   Spring — Knoppiesklimop

Deciduous climber, shrub or small tree; occurring in low-altitude bushveld (notably mopane veld) and thicket, often near rivers or on termitaria. Stems with **petiole bases often persisting as spines.** Leaves elliptic to elliptic-oblong, usually **about 60 x 30 mm**, fine-haired at first, becoming glabrous with age; apex tapering to rounded; base broadly tapering to rounded; principal lateral veins 5–9 pairs; petiole up to 5 mm long, basal portion **thickened**, often forming a curved spine. Flowers in dense **axillary spikes** up to 60 mm long, held horizontally and often produced before the leaves, showy, **white, often tinged with pink**, sweetly scented. Fruit (4)**5-winged, up to 20–30 x 20–25 mm**, briefly greenish tinged with pink, drying pale brown.

3 **Combretum nelsonii** — Waterberg bushwillow

SA: 540.2   Spring — Waterbergboswilg

Deciduous shrub or small tree, with reddish autumn and sometimes whitish spring colours; occurring mainly in bushveld, usually in rocky places. Leaves elliptic, obovate-elliptic or obovate, usually **40–80 x 25–45 mm**, essentially **hairless**, glossy **light to medium green** above, dull pale green below; apex and base tapering; venation with principal lateral veins 5–8 pairs, often with hairtuft domatia in axils, intersecondary veins **more or less plane below**; petiole up to 5 mm long. Flowers in axillary **subcapitate spikes** up to 20 mm long, greenish yellow. Fruit 4-winged, about **16 x 15 mm** with wings up to 8 mm wide, ripening ones **greenish brown**, usually partly or completely **tinged pink to dark red**.

Related to *C. kraussii* (p. 332), a medium to large forest tree with dark green leaves and flowers in more elongated spikes. *C. vendae*, a close relative confined to the Soutpansberg range, has leaves that are greyish green with the intersecondary veins conspicuously raised below, often with the lower surface covered with dense whitish or greyish hairs. Also likely to be confused with the associated *C. apiculatum* subsp. *apiculatum*, whose leaf apex is usually conspicuously twisted.

C. molle: flowers

C. molle: fruit

C. mossambicense: fruit

C. mossambicense: flowers

C. nelsonii: fruit

1 **Combretum paniculatum** (= *C. microphyllum*)   **Flame creeper**
SA: 545; Z: 779   Spring   **Vlamklimop**
Robust deciduous or evergreen (subsp. *paniculatum*) **climber**, sometimes a **scrambling** shrub or small tree; occurring in bushveld and forest, often along rivers. Stems with petiole bases often persisting as spines. Leaves **ovate, oblong-elliptic to almost circular**, usually about 120 x 80 mm; principal lateral veins 4–6 pairs, **yellowish**; petiole, **basal portion thickened, often persistent after the leaf falls to form a blunt spine**. Flowers in showy terminal or axillary panicles, produced before the new leaves (subsp. *microphyllum*), **crimson-red**. Fruit 4-winged, 20–25 x 15–20 mm with wings up to 9 mm wide, **green tinged with red or pink when young**, drying to pale yellowish brown. Subsp. *paniculatum* (mainly Eastern Highlands of Zimbabwe) occurs in evergreen forest and has relatively **large leaves (up to 180 x 95 mm)** usually **without hairs**. Subsp. *microphyllum*, with smaller hairy leaves, is more widespread, occurring in dryer bushveld areas.
    The plant is browsed by game. Root used medicinally. A decorative, but frost sensitive, garden subject. Larval food plant for the butterfly *Aterica galene theophane*.

2 **Combretum psidioides**   **Savanna bushwillow**
SA: 543; Z: 780   Spring   **Savanneboswilg**
Semi-deciduous shrub or small to medium-sized tree; young growth flushed orange-red; occurring in arid, low-altitude bushveld, often on Kalahari sand. Branchlets with bark peeling off in **large, more or less cylindrical or hemicylindrical pieces**, exposing a **reddish brown** surface. Leaves narrowly elliptic to oblong, 50–150 x 30–100 mm, covered in dense **silvery hairs when young** (except subsp. *glabrum*), becoming less hairy with age; apex usually rounded with a sharp tip; base rounded to almost heart-shaped; principal lateral veins 8–16 pairs; reticulation **rather prominent below**; petiole up to 10 mm long. Flowers in dense, hairy, axillary **spikes up to 100 mm long**, greenish yellow. Fruit 4-winged, **20–30 x 20–30 mm** with wings up to 13 mm wide, **glutinous when young**, ripening through **brilliant red** to dark brown. Lower surface of leaves with hairs spread all over in subsp. *dinteri*, mainly confined to the venation in subsp. *psidiodes*, absent in subsp. *glabrum*.
    The wood is used for axe-handles and smaller household items. Gum from stem wounds is edible. Roots are used to weave baskets; also in traditional medicine.
    Can be confused with *C. molle*, young branchlets whose bark comes off in untidy, irregular, fibrous strips or threads.

3 **Combretum wattii**   **Water bushwillow**
SA: 544   Spring–Summer   **Waterboswilg**
Deciduous, scrambling, semi-scandent shrub or small tree; restricted to the semi-desert Kaokoveld and adjacent Angola, usually occurring along watercourses. Branchlets densely covered with **yellowish hairs**. Leaves mainly on short lateral shoots, **subcircular**, about 40 x 40 mm, **bluish or greyish green, densely hairy**; apex and base rounded; principal lateral veins 4 or 5 pairs; petiole up to 8 mm long, with woolly hairs. Flowers in 1- or few-flowered axillary clusters, **unusually large (up to 45 x 15 mm), reddish to deep pink with long green stamens**, basal parts covered with yellowish brown woolly hairs. Fruit **5-winged**, 30–40 x 30–40 mm, greenish yellow, ripening to pale brown, with short velvety hairs.
    The plant is browsed by stock and game. Wood used to fashion knobkerries.

C. paniculatum: flowers

C. paniculatum: fruit

C. psidioides: fruit

C. wattii: fruit

C. paniculatum: flowers

C. wattii: flowers

1 Combretum zeyheri   Large-fruited bushwillow
SA: 546; Z: 781   Spring   Raasblaar
Small to medium-sized deciduous tree, with yellowish autumn colours; occurring in bushveld. Ultimate branchlets **minutely whitish hairy**. Leaves elliptic to oblong, usually about 70–100 x 30–50 mm, finely hairy particularly when young; apex and base broadly tapering to rounded; principal lateral veins raised below, **with domatia**; net-veining **slightly raised** below; petiole up to 10 mm long, often purplish black. Flowers in axillary **spikes** up to 70 mm long, often appearing before or with the new leaves, greenish yellow. Fruit 4-winged, **up to 80 x 80 mm** with wings up to 40 mm wide, yellowish green, ripening to pale brown.

The wood is pale yellowish brown, hard, tough, termite- and borer-proof; suitable as a general purpose timber. The gum is edible. Roots used to weave baskets and fishing traps. Various parts used in traditional medicine. Hornbills eat the seeds from fallen fruit. Larvae of the butterfly *Deudorix dinochares* feed on the seeds.

Easily confused with *C. mkuzense* (**1.1**), a scrambling shrub or small tree with curved branches, endemic to the Maputaland Centre. The plant has almost glabrous ultimate branchlets and slightly smaller fruit (about 50 x 50 mm). *C. kirkii*, which also has a very large fruit (up to 55 x 45 mm), is a creeper, mainly confined in southern Africa to the Zambezi River and its tributaries.

2 Pteleopsis anisoptera   Hairy stink bushwillow
SA: 547.1; Z: 783   Spring–Summer   Harige stinkboswilg
Semi-deciduous shrub or, more typically, a medium-sized tree with a single trunk; occurring in hot, low-altitude bushveld and thicket. Leaves elliptic, up to 70 x 35 mm, usually dull green above, **silvery hairy** when young, becoming more or less hairless above; apex usually **broadly tapering with a short, sharp tip**; **axillary buds usually conspicuous** in the axils of old or fallen leaves, **elongated, up to 3 mm long**; petiole up to 6 mm long. Flowers in axillary, subcapitate heads, white to yellowish. Fruit **3–4(5)-winged**, usually about 10 mm long or shorter, greenish yellow, drying to pale brown, usually with a distinct **apical peg up to 4 mm long**.

3 Pteleopsis myrtifolia   Stink bushwillow
SA: 547; Z: 784   Spring–Summer   Stinkboswilg
Deciduous shrub or small to medium-sized tree; occurring in hot, low-altitude sand forest, bushveld and thicket, usually on **sandy soil**. Leaves elliptic, up to 95 x 35 mm, somewhat shiny green above, **silvery hairy** when young, becoming more or less hairless, occasionally with a pair of **widely spaced, minute yellowish spots** in the middle part of the blade (extrafloral nectaries), midway between the midrib and margin; apex usually **narrowly tapering**; margin with a **minute fringe of hairs**; petiole up to 10 mm long, slender. Flowers in axillary, subcapitate heads, white to yellowish. Fruit **2–3(4)-winged**, usually about 15 mm long or longer, greenish yellow, drying to pale brown, usually **without an apical peg**.

The wood is reddish brown to pale brown, hard, and excellent for furniture; also used in hut construction and for smoking edible *Strychnos madagascariensis* fruit pulp (in Maputaland). Browsed by game. Pliable stems used for fishing baskets.

Easily confused with *Hymenocardia ulmoides* (Group 10, p. 192), which has alternate, less hairy leaves (usually only a few hairs on the midrib) and fruit fringed by a single, papery wing. The young leaves are reddish.

C. zeyheri: flowers

P. anisoptera: fruit

C. zeyheri: fruit

C. mkuzense: fruit

P. anisoptera: flowers

P. myrtifolia: flowers

P. myrtifolia: fruit

EBENACEAE (see page 24)
The leaf arrangement in some species of *Euclea* is very variable and may be opposite to subopposite, alternate or whorled, even on the same plant. Compare, therefore, those members of the genus included in Group 10.

1 *Euclea crispa*   **Blue guarri**
SA: 594; Z: 846 Spring–Summer   **Bloughwarrie**
Much-branched evergreen shrub or small tree, usually with a dense, **grey-green** crown; sexes separate, on different plants; occurring in bushveld, forest margins and sheltered places in grassland, often in rocky places. Young growth usually with **minute rusty brown granules (glands)**. Leaves variable in shape, **grey- to blue-green** above, paler below, leathery, **rigid, with a papery texture**; margin slightly or strongly wavy; petiole up to 2 mm long. Flowers in short axillary racemes, whitish, drooping. Fruit thinly fleshy, globose, up to 5 mm in diameter, ripening through reddish brown to black, single-seeded. The leaves of var. *crispa* are variable in shape, rather small and narrow, apex broadly tapering or rounded and the margin slightly wavy, whereas those of var. *ovata* (restricted to arid karroid areas) are ovate, apex sharply tapering and the margin conspicuously wavy.
Branches are used to beat out veld fires. Bark and leaves browsed by black rhino. The chewed ends of the twigs serve as toothbrushes. Bark and fruit used medicinally. The root yields a dark brown dye, used in basket weaving. Fruit edible.
Var. *ovata* resembles *E. coriacea* (found in the eastern Free State, western Lesotho and bordering karroid areas), which tends to have alternate leaves, flowers with the corolla tube slightly lobed at the mouth only, and larger fruit (up to 15 mm in diameter).

2 *Euclea divinorum*   **Magic guarri**
SA: 595; Z: 847 Winter–Summer   **Towerghwarrie**
Evergreen shrub or small tree; sexes separate, on different plants; occurring in bushveld, often on brackish floodplains along rivers or on termitaria. Leaves **elliptic, 35–80 x 10–25 mm**, **dark green to greyish green** above, paler below, leathery, **rigid, with a papery texture**; margin **conspicuously wavy**. Flowers in short, contracted, axillary heads, small, white to cream, somewhat drooping. Fruit thinly fleshy, globose, up to 7 mm in diameter, purplish black, single-seeded.
The frayed ends of twigs are used as toothbrushes. Branches used to fight veld fires. Fruit edible but not sweet-tasting; also used medicinally and to make a black ink. Root used medicinally; it also yields a brown dye used for basketware.

3 *Euclea undulata*   **Common guarri**
SA: 601; Z: 851 Summer–Autumn   **Gewone ghwarrie**
Evergreen, densely leafy shrub or small tree; sexes separate, on different plants; occurring in bushveld, grassland and semi-desert areas, often on rocky ridges. Young growth usually with **minute rusty brown granules (glands)**. Leaves **obovate to narrowly elliptic**, relatively **small (20–40 x 5–15 mm)**, **dark green** to blue-green above, paler below, sometimes tinged rusty brown owing to the presence of the minute glands, **stiff, with a papery texture**; margin usually **conspicuously wavy**. Flowers in short axillary sprays, small, whitish. Fruit thinly fleshy, globose, up to 6 mm in diameter, ripening through reddish brown to black, single-seeded.
The wood is tough and durable, and is used for fencing posts. Browsed by game and stock. Bark and root used medicinally. Fruit edible but not very tasty.

E. crispa: flowers

E. crispa: fruit

E. divinorum: flowers

E. divinorum: flowers

E. divinorum: fruit

E. undulata: flowers

E. undulata: fruit

HAMAMELIDACEAE (see page 25)

1 *Trichocladus crinitus*   Black hazel
SA: 142   Autumn–Winter   Swarthaselaar
Shrub or small tree; occurring in the understorey of evergreen forest. Branchlets and young leaves densely covered with **dark brown to blackish hairs**. Leaves elliptic, dark shiny green above, with **dark brown hairs, particularly on the midrib below**; base square to slightly lobed with petiole often attached **inside the margin** (peltate). Flowers in stalked axillary heads, **creamy green with orange** towards base. Fruit a capsule, up to 7 mm long, borne in dense heads, reddish brown.
     The wood is white, very hard, and is used for household implements. A decorative shade plant.

2 *Trichocladus grandiflorus*   Green hazel
SA: 144   Spring–Summer   Groenhaselaar
Deciduous shrub or small to medium-sized tree; occurring on the margins of forest or in wooded ravines. Branchlets **reddish**, hairy. Leaves **ovate to lanceolate**, at first downy with **reddish brown star-shaped hairs**, becoming **hairless with age**, glossy green above, paler with **prominent venation** below; apex and base tapering. Flowers in loose axillary or terminal heads, attractive, white **tinged with pinkish purple** towards base; petals **crinkly**. Fruit a capsule, dark brown, dehiscent.

LYTHRACEAE (see page 26)

3 *Galpinia transvaalica*   Transvaal privet
SA: 523; Z: 761   Spring–Winter   Transvaalliguster
Small to medium-sized evergreen tree, usually multistemmed with a rather sparse and twiggy crown; occurring in bushveld, mainly associated with the Lebombo Mountains and nearly always confined to rocky places. Branchlets **square** in transverse section. Leaves leathery, shiny dark green above, dull pale green below, lower surface with a **conspicuous gland terminating the midrib before the apex**; margin conspicuously **wavy**. Flowers in dense terminal and axillary panicles, small, white, with **crinkled** petals. Fruit a capsule, globose, about 5 mm in diameter, pink to reddish brown, produced in dense clusters, many-seeded.
     The wood is pale brown, fairly heavy, fine-grained, and suitable for turnery. Browsed by game. A decorative garden plant, but the flowering period is very brief.

MELASTOMATACEAE (see page 26)

4 *Memecylon natalense*   Natal rose-apple
SA: 560   Spring–Summer   Natalroosappel
Evergreen shrub or small tree with horizontally spreading branches; occurring in **understorey** of forest. Young growth purplish green. Leaves **broadly ovate**, 30–50 x 15–30 mm, **stiff and leathery**, **shiny** bright green above, paler below; base tapering; margin rolled under. Flowers in axillary clusters, white, often **tinged with purple**. Fruit globose, fleshy, purplish black, tipped by persistent calyx.
     Similar to *Eugenia natalitia* (Group 22), whose leaves have secretory cavities.
     M. bachmannii (= *M. grandiflorum*) is a shrub or small understorey tree confined mainly to forest in the Pondoland Centre. Its leaves are larger (40–90 x 30–50 mm) and they have a more rounded base. The leaves of *M. sousae* (Group 12, p. 254) are distinctly 3-veined from the base.

1

T. crinitus: fruit

1

T. crinitus: flowers

2

T. grandiflorus: flowers

2

T. grandiflorus: fruit

3

G. transvaalica: flowers

3

G. transvaalica: fruit

4

M. natalense: fruit

343

OLEACEAE (see page 28)

1 *Chionanthus foveolatus*   **Pock ironwood**

SA: 615; Z: 867   Spring–Summer   **Pokysterhout**

Small to medium-sized evergreen tree; occurring in forest and wooded ravines. Leaves **ovate-oblong, 20–70 x 13–40 mm**, glossy dark green above; dull pale green below; margin rolled under; **domatia usually present** in axils of side veins below; blade with fibrous edges when pulled apart. Flowers in **short, lax, axillary sprays** up to about 20 mm long, white to cream, sometimes tinged with pink, fragrant; petals with **hood-shaped** (cucullate) tips. Fruit a drupe, ovoid, purplish black to black. Subsp. *foveolatus* has ultimate branchlets **without hairs**, leaves more than twice as long as broad with base rounded to heart-shaped on coppice shoots, and fruit **up to 20 mm long**. The ultimate branchlets of subsp. *tomentellus* are **densely hairy** and the leaves **smaller (20–60 x 10–30 mm)**, usually less than twice as long as broad. Subsp. *major* is a large forest tree with the ultimate twigs **hairless**, its leaves usually **more than twice as long as broad**, and fruit which is **up to 30 mm long**.

The wood is pale brown, hard, heavy and strong. Fruit eaten by monkeys, bush-pigs, bats and birds.

Large fruit of subsp. *major* resembles that of *C. peglerae* (**1.1**) (large tree from coastal and montane forest; mainly Eastern Cape and KwaZulu-Natal), which has leaves up to 130 mm long as against the former's 70 mm. *C. battiscombei* (mainly from the Eastern Highlands of Zimbabwe, Maputaland and the Soutpansberg range) is very similar to subsp. *foveolatus*, but is distinguished by the almost stackless flowers which are borne in tight axillary clusters.

2 *Olea capensis*   **Ironwood**

SA: 618; Z: 869   Spring–Summer   **Ysterhout**

A very variable complex of evergreen shrubs and trees from a wide variety of habitats. Branchlets **4-angled**. Flowers in predominantly **terminal** heads with the leaves that are never linear oblong but usually more than 10 mm wide; blade has **fibrous edges** when pulled apart; petiole often **purplish**. Fruit a drupe, oval, purplish black. Three subspecies are distinguished:

Subsp. *capensis*: shrubs or **small** trees; occurring in coastal bush and forest. Leaves very variable; apex often rounded; midrib **prominent below from base to apex**. Inflorescences compact. Fruit **not more than 10 mm long**.

Subsp. *enervis*: shrub or **small** bushy tree; occurring in bushveld, usually on rocky outcrops. Leaves **broadly oval or oblong** (40–50 x 15–25 mm), **flat** (not curled downward along midrib); apex tapering; midrib usually **raised below in bottom half only**. Inflorescences **compact**. Fruit **not more than 10 mm long**.

Subsp. *macrocarpa*: medium to **tall** tree; occurring in coastal and montane forest. Leaves usually **narrowly elliptic, tapering** to the base and apex; blade flat; margin **wavy**. Inflorescences **lax**. Fruit **15–25 mm long**.

The heartwood of subsp. *macrocarpa* is dark brown and attractively figured, very hard, heavy and extremely difficult to work; once used extensively for railway sleepers and firewood, less frequently for furniture and in construction work. Subsp. *macrocarpa* is easily confused with *Chionanthus peglerae*, which has coppice leaves whose venation is markedly depressed above, the mature leaves often with small domatia in the axils of the side veins below.

C. foveolatus: flowers

C. foveolatus: fruit

C. peglerae: flowers

O. capensis: fruit

O. capensis: flowers

O. capensis: flowers

O. capensis: fruit

O. capensis: flowers

O. capensis: fruit

1 *Olea europaea* subsp. *africana* (= *O. africana*)   **Wild olive**
SA: 617; Z: 868   Spring–Summer   **Olienhout**
Small to medium-sized evergreen tree with a dense **rounded crown** and **greyish green foliage**; occurring in a wide range of habitats, usually on rocky hillsides or on stream banks. Branchlets **4-angled**, greyish. Leaves **narrowly oblong-elliptic, 7–17 mm wide**, shiny dark green above, often with minute whitish scales, **greyish** below due to a dense cover of silvery or brown scales; apex sharply pointed; margin entire, rolled under; side veins **indistinct**; blade with a tendency to **curl downwards** along the midrib, with fibrous edges when pulled apart. Flowers in **loose, axillary** or occasionally terminal heads, very small, white or cream, sweetly scented; stamens **2**. Fruit a drupe, ovoid, about 10 x 8 mm, purplish black.
    The tree has brown, richly figured heartwood and yellowish brown sapwood, very attractive, hard and heavy; extensively used for furniture and ornaments, although available only in limited quantities due to the relatively short, often gnarled and twisted trunks. Leaves browsed by game and stock. Fruit edible but not very tasty. Leaves and bark used in traditional medicine. A decorative garden subject, drought-resistant and frost-tolerant. Suitable for bonsai cultivation.
    Similar to *Buddleja saligna* (Group 23, p. 324), the lower surface of whose leaves are white and prominently veined. *O. woodiana*, an often tall canopy tree from mainly coastal forest, also has flowers in loose axillary or occasionally terminal heads. It differs in that the leaves are somewhat broader (10–35 mm) and sparsely dotted with minute scales below.

2 *Olea exasperata*   **Dune olive**
SA: 619   Spring   **Duine-olienhout**
Straggling shrub or small tree; occurring in **coastal bush**, usually on sand dunes or limestone hills. Branchlets **4-angled** with conspicuous **white lenticels** and prominent leaf scars. Leaves **linear-oblong, 3–10 mm wide**, broader in upper two-thirds, dark shiny green above, dull green below, with **minute pits** (rather than scales) on both surfaces; base narrowly and gradually tapering; margin entire, rolled under; blade with a tendency to **curl downwards** along the midrib, and with fibrous edges when pulled apart. Flowers in **loose, predominantly terminal** heads, very small, white, sweetly scented. Fruit a drupe, ovoid, about 10 x 8 mm, purplish black.
    The root is used for medicinal purposes.

3 *Schrebera trichoclada*   **Sand jasmine**
SA: 613; Z: 865   Summer   **Sandjasmyn**
Shrub or small tree, with a rounded or spreading crown; occurring in hot, low-altitude bushveld and thicket, often on Kalahari sand. Branchlets covered in **whitish hairs**, with **prominent corky lenticels**. Leaves elliptic to oblong-elliptic, **45–140 x 25–75 mm**, hairy when young, becoming hairless with age, except for principal veins below; reticulate venation **prominent on both surfaces**; petiole up to 15 mm long. Flowers in terminal clusters, creamy white to yellow, with **brownish hairs** at throat of corolla, extending almost to margins of corolla lobes. Fruit a capsule, **pear-shaped**, not laterally flattened, **up to 60 x 30 mm**, pale brown, often warty, splitting into 2 valves to release the flattish winged seeds.
    The root is used medicinally.

O. europaea: flowers

O. exasperata: flowers

O. europaea: fruit

S. trichoclada: flowers

O. exasperata: fruit

S. trichoclada: fruit

S. trichoclada: fruit (old)

OLINIACEAE (see page 28)

1 *Olinia emarginata*   Mountain hard pear
SA: 514   Spring–Summer   Berghardepeer
Small to medium-sized evergreen tree with a dense, glossy green crown; found in montane forest, protected wooded ravines and riverine fringes. Branchlets **4-angled**. Leaves **oblong to lanceolate, 20–50 x 7–20 mm**, glossy dark green above, pale green and dull below, **hairless**, often with a **faint almond scent** when crushed; apex rounded, notched, usually **tinged with pink or red**; petiole very short, **pink to red**. Flowers in loose axillary heads which are usually **more than half as long as the leaves**, very small, pale to dark pink. Fruit a drupe, thinly fleshy, globose, about 10 mm in diameter, bright red with a **circular scar** left by the deciduous floral tube.
The attractive fruit is eaten by birds. A decorative, frost-resistant garden subject.

2 *Olinia rochetiana*   Rock hard pear
SA: 516   Spring–Summer   Rotshardepeer
Shrub to small evergreen tree; occurring in montane forest and associated bush clumps, often among rocks. Branchlets **4-angled**. Leaves **elliptic to obovate, 15–60 x 8–25 mm**, glossy dark green above, **bluish green and dull** below, **hairless**, usually with a **strong almond scent** when crushed; apex broadly tapering and finely notched; venation **conspicuous on lower surface**; petiole very short, **purple-tinged**. Flowers in short dense axillary heads (which are **shorter** than the subtending leaf), relatively large (5–8 mm long), white changing to pale or dark pink with age. Fruit a drupe, thinly fleshy, globose, about 6–8 mm in diameter, red to reddish brown with a **circular scar** left by the deciduous floral tube.
This species is replaced by the closely related (perhaps conspecific) *O. vanguerioides* in the Eastern Highlands of Zimbabwe.

3 *Olinia ventosa* (= *O. cymosa*)   Hard pear
SA: 513   Spring   Hardepeer
Medium to tall evergreen tree, stem often **fluted**; occurring in forest, usually at low altitude. Branchlets **4-angled**. Leaves **ovate to elliptic, 25–80 x 10–50 mm**, glossy dark green above, pale green and dull below, **hairless**, usually with a **strong almond scent** when crushed; apex and base **tapering**; margin usually somewhat **wavy**. Flowers in dense axillary branched heads which are **as long or longer than the leaves**, very small, white to pale pink. Fruit a drupe, thinly fleshy, globose, about 10 mm in diameter, bright red with a **circular scar** left by the deciduous floral tube.
The wood is hard, heavy and strong. Fruit eaten by birds.
O. radiata, a tall evergreen tree with a straight trunk and reddish brown flaky bark, is a rare constituent of the coastal and mistbelt forests of KwaZulu-Natal and the Eastern Cape. Flowers are borne in compact heads, which are much shorter than the subtending leaves and densely clustered round the petiole. Leaves and bark smell strongly of almonds when crushed.

O. emarginata: flowers

O. rochetiana: fruit

O. emarginata: fruit

O. ventosa: fruit

O. ventosa: flowers

RHAMNACEAE (see page 30)

1 *Berchemia discolor*   **Brown ivory**
SA: 449; Z: 620   Spring–Summer   **Bruinivoor**
Medium to large deciduous or evergreen tree; occurring in low-altitude bushveld. Leaves elliptic or elliptic-oblong, **50–140 x 25–60 mm, shiny dark green** above, pale green below, essentially hairless; principal lateral veins **prominently raised below, ending at the margin**. Flowers in **loose** axillary clusters, small, greenish yellow. Fruit a drupe, ovoid, **yellow to pale orange**, with a single stone.
    The tree is browsed by game. Bark and leaves are used medicinally. Wood yellow-brown, hard, attractive, suitable for furniture. Fruit edible, sweet-tasting and used in making beer; also boiled in water which, after the fruit is removed, is used to make a pleasantly flavoured porridge.

2 *Berchemia zeyheri*   **Red ivory**
SA: 450; Z: 621   Spring–Summer   **Rooi-ivoor**
Small to medium-sized deciduous tree; occurring in bushveld. Leaves elliptic, **12–40 x 6–25 mm, shiny greyish green** above, pale green below, essentially hairless; principal lateral veins **prominently raised below, ending at the margin**. Flowers in **tight** axillary clusters, small, greenish yellow. Fruit a drupe, ovoid, **yellow to brownish red**, with a single stone.
    The tree is browsed by game and stock. The heartwood has unusual bright pink to red shades, and is hard, attractive, suitable for furniture and widely used for ornaments and curios. Bark used for medicinal and magical purposes. Fruit edible, sweet-tasting, often stored, eventually forming a thick, brown, sugary mass.

3 *Scutia myrtina*   **Cat-thorn**
SA: 451; Z: 622   Spring–Summer   **Katdoring**
Climber, scrambling shrub or small to medium-sized tree, usually **multistemmed**; occurring along forest margins, in bush clumps or thicket. Branchlets **4-angled**, with single or paired, **strongly hooked, axillary spines**. Leaves usually suboppo-site, ovate to elliptic, **glossy green** above, paler below; apex often **bristle-tipped**. Flowers in dense axillary clusters; small, yellowish or greenish white. Fruit a drupe, globose, up to 8 mm in diameter, ripening through **reddish to purple-black**.
    Browsed by game and stock. The fruit is edible but not tasty. Leaves used medicinally. An effective hedge plant. Larval food plant for the butterflies *Charaxes xiphanes*, *Charaxes ethalion ethalion* and *Eagris nottoana knysna*.

SALVADORACEAE (see page 31)

4 *Salvadora australis*
(= *S. angustifolia* var. *australis*)   **Narrow-leaved mustard tree**
SA: 621; Z: 877   Winter–Spring   **Smalblaarmosterdboom**
Shrub to small evergreen tree with a **greyish green** crown and branches usually drooping to the ground; occurring in hot, arid bushveld, particularly on floodplains, brackish flats and termitaria. Leaves **long and narrow, grey- to blue-green**, covered with **fine soft grey hairs, semi-succulent** with a salty taste; petiole 1 mm or shorter. Flowers in loose terminal or axillary heads, very small, greenish white. Fruit a drupe, oval, 5–10 mm long, greenish pink, finely velvety.
    Leaves browsed by stock (they taint the milk) and game, particularly impala; also used in traditional medicine. Fruit not tasty, but eaten by various animals.

1

B. discolor: flowers

1

B. discolor: fruit

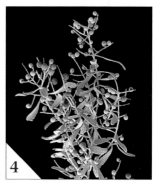

4

S. australis: fruit

2

B. zeyheri: flowers

2

B. zeyheri: fruit

3

S. myrtina: flowers

3

S. myrtina: fruit

4

S. australis: flowers

1 *Salvadora persica*   **Mustard tree**
SA: 622; Z: 878   Winter–Spring   **Mosterdboom**
Sprawling, low-growing shrub to small evergreen tree; occurring in hot, arid bushveld and semi-desert areas, often on floodplains along rivers and on termitaria; sometimes gregarious. Leaves **oblong-elliptic to almost circular**, broadly tapering to apex and base, **bright green, rather fleshy**; petiole **up to 10 mm long**. Flowers in branched axillary or terminal sprays, very small, yellowish green. Fruit a drupe, spherical, ripening pink to bright red.

Browsed by stock and game. The fruit is edible, with a sweet, rather pungent and peppery taste. Leaves and root used medicinally; the latter also used to clean teeth. Khorixas, a town in Namibia, derives its name from the local vernacular name for this tree.

SANTALACEAE (see page 31)

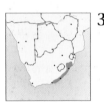

2 *Osyris compressa* (= *Colpoon compressum*)   **Cape sumach**
SA: 99   Autumn–Winter   **Pruimbas**
Shrub to small evergreen tree; a root hemiparasite occurring mostly on **coastal dunes**. Branchlets longitudinally ribbed. Leaves oval, **blue-green** with a **grey bloom, stiff and leathery**; apex broadly tapering with a sharp tip. Flowers in terminal clusters, small and inconspicuous, yellowish green. Fruit fleshy, oval, ripening shiny red to purplish-black.

The fruit is edible; favoured by birds. Bark has been extensively used for tanning.

Very similar to *Osyris quadripartita* (Group 10), an inland species which has alternate leaves.

SCROPHULARIACEAE (see page 31)

3 *Anastrabe integerrima*   **Pambati tree**
SA: 671   Summer–Autumn   **Pambatieboom**
Evergreen shrub or small to medium-sized tree, often multistemmed with a rather **untidy** crown; occurring on the margin of evergreen forest, rocky outcrops and along streams. Stems flattish and **hairy when young**. Leaves **elliptic to ovate-elliptic, stiff**, shiny dark green above, **creamy-grey to creamy-brown felty below**, tapering to a bristle tip; margin finely serrated or entire, **rolled under**. Flowers in small axillary clusters, yellow with throat tinged red, **bell-shaped and 2-lipped**. Fruit a capsule, ovoid, up to 8 mm long, splitting into **2 valves** to release numerous seeds.

Wood hard and termite-resistant, used for building poles and such carved household utensils as spoons. Worth cultivating as a foliage or flowering shrub in frost-free areas; can be trimmed, and does well in a pot.

4 *Freylinia lanceolata*   **Honey-bell bush**
SA: 670.1   All year   **Heuningklokkiesbos**
Shrub to small evergreen tree with a **slender** crown and somewhat **drooping** habit; occurring in damp places, particularly along the **banks of mountain streams**. Leaves **leathery, narrowly elliptic to lanceolate, 4–13 mm wide**, slightly curved, usually hairless; midrib raised below. Flowers in terminal heads, creamy-yellow, honey scented, often produced in abundance. Fruit a small capsule.

An attractive garden subject, especially near water. The plants are easily grown, can tolerate moderate frost, and do well in both winter- and summer-rainfall areas.

S. persica: fruit

O. compressa: flowers

O. compressa: fruit

A. integerrima: flowers

F. lanceolata: flowers & fruit

A. integerrima: flowers

F. lanceolata: flowers

THYMELAEACEAE (see page 32)

1 *Dais cotinifolia*   **Pompon tree**
SA: 521; Z: 760   Summer   **Basboom**
Small to medium-sized, tardily deciduous tree; usually slender, with a rounded crown; occurring on forest margins and in sheltered areas in grassland, often along streams and in ravines. Bark **tough and fibrous**; **branchlets difficult to break**. Leaves oblong-elliptic to obovate, dull dark green with a **bluish tinge** above, paler green below, **hairless**; venation somewhat **translucent and prominent below**; petiole up to 5 mm long. Flowers in dense **subspherical heads** up to 40 mm in diameter and with **4 broad green or brownish bracts at base**, pale pink to pinkish mauve, tubular, often produced in profusion. Fruit a small nutlet, enclosed by the shrivelled floral tube and concealed within the persistent, dry, inflorescence bracts.

The bark can be stripped and plaited into a good quality rope. Decorative when in flower (although flowering period very brief) and a popular garden plant.

2 *Englerodaphne pilosa*   **Silky fibre-bush**
SA: 518   Summer–Autumn   **Syhaarveselbos**
Shrub or small tree with **slender**, rather **drooping** branches; occurring in the **understorey of dense evergreen forest** and in riverine fringe forest, usually in high-altitude and mistbelt areas. Branchlets have tough bark and are **difficult to break**, with sparse, **white**, **spreading hairs**; tips with young leaves **silvery**, **drooping**. Leaves, **ovate to lanceolate, 25–80 x 13–40 mm**, pale green, **thinly** textured, with **long**, **soft**, **whitish hairs**, particularly below; petiole very short. Flowers in axillary, **drooping**, 2–5-flowered heads that hang below the leaves, pale orange-yellow, tubular. Fruit a small nut, inconspicuous.

Similar to *E. ovalifolia*, which is an understorey shrub found in coastal forest in KwaZulu-Natal and the Transkei region, and which has much less hairy leaves. *E. subcordata* is a white-flowered shrub or small tree occurring in coastal forest, thornveld and riverine thicket in the Eastern Cape. It has relatively small (13–40 x 8–18 mm), hairless leaves.

VERBENACEAE (see page 33)

3 *Avicennia marina*   **White mangrove**
SA: 669   Spring–Summer   **Witseebasboom**
Small to medium-sized tree; a mangrove occurring in **estuaries and intertidal areas** along subtropical and tropical coastlines, often dominant on the edges of mangrove swamps. Trunk surrounded by an extensive area of **slender, pencil-like, breathing roots** sticking up from the mud. Leaves ovate to elliptic, **green and hairless above, pale grey and hairy below**. Flowers in dense axillary or terminal heads, small, creamy yellow, sweetly scented. Fruit a capsule, greyish green, dehiscing by **2 valves**.

Wood grey to yellowish brown, dense and durable. The bark is rich in tannin and yields a brown dye. In Maputaland, the leafy branches are used in the construction of fish kraals.

D. cotinifolia: flowers

D. cotinifolia: flowers

E. pilosa: flowers

A. marina: breathing roots

A. marina: fruit

GROUP 24
Leaves simple, 3- or more whorled. Latex present.

ANACARDIACEAE (see page 19)

1 *Ozoroa engleri*   **White resin tree**
SA: 371   Spring–Summer   **Witharpuisboom**
Shrub or small semi-deciduous tree, usually with a short crooked stem and somewhat **drooping** crown; sexes separate, on different trees; occurring in bushveld,
often on sandy flats; confined mainly to the Maputaland Centre. Leaves usually in
whorls of 3, more or less **drooping, grey-green above, silvery (due to densely
appressed hairs) below**, narrowly tapering with a **bristle-like tip**; main side veins
parallel, prominent below. Flowers in terminal sprays, creamy white, sweetly
scented. Fruit a drupe, thinly fleshy, kidney-shaped or rounded, initially green with
a few minute reddish brown spots, ripening **black and wrinkled**.
  The leaves browsed by game and stock. Bark, leaves and roots used medicinally.

2 *Ozoroa insignis*   **African resin tree**
SA: 376; Z: 545   Spring   **Afrikaanse harpuisboom**
Small to medium-sized deciduous tree, much-branched; sexes separate, on different
trees; occurring in bushveld, often among rocks and on termitaria. Leaves usually
in **whorls of 3, spreading**, about **4 times as long as broad**, dark green and **rough
above**, densely covered with **coarse, woolly, yellowish or rusty hairs below**, apex
often with a **bristle-like tip**; main side veins **parallel**, these and interconnected tertiary veins **prominent below**. Flowers in terminal sprays, small, creamy white,
sweetly scented. Fruit a drupe, thinly fleshy, kidney-shaped, initially green with a
few reddish brown spots, ripening **black and wrinkled**. Most of the material from
southern Africa belongs to subsp. *reticulata*. Subsp. *grandifolia* has been recorded
only from Mozambique.
  The wood is reddish brown and suitable for small items of furniture. Bark, leaves
and roots used medicinally. Sticky latex from bark used for bird lime.

3 *Ozoroa obovata*   **Broad-leaved resin tree**
SA: 374; Z: 543   Summer–Autumn   **Breëblaarharpuisboom**
Much-branched shrub or small semi-deciduous tree; sexes separate, on different
trees; usually associated with coastal dune bush (var. *obovata*), but also occurs further inland in bushveld (var. *elliptica*). Leaves usually in **whorls of 3, spreading**,
usually **obovate or elliptic, dark green above, silvery (due to densely appressed
hairs) below**, apex **broadly tapering or rounded** with a **bristle-like tip**; main side
veins parallel, but not prominently raised below. Flowers in terminal sprays,
small, creamy white, sweetly scented. Fruit a drupe, thinly fleshy, kidney-shaped,
initially green with a few dark green spots (extrafloral nectaries), ripening **black
and wrinkled**. The taxonomic status of the two varieties is debatable.
  The bark is eaten by elephant and the leaves browsed by game. Fruit eaten by
hornbills. Nectaries on green fruit usually visited by numerous ants.

O. *engleri*: flowers

O. *engleri*: fruit

O. *insignis*: flowers

O. *obovata*: flowers

O. *insignis*: fruit

O. *obovata*: fruit

1 *Ozoroa paniculosa*   **Common resin tree**
SA: 375; Z: 544   Summer   **Gewone harpuisboom**
Small to medium-sized deciduous tree; sexes separate, on different plants; occurring in bushveld, often on rocky hillsides. Leaves usually in **whorls of 3**, more or less **elliptic, grey- to blue-green above, silvery to silky (due to densely appressed hairs) below**; apex narrowly or broadly tapering with a **bristle-like tip**; margin entire. Flowers in terminal sprays, small, creamy white, sweetly scented. Fruit a drupe, thinly fleshy, **elliptic or kidney-shaped**, initially green with a few small reddish brown spots, ripening **black and wrinkled**.
    Browsed by elephant and black rhino. The fruit is used for dyeing leather. Often confused with *O. sphaerocarpa* (below).

2 *Ozoroa sphaerocarpa*   **Currant resin tree**
SA: 377   Summer   **Korenteharpuisboom**
Small to medium-sized deciduous tree; sexes separate, on different plants; occurring in bushveld, often on rocky hillsides. Rather similar to *O. paniculosa* (with which it is often confused) but differs in its leaves, which are **roughly hairy** and not silvery or silky below, with the margin **thickened and uneven (minutely scalloped)**. It also differs in its fruits, which are elliptical or **almost spherical**. The two species are usually mutually exclusive.
    The leaves, root and bark are used medicinally. Sticky latex from bark used for bird lime.

APOCYNACEAE (see page 20)
3 *Gonioma kamassi*   **Kamassi**
SA: 641   Spring–Autumn   **Kamassie**
Shrub or small evergreen tree; occurring as an **understorey** constituent in afromontane forest, and particularly in the Tsitsikamma area of the Eastern Cape. Leaves usually in **whorls of 4**, occasionally 3 or opposite, **shiny dark green above**, dull and pale green below. Flowers in terminal clusters, white, **sweetly scented**. Fruit of **2 follicles**; seeds papery, winged.
    The wood is yellowish brown, fine-grained, used for turnery, carving and fine inlay work, but its uses are limited by its small size. Bark poisonous.

4 *Rauvolfia caffra*   **Quinine tree**
SA: 647; Z: 920   Winter–Spring   **Kinaboom**
Medium to tall deciduous to evergreen tree with a distinct trunk and spreading, rather upright and rounded crown; occurring in riverine bush and along forest margins. Latex **milky**. Leaves in whorls of **3–6**, glossy bright green above, dull pale green below; axils with a dense fringe of minute glands. Flowers in **terminal sprays**, small, white, sweetly scented. Fruit fleshy, almost spherical, green with **white spots**, becoming black and wrinkled when mature; 1- or 2-seeded.
    The flowers, leaves and fruit are eaten by monkeys. Wood whitish or pale brown, soft, light and with a rather featureless grain; used in general carpentry and for carved drums and kitchen utensils. Latex and various parts used medicinally; poisonous. Bark, especially that of the root, rich in alkaloids and widely used in traditional medicine. A decorative garden subject, frost-tender.
    Easily confused with *Breonadia salicina* (Group 25), but the latter lacks latex.

O. paniculosa: flowers

O. paniculosa: fruit

G. kamassi: fruit

O. sphaerocarpa: flowers

O. sphaerocarpa: fruit

G. kamassi: flowers

G. kamassi: fruit (dehisced)

R. caffra: flowers

R. caffra: fruit

1 *Strophanthus speciosus*   Common poison rope
SA: 647.2; Z: 932   Spring   Gewone giftou
Robust **climber**, scrambling shrub or small tree; occurring along forest margins.
Latex **watery**. Leaves **3-whorled, shiny dark green above**, dull pale green below;
axils with 3 minute, scale-like glands. Flowers in terminal clusters, **yellow with
reddish patch at base of each corolla lobe**, sweetly scented. Fruit **paired** and
borne **at right angles, long, slender**, maturing to pale brown, dehiscent; seeds
numerous, each with a tuft of hairs at one end.
    The seeds and latex are poisonous (they contain cardiac glucosides) and were
once used to prepare arrow poison. Roots used in traditional medicine.

CLUSIACEAE (see page 23)

2 *Garcinia livingstonei*   African mangosteen
SA: 486; Z: 716   Spring   Laeveldse geelmelkhout
Small to medium-sized semi-deciduous tree with **rigid branches** rising at a sharp
angle; sexes separate, on different trees; young growth often bright red; occurring
in low-altitude bushveld and subtropical coastal grassland, often on floodplains of
rivers. Latex **yellow**. Branches **short and thick**, in **3's or opposite**. Leaves
3-whorled or occasionally in 4s or opposite, **blue-green, thick, stiff and leathery**;
margin entire or with shallow teeth. Flowers clustered in leaf axils or on knobby
side spurs on older stems, cream to greenish yellow, sweetly scented. Fruit fleshy,
spherical or elliptical, up to 35 mm in diameter, **bright orange-red when ripe, peel
contains sticky yellow latex**, often produced in profusion; usually single-seeded.
    Fruit edible, with a delicious acid-sweet taste; also used in the preparation of an
alcoholic beer. Various parts used medicinally; leaves and flowers have proven
antibiotic properties. Wood yellowish white and suitable as a general purpose timber, although use is limited by small size.

S. speciosus: flowers

S. speciosus: fruit & seeds

S. speciosus: flowers

G. livingstonei: flowers

G. livingstonei: fruit

GROUP 25
Leaves simple, 3 or more-whorled. Latex absent.

See also Group 9: *Cassine transvaalensis* (p. 138); Group 19: *Premna mooiensis* (p. 304); Group 23: *Combretum adenogonium* (p. 326).

EUPHORBIACEAE (see page 24)

1 *Hyaenanche globosa*   Hyaena poison
SA: 319   Winter–Spring   **Gifboom**
Shrub or small evergreen tree; sexes separate, on different plants; occurring in fynbos, usually in rocky places; restricted to mountains in the vicinity of Vanrhynsdorp in the Western Cape. Leaves **4-whorled, dark green, stiff and leathery**; petiole short and thickset, **reddish**. Flowers in axillary clusters (male) or in groups of 2 or 3 (female); female ones greenish; male ones often **tinged deep red and with abundant, powdery pollen**. Fruit a **globose capsule, 3- or 4-lobed**, brownish yellow when mature, dehiscent; seeds black.

The seeds (possibly also other parts of the plant) contain a deadly toxin with a strychnine-like action; used as an arrow poison and to kill hyaenas and other predators. The Gifberg ('poison mountain') near Vanrhynsdorp derives its name from the tree. One of the few wind-pollinated trees native to southern Africa.

LOGANIACEAE (see page 26)

2 *Nuxia congesta*   Common wild elder
SA: 633; Z: 895   Summer–Winter   Gewone wildevlier
Shrub or small to medium-sized evergreen tree; occurring in grassland, bushveld and forest, usually in rocky places. Leaves **3-whorled**, crowded at ends of branches, very variable in shape and size, elliptic to almost circular, glabrous or **variously hairy**; margin entire or coarsely toothed; reticulate venation **obscure when viewed against the light**; petiole **2–10 mm long**. Flowers in **dense, congested** terminal heads, small, white, often tinged with mauve, fragrant. Fruit a capsule, about 3 mm long, hairy, brownish; seeds fine, inconspicuous.

The wood is whitish yellow, hard and heavy, but its practical uses are limited by the small size. It makes durable fence posts.

Similar to *N. glomerulata*, whose leaves are more elliptic and leathery, glabrous and with the reticulate venation translucent when viewed against the light. The plant has a restricted distribution between Pretoria and Zeerust.

3 *Nuxia floribunda*   Forest elder
SA: 634; Z: 896   Autumn–Winter   Bosvlier
Small to medium-sized evergreen tree with a densely leafy, somewhat rounded crown; occurring in and around forest. Twigs **angled with swollen nodes**. Leaves **3-whorled or opposite**, somewhat **drooping, more than 3 times as long as broad, hairless**; margin entire or obscurely toothed, particularly in coppice shoots, often wavy; midrib often **purplish** in young leaves; petiole slender, **15–45 mm long**. Flowers in **large, much-branched** terminal sprays, small, white, fragrant. Fruit a capsule, about 4 mm long, brownish when mature; seeds fine, inconspicuous.

The wood is pale yellowish, hard and heavy, used for fencing and in general carpentry. Leaves browsed by game. Bark used medicinally. A decorative garden plant.

H. globosa: female flowers

H. globosa: male flowers

H. globosa: fruit

N. congesta: flowers

N. floribunda: tree

N. floribunda: flowers

PROTEACEAE (see page 29)

1 *Brabejum stellatifolium* **Wild almond**
SA: 72   Summer **Wilde-amandel**

Shrub or medium-sized tree, often multistemmed with spreading branches; occurring in fynbos, along streams and in sheltered valleys. Young growth **densely covered with rusty to golden-brown hairs**. Leaves **4–9-whorled, dark green, hard and leathery**; margin irregularly, roughly and often sharply toothed. Flowers numerous, in dense axillary spike-like racemes up to 80 mm long near ends of branches, small, white, fragrant. Fruit almond-shaped, single-seeded, initially magenta, becoming **densely covered with rusty-brown hairs**, indehiscent.

The wood is reddish brown, attractive, and suitable for ornamental work. Roasted kernels were once used as a coffee substitute, but are said to be poisonous unless well soaked. Planted as a hedge in the Cape by the early Dutch settlers. Sections of the latter, known as Van Riebeeck's hedge and now more than 300 years old, can still be seen on the slopes of Cape Town's Table Mountain (notably in Kirstenbosch Botanic Garden).

RHIZOPHORACEAE (see page 30)

2 *Cassipourea gummiflua* **Large-leaved onionwood**
SA: 530; Z: 763   Summer–Autumn **Grootblaaruiehout**

Medium to large tree with a spreading crown and horizontal branching; occurring in forest, usually near the coast. Branchlets with scattered, **raised white dots** (lenticels); terminal buds covered with a **sticky, yellowish resin**. Leaves **3-whorled or opposite**, leathery, **shiny dark green above**, paler below; margin entire or with shallow serrations in upper half; venation **yellowish**, prominent below. Flowers in axillary clusters, greenish white, about 6 mm in diameter; stamens up to 14, conspicuous. Fruit an oval capsule, yellowish green when mature; seeds small with a yellow aril. All the material from southern Africa belongs to var. *verticillata*.

The freshly cut wood has a strong onion-like smell. Flowers attract many insects. Bark extensively used in traditional medicine.

RUBIACEAE (see page 30)

3 *Breonadia salicina* (= *Adina microcephala*) **Matumi**
SA: 684; Z: 1057   Summer **Mingerhout**

Small to **very large (up to 40 m)** evergreen tree with a tall, straight trunk and rather narrow crown; occurring in **riverine fringe forest** and **along the banks of permanent rivers and streams**. Leaves usually **4-whorled**, clustered towards ends of branches, tough, leathery, **glossy dark green above**, pale green below, hairless; petiole **thickset, up to 20 mm long**. Flowers in **compact round** axillary heads, small, pale yellow tinged with red, fragrant. Fruit a very small capsule, clustered in fruiting heads; seeds very small, 2-winged.

The wood is pale to dark brown with pale flecks, hard, heavy, somewhat oily with a fine grain; very durable, and used for furniture, boats, floors and various types of construction work. Leaves browsed by game. Bark used medicinally.

Can be confused with *Rauvolfia caffra* (Group 24, p. 358), which has milky latex and leaves with translucent veins.

B. stellatifolium: flowers

B. stellatifolium: young fruit

C. gummiflua: flowers

C. gummiflua: flower buds

B. stellatifolium: fruit

B. salicina: flowers

1 *Gardenia cornuta* Natal gardenia
SA: 690.1 Summer Natalkatjiepiering
Multistemmed shrub or small tree, with short, **rigid branches**; occurring in bushveld and thicket, mainly in the Maputaland Centre. Leaves **clustered** at the ends of short lateral twigs, usually **3-whorled**, obovate, **20–50 x 15–27 mm, hairless**; margin **wavy**. Flowers axillary, solitary, large and showy, white fading to cream; calyx tube **extended as a ribbed sleeve beyond the insertion of the lobes**. Fruit oval, up to 54 x 20 mm, **smooth**, woody, yellow, tipped with persistent calyx.

The plant is browsed by game. Young fruit much favoured by nyala, and also eaten by monkeys. The fruit and root are used medicinally.

2 *Gardenia resiniflua* subsp. *resiniflua* Resin gardenia
SA: 690.2; Z: 1073 Summer Harpuiskatjiepiering
Much-branched shrub or small tree, with short, **rigid** branches; occurring in hot, low-altitude bushveld and thicket, particularly associated with mopane. Leaves stalkless, **clustered** at the ends of short lateral twigs, usually **3-whorled**, obovate, 20–80 x 15–50 mm, young leaves **softly velvety**, mature ones sparsely haired above, **densely velvety below**, harsh to the touch; venation **submerged above, raised below**. Flowers axillary, solitary, white fading to cream. Fruit oval, about **13 mm in diameter**, smooth or covered in short hairs, woody, yellow, tipped with persistent calyx.

The wood is used for carving. Fruit used medicinally.

3 *Gardenia ternifolia* subsp. *jovis-tonantis* Yellow gardenia
SA: 690.3; Z: 1071 Spring–Summer Geelkatjiepiering
Shrub or small tree, with short, **rigid** branches; occurring in bushveld and thicket, often on termitaria. Branchlets often covered with **brownish powder**. Leaves **clustered** at the ends of short lateral twigs, usually **3-whorled**, oblanceolate to narrowly obovate, **up to 130 x 80 mm**, both surfaces covered in short, rough hairs, hairtuft **domatia often present** in axils of lateral veins; margin **wavy**. Flowers axillary, solitary, large and showy, white fading to cream. Fruit oval, **up to 50 x 35 mm, fine-haired**, woody, yellow-brown, tipped with persistent calyx.

The wood is yellowish or pinkish brown, hard and very fine-grained.

G. imperialis, from the Eastern Highlands of Zimbabwe and adjacent Mozambique, has very large (100–250 x 50–140 mm), more or less smooth leaves, very large white flowers (about 120 mm long x 130 mm in diameter) and resembles *Uapaca kirkiana* (Group 5, p. 90).

4 *Gardenia thunbergia* White gardenia
SA: 692 Spring–Summer Witkatjiepiering
Shrub or small tree, with short, **rigid** branches; occurring in forest and coastal thicket. Leaves **clustered** at the ends of short lateral twigs, usually **3- or 4-whorled**, elliptic to obovate, **76–150 x 38–100 mm, glossy dark green above** and below, **hairless**, usually with **domatia in axils of lateral veins**; margin **wavy**; petiole up to 25 mm long. Flowers axillary, solitary, large and showy, white fading to cream; calyx tube terminating in lobes. Fruit oval, usually about 70 x 35 mm, **without ribs**, woody, greyish green with **raised white dots**, tipped with persistent calyx.

The wood is very hard, tough, and used for small objects such as tool handles. Root and leaves used medicinally.

1

G. cornuta: flowers

1

G. cornuta: fruit

1

G. cornuta: fruit

2

G. resiniflua: fruit

4

G. thunbergia: flower

2

G. resiniflua: flowers

3

G. ternifolia: flower

3

G. ternifolia: fruit

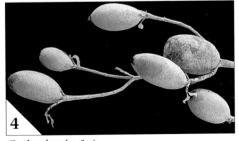

4

G. thunbergia: fruit

GROUP 25

1 **Gardenia volkensii** *(= G. spathulifolia)*   **Savanna gardenia**
SA: 691; Z: 1074   Spring–Summer   **Bosveldkatjiepiering**
Shrub or small tree, with short, **rigid** branches; occurring in bushveld. Leaves **clustered** at the ends of short lateral twigs, usually **3-whorled, broadly obovate, 30–50 x 25–40 mm, hairless**, rarely with rough hairs above and below, **domatia present** in axils of lateral veins; margin wavy. Flowers axillary, solitary, large and showy, white fading to cream. Fruit **oval, about 60 x 30–50 mm, shallowly ribbed longitudinally**, greyish green with **raised whitish dots**, tipped with persistent calyx.

The fruit and root are used medicinally. Wood very hard, heavy, fine-grained, and suitable for carving. Plants often left near villages as a protection against lightning.

G. posoquerioides, a forest species from the Eastern Highlands of Zimbabwe, has mainly opposite leaves and narrowly ellipsoidal fruit (up to 55 x 20 mm), with distinct ridges.

SCROPHULARIACEAE (see page 31)

2 **Bowkeria cymosa**   **Transvaal shell-flower bush**
SA: 672   Summer–Autumn   **Transvaalse skulpblombos**
Single or multistemmed shrub or small tree; occurring in bushveld and montane grassland in forest areas, usually **along stream banks**, rarely in moist places on hill slopes. Leaves usually **3-whorled**, upper surface **shallowly wrinkled**, with or without fine hairs, lower surface with **short soft hairs**; margin entire or finely toothed; venation **sunken above, prominently raised below**. Flowers in **few-flowered** branching axillary sprays, **white with reddish to yellowish streaks** in throat. Fruit a narrowly elliptic capsule tipped by the remains of the style, splitting into 2 or 3 valves; seeds numerous, minute.

3 **Bowkeria verticillata**   **Natal shell-flower bush**
SA: 673   Spring–Autumn   **Natalse skulpblombos**
Shrub or small evergreen tree, single or multistemmed; occurring in montane grassland and forest areas, mainly **along streams and on forest margins**. Leaves usually **3-whorled**, upper surface dark green and **conspicuously wrinkled**, finely **hairy or woolly below**; margin **toothed**; venation **sunken above, prominently raised below**. Flowers in axillary **pairs, pure white**, scented and sticky to the touch. Fruit an oval capsule tipped by the remains of the style, splitting into 3 valves; seeds numerous, minute.

An attractive garden plant that can tolerate considerable frost.

B. citrina is a rare shrub from the stream banks and forest margins of northwestern KwaZulu-Natal. It has bright yellow flowers borne singly in leaf axils.

G. volkensii: flowers

G. volkensii: fruit

B. cymosa: fruit

G. volkensii: flowers

B. cymosa: flowers

B. verticillata: flowers

B. verticillata: fruit

VERBENACEAE (see page 33)

1 *Clerodendrum glabrum* **Tinderwood**

SA: 667; Z: 994   All year (coast); Summer–Autumn (inland) **Tontelhout**

Shrub or small to medium-sized deciduous tree, crown often **drooping**; occurring in bushveld and along forest margins. Branchlets with **small raised whitish dots.** Leaves **3–6-whorled** or opposite, often **drooping**, variable in texture but usually thin and soft, very variable in shape and size, hairiness variable but usually covered with **short soft hairs below**, with or without a pungently foul smell when crushed. Flowers in dense, rounded, **terminal heads**, white to pinkish, foul- or sweet-scented. Fruit fleshy, round, **yellowish white**, surrounded by the withered persistent cup-like calyx.

The flowers attract numerous insects, particularly butterflies. Leaves used medicinally for a wide range of treatments. Fruit eaten by birds. Poles made from the tree are used in the construction of huts and fish kraals. Wood white to pale brown, hard and used for utility carving and small pieces of furniture. Once used as tinder-wood to start fires, hence the common names. Larval food plant for the butterflies *Hypolycaena philippus philippus* and *Spindasis natalensis*.

A heterogeneous species that needs to be further subdivided.

2 *Clerodendrum myricoides* **Blue-flowered tinderwood**

SA: 667.1; Z: 996   Spring–Summer **Bloutontelhout**

Deciduous shrub or small tree; occurring in bushveld and coastal bush, often in rocky places or on termitaria. Leaves **ovate, opposite or 3- or 4-whorled, softly textured, velvety hairy above** and often **more densely so below**, unpleasantly scented when crushed; margin **coarsely toothed**, mainly in the upper half. Flowers in few-flowered axillary and terminal clusters, either with **all petals bright blue to purple**, or with **4 upper corolla lobes white and the fifth, lower and larger lobe, bright blue to purple**. Fruit fleshy, **2–4-lobed**, yellowish red ripening black, each lobe single-seeded.

The fruit is edible and used medicinally, as are other parts of the tree.

The two colour forms may merit recognition as separate taxa.

C. glabrum: flowers

C. glabrum: fruit

C. myricoides: flowers

C. myricoides: fruit

GROUP 26
Leaves simple, bilobed.

CAESALPINIACEAE (see page 22)

1 Adenolobus garipensis **Blue neat's foot**
SA: 208   Spring–Summer **Latjiesbos**
Shrub or small tree; occurring in semi-desert and desert areas, often on rocky hills or along dry watercourses. Branchlets **long and slender**, with a **whitish bloom**. Leaves clustered on dwarf side shoots, dark green, often tinged with blue, rather thick and fleshy. Flowers **1–3** on short side shoots; petals **greyish, streaked with red or maroon**. Pods pale yellowish brown to pinkish red, shiny.
   Heavily grazed by stock and game, particularly kudu.
   A. pechuellii (**1.1**) is usually a small shrub with more than five flowers per inflorescence and yellow petals without the conspicuous reddish venation, but some often with red spots.

2 Bauhinia galpinii **Pride-of-De Kaap**
SA: 208.2; Z: 261   Summer **Vlam-van-die-vlakte**
Climber, **scrambling** shrub or small tree; occurring in bushveld and thicket, usually in rocky areas or near streams. Leaves deeply notched at the apex; venation prominently raised below. Flowers in **large, branched sprays** near ends of branches; the only **red-flowered** *Bauhinia* found in the region. Pods brown, dehiscent.
   Widely planted as an ornamental shrub in subtropical areas. Two butterflies, *Charaxes jasius saturnus* and *Deudorix diocles*, breed on the plants leaves leaves and pods respectively.

3 Bauhinia petersiana **Coffee neat's foot**
SA: 208.3; Z: 263   Summer **Koffiebeesklou**
Shrub or small tree, sometimes scrambling; occurring in bushveld, usually on Kalahari sand. Leaves **lobed for about half their length**; base deeply lobed. Flowers **large**, fragrant; petals **white, crinkly**; fertile stamens 3–6, pinkish. Hairs on lower surface of leaf appressed in subsp. *petersiana*, curved or spreading in subsp. *serpae*.
   The roasted beans are used as a coffee substitute or pounded into a meal to make a palatable porridge. Leaves and roots utilized medicinally.
   B. urbaniana, from the extreme north of Namibia and Botswana, has flower buds densely covered with reddish brown woolly hairs, and attractive flowers ranging from white through pink to purple. *B. bowkeri*, with smaller white flowers, has a restricted distribution in the Eastern Cape. *B. natalensis*, a shrub from southern KwaZulu-Natal and the Eastern Cape, has almost completely divided leaves and white flowers, often with a thin longitudinal red line in the middle of each petal.

A. garipensis: flowers

A. garipensis: fruit

A. pechuellii: flowers

B. galpinii: flowers

B. galpinii: fruit

B. petersiana: flowers

B. petersiana: fruit

373

1 *Bauhinia tomentosa*   Bush neat's foot
SA: 208.1; Z: 264   Summer   Bosbeesklou
Shrub or small tree; occurring in coastal forest and bushveld. Leaves deeply **divided for one-third to half their length**; lower surface **with or without hairs**. Flowers bell-shaped, sulphur-yellow, with or without a dark brown or maroon central blotch; the only yellow-flowered *Bauhinia* in southern Africa. Pods pale brown, **velvety**, dehiscent.
     An attractive garden plant. Widely used for a diversity of medicinal purposes.

2 *Bauhinia urbaniana*   Sand neat's foot
SA: –   Autumn–Spring   Sandbeesklou
Shrub or small tree, often multistemmed; occurring in dry woodland, on sandy soil. Branchlets slender, with **golden-brown, velvety hairs**. Leaves with blade often wider than long, lobed for about half its length; venation **conspicuously raised below, with reddish brown, velvety hairs**, particularly on the principal veins; base shallowly lobed. Flowers **large**, very attractive, **pink to purple**, rarely white flushed with pink or veined with pink; fertile stamens 5, pinkish. Pods narrow, dark brown, velvety, particularly when young, dehiscent.

3 *Piliostigma thonningii*   Camel's foot
SA: 209; Z: 265   Summer   Kameelspoor
Shrub or medium-sized tree; sexes usually separate, on different plants; occurring in bushveld, usually on sandy soil. Branchlets and lower surface of leaves with **reddish brown hairs**. Leaves **large (up to 120 mm long), thick and leathery**; venation **prominently raised below**. Flowers in axillary, leaf-opposed or terminal sprays; petals white or pinkish, **crinkly**; basal parts with dark brown, velvety hairs. Pods **large, woody** and indehiscent.
     Fibre from the bark is used as twine. Both the leaves and the fruit are eaten by stock and game. Macerated and boiled roots and bark yield a reddish dye; a blue-black dye is obtained from the pods and seeds. Pods are pounded to make a meal rich in ascorbic acid (vitamin C). Widely used medicinally. The butterfly *Charaxes achaemenes achaemenes* breeds on the plant.

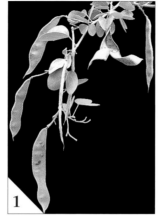

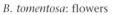

B. tomentosa: flowers

B. tomentosa: fruit

P. thonningii: flowers

B. tomentosa: flowers

B. urbaniana: flowers

P. thonningii: fruit

P. thonningii: tree

GROUP 27
Leaves compound, with 2 leaflets (bifoliolate).

BALANITACEAE (see page 20)

1 *Balanites aegyptiaca*   Simple-thorned torchwood
SA: –; Z: 380   Spring   Enkeldoring-fakkelhout
Small evergreen tree; occurring in dry bushveld, around pans and on alluvial flats along rivers. Branchlets **grey-green, stiff and brittle**, armed with **stout, unbranched, green or yellow spines.** Leaflets **shortly but distinctly stalked,** bright green, leathery, hairy when young, **hairless (at least above) with age**; petiole 8–20 mm long. Flowers clustered in axils of leaves, small, greenish white. Fruit thinly fleshy, up to 50 x 25 mm, yellowish red.

The fruit is edible, bitter-sweet when ripe; used in traditional medicine. Bark, fruit and roots contain an effective fish and snail poison.

2 *Balanites maughamii*   Green thorn
SA: 251; Z: 381   Spring   Groendoring
Tall deciduous tree with the trunk **distinctively and deeply fluted** in old specimens; occurring in dry bushveld and sand forest, often along riverbanks. Branchlets **grey-green, zigzag; spines usually unequally forked.** Leaflets **shortly stalked,** grey-green, leathery, **velvety hairy**, at least below; petiole up to 70 mm long. Flowers in axillary clusters, small, yellowish green; petal densely hairy on outer surface. Fruit with a thin fleshy layer surrounding the hard kernel, 40–60 x 20–30 mm, yellowish.

The green fruit yields a powerful fish and snail poison. Seeds contain large quantities of a colourless oil that burns well and has good lubricative qualities. Bark used medicinally.

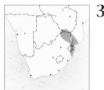

3 *Balanites pedicellaris*   Small green thorn
SA: 252; Z: 382   Spring   Kleingroendoring
Much-branched **shrub or small tree**; occurring in dry bushveld, often on alluvial flats near rivers. Spines **unbranched.** Leaflets **stalkless,** pale green, often tinged brownish, rather fleshy, **velvety, at least when young**; petiole up to 60 mm long. Flowers in axillary clusters, small, greenish white. Fruit with a thin fleshy layer surrounding the hard kernel, up to 25 x 20 mm, orange.

The fruit is edible but not greatly sought after.

Resembles *B. welwitschii* from the Kaokoveld, Namibia: a shrub or tree with very small, grey-green leaves.

B. aegyptiaca: fruit

B. maughamii: fruit

B. maughamii: trunk

B. maughamii: flowers

B. pedicellaris: flowers

B. pedicellaris: fruit

CAESALPINIACEAE (see page 22)

1 *Colophospermum mopane*   Mopane
SA: 198; Z: 246   Spring–Summer   Mopanie
Shrub or medium-sized to tall deciduous tree; occurring in **almost pure stands** in hot, low-lying areas, often on alluvial or lime-rich soils. Leaflets **stalkless**, resembling two butterfly wings, with a **minute protuberance between the pair**, hairless, smelling strongly of turpentine when crushed; petiole 20–40 mm long. Flowers in short axillary racemes or sprays, inconspicuous, greenish. Pods flattened, oval, **indehiscent**.

The heartwood is attractive, dark reddish brown, hard, heavy, very durable and extensively used for ornaments, furniture and fire wood. Browsed by cattle and game, particularly elephants. Caterpillars of the emperor moth, *Imbrasia belina*, feed on the leaves. The latter are known as mopane worms, and are widely used as food by man and beast.

2 *Guibourtia coleosperma*   Copalwood
SA: 199; Z: 244   Summer   Bastermopanie
Evergreen tree with a **large, rounded, drooping crown**; occurring in bushveld, almost exclusively on deep Kalahari sand. Young branchlets red. Leaflets **shortly stalked**, rather **sickle-shaped, glossy dark green**, hairless; petiole 15–35 mm long. Flowers in axillary or terminal panicles, small, creamy white. Pods thickly woody, almost circular, brown to dark brown, **splitting down one side to reveal a reddish-brown seed covered by a conspicuous scarlet aril** and hanging down on a slender stalk.

The wood is attractive, soft, pinkish brown and fine-grained. Seeds are roasted, pounded and eaten as meal. The aril is oily, providing a food in times of famine; it also yields a red dye used to stain furniture. Various parts of the tree have medicinal application.

3 *Guibourtia conjugata*   Small copalwood
SA: 200; Z: 245   Spring–Summer   Kleinbastermopanie
Small to medium-sized deciduous tree; occurring in hot, dry bushveld, usually in deep sand or along rivers. Leaflets **subsessile**, obliquely ovate, shiny green above, with 3–6 basal veins, **without a small appendage** between the pair (unlike mopane); apex **rounded**; petiole 8–18 mm long. Flowers in axillary or terminal panicles, small, white or cream. Pods flat, almost circular, leathery, **indehiscent**.

The heartwood is dark brown, hard and heavy. Leaves browsed by game.

C. *mopane*: flowers

C. *mopane*: fruit

G. *coleosperma*: flowers

G. *coleosperma*: fruit & seeds

G. *conjugata*: flowers

G. *conjugata*: fruit

GROUP 28
Leaves compound, with 3 leaflets (trifoliolate). Latex present.

See also Group 6: *Commiphora glandulosa* (p. 102); Group 35: *C. angolensis* (p. 434).

Certain Anacardiaceae, notably members of the genus *Rhus*, are inconsistent in showing a watery or cloudy resin (latex) exuding from the broken end of a freshly picked leaf. All these species were therefore included in Group 31 (see page 398), which should be consulted if the plant in hand has trifoliolate leaves with a liquid exudate, but does not appear to be a *Commiphora*.

BURSERACEAE (see page 21)

1 Commiphora africana   Hairy corkwood
SA: 270; Z: 407   Spring   Harige kanniedood
Shrub or small deciduous tree; sexes separate, on different plants; occurring in hot arid bushveld, often among rocks or on Kalahari sand. Bark grey to **green, smooth, peeling in papery scrolls**, rather succulent. Branchlets often **spine-tipped**. Leaflets usually obovate, side-leaflets about **a third the size of the terminal one**, both surfaces **finely velvety**; margin **coarsely toothed**; petiole up to 45 mm long. Leaves **bright yellow before falling**. Flowers in compact axillary clusters, small, greenish pink. Fruit a fleshy drupe, subglobose, pinkish red; stone partly enveloped by a **4-lobed, red pseudo-aril**.

Cuttings root easily and plants are often used as a live fence. Bark and fruit used in traditional medicine. Gum and resin also used medicinally and as an insecticide, especially against termites. Fruit eaten by yellowbilled hornbills. Larval food plant for *Diamphidia nigroornata*, one of several species of beetle whose pupae were used by the San to prepare arrow poison.

C. dinteri, a thick-stemmed, spineless shrub or small tree restricted to stony desert mountainsides in Namibia, has very small (up to 7 x 5 mm) leaflets clustered on dwarf, knobby side shoots.

2 Commiphora mossambicensis   Pepper-leaf corkwood
SA: 281; Z: 415   Spring–Summer   Peperblaarkanniedood
Small to medium-sized deciduous tree with **bright yellow autumn colours**; sexes separate, on different plants; occurring in hot arid bushveld, often on rocky hills. Bark brown or greyish, **smooth, not conspicuously peeling**. Branchlets **velvety**, not spine-tipped. Leaves most characteristic with **petiole usually erect and the leaflets drooping symmetrically around it**; leaflets almost **circular**, light green, shiny, apex **rounded with an abrupt narrow point**, both surfaces more or less velvety; margin **entire**, finely hair-fringed when young; petiole up to 45 mm long. Leaves bright yellow before falling. Flowers in compact axillary clusters interspersed with leafy bracts, small, yellowish pink. Fruit a fleshy drupe, subglobose, red to blackish; stone partly enveloped by a **red pseudo-aril**.

The wood is used for making household utensils.

C. africana: flowers

C. mossambicensis: fruit

C. africana: fruit

C. mossambicensis: bark

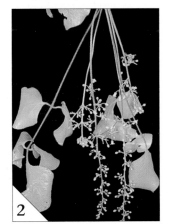

C. mossambicensis: flowers

1 *Commiphora neglecta*   Green-stem corkwood
SA: 283; Z: 415,1 Spring   Groenstamkanniedood
Small to medium-sized deciduous tree, usually multistemmed with an intricately
branched crown; sexes separate, on different plants; occurring in bushveld and sand
forest, often on rocky hillsides and in pure stands. Bark **peeling in brownish
papery strips to reveal a green underbark**. Branchlets often **spine-tipped**.
Leaflets usually **obovate**, with a few scattered hairs; margin **shallowly toothed in
upper half**; petiole long and slender. Leaves yellow before falling. Flowers in compact axillary clusters with the new leaves, small, greenish yellow. Fruit a fleshy
drupe, subglobose, red; stone partly enveloped by a **4-lobed, red pseudo-aril**.
   The fruit is favoured by birds. The root is sweet-tasting, edible to humans and also
eaten by such animals as bushpigs. Wood buoyant and used for fishing-net floats.
Easily grown from poles and often planted as a live fence.
   Similar to *C. discolor*, whose leaflets are conspicuously paler green below than
above. The plant is restricted to arid rocky desert areas in the Kaokoveld, Namibia.
It usually produces simple leaves.

2 *Commiphora schimperi*   Glossy-leaved corkwood
SA: 287; Z: 417 Spring   Blinkblaarkanniedood
Shrub or small deciduous tree with a sparse, rather drooping crown; sexes separate,
on different plants; occurring in hot arid bushveld, usually on sandy soil. Bark
green, smooth, peeling in yellowish brown papery flakes. Branchlets often
spine-tipped, reddish when young. Leaflets often in clusters at ends of side shoots,
usually **narrowly obovate**, side-leaflets **about half the size of the terminal one**,
shiny green with **both surfaces hairless**; margin coarsely **scalloped or toothed**;
petiole up to 25 mm long. Flowers in compact axillary clusters before the leaves,
small, greenish yellow, almost stalkless. Fruit a fleshy drupe, subglobose, pale pink;
stone almost completely enveloped by a **red pseudo-aril**.
   The leaves, bark and roots are eaten by game, notably elephant and warthog. Bark
used medicinally. Twigs once used to produce fire by friction.
   Often confused with *C. africana* (p. 380), which has densely hairy leaves.

3 *Commiphora tenuipetiolata*   White-stem corkwood
SA: 289; Z: 418 Summer   Witstamkanniedood
Small to medium-sized deciduous tree; sexes separate, on different plants; occurring in hot arid bushveld, often on sandy soil. Bark pale grey to yellowish green,
smooth, peeling in silver-white papery flakes. Branchlets **not spine-tipped**.
Leaves 3-foliolate or with 2–4 pairs of leaflets plus a terminal one; leaflets **elliptic**,
more or less **hairless**; margin **entire** or with very few scallops; petiole **up to 45 mm
long**. Flowers in loose axillary clusters with the new leaves, small, greenish yellow.
Fruit a fleshy drupe, subglobose, dark red; stone partly enveloped by a **red, cup-
shaped pseudo-aril**.
   Similar to *C. angolensis* (Group 35, p. 434), which is usually multistemmed with
hairy branchlets and leaves.

C. neglecta: flowers & fruit

C. schimperi: bark

C. schimperi: flowers

C. neglecta: flowers

C. tenuipetiolata: fruit

C. schimperi: fruit

C. tenuipetiolata: bark

C. tenuipetiolata: flowers

GROUP 29
Leaves compound, with 3 leaflets (trifoliolate). Stipules present.
Latex absent.

See also Group 39: *Bachmannia woodii* (p. 472).

BIGNONIACEAE (see page 21)

1 *Rhigozum obovatum* Yellow pomegranate
SA: 675   Spring Geelberggranaat
Rigid, compact shrub or small tree; occurring in karroid vegetation and valley
bushveld, often in rocky places. Leaves opposite or in clusters, 3-foliolate or apparently simple, borne on **short, spine-tipped side shoots**. Leaflets **obovate**, 5–13 x
2–5 mm, greyish green; apex **tapering**, often finely notched. Flowers in axillary
clusters, showy, bright yellow. Fruit a flattened, **pod-like capsule**, up to 80 mm
long, dehiscent; seed with **papery wings**.
Heavily browsed by game and stock, particularly goats.
R. brevispinosum, with a more northerly to westerly distribution, has leaves that
are predominantly simple. Also compare *R. zambesiacum* (Group 32, p. 416).

CAPPARACEAE (see page 22)

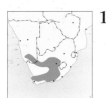

2 *Cladostemon kirkii* Tonga-kerrie
SA: 131; Z: 124   Spring Tongakierie
Small deciduous tree; occurring in bushveld and sand forest. Leaflets ovate to obovate, **40–150 x 30–70 mm**, leathery; petiole **up to 200 mm long**. Flowers in terminal clusters, large and very attractive; petals at first greenish, then **white with
pinkish venation**, becoming **yellowish with age**; stamens borne **near the tip of a
long stalk** (androphore). Fruit **pendulous, globose (80–120 mm in diameter)** with
a hard, pale brown shell, borne on a **thick, jointed stalk (up to 150 mm long)**, with
a pervasive, unpleasant odour when picked.
The root is used medicinally; also eaten by bushpigs. Shed fruit eaten by monkeys
and rodents. Decorative garden plant for frost-free areas.

3 *Maerua cafra* Common bush-cherry
SA: 133; Z: 143   Spring Gewone witbos
Evergreen, shrub or small tree; roots thick and tuberous; occurring in bushveld,
wooded grassland and along forest margins, often in rocky places. Leaflets usually
3 (rarely 4 or 5), **elliptic to obovate**, leathery to almost succulent (coastal forms);
apex with a **hair-like tip**; petiole **up to 60 mm long**. Flowers in terminal clusters,
comprised mainly of a **tuft of spreading white stamens (30–45)** up to 30 mm long.
Fruit oval, up to 45 mm long, **pendulous** on stout stalks, pale green with **dark
green longitudinal lines**.
Root used medicinally and as a chicory substitute.
Similar to *M. nervosa*, from coastal areas of KwaZulu-Natal and southern
Mozambique. This plant has leaflets whose venation is conspicuously raised below,
and flowers with fewer stamens (18–30). *M. pritwitzii*, from *Brachystegia* woodland
in the western Zambezi River Valley, has leaflets with prominent venation, broadly
tapering to rounded apices and almost spherical, warty fruit with a woolly covering.
M. triphylla, from the eastern Zambezi Valley, also has leaflets with prominent venation, but with relatively few stamens (12–16) and pod-like fruit up to 100 mm long.

R. obovatum: flowers

R. obovatum: fruit

C. kirkii: flowers

C. kirkii: fruit

M. cafra: flowers

M. cafra: fruit

1 *Maerua rosmarinoides*　　　　　　　　　**Needle-leaved bush-cherry**
SA: 135　Spring–Summer　　　　　　　　　　　**Naaldblaarwitbos**
Much-branched shrub or **small slender** tree; occurring in bushveld and coastal bush, often in stream-bank scrub. Leaves 3-foliolate (occasionally 1–5), dark green, **drooping**; petiole up to 25 mm long. Leaflets **long and very narrow, about 15 x 1 mm**, hairless; apex sharp-tipped; margin entire, slightly rolled under. Flowers in small, few-flowered heads on short side shoots, comprised mainly of a **tuft of spreading white stamens up to 20 mm long**. Fruit **cylindrical**, up to 20 mm long, **slightly constricted** between the seed, orange when ripe.

　　　Larval food plant for several butterflies of the family Pieridae (Whites).

　　　Closely related to *M. brevipetiolata*, a rare scrambling shrub endemic to the Maputaland Centre, which has slightly broader, more spreading, leaflets (12–32 x 2–4 mm) and much shorter petioles (0,5–7 mm).

CUNONIACEAE (see page 23)

2 *Platylophus trifoliatus*　　　　　　　　　　　　**White alder**
SA: 141　Summer　　　　　　　　　　　　　　　　**Witels**
Small to large evergreen tree; occurring in forest, often along stream-banks. Leaves **opposite**; petiole up to 40 mm long. Leaflets **sessile**, **lanceolate**, dark green above, slightly paler below, hairless, with conspicuous venation; margin **toothed**, rarely entire. Flowers in stalked, axillary, many-flowered heads or panicles, small, white, sweetly scented. Fruit a capsule, tipped with the persistent styles, dark brown, about 10 mm long, produced in abundance.

　　　This is only tree species in southern Africa with trifoliolate, opposite leaves with toothed margins. Wood pale yellowish white to dark brown, durable, suitable for furniture. The flowers are highly attractive to honey bees and other insects; yields an excellent honey.

FABACEAE (see page 25)

3 *Erythrina abyssinica*　　　　　　　　　**Red-hot poker coral tree**
Z: 366　Winter–Spring　　　　　　　　　　　　**Vuurpylkoraalboom**
Medium-sized, **thickset** deciduous tree with a rounded, spreading crown; occurring in bushveld and wooded grassland. Branchlets sometimes with prickles. Leaflets almost as **broad as long**, terminal one **55–140 x 60–140 mm**, lateral ones slightly smaller, densely woolly when young, becoming less hairy with age, **prickles often present** on midrib and principal lateral veins below, with two glands (stipels) at point of attachment; apex **rounded**; venation **prominently raised below**; stipules fall early. Flowers in sturdy axillary or terminal racemes, usually appearing before the new leaves, scarlet; standard **30–35 mm long**, enclosing the stamens; calyx with **long, slender, distinctive lobes at apex**. Fruit a cylindrical pod, up to 100 mm long, **deeply constricted between the seeds,** densely **furry**, dehiscent; seeds **red with black spot** at point of attachment.

　　　The wood is whitish, light, soft, used for drums, fishing-net floats, pestles and brake blocks. The seeds are made into necklaces. Larval food plant for the butterflies *Charaxes bohemani*, *C. castor flavifasciatus* and for for the hawk moth *Polyptychus falcatus*.

　　　Similar to *E. latissima* (p. 390), which has larger leaves and flowers (standard petal 40–55 mm long) and is more cold-tolerant.

M. rosmarinoides: flowers

M. rosmarinoides: fruit

P. trifoliatus: flowers

E. abyssinica: flowers

P. trifoliatus: fruit

E. abyssinica: fruit

1 *Erythrina caffra*
SA: 242 Spring

Coast coral tree
Kuskoraalboom

Medium to large deciduous tree with a spreading rounded crown; occurring in coastal forest and bush, often along rivers. Branchlets with **prickles**. Leaflets broadly **ovate to elliptic**, terminal one 80–160 x 80–180 mm, lateral ones slightly smaller, **hairless**, **without prickles**, with two glands (stipels) at point of attachment; apex **tapering**; stipules fall early. Flowers in stalked axillary or terminal racemes up to 100 mm long, usually appearing before the new leaves, orange-scarlet, rarely cream; standard petal relatively short and broad, **curved back to display stamens**; keel petal 20–25 mm long. Fruit a cylindrical pod, up to 65 mm long, deeply **constricted between the seeds**, hairless, dehiscent; seeds **red with black spot** at point of attachment.

Various parts of the plant are used for medicinal and magical purposes. Attractive garden tree, but frost tender.

Differs from *E. lysistemon* (p. 390) in its broader leaflets, backward curving standard petal and exposed stamens.

2 *Erythrina decora*
SA: 243 Spring–Summer

Namib coral tree
Namibkoraalboom

Shrubby, small to medium-sized deciduous tree; occurring in warm, arid bushveld, often in rocky places. Branchlets with **greyish white, woolly hairs**, occasionally with prickles. Leaflets **ovate to broadly ovate**, terminal one often broader than long, 30–180 mm long and wide, lateral ones slightly smaller, **densely velvety** when young, becoming smoother with age above, with two glands (stipels) at point of attachment, often with **prickles along the midrib, rachis and petiole**; apex **broadly tapering to rounded**; stipules fall early. Flowers in sturdy axillary or terminal racemes up to 150 mm long, usually appearing before the new leaves, scarlet; standard petal 30–40 mm long. Fruit a cylindrical pod, up to 120 mm long, deeply **constricted between the seed**, slightly hairy, dehiscent; seeds **red with black spot** at point of attachment.

In Namibia's Kaokoveld the seeds decorate a special type of gemsbok-horn trumpet used in herding cattle.

3 *Erythrina humeana*
SA: 243.1 Summer–Autumn

Dwarf coral tree
Kleinkoraalboom

Shrub to small deciduous tree, often **multistemmed** with a sparse crown; occurring in coastal grassland and bushveld, often on rocky outcrops. Branchlets **with prickles**. Leaflets **3-lobed, markedly triangular**, terminal one 90–130 x 80–120 mm, lateral ones slightly smaller, **hairless, with prickles on midrib, principal lateral veins, rachis and petiole**, with two glands (stipels) at point of attachment; apex **long and narrow**; stipules fall early. Flowers in long-stalked (up to 100 mm long) axillary or terminal racemes (flowering portion up to 100 mm long), usually appearing during **summer/autumn when already in leaf**, often in clusters towards ends of shoots, scarlet, fading to wine red; standard petal enclosing the stamens. Fruit a slender cylindrical pod, up to 150 mm long, **deeply constricted between the seeds**, hairless, dehiscent; seeds **red with black spot** at point of attachment.

A root extract and the ash from the bark are used medicinally. An attractive garden plant, although sensitive to frost.

E. caffra: leaf

E. decora: fruit & seed

E. caffra: flowers

E. caffra: fruit

E. decora: flowers

E. humeana: flowers

E. humeana: fruit

1 *Erythrina latissima*   **Broad-leaved coral tree**
SA: 244; Z: 364   Winter–Spring   **Breëblaarkoraalboom**
Sturdy small to medium-sized deciduous tree with a spreading rounded crown; occurring in wooded grassland and scrub forest, often on hillsides. Branchlets **woolly grey-brown hairy, with prickles.** Leaflets **ovate, very large, terminal one 60–300 x 70–320 mm**, lateral ones slightly smaller, **densely covered with woolly hairs when young,** becoming smooth with age, occasionally with a few scattered prickles; venation **prominently raised below.** Flowers in sturdy axillary or terminal heads up to 110 mm long, borne on bare stalks of about the same length, usually appearing before the new leaves, scarlet; standard 40–55 mm long, enclosing the stamens; calyx with **long, slender, distinctive lobes at apex.** Fruit a cylindrical pod, up to 300 mm long, deeply **constricted** between the seed, **woolly** when young, dehiscent; seeds **orange to red with black spot.**
   The leaves and bark are eaten by elephant. Ash from the tree's bark is used medicinally. A decorative garden tree, tender to frost.
   Similar to *E. abyssinica* (p. 386), which has slightly smaller leaves and flowers.

2 *Erythrina livingstoniana*   **Aloe coral tree**
Z: 365   Summer   **Aalwynkoraalboom**
Medium to large, sturdy, deciduous tree with a spreading crown; occurring at low altitude in hot, arid bushveld; uncommon. Branchlets with **prickles.** Leaflets **deeply divided into 3 lobes,** apical one **triangular and tapering to the apex,** lateral lobes blunt or broadly notched (almost 2-lobed), terminal one nearly as broad as long, up to 170 x 170 mm, lateral ones slightly smaller, **hairless, without prickles.** Flowers in **elongated, *Aloe*-like, axillary or terminal racemes,** extending along the main axis for up to 200 mm, usually appearing after good rains in **midsummer,** bright scarlet. Fruit a cylindrical pod, up to 350 mm long, **deeply constricted** between the seeds, **hairless,** dehiscent; seeds **bright red with white spot** at point of attachment.
   The most attractive of the region's coral trees, but very frost sensitive.

3 *Erythrina lysistemon*   **Common coral tree**
SA: 245; Z: 366   Winter–Spring   **Gewone koraalboom**
Small to medium-sized deciduous tree with a spreading crown; occurring in bushveld and coastal bush, often on warm, north-facing aspect of rocky ridges. Leaflets **ovate,** terminal one up to 125 x 85 mm, lateral ones slightly smaller, **hairless,** occasionally **with prickles along midrib, rachis and petiole;** apex **tapering.** Flowers in stalked axillary or terminal racemes up to 100 mm long, usually appearing before the new leaves, bright red, rarely pink or white; standard petal relatively **long and narrow, enclosing the stamens;** keel petal 9–18 mm long. Fruit a slender cylindrical pod, up to 150 mm long, **deeply constricted** between the seeds, **hairless,** dehiscent; seeds **red with a black spot.**
   The flowers attract many insects and bird species. Leaves often have globose insect galls. Leaves and bark browsed by game. Branches used as live fence poles. Various parts of the plant are used for medicinal and magical purposes. The seeds contain toxic alkaloids as well as anti-bloodclotting substances that may be of value in the treatment of thromboses (a property probably shared by other members of the genus). A decorative garden plant, but frost tender.
   In *E. caffra* (p. 388) the standard petal curves back to expose the stamens.

E. *latissima*: flowers & fruit

E. *livingstoniana*: fruit

E. *livingstoniana*: flowers

E. *lysistemon*: tree

E. *lysistemon*: flowers

E. *lysistemon*: fruit & seeds

VITACEAE (see page 33)

1 *Rhoicissus digitata*   **Baboon grape**
SA: 456.2   Summer   **Bobbejaandruif**
Woody **climber, scrambling** shrub or small tree; tendrils **opposite** leaves; occurring in grassland and bushveld, also along forest margins. Branchlets with **reddish brown** hairs. Leaflets **3–5, almost sessile, elliptic**, dark green and hairless above, finely **reddish brown hairy below**; margin **entire, rolled under**. Flowers in shortly stalked, **leaf-opposed** heads, greenish yellow. Fruit fleshy, oval, reddish brown to purplish black.
    The plant is browsed by game. Swollen roots eaten by bushpig.

2 *Rhoicissus revoilii*   **Bitter forest grape**
SA: 456.3; Z: 631   Summer   **Bitterbosdruif**
Scrambling shrub or small tree with somewhat **drooping** branches; tendrils **opposite** leaves; occurring in bushveld, often in rocky places. Young growth with dense **rust-brown hairs**. Leaflets **3, very variable in shape**, glossy dark green and usually hairless above, **densely reddish brown to greyish hairy below**; apex tapering to rounded; base tapering, often **markedly asymmetric in lateral leaflets**; margin usually **entire**. Flowers in shortly stalked, **leaf-opposed** heads, yellowish green, stalks and calyces densely covered with rust-coloured hairs. Fruit fleshy, 2-lobed, reddish to black.
    The stem contains a watery, acid sap and is chewed to relieve thirst. The pulpy part of the fruit is edible, reminiscent of grapes and rich in vitamin C (the skin and seeds are discarded). A refreshing drink is prepared by boiling the fruit in water and straining off the liquid; also used medicinally. A tasty jelly is obtained by adding sugar and boiling further.

3 *Rhoicissus tridentata*   **Bushman's grape**
SA: 456.6; Z: 634   Summer–Autumn   **Boesmansdruif**
Scrambling deciduous shrub or small bushy tree; tendrils **opposite** leaves; occurring in wooded grassland, bushveld and along forest margins, often on rocky ridges. Branchlets with **greyish or rusty** hairs. Leaflets **3**, nearly sessile, **narrowly to broadly obovate**, lateral ones usually **asymmetrical**, dark green to blue-green and hairless above, with or without hairs below, reddish in autumn; apex square to broadly rounded; margin toothed to almost entire, **each tooth with a minute point, 0,5 mm long**. Flowers in shortly stalked, **leaf-opposed** heads, greenish yellow. Fruit fleshy, spherical, ripening through red to black.
    The fruit is edible but has a sour taste. Roots tuberous, eaten by bushpig, baboons and porcupine; used in traditional medicine. The plant is browsed by game.
    A very variable species in regard to leaf characters: some of its several forms are recognized as subspecies, but others probably deserve specific status. *R. rhomboidea*, a vigorous climber of coastal and inland forest, has leaflets which are glossy dark green above, with tapering tips and toothed margins, each tooth tip with a minute point at least 1 mm long; lateral leaflets shortly stalked (1–4 mm long) and markedly asymmetrical.

R. digitata: fruit

R. revoilii: fruit

R. tridentata: fruit

R. tridentata: flowers

R. tridentata: fruit

GROUP 30

Leaves compound, with 3 leaflets (trifoliolate). Secretory cavities present. Stipules absent. Latex absent.

RUTACEAE (see page 30)

1 *Oricia bachmannii*   **Twin-berry tree**
SA: 257; Z: 392   Winter–Spring   **Tweelingbessieboom**
Small to medium-sized evergreen tree with a much-branched crown; occurring in coastal and montane forest. Leaflets **leathery**, shiny dark green, **rather drooping, shortly and distinctly stalked**, aromatic when crushed; apex rounded to pointed; petiole **up to 50 mm long**. Flowers in dense, branched, drooping, axillary or terminal heads, small, creamy white; sexes separate on the same tree. Fruit oval to round, usually **with an undeveloped lobe (carpel) at the base**, fleshy, about 20 mm long, yellow to orange, gland-dotted.
A larval food plant for several swallowtail butterflies (Papilionidae).

2 *Teclea gerrardii*   **Zulu cherry-orange**
SA: 263   Spring   **Zoeloekersielemoen**
Small to medium-sized evergreen tree; sexes separate, on different plants; occurring in coastal and inland forest. Leaflets **leathery**, dull green above, paler below, **lateral ones stalkless**, aromatic when crushed; apex **rounded**, sometimes notched; petiole grooved, sometimes narrowly winged. Flowers in **short axillary clusters** up to 50 mm long, small, yellowish green. Fruit almost spherical, fleshy, **about 10 mm in diameter**, velvety green, ripening bright reddish orange and **hairless** with an **uneven**, gland-dotted surface.
The fruit is eaten by birds and monkeys.
T. trichocarpa, from southeastern Zimbabwe and adjacent Mozambique, is very similar but its ripe fruit is densely velvety. *T. myrei* has ovoid fruit and leaflets with more tapering apices; in southern Africa it has been reported from dry thicket in southeastern Zimbabwe and central Mozambique.

3 *Teclea natalensis*   **Natal cherry-orange**
SA: 264   Spring   **Natalkersielemoen**
Small to medium-sized evergreen tree; sexes separate, on different plants; occurring in coastal and inland forest. Leaflets **leathery**, glossy dark green above, paler below, **distinctly stalked**, rather **drooping**, aromatic when crushed; apex **tapering**; petiole up to 10 mm long. Flowers in **branched axillary or terminal heads or panicles**, small, yellowish green. Fruit oval, fleshy, **about 10 mm long**, ripening through yellow to orange, gland-dotted.
A larval food plant for several swallowtail butterflies (Papilionidae).
T. nobilis is a large forest tree from the Eastern Highlands of Zimbabwe. It has narrowly elliptic, shortly stalked leaflets with very wavy margins, and small (up to 6 mm in diameter) fruit which is produced in great abundance.

O. bachmannii: flowers

O. bachmannii: fruit

T. gerrardii: fruit

T. gerrardii: flower

T. natalensis: flowers

1 *Toddaliopsis bremekampii*   **Wild mandarin**
SA: 262; Z: 397   Spring   **Wildenartjie**
Shrub or small evergreen tree, usually **multistemmed**; occurring in hot, dry bushveld and in sand forest, often associated with *Androstachys johnsonii* (Group 13, p. 258). Leaflets **leathery**, shiny dark green above, yellowish green below, **shortly and distinctly stalked**, **lemon-scented** when crushed; apex **tapering**; petiole up to 40 mm long. Flowers in short axillary or terminal clusters, small, creamy white; sexes separate on the same plant. Fruit **globose**, fleshy, about 14 mm in diameter, orange-green to reddish brown, **gland-dotted and rough-skinned**. The wood is used in hut-building.

2 *Vepris lanceolata* (= *V. undulata*)   **White ironwood**
SA: 261; Z: –   Summer   **Witysterhout**
Small to large evergreen tree with a **slender erect trunk** and wide, rounded crown; sexes separate, on different plants; occurring in forest and riverine bush. Leaflets leathery, **spreading**, **stalkless**, aromatic when crushed; apex tapering; margin **markedly wavy**. Flowers in branched terminal heads, small, greenish yellow. Fruit round, thinly fleshy, **about 5 mm in diameter, black**, gland-dotted.

    The wood is white, hard, strong and elastic; used in the making of implement handles, wheel spokes and roof beams. Bark eaten by porcupine. Root used medicinally. Several swallowtail butterflies (Papilionidae) breed on the tree.

    V. zambesiaca, a rather rare deciduous shrub or small tree from woodland in Zimbabwe and northern Mozambique, has branches and leaves which are densely hairy, with markedly winged petioles. *V. carringtoniana*, a deciduous shrub or small tree endemic to the Maputaland Centre, also has winged petioles, but the branchlets and leaves are hairless.

3 *Vepris reflexa*   **Bushveld white ironwood**
SA: 260; Z: 394   Spring–Summer   **Bosveldwitysterhout**
Shrub or small tree, **branching low down**; sexes separate, on different plants; occurring in dry bushveld, often along rivers or on rocky hillsides. Leaflets leathery, **drooping**, more or less **folded upward along midrib**, **shortly stalked**, aromatic when crushed; apex tapering; margin plane. Flowers in short axillary heads, small, greenish yellow. Fruit round, fleshy, **up to 12 mm in diameter, orange-red**, gland-dotted.

    The plant is browsed by elephant. Fruit eaten by birds. Several swallowtail butterflies (Papilionidae) breed on the tree.

T. bremekampii: flowers

T. bremekampii: fruit

V. lanceolata: flowers

V. lanceolata: fruit

V. reflexa: flowers

V. reflexa: fruit

GROUP 31

Leaves compound, with 3 leaflets (trifoliolate). Secretory cavities absent. Stipules absent Latex absent, or if present, then watery or cloudy, with flow inconspicuous or inconsistent.

See also Group 8: *Rhigozum brevispinosum* (p. 120); Group 29: *R. obovatum* (p. 384); Group 38: *Heteromorpha trifoliata* (p. 450).

The presence of resin ducts in members of the Anacardiaceae is often revealed by watery or cloudy liquid exuding from the base of a freshly picked leaf. Although all species of *Rhus* contain such ducts, the flow of resin from wounds may be either inconspicuous, or inconsistent, often varying from plant to plant, and between different leaves on the same plant, and from season to season. Thus those members of the family with trifoliolate leaves have been included in this group rather than, as might have been expected, in Group 28.

In the absence of fertile material, species of *Rhus* can easily be confused with members of the genus *Allophylus*. However, *Rhus* can usually be distinguished by the resinous smell of its crushed leaves, by resin exuding from the base of the leaf stalk, by branchlets that often have brownish lenticels, and by the lack of conspicuous hairtuft domatia in the axils of the principal lateral veins on the lower leaflet surface.

ANACARDIACEAE (see page 19)
Species of *Rhus* have minute, rather similar-looking, greenish or yellowish white flowers in axillary or terminal panicles or racemes. They are usually either male or female and are borne on separate trees. In all species the fruit is a drupe.

1 ***Rhus burchellii*** (= *R. undulata* var. *tricrenata*)   **Karoo kuni-bush**
SA: 379   Summer–Autumn   **Karookoeniebos**
Intricately branched evergreen shrub or small bushy tree, sometimes spiny; occurring in arid grassland and karroid vegetation, usually on rocky hills. Branchlets with prominent **brownish lenticels**. Leaflets **sessile**, crowded on reduced side shoots, olive- to blue-green on both sides, **hairless**; petiole up to 10 mm long. Terminal leaflet **obtriangular, 8–20 x 3–12 mm**; apex often **notched**; margin entire. Drupe somewhat rectangular, slightly compressed, chestnut brown, hairless.
The branches were once used by the San for bows.
R. longispina is a dense shrub with pale grey-brown to dull yellowish spinous branchlets, and oblanceolate to narrowly obovate leaflets crowded on pale spurs.

2 ***Rhus chirindensis***   **Red currant**
SA: 380; Z: 546   Summer   **Bostaaibos**
Medium to **large** evergreen or deciduous tree; young and coppicing stems often spinous; occurring in coastal and inland forest. Leaflets shortly stalked, dark green on both sides, **hairless**, often turning red before falling; petiole **up to 80 mm long**, pinkish red. Terminal leaflet ovate to ovate-lanceolate, 40–100 x 15–50 mm; apex **sharply tapering**; margin entire or minutely scalloped, usually **wavy**. Drupe spheroidal, **shiny, dark reddish brown**, hairless.
This is the largest member of *Rhus* in southern Africa. The wood is dark reddish brown, suitable for furniture. Bark used medicinally.
Similar to *R. acocksii*, a scandent shrub or woody climber endemic to the Pondoland Centre; spines short, backward-facing.

R. burchellii: flowers

R. burchellii: fruit

R. chirindensis: fruit

R. chirindensis: flowers

R. chirindensis: fruit

1 ***Rhus crenata***   **Dune crow-berry**
SA: 380.1 Summer   **Duinekraaibessie**
Much-branched, evergreen shrub or small tree; occurring on coastal and adjacent inland dunes. Leaflets sessile, dark green above, slightly paler below, **hairless**; petiole up to 5 mm long. Terminal leaflet **inversely triangular to obovate, 8–25 x 6–15 mm**; apex **blunt or rounded**; margin with **upper third toothed**. Drupe spheroidal, slightly compressed, shiny, **blueish dark brown**, hairless.

2 ***Rhus dentata***   **Nana-berry**
SA: 381; Z: 548 Spring   **Nanabessie**
Much-branched, deciduous shrub or small tree; occurring in sheltered places in grassland, along forest margins and in scrub forest and bushveld, often in rocky places and along streams. Leaves with sessile leaflets, **membranous**, pale to dark green above, paler below, turning dull yellow to orange-red in autumn; petiole up to 30 mm long. Terminal leaflet **widely obovate, 15–40 x 10–30 mm**; apex **pointed**; margin **prominently toothed**. Drupe **spheroidal**, shiny, pale to dark brown, hairless.
    The plant is browsed by game. Fruit edible. An attractive garden subject.

3 ***Rhus engleri***   **Velvet karree**
SA: 382 Spring–Summer   **Fluweelkaree**
Spiny, much-branched shrub or small tree; occurring in bushveld, usually on calcareous substrates and chromate hills. Leaflets sessile, **dull green above, densely whitish hairy below**. Terminal leaflet **oblanceolate to obovate, 15–30 x 5–10 mm**; apex **rounded or notched**; margin entire or with a few teeth towards apex. Drupe somewhat **diamond-shaped, strongly compressed, shiny chestnut brown**, hairless.
    The wood is reddish brown, tough, used for implement handles.

4 ***Rhus erosa***   **Broom karree**
SA: 383 Spring–Summer   **Besembos**
Much-branched, evergreen, **rounded** shrub; multistemmed with **wiry branches**; occurring in karroid areas, usually in large numbers on rocky koppies. Branchlets with **numerous brownish lenticels**. Leaflets sessile, leathery, olive-green above, slightly paler below, **hairless**, covered with a **shiny exudate**; petiole up to 30 mm long. Terminal leaflet **long and narrow, 25–90 x 3–10 mm**; apex **sharply pointed**; margin **shallowly to deeply toothed**. Drupe spheroidal, shiny, light brown, hairless.
    The branches and leaves are used as brooms, and are also suitable for thatching buildings. Various parts used for medicinal and magical purposes.

5 ***Rhus glauca***   **Blue kuni-bush**
SA: 383.2 Winter   **Bloukoeniebos**
Intricately branched, evergreen shrub or small tree; occurring mainly on coastal dunes and in adjacent areas. Leaflets sessile, semi-leathery, olive-green above and below, **hairless**, covered with a **shiny exudate**; petiole up to 20 mm long, often **slightly winged**. Terminal leaflet **obcordate to obovate, 10–30 x 5–15 mm**; apex **notched or rounded**, tipped by a **short, abrupt point**; margin **entire**, slightly rolled under. Drupe spheroidal, slightly compressed, shiny, chestnut-brown, hairless.
    One of the favoured hosts for the hemiparasitic shrub, *Viscum capense* (Viscaceae). Suitable for stabilizing coastal dunes.

R. crenata: fruit

R. dentata: flowers

R. dentata: fruit

R. engleri: fruit

R. erosa: flowers

R. engleri: flowers

R. erosa: fruit

R. glauca: flowers

1 *Rhus gueinzii*   **Thorny karree**
SA: 384; Z: 549   Summer   **Doringkaree**
Multistemmed, shrub or medium-sized tree, usually with **spinescent shoots**; occurring in bushveld. Branchlets with numerous **brownish lenticels**. Leaflets sessile, membranous, **dark green above, slightly paler below, hairless**; petiole up to 40 mm long. Terminal leaflet usually **lanceolate to narrowly elliptic**, 15–100 x 5–25 mm; apex **round or blunt with a shallow notch**; margin usually **entire**, often **wavy**. Drupe spheroidal, slightly compressed, shiny, light brown to brown, hairless.
   The reddish brown, hard wood is used for carved sticks and for firewood. Browsed by stock and game. Various parts used in traditional medicine.
   A taxonomically complex species with numerous forms, some of which have at times been given specific status. A form with orange veins occurs in Maputaland.

2 *Rhus incisa*   **Rub-rub berry**
SA: 385   Winter–Spring   **Baardbessie**
Much-branched, deciduous to evergreen shrub or small tree; occurring in dune scrub, shrublands and karroid areas, usually on clay-rich soils and along rivers. Branchlets with **brownish lenticels**. Leaflets sessile, leathery, **dark green, wrinkled and shortly hairy above**, densely **whitish hairy below**; petiole up to 12 mm long. Terminal leaflet **ovate to obovate, 12–40 x 8–18 mm**; apex blunt to rounded with a shallow notch; margin **irregularly incised or cleft and/or toothed**. Drupe spheroidal, slightly compressed, **densely covered with long creamy to pinkish brown hairs**, often splitting open. Var. *incisa* has leaflets which are deeply incised whereas those of var. *effusa* are merely irregularly and shallowly toothed.
   The plant is browsed by stock. Larval food plant for the butterfly *Phasis thero*.

3 *Rhus laevigata*   **Dune currant**
SA: 385.2   Summer   **Duinetaaibos**
Much-branched, multistemmed deciduous shrub or small tree; occurring in fynbos and karroid areas, often in dense stands and on coastal dunes. Leaflets sessile; petiole up to 30 mm long, **narrowly winged**: in forma *laevigata* more or less leathery, dark green above, slightly paler below, hairless; in forma *cangoana* more leathery to almost rubbery, blue-green with yellowish to reddish venation below, hairless (usually on limestone); in var. *villosa* with long straight hairs. Terminal leaflet widely **obovate to lanceolate, 10–65 x 5–35 mm**; apex more or less **rounded**; margin **entire**. Drupe spheroidal, shiny, dull yellow, reddish to brown, hairless.

4 *Rhus lancea*   **Karree**
SA: 386; Z: 550   Winter–Spring   **Karee**
Small to medium-sized evergreen tree; occurring in a wide range of habitats, often on calcareous substrates. Bark **rough, dark brown to blackish**. Leaflets sessile, semi-leathery, **dark olive-green** above, pale green below, **hairless**, covered with a **shiny exudate (particularly when young)**; petiole up to 30 mm long. Terminal leaflet **linear to lanceolate, 25–120 x 5–12 mm**; apex narrowly tapering; margin entire. Drupe spheroidal, slightly compressed, shiny, dull yellow to brown, hairless.
   The wood is reddish brown, hard, tough and durable. Bark used for tanning. Branchlets once used to make bows. Fruit pounded with water and brewed into a tasty beer. Widely cultivated as a garden ornamental; drought- and frost-resistant.

R. gueinzii: fruit

R. gueinzii: fruit

R. incisa: old fruit

R. incisa: fruit

R. laevigata: fruit

R. lancea: flowers

R. lancea: fruit

1 *Rhus leptodictya*   **Mountain karree**
SA: 387; Z: 551   Summer–Autumn   **Bergkaree**
Small to medium-sized evergreen tree with somewhat **drooping** branches; occurring in bushveld and grassland, often on rocky (particularly granite) ridges. Leaflets sessile, membranous to semi-leathery, **dull fresh green above**, slightly paler below, **hairless**; petiole up to 45 mm long. Terminal leaflet **lanceolate, 30–110 x 6–25 mm**; apex narrowly tapering; margin **shallowly to deeply toothed**, rarely entire. Drupe somewhat **diamond-shaped, strongly flattened**, shiny, light to dark brown, hairless.
    Beer is brewed from the fruit. Various parts are used in traditional medicine. A decorative garden subject, but sensitive to severe frost.

2 *Rhus lucida* forma *lucida*   **Glossy currant**
SA: 388.1; Z: 554   Spring   **Blinktaaibos**
Much-branched, evergreen shrub or small tree; occurring at the edge of bush clumps, scrub forest and in protected places in grassland. Leaves with sessile leaflets, semi-leathery, glossy dark olive-green above, slightly paler below, **hairless**, covered with a **shiny exudate**, often turning orange before they fall; petiole up to 22 mm long, often slightly winged. Terminal leaflet **obovate to oblong, 15–65 x 5–35 mm**; apex usually **rounded with a small notch**; margin **entire**. Drupe spheroidal, shiny, dark brown, hairless. Forma *scoparia* (occurring in the southern coastal region) has sessile to subsessile leaves with margin rolled under and the terminal leaflet usually shorter than 20 mm. Forma *elliptica* (rocky places from the Cape Peninsula eastward to Hermanus) rarely exceeds 1 m in height and has sessile to subsessile and more blue-green leaves, with margin strongly rolled under.

3 *Rhus natalensis*   **Natal karree**
SA: 390; Z: 555   Autumn   **Natalkaree**
Woody creeper, semiscandent evergreen shrub or small tree; occurring in coastal scrub and dune forest. Leaflets sessile, somewhat **drooping**, semi-leathery, dark green above, light green below, **hairless**, often **smelling somewhat like apples** when crushed; petiole up to 30 mm long. Terminal leaflet more or less **elliptic, 20–80 x 10–30 mm**; apex **broadly tapering to rounded**, often slightly notched; margin entire or shallowly toothed in upper two thirds, **slightly wavy**. Drupe spheroidal, slightly compressed, **reddish brown**, hairless.
    Sterile material can be confused with *Allophylus natalensis* (p. 412), a species from the same habitat which has more spreading leaves and which lacks the resinous or apple-like smell when crushed.

4 *Rhus nebulosa* forma *nebulosa*   **Sand currant**
SA: –   Summer   **Sandtaaibos**
Scandent shrub to small slender tree, rarely spinous; occurring mainly in coastal dune scrub and forest, occasionally more inland. Leaflets sessile, membranous to semi-leathery, **shiny dark green above**, slightly paler below, **hairless**; petiole up to 30 mm long. Terminal leaflet **obovate to broadly elliptic, 15–70 x 7–35 mm**; apex **rounded**, usually with a short **hair-like tip**; margin **entire**. Drupe spheroidal, shiny, brown to reddish brown, hairless. Forma *pubescens* (restricted to the Eastern Cape) has all its parts densely covered in short hairs.
    An excellent pioneer for stabilizing coastal dunes.

R. *leptodictya*: flowers

R. *leptodictya*: fruit

R. *lucida* forma *lucida*: flowers

R. *lucida* forma *lucida*: fruit

R. *natalensis*: flowers

R. *nebulosa*: flowers

R. *natalensis*: fruit

R. *nebulosa*: fruit

1 Rhus pendulina (= *R. viminales*)   **White karree**
SA: 396   Spring–Summer   **Witkaree**
Much-branched, semi-evergreen tree, usually single-stemmed with side shoots on **young stems often spinous**; occurring in karroid and semi-desert areas, mainly along the banks of the Orange River and a short distance up some of its tributaries. Bark grey-brown, **relatively smooth, rough and scaly when old**. Leaflets sessile, membranous, **dull fresh green above**, slightly paler below, **hairless**; petiole up to 40 mm long. Terminal leaflet **lanceolate, 25–95 x 6–15 mm**; apex **narrowly tapering**; margin **entire**. Drupe spheroidal, slightly compressed, reddish, drying black, hairless.

The wood is durable, suitable for fencing posts and hut construction. Slender branchlets woven into fish traps. Leaves used medicinally. Widely cultivated as an attractive shade tree, fast growing but relatively short-lived.

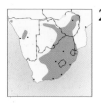

2 Rhus pyroides   **Common wild currant**
SA: 392; Z: 556   Spring–Summer   **Gewone taaibos**
Very variable, multistemmed, deciduous shrub or small to medium-sized tree; frequently **spiny**; occurring in a wide range of habitats, from coastal dunes through montane grassland and bushveld to semi-desert areas. Branchlets often with **velvety** hairs. Leaves with sessile leaflets, **membranous to semi-leathery, dull olive-green** above, slightly paler below, **variously hairy above and below**; secondary veins **prominently raised below**; petiole up to 40 mm long. Terminal leaflet **lanceolate to obovate, 30–80 x 10–23 mm**; apex **very broadly tapering to rounded, ending in a sharp point**; margin entire or irregularly toothed. Drupe spheroidal, shiny, ripening through dull yellow to dark brown, hairless. A taxonomically complex species with several varieties.

Roots are used for medicinal purposes. The fruit is edible, with a pleasant, sweet-acidic taste. Branchlets in var. *pyroides* occasionally parasitized, with characteristic green and hairy spherical galls produced in clusters just below the bark. Eventually the bark ruptures, the galls burst open, each releasing a hard-shelled egg-like structure with a tiny larva. Through contractions of the body of the larva, these 'eggs' jump up and down on the ground until buried in the litter below the tree, from where the mature insect eventually emerges.

3 Rhus rehmanniana   **Blunt-leaved currant**
SA: 393.1   Summer–Autumn   **Stompblaartaaibos**
Much-branched shrub or small tree; occurring in high-rainfall grassland, often on forest margins, also in bushveld, notably *Acacia* thornveld in KwaZulu-Natal. Leaves with sessile leaflets, **leathery, olive-green above**, slightly paler below, **wrinkled and hairless to hairy above**, velvety below; petiole 7–30 mm long. Terminal leaflet **widely obovate, 17–62 x 8–47 mm**; apex **blunt or broadly rounded**, occasionally more tapering; margin around apex **irregularly toothed**, otherwise entire. Drupe spheroidal, shiny, yellowish, hairless. Var. *rehmanniana* is usually a tree with rough, blocky bark and the irregularly toothed leaflet apices blunt or broadly rounded (Eastern Cape to Northern Province). Var. *glabrata* has a shrubby spreading habit with drooping branchlets, granular bark and more tapering terminal leaflets (common along fences and roads in the Eastern Cape and the Overberg region of the Western Cape, particularly on clay soils).

406

R. pendulina: flowers

R. pyroides: flowers

R. pyroides: fruit

R. rehmanniana: flowers

R. rehmanniana: fruit

1 Rhus tenuinervis   Kalahari currant
SA: 393.2; Z: 558   Summer–Autumn   Kalaharitaaibos
Much-branched rounded deciduous shrub or small bushy tree, occasionally spinescent; occurring in bushveld, usually on sandy soils, rocky hillsides or termitaria, often gregarious. Branchlets **velvety**. Leaves with sessile leaflets, leathery, olive-green above, slightly paler below, sparsely hairy above, **densely velvety below**; venation **prominent below**; petiole usually about 13 mm long. Terminal leaflet **obovate to widely obovate**, rarely elliptic, 10–84 x 6–45 mm; apex **broadly tapering to rounded**; margin **single or double toothed towards apex**. Drupe **diamond-shaped, strongly flattened**, at first with a whitish powdery coating, later shiny, dark brownish red, hairless.
     The heartwood is pink or reddish brown, dense and hard, very attractive, and excellent for carving. Bark rich in tannin and used for tanning. Bark, twigs and leaves yield a yellow dye. Leaves used by the San to flavour meat. Ripe fruit eaten by children, or pounded and allowed to ferment as a type of beer.

2 Rhus tomentosa   Real wild currant
SA: 394; Z: 560   Winter–Spring   Korentebos
Much-branched shrub or small tree; occurring on the margins of scrub forest, usually in rocky places. Branchlets **red and hairy**. Leaflets **shortly stalked** (3–5 mm long), leathery, dark **grey-green and hairless above, creamy velvety below**; petiole up to 35 mm long, often reddish. Terminal leaflet widely lanceolate, elliptic or obovate, 30–80 x 10–45 mm; apex usually tapering, occasionally rounded; margin entire or coarsely toothed in upper two thirds. Flowers in **dense, furry and conspicuous terminal heads**, unpleasantly scented. Drupe spheroidal, slightly compressed, **densely covered with creamy or greyish furry hairs**.
     The wood is hard and tough, but its use is limited by the small size. Bark used in tanning and as twine. Naturalized in India.

3 Rhus tumulicola (= *R. dura, R. culminum*)   Hard-leaved currant
SA: 381.1; Z: 547   Spring   Hardeblaartaaibos
Straggling shrub or small tree with a twisted and gnarled trunk; occurring in high-rainfall mountainous regions, often along forest margins or on rocky outcrops in grassland. Leaflets sessile or shortly stalked, **hard and leathery**, olive-green above, slightly paler below, hairless (var. *tumulicola*) or densely hairy, at least below (var. *meeuseana*); midrib and principal lateral veins **pale yellow, prominently raised above and below**; petiole up to 55 mm long, rather rigid. Terminal leaflet widely elliptic, elliptic to obovate, **20–108 x 13–50 mm**; apex broadly tapering to rounded; margin entire or irregularly toothed towards apex. Drupe spheroidal, shiny, brown, hairless. Var. *meeuseana* forma *pumila* is usually less than 0,5 m high with the terminal leaflets 10–25 x 6–15 mm (confined to cracks in rocks in cold, high-altitude areas).

R. tenuinervis: fruit

R. tenuinervis: fruit

R. tomentosa: flowers

R. tomentosa: fruit

R. tumulicola: flowers

R. tumulicola: fruit

1 Rhus undulata   **Namaqua kuni-bush**
SA: 389   Summer–Autumn   **Namakwakoeniebos**
Much-branched, multistemmed, evergreen shrub or small tree, occasionally spinous towards north of its range; occurring in semi-desert and karroid areas, often in rocky places. Branchlets often ending in **stiff spurs**. Leaflets sessile, membranous, olive-green above and below, **hairless**, often **covered with a shiny exudate when young**, with a distinct odour; petiole up to 25 mm long, often slightly winged. Terminal leaflet **oblanceolate to widely obovate, 6–50 x 1–18 mm**; apex **rounded or blunt**, notched or sharp-tipped, sometimes folded like a fan; margin entire or shallowly scalloped in upper half and apex, **not rolled under**, often **markedly undulate**. The drupe is spheroidal, slightly compressed, shiny, dull yellow to cream in colour, hairless.

The leaves are used in traditional medicine. Favoured host of the hemiparasitic shrub *Moquiniella rubra* (Loranthaceae). Larval food plant for the butterfly *Phasis thero cedarbergae*.

Previously often treated in a much broader sense to include *R. burchellii* (p. 398), a species with the terminal leaflets usually shorter than 15 mm. Very similar to *R. pallens*, from which it differs in its leaflet margins, which are not rolled under, and in its paler, slightly less compressed drupes.

2 Rhus zeyheri   **Blue currant**
SA: 396.1   Spring   **Bloutaaibos**
Multistemmed, much-branched deciduous shrub or small tree; occurring in bushveld, often on dolomite and in rocky places. Leaflets sessile, **leathery to almost rubbery, blue-green above and below**, often with a **powdery white coating**, hairless; petiole up to 30 mm long. Terminal leaflet obovate, 10–50 x 5–30 mm; apex **rounded, often sharp-tipped**; margin **entire**, slightly rolled under. Drupe spheroidal, shiny, dark brown to reddish brown, hairless.

A decorative garden shrub.

3 Smodingium argutum   **Rainbow leaf**
SA: 367   Summer   **Pynbos**
Deciduous shrub or small tree with somewhat **drooping branches and foliage**; crown usually with a few scattered **red leaves**; sexes separate, on different plants; occurring in *Acacia*-dominated bushveld or along forest margins in high-rainfall grassland. Leaflets narrowly ovate, up to 90 x 40 mm, dark green above, slightly paler below, leathery, hairless, turning yellow to reddish in autumn; **apex narrowly tapering and finely pointed**; margin **coarsely toothed**; petiole 50–80 mm long, slender, finely hairy. Flowers in large, branched, terminal sprays, very small, cream. Fruit a small **flattened nut encircled by a reddish papery wing**, produced in abundance, hairless, indehiscent.

The plants should be handled with extreme care as some people are highly allergic to it. Contact may result in painful and persistent blisters on the skin, which in severe cases may require hospitalization. Attractive autumn colours make this plant a decorative garden subject, even in areas with mild frost. Because of its poisonous properties, however, it should never be planted in public places or in those where the chances of people-contact are high.

R. undulata: flowers

R. undulata: fruit

R. zeyheri: flowers & fruit

R. zeyheri: fruit

R. zeyheri: fruit

S. argutum: flowers

S. argutum: fruit

411

SAPINDACEAE (see page 31)

1 *Allophylus africanus*   **Black false currant**
SA: 425; Z: 597   Summer   **Swartbastertaaibos**
Shrub or small to medium-sized tree; occurring on forest margins, in riverine thicket and bushveld, often on termitaria in *Brachystegia* woodland. Leaflets **obovate to elliptic, 70–150 x 40–80 mm**, membranous to leathery, hairless or variously hairy on one or both sides, **axils of secondary veins with domatia**; apex tapering, sometimes slightly notched; margin entire or broadly toothed or scalloped; petiole **up to 70 mm long**. Flowers in slender, usually branched, axillary spike-like racemes up to 260 mm long, small, creamy yellow. Fruit spherical to ovoid, fleshy, about 6 mm in diameter, ripening orange, red to black.
 The wood is white, hard, dense, but its usefulness is limited by the small size. Flowers attract numerous insects. Bark used medicinally and magically. Larval food plant for the butterflies *Charaxes varanes vologeses* and *C. acuminatus vumba*.
 A taxonomically complex species with several different forms. Sometimes difficult to distinguish from *A. decipiens* (mainly Northern Province to Eastern Cape) which tends to have leaves with smaller (15–70 x 5–25 mm) leaflets and a shorter (up to 40 mm long) petiole.
 A. abyssinicus (leaves finely hairy) and *A. chirindensis* (leaves without hairs except along the veins) are medium to large forest trees, recorded in southern Africa only in the Eastern Highlands of Zimbabwe. *A. chaunostachys*, a shrub or small tree from the same area, has branchlets with conspicuous lenticels, leaves hairless except for domatia, and the stalk of the terminal leaflet up to 15 mm long.

2 *Allophylus alnifolius*   **Lowveld false currant**
Z: 598   Summer   **Laeveldbastertaaibos**
Much-branched shrub or small tree; occurring at low altitude in bushveld, thicket and riverine bush, often on granite koppies. Leaflets obovate to elliptic, **30–80 x 20–40 mm, membranous** to leathery, **glossy dark green** above, paler below, with or without fine hairs; apex **rounded, notched**; margin **bluntly toothed to scalloped**; petiole up to 55 mm long. Flowers clustered along branched or unbranched, axillary spike-like racemes up to 120 mm long, small, whitish green. Fruit more or less spherical, fleshy, about 6 mm in diameter, bright red.

3 *Allophylus natalensis*   **Dune false currant**
SA: 426   Autumn   **Duinebastertaaibos**
Shrub or small tree with dense, spreading crown; occurring in coastal dune forest and bush. Leaflets with stalks **up to 5 mm long**, narrowly elliptic, 35–85 x 10–25 mm, **stiff and leathery**, shiny dark green above, paler below, essentially **hairless**; apex broadly tapering; base narrowly tapering; margin **shallowly toothed**; petiole up to 30 mm long. Flowers clustered along branched, spike-like axillary racemes up to 90 mm long, small, whitish yellow. Fruit more or less spherical, fleshy, about 7 mm in diameter, bright red, produced in abundance.
 The flowers attract numerous insects. The fruit is edible to humans and is also eaten by birds. The plant is browsed by bushbuck. Larval food plant for the butterfly *Charaxes varanes vologeses*.
 Similar to the associated *Rhus natalensis* (p. 404), which has more drooping leaves with a characteristic resinous, sometimes apple-like, smell when crushed.

A. africanus: flowers   *A. africanus*: fruit

A. alnifolius: flowers   *A. alnifolius*: fruit   *A. natalensis*: fruit

A. natalensis: flowers

GROUP 32
Leaves pinnately compound, opposite or whorled. Leaflets more than 3.

BIGNONIACEAE (see page 21)

1 *Kigelia africana*   Sausage tree
SA: 678; Z: 1035   Spring   Worsboom
Medium to large tree with a rounded crown: occurring in bushveld. Leaves **3-whorled**. Leaflets with **basal pair much smaller than the more terminal ones, hard**, leathery; margin **wavy**, toothed in young plants. Flowers in lax, 6–12-flowered, drooping sprays, dark maroon with yellow venation. Fruit **very large (up to 1 000 x 180 mm)**, heavy (up to 10 kg), sausage-shaped, **hanging down** on long, sturdy stalks.
   Bats are thought to be the main pollinators. The fruit is toxic and widely used in traditional medicine, particularly for skin disorders. An extract of the bark is effective in treating wounds and sores. Seeds are roasted and eaten during famine.

2 *Markhamia obtusifolia*   Golden bean tree
Z: 1032   Summer–Autumn   Goue boontjieboom
Shrub to small bushy tree; occurring in woodland and margins of montane forest, often on Kalahari sand. Young growth covered with **dense long golden hairs**. Leaflets 5 pairs plus a terminal one, hairless with age above, remaining **densely woolly below**; petiole **up to 80 mm long**. Flowers in branched panicles **at the ends of shoots, bright yellow with reddish streaks**. Fruit a slender, pendulous capsule **up to 800 mm long**, with **dense golden hairs**, splitting into 2 valves.
   Various parts of the plant are used in traditional medicine.

3 *Markhamia zanzibarica* (= *M. acuminata*)   Bell bean tree
SA: 677; Z: 1031   Spring–Summer   Klokkiesboontjieboom
Small slender tree with crooked branches; occurring in bushveld, usually on rocky hillsides and in riverine fringes. Branches **very brittle**. Leaflets 2 or 3 pairs plus a terminal one; margin smooth or toothed; petiole **40–90 mm**. Flowers in terminal or axillary racemes, attractive, varying from **yellow densely flecked with maroon to dark maroon on inside** and paler outside. Fruit a slender, pendulous capsule **up to 600 mm long**, hairless with **pale dots (lenticels)**, splitting into 2 valves.
   The roots are used in traditional medicine.

4 *Podranea brycei*   Zimbabwe creeper
Z: –   Spring–Summer   Zimbabwe-klimop
Robust, woody climber; occurring in bushveld. Branchlets **4-angled**, with **whitish lenticels**. Leaves usually with 5 pairs of leaflets, plus a terminal one, about 3 times as long as broad, **glossy pale green above**, paler below; apex **long and narrowly tapering**; petiole 20–60 mm long. Flowers in terminal panicles, pink-purple streaked with dark red on the inside; corolla tube **somewhat flattened and bell-shaped**. Fruit a slender, pendulous capsule up to 400 mm long, splitting into two valves.
   An attractive and widely cultivated garden subject; frost-sensitive.
   Closely related to *P. ricasoliana*, a woody climber confined to a small area in the Eastern Cape (vicinity of Port St Johns). Associated with forest margins, this plant has broader, darker green leaflets (twice or less as long as broad) with more abruptly tapering apices and a more spreading corolla tube.

K. africana: fruit

M. obtusifolia: flowers

M. obtusifolia: fruit

K. africana: flowers

M. zanzibarica: flowers

M. zanzibarica: fruit

P. brycei: flowers

1 *Rhigozum zambesiacum*   Mopane pomegranate
SA: 676; Z: 1028   Spring   Mopaniegranaat
Rigid shrub or small tree; occurring in hot, low-altitude bushveld, often on brackish or granitic soils. Branches often with **spinescent side shoots**. Leaves opposite or in tufts below the spines. Leaflets usually with 3–5-pairs plus a terminal one, sessile, **about 5 x 3 mm**, dark green; apex **rounded**; petiole **up to 5 mm long**. Flowers in axillary clusters, showy, bright yellow with **crinkled petals**, usually flowering in profusion after the first rain in spring, sweetly scented. Fruit a flattened, **pod-like capsule**, up to 70 mm long, **thin-walled**, pale brown, dehiscent; the seeds have papery wings.
   R. obovatum (Group 29, p. 384) usually has trifoliolate leaves.

2 *Stereospermum kunthianum*   Pink jacaranda
Z: 1033   Spring   Pienkjakaranda
Small to medium-sized deciduous tree with a rounded crown; occurring in woodland, frequently on rocky hillsides or termitaria. Bark smooth, **flaking in round patches (dippled-scaly)**. Leaflets 4 pairs plus a terminal one, **stiff and brittle, snap audibly in two when folded**; petiole up to 70 mm long. Flowers in large panicles, produced before the leaves, showy, **pale pink with red streaks** on lower corolla lobe. Fruit a capsule, **long and narrow, pendulous**, reddish brown, remaining on the tree for a long time, eventually splitting into 2-valves.
   The fruit is used medicinally. A potential garden plant, but apparently difficult to rear successfully.

3 *Tecomaria capensis*   Cape honeysuckle
SA: 673.1   Winter–Spring   Kaapse kamperfoelie
Many-stemmed scrambling shrub or rarely a small tree; occurring in valley bushveld, bushveld and along forest margins. Leaflets 2–5 pairs plus a terminal one, glossy green above with **small hairtufts (domatia) in axils of principal side veins** below; margin **scalloped or toothed**. Flowers in **terminal** racemes or panicles, attractive, orange to scarlet, with a yellow form in gardens. Fruit a capsule, slender, pendulous, up to 130 mm long, splitting into 2 valves.
   A widely cultivated ornamental plant. The bark is used medicinally.

CUNONIACEAE (see page 23)

4 *Cunonia capensis*   Red alder
SA: 140   Autumn   Rooiels
Shrub to tall evergreen tree; occurring in montane forest, usually in **wet places and along streams**. Young shoots and leaf stalks usually reddish. Growing buds of shoots **covered by two large, tightly appressed, spoon-shaped stipules**. Leaflets usually 3–5 pairs plus a terminal one, glossy dark green; margin **sharply toothed**. Flowers in long, erect, densely flowered axillary spikes towards ends of shoots, small, white to cream. Fruit a leathery capsule, small, 2-horned.
   The wood is reddish brown, even-grained, fairly hard and used for turning, and for household utensils and furniture.

R. zambesiacum: flowers

S. kunthianum: flowers

T. capensis: flowers

T. capensis: flowers

T. capensis: fruit

C. capensis: flowers

C. capensis: flowers

OLEACEAE (see page 28)

1 *Schrebera alata*   **Wild jasmine**
SA: 612; Z: 864   Summer   **Wildejasmyn**
Small tree; occurring in bushveld, coastal and montane forest. Vegetative parts smooth or variously hairy. Leaflets 1 or 2 pairs together with a terminal one, **shiny dark green above, pale green below**, smooth or hairy; rachis **winged**; petiole **distinctly winged** and **stem-clasping** at the base. Flowers in terminal clusters, white, often flushed with pink; petals **6**. Fruit a woody capsule, somewhat **wedge-shaped, flattened**, dehiscent.
The wood is pale brown, hard, heavy and durable.
Related to *S. trichoclada* (Group 23, p. 346), which has creamy white to yellow flowers, pear-shaped capsules and simple leaves. Can be confused with *Ekebergia pterophylla* (Group 38, p. 466), which has alternate leaves.

PTAEROXYLACEAE (see page 29)

2 *Ptaeroxylon obliquum*   **Sneezewood**
SA: 292; Z: 613   Spring–Summer   **Nieshout**
Deciduous or evergreen shrub to large tree, very variable in habit, size and colour of the leaves; sexes separate, on different plants; occurring in diverse habitats, including coastal, montane and sand forest as well as bushveld. Leaves dark green to blue-green. Leaflets **opposite, 3–7 pairs, without a terminal one**; base **markedly asymmetric**. Flowers in axillary clusters, small, yellowish with a **bright orange centre (disc)**. Fruit a capsule, about 20 x 15 mm, splitting into 2 valves; seeds winged.
The timber is extremely durable, attractively pinkish to golden brown with a fine grain and beautiful satin lustre. Heavily utilized in the past, particularly for railway sleepers. Sawdust from dry wood causes violent sneezing. The citrus swallowtail butterfly, *Papilio demodocus*, breeds on the tree. The plant is widely used in traditional medicine.
The only indigenous tree with opposite, paripinnate leaves in southern Africa. May be confused with *Haplocoelum gallense* (Group 34, p. 430), which has relatively small, alternate leaves in terminal clusters, and is restricted to Maputaland.

RUTACEAE (see page 30)

3 *Fagaropsis angolensis*   **Fagaropsis**
Z: 390   Spring   **Fagaropsis**
Small to medium-sized deciduous tree; sexes separate, on different plants; occurring in woodland, often in rocky places or on termitaria. Axillary buds **densely covered with silvery grey hairs**. Leaflets 2–4 pairs, plus a terminal one, **aromatic** when crushed, **soft velvety** on both surfaces; distinct **secretory cavities present**, visible when viewed against the light. Flowers in heads or panicles on the previous year's wood and before the new leaves, small, greenish yellow. Fruit globose, impressed gland dotted. All material in southern Africa is assigned to var. *mollis*.
The wood is often highly figured, very decorative and suitable for cabinet-work.
This is the only southern African tree with opposite, imparipinnate leaves with secretory cavities.

S. alata: flowers

S. alata: fruit

P. obliquum: flowers

P. obliquum: fruit

F. angolensis: male flowers

F. angolensis: fruit

GROUP 33

Leaves pinnately compound, alternate or in tufts. Leaflets more than 3, terminal one absent (paripinnate). Stipules present.

CAESALPINIACEAE (see page 22)

1 *Afzelia quanzensis*   Pod mahogany
SA: 207; Z: 259   Winter–Spring   Peulmahonie
Medium to tall deciduous tree with a **spreading crown**; occurring in hot, arid bushveld and sand forest, usually on deep sand. Bark flaking in **thick roundish scales**. Leaflets hairless, **glossy dark green** above; margin **wavy**; petiolules **twisted**. Flowers with a single large, streaked, pinkish-red petal. Pods large, **flat, woody**, dehiscing whilst on the tree; seeds black with a scarlet aril.
    The wood is reddish brown, strong and heavy; commercially traded under the name 'chamfuti'. Bark and roots used medicinally. Several *Charaxes* butterflies breed on the tree. Seeds eaten by rodents, and birds; also used for curios.

2 *Baikiaea plurijuga*   Zambezi teak
SA: 206; Z: 257   Summer–Autumn   Zambezikiaat
Medium to large deciduous tree with a dense spreading crown; occurring in open woodland, on **deep Kalahari sand**. Leaflets hairy, at least when young and especially beneath; tips usually **slightly indented and with a short bristle**. Flowers attractive, in long axillary racemes, pinkish mauve; buds **velvety, dark or golden brown**. Pods flattened, woody, velvety hairy, dehiscing explosively.
    An important timber tree, often known as 'Zimbabwean teak' (formerly known as 'Rhodesian teak'). The wood is dark red-brown, hard, strong and durable.

3 *Brachystegia boehmii*   Mfuti
Z: 248   Spring   Mfuti
Sturdy medium-sized deciduous tree with a spreading **flat-topped crown** and attractive **feathery foliage**; occurring in woodland, particularly on poorly drained soils and rocky slopes. Emerging young leaves very attractively flushed with **bright pink or red**. Stipules on mature growth **brown and shrivelled**, long, narrow. Leaflets **14–28 pairs** per leaf, **30–60 x 10–15 mm**, closely spaced and **overlapping, blue-green** below. Flowers inconspicuous. Pods hairless, upper margin with **broad flat ridge**.
    The bark is used for tanning; the inner bark yields an excellent strong fibre for ropes. Heartwood suitable as railway sleepers after treatment with preservatives.

4 *Brachystegia glaucescens*   Mountain acacia
Z: 249   Spring   Berg-mfuti
Beautiful large deciduous tree with a flat spreading crown and **delicate feathery foliage**; occurring on the slopes and summits of rocky hills. New spring growth attractively coloured in many coppery hues. Leaflets **10–16 pairs** per leaf, **13–30 x 4–10 mm, bluish to dark green above**, base **asymmetric** with the inner side tapering. Flowers inconspicuous. Pods **purplish**, hairless, upper margin with **broad flat ridge**.
    The heartwood is red-brown and durable, suitable as a general purpose timber. The tree is a good source of pollen and nectar for honey-bees.
    Hybrids with *B. spiciformis* (p. 422) are common. Closely related to *B. microphylla*, which has 25–55 pairs of smaller leaflets (about 3 mm wide); in southern Africa the plant is confined to the Eastern Highlands of Zimbabwe.

A. quanzensis: flowers

A. quanzensis: fruit & seeds

B. plurijuga: flowers

B. plurijuga: fruit

B. boehmii: young leaves

B. boehmii: fruit

B. glaucescens: fruit

B. boehmii: flowers

B. glaucescens: flowers

1 Brachystegia spiciformis   Msasa
Z: 252   Spring   Msasa
Medium to large deciduous tree with a somewhat layered crown; occurring in woodland and dominant over large areas of its range. Spring flush with shades of pink to intense red. Leaves **drooping, dark green, shiny**; leaflets usually in 4 pairs, the terminal pair being the largest, base markedly **asymmetric**; **two small, elongated stipellar expansions present below each pair of leaflets**. Flowers in racemes, greenish with red anthers. Pod **hairless**, the upper margin with **broad flat ridge**.

Characteristic tree of the so-called miombo woodlands of south-central Africa, often growing in association with *Julbernardia globiflora* (p. 424). The heartwood is pale reddish brown, suitable as general purpose timber. Bark fibre used for ropes. Flowers produce an excellent honey. Several *Charaxes* butterflies breed on the tree.

Easily confused with *Julbernardia globiflora*, which lacks stipellar expansions, has velvety pods and leaves whose terminal pair of leaflets is not the largest. It also hybridizes with *Brachystegia glaucescens* (p. 420) and *B. microphylla*.

2 Brachystegia utilis   **False mfuti**
Z: 253   Spring   **Vals-mfuti**
Slender medium-sized deciduous tree that from a distance resembles *B. boehmii*; occurring in mixed woodland, often on rocky slopes in mountainous regions. Stipules **leaf-like, shed early**. Leaflets usually 7–12 pairs per leaf, 20–40 x 5–15 mm and differ from *B. boehmii* in that they are more rounded and **not overlapping**. Flowers greenish, inconspicuous. Pods hairless, pinkish or dark purple, upper margin with **broad flat ridge**.

3 Cassia abbreviata   **Sjambok pod**
SA: 212; Z: 267   Spring   **Sambokpeul**
Small to medium-sized tree; occurring in bushveld, frequently associated with termitaria. Leaflets **5–20 pairs** per leaf, **dull green, thinly textured**, tips **rounded**; petiolules present, slender; rachis **without glands**. Flowers in large, loose sprays, yellow. Pods **pendulous, up to 0,9 m long, cylindrical, velvety**, remaining on the trees for a long time. Subsp. *beareana* is more common and has the hairs on the under surface of the leaflets pressed flat against the surface, whereas those of subsp. *abbreviata* (eastern Zimbabwe) are more spreading, even curly.

Various parts of the tree are used in traditional medicine. A decoction of the roots is said to be effective against blackwater fever.

Flowers resemble those of *Senna*, but the leaves of the latter group have conspicuous glands on the rachis between each pair of leaflets.

B. spiciformis: flowers

B. spiciformis: fruit

B. utilis: flowers

B. utilis: fruit

C. abbreviata: fruit

C. abbreviata: flowers

423

1 *Julbernardia globiflora*

Munondo
Z: 260   Summer–Autumn   **Dubbelkroon-boom**

Medium to large deciduous tree with a rounded crown; occurring in mixed woodland, frequently co-dominant with *Brachystegia spiciformis* in miombo woodland. Spring flush in shades of pale pink and fawn. Leaflets usually 6 pairs per leaf, the **largest being the third or fourth pair**; **stipels at base of leaflets absent**; petiolule flattened, yellowish. Flowers tightly clustered in **large, branched, terminal heads, white**. Pods dark brown, **velvety**, borne in a **distinct layer above the leaves**.

The wood is reddish brown, hard, very durable and used as a general purpose timber. A low-quality fibre is obtained from the bark.

Easily confused with *Brachystegia spiciformis* (p. 422), under which some of the differences are given. *Julbernardia paniculata* has larger leaflets (90 x 50 mm) and, in our region, has only been recorded from northeastern Mozambique.

2 *Schotia afra* var. *afra*

Karoo boer-bean
SA: 201   Spring–Summer   **Karooboerboon**

Much-branched shrub or small tree, often with **rigid** branchlets and a gnarled trunk; occurring in valley bushveld and wooded communities in dry broken country. Leaflets usually **6–11 pairs** per leaf, **10–17 x 4–10 mm**. Flowers congested in many-flowered **globose** inflorescences, usually on short side shoots; **petals 5**, stalked, red to pink. Pods woody, compressed, with a **hard margin along the upper edge which persists** after dehiscence of the valves, often with seed attached. Seeds **without conspicuous yellow aril**.

The leaves are browsed by stock. Seeds edible, either green or, if mature, roasted in the fire and ground to a meal. The butterfly *Deudorix antalis* breeds on the tree.

3 *Schotia afra* var. *angustifolia*

Small-leaved Karoo boer-bean
SA: 201.1   Spring–Summer   **Fynblaarkarooboerboon**

Much-branched shrub or small slender tree with a disjunct distribution; occurring in hot semi-desert areas (north west) or valley bushveld (east). Leaflets usually **12–18 pairs per leaf, 5–17 mm long, 1–3 mm wide**. Otherwise the plant is similar to var. *afra*.

4 *Schotia brachypetala*

Weeping boer-bean
SA: 202; Z: 255   Spring   **Huilboerboon**

Medium-sized semi-deciduous tree with a densely branched, somewhat rounded crown; occurring in bushveld and scrub forest, often on riverbanks or on termitaria. Leaflets **4–7 pairs per leaf, 25–85 x 12–45 mm**, the **upper leaflets largest**. Flowers in dense, branched heads, **mainly on the old wood**, deep red or scarlet; **all or some petals reduced to thread-like filaments**. Seeds pale brown **with a yellow basal aril**.

The leaves are browsed by game. Flowers produce abundant nectar which attracts several species of birds, particularly sunbirds. Heartwood dark brown to almost black, hard, heavy and fine-textured. Bark used medicinally and for tanning.

Similar to *S. latifolia* from the Eastern Cape, a forest species whose petals are well developed and usually pale pink rather than bright red. *S. capitata* (**4.1**), a scandent shrub or small tree (particularly common in Lebombo Mountains and northern KwaZulu-Natal), has smaller leaflets with mucronate tips. The flowers have well-developed petals and are clustered in dense, almost spherical, branched heads.

1

J. globiflora: fruit

2

S. afra var. *afra*: flowers & fruit

1

J. globiflora: flowers

3

Var. *angustifolia*: flowers

4

S. brachypetala: fruit

4

S. brachypetala: flowers

4.1

S. capitata: flowers

1 •*Senna didymobotrya* (= *Cassia didymobotrya*)   **Peanut butter cassia**
SA: – ; Z: –   All year   **Grondboontjiebotterkassia**
Evergreen, rounded shrub or small tree, most parts **unpleasantly scented** (some-times reminiscent of peanut butter) when bruised; invading grassland, coastal bush, bushveld, roadsides, riverbanks and disturbed places. Leaflets 10–22 pairs, ovate-oblong, dark green; apex **rounded with a tiny, sharp tip**; base asymmetric; stipules ovate, tip sharply pointed. Flowers in many-flowered, **erect racemes** borne in axils of upper leaves, bright yellow; **buds and bracts dark brownish green**, somewhat sticky. Pods **flattened, about 100 x 20 mm**, dark brown, softly downy.
    A native of tropical Africa; cultivated for ornament and hedging.

2 *Senna petersiana* (= *Cassia petersiana*)   **Monkey pod**
SA: 213   Summer–Autumn   **Apiespeul**
Shrub or small tree; occurring in bushveld and sand forest, particularly on sandy soils and alluvium along rivers. Stipules very conspicuous, **large, leafy, heart- to kidney-shaped**. Leaflets 7–12 pairs per leaf, **dark green above, densely hairy, glandular and pale green below**; rachis with a conspicuous stalked gland between all or most pairs of leaflets. Flowers in large, loose, branched sprays, yellow. Pods **flattened**, dark brown, with **transverse partitions** between the seeds; indehiscent with one- or more-seeded segments shed from between the **sutures that persist for some time**.
    Various parts used medicinally. Pod valves used in preparing a fermented bever-age, and are relished by birds. The butterfly *Catopsilia florella* breeds on the tree.
    S. singueana (**2.1**), with small stipules, flowers winter–spring, often when leafless.

3 *Tamarindus indica*   **Tamarind**
SA: 206.1; Z: 258   Spring–Summer   **Tamarind**
Medium to large evergreen tree with a somewhat **rounded crown**; occurring in woodland, often on termitaria or associated with deep alluvial soil along rivers. Leaflets usually **10–18 pairs per leaf, terminal pair points forward**, base asym-metric, tips **rounded**. Flowers in short racemes, red in bud; petals yellow with red veins. Pods **sausage-like**, indehiscent, with a dry outer shell **closely covered by minute brown scales** and a pulpy inner layer.
    The acid-sweet fruit pulp is edible and used for preserves, jams, sweets, refresh-ing drinks and in curries and chutneys. Flowers, leaves and crushed seeds are added to relishes and side dishes. Over-ripe fruit is used to polish silver, copper and brass ornaments. Wood dark-brown, suitable for general carpentry. Most probably intro-duced from India into our region by traders many centuries ago.

FABACEAE (see page 25)

4 •*Sesbania punicea*   **Sesbania**
SA: X564; Z: –   Spring–Autumn   **Sesbania**
Deciduous shrub or small tree, with slender branches; invading riverbanks, riverbeds, wetlands, roadsides and disturbed places. Leaves **drooping**, 100–200 mm long; leaflets **10–14 pairs, oblong, ending in a minute, pointed tip**, margin **entire**. Flowers in showy axillary clusters, red or orange. Pods **4-angled, with short wings on the angles**, tip **sharply pointed**; seeds separated by cross-partitions.
    A native of South America; cultivated for ornament. Most parts, including the seeds, are highly toxic to man and beast. This is a declared weed in South Africa.

S. didymobotrya: flowers

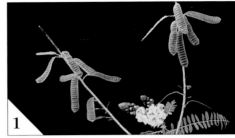

S. didymobotrya: flowers & fruit

S. singueana: flowers

S. singueana: flowers

S. petersiana: flowers

S. petersiana: fruit

T. indica: fruit

T. indica: flowers

S. punicea: flowers

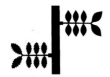

GROUP 34

Leaves pinnately compound, alternate or in tufts. Leaflets more than 3, terminal one absent (paripinnate). Stipules absent.

MELIACEAE (see page 26)

1 *Entandrophragma caudatum* Mountain mahogany
SA: 293; Z: 423 Spring Bergmahonie
Large deciduous tree, usually with a **long and straight bole**; occurring in dry bushveld, often in river valleys, on rocky hill slopes or Kalahari sand. Leaflets 5–8 pairs per leaf, ovate or lanceolate, gradually **tapering from near the base to a sharp, bristle-like tip**, hairless; base very asymmetric in terminal leaflets; venation indistinct. Flowers in axillary panicles, inconspicuous, pale green. Fruit a **cigar-shaped woody capsule up to 200 mm long, splitting into 5 valves which curve back** from a **large central column**, giving the appearance of a partly peeled banana; seeds with a large wing on one side.
A characteristic component of *Baikiaea plurijuga* woodland on Kalahari sand. The reddish brown, mahogany type timber is attractive and the wood is suitable for furniture and cabinet work. Bark used for dyeing and tanning.
E. spicatum has very similar fruit but its leaflets are more rounded, with blunt tips, and is only known to occur in the south of Angola and the north of Namibia.

2 *Khaya anthotheca* (= *K. nyasica*) Red mahogany
Z: 422 Spring Rooimahonie
Large to very large evergreen tree, trunk buttressed in old specimens; occurring in forest and riverine fringe forest. New growth red. Leaflets 2–7 pairs per leaf, up to **170 x 70 mm**, dark glossy green above, pale green below; tips **abruptly and shortly pointed**. Flowers in large, many-flowered, axillary panicles, inconspicuous, white, fragrant. Fruit a woody capsule, **ovate, 30–50 mm in diameter, splitting into 4 or 5 valves**; seeds winged.
The famous 'big tree' in the Chirinda Forest, near Mount Selinda in eastern Zimbabwe, is probably the tallest member of the species in southern Africa. This buttressed tree is about 65 m high, with a girth of almost 16 m at breast height. The wood is reddish brown, durable and excellent for furniture. The bark is bitter-tasting, and is used medicinally.

SAPINDACEAE (see page 31)

3 *Atalaya alata* Lebombo krantz ash
SA: 427 Spring–Summer Lebombokransesseboom
Small to medium-sized deciduous tree with a sparsely branched crown; occurring in bushveld on rocky hillsides, mainly associated with the Lebombo Mountains. Leaflets 5–7 pairs per leaf, **markedly asymmetrical, often almost sickle-shaped**; margin **toothed**, particularly along the upper edge. Flowers in loose terminal panicles, small, white. Fruit a nut, usually with **3 wings**.
The tree is browsed by elephant.
A. capensis, a rare plant confined to the Eastern Cape, has weakly asymmetrical leaflets, usually with smooth margins. *A. natalensis*, a tall and very rare forest tree from KwaZulu-Natal and the Transkei region, also has more symmetrical leaflets with untoothed margins.

E. caudatum: fruit

E. caudatum: fruit

K. anthotheca: flowers

K. anthotheca: fruit

K. anthotheca: old fruit

A. alata: flowers

E. caudatum: flowers

A. alata: fruit

1 ***Blighia unijugata***   **Triangle tops**
SA: 436; Z: 608   Spring–Summer   **Driehoektolletjies**
Medium to large tree with a dense round crown; sexes separate, on different plants; occurring in coastal, dune and riverine fringe forest and in woodland, often on termitaria. Young branchlets and leaf buds with **soft pale brown hairs**; **young leaves bright red**. Leaflets usually 2 or 3 pairs per leaf, uppermost pair the largest, smooth with minute **hairtufts in the axils of the side veins** below; tips **narrowly tapering**; margin often **wavy**. Flowers in drooping axillary racemes, white. Fruit a **3-lobed capsule, bright pink when ripe**, valves opening by curling strongly backwards.
    The heartwood is reddish brown, durable and suitable for carpentry. Sometimes cultivated in tropical gardens for its ornamental fruit. Larval food plant for several butterflies, including members of *Charaxes*, *Euphaedra* and *Euxanthe*.

2 ***Deinbollia oblongifolia***   **Dune soap-berry**
SA: 430   Autumn   **Duineseepbessie**
Slender erect shrub or small tree; occurring in dune forest and coastal bushveld. Leaves in terminal **clusters, up to 500 mm long**. Leaflets 5–10 pairs, more or less symmetrical, **hard-textured**; margin smooth; petiole **up to 90 mm long**. Flowers in **many-flowered**, dense, axillary racemes, white to cream; buds and flower stalks **with brownish velvety hairs**. Fruit a berry, pale yellow when ripe.
    The leaves are cooked as a relish, and are browsed by game. Fruit also edible. Seeds, which foam when rubbed in water, are used as soap. Root and bark used in traditional medicine. Flowers visited by numerous insects, including several species of butterfly that breed on the tree, among them the beautiful *Euphaedra neophron neophron*, *Euxanthe wakefieldi* and *Charaxes violetta melloni*.

3 ***Haplocoelum gallense***   **Galla plum**
SA: 432   Winter   **Gallapruim**
Shrub or small tree, with **very tough, rigid branches**; sexes separate, on different plants; endemic to Maputaland, occurring in sand and dune forest. Leaflets **4 pairs** per leaf, **up to 20 x 10 mm**, base markedly **asymmetric**; rachis **narrowly winged**. Flowers in clusters at ends of side shoots, inconspicuous, brownish green. Fruit fleshy, spherical, about 13 mm in diameter, **bright pink to red** when ripe.
    The stems are used both in hut construction and as fighting-sticks. Fruit edible; also eaten by birds and antelope. Roots used medicinally.
    Can be confused with *Ptaeroxylon obliquum*, which has larger, opposite leaves.

4 ***Hippobromus pauciflorus***   **False horsewood**
SA: 438   Autumn–Spring   **Basterperdepis**
Shrub or small, densely leafy semi-deciduous tree; occurring at margins of forest, along streams or in bushveld, often on rocky ridges. Leaflets 3–6 pairs per leaf, sub-opposite, **dark green above, pale green below**, sometimes with a strong resinous smell when crushed; margin smooth or toothed; **rachis winged, terminating in a short slender point**. Flowers in axillary, **golden velvety** heads or panicles, creamy white to yellowish, often tinged with red. Fruit globose, fleshy, up to 10 mm in diameter, dark red to black when ripe, not edible.
    The plant is browsed by game. Leaves, bark and root are used medicinally. Leaf and root known to be poisonous.

B. unijugata: young leaves

B. unijugata: male flowers

D. oblongifolia: flowers

B. unijugata: fruit

D. oblongifolia: fruit

H. gallense: flowers

H. gallense: fruit

H. pauciflorus: flowers

H. pauciflorus: fruit

1 *Lecaniodiscus fraxinifolius*   River litchi
Z: 603   Spring–Summer   Rivierlitchi
Small or medium-sized, densely leafy tree; sexes separate, on different plants; occurring at low altitude in **riverine fringes**, often in almost pure stands. Leaflets **3–7 pairs** per leaf, **almost stalkless**, thinly textured, hairless above, with minute glandular hairs on the veins below; margin entire, **very wavy**. Flowers in **axillary, spike-like racemes** up to 100 mm long (female ones shorter), yellowish or greenish. Fruit ovate, 15 x 13 mm, **velvety**, yellow, orange or pinkish when ripe, splitting irregularly from the base to reveal a single seed **completely covered by bluish-white, fleshy tissue.**
   The fleshy covering of the seed is edible. Several butterflies breed on the tree, among them *Euphaedra neophron neophron*, *Euxanthe wakefieldi* and *Charaxes jahlus argynnides*.

2 *Pancovia golungensis*   False soap-berry
SA: 430.2; Z: 601/1   Spring   Basterseepbessie
Shrub or small slender tree; sexes separate, on different plants; occurring in coastal and dune forest, often in shade. Young branchlets with **reddish brown hairs**. Leaflets usually 3 or 4 pairs, **pink to red and drooping when young, thin-textured**; apex tapering, **often forming a drip-tip**; margin smooth, often wavy; **petiolules curved forward.** Flowers in spikes or racemes on the **old wood and on the main stem**, small, cream, sweetly scented. Fruit berry-like, comprising 1–3 units joined at the base, velvety or smooth, orange when ripe.

3 *Stadmannia oppositifolia*   Silky plum
SA: 435; Z: 606   Spring–Summer   Sypruim
Small to medium-sized deciduous tree; sexes separate on the same tree; occurring in bushveld, usually in rocky places. Leaflets **2 or 3 pairs** per leaf, **elliptic, up to 85 x 35 mm**, shiny deep green and hairless above, **dull green with minute soft hairs below**, leathery; apex **rounded**, usually indented; margin somewhat rolled under. Flowers in axillary racemes, small, greenish yellow. Fruit berry-like, 1–3-lobed, velvety, green to red when ripe. Seed enveloped in a thin olive-green fleshy tissue. All material from southern Africa belongs to subsp. *rhodesica*.
   The leaves are browsed by elephant, the fruit favoured by birds.

4 *Zanha africana*   Velvet-fruited zanha
Z: 610   Spring–Summer   Fluweelvrug-zanha
Medium-sized deciduous tree; sexes separate, on different plants; occurring in woodland and riverine forest, often on granite hills. Leaflets **3–5 pairs** per leaf, **elliptic, leathery, brownish hairy, particularly below**; venation **conspicuous, especially above**; margin smooth, **scalloped or bluntly toothed**; petiole and rachis with **yellowish tawny hairs**. Flowers in dense heads before the new leaves, small, greenish white, sweetly scented. Fruit ovate, **velvety**, fleshy, bright orange when ripe.
   The bark and roots are toxic, and used medicinally. The fruit is edible, but the seeds are reputed to be poisonous and should not be swallowed. Seedlings have leaves with the rachis markedly winged.
   Z. golungensis (**4.1**) is a large spreading tree from open woodland and forest in eastern Zimbabwe and adjacent parts of Mozambique. It has hairless leaves and fruit.

L. *fraxinifolius*: female flowers

L. *fraxinifolius*: male flowers

P. *golungensis*: branchlet

S. *oppositifolia*: flowers

S. *oppositifolia*: fruit

Z. *africana*: flowers

Z. *africana*: fruit

Z. *golungensis*: fruit

GROUP 35

Leaves pinnately compound, alternate or in tufts. Leaflets more than 3, terminal one present (imparipinnate); margin toothed or lobed. Latex present.

See also Group 28: *Commiphora tenuipetiolata* (p. 382).

ANACARDIACEAE (see page 19)

1 •*Schinus molle*   **Pepper tree**
SA: X638   Spring–Summer   **Peperboom**
Medium to large evergreen tree with a short, gnarled trunk and **milky latex**; crown large, spreading, with **drooping branches and foliage**; sexes separate, on different trees; invading grassland, semi-desert shrubland, roadsides, riverbanks and disturbed places. Leaflets **up to 18 pairs plus a terminal one**, narrowly lanceolate, up to 70 mm long, greyish or light green, more or less hairless when mature, producing a strong peppery smell when crushed; margin entire or toothed. Flowers in terminal and axillary **drooping clusters**, very small, creamy white. Fruit a drupe, globose, about 5 mm in diameter, **pinkish red**, single-seeded.
    A native of South America; cultivated for ornament and shade. Dried fruit has a peppery taste; both leaves and fruit are used in curries.

BURSERACEAE (see page 21)

2 *Commiphora angolensis*   **Sand corkwood**
SA: 272; Z: 408   Spring   **Sandkanniedood**
Multistemmed shrub or small deciduous tree; sexes separate, on different plants; occurring, often gregariously, in hot arid bushveld, usually on Kalahari sand. Bark **peeling in whitish to yellowish papery pieces to reveal green underbark**, or brownish and flaking in polygonal scales. Branchlets **velvety**, not spine-tipped. Leaflets 2–4 pairs plus terminal one, sometimes 3-foliolate, **both surfaces finely velvety**; margin **finely scalloped or toothed**; petiole up to 50 mm long. Flowers in sparse axillary clusters with the new leaves, small, yellowish; stalks long, slender. Fruit a fleshy drupe, subglobose, pinkish red; stone partly enveloped by a **cup-shaped pseudo-aril**.
    The root is edible; wood used for carving household utensils.
    Similar to *C. tenuipetiolata* (Group 28, p. 382), which usually has a single trunk, hairless branchlets and leaves.

3 *Commiphora harveyi*   **Red-stem corkwood**
SA: 277   Spring–Summer   **Rooistamkanniedood**
Small to medium-sized, unarmed, deciduous tree; sexes separate, on different plants; occurring in valley bushveld and coastal forest, often in rocky places. Bark **greenish, smooth, peeling in large bronze or reddish brown, papery flakes**. Leaflets usually **2 or 3 pairs per leaf, plus a terminal one**, with a few **very short hairs**; leaflets turn bright yellow before falling. Flowers in short axillary inflorescences, small, whitish. Fruit a fleshy drupe, subglobose, red when ripe; stone partly enveloped by a **pale red pseudo-aril**.
    The fruit is eaten by monkeys and birds. Wood white, soft, used for carved spoons and other small articles. Grows easily from pole cuttings, which are often planted as fencing posts.

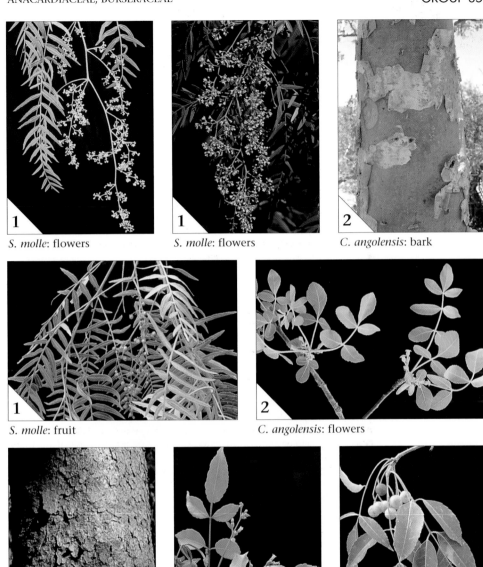

S. molle: flowers

S. molle: flowers

C. angolensis: bark

S. molle: fruit

C. angolensis: flowers

C. harveyi: bark

C. harveyi: flowers

C. harveyi: fruit

1 *Commiphora marlothii*   Paperbark corkwood
SA: 278: Z: 412   Spring   Papierbaskanniedood
Small to medium-sized, unarmed, deciduous tree with an often thickset trunk; sexes separate, on different plants; occurring in arid bushveld, usually on mountain slopes or granite hills. Bark **green, smooth, peeling in large yellowish papery pieces.** Leaflets **3–5 pairs per leaf plus a terminal one, densely and softly hairy.** Flowers in axillary inflorescences that appear with the new leaves, small, yellowish. Fruit a fleshy drupe, subglobose, **furry**, green or reddish; stone partly enveloped by a **yellow pseudo-aril.**

The bark has been made into writing paper, although the product is rather brittle and easily torn. The tree yields a lightweight wood of good texture. Fruit pulp edible, either fresh or made into jam or jelly. The root is scraped clean and chewed raw for its sweet juice.

C. ugogensis is a small spiny tree from dry bushveld in the Zambezi Valley, usually growing on alluvial flats along rivers, often in dense stands. It has green to reddish brown bark which peels in small flakes. Young branches are angular, inclined to zigzag and often spine-tipped.

2 *Commiphora woodii*   Forest corkwood
SA: 291   Spring–Summer   Boskanniedood
Small to medium-sized, much branched, unarmed, deciduous tree; sexes separate, on different plants; occurring in coastal and mist-belt forest, often in rocky places. Bark **grey, not peeling.** Leaflets **3–5 pairs plus a terminal one, hairless,** red when young. Flowers in **short (about 20 mm long)**, dense, axillary sprays, yellowish green. Fruit a fleshy drupe, subglobose, red when ripe; stone partly enveloped by a **red pseudo-aril.**

The light wood is used for fishing floats. Grows easily from pole cuttings, which are often planted as fencing posts. A gum is obtained from the bark.

Leaves resemble those of *C. harveyi* (p. 434), which have very short hairs. Also rather similar to *C. zanzibarica*, whose leaflet margin is usually smooth and the inflorescences up to 250 mm long.

C. *marlothii*: flowers

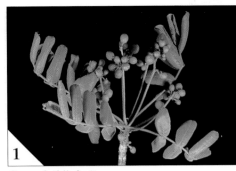

C. *marlothii*: fruit

C. *marlothii*: bark

C. *woodii*: fruit

GROUP 36

Leaves pinnately compound, alternate or in tufts. Leaflets more than 3, terminal one present (imparipinnate); margin toothed or lobed. Latex absent.

APIACEAE (see page 20)

1 *Steganotaenia araliacea*   **Carrot tree**
SA: 569; Z: 817   Spring   **Geelwortelboom**
Small, slender, deciduous tree; foliage **fresh to yellowish green, smelling of carrots when crushed**; occurring in hot, dry bushveld, often in rocky places. Bark grey-green and **peeling in small papery flakes**. Leaves crowded near ends of branches; leaflets with margin **conspicuously and jaggedly toothed**, tips **tapering to a fine point**; petiole with base broadened and **clasping the stem**. Flowers in compound **umbels**, usually before the new leaves, greenish. Fruit dry, flattened, with papery wings.

The root and bark are used in traditional medicine. In the Kaokoveld (Namibia), the straight stems serve as sacred fire sticks.

MELIANTHACEAE (see page 27)

2 *Bersama abyssinica*   **Winged bersama**
Z: 614   Summer   **Gevleuelde witessenhout**
Medium to large tree with **dark green foliage**; occurring in montane forest and associated woodland, often on termitaria. Leaves with the **rachis usually winged**; leaflets with side veins **conspicuously sunken above, raised below**, margin toothed or smooth. Flowers in **erect, spike-like racemes** up to 350 mm long, cream, often tinged with pink, hairy. Fruit a **smooth**, spherical capsule; seed bright red, partly enveloped by a fleshy, yellow aril. In subsp. *nyassae*, the lower surface of the leaflets is often covered with long, spreading, golden hairs. These are absent or sparsely present in subsp. *englerana*, a taxon found mainly in Mozambique.

Various parts, and particularly the bark, are used medicinally. The butterfly *Charaxes pollux gazanus* breeds on the tree.

PROTEACEAE (see page 29)

3 •*Grevillea robusta*   **Silky oak**
SA: X347; Z: –   Spring   **Silwereik**
Large evergreen to semi-deciduous tree, with a straight trunk and more or less upright crown; invading forest margins, moist bushveld and riverbanks. Leaves distinctive, **repeatedly deeply divided and fern-like**, 150–250 x 80–120 mm long, pinnately divided with 11–23 primary segments (leaflets), each segment may again be divided or lobed, **dark green and hairless above, silky silver-grey below**, margins rolled under, fallen leaves grey, slow to decompose. Flowers in large clusters of 1-sided racemes, **mainly on older wood**, golden-orange, showy, with copious nectar. Fruit a dark boat-shaped capsule (follicle) with a slender beak, about 20 mm long, leathery, 1- or 2-seeded.

A native of Australia; cultivated for ornament, shade, windbreaks, timber and shelter. The wood is pale yellow-brown, heavily mottled with dark rays, tough and durable, very attractive, and suitable for quality furniture.

S. araliacea: flowers

S. araliacea: fruit

S. araliacea: bark

B. abyssinica: flowers

B. abyssinica: fruit & seeds

B. abyssinica: fruit

G. robusta: flowers

G. robusta: fruit

ROSACEAE (see page 30)

1 *Leucosidea sericea*   Oldwood
SA: 145; Z: 161   Spring–Summer   Ouhout
Shrub or small tree, often with **gnarled twisted trunk and shaggy appearance**; occurring in high-altitude grassland, often in dense stands in the open or along streams. Young shoots **reddish, covered with persistent hairy stipules**. Leaflets dark green above, greyish green with silky hairs below, strongly scented when crushed. Flowers in dense, usually **erect spikes**, yellow; calyx persistent. Fruit dry, enclosed in the base of the old flowers.

     The tree is a useful source of firewood, particularly in mountainous areas. Tends to proliferate in overgrazed and disturbed areas. Leaves used medicinally.

2 •*Rosa eglanteria*   Sweetbriar
SA: –   Spring–Summer   Wilderoos
Compact deciduous shrub with somewhat **arching branches**; invading high-altitude grassland, particularly common in parts of Lesotho. Branchlets armed with **stout, hooked thorns**. Leaflets 2 or 3 pairs, plus a terminal one; margin **toothed**. Flowers in groups of 1–3, large, pink to white. Fruit somewhat fleshy, **oval, up to 20 mm long**, **orange to bright red**, crowned with the persistent remains of the calyx.

     A native of Europe and Asia; cultivated for ornament and hedging. The fruit is harvested for its juice, which is rich in vitamin C (rose-hip syrup).

RUTACEAE (see page 30)

3 *Clausena anisata*   Horsewood
SA: 265; Z: 402   Spring   Perdepis
Shrub or small, slender, unarmed tree; occurring in the under-canopy or along margins of coastal and inland forest, often near streams. Leaflets dark green, clearly **gland-dotted when held against the light**, base **asymmetric, strongly and unpleasantly scented when crushed**. Flowers in branched axillary sprays, small, white or yellowish. Fruit globose, fleshy, ripening red, purple-black to black.

     The aromatic qualities of the tree are an important element in medicinal and magical practices. The leaves are used to flavour curries. Several swallowtail butterflies (family Papilionidae) breed on the tree.

4 *Zanthoxylum capense* (= *Fagara capensis*)   Small knobwood
SA: 253; Z: 383   Summer   Kleinperdepram
Shrub or small tree armed with prickles; sexes separate, on different plants; occurring in grassland, bushveld and along forest margins, usually associated with bush clumps and rocky places. Trunk and stems often armed with **corky knobs that are spine-tipped**. Leaflets **10–40 x 10–20 mm, gland-dotted, especially near the margin, citrus-scented** when crushed; base tapering with **two minute sack-shaped lobes (domatia) against the petiolule**; main lateral veins 4–8 pairs. Flowers in short terminal branched sprays, greenish white. Fruit brownish red, gland-dotted, splitting when ripe to reveal a shiny black seed.

     The leaves, fruit and bark are used medicinally. Food plant for the larvae of several swallowtail butterflies (family Papilionidae).

     Z. chalybeum, from dry woodland in Zimbabwe, has leaves with less than 5 pairs of leaflets. The latter are larger (25–70 x 10–25 mm) and less prominently scalloped, with scattered gland dots.

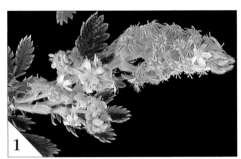

L. *sericea*: flowers

L. *sericea*: flowers

R. *eglanteria*: flowers

R. *eglanteria*: fruit

C. *anisata*: flowers

C. *anisata*: fruit

Z. *capense*: flowers

Z. *capense*: fruit

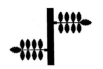

1 Zanthoxylum davyi (= *Fagara davyi*) **Knobwood**
SA: 254; Z: 385   Spring–Summer **Perdepram**
Medium to large tree; sexes separate, on different plants; occurring as a **canopy constituent, particularly in montane forest**. Bark with conspicuous **thorn-tipped knobs**. Leaflets with **pellucid glands** confined mainly to the margin, strongly **citrus-scented** when crushed; main lateral veins **16–20 pairs or more**; base with **two minute, sack-shaped domatia**; petiole and rachis often **with scattered prickles**. Flowers in small, terminal sprays, greenish yellow. Fruit spherical, reddish brown, splitting when ripe to reveal a shiny black seed.

The timber of this tree is fine-textured, strong, elastic, and useful.

Z. gilletii (= *Fagara macrophylla*) is a very large forest tree from the Eastern Highlands of Zimbabwe. Its leaflets are large (80–170 x 35–55 mm), robust, thick and leathery, with asymmetrical bases and a markedly rolled-under margin.

2 Zanthoxylum leprieurii (= *Fagara leprieurii*) **Sand knobwood**
SA: 255.1; Z: 387   Spring **Sandperdepram**
Small to medium-sized tree with somewhat **drooping crown**; sexes separate, on different plants; occurring in **dry bushveld and sand forest, usually on deep sand**, alluvial soils near rivers and on termitaria. Trunk and branches usually with **spine-tipped knobs**. Leaflets **gland-dotted** with a strong **citrus smell** when crushed, tapering to a **slender tip**; petiole and rachis often with scattered prickles. Flowers in **lax, terminal, branched panicles up to 60 mm long**, creamy white. Fruit in **pendulous** sprays, **orange red**, splitting when ripe to reveal a **shiny black** seed.

SIMAROUBACEAE (see page 31)

3 Kirkia acuminata **White seringa**
SA: 267; Z: 406   Spring **Witsering**
Medium-sized to large deciduous tree, usually with a **clean erect trunk and spreading rounded crown**; occurring in bushveld, often on rocky outcrops. Leaflets usually **6–9 pairs** per leaf, 10–24 mm wide, apex **acuminate**, base slightly oblique; becoming **bright yellow to scarlet in autumn**. Flowers in branched axillary inflorescences, white or cream. Fruit an elongated, dry, 4-sided capsule, **separating into 4 one-seeded units**, each attached by a strip of tissue to the top of a central column.

The wood is light, not durable, and difficult to work due to the presence of silica.

Superficially resembles *Commiphora crenato-serrata* from the Kaokoveld, Namibia, whose broken branches and leaves exude an aromatic pale milky resin.

4 Kirkia wilmsii **Mountain seringa**
SA: 269   Spring–Summer **Bergsering**
Small to medium-sized deciduous tree with rounded crown, trunk **often branching near base**; occurring on granitic and dolomitic soils in dry bushveld, usually in rocky places. Leaves **crowded at the ends of branchlets**; leaflets **10–22 pairs** per leaf, **small (15 x 3 mm)**, hairless; margin minutely crenate or smooth; becoming **reddish to bright scarlet in autumn**. Flowers in branched axillary sprays, greenish white. Fruit a capsule, **splitting into 4 valves** which remain joined at the apex.

The bark yields a strong fibre. An excellent garden subject: tolerates mild frost.

K. dewinteri is restricted to rock outcrops (often dolomite) in the Kaokoveld, Namibia. It has a yellowish bark with blackish spots and fruit that splits into 8 valves.

Z. *davyi*: fruit

Z. *davyi*: bark

Z. *leprieurii*: flowers

Z. *leprieurii*: fruit & seeds

K. *acuminata*: flowers

K. *acuminata*: fruit

K. *wilmsii*: flowers

K. *wilmsii*: fruit

GROUP 37

Leaves pinnately compound, alternate or in tufts. Leaflets more than 3, terminal one present (imparipinnate); margin smooth. Latex present.

See also Group 28: *Commiphora tenuipetiolata* (p. 382); Group 35: *Schinus molle* (p. 434).

ANACARDIACEAE (see page 19)

1 *Harpephyllum caffrum*   **Wild plum**
SA: 361   Summer   **Wildepruim**
Medium to large evergreen tree; sexes separate, on different trees; occurring in coastal forest. Leaves crowded **at ends of thick branchlets**, often with an odd **bright red** one; leaflets **sickle-shaped**, hairless, dark shiny green, base markedly asymmetric, margin **slightly wavy**. Flowers in much-branched sprays near the ends of branches, small, whitish. Fruit oblong, fleshy, bright red when ripe.

The fruit is edible, widely used to make a jelly preserve. Wood pale reddish brown, suitable as a general purpose timber. Bark used in traditional medicine. Cape parrots open the stone and eat the kernel. Attractive tree for frost-free gardens.

Vegetatively very similar to *Ekebergia capensis* (only the form in the Western Cape and southern parts of the Eastern Cape), a species which lacks the odd red leaf and does not produce watery resin at the base of a detached petiole (Group 38, p. 466).

2 *Lannea discolor*   **Live-long**
SA: 362; Z: 538   Spring   **Dikbas**
Small to medium-sized deciduous tree; sexes separate, on different trees; occurring in bushveld, often on rocky ridges or termitaria. Branchlets **rather thick**, densely covered with **whitish hairs**. Leaves with 3–5 pairs of leaflets plus a terminal one, **dark green above, velvety whitish grey below**. Flowers in spike-like inflorescences before the leaves in spring, small, creamy yellow. Fruit fleshy, ovoid, tipped with four minute style-remnants, reddish to purple-black when ripe.

The fruit is edible, having a pleasant grape-like flavour (the hard skins are discarded), and is also favoured by birds. Bark used medicinally, for tanning, for twine, and as the source of a red dye. Roots are split and used in basket making. Wood rather unattractive, often used for making household objects.

3 *Lannea schweinfurthii* var. *stuhlmannii* (= *L. stuhlmannii*)   **False marula**
SA: 363; Z: 538   Spring–Summer   **Bastermaroela**
Small to medium-sized deciduous tree; sexes separate, on different trees; occurring in riverine bush, dry bushveld and woodland, often on rocky outcrops or termitaria. Leaflets **1–3 pairs plus a terminal one, the latter always the largest, hairless** when mature, fresh pale green, tips **abruptly but broadly tapering**. Flowers produced with the new leaves in rather loose, drooping spikes, small, creamy white. Fruit oblong, fleshy, reddish to dark brownish black when ripe.

The fruit is· edible, pleasantly flavoured. Leaves browsed by cattle and game. Various parts used for medicinal and magical purposes. Wood suitable as a general purpose timber. Bark produces a purplish dye, and is used for tanning.

Easily confused with *L. antiscorbutica*, which in our region is mainly restricted to sand forest in Maputaland. It has relatively small leaflets (2–4 pairs) with more tapering tips, the terminal one the same size or slightly smaller than the others.

H. caffrum: fruit

L. discolor: flowers

H. caffrum: flowers

L. schweinfurthii: flowers

L. schweinfurthii: fruit

L. discolor: flowers

L. discolor: fruit

L. discolor: flowers

1 *Loxostylis alata*   Tarwood
SA: 365   Spring–Summer   Teerhout
Small to medium-sized evergreen tree; sexes separate, on different plants; occurring along forest margins and on **outcrops of sandstone and quartzite**. Young growth often conspicuously yellowish to coral pink. Leaflets stalkless, **hairless**, glossy dark green; **rachis markedly winged**. Flowers in dense terminal sprays; petals small, white; **sepals enlarging in fruit, becoming petal-like and bright pink to red**. Fruit small, enclosed by the persistent sepals.
   The bark and leaves are used medicinally. An attractive garden subject; fast growing and capable of tolerating mild frost.

2 *•Schinus terebinthifolius*   Brazilian pepper tree
SA: X640; Z: –   Spring–Summer   Brasiliaanse peperboom
Evergreen shrub or small tree, **with wide-spreading horizontal branches**; sexes separate, on different plants; invades coastal bush, roadsides and riverbanks. Leaflets 3 or 4 pairs, plus a terminal one, dark green with prominent pale veins above, **hairless**; **rachis distinctly winged**. Flowers in terminal and axillary clusters, very small, creamy white. Fruit fleshy, globose, **bright red**.
   A native of South America; cultivated for ornament, shelter and hedging.

3 *•Sclerocarya birrea* subsp. *caffra*   Marula
SA: 360; Z: 537   Spring   Maroela
Medium to large deciduous tree with an **erect trunk** and **spreading, rounded crown**; sexes separate, on different plants; occurring in bushveld and woodland. Leaflets usually 3–7 pairs plus a terminal one, **dark green above, much paler and bluish green below**; margin smooth, but distinctly toothed in juvenile growth and coppice shoots; petioles often tinged with pink. Flowers in unbranched sprays before the new leaves, yellowish, tinged with pink. Fruit fleshy, almost spherical, ripening to yellow after falling to the ground; stone very hard, with two or three lids.
   The fruit is edible, eaten either fresh or made into a delicious jelly; also makes a popular alcoholic beer; a marula liqueur is available commercially. Kernels of the stones are edible and highly nutritious, but difficult to remove intact. Leaves browsed by game and the bark stripped by elephants. Bark widely used for medicinal purposes (proven antihistamine and anti-diarrhoea properties) and to obtain a pale brown dye. Wood used for making household utensils. Several moths breed on the tree, including the beautiful green African moon moth (*Argema mimosae*).

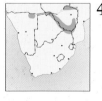

BURSERACEAE (see page 21)
4 *Commiphora edulis*   Rough-leaved corkwood
SA: 275; Z: 410   Spring–Summer   Skurweblaarkanniedood
Many-stemmed shrub or small deciduous tree; sexes separate, on different plants; occurring in hot, dry bushveld, often on rocky hillsides and in well-drained, sandy soil. Bark whitish, **flaking in small, yellowish, papery pieces** and locally as large blackish scales. Young branchlets **densely hairy**. Leaflets 1–4 pairs per leaf plus a terminal one, greyish green, **roughly hairy above**. Flowers in axillary inflorescences up to 150 mm long, small, cream. Fruit a fleshy drupe, subglobose, **orange-red** when ripe; stone partly enveloped by a **red pseudo-aril**.
   The fruit is eaten by birds, rodents and baboons. Easily grown from pole cuttings.

1 L. *alata*: male flowers

1 L. *alata*: female flowers

1 L. *alata*: fruit

2 S. *terebinthifolius*: flowers

2 S. *terebinthifolius*: fruit

3 S. *birrea*: flowers

3 S. *birrea*: fruit

4 C. *edulis*: flowers

4 C. *edulis*: fruit

1 Commiphora mollis   **Velvet corkwood**
SA: 280; Z: 414   Spring–Summer   **Fluweelkanniedood**
Small to medium-sized, deciduous tree; sexes separate, on different plants; occurring in hot, dry bushveld, often on rocky outcrops. Bark **greenish to silvery grey, usually flaking in thick discs**. Leaflets 2–6 pairs per leaf plus a terminal one, sparsely covered with **short, velvety hairs, paler green and more densely hairy below**; yellow in autumn. Flowers in axillary clusters before or with the new leaves, small, yellowish to pinkish. Fruit a fleshy drupe, subglobose, densely furry, reddish or brownish green when ripe; stone black, partly enveloped by a **scarlet pseudo-aril**.
    The tree is easily grown from truncheons. Browsed by cattle and game. Elephants dig up and eat the juicy roots.
    Resembles *C. karibensis* (**1.1**) (mainly from northern and western Zimbabwe) a small unarmed tree with the bole and branches strongly angular, ridged and often twisted. It has watery rather than milky latex. *C. zanzibarica* is a small unarmed tree with drooping, hairless foliage, from deep sandy soil in dry bushveld, thicket and sandforest (Maputaland northwards to Zambezi Valley). It has pale grey, rather smooth bark, which does not peel in papery flakes. The flowers and fruit are produced in pendulous bunches, up to 250 mm long.

2 Commiphora multijuga   **Purple-stem corkwood**
SA: 282   Spring   **Persstamkanniedood**
Shrub or small deciduous tree with **graceful, pale green, drooping foliage**; sexes separate, on different plants; restricted to hot, arid parts of northwestern Namibia and southwestern Angola, usually on rock outcrops. Bark **purplish grey to dark grey, smooth and not peeling**. Leaflets **4–10 pairs** per leaf plus a terminal one, essentially **hairless**, broadly **elliptic to rotund, abruptly pointed at both ends**, aromatic; petiolules 5–15 mm long, slender. Flowers in few-flowered axillary clusters, small, creamy yellow. Fruit a fleshy drupe, subglobose; stone partly enveloped by a **red pseudo-aril**.
    This tree holds special religious significance for the local people. Also, the fragrant watery resin is blended with animal fat and used as a perfume. Twigs pleasant-tasting and used as toothbrushes. The strongly aromatic leaves are browsed by stock and game, particularly elephants.

CAESALPINIACEAE (see page 22)

3 Cordyla africana   **Wild mango**
SA: 216; Z: 281   Winter–Spring   **Wildemango**
Large deciduous tree with **spreading, rather flat-topped crown**; occurring in hot, dry bushveld, riverine and sand forest, often on sandy soil. Leaflets **11–28**, alternate, plus a terminal one, **oblong, rounded at both ends, thin, hairless**, with **pellucid dots and streaks**; rachis and petiole conspicuously **grooved above**. Flowers in short, dense sprays that appear with the leaves on new shoots, orange-yellow. Fruit fleshy, oval, 1- or 2-seeded, **40–80 x 30–60 mm**, indehiscent, ripening to yellow after falling to the ground; seed pale brown, very large, often germinating while still in the fruit.
    The flowers contain abundant nectar and attract sunbirds. The fruit pulp is edible and rich in vitamin C, though not very tasty. Heartwood brown, hard, suitable for general carpentry but not very durable. Decorative plant for frost-free gardens.

C. *mollis*: flowers

C. *mollis*: fruit & stone with red pseudo-aril

C. *karibensis*: fruit

C. *multijuga*: fruit

C. *multijuga*: bark

C. *africana*: flowers

C. *africana*: fruit

GROUP 38

Leaves pinnately compound, alternate or in tufts. Leaflets more than 3, terminal one present (imparipinnate); margin smooth. Latex absent.

APIACEAE (see page 20)

1 *Heteromorpha trifoliata* (= *H. arborescens*)   **Parsley tree**
SA: 568; Z: 816   Summer   **Wildepietersieliebos**
Shrub or small to medium-sized deciduous tree; occurring in wooded grassland, bushveld and on forest margins. Bark **satiny-smooth, glossy, coppery-brown, peels off horizontally in papery pieces.** Leaves simple to variously compound, varying even on the same branch, **thinly textured; smelling of parsley** when crushed; petiole, base broad and **stem-clasping.** Flowers in **compound** spherical terminal **umbels**, small, greenish yellow. Fruit dry, laterally flattened, creamy brown. Leaves simple with petiole 6–27 mm long in var. *arborescens* (eastern Karoo and southern part of Western Cape), 3-foliolate or pinnately compound in var. *abyssinica* (from Free State northwards).
The leaves and root, and the smoke from burning wood, are used medicinally.

ARALIACEAE (see page 20)

2 *Polyscias fulva*   **Parasol tree**
Z: 812   Summer–Autumn   **Sambreelboom**
Large tree with a **clear straight trunk** and an **umbrella-shaped crown**; occurring as a canopy tree in montane forest. Leaves **very large, up to 800 mm long**; leaflets leathery, dark green and hairless above, densely **covered with creamy brown star-shaped hairs below, drooping.** Flowers in loose axillary heads, small, greenish yellow. Fruit subglobose, closely clustered, fleshy, crowned with 2 persistent styles.

CAESALPINIACEAE (see page 22)

3 *Dialium engleranum*   **Kalahari podberry**
SA: 210; Z: 266   Autumn–Winter   **Kalaharipeulbessie**
Medium-sized tree with a somewhat rounded crown; occurring in bushveld and woodland, usually on deep **Kalahari sand.** Leaflets usually **7–9 per leaf**, glossy dark green above, **sparingly or densely yellow, velvety hairy below.** Flowers in loose panicles, creamy white within, **golden-brown, velvety hairy** outside. Pods **ovoid**, dark brown, indehiscent; seeds 1 or 2, **bright reddish brown**, embedded in a mealy pulp.
The fruit is edible, either soaked in water and eaten fresh or with milk, or mixed with meal and made into a porridge. Various parts used medicinally.

4 *Dialium schlechteri*   **Zulu podberry**
SA: 211   Spring   **Zoeloepeulbessie**
Medium-sized tree with a somewhat rounded crown, often several-stemmed; occurring on deep sandy soils in dry bushveld and sand forest; near-endemic to the Maputaland Centre. Leaflets **7–13 per leaf**, shiny green, **essentially hairless** when mature, base **markedly asymmetric**, margin often **wavy.** Flowers in many-flowered panicles, white, sweetly scented, buds and outside covered with **golden brown, velvety hairs.** Pods **ellipsoid to subglobose**, indehiscent; seeds 1 or 2, **brown**, embedded in a dry orange-brown mealy pulp.
The fruit pulp is edible and makes a refreshing drink when mixed with milk or water. Wood reddish brown, hard, heavy and very durable. Bark used medicinally.

H. trifoliata: flowers & fruit

H. trifoliata: fruit

H. trifoliata: bark

P. fulva: tree

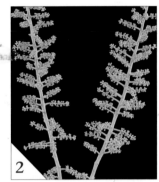

P. fulva: male flowers

P. fulva: branchlet

D. engleranum: flowers

D. schlechteri: flowers

D. schlechteri: fruit

1 *Parkinsonia africana* Wild green-hair tree
SA: 214   Spring Wildegroenhaarboom
Shrub or small, **slender**, **sparsely branched** tree, armed with **stout spines** which are modified lateral shoots; occurring in arid semi-desert and desert areas, especially on sandy plains near watercourses. Young branchlets greenish yellow or yellowish brown. Leaves **reduced to hair-like rachides**, occasionally with minute **scale-like leaflets**. Flowers in lax racemes, yellow. Pods brown, flattened, hairless, indehiscent; seed light brown with dark brown markings.
The leaves are browsed by stock and game. Seeds used as a coffee substitute.
Resembles *P. aculeata*, a Mexican species occasionally naturalized in the eastern parts of southern Africa, and which is more densely branched and more foliose.

2 *Swartzia madagascariensis* Snake bean
SA: 217; Z: 282   Spring–Summer Slangboom
Small to medium-sized, semi-deciduous tree, often with a **gnarled trunk**; occurring in hot bushveld and woodland, often on sandy soil. Bark dark grey, **rough, longitudinally fissured**. Leaflets 8–12, elliptic with **rounded tip**, dark green and hairless above, **densely yellowish hairy below**; petiolules **short and thick**. Flowers in sparsely flowered sprays, with a single white, crinkled petal with grey edging. Pods **cylindrical, up to 300 mm long**, indehiscent, **pendulous**, dark brown.
The pods are eaten by cattle; also used as a mild fish-poison. Ground pods have insecticidal properties. Various parts of the tree used in traditional medicine. Heartwood reddish brown to purplish black, dense, durable, very decorative and used for ornaments and curios; sapwood whitish.

FABACEAE (see page 25)
3 *Bolusanthus speciosus* Tree wisteria
SA: 222; Z: 287   Spring–Summer Vanwykshout
Small deciduous tree, usually **multistemmed** with narrow crown and **drooping foliage**; occurring in bushveld, often on heavy alkaline soils. Bark **rough and deeply fissured longitudinally**. Leaflets lanceolate, **greyish green** with minute silvery hairs above, dull green below, tip **narrowly tapering**, base markedly **asymmetric**. Flowers in loose hanging racemes, pale blue to violet. Pods flat, tardily dehiscent.
The wood is attractive, and durable, but its use is limited by the small pieces available. A decorative garden subject, although short-flowered. Bark used medicinally.

4 *Calpurnea aurea* Wild laburnum
SA: 219 & 220; Z: 286   All year Geelkeurboom
Shrub or small slender tree; occurring in forest areas, often associated with forest margins, stream vegetation and associated regenerative growth in clearings. Leaflets **11–31**, ovate to oblong, tip **rounded, light green above, silvery grey below, thin and soft-textured**. Flowers in **pendulous** sprays, yellow. Pods flat, thin, pale brown, indehiscent. Subsp. *sylvatica* has the ovary silky hairy and is confined to the Eastern Cape. Subsp. *aurea* has the ovary hairless and is more widespread.
An attractive garden ornamental. Roots and leaves used medicinally.
C. sericea, a hairy shrub from stream-banks in high-altitude grassland, has more erect inflorescences. Its hairless counterpart is *C. glabrata*. *C. robinioides*, from the eastern Free State and Drakensberg region, is a small tree with 7–9 leaflets.

P. *africana*: branchlet

P. *africana*: flowers

S. *madagascariensis*: flowers

S. *madagascariensis*: fruit

B. *speciosus*: tree

B. *speciosus*: flowers

B. *speciosus*: fruit

C. *aurea*: flowers

C. *aurea*: fruit

1 Craibia brevicaudata   **Northern peawood**
Z: 324   Spring–Summer   **Noordelike ertjiehout**
Medium to large evergreen tree with a rounded crown; occurring in coastal and montane forest, often in dense stands. Young shoots with **golden-brown velvety hairs**. Leaflets 6–8, alternate, **deep green**, leathery, **essentially hairless, tip tapering, base broadly tapering to rounded, margin wavy**; petiolules thick and wrinkled; petiole **very thick, grooved along the top**, conspicuously **swollen at base**. Flowers in short racemes near ends of shoots, pink to white; stalks and calyces densely covered with **golden-brown, velvety hairs** (subsp. *baptistarum*). Pods flat, creamy grey, dehiscent. Subsp. *schliebenii* has leaflets with a long, narrow drip-tip and floral parts covered with velvety black hairs (in southern Africa known only from Mt Gorongosa in Mozambique).
Several *Charaxes* butterflies breed on the tree.
C. zimmermannii (**1.1**), from Maputaland and Mozambique, is an often multi-stemmed small tree from sand and dune forest, often growing in groves. It has leaves with 4–6 alternate leaflets, each shiny, dark green, with a long and narrowly tapering tip. The flowers are white, becoming pinkish with age, and the calyx and flower stalk are almost hairless.

2 Dalbergia melanoxylon   **Zebrawood**
SA: 232; Z: 348   Spring–Summer   **Sebrahout**
Deciduous shrub or small, much-branched tree, armed with **spinescent shoots** and usually **several-stemmed**; occurring in bushveld and thicket, often on rocky outcrops and termitaria. Leaves often **clustered** on (spinescent) side shoots; leaflets 6–13, alternate, heart-shaped to oval, usually about 15 x 10 mm, dark green, tip **rounded**. Flowers appearing with new leaves in spring, small, white, sweetly scented. Pods thin, up to 70 x 15 mm, **flat, papery**, hairless, indehiscent; seeds 1 or 2.
The heartwood is attractive, dark purple-black to black, dense, very hard and, despite the small size, much sought after for ornaments, walking sticks and wood-wind musical instruments; sapwood yellowish white. Root used medicinally.
D. armata, a robust woody climber with strong spines (up to 100 mm long and often in clusters) on the main stem and branches, has 21–41 fine leaflets and is usually associated with coastal and montane forest.

3 Dalbergia nitidula   **Glossy flat-bean**
SA: 234; Z: 349   Spring   **Blinkplatboontjie**
Much-branched, unarmed, deciduous shrub or medium-sized tree; usually in bushveld and sand forest, occasionally associated with forest margins. Leaflets **5–15**, opposite to subopposite, **grey-green, oval with rounded tip and base**, hairless above, sometimes hairy below. Flowers produced with or after the new leaves, small, white, sweetly scented. Pods **flat, papery**, produced in profusion; young fruit often deformed by insects into round, **spiny galls**.
The heartwood is dark purple, used for making walking sticks, ornaments and small carvings. The roots are reputed to be toxic. Larval food plant for the butterflies *Charaxes bohemani* and *C. achaemenes achaemenes*.

C. brevicaudata: flowers

C. brevicaudata: fruit

C. zimmermannii: flowers

D. melanoxylon: flowers

D. melanoxylon: fruit

D. nitidula: fruit

D. nitidula: flowers

D. nitidula: insect gall

1 *Dalbergia obovata*   Climbing flat-bean
SA: 235   Spring   Rankplatboontjie
Unarmed robust woody climber or small tree; occurring in coastal forest and associated bush. Leaflets **5–9, shiny green above**, greyish green and prominently veined below, margin **wavy**; petiole with **velvety brown hairs**. Flowers in dense, many-flowered inflorescences, small, creamy white, sweetly scented. Pods **flat, thin, heavily veined**, indehiscent, usually **single-seeded**; fruit in KwaZulu-Natal often transformed into neat, oval, hollow insect galls, each containing a small larva.

The heartwood is reddish brown, attractive and used for walking sticks and small domestic items. Flexible stems used for woven hut walls and for fishing baskets. Bark yields twine; the ash of the bark is used medicinally (in snuff). Roots used for magical purposes. The butterfly *Neptis laeta* breeds on the tree.

D. martinii, from the upper Zambezi River Valley and adjacent areas, has well-developed coiled stem tendrils, and rough, often sticky twigs and leaves.

2 *Dalbergiella nyasae*   Mane-pod
Z: 351   Spring   Maanhaarpeul
Small to medium-sized deciduous tree; occurring in woodland and thicket. Young shoots rather **thick and corky, with short brown hairs**. Leaves **crowded near ends** of branches; leaflets 13–19, oval, greyish green, tip and base rounded; petiole with base swollen and covered with **short golden-brown hairs**. Flowers in profusion on long racemes, whitish cream to pink with large mauve spot at base of standard. Pods **flat, oblong with one side notched** (elongated kidney-shaped), velvety, **edged by a most distinctive fringe of dense, long, brown, plumose hairs**.

3 *Indigofera* sp. novum   River indigo
SA: 225.4   Summer   Rivierverfbos
Shrub to small slender tree; occurring in riverine forest, along forest margins and between rocks in grassland. Leaflets **4–7 pairs** plus a terminal one, **8–25 x 5–13 mm**, dark green, **hairless**; apex **rounded, notched**. Flowers in **short axillary spikes**, somewhat **bicoloured**, dark pink combined with pale pink to white, very attractive; back of standard covered in **fine whitish hairs**. Pods cylindrical, **40 x 3 mm, reflexed**, reddish brown, **hairy**, dehiscent.

This is an undescribed species, hitherto incorrectly referred to under the name *I. frutescens* or its synonym, *I. cylindrica*.

I. swaziensis has flowers with the back of the standard covered by dark brown, appressed hairs, and pods which are spreading and hairless. It occurs along the northeastern Drakensberg Escarpment and in Zimbabwe. Also very similar to some of the species of *Indigofera* in the Western Cape (e.g. *I. cytisoides, I. frutescens, I. superba*), but these all have flowers uniformly bright pink.

4 *Indigofera lyallii*   Venda indigo
SA: 225.7; Z: 306   Autumn   Vendaverfbos
Shrub to small slender tree; occurring in forest margins, ravine forest and protected places in montane grassland, often gregarious. Leaflets **8–12 pairs** plus a terminal one, up to **20 x 5–8 mm, finely velvety**. Flowers in short, compact racemes, small, dark wine-red. Pods cylindrical, about **3 x 0,3 mm, sharply reflexed**, reddish brown, **hairless**, dehiscent.

1

D. obovata: flowers

2

D. nyasae: fruit

1

D. obovata: fruit

2

D. nyasae: flowers

4

I. lyallii: flowers

3

Indigofera sp. novum: flowers

4

I. lyallii: fruit

GROUP 38

1 *Indigofera natalensis*   Forest indigo
SA: 225.6   Summer   **Bosverfbos**
Shrub or small slender tree; occurring in the **understorey of forest**, usually in dense shade. Leaflets 1–2 pairs plus a terminal one, **15–40 x 8–15 mm**, shiny dark green, with **long tapering tip**. Flowers in slender axillary sprays or racemes, **small (up to 5 mm long)**, white. Pods cylindrical, 40–50 x 4 mm, reddish brown, dehiscent.
    I. rhynchocarpa has larger white flowers (up to 8 mm long), pods with a conspicuous beak-like hook at the tip, and occurs in *Brachystegia* woodland in Zimbabwe.

2 *Lonchocarpus bussei*   Small apple-leaf
SA: 238.1; Z: 256   Spring   **Kleinappelblaar**
Small to medium-sized tree with a rather slender crown; occurring in woodland and thicket, often on rocky outcrops. Leaflets 3–7, usually **shorter than 70 mm**, dark green above, **almost hairless when mature**, tip and base **tapering**. Flowers in lax panicles **before** the new leaves appear, mauve to purple. Pods flat, narrowly oval, **relatively small (40–100 x 10–15 mm)**, hairless, usually single-seeded, indehiscent.

3 *Lonchocarpus capassa*   Apple-leaf
SA: 238; Z: 357   Spring   **Appelblaar**
Small to medium-sized deciduous or semi-deciduous tree with a rather sparse crown; occurring in bushveld and woodland, often at low altitude along rivers. Bark exudes a sticky red sap when cut. Leaves with **1 or 2 pairs of opposite** leaflets plus a terminal one; leaflets usually **longer than 80 mm**, shiny above, **grey-green below**, densely velvety when young, tip **broadly tapering or rounded with a hair-like tip**; **hair-like stipels present at base of petiolules**. Flowers small, mauve-purple, short-lived, borne in many-flowered panicles before or with the new leaves. Pods **flat**, relatively large (70–150 x 20–35 mm), hairless, **single- or 2-seeded**, indehiscent.
    The wood is attractive, hard and dense, and carved into handsome ornaments. Leaves browsed by stock and game. Roots and leaves used medicinally. Watery excretions by the sap-sucking nymphs of *Ptyelus grossus* (Hemiptera) cause the trees to 'rain' during certain times of the year. The butterflies *Charaxes bohemani* and *Coeliades forestan forestan* breed on the tree.

4 *Millettia grandis*   Umzimbeet
SA: 227   Summer   **Umzimbeet**
Small to medium-sized deciduous tree with a somewhat **flattened crown**; occurring in coastal forest and on forest margins. Bark pale grey-brown, flaking. New growth covered in **reddish brown hairs**. Leaflets 13–15, dark to bluish green above, yellowish green, **often with reddish brown hairs below**; venation **prominent below**, often reddish brown; pair of **minute hair-like stipels present at base of each pair of leaflets**. Flowers in erect, **terminal racemes**, purple to mauve; buds densely hairy, reddish brown. Pods flat, **velvety brown**, borne more or less erect, dehiscent.
    The heartwood is dark reddish brown, heavy, hard, durable and much favoured for making walking sticks. Roots and seeds used medicinally. An attractive garden plant. The butterflies *Deudorix diocles* and *Charaxes pondoensis* breed on the tree.
    M. sutherlandii is a large forest tree with smaller and fewer leaflets (7–9). It has a restricted, disjunct distribution in Swaziland, KwaZulu-Natal and the Eastern Cape (most common in Pondoland).

I. natalensis: flowers & fruit

I. natalensis: fruit

L. bussei: flowers

L. bussei: fruit

L. capassa: flowers

L. capassa: fruit

M. grandis: flowers

M. grandis: fruit

1 *Millettia stuhlmannii*
SA: 228.1; Z: 322   Summer

Panga panga
Panga-panga

Medium to large deciduous tree with a spreading crown; occurring in bushveld and forest, often on rocky hillsides. Bark yellow or greenish grey, **smooth**. Leaflets 7–9 opposite pairs plus a terminal one, **pale green above, bluish green below**, tip usually rounded; pair of minute **hair-like stipels present at base of each pair of leaflets**. Flowers in lax racemes up to 350 mm long, pinkish purple. Pods flat, woody, **golden-brown, velvety**, dehiscent.

The timber is dark brown to almost black, fine-grained, durable and available commercially. Root used for medicinal and magical purposes.

M. usaramensis subsp. *australis* is a shrub or small tree found in hot, arid bushveld in Zimbabwe and Mozambique. It has relatively small and narrow leaflets (20–55 x 15–25 mm) with tapering tips.

2 *Mundulea sericea*
SA: 226; Z: 231   Spring–Summer

Cork bush
Kurkbos

Shrub or small semi-deciduous tree; occurring in bushveld or wooded grassland, often in sandy soils and on rocky ridges. Bark pale grey, **deeply furrowed, thick and corky**. Leaflets 9–13, **grey-green, covered with silvery, silky hairs**. Flowers produced with the new leaves in spring, pale to dark purple, occasionally white. Pods flat, densely covered with **golden-brown velvety hairs**, tardily dehiscent.

The bark contains rotenone and is used as a fish poison. Leaves, bark and roots are used for medicinal and magical purposes. Leaves browsed by game and stock. The butterflies *Spindasis natalensis* and *Cyclyrius pirithous* breed on the tree.

3 *Pericopsis angolensis* (= *Afrormosia angolensis*)
Z: 284   Spring

Mwanga
Mwanga

Medium to large deciduous tree with a somewhat **crooked symmetry**; occurring in open or closed woodland, often associated with *Brachystegia boehmii*. Bark **greyish**. Leaflets 7–13, **ovate to elliptic, leathery, hairless**, tip rounded. Flowers whitish with a pink or mauve flush, appearing with the new leaves, rest of **inflorescence and outside of calyx rusty-brown**. Pods **flattened, narrowly winged along one or both margins**, indehiscent, borne in loose, pendulous bunches; seeds red.

Commercially known as 'afrormosia', the wood is attractive, hard, extremely durable and esteemed as general purpose timber and for carvings. It is also termite-proof and suitable for fence poles. Bark, root and leaves are used medicinally.

4 *Psoralea pinnata*
SA: 225.8   All year

Fountain bush
Fonteinbos

Shrub or **small slender** tree; occurring along streams and in moist places along forest margins. Leaflets 7–15, **very fine and slender (1–4 mm wide)**, dotted with **small black glands**, aromatic when crushed. Flowers in bunches in axils of terminal leaves, dark blue or mauve, rarely white. Pods small, about 5–3 mm, **partly surrounded by the persistent calyx.**

M. stuhlmannii: flowers   *M. stuhlmannii*: fruit   *M. sericea*: flowers

M. sericea: flowers   *M. sericea*: flowers & fruit

P. angolensis: flowers   *P. angolensis*: fruit   *P. pinnata*: flowers

1 *Pterocarpus angolensis*   **Wild teak**
SA: 236; Z: 352   Spring   **Kiaat**
Medium to large deciduous tree with an **open spreading crown**; occurring in bushveld and woodland, usually on deep sandy soil or rocky hillsides. Bark **rough, reticulate and fissured**, exuding a blood-red sticky sap when injured. Leaflets 11–25 pairs plus a terminal one, **hairless at maturity**, tip **tapering to a narrow bristle-tipped point**, base **rounded**, margin wavy, side veins **parallel, prominent above**; petiolules and petiole velvety. Flowers in large panicles, orange-yellow. Pods very distinctive, circular, central seed case indehiscent, **densely covered with coarse bristles, surrounded by a broad, thin, wavy wing**.

The heartwood is attractive, moderately dense, easily worked and widely used for high-quality furniture and ornaments. Leaves browsed by game, particularly elephant. Bark and root extensively used for magical and medicinal purposes. Pods eaten by baboons and monkeys. The butterfly *Charaxes achaemenes achaemenes* breeds on the tree.

P. brenanii, a shrub or small tree from eastern Zimbabwe and Mozambique, has similar circular pods but lacks the bristles on the seed case. It also has conspicuous leafy stipules and larger leaflets (usually 120 x 80–120 mm).

2 *Pterocarpus lucens* subsp. *antunesii*   **Thorny teak**
SA: 236.1; Z: 353   Spring–Summer   **Doringkiaat**
Small to medium-sized deciduous tree, often multistemmed with **stiff spine-like side shoots**; occurring in hot dry bushveld and thicket, usually on deep, sandy soils. Bark grey to greyish green and mottled, **smooth, locally exfoliating in thin scales**, exudes a red-brown sap when cut. Leaves **drooping**; leaflets 2–9, oval to oblanceolate, pale glossy green, **relatively small (20–30 x 10–20 mm)**, margin **wavy**. Flowers in slender axillary racemes, pale yellow. Pods **elliptic, flattened, with a swelling over the seed case and surrounded by a membranous wing**, hairless and often reddish-tinged, indehiscent.

The wood is pale brown, hard, strong, and used for axe handles and, in former times, for wagon wheel rims. The plant is browsed by game. The butterfly *Charaxes achaemenes achaemenes* breeds on the tree.

3 *Pterocarpus rotundifolius*   **Round-leaved teak**
SA: 237; Z: 355   Spring–Summer   **Dopperkiaat**
Small to medium-sized deciduous tree, often multistemmed; occurring in bushveld and woodland. Bark **rough and longitudinally fissured**. Leaflets 3–7, oval to elliptic, **35–150 x up to 110 mm**, tip **rounded and notched**, margin **wavy**; side veins **conspicuous, parallel**. Flowers in large panicles, deep yellow with crinkly petals. Pods flat, subrotund, thickened over the usually single seed, **without bristles**, indehiscent. Subsp. *rotundifolius* is the most widespread form in southern Africa. Subsp. *polyanthus*, which has 4–8 pairs of rather hairy leaflets, does not extend very far south of the Zambezi Escarpment.

The wood is pale brown with a featureless grain, and is used for household utensils; unpleasantly scented when cut. Larval food plant for the butterflies *Charaxes achaemenes achaemenes* and *Abantis venosa*.

P. angolensis: flowers

P. angolensis: fruit

P. lucens: flowers

P. lucens: fruit

P. rotundifolius: flowers

P. rotundifolius: fruit

1 **•*Robinia pseudoacacia***   **Black locust**
SA: X562   Spring   **Witakasia**
Deciduous tree with an oval or rounded crown; invading riverbanks, dongas, road-sides and urban open space. Branchlets **reddish brown**, with **pairs of short, straight spines** at the nodes. Leaflets 3–9 pairs plus a terminal one, **oval, 38–50 x 12–18 mm**, dull dark green. Flowers in **drooping** racemes, **100–200 mm long, white with a yellow blotch** on the upper petal, fragrant. Pods elongate, flat, 75–100 x 11–13 mm, reddish brown, dehiscent and **remaining on branches during winter**. A native of North America; cultivated for fodder and ornament.

2 ***Virgilia oroboides***   **Blossom tree**
SA: 221   Spring–Summer   **Keurboom**
Medium-sized, semi-deciduous tree with a somewhat rounded crown; occurring on forest edges, usually as a pioneer. Leaflets usually **13–25, glossy green above, densely hairy below**, tip **broadly tapering** with a **hair-like tip**. Flowers in short racemes, pale or dark pink. Pods flat, brown, **velvety**, dehiscent. Subsp. *oroboides* has pale pink or white flowers with the leaflets whitish hairy below, whereas subsp. *ferruginea* has rose-violet or violet-purple flowers with leaflets rusty-hairy below.
    The larvae of *Leto venus*, a very large and beautiful moth, live as borers in the trunk and stems. A fast-growing and attractive garden tree, though short-lived.
    Similar to *V. divaricata*, which has pinnae with more rounded tips, the lower sur-face more or less hairless, and attractive rose-violet or purple-violet flowers.

3 ***Xanthocercis zambesiaca***   **Nyala tree**
SA: 241; Z: 283   Spring   **Njalaboom**
Very large evergreen tree with heavy rounded crown and **somewhat drooping branchlets**; occurring in hot, dry bushveld, usually on deep alluvial soils near rivers and on termitaria. Leaflets up to 7 pairs plus terminal one, **oval, up to 55 x 20 mm, dark glossy green above**, pale dull green below. Flowers in short sprays, small, white. Fruit **fleshy, single- or 2-seeded**, yellowish brown when ripe; seeds black.
    The fruit is eaten fresh or dried and ground into a meal. Leaves browsed by game. Wood attractive, dust may cause irritation of the nose and throat.

4 ***Xeroderris stuhlmannii***   **Wing bean**
SA: 240; Z: 360   Spring   **Vlerkboon**
Medium to large deciduous tree with a spreading crown; occurring in hot dry bushveld, often on sandy soils. Bark exudes a red sap when cut. Leaflets about 15, **oblong to ovate, folded upward along midrib**, fresh green, **initially covered with fine golden or silvery hairs**, almost hairless later, tip and base rather rounded, mar-gin wavy, slightly rolled under; **petiolule of terminal leaflet articulated**. Flowers in terminal panicles, small, white to greenish white; calyces and stalks **densely covered with creamy to rusty velvety hairs**. Pods flat, conspicuously swollen over the seeds, the **seed-containing part surrounded by a rim and then a membranous wing**, up to 4-seeded; often parasitized by insects to form globose fruit-like galls.
    The wood is dark yellow, hard, and yields a useful timber. The red sap is used as a dye and for tanning leather. Fruits and leaves browsed by stock and game. Root used medicinally. Seeds ground to produce a meal. The butterfly *Charaxes bohe-mani* breeds on the tree. Host for the hemiparasitic shrublet *Vanwykia remota*.

R. pseudoacacia: flowers

V. oroboides: flowers

R. pseudoacacia: fruit

V. oroboides: fruit

X. stuhlmannii: flowers

X. zambesiaca: flowers

X. zambesiaca: fruit

X. stuhlmannii: fruit

MELIACEAE (see page 26)

1 *Ekebergia benguelensis*   Woodland dogplum
Z: 431   Spring   Bosveldessenhout
Small to medium-sized, semi-evergreen tree; sexes separate, on different plants;
occurring in open woodland. Young branchlets **stout, thick** (usually more than
7 mm), with **rough corky bark** and many crowded leaf scars. Leaflets **bluish green
above, whitish green below**; petiole, rachis and venation usually **reddish**. Flowers
in many-flowered panicles, white, often tinged with pink, sweetly scented. Fruit
fleshy, subglobose, pink to bright red when ripe.
  The fruit is edible. Root used medicinally.
  May be mistaken for *Lannea discolor* (Group 37, p. 444), which has leaves that
are densely whitish hairy below.

2 *Ekebergia capensis*   Cape ash
SA: 298; Z: 432   Spring   Essenhout
Medium to large semi-deciduous tree; sexes separate, on different plants; occurring in coastal and montane forest. Young branchlets dotted with **whitish lenticels**.
Leaflets 9–13 per leaf, glossy green, variable in shape and size, **usually hairless**,
base **asymmetric**. Flowers in **lax** axillary panicles, white, often tinged with pink.
Fruit fleshy, subglobose, pink to bright red when ripe. Two distinct variants
(worthy of specific recognition) occur. The southern or Cape variant has thickset
branchlets with prominent leaf scars, almost stalkless leaflets, a narrowly winged
rachis and yellowish autumn colours. The northern variant has more slender branchlets, clearly stalked leaflets, a wingless rachis, and reddish autumn colours.
  The wood is pale brown, light, soft, and suitable for furniture. Bark, root and
leaves are used medicinally.
  The Cape variant resembles *Harpephyllum caffrum* (Group 37, p. 444), but lacks
the watery secretion at the base of a detached leaf.

3 *Ekebergia pterophylla*   Rock ash
SA: 299   Spring   Rotsessenhout
Shrub or **small**, stout, evergreen tree; sexes separate, on different plants; occurring
in montane and coastal forest regions, usually associated with rocky outcrops and
forest margins. Leaflets 3–5, **leathery, tips usually rounded**, margin recurved;
rachis **broadly winged**. Flowers in short panicles, white, often tinged with pink.
Fruit fleshy, subglobose, 7–9 mm in diameter, pale yellow to red when ripe.
  Superficially similar to *Schrebera alata* (Group 32), which has opposite leaves.

E. benguelensis: flowers

E. benguelensis: fruit

E. capensis: flowers

E. capensis: fruit

E. pterophylla: flowers

E. pterophylla: fruit

1 *Trichilia dregeana*   Forest mahogany
SA: 300; Z: 434   Spring   Bosrooiessenhout
Medium to large evergreen tree with a **dense, spreading crown**; sexes separate, on different plants; occurring in coastal and montane forest. Leaflets 7–11, dark glossy green above, tips **more or less sharply pointed**, lower surface **essentially hairless**; principal side veins **7–12 pairs, widely spaced**. Flowers creamy white. Fruit a dehiscent capsule, 30–50 mm in diameter, green or bright purple (in parts of Soutpansberg), **without a neck (stipe) and thus joined directly to the stalk**, or with an indistinct one up to 3 mm long; seeds **black**, completely enveloped by a **bright red aril**.

The tree yields a general purpose timber that should be treated against borer attack. Bark extensively used in traditional medicine. Seeds contain a superior quality oil that is used for cooking and various other purposes; they are also eaten after removal of the seed coat. Scarlet arils eaten or crushed to extract a milky juice, used as a sweet drink or with side dishes. An attractive shade tree for frost-free gardens.

2 *Trichilia emetica*   Natal mahogany
SA: 301; Z: 435   Spring   Rooiessenhout
Medium to large evergreen tree with a **dense, spreading crown**; sexes separate, on different plants; occurring in riverine forest and bushveld. Leaflets 9–11, dark glossy green above, tips **more or less rounded or broadly pointed**, lower surface **sparsely to densely hairy**; principal side veins **11–18 pairs, closely spaced**. Flowers creamy green. Fruit a dehiscent capsule, 18–25 mm in diameter, sharply differentiated from a **5–10 mm long neck (stipe), by which it is joined to the stalk**; seed **black**, completely enveloped by a **bright red aril**.

Used in the same way as *T. dregeana* (above).

T. capitata is a scrambling shrub or small tree with leaves usually shorter than 200 mm and fruit about 15 mm in diameter. It occurs in bushveld and thicket in the northeast of Zimbabwe and in central Mozambique.

MELIANTHACEAE (see page 27)
3 *Bersama lucens*   Glossy white ash
SA: 439   Winter–Spring   Blinkblaarwitessenhout
Shrub to medium-sized tree; occurring in forest areas and associated bushveld, often in rocky places or on coastal dunes. New growth reddish brown. Stipules present, **intrapetiolar**. Leaflets **3–7, hairless, glossy green above**, tips **rounded or bluntly pointed**, margin **thickened and usually wavy**; venation **yellowish, conspicuous**. Flowers in erect racemes, cream. Fruit a capsule, subglobose, **wrinkled**, shortly hairy; seeds **bright scarlet**, partly enveloped in a **yellowish aril**.

The bark is extensively used in traditional medicine. Seeds eaten by monkeys and birds. An attractive garden subject with glossy brownish purple new leaves.

B. swynnertonii has dark, glossy green leaves with more than three pairs of leaflets; petiolules, rachis and petiole often pinkish red to dark purple; capsules wrinkled, hairless. The plant occurs in montane forest in the Eastern Highlands of Zimbabwe.

468

1

T. dregeana: fruit

2

T. emetica: fruit & seeds

3

B. lucens: fruit & seeds

2

T. emetica: flowers

3

B. lucens: fruit

1 *Bersama swinnyi*　　　　　　　　　　　Coastal white ash
SA: 441　Summer　　　　　　　　　　　　Kuswitessenhout
Small to medium-sized tree; occurring on margins of coastal forest, often on sandstone outcrops. Leaflets **crowded at ends of rather stout branches**; stipules present, **intrapetiolar**; leaflets **about 11**, tip **more or less rounded**, margin not conspicuously wavy. Flowers in stout axillary racemes, greenish white, **interspersed with silvery, silky bracts**. Fruit subglobose, **conspicuously warty**; seeds **brownish**, partly enveloped by a **yellowish aril**.
　　The bark is extensively used in traditional medicine.

2 *Bersama tysoniana* (= *B. stayneri*)　　　Common white ash
SA: 443　Spring–Summer　　　　　　　　Gewone witessenhout
Small to medium-sized tree; occurring at margins of coastal and montane forest. Stipule present, **intrapetiolar**. Leaflets 9–11, hairless when mature, sometimes with hairtuft domatia in the axils of the side veins below. Flowers in dense erect spike-like racemes, cream. Fruit a capsule, subglobose, covered with **woody protuberances**; seeds **reddish brown**, enveloped by a **yellow aril** at the base.
　　The bark is used medicinally.

SAPINDACEAE (see page 31)
3 *Erythrophysa alata*　　　　　　　　　Namaqua red balloon
SA: 436.1　Autumn　　　　　　　　　　Namakwarooiklapperbos
Shrub or small tree; occurring in semi-desert areas, often on rocky hillsides. Leaves with **4 pairs** of **opposite** leaflets plus a terminal one; leaflets dark green, **stalkless**; rachis **conspicuously winged**. Flowers red; petals spurred; stamens prominent. Fruit a **3-angled, inflated capsule** with a **slender pointed beak, red**, indehiscent.
　　The leaves are browsed by stock.

4 *Erythrophysa transvaalensis*　　　　　Transvaal red balloon
SA: 436.2; Z: 608/1　Spring　　　　　　Transvaalse rooiklapperbos
Shrub or small deciduous tree with a **sparsely branched** crown; occurring on rocky ridges in bushveld, often associated with outcrops of red syenite. Leaves with about **7 pairs** of leaflets plus a terminal one, dark glossy green; rachis **prominently winged**. Flowers green tinged with red, borne **before the appearance of the new leaves**. Fruit a **large, 3-angled, inflated capsule**, green flushed with red or completely red; seed slightly flattened, smooth, purplish black.
　　The seeds are used as beads. An attractive shrub for frost-free gardens.

B. *swinnyi*: fruit

B. *swinnyi*: fruit & seeds

B. *tysoniana*: flowers

B. *tysoniana*: fruit

E. *transvaalensis*: flowers

E. *alata*: buds & flowers

E. *transvaalensis*: fruit

GROUP 39
Leaves palmately compound, once-divided, alternate. Leaflets more than 3.

See also Group 2: *Cussonia arborea* (p. 48); Group 29: *Maerua cafra* (p. 384) and *Rhoicissus digitata* (p. 392).

ARALIACEAE (see page 20)

1 *Cussonia thyrsiflora*   Cape coast cabbage
SA: 565   Summer   Kaapse kuskiepersol
Scrambling shrub, rarely a small slender tree; occurring in coastal forest, particularly on dunes. Leaflets **5–8, leathery, glossy dark green above**; margin smooth or slightly toothed towards tip, rolled under. Flowers in dense **spikes**, 6–12 of these grouped together in a **terminal umbel**, greenish yellow, stalked. Fruit fleshy, purplish black.

2 *Schefflera umbellifera*   False cabbage tree
SA: 566; Z: 811   Summer   Basterkiepersol
Medium to large evergreen tree with a **tall trunk** and much-branched, **rounded crown**; occurring in coastal and montane forest. Leaves clustered at ends of branches; leaflets **3–5, glossy dark green above**, paler below, margin smooth or toothed in upper half, **very wavy**. Flowers in **large, branched, terminal heads**, small, pale yellow to white. Fruit fleshy, round, about 3 mm in diameter, red.
   The bark and leaves are used medicinally.
   S. goetzenii is a robust climber in the mountain forests of eastern Zimbabwe.

BOMBACACEAE (see page 21)

3 *Adansonia digitata*   Baobab
SA: 467; Z: 684   Spring–Summer   Kremetart
Grotesque, comparatively short, deciduous tree with hugely **swollen trunk**; occurring at low altitudes in hot dry bushveld. Bark **smooth**, folded. Leaves with **3–9** leaflets in mature plants, simple in seedlings and juveniles. Flowers solitary in leaf axils, **large, pendulous, white**; stamens numerous, spreading from a central column. Fruit ovoid to elliptic, **about 120 mm long, with hard woody shell**, densely covered with **yellowish grey hairs**; seeds numerous, embedded in a white, powdery pulp.
   The bark yields an excellent fibre, used for making floor mats and other woven articles. Young leaves are cooked as a green vegetable. Seeds edible, and a good coffee substitute when roasted. The white powdery pulp surrounding the seeds is rich in vitamin C and makes a refreshing drink when mixed with water or milk. Bark and other parts of the tree used in traditional medicine.

CAPPARACEAE (see page 22)

4 *Bachmannia woodii*   Four-finger bush
SA: 121   Autumn–Spring   Viervingerbos
Scrambling shrub or small tree; occurring in the **understorey of coastal forest**, particularly on sandstone. Leaflets **1–5, thick and leathery**; venation **prominently raised below**. Flowers in pendulous clusters on **old stems**, lilac pink with green basal portion. Fruit oval, up to 30 mm long, **pendulous** on a **jointed stalk** up to 25 mm long, yellowish when ripe.

1

C. *thyrsiflora*: flowers

1

C. *thyrsiflora*: fruit

2

S. *umbellifera*: flowers

3

A. *digitata*: tree

3

A. *digitata*: trunk

2

S. *umbellifera*: fruit

3

A. *digitata*: fruit

4

B. *woodii*: flowers

3

A. *digitata*: flower

4

B. *woodii*: fruit

473

EUPHORBIACEAE (see page 24)

1 Schinziophyton rautanenii (= *Ricinodendron rautanenii*)   **Manketti tree**
SA: 337; Z: 511   Spring   **Mankettiboom**
Large tree with a **spreading rounded crown**, sexes separate, on different plants; occurring in bushveld on Kalahari sand, sometimes in almost pure stands. Young branchlets, leaf buds and stalks with **reddish brown furry hairs. Latex present.** Leaflets **5–7, pale velvety-grey below**, with **1–3 flat, dark-coloured glands** present at junction with the leaf stalk. Flowers in slender, loose sprays, yellowish. Fruit egg-shaped, up to 35 x 25 mm, velvety; seeds with very **thick woody wall containing numerous pits.**

The dried fruit-pulp is pleasantly scented and used to make a porridge. The kernel of seeds is rich in oil and protein, tasty and very nutritious. Wood comparable with balsa wood; pale yellowish white, lightweight and strong.

MORACEAE (see page 27)

2 Myrianthus holstii   **Myrianthus**
Z: 71   Spring–Summer   **Myrianthus**
Medium-sized deciduous tree with separate male and female plants, occasionally with stilt-roots; occurring in the **understorey** of montane forest. **Watery latex present.** Leaves **very large, divided into 5–7 leaflets**, margin **finely toothed**; lower surface **velvety grey with venation very conspicuous**. Male flowers in staghorn-like heads, female ones in round heads. Fruit round, about 40 mm in diameter, fleshy, consisting of **tightly packed segments (like a small pineapple)**, bright yellow when ripe.

The seeds are embedded in a slightly acid, edible pulp. The rare butterfly *Hyalites pentapolis epidica* breeds on the tree.

STERCULIACEAE (see page 32)

3 Sterculia murex   **Lowveld chestnut**
SA: 475   Winter–Spring   **Laeveldkastaiing**
Medium-sized deciduous tree with attractive bronze spring foliage; occurring in bushveld, usually on rocky ridges. Petiole **100–230 mm long.** Leaflets **5–9**, soft-textured, **both sides hairy**, margin smooth. Flowers in axillary sprays near ends of branches, yellowish brown, usually **produced before the leaves**. Fruit comprising **1–5 carpels**, each covered with **spiny protuberances,** dehiscent along the upper surface; seeds embedded between **irritating hairs.**

The empty fruit shells can be used as ashtrays. The seeds are rich in oil, edible, and delicious when fried on coals. Green seeds are relished by baboons.

Related to *S. alexandrii*, which has smooth, leathery leaves, and is a rare species restricted to the Eastern Cape.

S. rautanenii: flowers

S. rautanenii: fruit

S. rautanenii: nuts

M. holstii: flowers

M. holstii: fruit

S. murex: flowers

S. murex: fruit

S. murex: fruit & seeds

GROUP 40
Leaves palmately compound, once-divided, opposite or whorled.
Leaflets more than 3.

VERBENACEAE (see page 33)

1 *Vitex doniana*   Black plum
Z: 984   Spring   Blinkvingerblaar
Medium-sized deciduous tree with a round canopy; occurring on the margins of
montane forest or associated riverine fringes and woodland. Leaflets **5**, relatively
large (up to 140 x 80 mm), dark green above, **thick and leathery**, essentially **hairless**. Flowers in sparse, branched, axillary heads, small, pale blue to white, 2-lipped.
Fruit fleshy, **up to 30 mm in diameter**; calyx **persistent** at base and **remaining on
tree after fruit has fallen.**
    The fruit is edible, with a taste reminiscent of prunes. The roots are used medi-
cinally. Although not very strong, the timber has some resemblance to teak and is
widely used in tropical Africa.

2 *Vitex ferruginea* subsp. *amboniensis*   Plum fingerleaf
SA: 659; Z: 983   Spring   Pruimvingerblaar
Shrub or small deciduous tree; occurring in bushveld, thicket and sand forest, usually on deep sand. Leaves aromatic; leaflets **3–7, clearly stalked**, median one narrowly ovate, obovate or elliptic, **55–145 mm long**, upper **surface smooth or
slightly hairy on veins, rusty velvety below.** Flowers in branched axillary heads,
blue to white with a yellow throat; ovary **densely hairy in upper half**; flowering
mainly late November early December. Fruit fleshy with calyx persistent at base.
    In *V. patula*, with which its distribution overlaps, the tip of the ovary is hairless
and the upper surfaces of the leaflets are rough to the touch (due to sparsely
arranged hairs). Flowering time of *V. patula* tends to peak slightly later in
December. It also resembles *V. angolensis*, from the Caprivi region and Angola,
whose upper leaf surface is hairy, and whose median leaflet is 25–50 mm long.

3 *Vitex harveyana*   Three-fingerleaf
SA: 660   Spring   Drievingerblaar
Shrub or small deciduous tree; occurring in bushveld and along streams, often in
sandy soil or among rocks. Young stems longitudinally ribbed. Leaflets usually **3**,
rarely 5, upper surface **hairless, dark glossy green**, tufts of hairs (domatia) present
in axils of veins below; margin **smooth or toothed in upper half.** Flowers in
branched axillary heads, **relatively large, 16–18 mm long**, violet-blue, 2-lipped;
ovary smooth. Fruit fleshy, black.
    The fruit is edible.

4 *Vitex mombassae*   Poora-berry
SA: 663; Z: 987   Spring–Summer   Poerabessie
Shrub or small deciduous tree; occurring in bushveld, often on rocky outcrops or
Kalahari sand. Leaves aromatic; leaflets **3–5, stalkless, both sides hairy**, terminal
one widely obovate to elliptic with **rounded tip**. Flowers in branched, axillary
heads, pale blue to white, 2-lipped; ovary with **upper half densely hairy**. Fruit
fleshy, with calyx persisting as a rim at base.
    The ripe fruit is edible, but has a very unpleasant smell.

1

V. doniana: flowers

1

V. doniana: fruit

2

V. ferruginea: flowers

2

V. ferruginea: fruit

3

V. harveyana: fruit

3

V. harveyana: flowers

4

V. mombassae: fruit

1 Vitex obovata   **Kei fingerleaf**
SA: 661   Spring   **Keivingerblaar**
Shrub or small deciduous tree; occurring in bushveld, coastal scrub and riverine bush. Leaves aromatic; leaflets **3–5**, **shortly stalked**, median one usually **20–30 mm wide** with upper surface essentially hairless in subsp. *obovata*, 35–40 mm wide and shortly hairy in subsp. *wilmsii*. Flowers in branched heads, pale blue to white, **weakly 2-lipped**. Fruit dry **(nut)**, enclosed by **persistent**, papery, bell-shaped calyx.

2 Vitex payos   **Chocolate berry**
Z: 988   Summer   **Bruinbekvingerblaar**
Small to medium-sized tree with rounded crown; occurring in woodland, often on rocky outcrops and termitaria. Leaves aromatic; leaflets **3–5**, almost stalkless, finely hairy above, lower surface **densely covered with woolly reddish hairs** and with **venation prominently raised**; margin rolled under. Flowers in branched, axillary heads, blue to white, weakly 2-lipped. Fruit **fleshy** with calyx persisting as a shallow cup or plate at base.

    The fruit is edible when very ripe, and much sought after, though it has an unpleasant scent and distinctive coffee-like flavour. The juice leaves a brown stain in the mouth. Leaves used medicinally.

3 Vitex pooara   **Waterberg poora-berry**
SA: –; Z: –   Spring   **Waterberg-poerabessie**
Shrub or small deciduous tree; occurring on rocky hillsides, usually in sandy soil. Leaves aromatic. Leaflets **3–5**, **velvety-hairy** above and below. Flowers in branched, axillary heads, **relatively small, 5–10 mm long**, blue to white, 2-lipped; ovary more or less **hairless at the apex**. Fruit **fleshy**, unpleasantly scented when ripe.

    The fruit is edible.

    Previously confused with *V. mombassae*, the apical part of whose ovary is hairy.

4 Vitex rehmannii   **Pipe-stem tree**
SA: 664   Summer   **Pypsteelboom**
Shrub or small deciduous tree with somewhat **drooping** habit; occurring in bushveld, on stony hillsides, rocky outcrops or deep sand. Leaves aromatic; leaflets **3–5**, essentially **hairless, long and narrow (less than 15 mm wide)**. Flowers in branched, axillary heads, pale blue to white, weakly 2-lipped. Fruit **dry (nut)**, enclosed by **persistent**, papery, bell-shaped calyx.

    An infusion of the leaves is widely used medicinally, and has proven antimicrobial properties. Wood yellowish grey, medium hard and termite resistant. The centres of the young stems are soft and suitable for the stems of tobacco pipes.

5 Vitex zeyheri   **Silver pipe-stem tree**
SA: 666   Summer   **Vaalpypsteelboom**
Shrub or small deciduous tree with **silver-grey foliage**; occurring in bushveld on rocky hillsides. Leaves aromatic; leaflets **3–5**, **grey-green**, upper surface densely **velvety with white hairs**. Flowers in loose, branched, axillary heads, pale mauve to white, weakly 2-lipped. Fruit **dry (nut)**, enclosed by **persistent,** papery, bell-shaped calyx.

1

V. obovata: flowers & fruit

1

V. obovata: fruit

2

V. payos: flowers

2

V. payos: fruit

3

V. pooara: flowers

3

V. pooara: fruit

4

V. rehmannii: flowers & fruit

5

V. zeyheri: flowers & fruit

GROUP 41
Leaves bipinnately compound (twice-divided). Spines present, at least some, if not all, recurved.

CAESALPINIACEAE (see page 22)

1 •*Caesalpinia decapetala*   **Mauritius thorn**
SA: – ; Z: –   Autumn–Spring   **Kraaldoring**
Robust, evergreen **scrambling shrub or climber**, usually forming dense, **impenetrable thickets**; invading forest margins and gaps, commercial plantations, roadsides and watercourses. Branchlets with numerous, **randomly scattered, straight to hooked thorns**. Leaflets up to 8 mm wide, dull dark green above, paler green below. Flowers in elongated, **erect, axillary racemes**, pale yellow. Pods woody, flattened, unsegmented, brown, hairless, **sharply pointed** at apex.
    A native of Asia; cultivated for security hedging and ornament. This is a declared weed in South Africa.

MIMOSACEAE (see page 27)

2 *Acacia ataxacantha*   **Flame thorn**
SA: 160; Z: 191   Summer   **Vlamdoring**
Very spiny scandent shrub, non-climbing shrub or medium-sized tree; occurring on rocky ridges, forest margins and in riverine bush, often forming **impenetrable thickets**. Thorns **hooked**, purple-brown, **scattered along the branches**. Leaves with 8–18 pairs of pinnae; leaflets 18–60 pairs per pinna; petiolar glands 1 or 2, **stalked**; glands present at base of at least upper pinnae pairs. Flowers in **elongated spikes** towards tips of branches, cream. Pods attractive, **flat, reddish to purplish brown**, brittle, dehiscent.
    Larval food plant for the butterfly *Charaxes ethalion ethalion*.
    Resembles *A. caffra* (p. 482), which has prickles in pairs at the base of the leaves (nodes), sessile petiolar glands and brownish pods. *A. eriocarpum*, a shrub or small tree from low-altitude bushveld and thicket in the Zambesi River Valley, also has thorns (prickles) scattered irregularly along the branches, and spicate inflorescences. It is distinguished by large (7–18 x 3–9 mm) leaflets, and thinly textured pods which are densely covered in brownish matted hairs.

3 *Acacia burkei*   **Black monkey thorn**
SA: 161; Z: 193   Spring   **Swartapiesdoring**
Medium to large tree; occurring in bushveld, often on sandy soil. Thorns **in pairs** below the nodes, hooked, **blackish**. Leaves with 3–13 pairs of pinnae; leaflets 4–19 pairs per pinna, linear-oblong, obovate to almost rounded, 1,2–20 x 0,8–13 mm; petiolar gland usually present; glands present or absent at base of at least upper pinnae pairs. Flowers in **elongated spikes**, cream **or white**. Pods **flat, reddish to purplish brown, leathery**, straight, dehiscent.
    The tree is browsed by stock and game. Bark and leaves used medicinally. Wood golden brown, very hard and difficult to work.
    Resembles *A. welwitschii* (p. 488), which has more slender thorns, hairless leaves with smaller, darker green pinnae, and hairless flower buds. Some forms difficult to distinguish from *A. nigrescens* (p. 486).
    An extremely variable species, particularly in leaflet size, shape and number.

C. decapetala: fruit

A. ataxacantha: fruit

A. ataxacantha: fruit

C. decapetala: flowers

A. ataxacantha: flowers

A. burkei: flowers

A. burkei: fruit

1 Acacia caffra   Common hook-thorn
SA: 162   Spring   Gewone haakdoring
Shrub to medium-sized deciduous tree with a somewhat rounded crown and **drooping foliage**; occurring in bushveld, grassland and coastal scrub, often on rocky ridges. Thorns in **pairs below the nodes**, hooked, rather sparse. Leaves with 8–35 pairs of pinnae, **fresh green and feathery**; leaflets 13–50 pairs per pinna; petiolar gland usually present; glands on rachis variable. Flowers in **elongated spikes**, yellowish white. Pods flat, pale brown to reddish brown, straight, dehiscent.
    The leaves and pods are browsed by stock. Various parts are used for medicinal purposes. The butterflies *Deudorix vansoni* and *D. penningtoni* breed in galls on the branches of the tree.
    Resembles *A. hereroensis* (p. 484), which has smaller, erect leaves and a more westerly distributional range; and *A. ataxacantha* (p. 480), which has the prickles scattered on the stems, and reddish to purplish brown pods.

2 Acacia erubescens   Blue thorn
SA: 164; Z: 199   Spring   Blouhaak
Many-stemmed shrub or small tree with a somewhat flattened and spreading crown; occurring in dry bushveld, often on rocky outcrops or along sandy banks of dry watercourses. Bark **rough, peeling in yellow paper layers**. Thorns **in pairs below the nodes**, hooked, **dark-tipped**. Leaves with **3–7 pairs** of pinnae, each recurved downwards; leaflets 10–30 pairs per pinna, usually 3–7,5 x 1–2 mm; petiolar gland present or absent; glands on rachis variable but **present at least at top pair of pinnae**. Flowers in **elongated spikes**, creamy white, sometimes pink. Pods flat, brown, leathery, dehiscent.
    Similar to *A. fleckii*, whose leaves have 8–20 pinnae pairs and smaller leaflets.

3 Acacia fleckii   Plate thorn
SA: 165; Z: 201   Summer   Bladdoring
Many-stemmed shrub or small tree with a somewhat rounded or flattened and spreading crown; occurring in dry bushveld, often along sandy banks of dry watercourses or on Kalahari sand. Bark **rough, peeling in yellowish or greyish papery layers**. Thorns in **pairs below the nodes**, hooked, **dark coloured**, broad based. Leaves with **8–20 pairs** of pinnae; leaflets 9–30 pairs per pinna, usually 2–5 x 0,5–1,2 mm; petiolar gland absent or present; **rachis without glands**. Flowers in **elongated spikes**, yellowish white. Pods flat, pale brown, leathery, dehiscent.
    Similar to *A. erubescens*, whose leaves have 3–7 pinnae pairs and larger leaflets.

4 Acacia galpinii   Monkey thorn
SA: 166; Z: 202   Spring   Apiesdoring
Medium to large deciduous tree with a somewhat rounded crown; occurring in bushveld, usually along riverbanks. Bark yellowish to brown. Thorns in **pairs below the nodes**, hooked to almost straight. Leaves with 7–14 pairs of pinnae; leaflets 12–40 pairs per pinna; petiolar gland usually present; glands on rachis present but variable in position. Flowers in **elongated spikes before the new leaves**, creamy white with the buds tinged reddish purple. Pods flat, reddish to purplish brown, straight, brittle, dehiscent.
    Often cultivated in gardens, particularly in areas with little frost.

A. *caffra*: flowers

A. *caffra*: fruit

A. *erubescens*: flowers

A. *erubescens*: flowers

A. *erubescens*: fruit

A. *fleckii*: flowers

A. *fleckii*: fruit

A. *galpinii*: flowers

A. *galpinii*: fruit

1 *Acacia hebeclada*   **Candle thorn**
SA: 170.1 & 170.2; Z: 206   Winter–Spring   **Trassiebos**
Low **spreading shrub** (subsp. *hebeclada*) or small tree with a flattened and somewhat spreading crown; occurring in dry grassland and bushveld. Young stems **velvety**. Thorns **paired below the nodes, straight, slightly recurved or straight with
slightly recurved tips, hairy when young**. Leaves with 5–9 pairs of pinnae,
slightly to densely hairy; leaflets 6–18 pairs per pinna; petiolar gland present or
absent; glands present at base of upper pinnae pairs. Flowers in **globose heads,
cream to white**. Pods straight with **thick, woody valves, densely greyish hairy**,
longitudinally veined, dehiscent. Pods **erect** in subspp. *hebeclada* (less than 25 mm
wide) and *chobiensis* (more than 25 mm wide), but pendulous in subsp. *tristis*.

2 *Acacia hereroensis*   **False hook-thorn**
SA: 171; Z: 207   Summer   **Valshaakdoring**
Shrub to small deciduous tree with a somewhat erect and slightly spreading crown;
occurring in dry grassland and bushveld. Thorns in **pairs just below the nodes**,
hooked. Leaves usually with 8–14 pairs of pinnae; leaflets 16–48 pairs per pinna;
petiolar gland present; glands present at base of at least upper pinnae pairs. Flowers
in **elongated spikes**, creamy white. Pods flat, reddish brown or brown, leathery,
often hairy, dehiscent.
    Distinguished from *A. caffra* (p. 482) by its smaller, more erect leaves, later flow-
ering time and more westerly distribution range.

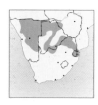

3 *Acacia luederitzii*   **False umbrella thorn**
SA: 174 & 174.1; Z: 210   Summer   **Basterhaak-en-steek**
Many-stemmed shrub or medium-sized tree with a flattened, spreading or somewhat rounded crown; occurring in bushveld, often on sandy soils. Spines **hooked,
usually intermixed with some straight ones, the latter often inflated**. Leaves
with 3–9 pairs of pinnae, sparsely or densely hairy, **margin with a fringe of hairs**,
particularly towards the tip; leaflets 10–26 pairs per pinna; petiolar gland usually
absent, glands may be present at base of the pinnae pairs. Flowers in **globose heads**,
yellowish white. Pods flat with thin and rather brittle valves, brown to reddish
brown, straight, longitudinally veined, dehiscent. Straight spines not inflated in var.
leuderitzii (found in Namibia, Botswana, Zimbabwe, Northern Cape), conspicuously so in var. *retinens* (eastern parts of South Africa, Swaziland, Mozambique).

4 *Acacia mellifera*   **Black thorn**
SA: 176 & 176.1; Z: 213   Spring   **Swarthaak**
Very thorny shrub to small tree with rounded or spreading flat crown; occurring in
bushveld and semi-desert areas, often on Kalahari sand and forming **impenetrable
thickets** in overgrazed areas. Thorns **in pairs below each node**, hooked, **blackish**.
Leaves with 2–4 pairs of pinnae; leaflets 1–3 pairs per pinna, **relatively large,
3,5–22 x 2–16 mm**; petiolar gland usually present; glands present at base of at least
upper pinnae pairs. Flowers in subglobose to elongated spikes, **cream, yellowish
white or rarely pink**. Pods flat, pale brown, papery, dehiscent. Subsp. *mellifera*
usually has 2 pinnae pairs and hairless leaflets, whereas subsp. *detinens* has 3 pinnae pairs and leaflets with a fringe of marginal hairs.
    Browsed by stock and game. The wood is attractive, hard, and used as fuel.

A. *hebeclada*: fruit

A. *hebeclada*: fruit

A. *hebeclada*: flowers

A. *hereroensis*: fruit

A. *luederitzii*: spines

A. *hereroensis*: flowers

A. *mellifera*: fruit

A. *luederitzii*: flowers

A. *luederitzii*: fruit

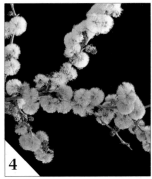

A. *mellifera*: flowers (2 forms)

1 *Acacia nigrescens*   Knob thorn
SA: 178; Z: 215   Winter–Spring   Knoppiesdoring
Medium to large tree with ascending branches and a somewhat rounded crown; occurring in bushveld, often on heavy soils. Trunk usually with **persistent thorns arising from raised knobs**, particularly in young trees. Thorns **in pairs below the nodes**, hooked. Leaves with 2–3 pairs of pinnae; leaflets **1 or 2 pairs per pinna, large (usually 10–30 x 7–30 mm)**; petiolar gland usually present; glands on rachis present at base of each pinna pair. Flowers in **elongated spikes**, yellowish white, buds often tinged reddish or purplish. Pods flat, 14–24 mm wide, dark brown to blackish, leathery, dehiscent.

The tree is browsed by stock and game, especially giraffe and elephant. Bark rich in tannin. Heartwood dark brown, tough, strong and close-grained. Larval food plant for the butterfly *Charaxes phaeus*.

Forms with small leaflets sometimes difficult to distinguish from *A. burkei* (p. 480). Resembles *A. galpinii* if flowering when leafless; flowers of the latter are usually minutely hairy and yellowish. *A. goetzei* (**1.1**), from bushveld and thicket mainly in Zimbabwe, differs from *A. nigrescens* in having more pairs (typically 8–10) of smaller (about 12 x 4 mm) leaflets, and broader (20–35 mm) pods.

2 *Acacia polyacantha*   White thorn
SA: 180; Z: 219   Spring–Summer   Witdoring
Medium to large tree with a relatively straight trunk and flattened, spreading crown; occurring in bushveld, usually on alluvial soils near rivers. Bark **yellowish to grey, peeling in corky flakes**. Thorns **in pairs below each node**, hooked. Leaves with 14–25 pairs of pinnae; leaflets 20–55 pairs per pinna; petiolar gland present; glands present at base of upper pinnae pairs. Flowers in **elongated spikes**, yellowish white. Pods flat, brown, leathery, dehiscent. All material from southern Africa belongs to subsp. *campylacantha*.

The tree yields a gum which is used as an adhesive and in confectionery. Bark used in tanning. Wood strong and termite resistant. Fresh roots have a strong odour and are used for medicinal and magical purposes. Larval food plant for the butterfly *Anthene crawshayi crawshayi*.

Distinguished from *A. caffra* (p. 482) by its larger size, relatively straight trunk, flattened, spreading crown and flaking bark. Resembles *A. sieberiana* (p. 498), which has straight spines and globose flower heads.

3 *Acacia robynsiana*   Whip-stick thorn
SA: 184   Spring   Sweepstokdoring
Shrub or small slender tree with a most **distinctive growth form, comprising a dense tangled growth of 1–2 m at the base, from which emerge one or more slender erect 8–15 m long stems that branch near the top into a few thin drooping branchlets**; occurring in arid areas, usually on rocky ridges and in ravines. Thorns absent, or paired at each node, hooked. Leaves with 1–2 pairs of pinnae; leaflets 6–13 pairs per pinna; petiolar gland present; glands present at base of each pinna pair. Flowers in elongated spikes, yellowish white (September–October, but may respond to rain). Pods flat, yellowish brown, dehiscent.

Farmers once attached their radio aerials to the long branches.

A. nigrescens: flowers

A. goetzei: flowers

A. nigrescens: fruit

A. nigrescens: stems

A. robynsiana: tree

A. polyacantha: flowers

A. polyacantha: fruit

A. robynsiana: flowers

A. robynsiana: fruit

1 *Acacia schweinfurthii*   River climbing thorn
SA: 184.1; Z: 222   Summer   Rivierrankdoring
Climber, scandent shrub or small spreading tree; occurring in riverine vegetation. Thorns **hooked, scattered along the branches and arising from dark-coloured longitudinal bands.** Leaves with 9–17 pairs of pinnae and **prickles scattered along the rachis**; petiole 26–55 mm long; leaflets 17–60 pairs per pinna; margin with **fringe of whitish hairs**; petiolar gland present, situated immediately above the base; glands present **at base** of at least upper pinnae pairs. Flowers in **globose heads in branched clusters** at ends of new shoots, yellowish white. Pods **flat with a raised area above each seed**, brownish, leathery, indehiscent or tardily dehiscent.
    Similar to *A. brevispica*, whose scattered thorns are arranged on pale ridges, with petioles shorter than 35 mm and leaflets that are usually hairy below. *A. kraussiana* (**1.1**) is a very thorny creeper from southern Mozambique and northern KwaZulu-Natal which has large, very green leaflets and is the only *Acacia* with tendrils.

2 *Acacia senegal*   Three-hook thorn
SA: 185 & 185.1; Z: 223   Winter–Spring   Driehaakdoring
Shrub or small tree with a slightly rounded or flattened and **somewhat spreading crown** (var. *rostrata*), or a **slender, upright, spindly** tree (var. *leiorhachis*); occurring in bushveld. Bark **flaking and papery, yellowish or orange-brown.** Thorns usually in **threes just below the nodes**, the central hooked downwards, the laterals curved upwards. Leaves with 3–8 pairs of pinnae; leaflets 7–24 pairs per pinna; petiolar gland usually present; glands present at base of all or at least upper pinnae pairs. Flowers in **elongated spikes**, white or cream. Pods flat, brownish, dehiscent.
    Produces a high-quality gum, which is commercially exploited in northern Africa as gum arabic. Browsed by game, especially black rhino.

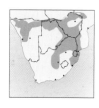

3 *Acacia tortilis*   Umbrella thorn
SA: 188 & 188.1; Z: 226   Spring–Summer   Haak-en-steek
Small or medium-sized tree with the crown **typically flattened and spreading or umbrella-shaped**; occurring in bushveld and grassland. Thorns in **pairs at nodes, short and hooked, mixed with long straight ones**, occurring in various proportions and combinations. Leaves with 2–10 pairs of pinnae; leaflets 6–22 pairs per pinna, **very small (usually 0,5–4 x 0,5–1 mm)**; petiolar gland usually present; glands on rachis present at base of lower and upper pinnae pairs. Flowers in **globose heads, white.** Pods **spirally twisted**, yellowish, hairless or nearly so in subsp. *heteracantha*, densely hairy and slightly curved in subsp. *spirocarpa*.
    The leaves and pods, which are browsed by stock and game, are very nutritious. Bark eaten by elephant, and also used medicinally.

4 *Acacia welwitschii* subsp. *delagoensis*   Delagoa thorn
SA: 163; Z: 227   Summer   Delagoa-doring
Small to medium-sized tree; occurring in bushveld. Thorns in **pairs below the nodes**, hooked. Leaves with 3–5 pairs of pinnae; leaflets **3–9 pairs per pinna**, 4–20 x 2–13 mm); petiolar gland usually present. Flowers in **elongated spikes**, yellowish white. Pods flat, reddish brown to grey, leathery, dehiscent.
    Differs from *A. burkei* in that most of its parts are hairless. *A. goetzei* (also see *A. nigrescens*) has broader pods and leaflets which are asymmetric basally.

A. schweinfurthii: fruit

A. kraussiana: fruit

A. schweinfurthii: flowers

A. senegal: flowers

A. senegal: fruit

A. tortilis: flowers

A. tortilis: fruit

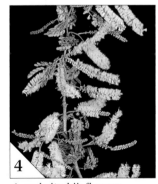

A. welwitschii: flowers

A. tortilis: tree

A. welwitschii: fruit

GROUP 42
Leaves bipinnately compound (twice-divided).
Spines present, all straight.

See also Group 41: *Acacia hebeclada* (p. 484), *A. luederitzii* (p. 484) and *A. tortilis* (p. 488); Group 43: *Albizia anthelmintica* (p. 506).

MIMOSACEAE (see page 27)

1 *Acacia abyssinica*   **Nyanga flat-top**
Z: 187   Spring   **Nyanga-platkruin**
Medium to large tree with a **conspicuous flat-topped crown**; occurring, often in groups, in high-altitude woodland, often in forest areas. Branchlets with **grey to yellowish hairs**. Spines **slender, usually white**. Leaves with 15–51 pairs of pinnae, with or without hairs; leaflets 20–40 pairs per pinna; petiolar gland present, glands absent at base of pinnae pairs. Flowers in **globose heads, white**. Pods flat, grey or brown, leathery, straight, longitudinally veined, usually hairless, dehiscent. All material from southern Africa belongs to subsp. *calophylla*.

2 *Acacia amythethophylla* (= *A. macrothyrsa*)   **Large-leaved thorn**
Z: 211   Summer   **Grootblaardoring**
Small to medium-sized tree with a somewhat rounded crown; occurring in woodland and bushveld, often in rocky areas and on termitaria. Spines **stout, dark brown**. Leaves **relatively large** with about 9–16 pairs of pinnae, hairless or with very short hairs; leaflets **12–70 pairs per pinna**; petiolar gland usually present, glands present at base of upper pinnae pairs. Flowers in **globose heads in large, much-branched, robust, terminal panicles, orange-yellow**. Pods flat, 15–25 mm wide, black, blackish purple or brown, glossy, hairless, straight, dehiscent.

   The heartwood is extremely attractive, dark reddish brown with orange-brown streaks and a beautiful grain, much valued for carvings. Flowerheads frequently galled. Several *Charaxes* butterflies breed on the tree.

3 *Acacia arenaria*   **Sand thorn**
SA: 186; Z: 190   Summer–Autumn   **Sanddoring**
Shrub to small tree, usually **multistemmed** or branching from near the ground; occurring in dry bushveld, usually on sandy soil. Spines **slender, often reddish**. Leaves with 15–36 pairs of pinnae, **sparingly to densely hairy**; leaflets 20–36 pairs per pinna; petiolar gland present or absent, glands present at base of upper pinnae pairs. Flowers in **globose heads, white** or pale pink. Pods pale to **deep reddish brown** with thin valves, long, slender, **curved**, dehiscent.

4 *Acacia davyi*   **Corky thorn**
SA: 163.1   Summer   **Kurkdoring**
Shrub or small tree with a somewhat untidy foliose crown; occurring in bushveld and grassland, often in high-rainfall mountainous regions in association with montane forest. Spines **slender, mostly ascending**. Leaves fresh green, **large and feathery with 14–27 pairs of pinnae**, with or without hairs; leaflets up to 44 pairs per pinna; petiolar gland usually present, glands present at base of one or more upper pinnae pairs. Flowers in **globose heads on the new season's growth, deep yellow to orange**. Pods pale brown, straight to slightly curved, hairless, dehiscent.

A. *abyssinica*: trees

A. *abyssinica*: flowers

A. *abyssinica*: fruit

A. *amythethophylla*: flowers

A. *amythethophylla*: fruit

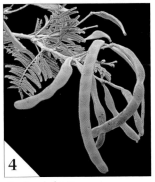

A. *davyi*: fruit

A. *arenaria*: flowers

A. *davyi*: flowers

1 Acacia erioloba (= *A. giraffae*)   **Camel thorn**
SA: 168; Z: 198   Winter–Spring   **Kameeldoring**
Medium or large tree with a **rounded or umbrella-shaped crown**; main branches often somewhat contorted in old trees; occurring in bushveld and grassland, usually on **deep sandy soils** or along watercourses in arid areas. Spines **stout, white or reddish, often swollen and fused together at the base**. Leaves with 2–5 pairs of pinnae, without hairs; leaflets 8–15 pairs per pinna, veins **prominent below**; petiolar gland **absent**, gland present at base of each pinna pair. Flowers in **globose heads** scattered along the branches, bright **golden-yellow**. Pods **velvety grey, large, thick and semi-woody, indehiscent;** seeds embedded in a spongy tissue.
    The pods are eaten by stock and game. Gum (from wounds) edible. The wood is strong and durable. Bark and pods used medicinally.
    Hybridizes with *A. haematoxylon* (p. 494).

2 Acacia exuvialis   **Flaky thorn**
SA: 164.1; Z: 200   Spring–Summer   **Skilferdoring**
Many-stemmed shrub or small slender tree; occurring in bushveld, often on gravelly soils. Bark with **smooth, shiny, yellowish or reddish areas, peeling off (at least in some forms) in thin strips or flakes**. Spines **slender** or slightly enlarged, straight or slightly deflexed. Leaves with 2–6 pairs of pinnae, usually without hairs; leaflets 3–6 pairs per pinna, **increasing in size from base to tip of pinnae,** tip more or less sharp-pointed; petiolar gland absent, glands present at base of pinnae pairs. Flowers in **globose heads** on younger shoots, **bright yellow**. Pods **flat**, pale to dark yellowish brown, **curved, slightly constricted between seeds**, hairless, dehiscent.

3 Acacia gerrardii   **Red thorn**
SA: 167; Z: 203   Spring–Summer   **Rooidoring**
Small to medium-sized tree with **ascending branches and a somewhat flattened crown**; occurring in bushveld, often in river valleys. Branchlets **densely hairy**, often with surface flaking or splitting to reveal an **orange-red colour**. Spines hairy when young. Leaves borne **on distinct cushions**, with 5–10 pairs of pinnae, **densely hairy**; leaflets 12–20 pairs per pinna; petiolar gland usually present, glands present at base of upper pinnae pairs. Flowers in **globose heads, creamy white**. Pods covered in **velvety grey hairs**, dehiscent.
    The tree is browsed by game. Bark used medicinally and to make twine.
    Resembles *A. robusta* (p. 498)*,* from which it differs in its hairy branchlets, later flowering time and much thinner velvety pods.

4 Acacia grandicornuta   **Horned thorn**
SA: 168.1; Z: 205   Summer   **Horingdoring**
Small to medium-sized tree with **ascending branches and somewhat rounded crown**; occurring in bushveld on deep brackish soils. Spines **sometimes stout and swollen**. Leaves with 2 or 3 pairs of pinnae, hairless or almost so; leaflets 8–18 pairs per pinna; petiolar gland present or absent, glands present at base of pinnae pairs. Flowers in **globose heads, white**. Pods flat, **curved, thin and brittle**, dehiscent.
    The tree is browsed by game.
    Resembles *A. robusta* (p. 498), which flowers earlier (August–October) and has broader, straight or only slightly curved pods and more slender spines.

A. *erioloba*: flowers

A. *erioloba*: fruit

A. *exuvialis*: bark

A. *exuvialis*: flowers

A. *exuvialis*: fruit

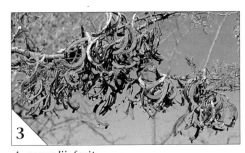

A. *gerrardii*: flowers

A. *gerrardii*: fruit

A. *grandicornuta*: flowers

A. *grandicornuta*: fruit

1 *Acacia haematoxylon*　　　　　　　　　　　　　　　**Grey camel thorn**
SA: 169　Summer　　　　　　　　　　　　　　　　　　**Vaalkameeldoring**
Shrub or small tree with somewhat drooping branches and an irregularly rounded crown with **grey foliage**; occurring in bushveld, usually **on deep Kalahari sand** between dunes or along dry watercourses. Spines **slender, not inflated**. Leaves with 6–26 pairs of pinnae, **densely covered with fine grey hairs**; leaflets **extremely small**, usually 12–24 pairs per pinna, **tightly compressed laterally**; petiolar gland usually absent, yellow glands present at base of some lower and upper pinnae pairs. Flowers in **globose heads, golden-yellow**. Pods **woody, velvety grey, 6–14 mm wide**, sometimes irregularly constricted between seeds, slightly curved, indehiscent.
　　　The species hybridizes with *A. erioloba* (p. 492).

2 *Acacia karroo*　　　　　　　　　　　　　　　　　　　**Sweet thorn**
SA: 172; Z: 208　Spring–Summer　　　　　　　　　　　　**Soetdoring**
Shrub to medium-sized tree, variable in shape but typically with a somewhat rounded crown; occurring in bushveld, grassland and associated with coastal dune forest. Spines **slender, white**, often more prominent on young trees. Leaves with 2–6 pairs of pinnae, typically hairless; leaflets 5–20 pairs per pinna; petiolar gland **usually present**, glands usually present at base of pinnae pairs. Flowers in **globose heads, bright yellow**. Pods flat, brown, smooth, **somewhat constricted** between seeds, **sickle-shaped**, dehiscent. A heterogeneous species best split into a number of distinct entities.
　　　The tree is browsed by game. Bark used in tanning, yields a strong rope, produces an edible gum and is used in traditional medicine, as is the root. Seeds roasted and used as coffee substitute. The wood is hard and heavy, but prone to borer attack. Trees often proliferate in overgrazed areas.
　　　Hybridizes with *A. tenuispina*, a multistemmed rhizomatous shrublet which forms dense thickets on black turf soils, particularly on the Springbok Flats north of Pretoria. Its shoots, leaves and pods are shiny, sticky, and covered with glands.

3 *Acacia kirkii*　　　　　　　　　　　　　　　　　　**Flood-plains thorn**
SA: 173; Z: 209　Winter–Summer　　　　　　　　　　　**Vloedvlaktedoring**
Shrub or medium-sized tree with a somewhat flattened crown; occurring in woodland, often in **seasonally flooded areas along rivers and around pans**. Bark **peeling or flaking off to reveal a greenish yellow surface**. Spines **slender**, greyish white. Leaves with 6–14 pairs of pinnae, with or without hairs; leaflets 9–18 pairs per pinna; petiolar gland usually absent, glands present at base of upper pinnae pairs. Flowers in **globose heads**, pinkish red in bud, **cream or white** when open. Pods flat, **reddish brown**, valves with a **prominent wart-like projection above each seed, prominently veined**, indehiscent. All material from southern Africa belongs to subsp. *kirkii* var. *kirkii*.
　　　The butterfly *Charaxes ethalion binghami* breeds on the tree.

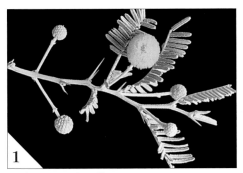

1

A. haematoxylon: flowers

1

A. haematoxylon: fruit

2

A. karroo: flowers

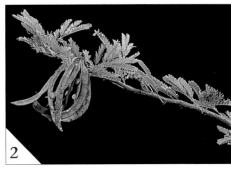

2

A. karroo: fruit

2

A. karroo: flowers

3

A. kirkii: flowers

3

A. kirkii: fruit

1 Acacia nebrownii   **Water thorn**
SA: 177.1; Z: 214   Spring   **Waterdoring**
Multistemmed shrub or small tree; occurring in hot, dry bushveld, on sandy soils and around pans or near riverbanks, often in dense stands. Branchlets **with numerous dark glands, sometimes sticky**. Spines slender, straight or slightly deflexed. Leaves with **mostly 1, rarely 2 or 3 pairs of pinnae**, hairless; leaflets 3–5 pairs per pinna, gland present at junction of the top or only pinna pair. Flowers in **globose heads, bright yellow**. Pods yellowish brown or chestnut, slightly to strongly curved, **strongly veined with numerous, scattered glands**, hairless, dehiscent.

The plant is related to a group of shrubby, straight-spined acacias characterized by glandular twigs and pods: *A. swazica* (from Swaziland and adjacent parts of Mpumalanga and Maputaland) is distinguished by the prominent venation on the lower surface of the leaflets; *A. permixta* (southwestern Zimbabwe and Northern Province) has spreading hairs on the young branchlets and leaf-rachides; *A. borleae* (Limpopo Valley, Lebombo Mountains and adjacent areas) has numerous sessile glands on the surface and margin of the leaflets, with pods curved and constricted between the seeds; *A. tenuispina* (Springbok Flats and southeastern Botswana) is a rhizomatous shrublet from black turf soils.

2 Acacia nilotica subsp. *kraussiana*   **Scented thorn**
SA: 179; Z: 216   Spring–Autumn   **Lekkerruikpeul**
Small to medium-sized tree with a somewhat flattened or rounded crown; occurring in bushveld. Spines slender, **usually deflexed backward**. Leaves with 5–11 pairs of pinnae, hairless or sparsely covered by hairs; leaflets 12–36 pairs per pinna; 1 or 2 petiolar glands usually present, glands present at base of upper pinnae pairs. Flowers in **globose heads, golden-yellow**. Pods **flat, black, smooth, deeply constricted between each seed**, the position of which is marked by a distinct **raised bump** on the valves, straight or slightly curved, **sweet-scented** when crushed, **indehiscent**, breaking up transversely between seeds after falling.

The wood is used for fencing posts and for firewood. Pods eaten by game and stock, but are toxic to goats. Bark exudes an edible gum, and is used medicinally.

Resembles *A. karroo* (p. 494), from which it can be distinguished by its small leaves and leaflets, deflexed spines, paler longitudinally fissured bark and distinct pods.

3 Acacia rehmanniana   **Silky thorn**
SA: 182: Z: 220   Summer   **Sydoring**
Shrub or small tree with a somewhat flattened spreading crown; occurring in bushveld and wooded grassland, often near rivers or on termitaria. Young stems with **bark often tinged orange-red**. Branchlets densely covered with **golden hairs that later become grey-white**. Spines hairy when young. Leaves with **15–40 pairs** of pinnae, **densely hairy, very shortly stalked (1–5 mm)**; leaflets 20–40 pairs per pinna; petiolar gland present, reddish brown, other glands variable. Flowers in **globose heads**, clustered into **terminal racemes, white or cream**. Pods flat, edges slightly raised, pale brown, straight, more or less hairless, dehiscent.

The bark is used for rope.

May be confused with *A. sieberiana* (p. 498), which has a more pronounced flattened crown, flaking bark, fewer pinnae, flowerheads that are not clustered into terminal racemes, and more robust pods.

A. *nebrownii*: flowers

A. *nilotica*: tree

A. *nebrownii*: fruit

A. *nilotica*: fruit

A. *rehmanniana*: fruit

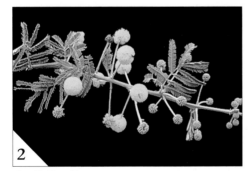

A. *nilotica*: flowers

A. *rehmanniana*: flowers

497

1 *Acacia robusta* Ankle thorn; Brack thorn
SA: 183 & 183.1; Z: 221 Winter–Spring Enkeldoring; Brakdoring
Robust small to medium-sized tree with sturdy ascending branches and an irregularly rounded or spreading crown; occurring in bushveld and grassland. Spines white, usually shorter than 12 mm. Leaves usually on distinct '**cushions**' and with 3–7 pairs of pinnae, hairless to densely hairy; leaflets 10–20 pairs per pinna; glands present at base of upper or lower pinnae pairs. Flowers in **globose heads, creamy white**, appearing **with new leaves in early spring**. Pods flat, dark brown to reddish brown, becoming grey with age, slightly curved or straight, **rather woody, without hairs, dehiscent**. Leaf rachis essentially hairless; pods more than 17 mm wide and straight in subsp. *robusta*; rachis sparsely to densely hairy, with pods less than 17 mm wide and usually slightly curved, in subsp. *clavigera*.

2 *Acacia sieberiana* Paperbark thorn
SA: 187; Z: 224 Spring Papierbasdoring
Medium to large tree with spreading branches and an **umbrella-shaped or flattened crown**; occurring in bushveld and grassland, often in deep soil and along rivers. Bark yellowish or greyish brown, **usually flaking in papery pieces**. Branchlets densely hairy. Spines white. Leaves with 8–28 pairs of pinnae, **densely hairy** to hairless; leaflets 12–40 pairs per pinna; petiolar gland present, glands present at base of upper pinnae pairs. Flowers in **globose heads, creamy white**. Pods yellowish to brown, **thick, woody, straight or slightly curved**, with or without hairs, tardily dehiscent, often only after falling to the ground. All material from southern Africa belongs to var. *woodii*.

The wood is strong but not very attractive, and prone to borer attack. Pods eaten by stock and game. A popular garden subject.

See *A. rehmanniana* for differences.

3 *Acacia xanthophloea* Fever tree
SA: 189; Z: 228 Spring Koorsboom
Medium to large tree with ascending branches and **a sparsely foliated**, rounded or flattened and somewhat spreading crown; occurring in bushveld, restricted to riverbanks and low-lying swampy areas, often gregarious. Bark **smooth, greenish yellow, powdery, green underneath**. Spines slender, white. Leaves with 3–6 pairs of pinnae, usually hairless; leaflets 8–20 pairs per pinna; petiolar gland usually present, glands present at base of upper pinnae pairs. Flowers in **globose heads, bright yellow**. Pods **flat with thin valves**, yellowish brown to brown, slightly constricted between seeds, hairless, more or less straight, indehiscent, breaking transversely into segments after being shed.

The tree is browsed by game. Wood provides a general purpose timber. Bark used medicinally. A decorative tree for gardens, though frost-sensitive.

A. robusta: flowers

A. robusta: fruit

A. sieberiana: flowers

A. sieberiana: fruit

A. sieberiana: bark

A. xanthophloea: tree

A. xanthophloea: bark

A. xanthophloea: flowers

A. xanthophloea: fruit

1 **Dichrostachys cinerea**   Sickle bush
SA: 190 & 190.1; Z: 230   Spring–Summer   Sekelbos
Shrub or small tree with a rather untidy crown, often **flat-topped**; occurring in bushveld, often invasive and thicket-forming, particularly in overgrazed areas. Spines **not paired**, similar in colour to the branchlets, **often leaf-bearing**. Leaves with 4–19 pairs of pinnae; leaflets up to 41 pairs per pinna; petiolar gland present, gland present at base of at least upper and basal pinna pairs. Flowers in an **elongated pendulous spike**, the **lower (basal) part with mauve or pink sterile flowers**, the **upper (apical) part with yellow fertile flowers**. Pods **curly and twisted**, densely clustered in bunches, indehiscent. Subsp. *nyassana* has at least some leaflets more than 2 mm wide, whereas all are less than 2 mm wide in subsp. *africana*. The former tends to grow larger and has less hairy leaves and leaflets.

Stock and game eat the pods. Various parts of the tree are used medicinally. Bark yields a strong fibre. The wood is hard and durable, used for fence poles and much sought after as firewood.

2 **Faidherbia albida** (= *Acacia albida*)   Ana tree
SA: 159; Z: 189   Winter–Spring   Anaboom
Medium to large tree with grey-green foliage and a wide, rounded crown in mature plants, slender and more upright in young ones; occurring in bushveld, usually on alluvial floodplains, riverbanks and along pans, swamps or dry watercourses with high water table. Branchlets **greenish white**, often drooping and somewhat zigzag. Spines **whitish, never swollen**. Leaves with 3–10 pairs of pinnae; leaflets 6–23 pairs per pinna; **petiolar gland absent**, conspicuous gland present at base of each pinna pair. Flowers in **elongated spikes**, pale cream. Pods **bright orange- to reddish brown**, flat, thick, hairless, conspicuously **curled into a circular coil or variously twisted**, indehiscent.

The pods are eaten by stock and game. Bark used medicinally.

3 **•Prosopis glandulosa** var. *torreyana*   Glandular mesquite
SA: X503   Winter–Spring   Suidwesdoring
Multistemmed shrub or small tree, resembling a species of *Acacia*; invading riverbanks, riverbeds, drainage lines in semi-desert and desert areas. Branches **reddish brown**, armed with **paired straight spines at the nodes**. Leaves with **1 pair of pinnae**, dark green; leaflets 7–18 pairs per pinna, **widely spaced**, 10–50 x 20–40 mm, **hairless**. Flowers in many-flowered **axillary spikes, yellow**. Pods **woody, slender, cylindrical, 100–250 mm long**, more or less **straight, slightly constricted** between the seeds.

A native of North and Central America; cultivated for fodder (pods), shade and firewood. Bees produce a good honey from the floral nectar. This is a declared invader in South Africa.

P. velutina is an invader of similar habitats in the same region as *P. glandulosa* var. *torreyana* and hybridizes with the latter, which makes it difficult to classify some of the plants reliably. All parts are (at least initially) covered with short, velvety hairs. *P. pubescens* has 5–8 pairs of leaflets per pinna, and peculiar, tightly spiralled pods, 30–50 mm long.

D. *cinerea*: flowers

D. *cinerea*: fruit

D. *cinerea*: flowers

F. *albida*: flowers

F. *albida*: fruit

P. *glandulosa*: flowers

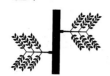

GROUP 43
Leaves bipinnately compound (twice-divided). Spines absent.

See also Group 11: *Acacia melanoxylon* (p. 230); Group 36: *Grevillea robusta* (p. 438).

1 BIGNONIACEAE (see page 21)
•*Jacaranda mimosifolia*   Jacaranda
SA: X971; Z: 1030   Spring   Jakaranda
Deciduous or semi-deciduous tree, with a rounded, spreading crown and yellowish autumn colours; spectacular when in full flower; invading bushveld, wooded ravines and riverbanks. Leaves **opposite, finely divided and fern-like**, with up to 20 pairs of pinnae, 200–400 mm long; leaflets dark green, **sharply pointed**. Flowers in loose, terminal panicles, usually before the appearance of the new leaves, mauve-blue, lilac or rarely white, bell-shaped, very showy. Fruit a **woody capsule, broadly oval**, up to 70 mm in diameter, **flat with a wavy edge**, splitting open to release the winged seed.
    A native of South America; cultivated for ornament (particularly as a street tree), shade and timber.

2 CAESALPINIACEAE (see page 22)
Burkea africana   Wild seringa
SA: 197; Z: 243   Spring   Wildesering
Medium-sized deciduous tree with a somewhat **flattened and spreading crown**; occurring in bushveld, often on **deep sandy soil**. Tips of branchlets with **velvety, reddish brown hairs**. Leaves clustered at tips of shoots, with 2 or 3 pairs of pinnae; leaflets **5–9 per pinna**. Flowers produced in drooping spikes with the new leaves. Pods **flat, elliptic**, wing-like, brown and woody, **single-seeded**, indehiscent.
    The dried and crushed bark is used as a fish poison. The wood is pale brownish to reddish brown, hard, heavy and tough, but prone to borer attack. Bark and root used in traditional medicine and for tanning. A red dye is obtained from the root. Several *Charaxes*, *Deudorix* and *Aphnaeus* butterflies breed on the tree. Caterpillars of the moth *Cirina forda* may occur in large numbers on the tree, often causing complete defoliation. Considered a delicacy, they are collected in large numbers, roasted and dried. The plants are extremely difficult to cultivate.

3 *Erythrophleum africanum*   Ordeal tree
SA: 194; Z: 241   Spring   Oordeelboom
Medium to large tree; occurring in hot, dry bushveld and riverine thicket, often on deep Kalahari sand. Leaves usually with 3 or 4 pinnae pairs; leaflets alternate, 8–15 per pinna, tip **broadly tapering to rounded; rachis with small gland present at junction of each pinna pair**. Flowers in dense spikes, greenish yellow or cream. Pods flat, brown, straight, leathery, **dehiscing simultaneously along both margins**; seeds 2–5.
    The bark, roots and leaves are poisonous. Bark exudes an amber-coloured gum comparable to gum arabic. The wood is reddish brown, heavy, hard, durable, and suitable as a general purpose timber.

J. mimosifolia: tree

J. mimosifolia: flowers

J. mimosifolia: fruit

B. africana: fruit

E. africanum: fruit

B. africana: flowers

1 *Erythrophleum lasianthum* Swazi ordeal tree
SA: 196   Spring Swazi-oordeelboom
Medium to large tree; occurring in hot, dry bushveld and sand forest, usually on deep sand. Leaves with usually 2–4 pinnae pairs, hairless; leaflets alternate, 9–13 per pinna, **up to 40 x 20 mm**, tip **narrowly tapering**, margin **wavy**; rachis with **small gland at junction of each pinna pair**. Flowers in dense spikes, greenish yellow or cream; stamen filaments **with woolly hairs**. Pods flat, brown, straight, thinly woody, dehiscing simultaneously along both margins; seeds 5–11.

The leaves and bark are poisonous; the latter is used for medicinal and magical purposes. Bark used as fish poison and the leaves to protect grain against insects.

E. suaveolens has larger leaflets (up to 50 x 25 mm) and hairless stamen filaments.

2 *Peltophorum africanum* Weeping wattle
SA: 215; Z: 280   Spring–Summer Huilboom
Small to medium-sized tree with a dense crown; occurring in bushveld, often on sandy soils. Young shoots densely covered with **fine, rusty brown hairs**. Leaves **feathery** with 4–9 pairs of pinnae; leaflets usually 8–22 pairs per pinna, **densely covered with hairs below**, sometimes also above. Flowers in **erect terminal racemes**; petals yellow, **crinkled**. Pods flat, winged, with **fine velvety hairs**.

The species is browsed by game. Bark and root used for medicinal purposes. Wood suitable for carving. Several butterflies of the genera *Charaxes* and *Axiocerses* breed on the tree. A decorative garden subject. Sap-sucking insects, known as spittle bugs, occur in large numbers on the branches during certain times of the year. They excrete almost pure water, which froths around the insect and drips constantly to the ground, thus causing the tree to 'rain' or 'weep'.

MIMOSACEAE (see page 27)

3 •*Acacia dealbata* Silver wattle
SA: X490; Z: 195   Winter Silwerwattel
Small to medium-sized evergreen tree, with an often **silvery grey** crown; invading grassland, roadsides and watercourses. Leaves with usually 10–20 pairs of pinnae, 25–100 mm long, **silvery grey** or light green; leaflets 17–50 pairs per pinna, 2–6 x 0,4–0,7 mm, **hairless**, sometimes hairy below; **gland present at junction of each pinnae pair**. Flowers in **globose heads**, borne in **axillary racemes or panicles**, **bright yellow**. Pods straight, greyish or purplish brown.

A native of Australia; cultivated for shelter, shade and firewood. This is a declared invader in South Africa.

4 •*Acacia mearnsii* Black wattle
SA: X494; Z: 212   Spring Swartwattel
Small to medium-sized evergreen tree with a **dark green** crown; invading grassland, forest gaps, roadsides and watercourses. Leaves with usually 8–21 pairs of pinnae, 40–120 mm long, **dark olive-green**; leaflets 15–70 pairs per pinna, 1,5–4 x 0,5–0,75 mm, hairless, sometimes appressed-hairy below; **gland present on rachis at and between the junctions of pinnae pairs**. Flowers in **globose heads**, in **terminal panicles**, **pale yellow or cream**. Pods straight, finely haired, dark brown.

A native of Australia; cultivated for tanbark, shelter, shade and firewood. Widely used in hut-building. This is a declared invader in South Africa.

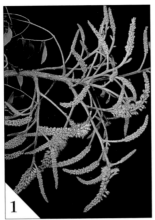

E. lasianthum: flowers

P. africanum: flowers

E. lasianthum: fruit

P. africanum: fruit

A. dealbata: flowers

A. mearnsii: flowers

1 *Albizia adianthifolia*   **Flat-crown**
SA: 148: Z: 172 Spring   **Platkroon**
Medium to large tree with a **flattened and spreading** crown; occurring in woodland, usually associated with coastal and montane forest. Bark usually **roughish**. Branchlets densely covered with **brown or greyish hairs.** Leaves with 4–8 pairs of pinnae; leaflets 6–15 pairs per pinna, usually **rectangular** in shape, **not 'heeled'**, **7–20 x 4–8 mm**, dark green above, yellowish hairy or rusty velvety below; petiolar gland present a short distance above the pulvinus; rachis with gland usually present at junction of top pinna pair. Flowers in globose heads, **whitish with staminal tube often tinged with pink, red or green**. Pods flat, **90–190 x 20–35 mm**, pale brown, hairy, **swollen above each seed**, dehiscent.

The leaves are browsed by elephant; the pods and seeds much favoured by blue duiker. Wood suitable as a general purpose timber. Bark and root used for medicinal purposes. Bark poisonous. Various *Charaxes* butterflies breed on the tree.

Resembles *A. gummifera*, a smooth-barked tree associated with montane forest in the Eastern Highlands of Zimbabwe. Its leaflets are dark glossy green, hairless, and usually with a distinct 'heel' at the base on the proximal side. Also similar to *A. schimperiana* from the Eastern Highlands of Zimbabwe, a species whose leaflets are less than 20 mm long and not as rectangular, and whose flowers are pure white.

A. procera, a native of India, has become naturalized in parts of KwaZulu-Natal and Zimbabwe. It has young branchlets which are hairless, larger (15–60 x 8–21 mm) leaflets and wider (30–45 mm) pods.

2 *Albizia amara*   **Bitter false-thorn**
SA: 149; Z: 173 Spring   **Bittervalsdoring**
Small to medium-sized tree with a rounded or somewhat flattened crown; occurring in bushveld, often on sandy soils. Young growth **golden velvety**. Leaves **feathery** with **12–44 pairs** of pinnae; leaflets **20–45 pairs** per pinna, 2–4 x 0,5–1 mm, **symmetrical**, not sickle-shaped, tip **bluntly pointed**, lateral veins **indistinct below**; petiolar gland present a short distance above the pulvinus. Flowers in globose heads, whitish or tinged with pink, buds golden-hairy. Pods flat, thin-valved, purplish when young, becoming brown to dark brown, **swollen above each seed**, apparently indehiscent. All material from southern Africa belongs to subsp. *sericocephala*.

Root used as soap substitute, the fruit in traditional medicine.

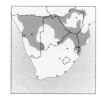

3 *Albizia anthelmintica*   **Worm-bark false-thorn**
SA: 150; Z: 174 Winter–Spring   **Wurmbasvalsdoring**
Shrub or small tree with a somewhat rounded crown, often multistemmed or branching near ground level; occurring in dry bushveld and sand forest. Young branchlets often forming **abbreviated spine-tipped side shoots**. Leaves with 2–4 pairs of pinnae; leaflets usually **2–4 pairs** per pinna, **ovate or almost circular**, usually 8–25 x 4–18 mm; petiolar gland present; rachis and rachillae usually **projecting at the ends as a short rigid deflexed hook**; stipels usually **present at base of pinnae pairs**. Flowers in large globose heads, white, usually produced before the new leaves. Pods flat, thin-valved, pale brown, **swollen above each seed**, dehiscent.

The leaves are browsed by goats and game. Bark and roots effective against intestinal parasites, especially tapeworm. Bark also used in basket-weaving.

Specimens from Namibia are often single-stemmed with a spreading crown.

A. adianthifolia: flowers

A. adianthifolia: fruit

A. anthelmintica: flowers

A. adianthifolia: tree

A. amara: flowers

A. amara: fruit

A. anthelmintica: flowers

A. anthelmintica: flowers

A. anthelmintica: fruit

1 *Albizia antunesiana* Purple-leaved false-thorn
SA: 151; Z: 175   Autumn–Spring   Persblaarvalsdoring
Small to medium-sized tree with a somewhat spreading crown; occurring in mixed woodland. Young growth **often purple**. Leaves with 1–4 pairs of pinnae, hairless; leaflets 3–8 pairs per pinna, **ovate with rounded tip**, usually **23–50 x 8–28 mm**, **blue-green above, paler below**; petiolar gland present. Flowers in large globose heads, creamy white. Pods flat, swollen above each seed, dehiscent.
   The heartwood is dark brown, hard, heavy, and makes very attractive furniture. Sawdust irritating to the nose and throat. Roots used medicinally.
   Resembles *A. glaberrima*, found in low-altitude mopane woodland in eastern Zimbabwe and in Mozambique, whose leaflets are bright green above and below. May be mistaken for *Burkea africana* (p. 502), but it lacks the brown velvety tips to the latter's branches. The blue-green foliage is reminiscent of *Ekebergia benguelensis* (Group 38, p. 466), which has once-pinnate leaves.

2 *Albizia forbesii* Broad-pod false-thorn
SA: 154; Z: 177   Summer   Breëpeulvalsdoring
Medium to large tree with a rounded, spreading crown and somewhat drooping branches; occurring in woodland and sand forest, often along stream and river banks. Young growth usually with **silver-grey, velvety hairs**. Leaves with 2–7 pairs of pinnae; leaflets 6–16 pairs per pinna, **oblong and closely ranked**, terminal pair **obovate, 3,5–8 x 1,5–4 mm**, hairless above, lateral veins usually **more or less raised below**; petiolar gland present. Flowers in small globose heads, creamy white, buds golden hairy. Pods flat, **prominently veined transversely**, indehiscent.

3 *Albizia harveyi* Common false-thorn
SA: 155; Z: 180   Spring   Bleekblaarboom
Small to medium-sized tree with a rather slender rounded crown; occurring in bushveld. Young growth **brown or golden velvety**. Leaves **feathery** with **6–22 pairs** of pinnae, often with golden spreading hairs; leaflets **12–28 pairs** per pinna, 2–6 x 0,5–1,5 mm, **asymmetric, slightly sickle-shaped**, tip **sharply pointed**, lower surface pale green with lateral veins **raised**. Flowers in globose heads, creamy white, buds golden-hairy. Pods flat, thin-valved, **swollen above each seed**, dehiscent.
   Compare *A. amara* (p. 506). *A. brevifolia* **(3.1)** usually has 6–10 pinnae pairs that are hairless or with appressed grey hairs, and leaflets that are not sickle-shaped.

4 *Albizia petersiana* subsp. *evansii* Many-stemmed false-thorn
SA: 153; Z: 181   Spring   Meerstamvalsdoring
Shrub or medium-sized deciduous tree, usually **branching freely near the base** with many branches ascending at a sharp angle; occurring in bushveld, often on sandy soils. Young branchlets densely hairy. Leaves usually with 2–4 pairs of pinnae; leaflets **2–5 pairs** per pinna, **obovate to heart-shaped**, usually 8–22 x 5–13 mm, lower surface pale green, **sparingly to densely hairy**; petiolar gland present. Flowers in rather **loose heads, whitish, usually tinged with red**. Pods flat, valves semi-woody, brown to deep reddish purple, dehiscent.
   The tree is browsed by game. Bark and root used medicinally.
   The leaves resemble those of *A. anthelmintica* (p. 506), but lack the hook at the tips of the rachis and rachillae, and the leaflets are more or less densely hairy below.

1

A. antunesiana: flowers

1

A. antunesiana: fruit

2

A. forbesii: flowers

2

A. forbesii: fruit

3

A. harveyi: flowers

3

A. harveyi: fruit

3.1

A. brevifolia: flowers

4

A. petersiana: flowers

GROUP 43

1 Albizia tanganyicensis
SA: 157; Z: 184   Spring

Paperbark false-thorn
Papierbasvalsdoring

Small to medium-sized tree with a somewhat sparse, rounded or flattened crown; occurring in bushveld, usually on rocky outcrops and in groups. Bark very distinctive, **smooth, creamy white, peeling off in large reddish or yellowish white, papery pieces.** Leaves with usually 3–6 pairs of pinnae; leaflets 4–13 pairs per pinna, usually **13–45 x 5–25 mm**, tip **tapering**, base **asymmetric**; petiolar gland present; rachis with glands present at junction of the top or top 1–5 leaflet pairs. Flowers in large globose heads, creamy white, usually produced before the new leaves. Pods flat, dark brown, dehiscent. All material from southern Africa belongs to subsp. *tanganyicensis*.

Sawdust from the wood, which is of no commercial value, irritates the nose and throat. Young pods, and to a lesser extent mature ones, are toxic and the cause of albiziosis in cattle; outbreaks usually occurring in late winter or early spring, when the pods are blown from the trees by high winds.

2 Albizia versicolor
SA: 158; Z: 185   Spring

Large-leaved false-thorn
Grootblaarvalsdoring

Medium to large tree with a somewhat spreading rounded crown; occurring in mixed woodland. Leaves with 1–3 pairs of pinnae; leaflets usually **2–5 pairs** per pinna, **elliptic to ovate, large (15–67 x 15–45 mm)**, hairy above, **rusty velvety below**; petiolar gland present a short distance above the pulvinus; rachis with glands usually present at junction of top or upper two pinnae pairs. Flowers in globose heads, creamy white. Pods flat, **glossy, brown to reddish brown**, more or less hairless, dehiscent.

The wood resembles that of *Pterocarpus angolensis* (Group 38, p. 462) and is exploited as a general purpose timber; sawdust causes sneezing. Leaves browsed by game. Root and bark used as a soap substitute. Bark employed in traditional medicine. Pods and seeds, particularly unripe ones, are highly toxic to stock. Seeds eaten by brown-headed parrots.

3 Amblygonocarpus andongensis
SA: 190.2; Z: 231   Spring

Scotsman's rattle
Skotseratel

Medium to large tree; **hairless throughout**; occurring in dry deciduous woodland, often on deep Kalahari sand or associated with mopane. Leaves with 2–5 pairs of pinnae; leaflets 5–9 on each side of the rachilla, **elliptic to obovate-elliptic, with indented tips**, 12–25 x 7–15 mm. Flowers in axillary racemes, 60–120 mm long, yellowish white. Pods very distinctive, **woody, straight, glossy brown, more or less square in cross section**, 80–170 x 18–30 mm.

Larval food plant for the butterflies *Charaxes guderiana guderiana* and *C. fulgurata*. Pods used as rattles.

A. tanganyicensis: flowers

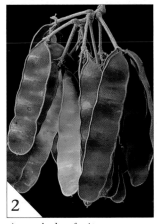

A. tanganyicensis: fruit

A. tanganyicensis: tree

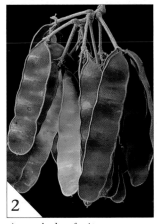

A. versicolor: fruit

A. andongensis: fruit

A. versicolor: flowers

A. andongensis: flowers

1 *Elephantorrhiza burkei*

Sumach bean

SA: 193; Z: 235   Spring

Basboontjie

Multistemmed deciduous shrub or small tree with **feathery foliage**; occurring in bushveld, usually on rocky hillsides. Leaves **blue-green, hairless**, with **4–8 pairs** of pinnae; leaflets about 12–23 pairs per pinna, midrib **central or almost so**, base **almost symmetric**. Flowers in axillary **spikes with the new leaves**, pale yellow, becoming darker with age; stalks with **minute reddish glands at base**. Pods flat, dark brown to reddish brown, dehiscing in a distinctive manner with the **valves peeling away from the margins, which remain as long threads on the tree**.

The roots are used medicinally.

E. goetzei has leaves with 14–41 pairs of pinnae, leaflets with strongly asymmetric bases and flowers that develop before the new leaves. *E. suffruticosa* has leaflets with the midrib running along the extreme inner edge rather than centrally.

2 *Entada abyssinica*

Tree entada

Z: 238   Spring

Boom-entada

Small to medium-sized tree with a somewhat rounded crown; occurring in woodland, often in mountainous regions. Leaves **feathery** with 2–20 pairs of pinnae; leaflets 22–55 pairs per pinna, 4–12 x 1–3 mm; petiole base **swollen with two small depressions above**. Flowers in **long fluffy spikes**, yellowish white. Pods **large (150–390 x 60–100 mm), flat, breaking transversely into 1-seeded segments** that fall away from the hard, woody rims, which remain on the tree for some time.

Larval food plant for some *Charaxes* and *Anthene* butterflies.

May be mistaken for *Acacia caffra* (Group 41, p. 482) from a distance, but unarmed.

3 *Newtonia buchananii*

Forest newtonia

Z: 232   Winter–Spring

Woud-newtonia

Large to very large tree with **tall upright trunk**, often buttressed at the base, and with **fine feathery foliage**; occurring in evergreen forest, often along streams and rivers. Leaves with **12–23 pairs** of pinnae, each bearing **38–67 pairs** of leaflets; rachis with raised gland present between each pair of pinnae. Flowers in axillary **spikes**, yellowish white. Pods flat, hairless, **dehiscing along one of the margins and opening out flat**; seeds flat, up to 75 mm long, surrounded by a reddish brown papery wing.

Larval food plant for the butterfly *Charaxes ethalion ethalion*.

4 *Newtonia hildebrandtii*

Lebombo wattle

SA: 191; Z: 233   Spring

Lebombowattel

Large tree with a rounded crown; occurring in low-altitude woodland and sand forest, usually on deep sandy soils. Leaves with **4–7 pairs** of pinnae; leaflets **6–19 pairs** per pinna; gland present on rachis at junction of each pinna pair. Flowers in axillary **spikes**, pale yellowish white. Pods flat, deep wine-red when young, becoming brown with age, hairless, **dehiscing along one of the margins and opening out flat**; seed flat, up to 60 mm long, surrounded by a **reddish brown papery wing**.

Var. *hildebrandtii* (confined to Maputaland) has more or less hairless leaflets, whereas those of var. *pubescence* are densely hairy.

The timber is dark brown and hard. Various parts of the tree are used for medicinal and magical purposes.

E. burkei: fruit   *E. abyssinica*: fruit   *N. hildebrandtii*: fruit & seeds

E. burkei: flowers   *N. buchananii*: flowers

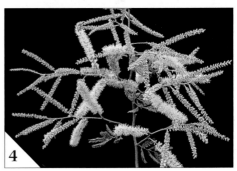

N. buchananii: fruit   *N. hildebrandtii*: flowers

1 *Xylia torreana*   **Sand ash**
SA: 192; Z: 234   Spring   **Sandessenhout**
Small to medium-sized tree, occurring in hot dry woodland and sand forest, often on deep sand. Young growth with **dense brownish hairs**. Leaves with **one pair of pinnae** and a **conspicuous gland just below their junction**; glands often present on rachis at junction of the leaflets; leaflets **hairy below** when mature. Flowers with stalks up to 15 mm long, borne in globose heads, yellow. Pods **large, flat, woody and broadly sickle-shaped**, covered with **brownish velvety hairs**; the seeds are without an aril.
   Pods resemble those of *Afzelia quanzensis* (Group 33, p. 420), but are hairy and the seeds lack a bright red aril. The young growth of *X. mendoncae*, from *Brachystegia* woodland in coastal Mozambique, is almost completely without hairs, and the flowers have no stalks.

MELIACEAE (see page 26)

2 **•*Melia azedarach***   **Seringa**
SA: X604; Z: 430   Spring   **Maksering**
Medium to large deciduous tree, with a rounded, spreading crown and yellowish autumn colours; invading bushveld, roadsides, disturbed places, riverbanks and urban open space. Leaves **clustered towards ends of branches**, somewhat drooping, **up to 400 mm long**, with **3-pairs** of pinnae, glossy dark green, **unpleasantly scented** when crushed; leaflets 5 per pinna, lanceolate, up to 80 mm long; margin **coarsely and irregularly toothed**. Flowers in showy axillary panicles, often before the new leaves are fully expanded, petals **pale lilac**, staminal tube **dark purple**. Fruit a drupe, globose, about 15 mm in diameter, yellow, with a single ribbed stone.
   A native of Asia; cultivated for ornament and shade. The fruit is extremely toxic, causing death among humans, poultry and stock. Seeds (stones) are cleaned, sometimes stained, and strung as beads to make attractive necklaces. A watery extract of the leaf, sprayed on kitchen-gardens and orchard crops, is an effective deterrent for various leaf-eating insects, notably grasshoppers. Various parts used medicinally.

MORINGACEAE (see page 27)
3 *Moringa ovalifolia*   **Phantom tree**
SA: 137   Spring–Summer   **Sprokiesboom**
Small tree with a distinctive, squat, **swollen stem** and branches; occurring in arid areas, usually on rocky hillsides, rarely on sandy flats. Bark **smooth, pale grey to whitish**. Leaves **crowded near ends of branches**, hairless. Flowers in large, many-flowered panicles. Fruit **pod-like** and **pendulous, 3-sided, up to 400 mm long**, splitting into 3 valves.
   The leaves and fruit are browsed by elephant, giraffe and springbok. Bark, wood and root eaten by small stock and porcupine. Root edible, but sour-tasting. Wood light, spongy and very brittle.

X. torreana: flowers

X. torreana: fruit

M. azedarach: flowers & fruit

M. azedarach: flowers

M. ovalifolia: tree

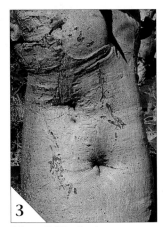

M. ovalifolia: bark

M. ovalifolia: flowers

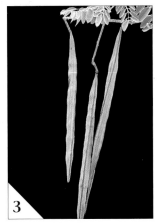

M. ovalifolia: fruit

Numbers in square brackets refer to the line drawings and photographs on pages 519 and 521. Synonyms commonly encountered in botanical works are supplied for some terms, and are given in round brackets at the end of the definition.

afromontane forest see **forest**.

alien a plant introduced from elsewhere and now more or less naturalized (= exotic). Compare **native**, **naturalized**.

alternate applied to leaves placed singly at different heights on a stem [9]. Compare **opposite**, **whorled**.

anastomosing rejoining after branching, and forming an intertwining network, as in some leaf veins.

anther the part of the stamen containing the pollen; usually borne on a slender stalk (= filament) [39].

anthesis the opening of the flower bud.

apex, **apical** the tip of a plant organ (plural: **apices**).

appressed lying close to or pressed flat against a surface or structure, as hairs are on certain leaves.

arcuate curved into an arch, like a bow.

aril a fleshy outer covering or appendage that encloses the whole or part of the seed, and usually develops from its stalk; often brightly coloured.

armed bearing thorns, spines, barbs or prickles.

axil the upper angle between the leaf and the stem on which it is carried; **axillary**: in, or arising from, an axil [1].

axis the main stem of a plant, or inflorescence, on which the plant's other organs are borne.

bacterial nodule a swelling or knob containing bacteria [60].

berry a many-seeded fleshy fruit with a soft outer portion, with the seeds embedded in the fleshy or pulpy tissue (e.g. the tomato). Compare **drupe**.

bifoliolate, 2-foliolate with two leaflets [3].

bilobed divided into two lobes [2].

bipinnate, bipinnately compound when the first divisions (pinnae or leaflets) of a leaf are further divided, i.e. with leaflets (pinnules) borne on branches of the rachis [8] (= twice pinnate). Compare **pinnate**.

blade the flat, expanded part of a leaf [1] (= lamina).

bloom 1. the flower, or process of flowering. 2. a thin layer of white waxy powder on some leaves and fruit.

bole the main stem or trunk of a tree (= trunk).

bract a usually small, leaf-like structure, in the axil from which arises a flower or a branch of an inflorescence; **bracteate** having bracts.

branchlet a twig or small branch.

bushveld used in the present work in a general sense to include any vegetation type in which both trees and grasses are conspicuous (= savanna, savannah). Compare **forest, miombo woodland, woodland, thicket**.

calyx collective term for all the sepals of a flower; the outer whorl of most flowers; usually green [39].

capitate head-like, or in a head-shaped cluster, as in the flowers of some species of *Acacia*.

capsule a dry fruit produced by an ovary comprising two or more united carpels and usually opening by slits or pores. Compare **follicle, pod**.

carpel one of the leaf-derived, usually ovule-bearing units of a pistil or ovary; sometimes free, but usually united to form a compound pistil or ovary. The number of carpels in a compound pistil is generally difficult to establish, but often equals the number of chambers or stigmatic lobes per pistil.

chamber the cavity of an ovary which contains the ovules [39] (= locule).

cladode, cladophyll a leaf-like structure formed by a modified stem, as in the genus *Opuntia* (prickly pears).

clasping used for leaf bases that partly or completely enclose the stem.

coastal forest see **forest**.

compound consisting of several parts; e.g. a compound leaf has two or more separate leaflets [3–8].

cone a rounded or elongate structure comprising, on a central axis, many overlapping bracts which bear pollen, spores or seeds; characteristic of many gymnosperms.

congested crowded.

coppice, coppicing vegetative shoots at the base of the stem; sprouts arising from a stump.

cordate heart-shaped, with the notch at the base [31].

corolla collective term for the petals of a flower; usually coloured [39].

crenate with rounded teeth along the margin [38]; in this book often simply described as toothed (= scalloped).

crisped curled, wavy or crinkled.

cucullate hooded or hood-shaped.

cyathium a flower-like inflorescence characteristic of the genus *Euphorbia*.

deciduous shedding leaves at the end of the growing season. Compare **evergreen**.

decoction liquid potion prepared from the extraction of the water-soluble substances of a medicinal plant by boiling in water.

dehiscent opening, as in anthers or fruit.

dichotomous branched or forked into two more or less equal divisions.

disc (disk) 1. the fleshy outgrowth developed from the receptacle at the base of the ovary or from the stamens surrounding the ovary, usually in the form of a ring or cushion, or of separate gland-like parts; often secreting nectar. 2. the central part of the head-like inflorescence of the Asteraceae.

domatia small structures in the forks of the midrib and the main lateral veins. They take two main forms: either conspicuous tufts of hairs, or small pits. These structures are formed by the plant to act as shelter for mites, who in return help clean the leaf surface and protect it against damage by plant-eating mites [57, 58] (singular: **domatium**).

drip-tip a long, gradually tapering tip of a leaf [18] (= attenuate).

drooping bending or hanging downwards, but not quite pendulous. Compare **pendulous**.

drupe a fleshy, indehiscent fruit with one or more seeds, each of which is surrounded by a hard stony layer formed by the inner part of the ovary wall (e.g. stone fruit such as peaches, olives). Compare **berry**.

ellipsoid a solid body elliptic in long section and circular in cross section.

elliptic oval and narrowed to rounded ends, widest at or about the middle [26].

entire see **smooth**.

epiphyte a plant that grows on another plant but is not parasitic on it; usually with its roots not in the ground. Compare **parasite**.

even-pinnate See **paripinnate**.

evergreen retaining green leaves throughout the year, even during winter. Compare **deciduous**.

exserted projecting beyond the surrounding parts, as with stamens protruding from a corolla; not included.

extrafloral nectaries nectar-secreting glands located outside the flower, as in leaves or bracts [55, 56].

felted closely matted with intertwined hairs.

filament see **flower**.

flower the structure concerned with sexual reproduction in flowering plants [39]. Generally interpreted as a short length of stem with modified leaves attached to it. Four sets of modified leaves may be present. The outermost are the **sepals**, usually green, leaf-like, in the bud stage enclosing and protecting the other flower parts, and collectively known as the **calyx**. Within the sepals are the **petals**, usually conspicuous and brightly coloured, collectively known as the **corolla**. Within the petals are the **stamens** which are the male reproductive organs, each comprising a **filament** (stalk) which bears an **anther**, in which pollen grains are produced. In the centre of the flower is the female reproductive organ, the **pistil(s)**. Each pistil consists of an **ovary** (derived from modified leaves called **carpels**) at its base, a slender, ± elongated projection (more than one in some species) called a **style**, and an often enlarged tip called a **stigma** which acts as the receptive surface for pollen grains. The ovary contains a varying number of **ovules**, which after fertilization develop into **seeds**. The male and female parts may be in the same flower (**bisexual**) or in separate flowers (**unisexual**). Compare **perianth**.

foliolate pertaining to or having leaflets; usually used in compounds, such as bifoliolate or trifoliolate [3, 4].

follicle a dry fruit which is derived from a single carpel and which splits open along one side only. Compare **capsule**, **pod**.

forest a tree-dominated vegetation type with a continuous canopy cover of mostly evergreen trees, a multi-layered understorey, and almost no ground layer. **Coastal forest** is found at low altitude, under humid, subtropical conditions along the east coast of southern Africa. **(Afro)montane forest** is generally found inland, at higher altitude under more temperate conditions. **Sand forest** is a rare and distinctive forest type with a unique species composition, comprising mainly deciduous to semi-deciduous trees and shrubs; in our region sand forest is restricted to ancient coastal dunes in the Maputaland Centre.

free not joined to each other or to any other organ (e.g. petals to petals, or stamens to petals). Compare **united**.

fruit the ripened ovary (pistil) and its attached parts; the seed-containing structure. Compare **seed**.

fused see **united**.

fynbos A vegetation type characterized by evergreen shrublets with hard, needle-shaped leaves. It is exceptionally rich in plant species diversity, especially among the Restionaceae, Ericaceae, Proteaceae and the bulbous plants. Closely associated with quartzitic and sandstone substrates of (mainly) the Western Cape, with large areas subjected to winter rains and summer drought (Mediterranean climate).

gall a localized abnormal growth on a plant induced by a fungus, insect or other foreign agent.

glabrous smooth; hairless.

gland an appendage, protuberance, or other structure which secretes sticky, oily or sugary liquid; usually found on the surface of, or within, an organ (e.g. leaf, stem or flower) [55, 56].

gland-dotted with small translucent or coloured dots when viewed against the light, usually descriptive of leaves with secretory cavities in its tissues [59] (= pellucid gland-dotted; glandular-punctate). Compare **secretory cavities**.

glandular hairs terminated by minute glands, often sticky to the touch.

globose spherical, rounded.

glutinous gluey; sticky; gummy; covered with a sticky exudate.

gregarious growing in groups or colonies.

heart-shaped see **cordate**.

heartwood the innermost, generally harder and somewhat darker wood of a woody stem; nonliving (= duramen). Compare **sapwood**.

hemiparasite a parasitic plant which contains chlorophyll and is thus partly self-sustaining, as in the Santalaceae. Compare **epiphyte**, **parasite**.

imparipinnate a pinnately compound leaf with an odd number of leaflets, and with a single terminal leaflet [6] (= odd-pinnate). Compare **paripinnate**, **bipinnate**.

indehiscent remaining closed; not opening when ripe or mature. Compare **dehiscent.**

indigenous see **native.**

inflorescence any arrangement of more than one flower; the flowering portion of a plant, e.g. head, spike, panicle, cyathium, raceme.

interpetiolar between the leaf stalks, as an interpetiolar stipule that extends from the base of one leaf stalk across the stem to the base of the stalk of the opposite leaf (e.g. a feature of many Rubiaceae) [50, 51]. Compare **intrapetiolar.**

intersecondary veins the veins in a leaf blade that interconnect the main lateral veins.

intramarginal vein a vein of constant thickness (but much thinner than the midrib) just inside the margin of the leaf blade, running from the base to the apex. Lateral veins run from the midrib to the intramarginal vein [1].

intrapetiolar between the petiole and the stem, as an intrapetiolar stipule that extends across the axil of the leaf (e.g. in members of the Melianthaceae). Compare **interpetiolar.**

involucral bracts one or more whorls of bracts or leafy structures (often sepal-like) that surround the base of an umbel or flower head, notably in the Asteraceae (= phyllaries).

irregular flowers that can be divided into two equal halves (mirror images) along only one plane, i.e. corolla lobes unequal [44] (= zygomorphic). Compare **regular.**

karroid pertaining to the vegetation of the Karoo in South Africa; an essentially treeless semi-desert vegetation type dominated mainly by dwarf xerophytic woody shrublets and succulents.

keel (petals) the two loosely united lower petals of the flowers of the Fabaceae [40] (= carina). Compare **standard, wing.**

lamina See **blade.**

lanceolate with the shape of a lance or spear; much longer than broad, tapering to the tip from a broad base, with the widest point below the middle [29] (= lance-shaped).

lateral borne on or at the side.

latex in this book used rather loosely for any copious liquid exudate, whether watery (clear), milky or any other colour [53, 54].

lax loose; with parts open and spreading, not compact.

leaf an aerial outgrowth from a stem, numbers of which make up the foliage of a plant. Characterized by an axillary bud. A leaf typically consists of a stalk (petiole) and a flattened blade (lamina), and is the principal food-manufacturing (photosynthetic) organ of a green plant [1].

leaflet the individual division of a compound leaf, which is usually leaf-like. It has a stalk of its own, but lacks an axillary bud in the axil with the rachis [3–7] (= pinna, pinnule).

lenticel a slightly raised, somewhat corky, often lens-shaped area on the surface of a young stem. Lenticels facilitate gaseous exchange between plant tissues and the atmosphere [45].

linear resembling a line; long and narrow, with more or less par-

allel sides [24]. Compare **oblong.**

lobe a part or a segment of an organ (e.g. leaf, petal) deeply divided from the rest of the organ but not separated; segments are usually rounded.

locule see **chamber.**

mangrove generally applied to several groups of highly specialized tropical trees that grow in the mud and silt of tidally flooded ground along coastal banks, especially in tidal estuaries and lagoons. Many are characterized by aerial 'breathing roots'.

-merous suffix meaning parts of a set. A 5-merous corolla would have five petals.

mesic moist, especially in reference to habitats or environments.

midrib the central or largest vein or rib of a leaf or other organ.

miombo woodland an attractive, very distinct kind of woodland dominated by species of *Brachystegia*, *Julbernardia* and *Isoberlinia*; common on acid, usually shallow soils over large parts of Zimbabwe, Mozambique and further northwards. Compare **bushveld, woodland.**

montane forest see **forest.**

mucro a short, sharp, abrupt point, usually at the tip of a leaf or other organ [23].

native a plant occurring naturally in an area and not introduced from elsewhere (= indigenous). Compare **alien, naturalized.**

naturalized a plant introduced from a foreign area (an alien) which has become established and is reproducing successfully in the new area. Compare **alien, native.**

nectar the sugary liquid produced by the flowers or other floral parts on which insects and birds feed; **nectary** any structure which produces nectar, such as glands or special hairs.

notched with a small V-shaped cut or indentation at the apex; usually referring to leaves [22] (= emarginate).

nut a dry, single-seeded and indehiscent fruit with a hard outer covering, e.g. acorns, walnuts; **nutlet** a small nut.

obconic(al) conical or cone-shaped, with the attachment at the narrow end.

ob- a prefix meaning opposite, inverse, or against.

obcordate inversely cordate (heart-shaped), with the attachment at the narrow end; sometimes refers to any leaf with a deeply notched apex.

oblanceolate inversely lanceolate (lance-shaped), with the attachment at the narrow end [32].

oblong an elongated but relatively wide shape, two to four times longer than broad with nearly parallel sides [25] (= strap-shaped). Compare **linear.**

obovate inversely egg-shaped; with the broadest end towards the tip [34]. Compare **ovate.**

obtriangular inversely triangular; with the broadest end towards the tip.

odd-pinnate See **imparipinnate.**

opposite applied to two organs (e.g. leaves) growing at the same

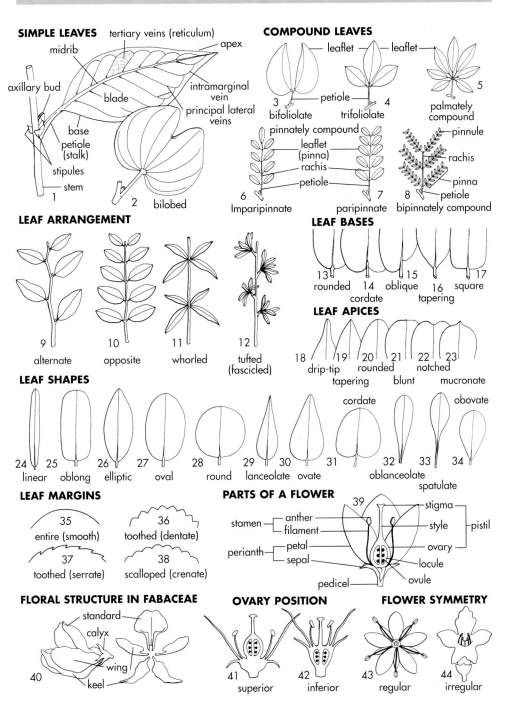

SIMPLE LEAVES

tertiary veins (reticulum)
midrib
apex
axillary bud
intramarginal vein
blade
principal lateral veins
base
petiole (stalk)
stipules
stem
1
2 bilobed

COMPOUND LEAVES

leaflet — leaflet
3 bifoliolate
petiole
4 trifoliolate
5 palmately compound

pinnately compound
leaflet (pinna)
rachis
petiole
6 Imparipinnate
7 paripinnate
pinnule
rachis
pinna
petiole
8 bipinnately compound

LEAF ARRANGEMENT

9 alternate
10 opposite
11 whorled
12 tufted (fascicled)

LEAF BASES

13 rounded
14 cordate
15 oblique
16 tapering
17 square

LEAF APICES

18 drip-tip
19 tapering
20 rounded
21 blunt
22 notched
23 mucronate

LEAF SHAPES

24 linear
25 oblong
26 elliptic
27 oval
28 round
29 lanceolate
30 ovate
31
32 cordate
oblanceolate
33
spatulate
34 obovate

LEAF MARGINS

35 entire (smooth)
36 toothed (dentate)
37 toothed (serrate)
38 scalloped (crenate)

PARTS OF A FLOWER

39
stigma
stamen — anther
filament
style — pistil
perianth — petal
sepal
ovary
locule
pedicel
ovule

FLORAL STRUCTURE IN FABACEAE

standard
calyx
40
wing
keel

OVARY POSITION

41 superior
42 inferior

FLOWER SYMMETRY

43 regular
44 irregular

519

level on opposite sides of the stem [10], or otherwise opposite each other, or when the one organ arises at the base of another (e.g. a stamen opposite a petal or sepal). Compare **alternate**, **whorl**.

oval broadly elliptic, the width more than half the length [27].

ovary the hollow basal portion of a pistil which contains the ovules within one or more chambers, and which produces the fruit if pollination and fertilization take place [39]. A **superior ovary** is borne on top of the receptacle and, as the sepals, petals and stamens are attached below its base, is visible when the flower is viewed from above [41]. Fruits from superior ovaries are not tipped by the remains of the perianth and stamens (e.g. avocados, oranges, grapes). An **inferior ovary** is completely enclosed by the receptacle and is usually visible as a swelling of the flower stalk below the attachment of the sepals, petals and stamens [42]. Fruits from inferior ovaries are often tipped by the remains of the perianth, or by a scar if it is deciduous (e.g. apples, guavas, pomegranates).

ovate egg-shaped in outline and attached at the broad end (applied to flat surfaces) [30]. Compare **ovoid**.

ovoid egg-shaped (applied to three-dimensional structures). Compare **ovate**.

ovule the minute roundish structure(s) within the chamber of the ovary. The ovule contains the egg cell and, after fertilization, develops into the seed [39].

palmate with three or more parts arising from a single point and radiating outward like the fingers of an open hand; as in palmately compound leaves [5] or palmate venation [2].

panicle an inflorescence with an axis that can continue to grow and does not end in a flower (i.e. the axis is indeterminate). It has many branches, each of which bears two or more flowers; often loosely applied to any complex, branched inflorescence.

parasite a plant which obtains its food from another living plant (the host) to which it is attached. Compare **hemiparasite**.

paripinnate a pinnately compound leaf with an even number of leaflets and terminated by a pair of leaflets [7] (even-pinnate). Compare **imparipinnate, bipinnate**.

pedicel the stalk of an individual flower [39].

peltate shield-shaped; a flat structure borne on a stalk attached to the lower surface (like the handle of an umbrella) rather than to the base or margin; usually used to describe leaves.

pendulous hanging downward (= pendant). Compare **drooping**.

perennial living for three or more years.

perianth the outer, sterile whorls of a flower, made up of sepals or petals or both [39].

persistent remaining attached and not falling off.

petal see **flower**.

petiolate leaves possessing a stalk (petiole).

petiole the leaf stalk [1].

petiolule the stalk of a leaflet of a compound leaf.

phyllode an expanded, leaflike petiole lacking a true leaf blade. Used to describe the 'leaves' of some Australian acacias.

pinna 1. the primary division of a pinnate leaf [3–7] (=leaflet). 2. the first series of branches within a bipinnate leaf which bears the pinnules [8].

pinnate, pinnately compound applied to a compound leaf whose leaflets are arranged in two rows along an extension (the rachis) of the leaf stalk [6, 7]. Compare **imparipinnate, paripinnate, bipinnate**.

pioneer species refers to the first plant species which colonize bare or disturbed areas; and the first tree species which start the orderly change in composition of vegetation (succession) towards the establishment of a climax forest.

plane with a flat surface.

pod a general term applied to any dry and many-seeded dehiscent fruit, formed from one unit or carpel. In this book the word is usually applied to a legume which is the product of a single pistil (carpel) and which usually splits open along one or both its two opposite sutures or seams (a characteristic of many Mimosaceae, Caesalpiniaceae and Fabaceae). Compare **capsule**, **follicle**.

prickle a small, sharp-pointed outgrowth of the epidermis or bark.

pseudo-aril a false aril. In this book used for the fleshy, often brightly coloured, covering of the stone in the Burseraceae, which develops from the fruit wall and not, as in a typical aril, the stalk of a seed.

raceme an inflorescence in which the flowers are borne consecutively along a single (unbranched) axis, the lowest on the axis being the oldest. Each flower has a stalk. Compare **spike**.

rachis (rhachis) 1. the axis of a compound leaf [6–8]; 2. the axis of an inflorescence.

rank a vertical row; leaves arranged in two ranks are in two vertical rows when viewed from the tip of the shoot.

receptacle the uppermost part of the flower stalk, on which the floral parts are borne.

regular radially symmetrical, as in a flower that can be divided into two identical halves (mirror images) along more than one plane (i.e. the corolla lobes are equal) [43] (= actinomorphic). Compare **irregular**.

sand forest see **forest**.

sapwood the outer, newer, usually softer and somewhat lighter wood of a woody stem; the wood that is alive and actively transporting water (= alburnum). Compare **heartwood**.

savanna(h) see **bushveld**.

scalloped applied to a leaf margin notched with rounded or broad and blunt teeth or projections [38] (= crenate, crenulate). Compare **toothed**.

scandent climbing.

secretory cavities roundish cavities within the leaf blade that

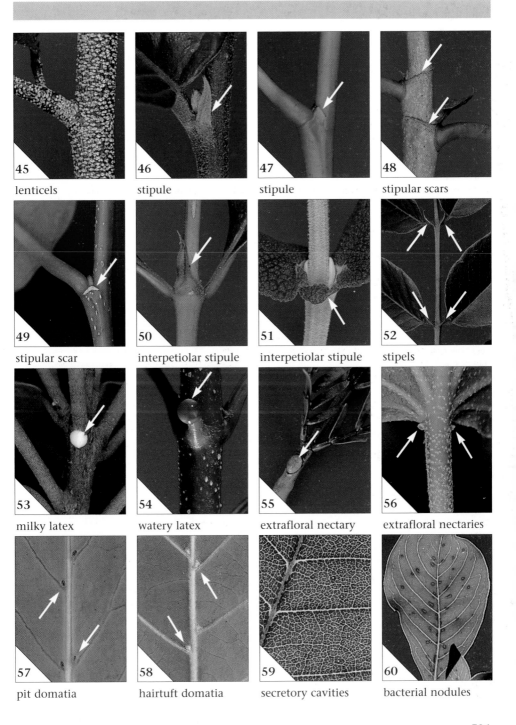

45 lenticels	**46** stipule	**47** stipule	**48** stipular scars
49 stipular scar	**50** interpetiolar stipule	**51** interpetiolar stipule	**52** stipels
53 milky latex	**54** watery latex	**55** extrafloral nectary	**56** extrafloral nectaries
57 pit domatia	**58** hairtuft domatia	**59** secretory cavities	**60** bacterial nodules

contain secretions such as resin, mucilage and oil [59]. Compare **gland-dotted**.

seed the ripened ovule containing an embryo. Compare **fruit**.

sepal see **flower**.

sessile attached directly, without a supporting stalk, as in a leaf without a petiole (= stalkless).

shrub a perennial woody plant with, usually, two or more stems arising from or near the ground; differs from a tree in that it is smaller and does not possess a trunk or bole. Compare **tree**.

simple leaf with only a single blade [1, 2]; the opposite of a compound leaf.

sinuate usually used to describe structures, such as leaf margins, with a number of regular curved indentations or small lobes. Compare **wavy** (= **undulate**).

smooth with an even and continuous margin; lacking teeth, lobes or indentations [35] (= entire). Compare **toothed**.

spatulate like a spatula in shape, with a rounded blade gradually tapering to the base [33].

spike an inflorescence with stalkless flowers arranged along an elongated, unbranched axis. Compare **raceme**.

spine a hard, straight and sharply pointed structure, often long and narrow. Usually a modified leaf or stipule. Compare **thorn**.

spinescent ending in a spine or in a very sharp hard point, as in a spinescent shoot (= thorn).

spray a slender shoot or branch together with its leaves, flowers, or fruit.

spreading extending outwards in all directions.

stamen one of the male reproductive organs of the flower, usually made up of a narrow stalk (filament), and an anther in which the pollen is produced [39].

standard the large upper petal of a flower in the Fabaceae [40] (= banner, vexillium). Compare **keel**, **wing**.

stem the main axis of the plant, or a branch of the main axis, that produces leaves and buds at the nodes. Usually above ground, but sometimes modified and underground (e.g. rhizomes).

sterile lacking functional sex organs; a sterile flower produces neither pollen nor functional ovules.

stigma the part of the pistil on which the pollen grains germinate, normally situated at the top of the style and covered with a sticky secretion [39].

stipel the equivalent of stipules but found on compound leaves near the point of attachment of leaflet stalks [52] (plural: stipellae).

stipule small scale- or leaf-like appendages at the base of the leaf stalk in some plants; generally found in pairs on each side of the stem at the junction of the leaf stalk and the stem. Stipules often fall off early in life, leaving scars on the stem. They are best seen on young, actively growing shoots [1, 46–51].

stone the hard, seed-containing pit of a drupe (e.g. the so-called 'seed' of a peach, cherry or olive). Compare **drupe**.

style a more or less elongated projection of the ovary which bears the stigma [39].

subtend to be below and close to, as a bract may subtend a flower.

taxon any taxonomic unit into which living organisms are classified, such as family, genus, species, or subspecies (plural: taxa).

taxonomy, taxonomic the science of the classification of organisms. More or less synonymous with the term systematics.

tendril a slender, usually coiling part of the leaf or stem that serves to support the stem; a climbing organ.

thicket a vegetation type characterized by thickly growing (almost impenetrable) deciduous or evergreen shrubs, occasionally with trees rising above, and lacking a conspicuous grassy ground layer; sometimes very thorny, or with many succulents. Common in hot, arid, river valleys in subtropical regions along the east coast. Compare **bushveld**.

thorn 1. a curved spine. 2. a sharply pointed branch. Often used synonymously with spine. Compare **spine**.

throat the opening of a tubular or funnel-shaped corolla.

toothed used in a generalized sense in this book to refer to leaf margins which are toothed in various ways, including dentate (with coarse sharp teeth perpendicular to the margin), serrate (with sharp, forward-pointing teeth) and crenate (with shallow, rounded teeth) [36–38]. Compare **smooth**.

trifoliolate, 3-foliolate referring to a compound leaf with three leaflets [4].

tree a perennial woody plant with a single (usually) main stem and a distinct upper crown. Compare **shrub**.

trunk the main stem of a tree below the branches (= bole).

umbel an umbrella-shaped inflorescence in which the stalks of the flowers all grow from the top of the main stem; the umbels themselves may be similarly arranged, in an inflorescence that is called a compound umbel.

unarmed lacking spines, thorns or prickles.

undulate with a wavy margin (= wavy).

united joined together (= fused). Compare **free**.

wavy a term used to describe the margins of leaves which are wavy (not flat), but not indented as in sinuate margins (= undulate). Compare **sinuate**.

whorl 1. the arrangement of three or more leaves or flowers at the same node of the axis, forming an encircling ring [11] (= verticil). Compare **alternate**, **opposite**. 2. more than two of any other organs (e.g. petals, stamens) arising at the same level.

wing 1. any thin, flat extension of an organ, as in winged fruit or seed. 2. each of the two side (lateral) petals of a Fabaceae flower [40] (= ala, alae). Compare **keel**, **standard**.

woodland an open, park-like vegetation type with scattered trees at least 8 m tall, a canopy cover of 40 per cent or more, and a grass-dominated ground layer. Compare **bushveld**.

woolly with long, soft, rather tangled hairs.

SELECTED REFERENCES AND CONTACT ADDRESSES

Coates Palgrave, K. 1984. *Trees of Southern Africa*, 2nd edition, 4th impression. C. Struik, Cape Town.

Coates Palgrave, M. 1996. *Key to the trees of Zimbabwe*. Modern Press, Gweru.

Davis, S.D., Heywood, V.H. & Hamilton, A.C. (Eds) 1994. *Centres of plant diversity; a guide and strategy for their conservation*. IUCN Publications Unit, Cambridge.

Drummond, R.B. 1981. *Common trees of the central watershed woodlands of Zimbabwe*. The Department of Natural Resources, Harare.

Goode, D. 1989. *Cycads of Africa*. Struik, Cape Town.

Henderson, L. 1995. *Plant invaders of southern Africa*. Plant Protection Research Institute, Pretoria.

Low, A.B. & Rebelo, A.G. (Eds) 1996. *Vegetation of South Africa, Lesotho and Swaziland* [with accompanied vegetation map]. Department of Environment Affairs & Tourism, Pretoria.

Palmer, E. & Pitman, N. 1972 & 1973. *Trees of southern Africa*. 3 Vols. A.A. Balkema, Cape Town.

Pooley, E. 1994. *The complete field guide to trees of Natal, Zululand & Transkei*. 2nd impression. Natal Flora Publications Trust, Durban.

Steyn, M. 1994. *S.A. Acacias: Identification guide*. Published by the author, Pietersburg.

Steyn, M. 1996. *SA Ficus: Identification guide for wild figs in S.A.* Published by the author, Pietersburg.

Van Wyk, B-E. & Smith, G. 1996. *Guide to the aloes of South Africa*. Briza Publications, Pretoria.

Van Wyk, P. 1996. *Field guide to the trees of the Kruger National Park*, 3rd ed., 2nd impression. Struik Publishers, Cape Town.

Von Breitenbach, F. 1989. *National list of introduced trees*. 2nd ed. Dendrological Foundation, Pretoria.

Von Breitenbach, F. 1995. *National list of indigenous trees*, 3rd ed. Dendrological Foundation, Pretoria.

West, O. 1992. *Aloes of Zimbabwe*, 2nd ed. Longman Zimbabwe, Harare.

White, F. 1983 *The vegetation of Africa*. UNESCO, Paris.

HERBARIA

Only a few of southern Africa's larger herbaria are listed in the next column; there are many other, smaller ones, one or more of which could well be more suitable, or more conveniently situated, for your purposes. A letter or telephone call to your regional herbarium will elicit the information you require.

BOTSWANA: The Herbarium, Department of Biological Sciences, University of Botswana, Private Bag X0267, Gaborone 0267.

LESOTHO: The Herbarium, Biology Department, National University of Lesotho, P.O. Box Roma 180.

MOZAMBIQUE: Herbário, Departamento de Botânica, Universidade Eduardo Mondlane, Caixa Postal 257, Maputo. • LMA Herbário, Departamento de Botânica, Instituto Naçional de Investigão Agronómica, F.P.L.M. Avenue-Mavalane, Caixa Postal 3658, Maputo 8.

NAMIBIA: The Herbarium, National Botanical Research Institute, Private Bag 13184, Windhoek.

SOUTH AFRICA: Bews Herbarium, University of Natal, P.O. Box 375, Pietermaritzburg 3200. • Bolus Herbarium, University of Cape Town, Private Bag, Rondebosch 7700. • C.E. Moss Herbarium, Department of Botany, University of the Witwatersrand, Private Bag 3, Wits 2050. • Compton Herbarium, Kirstenbosch, Private Bag X7, Claremont 7735. • Alexander McGregor Memorial Museum, P.O. Box 316, Kimberley 8300. • National Museum, P.O. Box 266, Bloemfontein 9300. • H.G.W.J. Schweickerdt Herbarium, Department of Botany, University of Pretoria, Pretoria 0002. • National Herbarium, Private Bag X101, Pretoria 0001. • Selmar Schonland Herbarium, P.O. Box 101, Grahamstown 6140. • Natal Herbarium, Botanic Gardens Road, Durban 4000.

SWAZILAND: Swaziland National Herbarium, Malkerns Research Station, P.O. Box 4, Malkerns.

ZIMBABWE: National Herbarium & Botanic Garden, P.O. Box CY550, Causeway, Harare.

SOCIETIES

Botanical Society of South Africa, Kirstenbosch, Claremont 7735, South Africa.
Dendrological Society, P.O. Box 104, Pretoria 0001, South Africa.
The Tree Society of Southern Africa, P.O. Box 70720, Bryanston 2021, South Africa.
Tree Society of Zimbabwe, P.O. Box 2128, Harare, Zimbabwe.

ACKNOWLEDGMENTS

We thank all those who made it possible for this book to be produced. For assistance with plant identification, we are indebted to the staff of the National Herbarium in Pretoria, Natal Herbarium in Durban, Stellenbosch Herbarium in Stellenbosch (now incorporated in the Compton Herbarium, Cape Town) and the National Herbarium in Harare, in particular to Bob Drummond and Thom Müller. Grateful thanks are extended to Martie Dednam, of the H.G.W.J. Schweickerdt Herbarium, University of Pretoria, who very effectively handled the administration of herbarium specimens and assisted with the preparation of the manuscript. We gratefully acknowledge the help of Juta and the late Fried von Breitenbach, who kindly allowed us access to the tree distribution maps of the Dendrological Society, Pretoria. We are also greatly indebted to the many people and institutions who have allowed us to visit their gardens, farms and nurseries to gather material and to take photographs, especially the Bvumba Botanic Garden, Kirstenbosch National Botanical Garden, KwaZulu-Natal Department of Nature Conservation, Natal Parks Board, National Parks Board of South Africa, Pretoria National Botanical Garden and the Lowveld National Botanical Garden. A special word of thanks to Anne Stadler, who prepared the line drawings for the glossary.

Our thanks and appreciation to many other individuals, for their help with research, accommodation, the provision of photographs and for inspiration and support, in particular Tony and Maggie Abbott, Win Andrews, Robert Archer, Mrs. Augustyn (Namibia), John and Debbie Binda, Daan Botha, Diane Bridson, Grant Burton, Bill Duthie, Gene Engelbrecht, Mike and André English, Neil Fairall, Ian Garland, Jonathan Gibson, Manie Grobler, Hazel Hayter, Meg Coates Palgrave, Gert Pienaar, Schalk and Joan du Plessis, Dave Hartung, Norbert Hahn, Humphrey and Margaret Hayes, Geoff Hemm, Lesley Henderson, Jeremy Hollmann, Marie Holstenson, Johan Hurter, Sandy Innes, David Johnson, Marie Jordaan, Pieter Jordaan, Giskin Kesterton, Johan Kluge, Edward Mabogo, Anthony Maddock, Deon Marais, Wayne Matthews, Dr. E.A. Mbise, Wally Menne, Hans Meyer, Roly and Paddy Morrison, Tina Mössmer, Steven Mostert, E.S. Murimba, Susan Myburgh, Geoff Nichols, Hugh Nicholson, Jan and Annetta Oelofse, Jo Onderstall, Willie Oosthuizen, Elsa Pooley, Mmabatho Phuduhudu, Elizabeth Retief, Veronica Roodt, Colin Saunders, Brian Schrire, Gideon Smith, Tim and Janet Snow, John Sullivan, Harold and Marita Thornhill, Manie and Wilma Uys, Ernst van Jaarsveld, Dave Varty, Irmgard von Teichman, Piet Vorster, Jill Wiley, Rosemary Williams, Lloyd Wilmot, Tommy and Molly Wrath, as well as various staff members at the National Parks Board of S.A., including former colleagues of one of the authors (PvW).

A publication of this kind entails extensive travelling and the consumption of vast quantities of photographic film and other materials, and the costs are enormous. We did, however, receive generous field-work support from three principal sponsors, namely Total SA (Pty) Ltd (fuel), Mazda Wildlife Fund (transport) and Agfa (films), and we take this opportunity to express our gratitude to them. Sincere thanks are also extended to individuals within these concerns, among them Barbara Garner (Agfa); Peter Frost and members of the Advisory Board (Mazda Wildlife Fund); and Andries van der Walt and Karen du Toit (Total SA). For financial and other assistance we are greatly indebted to the following companies, institutions and their representatives: APBCO Insurance Brokers, Pretoria (Kobus du Plessis); Letaba Tyres, Tzaneen (Dirk Robinson); Persetel (Pty) Ltd (Roux Marnitz, Louis Harding), VDO Architects, Pretoria (Willie Oosthuizen); Department of Botany, Rand Afrikaans University (Ben-Erik van Wyk); University of Pretoria (Heleen Visser, Willem van Biljon) and especially its Department of Botany (Albert Eicker, Elsa van Wyk).

We would like to express our appreciation to the staff of Struik Publishers, and specifically to Pippa Parker, Janice Evans, Dean Pollard (the designer) and Peter Joyce, who with great skill, patience and courtesy, edited this book.

Finally we would like to thank our respective families for their patience and forbearance during the long hours of field work and writing involved in the preparation of the book. To our wives, Elsa and Emmarentia, we owe a tremendous debt. Without their understanding, encouragement, help and support it would not have been possible to complete the task.

INDEX

Family names appear in capital letters; scientific names in italics; bold page numbers denote full species accounts; bullets (black dots) denote alien species.

Aalwynkoraalboom 390
Aartappelbos 194
Abiekwasgeelhout 68
Acacia abyssinica **490**
Acacia albida: see *Faidherbia albida*
Acacia amythethophylla **490**
Acacia arenaria **490**
Acacia ataxacantha 480;**482**
Acacia borleae **496**
Acacia brevispica **488**
Acacia burkei 480;486;488
Acacia caffra 480;**482**;484; 486; 512
•*Acacia cyanophylla*: see *A. saligna*
•*Acacia cyclops* **230**
Acacia davyi **490**
•*Acacia dealbata* **504**
Acacia eriocarpum 480
Acacia erioloba 492;**494**
Acacia erubescens **482**
Acacia exuvialis **492**
Acacia fleckii **482**
Acacia galpinii **482**;486
Acacia gerrardii **492**
Acacia giraffae: see *A. erioloba*
Acacia goetzei 486;488
Acacia grandicornuta **492**
Acacia haematoxylon 492;**494**
Acacia hebeclada **484**
Acacia hereroensis 482;**484**
Acacia karroo 494;**496**
Acacia kirkii **494**
Acacia kraussiana **488**
•*Acacia longifolia* **230**
Acacia luederitzii **484**
Acacia macrothyrsa: see *A. amythethophylla*
•*Acacia mearnsii* **504**
•*Acacia melanoxylon* **230**
Acacia mellifera **484**
Acacia nebrownii **496**
Acacia nigrescens 480;**486**;488
Acacia nilotica **496**
Acacia permixta 496
•*Acacia podalyriifolia* **202**
Acacia polyacantha **486**
•*Acacia pycnantha* **202**
Acacia rehmanniana 496;**498**
Acacia robusta 492;**498**
Acacia robynsiana **486**
•*Acacia saligna* **202**
Acacia schweinfurthii **488**
Acacia senegal **488**
Acacia sieberiana 486;496;**498**
Acacia swazica **496**
Acacia tenuispina 494;**496**

Acacia tortilis **488**
Acacia welwitschii 480;**488**
Acacia xanthophloea **498**
Acalypha glabrata **224**
ACANTHACEAE 19;296;324
Acokanthera oblongifolia **310**
Acokanthera oppositifolia **310**
Acokanthera rotundata **312**
Acokanthera schimperi: see *A. rotundata*
Adansonia digitata **472**
Adenium boehmianum 34
Adenium multiflorum 34
Adenium obesum var. *multiflorum*: see *Adenium multiflorum*
Adenolobus garipensis **372**
Adenolobus pechuelli 372
Adina microcephala: see *Breonadia salicina*
African dog-rose 196
African mangosteen 360
African osage orange 70
African resin tree 356
African star-chestnut 234
Afrikaanse harpuisboom 356
Afrikaanse hondsroos 196
Afrikaanse sterkastaiing 234
Afrika-soetlemoen 70
Afrocarpus falcatus: see *Podocarpus falcatus*
Afrormosia angolensis: see *Pericopsis angolensis*
Afzelia quanzensis 420;514
Alberta magna **278**
Albizia adianthifolia **506**
Albizia amara **506**;508
Albizia anthelmintica **506**;508
Albizia antunesiana **508**
Albizia forbesii **508**
Albizia glaberrima 508
Albizia gummifera **506**
Albizia harveyi **508**
Albizia petersiana **508**
•*Albizia procera* 506
Albizia schimperiana 506
Albizia tanganyicensis **510**
Albizia versicolor **510**
Alchornea hirtella 104
Alchornea laxiflora **104**
Aleppoden 64
Aleppo pine 64
Allophylus abyssinicus 412
Allophylus africanus **412**
Allophylus alnifolius **412**
Allophylus chaunostachys 412
Allophylus chirindensis 412
Allophylus decipiens 412
Allophylus dregeanus **154**
Allophylus natalensis 404;**412**
Aloe africana 42
Aloe arborescens **42**
Aloe bainesii: see *Aloe barberiae*
Aloe barberiae **42**
Aloe candelabrum **44**

Aloe coral tree 390
Aloe dichotoma **44**
Aloe ferox **44**
Aloe marlothii **44**
Aloe pillansii 44
Aloe ramosissima 44
Aloe thraskii **46**
Alsophila dregei: see *Cyathea dregei*
Amblygonocarpus andongensis **510**
Anaboom 500
ANACARDIACEAE 19;84;102;356;398;434;444
Anastrabe integerrima **352**
Ana tree 500
Ancylanthos monteiroi: see *Lagynias monteiroi*
Andrachne ovalis 190
Androstachys johnsonii **258**
Angolabrandnetel 246
Angola nettle 246
Ankle thorn 498
Annona brachypetalus 156
ANNONACEAE 19;156
Annona senegalensis **156**
Annona stenophylla 156
Anthocleista grandiflora **276**
Antidesma venosum **188**
Aphloia theiformis **144**
APIACEAE 20;438;450
Apiesdoring 482
Apiespeul 426
APOCYNACEAE 20;34;306;310;358
Apodytes abbottii 198
Apodytes dimidiata **198**
Apodytes geldenhuysii 198
Appelblaar 458
Apple-leaf 458
AQUIFOLIACEAE 20;160
ARALIACEAE 20;48;224;450;472
ARECACEAE 20 50
Argomuellera macrophylla 154
Artabotrys monteiroae **156**
Assegaai 292
Assegai 292
ASTERACEAE 20;34; 60;110;134;162, 296
Atalaya alata **428**
Atalaya capensis 428
Atalaya natalensis 428
Atriplex nummularia **170**
Avicennia marina **354**
Azanza garckeana **228**

Baardbessie 402
Baardsuikerbos 214
Baboon grape 392
Bachmannia woodii **472**
Baikiaea plurijuga 420;**428**
BALANITACEAE 20;376
Balanites aegyptiaca **376**
Balanites maughamii **376**

Balanites pedicellaris **376**
Balanites welwitschii 376
Baobab 472
Baphia massaiensis **194**
Baphia racemosa **196**
Barringtonia racemosa **200**
Basboom 354
Basboontjie 512
Basterassegaai 146
Basterblinkblaar 142
Basterbokdrol 262
Basterbospendoring 126
Basterbruidsbos 288
Basterhaak-en-steek 484
Basterkiepersol 472
Bastermaroela 444
Bastermopanie 378
Basterpendoring 124
Basterperdepis 430
Bastersaffraan 298
Basterseepbessie 432
Basterswartklapper 250
Bastertambotie 190
Bastervy 82
Basterwitstinkhout 244
Bauhinia bowkeri 372
Bauhinia galpinii **372**
Bauhinia natalensis 372
Bauhinia petersiana 372
Bauhinia tomentosa **374**
Bauhinia urbaniana 372;**374**
Bead-bean tree 168
Bearded sugarbush 214
Beefwood 60
Bell bean tree 414
Bell gardenia 286
Bequaertiodendron magalismontanum: see *Englerophytum magalismontanum*
Bequaertiodendron natalense: see *Englerophytum natalense*
Berchemia discolor **350**
Berchemia zeyheri **350**
Bergaalwyn 44
Bergbas 220
Bergbrandnetel 246
Berghardepeer 348
Bergkaree 404
Bergmahonie 428
Berg-mfuti 420
Bergmispel 274
Bergperske 144
Bergpopulier 90
Bergsering 442
Bergsipres 62
Bergvaalbos 110
Bergvy 74
Bersama abyssinica **438**
Bersama lucens **468**
Bersama stayneri: see *B. tysoniana*
Bersama swinnyi **470**
Bersama swynnertonii 468
Bersama tysoniana **470**

Besembos 400
Besemtrosvy 80
Bietou 134
BIGNONIACEAE
21;120;384;414;502
Big num-num 308
Bitteraalwyn 44
Bitter aloe 44
Bitterblaar 110
Bitterbosdruif 392
Bitter false-thorn 506
Bitter forest grape 392
Bitter-leaf 110
Bittervalsdoring 506
Black bird-berry 282
Black bitterberry 252
Black false currant 412
Black forest spike-thorn 122
Black hazel 342
Black locust 464
Black mangrove 276
Black monkey orange 250
Black monkey thorn 480
Black plum 476
Black star-apple 182
Black thorn 484
Black wattle 504
Blackwood 230
Bladder-nut 184
Bladdoring 482
Bleekblaarboom 508
Bleekwattel 230
Blighia unijugata 430
Blinkblaar 152
Blinkblaarkanniedood 382
Blinkblaarwag-'n-bietjie 232
Blinkblaarwitessenhout 468
Blinkplatboontjie 454
Blinktaaibos 404
Blinkvingerblaar 476
Blossom tree 464
Bloubessiebos 178
Bloubitterbessie 254
Bloubittertee 134
Bloublaarkanniedood 86
Bloubos 178
Bloughwarrie 340
Blouhaak 482
Blouklokkiesbos 296
Bloukoeniebos 400
Bloulipbos 296
Blousoetbessie 188
Blousuikerbos 216
Blousuurpruim 130
Bloutaaibos 410
Bloutontelhout 370
Blueberry bush 178
Blue bitterberry 254
Blue bitter-tea 134
Bluebush 178
Blue currant 410
Blue-flowered tinderwood 370
Blue guarri 340
Blue kuni-bush 400
Blue-leaved corkwood 86

Blue-lips 296
Blue neat's foot 372
Blue sourplum 130
Blue sugarbush 216
Blue sweetberry 188
Blue thorn 482
Blunt-leaved currant 406
Bobbejaandruif 392
Boereturksvy 36
Boesmansdruif 392
Boesmanstee 292
Bokappel 118
Bolusanthus speciosus 452
BOMBACACEAE 21;472
Boomaalwyn 42
Boom-entada 512
BORAGINACEAE 21;134;162;224
Borassus aethiopum 50
Bosbastertaaibos 154
Bosbeesklou 374
Bosbitterhout 160
Boscia albitrunca 164;166
Boscia angustifolia 164
Boscia foetida 164
Boscia mossambicensis 164;166
Boscia oleoides 166
Boscia salicifolia 166
Bosgeelmelkhout 316
Boskanariebessie 142
Boskanniedood 436
Boskokaboom 186
Boskoorsbessie 106
Boskoorsboom 276
Bosmelkbessie 94
Bosmispel 290
Bosnoemnoem 306
Bospaddaboom 314
Bosperske 144
Bosqueia phoberos: see
Trilepisium madagascariense
Bosrooiessenhout 468
Bosrosyntjie 240
Bosstamvrug 92
Bostaaibos 398
Bosvaderlandswilg 332
Bosvalsnetel 224
Bosveldessenhout 466
Bosveldkatjiepiering 368
Bosveldwitysterhout 396
Bosverfbos 458
Bosvlier 362
Bosvy 72
Boswaterhout 322
Bosysterpruim 190
Bottelboom 34
Bottle tree 34
Bowkeria citrina 368
Bowkeria cymosa 368
Bowkeria verticillata 368
Brabejum stellatifolium 364
Brachylaena discolor 110
Brachylaena elliptica 110
Brachylaena huillensis 110
Brachylaena ilicifolia 110
Brachylaena neriifolia 162

Brachylaena rotundata 110
Brachylaena transvaalensis 110
Brachystegia boehmii 420
Brachystegia glaucescens 420;422
Brachystegia microphylla 420;422
Brachystegia spiciformis 420;422
Brachystegia utilis 422
Brack thorn 498
Brackenridgea zanguebarica 148
Brakdoring 498
Brandbos 280
Brasiliaanse peperboom 446
Brazilian pepper tree 446
Breëblaarboekenhout 210
Breëblaarharpuisboom 356
Breëblaarkanferbos 112
Breëblaarkoraalboom 390
Breëblaarkweper 228
Breëblaarpluisbos 34
Breëblaarsuikerbos 214
Breëblaarwasbessie 146
Breëblaarwitgat 166
Breëpeulvalsdoring 508
Bredasdorp sugarbush 216
Bredasdorpsuikerbos 216
Breekhout 278
Breonadia salicina 358;364
Bridelia cathartica 188
Bridelia micrantha 188
Bridelia mollis 190
Broad-leaved beech 210
Broad-leaved camphor bush 112
Broad-leaved coral tree 390
Broad-leaved fluff bush 34
Broad-leaved quince 228
Broad-leaved resin tree 356
Broad-leaved shepherd's tree 166
Broad-leaved sugarbush 214
Broad-leaved waxberry 146
Broad-pod false-thorn 508
Broom cluster fig 80
Broom karree 400
Brown gonna 68
Brown ironwood 144
Brown ivory 350
Bruguiera gymnorrhiza 276
Bruinbekvingerblaar 478
Bruingonna 68
Bruinivoor 350
Bruinysterhout 144
Buddleja auriculata 256
BUDDLEJACEAE 21;256;324
Buddleja corrugata: see B. loricata
Buddleja dysophylla 256
Buddleja glomerata 256
Buddleja loricata 258;324
Buddleja pulchella 256
Buddleja saligna 324;346
Buddleja salviifolia 258
Buffalo-thorn 232
Bug tree 118
Burchellia bubalina 278
Burkea africana 502
BURSERACEAE
21;86;102;380;434;446

Bush bitterwood 160
Bushman's grape 392
Bushman's tea 292
Bush medlar 290
Bush neat's foot 374
Bush-tick berry 134
Bushveld white ironwood 396
BUXACEAE 21;324
Buxus macowanii 324
Buxus natalensis 316;324

CACTACEAE 21;36
Cadaba kirkii 166
Cadaba natalensis 166
Cadaba termitaria 166
CAESALPINIACEAE
22;372;378;420;448;
450;480;502
•Caesalpinia decapetala 480
•Callistemon viminales 204
Calodendrum capense 322
Calpurnea aurea 452
Calpurnea sericea 452
Calpurnia glabrata 452
Calpurnia robinioides 452
Camel's foot 374
Camel thorn 492
Candle thorn 484
Candlewood 170
Canthium ciliatum 260
Canthium frangula:
see C. glaucum
Canthium gilfillanii 270;278
Canthium glaucum 260
Canthium gueinzii: see Keetia
gueinzii
Canthium huillense: see Psydrax
livida
Canthium inerme 260
Canthium locuples: see Psydrax
locuples
Canthium mundianum 270;278
Canthium obovatum: see Psydrax
obovata
Canthium setiflorum 270
Canthium vanwykii 260
Canthium ventosum:
see C. inerme
Cape ash 466
Cape beech 202
Cape blackwood 138
Cape chestnut 322
Cape coast cabbage 472
Cape coffee 288
Cape gardenia 286
Cape holly 160
Cape honeysuckle 416
Cape myrtle 146
Cape plane 148
Cape quince 198
Cape saffron 298
Cape stock-rose 244
Cape sumach 352
Cape teak 248
Cape willow 116

CAPPARACEAE 22;120;164;384;472
Capparis sepiaria 120
Capparis tomentosa 120
Cardiogyne africana 70
Carissa bispinosa 306;308
Carissa edulis 306
Carissa haematocarpa 308
Carissa macrocarpa 308
Carissa tetramera 306;308
Carissa wyliei 306;308
Carrot tree 438
Cassia abbreviata 422
Cassia didymobotrya: see Senna
    didymobotrya
Cassia petersiana: see Senna
    petersiana
Cassine aethiopica:
    see Mystroxylon aethiopicum
Cassine crocea:
    see Elaeodendron zeyheri
Cassine eucleiformis 136;138
Cassine maritima 136
Cassine matabelicum: see
    Elaeodendron matabelicum
Cassine papillosa:
    see Elaeodendron croceum
Cassine peragua 298;300
Cassine tetragona 298
Cassine transvaalensis 138
Cassinopsis ilicifolia 294
Cassinopsis tinifolia 276
Cassipourea congoensis:
    see C. malosana
Cassipourea flanaganii 294;302
Cassipourea gerrardii:
    see C. malosana
Cassipourea gummiflua 364
Cassipourea malosana 294;302
Cassipourea mossambicensis 294
Cassipourea swaziensis 294
CASUARINACEAE 22;60
•Casuarina cunninghamiana 60
•Casuarina equisetifolia 60
Catha abbottii 292;298
Catha edulis 292
Catha transvaalensis 292
Catophractes alexandri 120
Cat-thorn 350
Catunaregam spinosa 262
CELASTRACEAE
    22;122;186;292;298;326
Celtis africana 244
•Celtis australis 244
Celtis durandii 244
Celtis gomphophylla:
    see C. durandii
•Celtis sinensis 244
Cephalanthus natalensis 280
Ceraria namaquensis 66
•Cereus jamacaru 36
•Cereus peruvianus:
    see C. jamacaru
Ceriops tagal 278
Chaetachme aristata 132

Cheesewood 206
CHENOPODIACEAE 22;60;170
Chinese lanterns 200
Chionanthus battiscombei 344
Chionanthus foveolatus 344
Chionanthus peglerae 344
Chocolate berry 478
Choristylis rhamnoides 142
Chrysanthemoides monilifera 134
CHRYSOBALANACEAE 22;112
Chrysophyllum gorungosanum 92
Chrysophyllum viridifolium 92
Cladostemon kirkii 384
Clausena anisata 440
Cleistanthus schlechteri 190
Cleistochlamys kirkii 156
Clerodendrum glabrum 370
Clerodendrum myricoides 370
Climbing flat-bean 456
Climbing raisin 238
Climbing saffron 298
Climbing turkey-berry 280
CLUSIACEAE 23;316;326;360
Cluster-head sugarbush 220
Cluster pine 64
Clutia pulchella 190
Coastal red milkwood 96
Coastal white ash 470
Coast coral tree 388
Coast silver oak 110
Cobas 46
Coddia rudis 280
Coffee neat's foot 372
Coffee pear 326
Cola greenwayi 222
Cola natalensis 222
Colophospermum mopane 378
Colpoon compressum: see Osyris
    compressa
COMBRETACEAE 23;126;172;326
Combretum adenogonium 326
Combretum apiculatum 328;334
Combretum caffrum 330
Combretum collinum 328
Combretum edwardsii 332
Combretum elaeagnoides 330
Combretum erythrophyllum 330
Combretum fragrans:
    see C. adenogonium
Combretum hereroense 332
Combretum imberbe 332
Combretum kirkii 338
Combretum kraussii 332;334
Combretum microphyllum:
    see C. paniculatum
Combretum mkuzense 338
Combretum molle
    196;270;334;336
Combretum mossambicense 334
Combretum nelsonii 328;332;334
Combretum paniculatum 336
Combretum psidioides 334;336
Combretum vendae 334
Combretum wattii 336
Combretum woodii 332

Combretum zeyheri 196;338
Commiphora africana 232;282;380
Commiphora angolensis 382;434
Commiphora crenato-serrata 442
Commiphora dinteri 380
Commiphora discolor 382
Commiphora edulis 446
Commiphora glandulosa 102
Commiphora glaucescens 86
Commiphora harveyi 434;436
Commiphora karibensis 448
Commiphora marlothii 436
Commiphora merkeri 102
Commiphora mollis 448
Commiphora mossambicensis 380
Commiphora multijuga 448
Commiphora neglecta 382
Commiphora pyracanthoides
    102;104
Commiphora pyracanthoides
    subsp. glandulosa:
    see C. glandulosa
Commiphora schimperi
Commiphora tenuipetiolata
    382;434
Commiphora ugogensis 436
Commiphora woodii 436
Commiphora zanzibarica 436;448
Common bride's bush 266
Common bush-cherry 384
Common cabbage tree 48
Common canary-berry 142
Common cluster fig 80
Common coca tree 186
Common coral tree 390
Common corkwood 104
Common false-thorn 508
Common forest grape 246
Common forest myrtle 318
Common guarri 340
Common hard-leaf 66
Common hook-thorn 482
Common lightning bush 190
Common onionwood 294
Common poison-bush 310
Common poison rope 360
Common resin tree 358
Common saffron 298
Common sourberry 226
Common spike-thorn 122
Common star-apple 176
Common star-chestnut 236
Common sugarbush 214
Common tree euphorbia 40
Common tree fern 54
Common turkey-berry 260
Common white ash 470
Common wild currant 406
Common wild elder 362
Common wild fig 82
Common wild pear 234
Condiment saffron 300
Copalwood 378
Cordia abyssinica 136
Cordia caffra 134

Cordia gharaf: see C. sinensis
Cordia grandicalyx 136;224
Cordia monoica 136
Cordia ovalis: see C. monoica
Cordia pilosissima 224
Cordia sinensis 136
Cordyla africana 448
Cork bush 460
Corky monkey orange 248
Corky thorn 490
CORNACEAE 23;292
Coshwood 222
Craibia brevicaudata 454
Craibia zimmermannii 454
Crassula arborescens 36
CRASSULACEAE 23;36
Crassula ovata 36
Crassula portulacea: see C. ovata
Crocodile-bark jackal-berry 180
Crocoxylon croceum:
    see Elaeodendron croceum 300
Cross-berry 240
Crossopteryx febrifuga 270
Croton gratissimus 86
Croton leuconeurus 104
Croton megalobotrys 104
Croton menyhartii 86
Croton pseudopulchellus 88
Croton scheffleri 104
Croton steenkampianus 86
Croton sylvaticus 106
Cryptocarya latifolia 228
Cryptocarya liebertiana 116
Cryptocarya myrtifolia 116
Cryptocarya woodii 198
Cryptocarya wyliei 116
Cunonia capensis 416
CUNONIACEAE 23;386;416
CUPRESSACEAE 23;62
Currant resin tree 358
Curry bush 326
Curtisia dentata 292
Cussonia arborea 48
Cussonia arenicola 50
Cussonia natalensis 224
Cussonia nicholsonii 50
Cussonia paniculata 48
Cussonia sphaerocephala 48
Cussonia spicata 48
Cussonia thyrsiflora 472
Cussonia transvaalensis 50
Cussonia zuluensis 50
Cyathea capensis 54
CYATHEACEAE 23;54
Cyathea dregei 54
Cyathea manniana 54
Cyathea thomsonii 54
Cyphostemma bainesii 46
Cyphostemma currorii 46
Cyphostemma juttae 46
Cyphostemma uter 46

Dais cotinifolia 354
Dalbergia armata 454
Dalbergia martinii 456

Dalbergia melanoxylon **454**
Dalbergia nitidula **454**
Dalbergia obovata **456**
Dalbergiella nyasae **456**
Deinbollia oblongifolia **430**
Delagoa-doring **488**
Delagoa thorn **488**
Deurmekaarbos 162
Dialium engleranum **450**
Dialium schlechteri **450**
Dichrostachys cinerea **500**
Didelta spinosa **296**
Dikbas 444
Diospyros austro-africana 178
Diospyros dichrophylla **176**
Diospyros glabra **178**
Diospyros kirkii **178**
Diospyros lycioides **178**
Diospyros mespiliformis **180**
Diospyros natalensis **180**
Diospyros quiloensis **180**
Diospyros rotundifolia **182**;318
Diospyros scabrida **182**;184
Diospyros simii 176
Diospyros usambarensis **182**
Diospyros villosa **182**
Diospyros whyteana **184**
Diplorhynchus condylocarpon **312**
DIPTEROCARPACEAE 24;114;176
Dodonaea angustifolia **220**
Dodonaea viscosa:
   see *D. angustifolia*
Dogwood 152
Dombeya autumnalis 234
Dombeya burgessiae **232**
Dombeya cymosa 234
Dombeya kirkii **234**
Dombeya pulchra 232
Dombeya rotundifolia 234
Dombeya shupangae 234
Dombeya tiliacea 234
Dopperkiaat 462
Doppruim 222
Doringbeenappel 262
Doringkaree 402
Doringkatjiepiering 262
Doringkiaat 462
Doringolm 132
Doringpeer 130
Doringslaaibos 296
Doringtrosblaar 126
Dovyalis caffra **126**;224
Dovyalis longispina 224
Dovyalis rhamnoides **226**
Dovyalis zeyheri **128**
Dracaena aletriformis **54**
DRACAENACEAE 24;54
Dracaena hookeriana:
   see *D. aletriformis*
Dracaena mannii **54**
Dracaena steudneri 54
Dracaena transvaalensis 54
Dracaena usambarensis:
   see *D. mannii*
Driehaakdoring **488**

Driehoektolletjies 430
Drievingerblaar 476
Drypetes arguta **142**
Drypetes gerrardii **190**
Drypetes natalensis **142**;144
Drypetes reticulata 190
Dubbelkroon-boom 424
Duiker-berry 108
Duikerbessie 108
Duinebastertaaibos 412
Duinebotterlepelbos 286
Duinebruidsbos 268
Duinegifboom 310
Duinekokoboom 140
Duinekraaibessie 400
Duinemirt 318
Duinemispel 272
Duine-olienhout 346
Duineseepbessie 430
Duinetaaibos 402
Duingonna 68
Duinjakkalsbessie 182
Dune bride's bush 268
Dune butterspoon bush 286
Dune crow-berry 400
Dune currant 402
Dune false currant 412
Dune gonna 68
Dune jackal-berry 182
Dune koko tree 140
Dune medlar 272
Dune myrtle 318
Dune olive 346
Dune poison-bush 310
Dune soap-berry 430
•*Duranta erecta* 304
•*Duranta repens*: see *D. erecta*
Duvernoia adhatodoides **324**
Dwarf bride's bush 266
Dwarf coral tree 388
Dwergbruidsbos 266

Eastern Cape cycad 58
Ebbeboom 184
EBENACEAE 24;176;340
Ebony tree 184
Ehretia amoena **162**
Ehretia obtusifolia 162
Ehretia rigida **162**
Ekebergia benguelensis **466**;508
Ekebergia capensis 444;**466**
Ekebergia pterophylla 418;**466**
Elaeodendron croceum **298**
Elaeodendron matabelicum **300**
Elaeodendron zeyheri **300**
Elephantorrhiza burkei **512**
Elephantorrhiza goetzei 512
Elephantorrhiza suffruticosa 512
Encephalartos altensteinii 58
Encephalartos natalensis 58
Encephalartos senticosus 58
Encephalartos transvenosus **58**
Englerodaphne ovalifolia 354
Englerodaphne pilosa **354**
Englerodaphne subcordata 354

Englerophytum magalismontanum 92
Englerophytum natalense **94**
Enkeldoring 498
Enkeldoring-fakkelhout 376
Enkeldoringnoemnoem 306
Ensete ventricosum **56**
Entada abyssinica **512**
Entandrophragma caudatum **428**
Entandrophragma spicatum 428
Enterospermum littorale:
   see *Tarenna littoralis*
Enterospermum rhodesiacum:
   see *Tarenna zimbabwensis*
Erica caffra **62**
Erica caffrorum 62
Erica canaliculata 62
ERICACEAE 24;62
Erica pleiotricha 62
Erica thryptomenoides:
   see *E. pleiotricha*
Erythrina abyssinica **386**;390
Erythrina caffra **388**;390
Erythrina decora **388**
Erythrina humeana **388**
Erythrina latissima 386;**390**
Erythrina livingstoniana **390**
Erythrina lysistemon 388;**390**
Erythrophleum africanum **502**
Erythrophleum lasianthum **504**
Erythrophleum suaveolens 504
Erythrophysa alata **470**
Erythrophysa transvaalensis **470**
ERYTHROXYLACEAE 24;186
Erythroxylum delagoense **186**
Erythroxylum emarginatum **186**
Erythroxylum pictum **186**
Erythroxylum zambesiacum 186
ESCALLONIACEAE 24;142
Essenhout 466
•*Eucalyptus camaldulensis* **204**
•*Eucalyptus cladocalyx* 204
•*Eucalyptus diversicolor* 204
•*Eucalyptus lehmannii* 204
Euclea coriacea 340
Euclea crispa **340**
Euclea divinorum **340**
Euclea linearis 184
Euclea natalensis **184**;318
Euclea pseudobenus **184**
Euclea racemosa **186**
Euclea tomentosa **186**
Euclea undulata **340**
Eugenia capensis 182;**318**
Eugenia natalitia 318;342
Eugenia simii 318
Eugenia umtamvunensis 318
Eugenia verdoorniae 318
Eugenia woodii 318
Eugenia zeyheri **318**
Eugenia zuluensis 318
EUPHORBIACEAE 24;38;86;104;142;188;224;258; 362;474
Euphorbia confinalis **38**

Euphorbia cooperi **38**
Euphorbia curvirama 42
Euphorbia espinosa **88**
Euphorbia evansii **38**
Euphorbia grandidens **40**
Euphorbia guerichiana **88**
Euphorbia ingens 36;**40**
Euphorbia matabelensis 88
Euphorbia sekukuniensis 38
Euphorbia tetragona **40**
Euphorbia tirucalli **40**
Euphorbia triangularis **42**
Euphorbia zoutpansbergensis 38
Excoecaria bussei **106**
Excoecaria simii 106

FABACEAE 25;194;386;426;452
Fagara capensis:
   see *Zanthoxylum capense*
Fagara davyi: see *Zanthoxylum davyi*
Fagara leprieuri: see *Zanthoxylum leprieurii*
Fagara macrophylla: see *Zanthoxylum gilletii*
Fagaropsis 418
Fagaropsis angolensis **418**
Faidherbia albida **500**
False assegai 146
False blackbark 182
False black monkey orange 250
False bride's bush 288
False buffalo-thorn 232
False cabbage tree 472
False dogwood 142
False fig 82
False forest spike-thorn 126
False gardenia 272
False hook-thorn 484
False horsewood 430
False lemon thorn 276
False marula 444
False medlar 274
False mfuti 422
False olive 324
False red pear 302
False soap-berry 432
False spike-thorn 124
False tamboti 190
False turkey-berry 262
False umbrella thorn 484
False white stinkwood 244
Faurea delevoyi 210
Faurea forficuliflora 210
Faurea galpinii 210
Faurea rochetiana 210
Faurea rubriflora **210**
Faurea saligna **210**
Faurea speciosa:
   see *F. rochetiana*
Feretia aeruginescens **270**
Fever pod 312
Fever tree 498
Ficus abutilifolia **70**
Ficus burkei: see *F. thonningii*

Ficus burtt-davyi 70
Ficus capensis: see F. sur
Ficus capreifolia 72
Ficus chirindensis 78
Ficus cordata 72;74;78
Ficus cordata subsp. salicifolia:
see F. salicifolia
Ficus craterostoma 72
Ficus exasperata 74
Ficus glumosa 74
Ficus hippopotami:
see F. trichopoda
Ficus ilicina 74
Ficus ingens 76
Ficus lutea 76;82
Ficus natalensis 72;76
Ficus nigropunctata 78
Ficus petersii: see F. thonningii
Ficus pretoriae: see F. salicifolia
Ficus pygmaea 72
Ficus salicifolia 72;76;78
Ficus sansibarica 78
Ficus smutsii: see F. tettensis
Ficus soldanella: see F. abutilifolia
Ficus sonderi: see F. glumosa
Ficus stuhlmannii 74;78
Ficus sur 80
Ficus sycomorus 80
Ficus tettensis 70;80
Ficus thonningii 76;82
Ficus trichopoda 76;82
Ficus vallis-choudae 80
Ficus vogelii: see F. lutea
Firebush 280
Fisantebessie 194
FLACOURTIACEAE
25;114;126;144;196;224;302
Flacourtia indica 128
Flaky thorn 492
Flame creeper 336
Flame thorn 480
Flat-crown 506
Flood-plains thorn 494
Flueggea virosa 192
Fluted milkwood 92
Fluweelboswilg 334
Fluweelkanniedood 448
Fluweelkaree 400
Fluweelklipels 270
Fluweelrosyntjie 238
Fluweelsoetbessie 190
Fluweelvrug-zanha 432
Fonteinbos 460
Forest bushwillow 332
Forest canary-berry 142
Forest coca tree 186
Forest corkwood 436
Forest elder 362
Forest false currant 154
Forest false-nettle 224
Forest fever-berry 106
Forest fever tree 276
Forest fig 72
Forest indigo 458
Forest ironplum 190

Forest mahogany 468
Forest mangosteen 316
Forest milkberry 94
Forest newtonia 512
Forest num-num 306
Forest peach 144
Forest raisin 240
Forest sandpaper fig 72;74
Forest toad tree 314
Forest waterwood 322
Forget-me-not tree 304
Fountain bush 460
Four-finger bush 472
Four-leaved bushwillow 326
Freylinia lanceolata 352
Friesodielsia obovata 158
Fringed cluster-leaf 172
Fynblaarbruidsbos 268
Fynblaarjakkalsbessie 180
Fynblaarkarooboerboon 424
Fynblaarkokaboom 186
Fynblaarrooihout 152
Fynblaarsaffraan 300

Galla plum 430
Gallapruim 430
Galpinia transvaalica 342
Garcinia buchananii 316
Garcinia gerrardii 316;324
Garcinia huillensis:
see G. buchananii
Garcinia kingaensis 316
Garcinia livingstonei 360
Gardenia amoena:
see Hyperacanthus amoenus
Gardenia cornuta 366
Gardenia imperialis 366
Gardenia posoquerioides 368
Gardenia resiniflua 366
Gardenia spathulifolia:
see G. volkensii
Gardenia ternifolia 366
Gardenia thunbergia 366
Gardenia volkensii 368
Geelberggranaat 384
Geelbitterbessie 252
Geelbrandbos 280
Geelbranddoring 116
Geelkatjiepiering 366
Geelkeurboom 452
Geellekkerbreek 148
Geelsuikerkan 214
Geelwortelboom 438
Geneesblaarboom 118
Gerrardina foliosa 144
Gevleuelde witessenhout 438
Gewone bliksembos 190
Gewone bokdrol 260
Gewone boomvaring 54
Gewone bosdruif 246
Gewone bosmirt 318
Gewone bruidsbos 266
Gewone drolpeer 332
Gewone ghwarrie 340
Gewone gifboom 310

Gewone giftou 360
Gewone haakdoring 482
Gewone hardeblaar 66
Gewone harpuisboom 358
Gewone kanariebessie 142
Gewone kanniedood 104
Gewone kiepersol 48
Gewone kokaboom 186
Gewone koraalboom 390
Gewone naboom 40
Gewone pendoring 122
Gewone saffraan 298
Gewone sterappel 176
Gewone sterkastaiing 236
Gewone suikerbos 214
Gewone suurbessie 226
Gewone taaibos 406
Gewone trosvy 80
Gewone uiehout 294
Gewone wildevlier 362
Gewone wildevy 82
Gewone witbos 384
Gewone witessenhout 470
Giant-leaved fig 76
Giant raisin 238
Gifboom 362
Gifbruidsbos 268
Gifolyf 222
Gland-leaf tree 264
Glandular mesquite 500
Glossy currant 404
Glossy flat-bean 454
Glossy white ash 468
Glossy-leaved corkwood 382
Goat apple 118
Goewerneurspruim 128
Golden bean tree 414
Gonioma kamassi 358
Goudwilger 202
Goue boontjieboom 414
Gourd bush milkwood 100
Governor's plum 128
Granietgeelmelkhout 316
Granietrooihout 150
Granite garcinia 316
Granite plane 150
Green-apple 158
Green cluster-leaf 172
Green hazel 342
Green monkey orange 254
Green resin tree 84
Green-stem corkwood 382
Green thorn 376
Green tree 284
•Grevillea robusta 438
Grewia bicolor 236
Grewia caffra 238
Grewia flava 238
Grewia flavescens 238
Grewia hexamita 238
Grewia hornbyi 240
Grewia lasiocarpa 240
Grewia microthyrsa 240
Grewia monticola 240
Grewia occidentalis 240

Grewia pachycalyx 242
Grewia pondoensis 240
Grewia praecox 242
Grewia retinervis 238
Grewia robusta 242
Grewia sulcata 242
Grewia tenax 242
Grewia villosa 242
Grey camel thorn 494
GREYIACEAE 25;226
Greyia flanaganii 226
Greyia radlkoferi 226
Greyia sutherlandii 226
Grey-leaved saucer-berry 136
Groenappel 158
Groenboom 284
Groendoring 376
Groenharpuisboom 84
Groenhaselaar 342
Groenklapper 254
Groenstamkanniedood 382
Groenvaalboom 172
Grondboontjiebotterkassia 426
Groot gewone kanniedood 102
Grootblaarbruidsbos 266
Grootblaardoring 490
Grootblaardrakeboom 54
Grootblaarrooihout 148
Grootblaarrotsvy 70
Grootblaarsterkastaiing 236
Grootblaaruiehout 364
Grootblaarvalsdoring 510
Grootblomwitbos 168
Grootblomwurmbos 166
Grootgeelbos 212
Grootkoorsbessie 104
Grootnoemnoem 308
Grootvrugsuurpruim 206
Grysappel 112
Grysblaarpieringbessie 136
Guava 320
Guibourtia coleosperma 378
Guibourtia conjugata 378
Gymnosporia buxifolia 122
Gymnosporia linearis 122
Gymnosporia mossambicensis
122
Gymnosporia nemorosa 124
Gymnosporia polyacantha 124
Gymnosporia senegalensis 124
Gyrocarpus americanus 228

Haak-en-steek 488
Hairy cluster-leaf 172
Hairy corkwood 380
Hairy star-apple 182
Hairy stink bushwillow 338
Hairy turkey-berry 260
Hairy violet-bush 154
•Hakea drupaceae 66
•Hakea gibbosa 66
•Hakea sericea 66
Halleria lucida 302
HAMAMELIDACEAE 25;114;342
Haplocoelum gallense 418;430

Hardeblaartaaibos 408
Hardekool 332
Hardepeer 348
Hard-leaved currant 408
Hard pear 348
Harige bokdrol 260
Harige kanniedood 380
Harige sterappel 182
Harige stinkboswilg 338
Harige vaalboom 172
Harige viooltjiebos 154
Harpephyllum caffrum **444**;466
Harpuiskatjiepiering 366
Harpuistrosblaar 176
Hartboom 192
Hartogiella schinoides 298;**300**
Harungana madagascariensis **316**
Healing-leaf tree 118
Heart tree 192
Heeria argentea **84**
Heinsia crinita **272**
Helikopterboom 228
Henkel-se-geelhout 208
Henkel's yellowwood 208
Hererosesambos 132
Herero sesame-bush 132
HERNANDIACEAE 25;228
Heteromorpha arborescens:
 see *H. trifoliata*
Heteromorpha trifoliata **450**
HETEROPYXIDACEAE 25;198
Heteropyxis canescens 198
Heteropyxis dehniae:
 see *H. natalensis*
Heteropyxis natalensis **198**
Heuningghwarrie 186
Heuningklokkiesbos 352
Heuningnaboom 40
Hexalobus monopetalus **158**
Heywoodia lucens **192**
Hibiscus diversifolius 228
Hibiscus tiliaceus **228**
Highveld cabbage tree 48
Hippobromus pauciflorus **430**
Hoëveldse kiepersol 48
Holarrhena pubescens **312**
Holmskioldia speciosa:
 see *Karomia speciosa*
Homalium abdessammadii 144
Homalium chasei 144
Homalium dentatum
Honey-bell bush 352
Honey euphorbia 40
Honey guarri 186
Hophout 244
Horingdoring 492
Horingpeultjieboom 312
Horned thorn 492
Horn-pod tree 312
Horsewood 440
Hotnotskersie 326
Hottentot's cherry 326
Houtmelkbos 88
Huilboerboon 424
Huilboom 504

Hyaenanche globosa **362**
Hyaena poison 362
Hymenocardia acida **192**
Hymenocardia ulmoides **192**;338
Hymenodictyon floribundum **280**
Hymenodictyon parvifolium 280
Hyperacanthus amoenus **262**
Hyperacanthus microphyllus 262
Hypericum revolutum **326**
Hypericum roeperianum 326
Hyphaene benguellensis:
 see *H. petersiana*
Hyphaene coriacea **50**
Hyphaene natalensis:
 see *H. coriacea*
Hyphaene petersiana **52**

I CACINACEAE 25;198;276;294
Ilex mitis **160**
Impalalelie 34
Impala lily 34
Indigofera cylindrica:
 see *I. frutescens*
Indigofera cytisoides 456
Indigofera frutescens 456
Indigofera lyallii **456**
Indigofera natalensis **458**
Indigofera sp. novum **456**
Indigofera rhynchocarpa 458
Indigofera superba 456
Indigofera swaziensis 456
Iron martin 102
Ironwood 344

J acaranda 502
•*Jacaranda mimosifolia* **502**
Jackal-berry 180
Jackal-coffee 288
Jacket-plum 222
Jakaranda 502
Jakkalsbessie 180
Jakkalskoffie 288
Jubaeopsis caffra 52
Jujube 232
Julbernardia globiflora 422;**424**
Julbernardia paniculata 424
Jumping-seed tree 106

K aapse boekenhout 202
Kaapse kamperfoelie 416
Kaapse katjiepiering 286
Kaapse kiaat 248
Kaapse koffie 288
Kaapse kuskiepersol 472
Kaapse kweper 198
Kaapse rooihout 148
Kaapse stokroos 244
Kaapse swarthout 138
Kaapse wilger 116
Kalahari-appelblaar 196
Kalahari apple-leaf 196
Kalahari currant 408
Kalaharipeulbessie 450
Kalahari podberry 450
Kalaharitaaibos 408

Kalbasbosmelkhout 100
Kamassi 358
Kamassie 358
Kameeldoring 492
Kameelspoor 374
Karee 402
Karomia speciosa **304**
Karomia tettensis 304
Karoo boer-bean 424
Karooboerboon 424
Karoo cross-berry 242
Karookoeniebos 398
Karookruisbessie 242
Karoo kuni-bush 398
Karoonoemnoem 308
Karoo num-num 308
Karoo sage 256
Karoosalie 256
Karoowitgat 166
Karree 402
Karroo shepherd's tree 166
Kasuarisboom 60
Kasuur 206
Katdoring 350
Keetia gueinzii **280**
Keiappel 126
Kei-apple 126
Kei fingerleaf 478
Keivingerblaar 478
Kerkeibos 36
Kerky-bush 36
Kerriebos 326
Kershout 170
Keurboom 464
Khaya anthotheca **428**
Khaya nyasica: see *K. anthotheca*
Kiaat 462
Kierieklapper 332
Kigelia africana **414**
Kiggelaria africana **114**
Kinaboom 358
Kirkia acuminata **442**
Kirkia dewinteri 442
Kirkia wilmsii **442**
Klapperbos 200
Kleinappelblaar 458
Kleinbastermopanie 378
Kleinbeenappel 280
Kleinblaardrakeboom 54
Kleinblaarkruisbessie 242
Kleinblaarrotsvy 80
Kleingroendoring 376
Kleinkoraalboom 388
Kleinlaventelkoorsbessie 88
Klein-mahobohobo 92
Kleinmuishondbos 304
Kleinperdepram 440
Kleinsuurpruim 206
Kleintrospeer 160
Kliertjiesboom 264
Klipels 278
Kliphout 84
Klipkershout 168
Klokkiesboontjieboom 414
Klokkieskatjiepiering 286

Knobbly creeper 334
Knobbly fig 78
Knob thorn 486
Knobwood 442
Knoppiesboontjieboom 168
Knoppiesdoring 486
Knoppiesklimop 334
Knoppiesvy 78
Knuppelhout 222
Kobas 46
Koeboebessie 140
Koedoebessie 194
Koejawel 320
Koffiebeesklou 372
Koffiepeer 326
Kokerboom 44
Kokoboom 140
Koko tree 140
Kooboo-berry 140
Koorsboom 498
Koorspeulboom 312
Korentebos 408
Korenteharpuisboom 358
Kortdoringgranaat 120
Kosi palm 52
Kosipalm 52
Kraaldoring 480
Kraalnaboom 40
Kraalpendoring 124
Kraal spike-thorn 124
Kransaalwyn 42
Kransbessie 144
Kranskwar 284
Krantz aloe 42
Krantz berry 144
Krantz quar 284
Kraussia floribunda **282**
Kremetart 472
Kreupelhout 212
Kreupelrooihout 150
Kringboom 168
Krinkhout 210
Krokodilbasjakkalsbessie 180
Kruisbessie 240
Kudu-berry 194
Kurkbasklapper 248
Kurkbos 460
Kurkdoring 490
Kuskoraalboom 388
Kusrooimelkhout 96
Kusvaalbos 110
Kuswitessenhout 470
Kwar 284

L aeveldbastertaaibos 412
Laeveldbittertee 162
Laeveldkastaiing 474
Laeveldmelkbessie 96
Laeveldnaboom 38
Laeveldse geelmelkhout 360
Laeveldse kamperfoelieboom 202
Laeveldvaalbos 110
Laeveldvy 78
Lagynias 272
Lagynias dryadum **272**

Lagynias lasiantha **282**
Lagynias monteiroi **272**
Lala palm 50
Lalapalm 50
Lance-leaved myrtle 320
Lance-leaved waxberry 146
Lannea antiscorbutica 444
Lannea discolor **444** 446
Lannea schweinfurthii **444**
Lannea stuhlmannii:
  see L. schweinfurthii
Lantana 304
•Lantana camara **304**
Large fever-berry 104
Large-flowered bush-cherry 168
Large-flowered worm-bush 166
Large-fruited bushwillow 338
Large-fruited sourplum 206
Large-leaved bride's bush 266
Large-leaved dragon tree 54
Large-leaved false-thorn 510
Large-leaved onionwood 364
Large-leaved plane 148
Large-leaved rock fig 70
Large-leaved star-chestnut 236
Large-leaved thorn 490
Latjiesbos 372
LAURACEAE 25;116;198;228
Laurel fig 74
Laurocerasus africana:
  see Prunus africana
Laurophyllus capensis **102**
Lavender fever-berry 86
Lavender tree 198
Laventelboom 198
Laventelkoorsbessie 86
Leadwood 332
Lebombo cluster-leaf 172
Lebombo euphorbia 38
Lebombo ironwood 258
Lebombokransesseboom 428
Lebombo krantz ash 428
Lebombo-naboom 38
Lebombo raisin 240
Lebomboorsyntjie 240
Lebombotrosblaar 172
Lebombowattel 512
Lebombo wattle 512
Lebombo-ysterhout 258
Lecaniodiscus
  fraxinifolius **432**
LECYTHIDACEAE 26;200
Lekkerbreek 204
Lekkerruikpeul 496
Lemoenhout 302
Lemoentjiedoring 294
Lemon thorn 294
Lemon wood 302
Lepelhout 300
Lesser mahobohobo 92
Leucadendron eucalyptifolium **212**
Leucosidea sericea **440**
Leucospermum
  conocarpodendron **212**
Leucospermum reflexum **212**

LILIACEAE 26;42
Lip-flower sugarbush 220
Lippeblomsuikerbos 220
Live-long 444
LOGANIACEAE
  26;248;276;302;362
Lonchocarpus bussei **458**
Lonchocarpus capassa **458**
Lonchocarpus nelsii **196**;328
Long-bud sugarbush 214
Lopholaena platyphylla **34**
Louriervy 74
Lowveld bitter-tea 162
Lowveld chestnut 474
Lowveld cluster-leaf 126
Lowveld euphorbia 38
Lowveld false currant 412
Lowveld fig 78
Lowveld honeysuckle tree 202
Lowveld milkberry 96
Lowveld silver oak 110
Loxostylis alata **446**
Luisboom 118
Lycium afrum 132
Lycium austrinum 132
Lycium hirsutum 132
Lye ganna 60
LYTHRACEAE 26;342

Maanhaarpeul 456
Maanhaarvaalboom 172
Macaranga capensis **88**
Macaranga mellifera **90**
Mackaya bella **296**
Maclura africana: see Cardiogyne
  africana
Maerua angolensis **168**
Maerua brevipetiolata 386
Maerua cafra **384**
Maerua kirkii **168**
Maerua nervosa 384
Maerua pritwitzii 384
Maerua rosmarinoides **386**
Maerua schinzii **168**
Maerua triphylla 384
Maesa lanceolata **146**
Magic guarri 340
Mahobohobo 90
Maksering 514
Mallow raisin 242
MALVACEAE 26;228
Malvarosyntjie 242
Mane-pod 456
Manica beechwood 210
Manicaboekenhout 210
Manilkara concolor **94**
Manilkara discolor **94**
Manilkara mochisia **96**
Manilkara nicholsonii 94
Mankettiboom 474
Manketti tree 474
Many-stemmed false-thorn 508
Margaritaria discoidea **194**
Markhamia acuminata:
  see M. zanzibarica

Markhamia obtusifolia **414**
Markhamia zanzibarica **414**
Maroela 446
Marula 446
Matumi 364
Mauritius thorn 480
Maurocenia frangula **326**
Maytenus abbottii 138
Maytenus acuminata **138**
Maytenus cordata 138
Maytenus heterophylla 122
Maytenus linearis:
  see Gymnosporia linearis
Maytenus lucida 140
Maytenus mossambicensis: see
  Gymnosporia mossambicensis
Maytenus nemorosa:
  see Gymnosporia nemorosa
Maytenus oleoides **168**;170
Maytenus oleosa 140
Maytenus peduncularis **138**
Maytenus polyacantha:
  see Gymnosporia polyacantha
Maytenus procumbens **140**
Maytenus senegalensis:
  see Gymnosporia senegalensis
Maytenus undata **140**
Meerstamvalsdoring 508
MELASTOMATACEAE 26;254;342
•Melia azedarach **514**
MELIACEAE 26;200;428;466;514
MELIANTHACEAE 27;438;468
Memecylon bachmannii 342
Memecylon grandiflorum:
  see M. bachmannii
Memecylon natalense 318;**342**
Memecylon sousae 254;342
Metalasia muricata **60**
Metrosideros angustifolia 320
Mfuti 420
Millettia grandis **458**
Millettia stuhlmannii **460**
Millettia sutherlandii 458
Millettia usaramensis 460
MIMOSACEAE
  27;202;230;480;490;504
Mimusops caffra **96**
Mimusops obovata **96**
Mimusops obtusifolia 96
Mimusops zeyheri **98**
Mingerhout 364
Mirtekweper 116
Mirting 146
Mitseeri 188
Mobola plum 112
Modjadjibroodboom 58
Modjadji cycad 58
Moepel 98
Moerasvy 82
MONIMIACEAE 27;302
Monkey pod 426
Monkey thorn 482
Monodora junodii **158**
Monotes engleri **114**
Monotes glaber **176**

Monotes katangensis 176
Mopane 378
Mopane pomegranate 416
Mopanie 378
Mopaniegranaat 416
MORACEAE 27;70;474
MORINGACEAE 27;514
Moringa ovalifolia **514**
Mosterdboom 352
Mountain acacia 420
Mountain aloe 44
Mountain cypress 62
Mountain fig 74
Mountain hard pear 348
Mountain karree 404
Mountain mahogany 428
Mountain medlar 274
Mountain nettle 246
Mountain peach 144
Mountain poplar 90
Mountain seringa 442
Mountain silver oak 110
Msasa 422
Mundulea sericea **460**
Munondo 424
MUSACEAE 28;56
Mustard tree 352
Mwanga 460
Myrianthus 474
Myrianthus holstii **474**
MYRICACEAE 28;146
Myrica microbracteata 146
Myrica pilulifera **146**
Myrica serrata **146**
MYRSINACEAE 28;146;202
Myrsine africana **146**
Myrsine pillansii 146
MYRTACEAE 28;204;318
Myrtle quince 116
Mystroxylon aethiopicum **140**

Naaldblaarwitbos 386
Nagblom 36
Namakwaharpuisboom 84
Namakwakoeniebos 410
Namakwarooiklapperbos 470
Namakwavy 72
Namaqua fig 72
Namaqua kuni-bush 410
Namaqua porkbush 66
Namaqua red balloon 470
Namaqua resin tree 84
Namib coral tree 388
Namibian resin tree 84
Namibiese
  harpuisboom 84
Namibkoraalboom 388
Nana-berry 400
Nanabessie 400
Narrow-leaved false bride's bush
  288
Narrow-leaved mahobohobo 90
Narrow-leaved mustard tree 350
Narrow-leaved spike-thorn 122
Natalappelkoos 224

Natal apricot 224
Natalbosmelkhout 100
Natalbosmispel 290
Natal bottlebrush 226
Natal box 324
Natal bush medlar 290
Natal bush milkwood 100
Natal camwood 196
Natal cherry-orange 394
Natal coca tree 188
Nataldrolpeer 234
Natal fig 76
Natal flame bush 278
Natal forest cabbage tree 48
Natal gardenia 366
Natalghwarrie 184
Natal guarri 184
Natal ironplum 142
Natalkaree 404
Natal karree 404
Natalkatjiepiering 366
Natalkersielemoen 394
Natalkokaboom 188
Natal mahogany 468
Natal medlar 282
Natalmelkpruim 94
Natal milkplum 94
Natalmispel 282
Natal plane 150
Natalrooihout 150
Natalroosappel 342
Natal rose-apple 342
Natalse baakhout 226
Natalse boskiepersol 48
Natalse buksboom 324
Natalse kamhout 196
Natalse skulpblombos 368
Natalse wildepiesang 56
Natal shell-flower bush 368
Natalvy 76
Natal wild banana 56
Natal wild pear 234
Natalysterpruim 142
Nectaropetalum capense 188
Nectaropetalum zuluense 188
Needle-leaved bush-cherry 386
Neorosea andongensis:
  see Sericanthe andongensis
Newtonia buchananii 512
Newtonia hildebrandtii 512
•Nicotiana glauca 222
Nieshout 418
Njalaboom 464
Noltea africana 152
Noordelike ertjiehout 454
Noordelike suikerbos 212
Northern peawood 454
Northern sugarbush 212
Notsung 302
Nuxia congesta 362
Nuxia floribunda 288;362
Nuxia glomerulata 362
Nuxia oppositifolia 302
Nyala tree 464
Nyanga flat-top 490

Nyanga-platkruin 490
Nymania capensis 200

Obetia carruthersiana 246
Obetia tenax 246
Ochna arborea 148
Ochna barbosae 148
OCHNACEAE 28;148;204
Ochna gambleoides 148
Ochna holstii 150
Ochna inermis 150
Ochna natalitia 150
Ochna pretoriensis 150
Ochna puberula 150
Ochna pulchra 204
Ochna schweinfurthiana 150
Ochna serrulata 152
Ocotea bullata 200
Octopus cabbage tree 48
OLACACEAE 28;130;206
Olax dissitiflora 206
Olax obtusifolia 206
Oldenburgia arbuscula:
  see O. grandis
Oldenburgia grandis 112
Old man's salt bush 170
Oldwood 440
Olea africana: see O. europaea
Olea capensis 344
OLEACEAE 28;344;418
Olea europaea 346
Olea exasperata 346
Oleasterboswilg 330
Oleaster bushwillow 330
Olea woodiana 346
Olienhout 346
OLINIACEAE 28;348
Olinia cymosa: see O. ventosa
Olinia emarginata 348
Olinia radiata 348
Olinia rochetiana 348
Olinia vanguerioides 348
Olinia ventosa 348
Oncoba spinosa 128
Oordeelboom 502
Oos-Kaapse broodboom 58
Opregte geelhout 208
Opregte suikerbos 218
Opregte waaierpalm 52
•Opuntia ficus-indica 36
•Opuntia lindheimeri 36
Orange-milk tree 316
Oranjemelkhout 316
Ordeal tree 502
Oricia bachmannii 394
Osyris compressa 220;352
Osyris lanceolata: see O. quadri-
  partita
Osyris quadripartita 220;352
Ouhout 440
Oumansoutbos 170
Outeniekwageelhout 206
Outeniqua yellowwood 206
Oxyanthus gerrardii:
  see O. speciosus

Oxyanthus latifolius 282
Oxyanthus natalensis:
  see O. pyriformis
Oxyanthus pyriformis 282
Oxyanthus speciosus 282
Ozoroa concolor 84
Ozoroa crassinervia 84
Ozoroa dispar 84
Ozoroa engleri 356
Ozoroa insignis 356
Ozoroa namaensis 84
Ozoroa obovata 356
Ozoroa paniculosa 358
Ozoroa sphaerocarpa 358

Pachypodium lealii 34
Pachypodium namaquanum 34
Pachystigma bowkeri 290
Pachystigma macrocalyx 274
Pachystigma triflorum 272
Paddaboom 312
Pale-fruited monotes 176
Pambatieboom 352
Pambati tree 352
Pancovia golungensis 432
Panga panga 460
Paperbark corkwood 436
Paperbark false-thorn 510
Paperbark thorn 498
Papierbasdoring 498
Papierbaskanniedood 436
Papierbasvalsdoring 510
Pappea capensis 222
Parasol tree 450
Parinari capensis 112
Parinari curatellifolia 112;114
•Parkinsonia aculeata 452
Parkinsonia africana 452
Parsley tree 450
Passerina falcifolia 68
Passerina filiformis 68
Passerina rigida 68
Patula pine 64
Pavetta bowkeri 264
Pavetta cataractarum 264
Pavetta catophylla 264
Pavetta edentula 264
Pavetta eylesii 266
Pavetta gardeniifolia 266
Pavetta gracilifolia 266
Pavetta harborii 268
Pavetta inandensis 266
Pavetta kotzei 266
Pavetta lanceolata 266
Pavetta natalensis 264
Pavetta revoluta 268
Pavetta schumanniana 268
Pavetta trichardtensis 268
Pavetta tristis: see P. lanceolata
Pavetta zeyheri 268
Pavetta zoutpansbergensis:
  see P. trichardtensis
Peanut butter cassia 426
PEDALIACEAE 29;132
Peddiea africana 222

Peeling plane 204
Peltophorum africanum 504
Peperblaarkanniedood 380
Peperboom 434
Pepersaadboom 106
Pepper-leaf corkwood 380
Pepper-seed tree 106
Pepper tree 434
Perdekop 212
Perdepis 440
Perdepram 442
Pericopsis angolensis 460
Persblaarvalsdoring 508
Persdrolpeer 232
Persstamkanniedood 448
Pers-trospeer 156
Petrolbos 62
Petrolbush 62
Peulmahonie 420
Phantom tree 514
Pheasant-berry 194
Philippia benguelensis 62
Philippia hexandra 62
Philippia mannii 62
Philippia simii 62
Phoenix reclinata 42
Phylica buxifolia 66
Phylica oleifolia 66
Phylica paniculata 66
Phylica purpurea 66
Phylica villosa 66
Phyllanthus discoideus:
  see Margaritaria discoidea
Phyllanthus reticulatus 192;194
Pienkjakaranda 416
Pienkjakkalsbessie 178
Pienkmonotes 114
Pienkvrugklipels 260
Pigeonwood 244
Piliostigma thonningii 374
PINACEAE 29;64
Pink-fruited monotes 114
Pink-fruited rock elder 260
Pink jacaranda 416
Pink jackal-berry 178
Pink wild pear 232
•Pinus canariensis 64
•Pinus elliottii 64
•Pinus halepensis 64
•Pinus patula 64
•Pinus pinaster 64
•Pinus pinea 64
•Pinus radiata 64
•Pinus taeda 64
Pipe-stem tree 478
Pistol bush 324
Pistoolbos 324
PITTOSPORACEAE 29;206
Pittosporum viridiflorum 206
Plate thorn 482
Platkroon 506
Platylophus trifoliatus 386
Plectroniella armata 262
Pleurostylia africana:
  see P. capensis

Pleurostylia capensis 326
Plum fingerleaf 476
Pock ironwood 344
Pod mahogany 420
Podalyria calyptrata 196
PODOCARPACEAE 29;206
Podocarpus elongatus 208
Podocarpus falcatus 206
Podocarpus henkelii 208
Podocarpus latifolius 208
Podranea brycei 414
Podranea ricasoliana 414
Poeierkwasboom 200
Poerabessie 476
Poison bride's bush 268
Poison olive 222
Pokysterhout 344
POLYGALACEAE 29;208
Polygala myrtifolia 208
Polyscias fulva 450
Pompon tree 354
Pondo bride's bush 264
Pondobruidsbos 264
Pondo-klipels 260
Pondo turkey-berry 260
Poora-berry 476
Porkbush 46
Port Jackson willow 202
PORTULACACEAE 29;46;66
Portulacaria afra 46
Potato bush 194
Pouzolzia hypoleuca: see P. mixta
Pouzolzia mixta 100;246
Powder-puff tree 200
Premna mooiensis 304
Premna senensis 304
Pride-of-De Kaap 372
Propeller tree 228
•Prosopis glandulosa 500
•Prosopis pubescens 500
•Prosopis velutina 500
Protea angolensis 212
Protea arborea: see P. nitida
Protea aurea 214
Protea barbigera: see P. magnifica
Protea caffra 214
PROTEACEAE 29;66;210;364;438
Protea compacta 214
Protea eximia 214
Protea gaguedi 220
Protea laurifolia 216
Protea magnifica 214
Protea mellifera: see P. repens
Protea multibracteata:
see P. caffra
Protea mundii 216
Protea neriifolia 216
Protea nitida 216
Protea obtusifolia 216
Protea petiolaris 218
Protea repens 218
Protea roupelliae 218
Protea rubropilosa 218
Protea subvestita 220
Protea susannae 216

Protea welwitschii 220
Protorhus longifolia 86
Pruimbas 352
Pruimvingerblaar 476
Prunus africana 152
Pseudolachnostylis maprouneifolia
194
Pseudoscolopia polyantha 302
•Psidium guajava 320
•Psidium littorale 320
Psoralea pinnata 460
Psychotria capensis 282
Psychotria mahonii 282
Psychotria zombamontana 284
Psydrax fragrantissima 284
Psydrax livida 284
Psydrax locuples 284
Psydrax obovata 284
PTAEROXYLACEAE 29;418
Ptaeroxylon obliquum 418;430
Pteleopsis anisoptera 338
Pteleopsis myrtifolia 192;338
Pterocarpus angolensis 462;510
Pterocarpus brenanii 462
Pterocarpus lucens 462
Pterocarpus rotundifolius 462
Pterocelastrus echinatus 170
Pterocelastrus rostratus 170
Pterocelastrus tricuspidatus
168;170
Purple cluster-pear 156
Purple-leaved false-thorn 508
Purple-stem corkwood 448
Putterlickia pyracantha 124
Putterlickia retrospinosa 126
Putterlickia verrucosa 126
Puzzle bush 162
Pynbos 410
Pypsteelboom 478
•Pyracantha angustifolia 116
•Pyracantha crenulata 116

Quar 284
Queen of the night 36
Quinine tree 358
Quiver tree 44

Raasblaar 338
Rainbow leaf 410
Rankbokdrol 280
Rankplatboontjie 456
Rankrosyntjie 238
Ranksaffraan 298
Rapanea gilliana 202
Rapanea melanophloeos 202
Raphia australis 52
Raphia vinifera 52
Rauvolfia caffra 358;364
Rawsonia lucida 144
Real fan palm 52
Real sugarbush 218
Real wild currant 408
Real yellowwood 208
Red alder 416
Red beech 86

Red bird-berry 284
Red bitterberry 250
Red bushwillow 328
Red candlewood 170
Red currant 398
Red eye 230
Red gum 204
Red-heart tree 192
Red hook-berry 156
Red-hot poker coral tree 386
Red ivory 350
Red-leaved fig 76
Red-leaved medlar 270
Red mahogany 428
Red mangrove 278
Red milkwood 96
Red pear 128
Red quince 116
Red spike-thorn 124
Red-stem corkwood 434
Red stinkwood 152
Red thorn 492
Renosterkoffie 282
Resin cluster-leaf 176
Resin gardenia 366
Reuseblaarvy 76
Reuserosyntjie 238
RHAMNACEAE 30;66;152;232;350
Rhamnus prinoides 152
Rhamnus staddo 152
Rhigozum brevispinosum 120;384
Rhigozum obovatum 384;416
Rhigozum zambesiacum 384;416
Rhino-coffee 282
RHIZOPHORACEAE
30;276;294;364
Rhizophora mucronata 276;278
Rhodesian gardenia 286
Rhodesiese katjiepiering 286
Rhoicissus digitata 392
Rhoicissus revoilii 392
Rhoicissus rhomboidea 392
Rhoicissus tomentosa 246
Rhoicissus tridentata 392
Rhus acocksii 398
Rhus burchellii 398;410
Rhus chirindensis 398
Rhus crenata 400
Rhus culminum: see R. tumulicola
Rhus dentata 400
Rhus dura: see R. tumulicola
Rhus engleri 400
Rhus eroŝa 400
Rhus glauca 400
Rhus gueinzii 402
Rhus incisa 402
Rhus laevigata 402
Rhus lancea 402
Rhus leptodictya 404
Rhus longispina 398
Rhus lucida forma lucida 404
Rhus natalensis 404;412
Rhus nebulosa forma nebulosa
404
Rhus pallens 410

Rhus pendulina 406
Rhus pyroides 406
Rhus rehmanniana 406
Rhus tenuinervis 408
Rhus tomentosa 408
Rhus tumulicola 408
Rhus undulata 410; see also
R. burchellii
Rhus viminales: see R. pendulina
Rhus zeyheri 410
Ricinodendron rautanenii:
see Schinziophyton rautanenii
Ringwood tree 168
Rinorea angustifolia 154
Rinorea convallarioides 154
Rinorea domatiosa 154
Rinorea ferruginea 154
Rinorea ilicifolia 144
River bells 296
River bushwillow 330
River climbing thorn 488
River cluster-leaf 174
River euphorbia 42
River honey-thorn 132
River indigo 456
River litchi 432
River wild pear 234
Rivierdrolpeer 234
Rivierkriedoring 132
Rivierlitchi 432
Riviernaboom 42
Rivierrankdoring 488
Riviervaalboom 174
Rivierverfbos 456
Robinia pseudoacacia 464
Robsonodendron 136
Rock alder 278
Rock ash 466
Rock cabbage tree 224
Rock candlewood 168
Rocket pincushion 212
Rock hard pear 348
Rockwood 84
Rondeblaargifboom 312
Rondeblaarpieringbessie 136
Rooibitterbessie 250
Rooiblaarmispel 270
Rooiblaarvy 76
Rooibloekom 204
Rooiboekenhout 86
Rooibos 328
Rooidoring 492
Rooiessenhout 468
Rooi-haakbessie 156
Rooihartboom 192
Rooi-ivoor 350
Rooikershout 170
Rooikrans 230
Rooikweper 116
Rooimahonie 428
Rooimelkhout 96
Rooipeer 128
Rooipendoring 124
Rooistamkanniedood 434

Rooistinkhout 152
Rooivoëlbessie 284
Rooiwortelboom 278
ROSACEAE 30;116;152;440
•*Rosa eglanteria* 440
Rosette cluster-leaf 174
Rosetvaalboom 174
Rothmannia capensis **286**
Rothmannia fischeri 286
Rothmannia globosa **286**
Rothmannia urcelliformis 286
Rotsessenhout 466
Rotshardepeer 348
Rotskiepersol 224
Rough-leaved corkwood 446
Rough-leaved shepherd's tree 164
Round-leaved poison-bush 312
Round-leaved saucer-berry 136
Round-leaved teak 462
Rubber euphorbia 40
RUBIACEAE
30;260;264;270;278;364
Rub-rub berry 402
Russet bushwillow 332
RUTACEAE 30;322;394;418;440

Saalpeultjieboom 314
Saddle pod 314
Sagewood 258
SALICACEAE 30;116;154
Saliehout 258
•*Salix babylonica* **154**
Salix capensis: see *S. mucronata*
Salix mucronata **116**
Salix subserrata:
    see *S. mucronata*
Salix woodii: see *S. mucronata*
Sallow wattle 230
Salsola aphylla **60**
Salsola arborea 60
Salvadora angustifolia:
    see *S. australis*
Salvadora australis **350**
SALVADORACEAE 31;350
Salvadora persica **352**
Sambokpeul 422
Sambreelboom 450
Sand ash 514
Sandbeesklou 474
Sand bride's bush 264
Sandbruidsbos 264
Sand camwood 194
Sand corkwood 434
Sand crown-berry 270
Sand currant 404
Sanddoring 490
Sandessenhout 514
Sand forest num-num 308
Sand jasmine 346
Sandjasmyn 346
Sandkamhout 194
Sandkaniedood 434
Sand knobwood 442
Sandkroonbessie 270
Sand neat's foot 374

Sandolien 220
Sand olive 220
Sand onionwood 294
Sandpaper bush 162
Sandpaper raisin 238
Sandperdepram 442
Sand plane 148
Sandrooihout 148
Sandtaaibos 404
Sand thorn 490
Sanduiehout 294
Sandwoudnoemnoem 308
SANTALACEAE 31;220;352,
SAPINDACEAE
    31;154;220;412;428;470
Sapium ellipticum **106**
Sapium integerrimum **108**
SAPOTACEAE 31;92
Sausage tree 414
Savanna bushwillow 336
Savanna dwaba-berry 158
Savanna gardenia 368
Savanneboswilg 336
Savannedwababessie 158
Scented thorn 496
Schefflera goetzenii 472
Schefflera umbellifera **472**
Schinus molle **434**
•*Schinus terebinthifolius* **446**
Schinziophyton rautanenii **474**
Schotia afra 424
Schotia brachypetala **424**
Schotia capitata 424
Schotia latifolia 424
Schrebera alata 418;466
Schrebera trichoclada 346;418
Sclerocarya birrea **446**
Sclerochiton harveyanus **296**
Sclerochiton odoratissimus 296
Scolopia flanaganii 128
Scolopia mundii **128**
Scolopia zeyheri **130**
Scotsman's rattle 510
SCROPHULARIACEAE
    31;302;352;368
Scutia myrtina **350**
Sea guarri 186
Sebrabaskanniedood 102
Sebrahout 454
Securidaca longipedunculata **210**
Securinega virosa: see *Flueggea
    virosa*
Seeghwarrie 186
Seekatkiepersol 48
Seepblinkblaar 152
Seepganna 60
Seepnetel 100
Sekelblaarsuikerbos 218
Sekelbos 500
Sekhukhuneboesmanstee 292
Sekhukhune Bushman's tea 292
•*Senna didymobotrya* **426**
Senna petersiana **426**
Senna singueana 426
Septeeboom 134

Septee tree 134
Septeeboom 134
Septemberbossie 208
September bush 208
Sericanthe andongensis **272**
Sericanthe odoratissima 272
Seringa 514
Sesamothamnus benguellensis
    132
Sesamothamnus guerichii **132**
Sesamothamnus lugardii **132**
Sesbania 426
•*Sesbania punicea* **426**
Shakama plum 158
Shakamapruim 158
Shepherd's tree 164
Short-thorn pomegranate 120
Sickle bush 500
Sickle-leaf sugarbush 218
Sideroxylon inerme **98**
Silky bark 138
Silky fibre-bush 354
Silky hakea 66
Silky oak 438
Silky plum 432
Silky thorn 496
Silver cluster-leaf 174
Silver pipe-stem tree 478
Silver raisin 240
Silver sugarbush 218
Silver wattle 504
Silwereik 438
Silwerhakea 66
Silwersuikerbos 218
Silwerwattel 504
SIMAROUBACEAE 31;442
Simple-spined num-num 306
Simple-thorned torchwood 376
Sjambok pod 422
Skilferdoring 492
Skotseratel 510
Skurweblaarbos 162
Skurweblaarkanniedood 446
Skurweblaarwitgat 164
Skurwerosyntjie 238
Skurwevy 72
Slangboom 452
Smalblaarbasterbruidsbos 288
Smalblaar-mahobohobo 90
Smalblaarmosterdboom 350
Smalblaarpendoring 122
Smalblaarwasbessie 146
Smalblad 320
Small apple-leaf 458
Small bone-apple 280
Small cluster-pear 160
Small copalwood 378
Small green thorn 376
Small knobwood 440
Small lavender fever-berry 88
Small-leaved bride's bush 268
Small-leaved coca tree 186
Small-leaved cross-berry 242
Small-leaved dragon tree 54
Small-leaved jackal-berry 180

Small-leaved Karoo boer-bean
    424
Small-leaved plane 152
Small-leaved rock fig 80
Small-leaved saffron 300
Small skunk bush 304
Small sourplum 206
Smodingium argutum **410**
Snake bean 452
Sneezewood 418
Snotappel 228
Snot apple 228
Snot berry 136
Snotbessie 136
Snuff-box tree 128
Snuifkalbassie 128
Soap dogwood 152
Soap-nettle 100
Soetdoring 494
SOLANACEAE 32;118;132;222
Solanum aculeastrum 118
Solanum giganteum **118**
•*Solanum mauritianum* **118**
Sourplum 130
Soutpansberg bride's bush 268
Soutpansbergbruidsbos 268
Sparrmannia africana **244**
Spekboom 46
Speserysafraan 300
Spine-leaved monkey orange 252
Spirostachys africana **108**
Spoonwood 300
Springsaadboom 106
Sprokiesboom 514
Stadmannia oppositifolia **432**
Stamvrug 92
Steganotaenia araliacea **438**
Stekelblaarklapper 252
Sterculia africana **234**
Sterculia alexandrii 474
Sterculia appendiculata 236
STERCULIACEAE 32;222;232;474
Sterculia murex 474
Sterculia quinqueloba 236
Sterculia rogersii **236**
Stereospermum kunthianum **416**
Sterkbos 126
Stinkbos 164
Stinkboswilg 338
Stink-bush 164
Stink bushwillow 338
Stinkebbehout 192
Stink ebony 192
Stinkhout 200
Stink shepherd's tree 164
Stinkwitgat 164
Stinkwood 200
Stompblaartaaibos 406
Strandaalwyn 46
Strand aloe 46
Strawberry bush 280
Strelitzia caudata 56 56
STRELITZIACEAE 32;56
Strelitzia nicolai **56** 56
Strophanthus speciosus **360**

Strychnos cocculoides 248
Strychnos decussata 248
Strychnos gerrardii 250
Strychnos henningsii 250
Strychnos innocua 250
Strychnos madagascariensis 250
Strychnos mitis 252
Strychnos potatorum 252
Strychnos pungens 252
Strychnos spinosa 248;254
Strychnos stuhlmannii:
see S. potatorum
Strychnos usambarensis 254
Stunted plane 150
Suidwesdoring 500
Sumach bean 512
Suregada africana 142
Suregada procera 142
Suregada zanzibariensis 142
Suurberg cushion bush 112
Suurbergse kussingbos 112
Suurpruim 130
Swamp fig 82
Swartapiesdoring 480
Swartbas 184
Swartbastertaaibos 412
Swartbitterbessie 252
Swartbospendoring 122
Swarthaak 484
Swarthaselaar 342
Swarthout 230
Swartklapper 250
Swartsterappel 182
Swartvoëlbessie 282
Swartwattel 504
Swartwortelboom 276
Swartzia madagascariensis 452
Swazi-oordeelboom 504
Swazi ordeal tree 504
Sweepstokdoring 486
Sweetbriar 440
Sweet prickly pear 36
Sweet thorn 494
Sybas 138
Sydoring 496
Syhaarveselbos 354
Sypruim 432
Syzygium cordatum 320
Syzygium gerrardii 322
Syzygium guineense 322
Syzygium legatii 322
Syzygium pondoense 322

Tabernaemontana angolensis:
see T. stapfiana
Tabernaemontana elegans 312
Tabernaemontana stapfiana 314
Tabernaemontana ventricosa 314
Tall common corkwood 102
Tall yellowbush 212
TAMARICACEAE 32;68
Tamarind 426
Tamarindus indica 426
•Tamarix chinensis 68
•Tamarix ramosissima 68

Tamarix usneoides 68
Tamboti 108
Tambotie 108
Tapiphyllum parvifolium 274
Tapiphyllum velutinum 274
Tarchonanthus camphoratus 112
Tarchonanthus trilobus 112
Tarenna barbertonensis:
see T. supra-axillaris
Tarenna littoralis 286
Tarenna pavettoides 288
Tarenna supra-axillaris 288
Tarenna zimbabwensis 286
Tarwood 446
Tassel berry 188
Teclea gerrardii 394
Teclea myrei 394
Teclea natalensis 394
Teclea nobilis 394
Teclea trichocarpa 394
Tecomaria capensis 416
Teerhout 446
Terminalia brachystemma 172
Terminalia gazensis 172
Terminalia mollis 172;174
Terminalia phanerophlebia 172
Terminalia prunioides 126
Terminalia randii 126;176
Terminalia sambesiaca 174
Terminalia sericea 174
Terminalia stenostachya 174
Terminalia stuhlmannii 176
Terminalia trichopoda 174
Thespesia acutiloba 230
Thespesia populnea 230
Thorn pear 130
Thorny bone-apple 262
Thorny cluster-leaf 126
Thorny elm 132
Thorny gardenia 262
Thorny karree 402
Thorny salad bush 296
Thorny teak 462
Three-fingerleaf 476
Three-hook thorn 488
THYMELAEACEAE 32;68;222;
354
TILIACEAE 32;236
Tinderwood 370
Toad tree 312
Toddaliopsis bremekampii 396
Tonga-kerrie 384
Tongakierie 384
Tongaroosappel 254
Tonga rose-apple 254
Tontelhout 370
Towerghwarrie 340
Transvaal beech 210
Transvaalboekenhout 210
Transvaal bottlebrush 226
Transvaal cabbage tree 50
Transvaal candelabra tree 38
Transvaalkiepersol 50
Transvaalliguster 342
Transvaal milkplum 92

Transvaal mountain sugarbush
218
Transvaal privet 342
Transvaal red balloon 470
Transvaal red milkwood 98
Transvaalsaffraan 138
Transvaal saffron 138
Transvaalse baakhout 226
Transvaalse bergsuikerbos 218
Transvaalse kandelaarnaboom 38
Transvaalse rooiklapperbos 470
Transvaal sesame-bush 132
Transvaalse sesambos 132
Transvaalse skulpblombos 368
Transvaalse wildepiesang 56
Transvaal shell-flower bush 368
Transvaal sumach 220
Transvaal wild banana 56
Trassiebos 484
Tree aloe 42
Tree entada 512
Tree fuchsia 302
Tree pincushion 212
Tree wisteria 452
Trema orientalis 244
Treurbruidsbos 266
Treurden 64
Treurperdestert 204
Treursalie 256
Treurwilger 154
Triangle tops 430
Tricalysia capensis 288
Tricalysia delagoensis 288
Tricalysia lanceolata 288
Tricalysia sonderiana 288
Trichilia capitata 468
Trichilia dregeana 468
Trichilia emetica 468
Trichocladus crinitus 342
Trichocladus ellipticus 114
Trichocladus grandiflorus 342
Trilepisium madagascariense 82
Trimeria grandifolia 226;240
Trimeria trinervis 226
Triplochiton zambesiacus 236
Trompetdoring 120
Trosden 64
Troshofiesuikerbos 220
Trumpet thorn 120
Turraea floribunda 200
Turraea nilotica 202
Tweelingbessieboom 394
Twin-berry tree 394

Uapaca kirkiana 90;92;366
Uapaca lissopyrena 90
Uapaca nitida 90
Uapaca sansibarica 92
Uitenhaagsaalwyn 42
Uitenhage aloe 42
ULMACEAE 32;132;244
Umbrella thorn 488
Umzimbeet 458
Urera tenax: see Obetia tenax
URTICACEAE 33;100;246

Uvaria caffra 160
Uvaria gracilipes 160
Uvaria lucida 160

Vaalboom 174
Vaalkameeldoring 494
Vaalmonotes 176
Vaalpypsteelboom 478
Vaalrosyntjie 240
Vaderlandswilg 330
Valleibosnaboom 40
Valley-bush euphorbia 40
Valshaakdoring 484
Valskatjiepiering 272
Valslemoentjiedoring 276
Vals-mfuti 422
Valsmispel 274
Valsrooipeer 302
Vals-swartbas 182
Valswag-'n-bietjie 232
Vangueria chartacea: see V. randii
Vangueria cyanescens 274;290
Vangueria esculenta:
see V. cyanescens
Vangueria infausta 274;290
Vangueria randii 290
Vangueriopsis lanciflora 274
Vanwykshout 452
Variable bushwillow 328
Variërende boswilg 328
Veld fig 70
Veldvy 70
Velvet bushwillow 334
Velvet corkwood 448
Velvet-fruited zanha 432
Velvet karree 400
Velvet raisin 238
Velvet rock alder 270
Velvet sweetberry 190
Venda bead-string 104
Venda coffee 272
Venda indigo 456
Vendakoffie 272
Vendakralesnoer 104
Vendaverfbos 456
Vepris carringtoniana 396
Vepris lanceolata 396
Vepris reflexa 396
Vepris undulata: see V. lanceolata
Vepris zambesiaca 396
VERBENACEAE
33;304;354;370;476
Vergeet-my-nie-boom 304
Vernonia ampla: see V. myriantha
Vernonia amygdalina 162
Vernonia colorata 162
Vernonia myriantha 134
Vernonia stipulacea:
see V. myriantha
Vierblaarboswilg 326
Viervingerbos 472
VIOLACEAE 33;154
Violet tree 210
Virgilia divaricata 464
Virgilia oroboides 464

INDEX

Viscum capense 400
VITACEAE 33;46;246;392
Vitellariopsis dispar 100
Vitellariopsis ferruginea 100
Vitellariopsis marginata 100
Vitex angolensis 476
Vitex doniana 476
Vitex ferruginea 476
Vitex harveyana 476
Vitex mombassae 476;478
Vitex obovata 478
Vitex patula 476
Vitex payos 478
Vitex pooara 478
Vitex rehmannii 478
Vitex zeyheri 478
Vlamdoring 480
Vlamklimop 336
Vlam-van-die-vlakte 372
Vlerkboon 464
Vloedvlaktedoring 494
Voacanga thouarsii 314
Voëlsitboom 188
Vuurpylkoraalboom 386

Waboom 216
Wagon tree 216
Waterbergboswilg 334
Waterberg bushwillow 334
Waterberg-poerabessie 478
Waterberg poora-berry 478
Water berry 320
Waterbessie 320
Water blossom pea 196
Waterboomheide 62
Waterboswilg 336
Water bushwillow 336
Waterdoring 496
Water elder 302
Water ironplum 142
Waterkeurtjie 196
Water pear 322
Waterpeer 322
Water thorn 496
Water tree heath 62
Watervlier 302
Water white alder 162
Waterwitels 162
Waterysterpruim 142
Weeping boer-bean 424
Weeping bottlebrush 204
Weeping bride's bush 266
Weeping sage 256
Weeping wattle 504
Weeping willow 154
Westelike houtmelkbos 88
Western woody milkbush 88
Whip-stick thorn 486
White alder 386
White-berry bush 192
White bristle bush 60
White candlewood 170
White climbing sage 256
White cross-berry 242
White forest spike-thorn 124

White gardenia 366
White hazel 114
White ironwood 396
White karree 406
White mangrove 354
White milkwood 98
White pear 198
White raisin 236
White resin tree 356
White seringa 442
White silky bark 136
White-stem corkwood 382
White stinkwood 244
White sugarbush 216
White thorn 486
White violet-bush 154
Widdringtonia
    cedarbergensis 62
Widdringtonia nodiflora 62
Widdringtonia schwarzii 62
Wild almond 364
Wild apricot 128
Wild banana 56
Wild camphor bush 112
Wild caper-bush 120
Wild cotton tree 228
Wild custard-apple 156
Wild date palm 52
Wild jasmine 418
Wilde-amandel 364
Wilde-appelkoos 128
Wildedadelpalm 52
Wildefrangipani 314
Wildegranaat 278
Wildegroenhaarboom 452
Wildejasmyn 418
Wildekamperfoelieboom 200
Wildekanferbos 112
Wildekaperbos 120
Wildekastaiing 322
Wildekatoenboom 228
Wildelukwart 282
Wildemango 448
Wildemirt 318
Wildemispel 274
Wildemoerbei 226
Wildenartjie 396
Wildeperske 114
Wildepiesang 56
Wildepietersieliebos 450
Wildepopulier 88
Wildepruim 444
Wilderoos 440
Wildesambreelblom 304
Wildesering 502
Wildesuikerappel 156
Wildetabak 222
Wildetulpboom 230
Wild frangipani 314
Wild green-hair tree 452
Wild honeysuckle tree 200
Wild jasmine 418
Wild laburnum 452
Wild loquat 282
Wild mandarin 396

Wild mango 448
Wild medlar 274
Wild mulberry 226
Wild myrtle 318
Wild olive 346
Wild parasol flower 304
Wild peach 114
Wild plum 444
Wild pomegranate 278
Wild poplar 88
Wild seringa 502
Wild tamarisk 68
Wild teak 462
Wild tobacco 222
Wild tulip tree 230
Wilgerblaarwitgat 166
Willow-leaved shepherd's
    tree 166
Wine-cup 236
Wing bean 464
Winged bersama 438
Witaarbeibos 280
Witakasia 464
Witbessiebos 192
Witbospendoring 124
Witdoring 486
Witels 386
Witgat 164
Witharpuisboom 356
Withaselaar 114
Without 160
Witkaree 406
Witkatjiepiering 366
Witkershout 170
Witkruisbessie 242
Witmelkhout 98
Witolienhout 324
Witpeer 198
Witranksalie 256
Witrosyntjie 236
Witseebasboom 354
Witsering 442
Witstamkanniedood 382
Witsteekbos 60
Witstinkhout 244
Witsuikerbos 216
Witsybas 136
Witviooltjiebos 154
Witysterhout 396
Wolftoon 66
Wollerige kapperbos 120
Wollerige piering-
    bessie 224
Wonderboom fig 78
Wonderboomvy 78
Woodland dogplum 466
Woody milkbush 88
Woolly caper-bush 120
Woolly saucer-berry 224
Worm-bark
    false-thorn 506
Worsboom 414
Woud-newtonia 512
Woudskurwevy 74
Wrightia natalensis 314

Wurmbasvalsdoring 506
Wynkelk 236

Xanthocercis zambesiaca 464
Xeroderris stuhlmannii 464
Xeromphis obovata:
    see Catunaregam spinosa
Xeromphis rudis:
    see Coddia rudis
Ximenia americana 130
Ximenia caffra 130
Xylia mendoncae 514
Xylia torreana 514
Xylopia aethiopica 160
Xylopia odoratissima 160
Xylopia parviflora 160
Xylotheca kraussiana 196
Xylotheca tettensis 196
Xymalos monospora 302

Yellow bitterberry 252
Yellow firebush 280
Yellow firethorn 116
Yellow gardenia 366
Yellow peeling plane 148
Yellow pomegranate 384
Ysterhout 344
Ystermartiens 102

Zambezikiaat 420
Zambezi plane 150
Zambezirooihout 150
Zambezi teak 420
ZAMIACEAE 33;58
Zanha africana 432
Zanha golungensis 432
Zanthoxylum capense 440
Zanthoxylum chalybeum 440
Zanthoxylum davyi 442
Zanthoxylum gilletii 442
Zanthoxylum leprieurii 442
Zebra-bark corkwood 102
Zebrawood 454
Zimbabwe creeper 414
Zimbabwe-klimop 414
Ziziphus abyssinica 232
Ziziphus mucronata 232
Ziziphus rivularis 232
Zoeloekersielemoen 394
Zoeloekiepersol 50
Zoeloelukwart 282
Zoeloemelkbessie 94
Zoeloepeulbessie 450
Zulu cabbage tree 50
Zulu cherry-orange 394
Zulu loquat 282
Zulu milkberry 94
Zulu podberry 450